Crowdfunding and Sustainable Urban Development in Emerging Economies

Umar G. Benna
Ahmadu Bello University, Nigeria

Abubakar U. Benna
Durham University, UK

A volume in the Advances in E-Business Research (AEBR) Book Series

IGI Global
DISSEMINATOR OF KNOWLEDGE

Published in the United States of America by
IGI Global
Business Science Reference (an imprint of IGI Global)
701 E. Chocolate Avenue
Hershey PA, USA 17033
Tel: 717-533-8845
Fax: 717-533-8661
E-mail: cust@igi-global.com
Web site: http://www.igi-global.com

Library of Congress Cataloging-in-Publication Data

Names: Benna, Umar G., 1942- editor. | Benna, Abubakar U., 1980- editor.
Title: Crowdfunding and sustainable urban development in emerging economies / Umar G. Benna and Abubakar U. Benna, editors.
Description: Hershey : Business Science Reference, [2018]
Identifiers: LCCN 2017024126| ISBN 9781522539520 (hardcover) | ISBN 9781522539537 (ebook)
Subjects: LCSH: Crowd funding--Developing countries. | City planning--Developing countries. | Sustainable development--Developing countries.
Classification: LCC HG4751 .C784 2018 | DDC 307.1/416091724--dc23 LC record available at https://lccn.loc.gov/2017024126

This book is published in the IGI Global book series Advances in E-Business Research (AEBR) (ISSN: 1935-2700; eISSN: 1935-2719)

British Cataloguing in Publication Data
A Cataloguing in Publication record for this book is available from the British Library.

For electronic access to this publication, please contact: eresources@igi-global.com.

Advances in E-Business Research (AEBR) Book Series

In Lee
Western Illinois University, USA

ISSN:1935-2700
EISSN:1935-2719

Mission

Technology has played a vital role in the emergence of e-business and its applications incorporate strategies. These processes have aided in the use of electronic transactions via telecommunications networks for collaborating with business partners, buying and selling of goods and services, and customer service. Research in this field continues to develop into a wide range of topics, including marketing, psychology, information systems, accounting, economics, and computer science.

The **Advances in E-Business Research (AEBR) Book Series** provides multidisciplinary references for researchers and practitioners in this area. Instructors, researchers, and professionals interested in the most up-to-date research on the concepts, issues, applications, and trends in the e-business field will find this collection, or individual books, extremely useful. This collection contains the highest quality academic books that advance understanding of e-business and addresses the challenges faced by researchers and practitioners.

Coverage

- Web advertising
- Economics of e-business
- E-CRM
- Valuing e-business assets
- E-Services
- Virtual organization
- Telework and Telecommuting
- Interorganizational information systems
- E-business models and architectures
- Evaluation methodologies for e-business systems

IGI Global is currently accepting manuscripts for publication within this series. To submit a proposal for a volume in this series, please contact our Acquisition Editors at Acquisitions@igi-global.com or visit: http://www.igi-global.com/publish/.

The Advances in E-Business Research (AEBR) Book Series (ISSN 1935-2700) is published by IGI Global, 701 E. Chocolate Avenue, Hershey, PA 17033-1240, USA, www.igi-global.com. This series is composed of titles available for purchase individually; each title is edited to be contextually exclusive from any other title within the series. For pricing and ordering information please visit http://www.igi-global.com/book-series/advances-business-research/37144. Postmaster: Send all address changes to above address.

Titles in this Series

For a list of additional titles in this series, please visit: www.igi-global.com/book-series

Mobile Platforms, Design, and Apps for Social Commerce
Jean-Éric Pelet (ESCE International Business School, Paris, France)
Business Science Reference • copyright 2017 • 411pp • H/C (ISBN: 9781522524694) • US $215.00 (our price)

The Internet of Things in the Modern Business Environment
In Lee (Western Illinois University, USA)
Business Science Reference • copyright 2017 • 340pp • H/C (ISBN: 9781522521044) • US $205.00 (our price)

Key Challenges and Opportunities in Web Entrepreneurship
Alexandru Capatina (Dunarea de Jos University of Galati, Romania) and Elisa Rancati (University of Milan – Bicocca, Italy & Beta Consulting, Italy)
Business Science Reference • copyright 2017 • 291pp • H/C (ISBN: 9781522524663) • US $205.00 (our price)

Apps Management and E-Commerce Transactions in Real-Time
Sajad Rezaei (Taylor's University, Malaysia)
Business Science Reference • copyright 2017 • 379pp • H/C (ISBN: 9781522524496) • US $210.00 (our price)

Driving Innovation and Business Success in the Digital Economy
Ionica Oncioiu (Titu Maiorescu University, Romania)
Business Science Reference • copyright 2017 • 321pp • H/C (ISBN: 9781522517795) • US $200.00 (our price)

Social Media Listening and Monitoring for Business Applications
N. Raghavendra Rao (FINAIT Consultancy Services, India)
Business Science Reference • copyright 2017 • 470pp • H/C (ISBN: 9781522508465) • US $205.00 (our price)

Analyzing the Strategic Role of Social Networking in Firm Growth and Productivity
Vladlena Benson (Kingston University, UK) Ronald Tuninga (Kingston Business School, UK) and George Saridakis (Kingston University, UK)
Business Science Reference • copyright 2017 • 525pp • H/C (ISBN: 9781522505594) • US $220.00 (our price)

Securing Transactions and Payment Systems for M-Commerce
Sushila Madan (University of Delhi, India) and Jyoti Batra Arora (Banasthali Vidyapeeth University, India)
Business Science Reference • copyright 2016 • 349pp • H/C (ISBN: 9781522502364) • US $205.00 (our price)

IGI Global
DISSEMINATOR OF KNOWLEDGE

701 East Chocolate Avenue, Hershey, PA 17033, USA
Tel: 717-533-8845 x100 • Fax: 717-533-8661
E-Mail: cust@igi-global.com • www.igi-global.com

Editorial Advisory Board

List of Reviewers

Table of Contents

Detailed Table of Contents

Collaborative consumption is a broader term encompassing emerging areas, such as crowdfunding and the sharing economy, which enhance consumer enablement through direct interaction. This chapter addresses opportunities and challenges of how to support small- and medium-scale farmers in developing countries. Traditional agriculture, as well as urban agriculture, is rising with the significant urbanization that is occurring in developing economies. There is currently limited research on the value of collaborative consumption as a catalyst for agricultural development. Consequently, the aim of this chapter is to provide an overview of how collaborative consumption in agriculture can be supported. The study is conducted based on the review of literature and case studies related to both agriculture and collaborative consumption. A few key observations are provided in order to assist with the formulation of strategies that increase producer and customer satisfaction, value addition, and engagement.

The contemporary process of urbanization prevalent in the countries of the Global South, especially in Africa and Asia, is characterized by an unprecedented rise in urban populations, exceeding the capacity of local authorities to provide essential services. In particular, local authorities lack the funding required to build adequate infrastructure. One striking feature of contemporary urbanization is the growth in informal urbanized settlements, called "census towns" in India, "urban villages" in China, and "townships" in South Africa. Compared to India, China and South Africa have been able to turn around their cities and revamp them within 10 years. These countries present similarities and differences in managing and providing basic urban services. In this chapter, an attempt is made to analyze and compare the urbanization process in these countries and to identify some financial alternatives and policy implications to foster inclusive growth by integrating informal settlements into mainstream urbanization with focus on India.

To efficiently manage growth and changes arising from rapidly increasing population and urbanization trends, developing countries need to employ appropriate tools to analyze the key issues involved. Globally, crowdsourcing is increasingly being applied to facilitate sustainable urban development (SUD) planning process. Crowdsourcing has already proved capable of generating new models for urban planning and governance that source and mobilize diverse social actors working toward sustainable and innovation-oriented urban space. However, few studies have explored crowdsourcing applications in SUD planning in developing countries. Therefore, based on desktop study, this chapter examines applications of crowdsourcing in SUD planning in developing countries. The chapter reviews the conceptual and historical foundation of crowdsourcing, and highlights some exemplary applications of crowdsourcing in SUD planning worldwide. It then discusses the challenges and potentials of crowdsourcing as a tool in planning for SUD in developing countries and concludes with future research directions.

Section 2
Opportunities and Challenges in Crowdfunding Markets

This chapter seeks to fill a gap in the regional analysis of online crowdfunding platforms and projects by examining selected platforms in Africa and in the Middle East. The authors considered the quantity and quality of the actors: fundraisers, funders, and other stakeholders; analyzed characteristics, quality, fees, and general value for money; and evaluated the capacity of the platforms in terms of system interface, projects, and customer crowds aiming to enhance their overall capacity to become nodes of local and regional crowdfunding activities. These are connected to other district and urban centers that would serve as a springboard to organize and network with overseas centers for the growth and development of the regional centers.

Developing countries will account for 90% of the new 2.5 billion urban population inflow projected by 2050. To provide decent urban environment new non-traditional financial sources such as crowdfunding are needed. In developing these sources, mutual learning experiences are the key to success but cross-cultural studies among cultures remain limited; this chapter seeks to address this issue. Africa and India are likely the key beneficiaries of future urban growth and most likely users of alternative finance tools to fund their growth. Both are slow starters in rapid urbanization and the use of crowdfunding but are making rapid progress.

This chapter compares the African and Chinese crowdfunding markets with a view to draw lessons from the two markets. China has a longer experience than Africa in the crowdfunding activities; crowdfunding processes in the country may not be directly applicable to the African states, but there are lessons that can be learnt by individual or group of African or Asian governments. These differing experiences identified

The utility of crowdfunding in promoting sustainable development is beyond doubt due to its popularity in the Global North. The application of this concept in the Global South, especially in Africa, is ill-understood and questionable considering the high levels of corruption, poverty, and poor governance. Applying the concept of crowdfunding in Africa then becomes problematic. The chapter aims to undertake a critical analysis of the concept of crowdfunding and its sustainability in advancing the success of urban-based projects in African cities. What can (or should) be the defining pillars for sustainable and inclusive crowdfunding? What are the known (or even unknown) limits and prospects to initiatives like crowdfunding? What are the answers to the colonial legacy derived scepticisms about self-worth and context? What options do the African cities have? The chapter engages a mix of methodologies including literature review, document review, and case studies. Thematic content analysis is applied in building up the discourse. From the study, five critical observations emerge.

The chapter studies and attempts to understand the idea of crowdfunding and the possibility of it being adopted and adapted within the urban Indian framework. It explores the potential of crowdfunding – the civic variety, which can supplement a small but meaningful percentage of financial resources required to provide urban services in Indian cities. The objective of using the crowdfunding platform is to create sustainable and livable cities. While the delivery of basic urban services is the responsibility of the urban local bodies, it is observed that the available financial resources at their disposal poses an impediment in service delivery. With the process of urbanization gaining momentum, India will require billions of dollars to build the much-needed urban infrastructure and provide basic urban services. It is envisaged that civic crowdfunding, which addresses the varied requirements of urban citizens, may be the appropriate solution to the problem.

Neither urban quality of life research nor effective urban energy policy research is new in Africa, but funding the future needs in these two areas requires exploring the new options, such as the emerging crowdfunding market. It is projected that by 2100 Africans will account for 40% of global population and majority urban residents, with huge workforce, a growing middle class, experiencing hyper-globalization, and increased innovation, all of which will enhance quality of urban life. For Africa to meet its large-scale energy-deficit and expected huge future demand triggered by rapid and massive urbanization, alternative renewable sources are considered in the supply policy options. Similarly, alternative visions of how energy can contribute to inclusive economic growth in Africa are examined and ways to fund them explored. To leap-frog Africa's development while the traditional funding mechanism helps, sustainable option lies in innovative alternative finance, especially crowdfunding markets in Africa and in diaspora.

Preface

The emerging economies of Africa, Asia and Latin America are facing transformations in their social, economic, environmental systems and processes triggered by the forces of rapid urbanization, confusing globalization and accelerating technological advances. UN-DESA projections show that by 2050 over two-thirds of humanity will be urban residents, up from the present half. The sheer scales of rural-urban and cross-border migration suggest that urbanization will be the converging force driving societies and economies worldwide in decades to come. The pressing issue tackled by the diverse authors in this book, is how to fund and accelerate sustainable urban development in these emerging economies given the prevailing gloomy financial climate and the competing demands in other areas.

AIMS OF THE BOOK

A number of objectives motivate the publication of this book; the first is to stress the transformative power of urbanization as a development tool. This can be highlighted in at least four areas. The first is that in the twenty-first century, cities have become dazzling containers of global activities in innovation, production, logistics and trade. Secondly, cities in many developing regions are increasingly offering substantial opportunities for both formal and informal jobs, thereby increasing the quality of life for a large numbers of households. Thirdly, urbanization has- as the Chinese examples show- facilitated the lifting of millions out of poverty due to prudent and effective socio-economic policies and programs by urban actors. Fourth, the rapid and widespread deployment and penetration of Information and Communications Technology has highlighted the transformative power of urbanization, especially in key emerging economies.

The second objective is to explore how to fund sustainable urbanization of acceptable quality. Hence, this book aims to provide relevant theoretical frameworks and the latest empirical research findings in the relationship between crowdfunding and sustainable urban development in emerging economies. Broadly, this book seeks to create the understanding of the emerging values and visions guiding the rise of new platforms for digital activities, concepts of sharing economy, collaborative economy, crowdsourcing, crowdfunding and others that are shaping new tools in the developing world.

At a more practical level, the book will highlight and sharpen the main development instruments including innovative resource mobilizing policies, plans, programs as well as investment strategies that are transforming the ways people work, learn and conduct affairs in the physical and digital space. It will highlight the changing mindset, culture, and behaviors that are successful in the digital age.

The more specific objectives of the book are:

1. To explore the theoretical foundation and development values influencing the choices by key development actors in developing countries of various types of activities, and the tools for undertaking them.
2. To highlight how public institutions use digital technologies to transform their activities in their cities and the results achieved.
3. To understand how private sector businesses and entrepreneurs use digital technologies to enhance the smartness of their activities.
4. To study how social sector organizations apply digital technologies to increase the quality of life of their members and the effects on urban growth.

ABOUT THE KEY CONCEPTS USED IN THE BOOK

Many of the key concepts used in the book are new and carry meanings valid to certain networked authors/publishers/audiences, or certain regions, and there are no internationally accepted definitions. Therefore, the authors have suggested definitions suited to their contexts. The key concepts used in this book relate to the funding process of sustainable urbanization in emerging economies in terms of the development resource types (Cash vs Non-Cash) and the location of resource mobilization (Online vs Offline; OnSite vs OffSite). The resource types consist of digital cash that usually flows through electronic networks and non-cash types in terms of volunteerism of labor, ideas, skills and others which can be virtual, online, electronic, or remote if digital; or alternatively physical onsite or offsite volunteering. The location for resource mobilization may be online or offline and may be delivered onsite of offsite.

The types and characteristics of the emerging funding concepts are explained below in terms of what is included or excluded and based on the current Statista (2017) data of worldwide transaction values in 2017 as well as rate of growth to 2021 with the projected figures.

- **FinTech:** This is short for "Financial Technology", which is an emerging concept without generally accepted definition, but recognized as the central concept of structural transformation and digitization within the financial services industry. It is quite broad in scope, as it encompasses all forms of digital payments (Digital Commerce, Mobile Payments, P2P Money Transfers), business finance that is all forms of crowdfunding and personal finance (Robo-Advisors, Marketplace Lending). FinTech is characterized by simplified access for end users through the Internet or mobile devices, higher processing speed using automated processes, cost reduction, strong attention to customer service, more convenience, better transparency and the effective use of networks to deliver services. Like most innovations, the FinTech market is characterized by rapid growth startups and businesses without bank licenses (non-banks). It is generally accepted that FinTech powers the emerging Alternative Finance market.
- **Alternative Finance:** Is the concept coined to represent forms of finance that stretch beyond the three traditional asset types of stocks, bonds and cash. The advantage of alternative finance for startups and SMEs includes lower costs and speed. Updated credit assessment processes enable profit-making businesses to respond quickly to both challenges and opportunities. The number of accessible alternative finance platforms is growing rapidly and they include reward-based crowdfunding, equity crowdfunding, peer-to-peer consumer, business lending and invoice trading third party payment platforms (CCAF, 2017). The way in which the digitization of the finance industry

is transforming access to finance for individuals, start-ups, SMEs or social enterprises - for example through online platforms for crowdfunding, marketplace (peer-to-peer) lending, and third-party payment systems - has already gained prominence and attention. Digitization is lowering barriers to entry, with the result that corporations and institutions whose activities have not traditionally encompassed finance provision, are being drawn into the arena.

- **Business Finance:** The "Business Finance" market segment relates to digital financial services for business customers and includes sub-segments of crowdfunding, crowdlending and crowd-investing. The scope of the market is focused on serving as alternative financing for small- and medium-sized enterprises (SMEs) and freelancers, marketplace lending from private or institutional investors (non-banks), and equity-based crowdfunding (or crowd-investing). On the other hand, it does not include traditional bank loans, donation-based crowdfunding, and the traditional venture capital investments by institutional or private investors. According to Statista (2017), the worldwide total transaction value in the "Business Finance" segment amounts to US$194,815m in 2017. The projected annual growth rate (CAGR 2017-2021) is 30.5% yielding total amounts of US$565,187million in 2021.
- **Lending-Based Crowdfunding:** Models include alternative financing for SMEs and freelancers, small business loans issued by single or multiple private and institutional investors (non-banks) and online loan request, scoring and approval. It does not, however, include traditional bank loans, consumer loans and credit card transactions, or business-to-business credit scoring and rating services. The transaction value in the "Crowdlending" segment totals US$181,895million in 2017 and according to Statista (2017), with the growth rate (CAGR 2017-2021) of 30.5% p.a., it will yield the total amount of US$526,894 million in 2021.
- **Reward-Based Crowdfunding:** Crowdfunding (also reward-based crowdfunding) is a financing form independent from financial institutions and from the investors. It normally includes reward-based crowdfunding, pre-financing of products, art, music and films, software or scientific research through platforms such as Kickstarter, Indiegogo. It does not include the traditional venture capital investments, equity-based crowdfunding (see Crowdinvesting), donation-based crowdfunding, or lending-based crowdfunding (see Crowdlending). Considering the scope of its worldwide transaction activities, the value in the "Crowdfunding" segment is expected to amounts to US$7,230m in 2017, with the annual growth rate (CAGR 2017-2021) of 27.3% resulting in the total amount of US$18,967 million in 2021 (Statista 2017).
- **Crowdinvesting:** This is another financing form independent from financial institutions, and the investors. The scope of activity includes funding of startup companies and SMEs by an unspecified number of investors in return for equity, or profit-related returns (e.g., royalties or convertible loans) through equity platforms such as EquityNet, CrowdCube and Seedrs. It normally excludes reward-based crowdfunding (see Crowdfunding), donation-based crowdfunding, and the lending-based crowdfunding (see Crowdlending). The scope of the transaction value in the "Crowdinvesting" segment worldwide amounts to US$5,690m in 2017. Based on Statista (2017) projections, the annual growth rate (CAGR 2017-2021) of 35.8% will yield the total amount of US$19,326 million in 2021.
- **Digital Commerce:** The "Digital Commerce" segment covers all consumer digital transactions relevant to online shopping for products and services. Online transactions use various payment methods (credit cards, direct debit, invoice, or online payment providers, such as PayPal and AliPay). The scope of activities includes the following categories: First, online consumer payment

transactions for physical goods and services. Secondly, various payment methods like credit card, bank transfer, invoice or online payment providers and thirdly consists of the following payment categories: e-Commerce goods, digital items or media contents, eServices, Online Travel, etc. The fourth consists of purchases processed on computers as well as on mobile devices (mCommerce: smartphone, tablet). The worldwide transaction value in the "Digital Commerce" segment amounts to US$2,372,681 million in 2017, according to Statista (2017), the projected annual growth rate (CAGR 2017-2021) of 11.1% will generate US$3,609,840 million in 2021. The estimated number of users of the "Digital Commerce" segment is 2,402.5 million by 2021.

- **Crowdsourcing:** This is a digital sourcing model applied by individuals or organizations to mobilize needed services or ideas from diverse sources. Its advantages include costs efficiency, speed, quality, flexibility, scalability, or diversity. It provides opportunities for innovation contests directed towards internal and external actors to organizations. It can incorporate tiresome "microtasks" executed in parallel by large volunteer crowds and it is used to develop common goods or services, such as Wikipedia.
- **Crowdmapping:** This subtype of crowdsourcing is used to aggregate crowd-generated inputs such as capturing data and social media feeds, combined with geographic data to create a digital map by people collaborating over the Internet. It provides up-to-date maps of on-going events such as wars, crime, and natural disasters.
- **Microfinance:** This initially restricted activity has emerged as a broader movement, the aim of which is to be inclusive of all social groups, particularly the poor and socially excluded. These groups are offered high quality financial products and services such as credits, savings, insurance and financial transfers that are speedy and cost-effective.
- **Micro-Volunteering:** This is an individual or a team of volunteers, completing small tasks that make up a larger project. These tasks of short durations often benefit research, charity, or an NGO. In the case of virtual or online volunteering, the tasks are usually distributed, completed and coordinated online, without lengthy recruiting or training procedures.
- **Virtual Volunteering:** This is the practice of volunteering online or off-site from the assisted organization. Virtual volunteering is also known as online volunteering, remote volunteering or e-volunteering. Some organizations, like the UN, offer online volunteering opportunities, which last from ten minutes to an hour. Locations of activities may be remote to the organization or people they are assisting via a computer or other Internet-connected device, such as: researching subjects (e.g., for Wikia projects), writing or fixing software, and similar activities.

TARGET AUDIENCE

The book targets a broad range of professionals and activist interested in cities and issues of sustainable urbanization. This includes professionals in the field of Urban Planning, Architecture, Urban studies, Sociology, Urban Geography, Economics, Public Health, Environmental studies, and Infrastructure Engineering. Others including teachers and students in higher educational and other institutions, researchers in public and private institutions, entrepreneurs and urban practitioners will find this book useful. The innovative ideas and concepts will attract many organizations in the public, private and social sectors of society including members and affiliates of multi-lateral agencies, regional development institutions, donor agencies, private sector organizations engaged in promotion of economic growth and poverty reduction, and voluntary social organizations working to promote social development.

ORGANIZATION OF THE BOOK

The book is organized into three thematic sections and has 14 chapters, of which eight are about Africa, seven on Asia, and a chapter discusses Latin America. Section 1 reviews opportunities and challenges that are influencing the mobilization of resources used in the growth of sustainable urbanization in the emerging economies of the world. Section 2 focuses on comparative analysis of the dynamics of crowdfunding and crowdsourcing in paired developing economies. Evolving Crowdfunding in Emerging Economies is analyzed in Section 3. Each of these sections is discussed in more detail below.

Section 1: Opportunities and Challenges in Crowdfunding Markets

In Chapter 1, Garcia focuses on knowledge as the force driving opportunities in Crowdfunding and in society. It views knowledge production, marketing, distribution, application through networks and crowds at various spatial scales (national, regional, urban) more especially in cities. These opportunities are exploited using not only the tools of knowledge markets (knowledge agents, social capita and learning), social media networks and cities but also wide array of others associated with them. The factors used to build the 'commons economy' include easy and quick access to funds, risk reduction, marketing, branding, crowd-building, data-building, loyalty-building, low-cost operation, pre-selling opportunities, mobile –based service, open source and web-access. The opportunities generated by knowledge units are by their nature not local-centered, they are easily and speedily, digitally transmitted and shared across borders and across regions.

Sulaiman, Yangora, and Salami, in Chapter 2, draw our attention to the role of IT as a driving force for crowdfunding growth, especially civic crowdfunding that can have direct bearing in shaping the scale and tempo of urban development, a pressing area of concern to the rapidly urbanizing developing countries. The authors suggest an integrative framework for which various IT trends can be harnessed to crowdfunding urbanization processes though the use of increasingly affordable mobile and other handheld devices for use in Web-tech, email-tech, social media-tech, SMS-tech, FinTech, 3D-tech. These technologies are destined to transform the financial system, and how urban actors work, live, shop and socialize.

Chapter 3 highlights the opportunities offered by sharing activities to realize the values derived from the crowd and the opportunities associated with the efficient use of underutilised assets, cost savings, environmental efficiency and the redistribution of wealth from corporations to individuals. Abubakar Benna highlights the impact that cohesive relationships of collaborative consumption based businesses is important in all contexts especially within the growing agricultural sector. At the nexus of smart cities and sharing economy, arise the sharing cities that optimize the mobilization and redistribution of financial resources using the efficiency of financial technologies. The efficient redistribution is possible through the application of mobile telecom that is already familiar to m-money, m-payments and alternative financing mechanisms, including, microfinance, social investment funds, crowdfunding, member owned financial institutions.

One striking feature of contemporary urbanization is the growth in informal urbanized settlements, which Chapter 4 shows to offer massive opportunities for transformation into a formal, innovative and inclusive urban system. Using India's example Jain, Sridharan and Korzhenevych advocate a strategy on how such transformation can be implemented. The strategy consists of financing instruments for infrastructure delivery, creating a decentralized infrastructure provision structure, and the introduction of innovative financial instruments. The financing instruments for infrastructure delivery components consists of "innovative value capture, user participation and the user-investor approach (crowdfunding), direct institutional investor engagement in a greenfield project, the multi-jurisdictional pooled approach, as well as socially-responsible financing.

Crowdsourcing offers opportunities in advancing Sustainable Urban Development (SUD) planning in Developing Countries. The crowdsourcing process has already generated innovative, broad-based, and inclusive models for urban planning and governance that gather and mobilize around heterogeneous social actors working toward sustainable, innovative and inclusive urban spaces. In Chapter 5, Abubakar reviews the conceptual and historical foundation of crowdsourcing, highlights some exemplary case studies of the utilization of crowdsourcing for SUD planning, and discusses the opportunities and challenges of crowdsourcing as a tool for creating exciting and sustainable urban systems in developing countries.

Section 2: Opportunities and Challenges in Crowdfunding Markets

In an increasingly globalized and interactive world fueled by knowledge and increasing application of networked digital technologies, comparative studies offer both benefits and drawbacks. They help draw teachable and practical lessons that can be shared across nations and cultures. Three of the four chapters compare African crowdfunding experiences with the global growth economies of Middle East, India and China. It is interesting to note that Africa shared varying periods of contact based on factors of religion (with the Middle East), common colonial experience (with India) and more recently resource-based investment relations (with China).

In Chapter 6, Sulaiman carries out a Comparative Analysis of Online Crowdfunding Platforms in Africa and the Middle East. These are among the fastest growing vital resource regions in the world and their future growth will likely influence world events. The two regions have much in common partly due to deep historic, cultural and religious interactions. The issues covered include the rise of the "crowd" as source of empowerment reflected by population size, level of urbanization, and the extent of human capital development resources needed to advance future growth. Although still in its nascent phase in both economies, donation crowdfunding, largely supported by foreign backers, seems more favored in Africa while equity model supported by local backers dominates the Middle East market, where multi-language portals are used, whereas application of local language is missing in Africa.

In Chapter 7, Dano and Benna compare the African and Indian Crowdfunding markets, whose key actors have grown over many decades with cumulative experiences spanning colonial, post-colonial nationalist fervor but without the real retooling necessary to deal with the demands of digital technology environments. Hence, most of public finance managers at the various levels of the public institutions, and to some extent the private, are new to the applications of digital technologies let alone how to manage them. Four main market models of crowdfunding -- donation, reward, peer-to-peer lending and equity – dominate both Africa and India. The growth drivers for crowdfunding include, but are not limited to the following: the real market need of alternative source of financing, the expansion of mobile technology, the use of online social media, platforms and networks, the rise of a middle class, and the active contribution of the Diaspora population.

Chirisa and Mukarwi provide a comparative analysis of African and Chinese crowdfunding markets in Chapter 8, to provide lessons in innovative urban development issues. The chapter finds the Africa markets lag behind their Chinese counterparts and suggest Africa can learn from the Chinese experience. It further argues that the low adoption of crowdfunding by Africa can be attributed to a number of factors, including national regulatory environments that are not conducive for crowdfunding of equity and debt, and unconducive technological environments where e-commerce is not widely utilized.

In Chapter 9, Indo Benna explores the use crowdsourcing as a tool for improving learning in tertiary institutions in developing countries, focusing on the Middle East. The increasing use of English to conduct global commerce, politics and knowledge development has increased its appeal among various cultures, where due to the rise in specialized knowledge, it is targeted for specific purposes in engineering, medicine, business and education. The author analyzes the process, evaluates the outcome of the crowdsourcing tool, and suggests that its application can keep higher education institutions in developing countries at the forefront of education and research innovation. It also prepares members in these institutions for innovative problem solving and for the challenges of the online world. After the rise of crowdsourcing in educational activities, the growing engagement of multilingual crowd, and the emergence of crowdsourcing culture, the author suggests a framework for curriculum development through crowdsoursing.

Section 3: Evolving Crowdfunding in Emerging Economies

As generally used by development actors, crowdfunding implies open online cash mobilization from individuals and groups. In Chapter 10, Abdullahi advocates the extension of the scope of crowdfunding to include the use of traditional offline and non-cash means to complement project development. While Information Technology has transformed conventional in-person volunteering on-site into online volunteering and civic participation, it has also reduced the scope of the application of human capital in many technologically challenged regions within Africa. The author points to studies showing active online volunteers are also active offline volunteers, suggesting that volunteering in one sphere can complement volunteering elsewhere and that volunteers can belong to multiple urban development agencies; thus maximizing the use of abundant human capital in areas of greatest needs of these emerging economies.

After accepting many potential benefits of crowdfunding in development process, Chirisa, Mukarwi, and Matamanda, in Chapter 11, suggest that the application of the concept in the Global South, is ill-understood and questionable considering the high levels of sleaze, poverty and ineffective governance. Perhaps the problem of overcoming these largely colonial legacies has resulted in slow progress of applying crowdfunding to generate adequate funds to emanate shortage of social services and facilities, let alone to plan and provide soft and hard infrastructure to match urban population growth. Africa has complex regional urbanization trends, development realities and growth directions. The disparities in level of urbanization, quality of cities, and culture and quality of urban actors suggest a uniform approach to policy is unworkable. In addition, there are regional levels of urban physical and socio-economic characteristics, levels of managerial resources to problems, and inadequate financial resources to tackle them.

With increased urbanization and more demand for urban services, many Indian cities are incapable of generating more than 50% of their resource demands. To enable them to face the future, substantial resource needs, Chandiramani and Patil in Chapter 12, advocate at least some of that has to come from civic crowdfunding sources. Part of its benefits is that civic crowdfunding allows citizens unprecedented access into infrastructure management through initial financing and decision-making. When civic projects compete for crowdfunding, success inherently relies on their popularity, appeal and marketability. It is envisaged that civic crowdfunding will also bring with it a much desired transparency and involvement of all stakeholders' in governance and a sense of ownership of the city. Moreover, to ensure the success of the models, it is necessary to prepare well-defined and detailed prototypes and operating plans that the authors feel will result in the cities being acknowledged for better delivery of urban services.

In Chapter 13, Ibrahim Benna draws attention to how crowdfunding can improve the quality of urban life; through enhanced energy policy in Africa. The quality of urban life can be enhanced greatly by means of careful urban design, which is achievable with high-energy efficiency using the traditional spatial tools that include selection of compact design, and urban management process that includes directed public participation, all of which can be funded through crowdfunding. As a late starter in the development process Africa has the distinct advantage of wider energy policies to choose from, a choice made relatively easy by sustainable development consideration and the rich potentials in renewable energy sources, especially solar because the Equator and rich agro-based energy sources bisect it.

Abdullahi complements his earlier chapter by exploring the application of volunteerism and use of alternative finance. In Chapter 14, he seeks to elaborate the possible roles of volunteer corps with respect to three broad development areas of national, regional and local significance; namely coordinating growth efforts in major development corridors across Nigeria, the reconstruction of urban centers in Boko-Haram affected areas, and the upgrading of city centers in each state. Through them, he explores potential impacts of all the volunteer corps in social, economic, and knowledge development in selected key sub-national and national development problem areas.

Umar G. Benna
Ahmadu Bello University, Nigeria

Abubakar U. Benna
University of Durham, UK

REFERENCES

Cambridge Centre for Alternative Finance (CCAF). (2017). *Africa and Middle East Alternative Finance Benchmarking Report*. Retrieved from https://www.jbs.cam.ac.uk/faculty-research/centres/alternative-finance/publications/africa-middle-east/#.Wd9nZFuCyvg

Statista. (2017). *Statista – The portal for statistics*. Retrieved from https://www.statista.com/

Acknowledgment

The development of an edited book of this nature—like crowdfunding a project—is not possible without the contributions of a truly global "crowd". The crowd, in this case, consists of a wide array of organizations, collaborative groups of scholars within and across-borders working together to produce chapters, the individual authors, the reviewers, and those who enhanced the quality of the book by copy-editing or testing manuscripts.

Specifically, we express our gratitude to the management of IGI-Global and in particular, Ms. Maria Rohde, Assistant Development Editor for this book and wish to thank the many universities and private organizations to which our authors are affiliated. We cannot quantify the contributions of our truly international "crowd" of authors, whose scientific approach to this innovative subject and the reviewers, whose critical comments, cogent corrections, and recommendations on the manuscripts assisted us to select the best from numerous papers submitted to the editorial board, to whose members we are also thankful. The full list of the members of the Editorial Board, the authors, and the reviewers is appended in this book. Finally, our sincere appreciation goes to all scholars in the emerging field of Alternative Finance, especially, Crowdfunding, who directly and indirectly made significant contributions to this book. We wish to acknowledge the valued intellectual resources that you invested in this field and together we have endeavored to contribute to the development of humankind.

And all praise be to God for guiding us through this project!

Umar G. Benna
Ahmadu Bello University, Nigeria

Abubakar U. Benna
Durham University, UK

Section 1

Opportunities and Challenges in Crowdfunding Markets

Chapter 1
Knowledge Networks, Crowds, and Markets:
A Social Entrepreneurship Project in Latin America

Blanca C. Garcia
El Colegio de la Frontera Norte (Colef), Mexico

ABSTRACT

In some knowledge-based urban contexts, a new way of conducting creativity and innovation is already operating quasi-independently of the current money system. Its chief ingredients are intangible assets such as time, imagination, knowledge, initiative, and trust, to which money has quickly moved from primary to secondary concern. In this context, this chapter explores their links to emerging models of Commons and Peer-to-Peer (P2P) economies in order to frame a recent crowdfunding experience in the Mexico-Texas borderland.

1. INTRODUCTION

As we move further onto the second decade of the millennium, a convergence of three key concepts: *urban networks, crowds*, and *markets* have increasingly gained emphasis both in theoretical and practical knowledge-based models in urban studies. This also could imply a more mature stage of understanding the dynamics of the *Commons*, and the challenges behind managing them. There is no easy path to it, but clearly, alternative regulating models are urgently needed as we further develop knowledge-based societies and economies, "at the center of which the logic of the *commons* would perform an essential role in how we handle organizations" (Vercellone,et.al., 2015:4). In such context, theoretical advancements from Elinor Ostrom's (2007), *Knowledge as a Commons*, to *cognitive capitalism, collaborative consumption,* or the more radical advancements of *Peer-to-Peer Economy* are urging us to develop *Commons*-based organization systems. They are above all, social constructions based on the value-creating capabilities of knowledge and self-governance logic, and not on the pre-assumed nature or value of goods. That is why practices for governance of commons loudly resonate, based on collaboration and

DOI: 10.4018/978-1-5225-3952-0.ch001

sharing. They portray elements of the *collaborative economy* and the *sharing economy* models in which shared resources and infrastructures promote the development of the commons, and they have started to act as a new significant form of economic and social organization. Emerging organizations like *Uber, Airbnb, Kickstarter, Cropital, Guardian Angels, Rockethub* and many others are examples of what some authors have already analyzed from the point of view of the *knowledge-based markets* model (Carrillo, et. al., 2014). Such organizations seem to thrive and actually address the emerging sustainability and resilience challenges of knowledge-based contexts, despite facing major difficulties in managing their key intangibles (knowledge, social relationships, rules and values, options) in order to keep the commons viable (Cantino, et. al., 2017).

In this context, this paper is aiming to dive into a literature review of Knowledge Cities as Knowledge Markets, and explore their links to emerging models of *Commons* and *Peer to Peer (P2P)* economies in order to frame a recent crowdfunding experience in the Mexico-Texas Borderland.

2. KNOWLEDGE CITY CONCEPTS

The *Knowledge City* concept is a subfield of Knowledge-based Development (KBD) and stems from a convergence of Urban Studies and Planning with Knowledge Management (KM) (Carrillo, 2006:xiii). In fact, KBD is the particularly distinctive third generation of KM, as shown in Table 1. While the first generation mainly addressed information storage, and the second generation made a clear shift "from collecting knowledge to connecting people" (Huysman and Wulf, 2005), the third KM generation is the generation of complex, deeply inter-connected systems of knowledge generation and knowledge exchange. It focuses on systemic, societal change analysis, which is becoming increasingly predominant: "in the next years, knowledge management theorists and practitioners will find themselves asking how revolutions can be managed" (Toumi, 2002). In such intriguing context, our globe is seemingly turning into a world of *parallel systems of meaning* (Toumi, 2004:1).

Within this multi-meaning universe, the emerging societies in different parts of our world are increasingly depending on international links and networks to live on: their communication activities become critically important in the social construction of *communities that learn* (Tuomi, 2004a:1). Hence, our unconventional exchanges of information, knowledge and experiences (i.e. over the Internet) are becoming permanent and personal processes of *meaning negotiation*. Message significance depends on who and where are the users at the moment of interaction. At the core of this complex makeover of the social, economic and technical sub-systems, sits the *system of learning* on which each of our societies rely on. Our systems of learning are historical societal structures now seemingly developing into *systems of meaning-creation* (Tuomi, 2004a:2) as the basis of learning systems in emerging knowledge-based societies. For the analysis of these knowledge-based contexts, emerging frameworks that could include the emerging complexities were critical to the sense-making process of prospective and development of cities. In a reflection on how value-based concepts develop in urban settings, some considerations on the progress and historic evolution of KM as a discipline are highly relevant as part of this study (as expressed in Table 1). The perspectives of Knowledge Management (KM) scholars (Tuomi, 2004; Huysman and Wulf, 2005; Carrillo, 2006) who have identified distinct and influential KM generations are essential to characterise the recent transformations in the discipline and their relevance in emerging research.

The third KM generation was triggered by notions such as *learning regions* that started to emerge as a framework for understanding development in a multi-dimensional, highly networked setting beyond

Table 1. Three generations of Knowledge Management (KM) vs. k-markets

Elements	First Generation of KM (ICT Systems)	2nd Generation of KM (Learning Orgs)	3rd Generation of KM (KBD, Knowledge Cities)	Transitional Generation of KM (K-Markets)
Agent	The individual and his/her capacity of knowledge transfer.	Communities (including emerging CoPs) and their potential for knowledge exchange.	Communities of Practice (CoPs) in cities and regions, linked for increased performance and knowledge-creation adding value to the knowledge-capitals of the city.	From Peer to Peer (P2P) or network to network, to clusters of networks. It is a multilevel macro-system of agents that interact simultaneously and between big and small units.
Support	Information Technologies supporting base repository systems	Information technologies supporting people's connectivity.	Networked information systems that enable people to permanently interact through conversations and knowledge moments.	Macro-systems of agents with specific roles: Seeker, Solver, Broker, Manager, Regulator (Carrillo, 2014) and 24/7 interaction.
Emphasis	Importance of systems that store and distribute knowledge.	Importance of systems that play a role in the construction and maintenance of the relational base of capital.	Importance of a system of systems that add value to interconnected capitals in order to raise human standards of living.	Importance of value transfer systems in which free and conscious agents engage in mutual satisfaction or in facilitating such satisfaction between third parties.
Objective	Distribution of instrumental capital	Human Capital Development.	Capital systems development.	Full Capital Systems Interplay. (Identity, Intelligence, Relational, Financial Human and Instrumental Capitals).
Context	Transfer	Transfer Exchange Use capacity	Transfer Exchange Use capacity Transaction regime	Transfer Exchange Use capacity Transaction regime Ownership

Source: Adapted from Huysman, M.H. and Wulf, V. (2005); and Carrillo, F. J. (2006, 2014).

city limits (Florida, 1995). Other parallel notions shaping this third generation are *intellectual capital systems* (Stewart, 1997), *innovation clusters* (Porter, 1995), *global networks* (World Bank, 2002), *capacity building strategies* (UNDP, 2002) and other related concepts. Such rich blend of theory and practice, is finding new theoretical expressions in frameworks such as the *Knowledge City* (KC): a city purposefully pursuing knowledge as a means for development (Carrillo, 2004), the *Ideopolis*: a city of Ideas and inclusive communities (Work Foundation, 2002); the *Creative City*, as a city driven by the creativity of its creative class and milieu; and the *Intelligent City* which heavily relies on social intellect, IC mapping, virtual connectivity and the strong capacities of its citizen story-tellers (Pricewaterhouse-Coopers, 2005).

In the context of the *Knowledge Economy* (Burt, 2000), from Weber's classical definition of a city as: "a settlement that does not live on agriculture but on trade and services" (Weber, 1958:66), cities as units of analysis for research are progressively being understood primarily as productive entities (Amin, et.al. 2003:3; Carrillo, 2004:29). In it, the *Knowledge City* (KC) concept is defined as "short hand for a regional economy driven by high value added exports created through research, technology and brain power (Melbourne City Council, 2002; in Ergazakis, et.al. 2004:6). A Knowledge City invests significantly more of the community's income (GDP) in education, training and research" (Melbourne City Council, 2002; in Ergazakis, et.al. 2004:6). In fact, It's

... a region that bases its ability to create wealth on its capacity to generate and leverage its knowledge capabilities. In a knowledge capital, enterprises and people link to form knowledge-based extended networks to achieve strategic goals, cultivate innovation and successfully respond to rapidly changing conditions. (Chatzkel, 2004:62).

In brief, a Knowledge city is a city 'purposefully designed to nurture knowledge" (Edvinsson, 2002; in Dvir and Pasher, 2004:17); a city "in which its citizenship undertakes a deliberate, systematic attempt to identify and develop its capital system, with a balanced and sustainable approach" (Carrillo, 2004:34).

But although the terminology is new, there are a number of historical examples of cities that follow the KC pattern. They evoke historical elements of core cities of the past, where open, informal places were the space for knowledge to be liberally shared. As modern Agora, *Knowledge Cities* encompass the underlying assumption that knowledge and ideas are created mainly through *conversations* (Dvir and Pasher, 2004:17, 21). Such assumption positions learning, innovation and clustering at the core of some theories of knowledge-creation, strongly influenced by Michael Porter's work (1995). Not surprisingly, recent literature on the role of universities in the knowledge-based economy tends to highlight three essential functions: the training of highly qualified personnel, the performance of research and the transfer of knowledge for economic growth (Wolfe, 2004). It is argued in this literature that "the joint production and transmission of new knowledge occurs most effectively amongst economic actors located close to each other" (Wolfe, 2004:16). It is also thought that 'synchronous face-to-face interactions matter for transmitting (non-bit string) knowledge' (Quah, 2002:39), as

Researchers must work somewhere and so might well cluster geographically because communication of tacit knowledge, not digital goods, is most efficient in close physical proximity. (Quah, 2002:36).

In emerging Knowledge Cities, the dynamics of learning and clustering are encouraging knowledge-intensive organizations and institutions, characterising them as 'engines of innovation' and major agents of change and economic growth (Wolfe, 2004:1). Innovation is progressively understood as "knowledge-based innovation" or the creation and application of marketable goods and services exchanged in ***knowledge-markets*** for the advancement of society as a whole (Dvir and Pasher, 2004:17, Carrillo, 2010).

3. KNOWLEDGE MARKETS, NETWORKS AND CROWDS IN CITIES

A lot of the measurable social capital of human communities is triggered by interactions in the marketplace. The internet, extranets, and intranets, are increasing those interactions exponentially (i.e. e-Bay, Amazon, FaceBook Marketplace etc.). That's also a promise for *knowledge markets* (Davis, 2007). This vision of *Knowledge Markets* is conglomerating notions of knowledge-based agents, social capital and learning through conversations, in which networks are the core basic structure and scaffolding of urban reality.

Such networks are part of cities' capitals (i.e. relational capital), and it can take different forms. With time, as the city's population grows and diversifies, so does its knowledge, and the channels and networks through which it is distributed. Portes indicates: "whereas economic capital is in people's bank accounts, and human capital is inside their heads, social capital inheres in the structure of their relationships... To possess social capital, a person must be related to others, and it is those others, not himself, who are the actual source of his or her advantage" (Portes,1998:7). Clearly, in the e-learning realm, social capital concepts like this have triggered swift advancements, with new dynamic and powerful forms of *network weaving*. Some scholars believe that "something ground-breaking is to emerge" with a critical mass of people now "aware of one another and adeptly making use of microblogging — talking *and* listening — to become acquainted with one another and building mutual trust and knowledge". People who purposefully create social capital are thought as first-rate *knowledge network weavers* (Paquet, 2010). In these emerging Knowledge Cities, new intersections of social capital, entrepreneurship, knowledge, innovation, money, and finance are at the forefront. However, innovation is no longer about financial investments. It is more about time, imagination, knowledge, initiative and trust. In these contexts, visionaries such as Sebastien Paquet see "an emerging set of tools and customs -- cognitive infrastructure, when you think about it -- that will give us the necessary scaffolding to grow a multitude of *virtual cities*". These cities will bring together people with shared values and orientations towards the future, and who are in a position to collaborate to bring something new into the world. "They are part and parcel of the emerging Relationship Economy" (Paquet, 2010).

Indeed, KM3 views learning as knowledge creation: a *collective, constructive* and *conversational knowledge-acquisition process* (Scott, 2005). Hence the underlying assumption is that learning is fundamentally the result of our social interactions. Moreover, conversations with knowledgeable peers can provide "a milieu which triggers and enables an intensive, on-going, rich, diverse, and complex flow of *Knowledge Moments*" (Dvir, 2006:245). The concept of a knowledge moment is still elusive in the literature on Knowledge Cities, but has been defined as "a conversation between (or even within) people in a particular place, using structured and unstructured processes aimed at explicit or implicit purposes" (Dvir, 2006:271). It is thought that a knowledge moment constitutes "a spontaneous or planned human experience in which knowledge is discovered, created, nourished, exchanged and transformed into a new form" (Dvir, 2006:245), intrinsically linked to collective learning experiences. Such notion of knowledge moments for knowledge creation and sharing will prove to be useful as this study on crowdfunding for social development progresses.

Hence, the notion of *crowd funding* comes naturally embedded in the social structures created by the knowledge markets and knowledge networks interactions. For the purposes of this chapter, it can be advanced that *crowdfunding is a type of knowledge market*, with some specific features. In the knowledge-based development literature on the subject, Carrillo (2014) has provided a consolidated typology of knowledge markets, on the basis of the following criteria: A knowledge market is a) Capital-inclusive, b) Translational, c) Formal, d) Flexible, e) Bottom-up and f) Transformative (Carrillo, 2014:250). This taxonomy can accommodate both face-to-face and virtual transactions, and can be grouped in ten main categories and subcategories, with some sample initiatives (shown in Table 2).

According to these criteria, *crowd funding* can be classified under the Crowd Dealing type of generic knowledge market which is seemingly "one of the most successful and rapidly evolving forms of market organization" (Carrillo, 2014: 253). *Crowd dealing* involves a collective effort in favor of political campaign funding, scientific research, venture capital raising, and social innovation. Hence, *crowd funding* can be defined as "the direct financial funding of projects by a community, brought together by common interests online" (Carrillo, 2014: 254). There are a good number of initiatives and websites for crowd funding, of which a well-known example is *Kickstarter*. Like many others, it conveys a funding platform for different creative projects, ranging from comics and videogames to fashion, film and food, with a time limit to raise the necessary funds for individuals projects. It is reputed to be a safe, user-friendly and effective platform. Other international crowd funding efforts are *Start some good*, (https://startsomegood.com/projects) and *Go fund me* (https://www.gofundme.com). This latter one was recently

Table 2. Knowledge markets typology

No.	Knowledge Market	Knowledge Submarket	Initiatives
a	Intellectual Capital Dealing	• IP Trading • Technology Trading • IC Trading • Intellectual Capital Partnerships	• Unit License Right Contract • WSJ Technology Sector Market Map • *JobsInAcademia.org* • Georgia IC Partnership Program
b	Open Dealing	• Peer-to-Peer • Customer-to-customer • Open Sourcing • Open innovation • Transparency	• P2P Foundation • *eBay.com* • *Linux; Mozilla Firefox; Wikipedia* • *Innocentive; Seeks Solutions* • *Opensecrets*
c	Crowd Dealing	• Crowd funding • Crowd Casting • Crowd Testing • Crowd working	• *Kickstarter; Indiegogo,* • *Crowdcast* • *Mob4Hire* • *Genius Rocket*
d	Cooperative Dealing	• Co-operativism • Collaborative Consumption • Co-housing • Co-sharing • Co-working	• *Co-Operation.org, the Co-operative Group* • *Zipcar; Taskrabbit* • *Cohousing.org* • *Refashioner* • *Co-working wiki; Citizen Space*
e	Non-monetary Dealing	• Frugal Innovation • Self-Sufficiency • Moneyless Initiatives • Pay-it-forward Initiatives • Cognitive surplus • Voluntarism	• *Mitti Cool Fridge* project in India • *DIY Network; DoItYourself.com* • Loyalty Programs, Blood Banks • Pifexperience.com • Wikipedia • Eurofund
f	Social Dealing	• Social Innovation • Social Entrepreneurship • Micro-entrepreneurship	• *Firefly; KinkaJou* • *Ashoka* • *Reuters Market Light*
g	Alternative Currencies & Incentive Regimes	• Digital Money • Local Currencies • Tokens • Incentive Regimes	• *Bitcoin; Mintchip* • *Fureai Kippu* in Japan. • *Tookets* • *Foldit*
h	Alternative Banking	• Barter • Pawn Brokering • State Lotteries • Food Banks • Time Banks • Skill Banks • Physical Assets Banks • Service Banks • Space Banks • Public Banking • Alternative Lending • P2P Lending	• *Skillsbarter* • (ancient practice) • *Norsk Tipping* (National Lottry in Norway) • *San Francisco Food Bank* • *Comunitats (Spain)* • *Taskrabbit* • *RelayRides* • *Vayable* • *Airbnb* • *Public Banking Institute* • *Coalition of Community Development* • *Zopa*
i	Open Social Learning	• Citilabs • Fablabs • Hacklabs • Living Labs • Tech Shops • Innovation Bootcamps	• *Citilab* Barcelona • *Fablab* Manchester • *Hackerspaces* • *European Network of Living Labs* • *Techshop* • *The Board of Innovation Bootcamp*
j	Social Network Markets	• Professional Social Networks • Social Media • Virtual Communities	• *Internations; Linked In* • *About.com* • *Coursera, Facebook, Wikis*

Source: Adapted from Carrillo, F. J., et. Al. (2014).

praised for the capabilities put in place in trying to save Charlie Gard's life, a UK born baby with a rare disease in urgent need for surgery in the US. Charlie's parents raised £1.2m through more than 34,000 donations by setting up a crowdfunding campaign in *Go fund me* to help take their son to the US. The amount raised was enough to finance his care in the United States. However, in June, London's Supreme Court ruled that Charlie could not be sent overseas, reasoning that any additional treatment would only prolong the child's suffering. This heartbreaking story highlights nevertheless the role and power of crowdfunding efforts for humanitarian and any other worthwhile causes.

4. CITIES IN THE COMMONS ECONOMY

At the macro level, there have been numerous attempts to generate awareness on international networks' social capital. These frameworks have now multiplied and streamed into converging paradigms, such as: *Fair Trade, Ethical Banking, Social Economy, Solidarity Economy, Commons Economy, Transition Town, Degrowth, Blue Economy, Circular Economy*, amongst many others. For the purposes of this chapter, we would like to mention only two of these concepts, as they will be useful for the kind of crowdfunding example we intend to build. Moreover, as traditional capitalism faces a series of structural crises, unsuspected social, political and economic dynamics are emerging. Along with *crowd dealing*, *open dealing* is an element that could develop a Peer-to-Peer (P2P) Economy. P2P ideally describes "systems in which any human being can contribute to the creation and maintenance of a shared resource, while benefiting from it" (Felber, 2012). There is an enormous variety of such systems: from free Wikipedia to free/open-software projects, to open design and hardware communities; also re-localization initiatives and community currencies (Bauwens, 2015). Seemingly, the key point of P2P social structure is that it has the capacity to allocate resources that do not involve any specific reciprocity between individuals, but only between the individuals and the collective resource. Now, the concept and action of *commoning*, is used in the sense that it describes the capacity to contribute to the creation and maintenance of any shared resource. Although there are multiple definitions of "the "commons", for the purposes of this paper we will adhere to David Bollier's characterization of the commons as "a shared resource, co-governed by its user community according to the rules and norms of that community" (Bollier, 2011[1]).

This view of commons includes water and land, but also shared assets or creative work such as digital commons, cultural and knowledge artefacts, also known as the *new commons*. In that sense, commons-based peer production, (P2P) are the seed of a new social model. Indeed, notions and typologies of knowledge markets are undoubtedly the foundational basis of city-building, and is taking unchartered shapes and forms as the next paragraphs will describe, with Latin American examples of crowdfunding platforms such as *Codeando México* (www.codeandomexico.org).

5. THE NATIONAL SCENARIO: CODEANDO MEXICO – HACKERS FOR CITIZEN PARTICIPATION

Codeando México is a non-governmental Mexican organization (ONG) dedicated to build a community of technologists and citizens who join efforts to develop technology in order to solve public and social problems on a permanent basis. It started up during the *Developing Latin America* conference in December 2012 and formally began its operations in July 2013.

According to *Codeando México*[2] (CMX)'s CEO, Miguel Salazar, *the organization* defines itself as "a hacking movement that does not need a lot of resources to show that there are other ways to exercise citizenship." CMX mission is to convene technologists, social scientists, artists and activists to work together, and coordinate their strengths. This can result in a powerful formula for cracking the problems of any given society. However, finding the ideal talent who shows commitment to join this cause has proven to be difficult. Finding those committed technologists has been one of the main obstacles to the growth of the *Codeando Mexico* organization, a core player in the Latin American horizon of Open Data initiatives. Unlike common belief, CMX believes Mexico has a lot of human capital in the area of technology. However, they are usually busy working and maybe looking to start their own projects. Those developers are the ones the organization aims to reach. CMX aims to have a positive impact on society in various ways. From creating more open governments, to transforming the ways citizens interact with government. Despite the talent availability obstacle, the organization has had impressive achievements. *Codeando México* gathers software developers, technologists, designers, citizens, public officials, scientists, artists and other organizations that find in technology a means to solve problems in Mexican society. A core full time team supports them all as to facilitate the processes of citizen participation through technology.

An example of CMX initiatives are *Public Challenges*, a platform where the technological community seeks to solve governance challenges. Fifteen challenges have been launched, from 10 federal agencies in Mexico, and there are more than 1,290 participating firms.

In parallel, the *Civic Challenges* initiative is also in place, in which citizens collaborate to solve social sector challenges. Over 50 challenges have been uploaded on the platform, from more than 13 organizations, and the number of participants exceeds 1,300. All this is done under a logic of open and collaborative work, as it is in the spirit and philosophy of Open Data.

Another of *Codeando México*'s projects is *Datamx*, where civil society organizations, citizens and technologists can open and share data or download them to develop civic applications. This project is the first and only citizen data platform open in Mexico, and thus obtained the first place in the National Award for Innovation in Transparency 2015. It has more than 1000 open datasets and the participation of more than 45 organizations. Civil society, business and government publishing data.

Lastly, *Codeando México*'s is also focusing on creating local communities of *civic hacking*. These are groups of citizens who come together to identify local problems, propose technological solutions to those problems, and develop collaborative solutions. They have communities in 10 different cities within Mexico, and anyone can start a community in their city, as a local chapter for *Codeando México*. In fact, *Hack Your City* is an exercise that seeks to promote civic hacking and the development of civic technology in college students. Initially the program was carried out at universities in cities like Monterrey (North of the country, see next paragraphs) and Guadalajara (West region of Mexico), and will soon reach more cities. This extensive collaborative work has been the result of the collaboration of government agencies and networks at all levels (federal, state and local), as well as with other civil society organizations, academia and the private sector. Financially, *Codeando México* is supported by Avina Foundation[3] and Microsoft Mexico.

Seemingly, at the Latin American level, Mexico is a benchmark in open data. This is a favourable circumstance for the CMX team. In fact, data.gob.mx is one of the largest open data repositories in the Latin American region. The fact that there is a strong political initiative to open up a greater amount of data facilitates part of the work. However, there are always organizations that are not open to change. Sometimes there is a very large generational gap between the CMX team and the people working in these organizations and it is difficult to come up and talk about civic technology and open data. However, some efforts are in place, such as the Latin American Open Data Initiative (ILDA), which helps create spaces for collaboration among organizations in different countries to put issues on the table for discussion.

Moreover, the *Codeando México*, main method of incidence is the development of technology that attacks specific problems, which qualify as "preaching by example". The kind of message that *Codeando Mexico* wants to give is the following: It is not necessary to invest millions, not to do a great research, nor to discuss an idea for months to be able to see its first outcomes and solutions. As CMX CEO points out, with a little talent, creativity and hours of programming, people are able to do quite good and useful things for other citizens.

6. THE REGIONAL SCENARIO: CODEANDO MONTERREY – OPEN SOURCE CITIES FOR CITIZEN PARTICIPATION AND PROJECT METHODOLOGY

As mentioned earlier, *Codeando México* has a few regional chapters in key cities around the country. The *Hack Your City* exercise was carried out at universities in cities like Monterrey, a Northern city located at a three-hour drive from the Mexico-Texas border. Monterrey is the capital city of Nuevo León, one of the four Mexico's border states near Texas, USA. The following is an account of my individual participation in an exercise that the Monterrey Tech students developed to support *Codeando Monterrey*[4] initiatives in the city.

Figure 1. Mexico border map
Source: Adapted from SEMARNAT (2011).

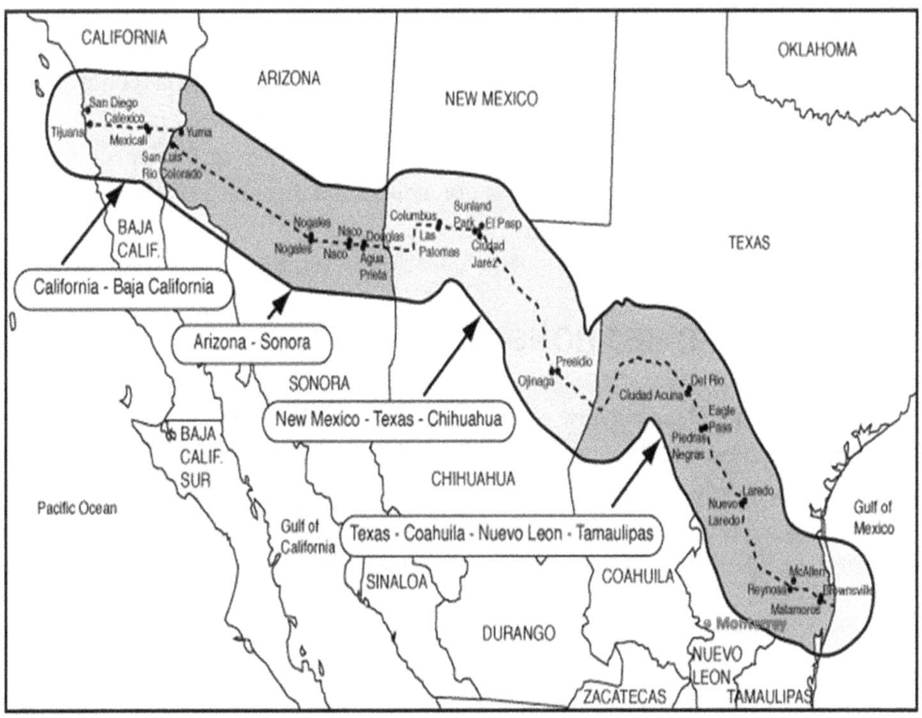

The research exercise consisted of creating a scenario analysis on the Open Source Cities prospective for the city of Monterrey by year 2021 (five years after the exercise took place). The students' strategy included collaboration with the *Codeando Mexico* organization within its Monterrey chapter. The project aimed to seek a solution for public and social problems using technology, by activating technological communities towards new forms of citizen participation. Research students used an Open Source (OS) Cities framework, which defined OS Cities as those who show these specific features: a) active and participatory citizenship, b) open and efficient government policies, c) public open data policies, d) a transverse economic development plan and also e) a center of innovation and f) Open Source private sector organizations. The feasibility of incorporating these characteristics into the development model of the city of Monterrey by the year 2021 would be evaluated by a panel of experts from four different areas, and would be done considering a five-year time frame, from survey administration date, and taking into account the exponential acceleration of information and communication technologies (ICTs).

In order to carry out this research work, the Regnier's Abacus method was used to identify possible scenarios and the IGO (Decision Matrix) technique to propose a concrete and relevant strategy for the *Codeando Monterrey* organization. It was expected that these tools would be the most adequate methodology for achieving the objectives of this prospective project and that it would facilitate the visualization of an ecosystem favourable to the exchange of positions and arguments among the experts participating in this collaborative work. The specific aim of the project was to generate a prospective study on the future possibilities of implementing the Open Code cities model in the Metropolitan Area of Monterrey by the year 2021. Moreover, a specific objective of the research was to identify realistic scenarios for the Open Code cities model in Monterrey by 2021, and propose a strategy to reach those scenarios. In this singular exercise, through the exchange of experiences and opinions, an enrichment on the perceptions of experts on the Open Source Model was sought after. The Regnier's Abacus allowed for remote participation and interaction of experts, which was crucial for the exercise. It helped to create an interactive environment that facilitated open participation, dialogue, negociation of meanings and internal reflection of the participants. Also, the operational nature of the technique allowed friendly facilitation, without the need to request extra time from experts. As for the Decision Matriz technique (IGO), it was particularly powerful offering a number of good alternatives to choose from, and many different factors to take into account. It was an adequate techinque to use in order to favour the decision-making process proposed by (junior) researchers, where there was not a clear and obvious preferred option for an Open Source City Model in the short term for Monterrey.

7. FUTURE RESEARCH DIRECTIONS

Open Source City Models are clearly a new research path in the Mexican community, emphasizing two core dimensions: significance and governance of emerging frameworks. And in *Codeando Monterrey* case, the team could choose which Open Source city model has better possibilities in view of Monterrey by 2021, as a future research direction. These circumstances, linked to the new and better technologies in the public sector, could trigger the possibility of exponential democratization in contexts like the Mexico-Texas border.

Ii ts thought that in the midst of technological acceleration, borderland regions can assume the connectivity that the Internet promises to trigger intense knowledge exchange, as well as real-time good practices happening in other parts of the world. This accelerated connectedness growth could provide unanticipated opportunities to its population, especially in terms of governance. Clearly, traditional means of maintaining contact are no longer enough, and this is blatantly true especially in the public sector. However, little by little, the Internet has made it easier for civil societies to follow and audit processes of transparency and accountability from their governments, as well as facilitating access to the Education through multiple free platforms. These are clearly the seeds for Open Source and Crowd Dealing models to take root in regios such as Latin America and the Northern region of Mexico.

The principles of the Commons Economy and the P2P Economy are ever more present in such contexts, even if their traditions and culture dictate otherwise. Recent events such as the discovery of the Panama Papers reflect the importance of free information flows and open source repositories, even if it generates hot debates. Clearly, there are still a lot of things to build for a more democratic Mexico, such as larger citizen participation. However, Monterrey is a city that has seen significant advancements in terms of civil society mobilization, led both by universities and civil society organizations. As a first timer, the independent governor has yet to prove that a democratically elected government actually works. But during his campaign and in the process of consolidating the State Development Plan, it was clear that he was making a impact in the Democracy history of Nuevo Leon (our State) and also in the eyes of the entire nation in Mexico. It created a certain expectation of the future. Hence, such small changes in the democratic atmosphere of Monterrey, the capital city of Nuevo León, are variables that Open Source initiatives could bank on. An optimism for a different future actually triggered a possibility to consolidate models such as the Open Source Cities model, and to move on building city features advanced by Civil society organizations such as *Codeando Monterrey*. Thus, they could become the main promoters of a collective effort to reach ruling of Open data public policies, leading to a truly Open government.

On the other hand, the interest of (local) large corporations in promoting technology, could also represent an opportunity for *Codeando Monterrey* to boost its vision for social problem solutions through technology with the financial support of the multiple corporations of the region. In brief, the identified strategies would allow *Codeando Monterrey* to push towards the model of Open Source cities quite significantly. Even if in 5 years access to widespread use of the Internet and other technological tools is not a 100% probability, a significant progress towards this specific goal can be expected to support the transformation of Monterrey's urban milieu.

8. CONCLUSION

Hence, as this chapter advances practical evidence of Knowledge City concepts embedded in the networks, markets and crowds universe within the KDB discipline, particular aspects of the Commons Economy models led us to identify new social forms of organization likely to emerge. Most importantly, the chapter has attempted to portray how Knowledge City definitions are intertwined in the rising of *P2P Economy* and *Relational Society* frameworks. In such context, a glimpse of the role played by different capital systems, has revealed them as articulators of Open Dealing and Crowd Dealing principles within Mexico's urban communities.

Also, following a deeper sense of urgency, this Chapter has aimed to contribute to the meaning creation of emerging forms of social organization, where K-City schemes for sustainable development are also more than ever likely to be revealed. In fact, as more radical networks, markets and crowds frameworks converge, they could portray a more balanced and realistic outlook of complex capital systems in the global KBD arena. Indeed, as notions of *Knowledge Markets* continue to be present in KBD practice, further theoretical aspirations could develop the social organization shapes here presented. The gap in the literature in regards of the understanding of how urban communities are built, still stands as how they thrive in emerging relational contexts such as the *Economy of the Commons*. As the challenges and findings of this research are on the table of discussions, further advancements of the *Knowledge City* and Open Source City frameworks in theory and practice is intently expected.

REFERENCES

Allen, S., Deragon, J. T., Orem, M., & Smith, C. F. (2009). *The Emergence of the Relationship Economy: The New Order of Things to Come*. Retrieved from http://www.happyabout.com/RelationshipEconomy.php

Bauwens, M. and Lievens, J. (2015). *Sauver le monde, Vers une société post-capitaliste avec le peer-to-peer*. Paris: Les liens qui liberent, Editorial.

Bollier, D. (2011). Intellectual Property in the Digital Age. In *Key Issues in the Arts and Entertainment Industry*. London: Goodfellow Publishers. Retrieved from http://bollier.org/ip-digital-age-book-chapter

Bourdieu, P. (1990) *Capital Social, Ecole et Space Culturel*. Paris: XXIe Siecle.

Brown, J. S., & Duguid, P. (1991). Organizational learning and communities of practice: Toward a unified view of working, learning and innovation. *Organization Science*, *2*(1), 40–57. doi:10.1287/orsc.2.1.40

Brown, J. S., & Duguid, P. (2000). *The Social Life of Information*. Boston, MA: Harvard Business School Press.

Burt, R. (2000). *The network structure of social capital. In Research in Organisational Behaviour* (Vol. 22). Greenwich, CT: JAI Press.

Cantino, V., Rossignoli, C., & Ricciardi, F. (2017). Organizational learning for the common good: an emerging approach to sustainability and resilience. In *IFKAD 2017 Special Tracks Proposal*. Retrieved from http://www.ifkad.org/Tracks/?track=01

Carrillo, F. J. (2002). Capital systems: implications for a global knowledge agenda. Journal of Knowledge Management, 6(4).

Carrillo, F. J. (2004). Capital cities: a taxonomy of capital accounts for knowledge cities. Journal of Knowledge Management, 8(5), 28-46. doi:10.1108/13673270410558738

Carrillo, F. J. (Ed.). (2006). Knowledge Cities. Approaches, Experiences and Perspectives. Burlington, MA: Butterworth-Heinemann (Elsevier).

Carrillo, J., Yigitcanlar, T., Garcia, B., & Lonnqvist, A. (2014). *Knowledge & the City. Concepts and Applications of Knowledge-Based Development*. Routledge.

Castells, M. (2004). *The Network Society: A Cross-Cultural Perspective*. Cheltenham, UK: Edward Edgar. doi:10.4337/9781845421663

Cervantes, M.E., Casillas, L., Weigend, J., & Hoppenstedt, S (2016). *Open Source Cities: Monterrey 2021*. Prospectiva Estratégica, ITESM.

Chatzkel, J. (2004). Greater Phoenix as a knowledge capital. *Journal of Knowledge Management, 8*(5), 28-46.

Cobo, C. (2013). Gobierno Abierto: de la transparencia a la inteligencia cívica. *Info DF*, 11.

Coopers, P. (2005). *Cities of the Future. Global competition Local leadership*. Available from www.pwc.com

Davenport, T., & Prusak, L. (1998). *Working Knowledge: How organisations manage what they know*. Boston: Harvard Business School Press.

Dewey, J. (1949). *Knowing and the Known*. American institute for Economic Research. Available on line at: http://www.aier.org/research

Dvir, R. (2006). Knowledge City seen as a collage of Human Knowledge Moments. In Knowledge Cities. Approaches, Experiences and Perspectives. Burlington, MA: Butterworth-Heinemann (Elsevier). doi:10.1016/B978-0-7506-7941-1.50022-1

Dvir, R., & Pasher, E. (2004). Innovation engines for knowledge cities: an innovation ecology perspective. Journal of Knowledge Management, 8(5), 16-27.

Easley, D., & Kleinberg, J. (2010). *Networks, Crowds and Markets. Reasoning about a Highly Connected World*. Cambridge, UK: Cambridge University Press. doi:10.1017/CBO9780511761942

Edvinsson, L. (2002). *Corporate Longitude*. Harlow: Pearson Education.

Edvinsson, L., & Grafstrom, G. (1999). *Accounting of Minds*. Stockholm, Sweden: Skandia.

Engeström, Y. (2004). New forms of learning in Co-configuration work. *Journal of Workplace Learning, 16*(1/2), 11–21. doi:10.1108/13665620410521477

Ergazakis, K., Metaxiotis, K., & Psarras, J. (2004). Towards knowledge cities: conceptual analysis and success stories. Journal of Knowledge Management, 8(5), 5-15.

Felber, C. (2012). *The economy of the common good*. Bilbao: Ed. Deusto.

Florida, R. (1995). Towards the Learning Region. *Futures, 27*(5), 527–536. doi:10.1016/0016-3287(95)00021-N

Fox, J. (2008). *Accountability Politics: Power and Voice in Rural Mexico*. Oxford Studies in Democratization Series.

Gándara, G. Y., & Osorio, F. (2014). *M étodos prospectivos. Manual para el estudio y la construcción del futuro*. Paidós.

Garcia, B. (2007, October). Working and Learning in a Knowledge City: A Framework for Knowledge Workers. *Journal of Knowledge Management*, *11*(5), 18–30. doi:10.1108/13673270710819771

García Nales, M. C. (2010). *Gobernanza local: alcances y limitaciones conceptuales*. San Luis Potosí: El Colegio de San Luis.

Giddens, A. (1984). *The Constitution of Society: outline of the theory of structuration*. Berkeley, CA: University of California Press.

Gundry, J. (2006). *Web 0.0 Social Media*. Paper from Knowledge Ability Ltd, Malmesbury, UK. Retrieved from www.knowab.co.uk/socialmedia.html

Halal, W. E. (2005). *Making sense of knowledge*. Bradford, UK: Emerald Publishing.

Huysman, M., & Wulf, D. (2005). The role of Information Technology in building and sustaining the relational base of communities. The Information Society, (21), 81-89. doi:10.1080/01972240590925285

Huysman, M. H. (2003). Communities of Practice: Towards a second generation of Knowledge Management. Human Resource Development, 4(4).

Huysman, M. H., & de Wit, D. (2004). Practices in Knowledge sharing: Towards a second generation of Knowledge Management. *Knowledge and Process Management*, *11*(2), 81–92. doi:10.1002/kpm.192

Kriščiūnas, K., & Daugeliene, R. (2006). The assessment models of knowledge-based economy penetration. *The Engineering Economist*, *50*(5), 36–46.

Lave, J., & Wenger, E. (1991). *Situated Learning. Legitimate Peripheral Participation*. Cambridge, UK: Cambridge University Press. doi:10.1017/CBO9780511815355

Melbourne City Council. (2002). *Melbourne City Plan 2010*. Melbourne City Council Official Documentation. Retrieved from http:www.melbourne.vic.gov.au/cityplan/infopage.cfm?tid=*1

Monge, P. R., & Contractor, N. S. (2003). *Theories of Communication Networks*. New York: Oxford University Press. Retrieved from www.uiuc.edu/ph/www/nosh

Moravec, J. (2008). *Knowmads in Web 3.0*. Retrieved from http://www.educationfutures.com/2008/11/20/knowmads-in-society-30/

Nonaka, I. (1991). The Knowledge Creating Company. Harvard Business Review, 69(6), 96-105.

Olson, M. (1965). *The Logic of Collective Action: Public Goods and the Theory of Groups*. Cambridge, MA: Harvard University Press.

Open Knowledge Foundation. (2011). *Open Knowledge Foundation*. Available from: http://web.archive.org/web/20131109174520/http://opendefinition.org/okd/esp anol/

Osborne, M., Kearns, P., & Yang, J. (2013). Learning Cities: Developing Inclusive, Prosperous and Sustainable Urban Communities. International Review of Education, 59(4), 409-423.

Ostrom, E. (1990). *Governing the Commons: The Evolution of Institutions for Collective Action*. Cambridge, MA: Cambridge University Press. doi:10.1017/CBO9780511807763

Ostrom, E., & Hess, C. (2007). *Understanding knowledge as a commons: from theory to practice*. Cambridge, MA: MIT Press.

Paquet, S. (2010). *What are Emergent Cities?* Retrieved on 3 Nov 2010, from: http://emergentcities.sebpaquet.net/what-are-emergent-cities

Porter, M. (1995, May). The Competitive advantage of the Inner City. *Harvard Business Review*.

Portes, A. (1998). Social Capital: its origins and applications in modern sociology. Annual Review of Sociology, 24.

Putman, R. (Ed.). (2002). *Democracies in Flux: The Evolution of Social Capital in Contemporary Society*. Oxford, UK: Oxford University Press.

Quah, D. (2002). *Digital goods and the New Economy*. Centre for Economic Performance, London School of Economics. Available at: http://cep.lse.ac.uk/pubs/download/dp0563.pdf

Sassen, S. (2002). *Global networks, Linked Cities*. New York: Routledge.

Savage, Ch. (1990). *Fifth Generation Management. Integrating enterprises through human networking*. Bedford: Digital Press.

Scott, B. (2005). *Introduction to conversation Theory: Applications in education and Epistemology*. Paper presented in the Higher Education Academy seminar: e-Learning, University of Manchester. Available on line at: http://www.omg.mcs.cranfield.ac.uk

Seufert, A., Krogh, G. von, & Back, A. (1999). Towards knowledge networking. *Journal of Knowledge Management, 3*(3), 180-190. Retrieved on 3 October 2011: http://citeseerx.ist.psu.edu/viewdoc/download?doi=10.1.1.116.9649&rep=rep1&type=pdf

Seufert, A., Krogh, G. von, & Back, A. (2003). Unleashing the power of networks for knowledge management: putting knowledge networks into action. In Knowledge management and networked environments. Amacom.

Seufert, A., & Seufert, S. (1998). Knowledge Creation and Transfer in Knowledge Networks. IO Management, 67, 77-84.

Siemens, G. (2006). *Knowing Knowledge*. Retrieved on 21st Nov 2006, from: http://www.elearnspace.org/KnowingKnowledge_LowRes.pdf

Stewart, T. (1997). *Intellectual Capital: The new wealth of Organisations*. New York: Doubleday/Currency.

Tuomi, I. (2002). The Future of Knowledge Management. *Lifelong Learning in Europe (LLinE), 7*(2), 69-79. Available at: http://www.meaningprocessing.com/personalPages/tuomi/articles/FutureOfKnowledgeManagement.pdf

Tuomi, I. (2004a). *Future Challenges of the European Knowledge Society*. Paper presented at Institute for Prospective Technological Studies. Available at: http://www.meaningprocessing.com/personalPages/tuomi/articles/TheFutureOfTheEuropeanKnowledgeSociety.pdf

Tuomi, I. (2004b). *Knowledge sharing and the idea of Public Domain*. Paper presented at the Unesco 21st Century Dialogue on Building Knowledge Societies. Available at: http://www.meaningprocessing.com/personalPages/tuomi/articles/KnowledgeSharingAndTheIdeaOfPublicDomain.pdf

United Nations Development Programme (UNDP). (2002). Developing Capacity through Technical Cooperation: Country Experiences. London: Overseas Development Institute.

Varnelis, K. (2010). *The meaning of network culture*. Retrieved on 14th January 2010, from: http://www.eurozine.com/articles/2010-01-14-varnelis-en.html

Vercellone, C., Bria, F., Fumagalli, A., Gentilucci, E., Giuliani, A., Griziotti, G., & Vattimo, P. (2015). *Managing the commons in the knowledge economy*. Retrieved from https://www.nesta.org.uk/publications/d-cent-managing-commons-knowledge-economy

Vygotsky, L. S. (1986). *Thought and Language*. Cambridge, MA: MIT Press.

Waag. (2015). *Waag*. Retrieved from https://waag.org/en/blog/hackablecity

Weber, M. (1958). *The City*. New York: The Free Press, Macmillan Publishing Co.

Wenger, E. (1998). *Communities of Practice: Learning, Meaning and Identity*. Cambridge, UK: Cambridge University Press. doi:10.1017/CBO9780511803932

Wolfe, D. (2004). The role of Higher Education in Regional Innovation and Cluster Development. In *Creating Knowledge, Strengthening Nations*. Toronto: Toronto University Press. Available on line at http://www.utoronto.ca /progris/pdf_files/higher_education_UofTPress.pdf

Work Foundation. (2002). *Manchester: Ideopolis? Developing a Knowledge Capital*. London: Prepared by Andy Westwood and Max Nathan. The Work Foundation.

Work Foundation. (2005). *The Ideopolis: Knowledge City Consortium*. Research Project. Available at: http://theworkfoundation.com/research/ideopolis.jsp

World Bank. (2002). *Global Development Learning Network*. Available at: www.globalknowledge.org

World Capital Institute (WCI). (2007). *The Most Admired Knowledge City (MAKCi) Report*. World Capital Institute & Teleos. Available at: http://www.worldcapitalinstitute.org/makci/history

KEY TERMS AND DEFINITIONS

Common Good: Either what is shared and beneficial for all or most members of a given community, or alternatively, what is achieved by citizenship, collective action, and active participation in the realm of politics and public service.

Crowd Funding: A specific kind of knowledge-based crowd sourcing. It is a trading technique wherein an investor follows the trades of a certain group of exchange members who are assembled around a trading post to make transactions. (Read more: http://www.investorwords.com/16309/crowd_trading.html#ixzz4v3LBhtnJ).

Crowd Sourcing: A generic type of knowledge market. Crowd sourcing involves obtaining work, information, or opinions from a large group of people who submit their data via the internet, social media, and smartphone apps. People involved in crowdsourcing sometimes work as paid freelancers, while others perform small tasks on a voluntary basis, in which transactions or relations with others are carried out.

Knowledge City (KC): An urban community that purposefully uses knowledge to leverage indogenous input to trigger its own development. Examples of KC are Ideopolis, Creative City, Smart City, Intelligent City.

Knowledge Market: A knowledge market is a mechanism for distributing knowledge resources. It can work under the construct of intellectual property or as a public good and hence encouraging free sharing of knowledge.

Knowledge-Based Development (KBD): Known as the third generation of knowledge management. KBD is a body of theory and methodology that uses a variety of knowledge management systems and network- based approaches for collaborative, value-driven strategies to capture new opportunities to advance development in regions.

Peer-to-Peer Economy: P2P economy is a decentralized model whereby two individuals interact to buy or sell goods and services directly with each other, without intermediation by a third party, or without the use of a company of business.

Value-Based Capital System: A systemic accountable base approach used by knowledge-based models or frameworks, capital system taxonomies, and knowledge cities benchmarking models. It stems from a capitalist economic system and view based on private ownership of the means of production and their operation for profit.

ENDNOTES

1 Bollier, 2011 en http://www.bollier.org/commons-short-and-sweet

2 www.codeandomexico.org; http://distintaslatitudes.net/codeando-mexico-hackers-la-participacion-ciudadana

3 http://www.avina.net/avina/informe-anual-avina-2013/

4 https://codeandomonterrey.github.io/

Chapter 2
Framework for IT Role in Crowdfunding Urbanization Process in Developing Countries

Muhammad A. Sulaiman
King Fahd University of Petroleum and Minerals, Saudi Arabia

Adam M. Yangora
Universiti Malaysia Sarawak, Malaysia

Hamza O. Salami
University of Hafr Al Batin, Saudi Arabia

ABSTRACT

The recent urbanization process is increasingly rapid and unplanned. With the current projection that seven out of ten people worldwide will be living in the cities by the year 2050, with the majority of the growth occurring in cities of the developing countries, information technology (IT) can be used to positively drive the urbanization process. This chapter provides an integrative framework for which various IT trends can be harnessed to crowdfunding urbanization process by focusing on the use of mobile and other handheld devices. Existing use of mobile phone in developing countries focus on e-education, e-commerce, and social media technologies. However, there is little evidence that researchers have analyzed the role of IT in crowdfunding. Consequently, this chapter develops a framework on how the capabilities of mobile devices can be harnessed for crowdfunding urbanization process in the developing countries.

INTRODUCTION AND BACKGROUND

Crowdfunding is a concept that involves raising finance from "crowd" for the purpose of achieving a specific goal. Inbuilt in this idea is a sense of inclusiveness, where individual persons (the "crowd") that took part in such an activity have a feeling of collective ownership of the project (Hufner, 2016). Even though crowdfunding is largely seen as private entrepreneurial projects and little attention has been paid to its used for civic projects (Schiller, 2014), The concept agreed with the UN post-2015 development

DOI: 10.4018/978-1-5225-3952-0.ch002

agenda, which have ICT and Urbanization among the key goals. In fact, sustainable urbanization is directly linked to Goal 11, which states "*make cities and human settlements inclusive, safe, resilient and sustainable.*" (Kamau & Donoghue, 2015). More so, with the advent of Internet, crowdfunding is now performed through the Internet with a large number of participants (infoDev, 2013). Moreover, with the ubiquitous number of mobile / other handheld devices and increasing access to the Internet, the potentials to reach a large number of participants in a quick and easy way is unprecedented. Thus, learning from the current usage of mobile devices in the developing countries like Africa, which is mainly focused on e-Education, e-Commerce and Social media technologies (Vosloo, 2014; Riaga, 2016) and learning from the civic projects crowdfunding experience in developed countries like US and UK (Davies, 2014), this chapter seeks to provide an integrative IT framework through which mobile devices will play a vital role in crowdfunding civic projects in the developing countries.

Recent studies by Google Inc. have indicated that global web traffic from mobile devices is on the rise and that the number of smartphones has surpassed the number of personal computers (Anonymous, n.d.). In another study, it is indicated that Africa is now the fastest growing and second largest mobile phone market in the world (Vosloo, 2014). These facts and more serve as motivation for the possible implementation of civic crowdfunding projects in the developing countries like Africa as is currently the case in the developed countries.

This chapter explores the mobile usages for virtually all ICT trends; mobile apps, social media technologies, software and web technologies, virtual reality, and etc., their roles to crowdfunding civic projects. Hence, this chapter is organized to include literature review; integrative IT framework; future trends and conclusion.

LITERATURE REVIEW

There are little or no evidences that crowdfunding for civic projects exist today in the developing world like countries in Africa, despite the growing use of crowdfunding in the recent years to successfully support civic projects in the developed countries (Davies, 2014; Schiller, 2014). However, with the experience of the developed countries, such solution can be reengineered and adopted for developing countries. Just like the emergence of microfinance as a means of soft loans to start a small business or expand an existing one among very low incomes earners in developing countries. This solution has been adopted by some developed countries as means of securing microloans to entrepreneurs with similar difficulties in accessing conventional loans. (Bruton, Khavul, Siegel, & Wright, 2014). Crowdfunding is believed to be largely developed-world phenomenon with support from development organization and governments, experts still believe that it could become a useful tool in the developing countries as well (infoDev, 2013).

To give a broader perspective on the role of IT in crowdfunding urbanization process in developing countries, the rest of this literature review will focus on three main issues. Firstly, it will highlight the transformative nature of urbanization process; secondly, it will review the literature on the nature of crowdfunding projects and processes; and thirdly it will focus on civic crowdfunding that has more direct impact on urban development.

Review of Urbanization Process

Urbanization could be seen as a long-term continuous process in the form of social transformation from traditional rural societies to modern urban communities (Kumar & Rai, 2014). It is defined as a process which reveals itself through temporal, spatial and sectoral changes in the demographic, social, economic, technological and environmental aspects of life in a given society (Lonavath, 2014). Davis (1965) sees urbanization as a progressive concentration of population in an urban unit. "Urbanization is not only accompanying to industrialization, but it is also interlinked with modernization and these three sometimes work in conjunction. The process of urbanization in developed countries has been very slow but steady and it has been accompanied by agricultural and industrial revolution, higher per capita income and high standard of living, whereas in developing countries the rate of urbanization is very fast and it is not accompanied by industrialization but rapid growth of service sector in the economies" (Macbeth & Collinson, 2002; Kumar & Rai, 2014). Urbanization is not merely a concomitant of industrialization, but a concomitant of the whole gamut of factors underlying the process of economic growth and social change (Gallion & Eisner, 1996).

Review of Crowdfunding Projects and Processes

Crowdfunding phenomenon is a collective effort by people who network and pool their money together, usually via the Internet, in order to invest in and support efforts initiated by other people or organizations (Ordanini A., 2009). Crowdfunding is an initiative undertaken to raise money for a new project proposed by someone, by collecting small to medium-sized investments from several other people (i.e., a crowd) (Ordanini A., 2009). There are three categories of subjects that are involved in a typical crowdfunding scheme, the first category is the subjects who propose ideas and/or projects to be funded. The intention of the first category of people is to use crowdfunding to get direct access to the market and to gather financial support from truly interested supporters. The second category of subjects is the crowd of people that decide to financially support such projects, bearing a risk and expecting a certain payoff. These supporters co-produce the output, selecting – and sometimes developing -- the offers they deem to be most promising or interesting (Ordanini et al., 2011). The third category of players is the crowdfunding organization that brings together the first two categories of players, that is those who want to deliver the new initiatives using crowdfunding mechanisms and those who may wish to support such initiatives through their investment efforts (Ordanini et al., 2011).

Historically, crowdfunding models involve collecting small amounts of money from many people in the form of charity and social cooperation. However, this model extended to investment portfolio (Lake, 2015), because the money is invested by consumers to obtain a return, mostly financial, but sometimes intangible (e.g., status, social esteem, identification, etc.) (Ordanini et al., 2011; Lake, 2015). In the same vein, "The crowdfunding mechanism is also related to social networking, where consumers actively participate in online communities to share information, knowledge, and suggestions about a new initiative and/or brand. However, crowdfunding goes beyond conventional social- network participation by incorporating more proactive roles for consumers, such as selecting new initiatives to support and providing financial backing for them. Therefore, crowdfunding, although sharing some characteristics of traditional resource-pooling and social-networking phenomena, has some unique elements related to creating service platforms through which individual consumers can pool monetary resources to support and sustain new projects initiated by others." (Ordanini, Miceli et al., 2011). Finally, even though crowdfunding is a developed world phenomenon, again experts believe that it draws inspiration from other innovations that have shaped enterprise in the developing countries (infoDev, 2013). Many of these initiatives leapfrogged the developed world, examples include mobile payment in East Africa, low-cost drip irrigation in India and alternative fuel adoption (ethanol) in Brazil (infoDev, 2013).

Review on Civic Crowdfunding Projects

Civic crowdfunding project is further reviewed separately, because of its direct connection to urbanization process. Civic crowdfunding project is defined in a broader sense as crowd-funded projects that provide services to communities. "Civic crowdfunding projects would be expected to produce goods that are non-rival and non-excludable — that once produced can be enjoyed by all members of a community equally, perpetually, and without regard for their contribution. In other words, the expected output of the civic project is a public good." (Davies, 2014; Barber, 2004). Tilburg (2015) view civic crowdfunding as:

... *Is about Raising Funds to Initiatives in the Public Domain, Like a Neighborhood Garden or a Community Art Project, or with a Common Social Goal, Like Activities for the Elderly in a Community Centre. Often Civic Crowdfunding Campaigns are Initiated by Citizens, Local Communities, Social Entrepreneurs or Social Organization.*

Civic crowdfunding could be the oldest kind of crowdfunding, many worship places, school, and sports clubs are built with crowdfunding. Also, the base of the State of liberty has been realized with a kind of crowdfunding that closely resembles '*modern*' digital crowdfunding campaigns (Tilburg, 2015).

Davies (2014b) extensively studied civil crowdfunding and presents four known features of civic crowdfunding as follows:

1. Civic crowdfunding is small scale but relatively successful and has big ambitions. As of 2014, on average the civic crowdfunding projects is small on the scale of $6,357 in the median amount raised. Tilburg (2015) equally identified civic crowdfunding campaign as small scale, and as one of the reasons that accelerate its growth. For example, Davies (2014b) reported that projects that were tagged "civic" on Kickstarter platform succeed 81% of the time. Most platforms and institutions have started to see civic crowdfunding as a new public-private partnership mechanism that is capable of realizing large-scale projects (Davies, 2014b). And to fulfill its big ambition all stakeholders which include governments, profit, and large non-profit sectors need to be comprehensively engaged with the process (Davies, 2014b).
2. Civic crowdfunding started as a hobby for green space projects by local non-profits organization, but have long attracted large organizations. 29% of the civic crowdfunding platform is used for park and garden related projects and other popular campaigns include event-based, education and training (Davies, 2014b). Various interest groups such as governments, corporate organizations and large foundations are exploring ways to supports crowdfunding wider ranges of community-oriented activities.

3. The concentration of civic crowdfunding in the cities. For example, in the US, five states account for 80% of the projects with New York and California at the top. The reasons for this could be associated with the proximity of where the platforms were located and lack of awareness (Davies, 2014b). Davies (2015b) argued that it requires a hard work to convince communities to use crowdfunding to get projects off the ground. However, apart from technological development, the trend of government withdrawal, cutbacks and demand of citizens to participate and take responsibility for their environment are additional reasons that accelerate the growth of civic crowdfunding (Tilburg, 2015).
4. Civic crowdfunding has the same highly unequal distributional tendencies as other crowd markets. "Most projects are small-scale, but a small number of high-value projects have taken a large share of the total revenue raised by civic crowdfunding." (Davies, 2014b). Typical successful civic crowdfunding projects on Kickstarter are in the range of $5,000 to $10,000 on average which is within the same closed intervals with the 47% of civic projects studied by Davies (2015b). However, civic crowdfunding projects such as 'Veronica Mars' and 'Wish I was Here' which hit $2 million targeted goals in less than a day (Strecker, 2013) and in 3 days (Fleming, 2013) respectively are examples of what is possible, but these examples are few exceptional cases that give the Long Tail of the distribution (Davies, 2014b). Nevertheless, the average amount spent per contributor on 'Veronica Mars' and 'Wish I was Here' campaigns was placed at $62 - $66, with 91,000 people and over 46,000 people raised a total of $5.7 million and $3.1 million for 'Veronica Mars' and 'Wish I was Here' respectively (Venable, n.d.).

One interesting feature of civic crowdfunding pointed out in Davies (2015) is the emergence of replicability of crowdfunding as a strategy. The three prominent ways enumerated in Davies (2015) are: (1) a single group using the technique repeatedly for different type of projects in the same geographic community, (2) a single group or individual crowdfunding repeated iterations of the same project (usually an event) over several years, and (3) groups crowdfunding projects in different locations based on a common model.

Innovative Use of Mobile Devices in the Developing World

A literature review has indicated that Mobile devices are innovatively used in the developing countries in the areas of e-Education, e-Commerce, and social media technologies (Trucano, 2011). One of the early mobile learning models for distance learning was designed and adopted for Africa has m-learning environment underpinned by traditional learning environment. It enables both learner-to-learner and learner-to-teacher communications (Barker et al., 2005). This model was successfully implemented at the University of Pretoria in 2002 (Gregson & Jordaan, 2009). The m-learning model integrates SMS messaging with a paper-based program to enhance administrative and motivational support to a group of students. It consists of bulk SMS, Instant Voice Response (IVR) and SMS assessment tools.

Another interesting m-learning project was Yoza project, it was designed to support reading and writing by youths in South Africa via Mobile phones. M-novel was the pilot phase of the project, it was written and published in September 2009 on MXit (Anonymous, About the Project, 2010). MXit is Africa's largest homegrown mobile social network (Vosloo, 2014). It is accessible in feature phones and used by more than 100 million people in emerging markets around the globe (MXit, n.d., para 2). A feature phone is a mobile phone that incorporates features such as the ability to access the Internet and store and play music but lacks the advanced functionality of a smartphone.

Another attempt to revolutionize access to information and knowledge particularly in the developing countries was made in the recent time by Wikimedia Foundation, the nonprofit organization that operates Wikipedia. Wikimedia Foundation has signed Wikipedia Zero partnership with three mobile operators in 2012 to bring free Wikipedia access to 230 million mobile users in 31 countries (Wadhwa, 2013). Wadhwa (2013) further highlighted that an additional partnership was signed to extend the project to at least 100 million more mobile users in five more countries in 2013. Wikipedia Zero partnership is based on providing mainly the feature phones users USSD and SMS access to Wikipedia. USSD protocol is used by GSM cellular telephones to establish communication with service provider's computer. A user will send a text request to Wikipedia and get access to the requested article on user's phone within seconds.

Mobile money is seen as an umbrella term, that defines an ecosystem which includes all forms of financial activities transacted via a mobile device (Debray et al., 2014). The ecosystem consists of Mobile banking, Mobile payments and Mobile Commerce (Debray et al., 2014). Bångens and Söderberg (2008, p. 14) defines m-banking as "… Financial Services Delivered via Mobile Networks and Performed on a Mobile Phone. These Services May or May not be Defined as Banking Services by the Regulator, depending on the Legislation of the Country in Question, as well as on which Services are offered".

Debray et al. (2014, p. 2) defined Mobile Payments Commonly Referred to as Mobile Money Transfer as "Payment Services Operated under Financial Regulation and Performed from or via a Mobile Device. This Ranges from Remittance Type Activities, both Domestic and International, Cash In/ Out, etc", and Mobile Commerce as The Buying and Selling of Goods and Services through A Mobile Device."

M-money is seen as a value-added service offered through telecom companies and both telecommunication and financial institutions have an interest in this prospective business. It is a strategy for telecommunication companies to keep churn rates low and retain customer loyalty and for the financial institutions, it helps to increase banking penetration, develop customer loyalty and reduce operational costs (Wishart, 2006; Bångens & Söderberg, 2008; Alampay, 2010). The previous investigation on branchless banking recognized the importance of mobile phones in some models (Lyman et al., 2008). M-money has the potential for expanding financial services to unbanked poor (Ahmad, 2006; Bångens & Söderberg, 2008; Alampay, 2010). Like any venture, there are challenges of striking the right balance where regulations do not hinder useful innovation and experimentation permit branchless banking to expand and thrive (Lyman, Pickens, & Porteous, 2008; Alampay, 2010).

M-Pesa is a case study of m-money in Kenya. It has been reported that Kenya is leading the world in m-money, with M-Pesa service it is easier to pay for taxi drive in Kenya than in New York (Anonymous, 2015). M-Pesa was launched in 2007 by Vodafone for Safaricom and Vodacom, the largest mobile network operators in Kenya and Tanzania (Anonymous, 2012), and by 2014 there were about 18 million M-Pesa active registered accounts in Kenya (Mutiga, 2014). With a successful implementation of M-PESA in 2007, it has been extended to Tanzania and Afghanistan in 2008, and from 2010 to 2015 M-Pesa has been extended to South Africa, India, Mozambique, Lesotho, Egypt, Eastern Europe (Romania and Albania) and by end of March, 2016 M-Pesa reported a total of 25 millions subscriber base globally (Anonymous, 2013; Tshabalala, 2015; Sarin, 2008; Ochieng, 2016).

M-Pesa was originally designed to serve as microfinance-loan service via a mobile phone and with its successful implementation, it was extended to a general money transfer scheme. M-Pesa process flow consists of three simple steps to complete a transaction using SMS as follows: (1) Customers register for free with M-Pesa authorized agent, usually a mobile phone dealer, gas station, Chemist, Supermarket or Shop. (2) Customers buy electronic value (3-value) to send text messages to any other Safaricom mobile phone users in Kenya. (3) Recipients can collect money at any M-Pesa registered agent after showing their mobile text and ID card.

FRAMEWORK DEVELOPMENT PROCESS

After the general review of the relevant literature, we shall now explore conceptual framework suited to the task of the crowdfunding urbanization process in developing countries. This is done, first, by exploring suitable framework for IT in crowdfunding urbanization process; second by identifying sound framework for IT in crowdfunding urbanization process; third by discussing various strategies for civic crowdfunding; and finally reviewing emerging trends in applying mobile devices in conducting civic crowdfunding activities.

In his proposed theory of Meaningful Learning, David Ausubel (1978) encourages that new ideas are acquired by adding questions and clarifications to the old ideas- "*the concept of reception learning*" (Tomei, 2004). Two methods were advocated: the first is *signaling*, which indicates 'important information'; the second is *advanced organizers*, which indicates the 'sequence between them' (Acharya & Sinha, 2014). These methods are the psychological foundations that have led to the creation of Concept Map Approach in 1972 (Novak & Cañas, 2006; Novak & Cañas, 2007). Concept Map can be defined as "*concept as a perceived regularity in events or objects, or records of events or objects, designated by a label.*" Within the field of learner-created knowledge models, the Cmaps are tools that are used to graphically organize and represent knowledge or ideas in a hierarchical style (Novak & Cañas, 2007). "*The hierarchical structure of a particular domain of knowledge also depends on the context in which that knowledge is being applied or considered*" (Novak & Cañas, 2007). The approach is based on the notion that "*true learning involves the learner to*" create "*relationships between the new information he or she acquires and*" the information that has been possessed already. The approach focuses on explicitly mapping "*out the relationships within a certain process or object that is being studied*" in order "*to have a deeper understanding of the concept*" that is being mapped out (Novak & Cañas, 2007). Concept maps consist of ideas that are usually enclosed as nodes or boxes. These ideas are connected by a line with linking words or linking phrases – written in semantic units, that link and specify the relationships between two concepts (Novak & Cañas, 2007). The concept map approach is used for design and development of the FITCUP.

FRAMEWORK FOR IT ROLE IN CROWDFUNDING URBANIZATION PROCESS (FITCUP)

Important to the sustainable urbanization through crowdfunding is IT trends. This section discusses FITCUP design and development process, various IT trends and strategies for crowdfunding civil projects using Mobile. From now on the term, Mobile is used to refer to all mobile technologies which include devices with or without default call capability and can be used to access the Internet or run social media/phone apps or both.

This section consists of three main subsections, the FITCUP development process, the civic crowdfunding strategies and the IT trends to enhance civic crowdfunding using Mobile. The framework development process provides the methodology through which the FITCUP model is developed and the remaining two subsections describe components of the FITCUP model.

FITCUP Conceptual Framework and Design

In order to develop FITCUP, first, we conceived the conceptual framework based on the review of various crowdfunding projects that exist in many online crowdfunding platforms as well as various relevant literature. Even though the public civic project is an old concept among various communities around the world, online civic crowdfunding is relatively new, it is becoming popular among the online crowdfunding platforms in the developed world only in the recent time (Davies, 2014c). Thus, this study focuses on the civic crowdfunding project because of its direct link with the urban development process. And when harnessed judiciously in the developing countries, it has great potential to lead the urbanization process as rightly said by Tilburg (2015, para. 8): "… the big impact of civic crowdfunding is not in the money that is raised. First and foremost, civic crowdfunding is a powerful campaign instrument. It is about building communities, promoting your project and can even be a political instrument to put pressure on local authorities and other key players". Similarly, Voor Je Buurt (n.d.) envisages the potential of civic crowdfunding to change the role of local governments, where civil society take charges by means of civic initiative without waiting for funding or permission from the local governments, a situation that will force the local government to see civil society as equal partner in realizing an initiative. To realize the full potential of civic crowdfunding in the developing world various strategies that depend on the existing and emerging IT trends need to be conceptualized. Henceforth, development of FITCUP follows a concept map methodology in which ideas are objects of the CMap (known as concepts) and concept are linked to each other using relationship (linking words) and all together give the overall framework.

Figure 1 is the conceptual process that resulted to the development of FITCUP model in Figure 3.

FITCUP is developed as two-level models:

1. Various features of civic crowdfunding projects from the relevant literature survey, extensive investigation and analysis of features from the various existing crowdfunding platforms and the studied

Figure 1. Process for developing the FITCUP

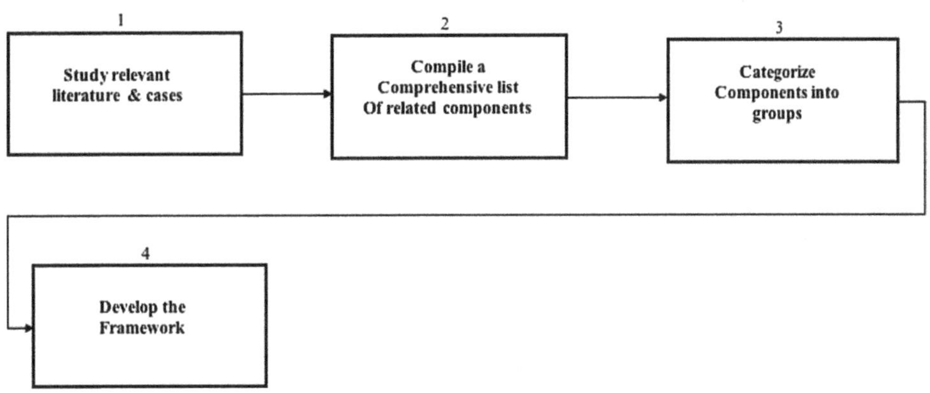

cases of mobile usage in both the developed and the developing world formed the root components that conceptualized and upgraded into Level 1 FITCUP Model as presented in Figure 2.

2. Further upgrade and expansion of the *Level 1 FITCUP model* give the final FITCUP as presented in Figure 3.

Subsequent subsections discuss various components of the final FITCUP model and how they can play role in enhancing crowdfunding urbanization process using Mobile.

CIVIC CROWDFUNDING STRATEGIES (CC STRATEGIES)

Based on the various existing crowdfunding platforms considered in this study; the authors recognize three crowdfunding strategies that can be used with various IT tools for civic crowdfunding projects. Namely, (1) peer-to-peer civic crowdfunding, (2) team civic crowdfunding and (3) corporate partnership civic crowdfunding.

Figure 2. Level 1 FITCUP model

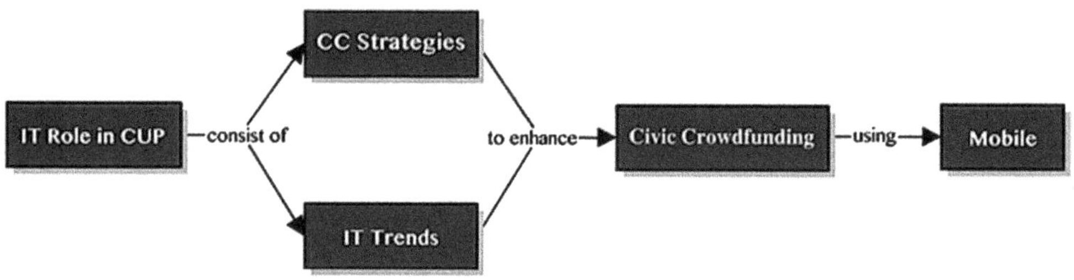

Figure 3. Level 2 FITCUP model

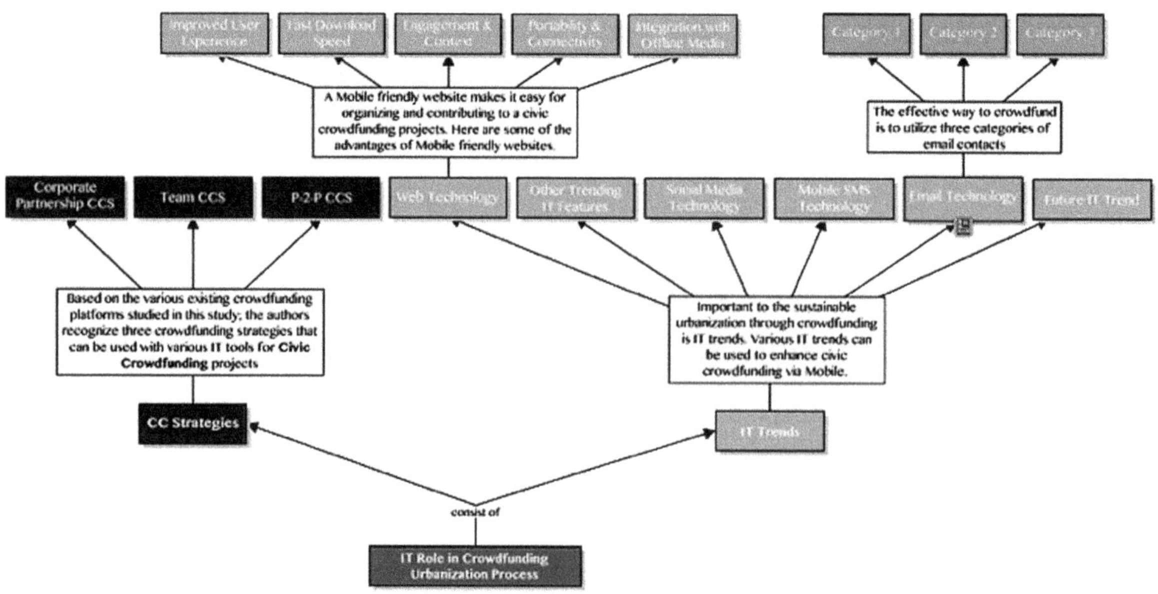

1. **Peer-to-Peer Civic Crowdfunding Strategy (P-2-P CCS):** Involves individuals contacting their close contacts or relations. This is usually done through family, friends and social networks using text message keyword or providing a donation page link to sign-up to the site to volunteer. Mobile provides an effective way to engage peers in a network, using text message in the form of SMS or simple chat message using mobile or social media apps. The peer-to-peer strategy is usually suitable for small or medium scale civic projects. The strategy is easy to initiate since it requires individual organizers to use their contacts from mobile phone, email account, and social media accounts directories. Those contacts formed the contact lists for the campaign and require to be grouped according to the level of closeness and/ or acquaintance. For example, close family contact list, close friend contact list, acquaintance contact list, and etc.
2. **Team Civic Crowdfunding Strategy (Team CCS):** Involves people with common interest in some particular social/ civic activities. A team civic crowdfunding strategy can make life much easier for crowdfunding campaign using IT facilities and it is suitable for medium to large scale civic projects. A team civic crowdfunding strategy can be seen for example in a campaign for crowdfunding the construction of a stadium for a community among people with common interest in sport. This strategy involves registration of various teams/clubs, and fund contribution towards the civic project (e.g. stadium project) is made based on registered teams. Each team generates funds among its team members and each team subsequently presents its part of funds for a common goal. Using Web technology, each team may have a crowdfunding campaign page and direct its members to donate through their page. Individual fundraiser's amount is automatically summed on the team's campaign page and subsequently, the total amount contributed by each team are summed up to the total amount of funds raised for the main campaign page. Relying on Mobile friendly tools such as SMS and social media chats, team civic crowdfunding campaign can be spread very fast. Also, Team civic crowdfunding can serve as a common control for campaign initiator.
3. **Corporate Partnership Civic Crowdfunding Strategy (Corporate Partnership CCS):** Involves corporation for much bigger (large scale) civic projects. This category of a civic project can be initiated by individuals or government (local, state or even federal) in the form of government-private or individuals (or group)-private civic crowdfunding campaign. Whichever the case, such civic project can be facilitated using Mobile tools. Partnership with companies could make a huge civic crowdfunding success, this strategy involves companies advertise a civic crowdfunding campaign to their customers as well as their employees to give a campaign a heightened exposure. For example, each corporate partner obtained their donation using customized branding campaign page embedded on their website. So, each donation from customers of the corporate partners and employees go directly to the campaigner and feedback sent to the corporate partner admin as when the donation is made.

IT TRENDS TO ENHANCE CIVIC CROWDFUNDING USING MOBILE

Various IT trends can be used to enhance civic crowdfunding via Mobile. This subsection provides a comprehensive list of those IT trends and how they can best be used for civic crowdfunding campaigns.

1. **Web Technology:** With the invention of www in the early 90s, website becomes the widest means of sharing information. And currently, most of the crowdfunding projects were done through the website owned and maintained by intermediaries known as funding portals or crowdfunding platforms. A Mobile friendly website makes it easy for organizing and contributing to civic crowdfunding projects. The mobile friendly website is design based on a simple and secure form that can be accessible from various Mobile platforms. Below we present some of the advantages of Mobile friendly websites:
   a. **Improved User Experience:** Research on Mobile website usability indicated that mobile-optimized website improved user experience and satisfaction (HUMAN SERVICE SOLUTIONS, n.d.; Budiu, 2015).
   b. **Fast Download Speed:** Mobile website is designed to provide optimal download speed, which translates to less waiting time and more browsing experience.
   c. **Engagement and Context:** Mobile website is engaging and convenient in providing features such as click-to-donate and click-to-call buttons. More interesting is the location-aware technology in Mobile, which can be utilized to connect users to civic crowdfunding project website when they are in a closed geographical location; this is a great opportunity to connect a civic project campaign to a concerned community where the project will likely take place and this will surely improve civic crowd participation.
   d. **Portability and Connectivity:** Mobile websites are accessible anytime and anywhere. This provides a consistent connection with target crowd everywhere.
   e. **Integration With Offline Media:** Mobile website closes the gap between online and offline media by means of IT trend such as the 2D matrix barcode called QR codes. QR codes display in print can be scanned with a Smart Mobile and translate into electronic messages such as website url, email address or SMS.

Mobile friendly crowdfunding website is the base on which other IT trends will provide a supporting role to enhance and improve any civic crowdfunding project. So, before embarking on any civic crowdfunding campaign, a project initiator needs to carefully choose crowdfunding platform with Mobile friendly web tools and support for various IT trends for successful civic crowdfunding. For example, many crowdfunding platforms allow campaigners to spread the word about their civic campaign right on the campaign social media page, by making it simple for crowds to donate with just a few clicks.

2. **Email Technology:** Prior to the popularity or availability of social media technologies, emails have been the most ubiquitous channels for fundraising. However, when effectively utilized it provides a unique way to successful civic crowdfunding projects. Emails can be used for small and medium scale civic project using peer-to-peer crowdfunding model. With Email civic crowdfunding campaign, you can control who sees the campaign first and effectively get your friends and family to come onboard for your civic crowdfunding project and as well the people or group of people you are able to bring together in the course of building civic crowdfunding project (Jekins, 2014). According to Brian Meece, the CEO of RocketHub,

There is a Strong Correlation with an Email Strategy and Our Data Indicates that Email is usually 5 Times more Effective than a FB Status or Tweet. There are Outliers Which Allow the Social Media Messaging to Carry Through New Networks, but for Most Users, Email is Still Tops. (Luzar, 2013).

Also, Julie Kresen, whose "Here You Go" civic project was designed to spread goodwill by handing a thousand umbrellas to people stuck in the rain has this to say about the email civic crowdfunding campaign:

Email was especially Important at the Very End because Right before Our Kickstarter Campaign Ended We did an Email Push… My Husband did it, and that Was Strictly Over Email. It was an Email to Maybe 75 People about 2 or 3 Days before the Kickstarter Campaign… 'Here's What We Have, Here's What We Still Need, Here's Our Deadline, It's Only Two Days Away.' That Was Where We Had the Final Push Where We Got about 30% of Our Money after that. (Luzar, 2013)

Jekins (2014) suggested that the effective way to crowdfunding using email is to collect a pool of email contacts from your email inbox archives and categorizing them into 4 or more groups namely:

Category 1: People who know what you are doing, and/or who are close to you.
Category 2: People who you are fairly close to, and who may or may not know what your project is all about.
Category 3: People who you haven't seen in a really long time and who have no idea what you are up to.
Category 4: People you don't know/are not on good terms with/tech support emails/emails you KNOW are dead etc.

It is expected that people in category 4 are to be removed completely from your contact lists for the civic campaign. The rest three categories will have a different email template since the first category are people that know what you are doing they should receive personal and individualized email; it is expected that those in Category 1 will make you achieve at least 10% of your goals. However, the remaining two categories (2 and 3) will have a common, but a personalized message. Using email features like Mail merger will enable sending customize emails with a specific template and email marketing tools such as Litmus, Mail Chimp and etc. enable campaigner to organize responses and take an audit of how a campaign is doing using your Mobile. The study has shown that 56% of all emails are read on a mobile device (Lewkowicz, 2016), composing a short email containing a link or wrapped with mobile friendly donation page will strengthen the effectiveness of email campaigns.

3. **Social Media Technology:** Social media has become de facto for a successful civic crowdfunding campaign. It helps in increasing online presence for a civic crowdfunding project. For a civic crowdfunding campaign to reach its goal, social media presence is a must before, during and after a campaign is started (Wu, 2015). A study by Georgetown University and Waggener Edstrom (2012) indicated that 56% of survey respondents said they were inspired to take further action for a cause after reading a story on social media. Social media technology has diverse channels and the channels are on increase every now and then, so choosing and focusing on selected channels is a key to a successful civic crowdfunding campaign. Wu (2015) suggested some questions be considered before picking the right channels:

a. On which channel do you have the most followers?
b. Where do your prospects (targeted crowd) converse and share?
c. What people have the greatest influence in your community?
d. Which platform are you most comfortable with?

Some of the most popular channels are (1) Facebook with 1.86 billion active users and 1.23 billion logging in every day (Hutchinson, 2017). (2) Twitter has 319 million average monthly active users as of February 2017 (Reuters, 2017; Smith, 2017). (3) LinkedIn as of September 2016 has 467 million accounts with 106 million active users (FORM 10-Q, 2016). (4) Instagram has 600 million users as of December 2016 (Instrgram, 2016; Smith, 2017). (5) and WhatsApp has grown to1 billion users by February 2016 (Statista, 2017; Statt, 2016). Each of these channels has a variety of features that can be used to enhance the success of a civic campaign project, this includes posting a picture, video, links and in the recent time live streaming features. For most crowdfunding campaigns, the right channels will typically be Facebook and Twitter, because they reach the most people and encourage the most interactivity (Wu, 2015). However, the LinkedIn network is more suitable for a civic campaign that targeted professionals and industries. Many business people engage on LinkedIn far more often than other social media, so take advantage of this tool by tailoring the civic crowdfunding that targets professionals and industries to that audience (Almerico, 2014). WhatsApp allows people to easily sent texts, photos, videos and voice to each other over the Internet without paying data charges. This makes WhatsApp suitable for peer-to-peer civic crowdfunding strategy. The appealing photo sharing and short video capabilities of Instagram is a useful means to visually engage potential donors for a civic crowdfunding project. In the recent time, Facebook and Instagram have introduced live event streaming which will serve as powerful tools to engage crowd directly in real-time.

Social media channels can be used for small, medium and large scale projects, this makes it one of the most powerful tools for a civic crowdfunding campaign. Indeed, it is a highly efficient way to let your wider network of friends, acquaintances, colleagues and business contacts know your project and its crowdfunding campaign (Canada Media Fund, n.d.). Best practice suggests that whichever channel is chosen, a fresh account/page different from personal account should be branded for the intended civic project campaign. A typical crowdfunding campaign period is within 30 to 60 days (Wang, n.d.; Almerico, 2014), so adding Category 1 contact should start at least a week before the campaign officially start. Once the campaign is launch regular time should be set to engage with potential donors or even campaign backers on a daily basis. Channels like WhatsApp require that basic information such as introductory text, donation page link to the campaign website, photos and videos be repeatedly posted each time a new contact is added to a project WhatsApp group, successful civic crowdfunding campaign through Twitter and Instagram require utilization of hashtag feature and regular status update and post pinning are required in Facebook page and LinkedIn network.

4. **Mobile SMS Technology:** Provides civic crowdfunding campaign with opportunities to reach out mainly to the donors who do not have smartphones. This categories of crowd are found mainly in the rural areas of developing world. Apart from reaching out to feature phones users, Mobile SMS is yet another best way to connect with donors on their personal mobile devices. Many crowdfunding platform partnering with telecommunication companies to provides text-to-donate keyword feature to crowdfunding project. Text-to-donate keywords provide campaigner and donor easy way to transact, campaigner instructs donors to text a unique campaign keyword known as a short code

to an *X*-digit phone number, and the donors receive an instant reply with a link to the campaign mobile-friendly donation page. Once donation is made an instant feedback is usually received by the campaign donor thanking them for their contribution.

5. **Other Trending IT Features in Crowdfunding:** Include (1) Credit card donation via the mobile-friendly page. (2) Radio program which provides additional ways to reach potential donor for a civic campaign. Donation process can be streamlined for radio announcer and campaign representatives with a simple way for listeners to make a donation such as via text-to-donate. (3) A direct mobile phone call to donor increases donor's connection to a civic crowdfunding campaign. Some crowdfunding platform provide a simple form through which a campaign representative can key in basic credit card information of donor to make donation or if the donor is unwilling to provide credit card information, trigger a Give Later text message that will send the person a link to campaign donation page to complete the process at a later time. Alternatively, campaign representative can provide text-to-donate instruction to the person through which he can securely donate to the civic campaign. (4) Real-time lives streaming in social media can be used to connect to donors directly in real time. (5) Video link can be provided to showcase an ongoing civic campaign; from campaign updates to event recaps and donation thank you. A link to the video can be conveniently sent to donors via SMS technology or social media. (6) Automated reminder via Bulk message services can be used to remind donors to donate before the deadline of a civic campaign. Such message will contain a link to a donation page. (7) Use of Widget to subscribe donor to subscriber lists. A mobile subscription widget can be embedded into mobile friendly campaign site, requesting visitors to signup and receive a text message directly from campaigner. Subscriber lists are used to send customized text message using bulk message technology.
6. **Future IT Trend That Can Be Used to Support Successful Civic Campaign:** Includes (1) Virtual reality 3D tour technology can be used to showcase a civic crowdfunding project. This technology provides project supporters an interactive/convincing prototype of a civic project. (2) Big data analytic technology can be used to analyze potential success of a civic project using social media threads and perception analysis.

FUTURE RESEARCH TRENDS AND CONCLUSION

The previous section of this chapter has provided a unified framework for IT role in enhancing crowdfunding urbanization process for sustainable urban growth in the developing world. The framework has captured the state of the art IT trends that are currently employed in crowdfunding platforms and provided a possible feature trends that can viably use to enhance successes of urban project crowdfunding. In its design, FITCUP provides more room for expansion and upgrade with new components/trends.

This study has demonstrated the features and potentials of civic crowdfunding projects via Mobile. The authors believed that civic crowdfunding experiences in the developed countries can be adopted as part of the tools for sustainable urbanization in the developing countries. From 2012 till date, developing world, particularly Africa have seen the rise of crowdfunding platforms. However, the online crowdfunding platforms in Africa have been characterized by AfrikStart (n.d.) as belong to one of the following operational phases in 2015: (i) Idea phase (platform has been launched online but without any crowdfunding activities), (ii) prototype phase (platform has been launched and early crowdfunding activities has started as experimental), (iii) pilot phase (platform has been launched and operational for less than a year; i.e. it has a list of crowdfunding projects on its site and have started raising money actively), and (iv) Early stage phase (platform exist for one year or more and have active crowdfunding projects). But unfortunately, many of these platforms have either remained stagnant in their operational phases of 2015 or are completely not reachable at all. Only a few platforms like M-Changa from Kenya, Thundafund from South Africa and few others can be said to have passed the early stage of operations.

This study believes that the suitable direction for future research regarding the use of Mobile in crowdfunding in developing the world is how to effectively and efficiently use the mobile money services for crowdfunding. M-Changa has already key in for the mobile crowdfunding platform using the well established mobile money ecosystem in Kenya. Integrating Mobile money into civic and none civic online crowdfunding will provide a lot of opportunities for both banked and unbanked individual of a community to take part in crowdfunding projects. However, currently in the most part of developing countries both online crowdfunding and mobile money concepts are facing a lot of common and varied challenges. Some of the challenges of online crowdfunding platform are:

1. **Regulation:** In many developing countries crowdfunding platforms are operating in an unregulated space, this raises the issue of trust among crowd and investors in the case of equity based platforms. Both crowd and investors need adequate protection of their contribution towards a project. Currently, crowdfunding platforms can not hold fundraiser accountable if they failed to fulfill their project campaign promises and objectives, the highest they could do is to blacklist a defaulter for the future launch of a campaign on their platform.
2. **Legislation:** Most crowdfunding platforms in developing countries have unclear legal status, most crowdfunding platforms. Currently, many crowdfunding platforms relied on existing money laundering and fraud legislations in their host countries. Unless a deliberate effort is made by the government to legislate laws that will cover the activities of crowdfunding, many crowds will find it unsaved or unlawful to back projects through online crowdfunding; since most of the online crowdfunding in developing countries is actually not licensed as financial services organization. Hence, this creates concerns among crowds of either being defrauded or breaking the law of the host country.
3. **Lack of Awareness:** Many young entrepreneurs or civil society in developing countries are unaware of how the of crowdfunding operates, and many others lack the skills and knowledge on what to do to invites backers or crowds to their campaign. Online crowdfunding is only popular among a fewer population with technical know-how. As for the online crowdfunding platforms, their founders lack the requisite financial capacity to aggressively engage communities to patronize the platforms, instead they relied on fewer individuals who have awareness of their platforms to invites many others to launch a campaign or limited their awareness campaign on social media and among their network of friends. And the reason for this is that many founders are either members of a civil society or a start-up entrepreneur.
4. **Lack of Transparency:** Another issue with the online crowdfunding platforms in the developing countries is a lack of transparency; a standard online crowdfunding platform operates "all or nothing" mode with a campaign period in the range of 30 to 90 days. This means if the amount raised reaches the set campaign goal before the deadline specified by the fundraiser, the campaign is successfully funded, otherwise, the money is returned to the funders. Many crowdfunding platforms in developing countries do not strictly follow the standard mode, in some platform, a campaign can still be opened for funding long after the specified period by fundraiser has elapsed.

Other challenges of crowdfunding in developing world is absent of mobile money system in many countries, and where it exists, it faces at least the first three challenges of crowdfunding discussed above and in addition to the above, there are security concerns associated with data protection. Unless and until some of these challenges are mitigated, developing countries will continue to have low growth. In another word, deliberate efforts to mitigate these challenges through research and government policies will bridge the gap between urban-rural divides and effectively improved civic crowdfunding as the developing world is more urbanized and populated.

FITCUP consists of civic crowdfunding strategies and IT trends, each "*CC strategy – IT trends*" mix can not be fit to all forms of civic crowdfunding projects. Future upgrade or expansion of FITCUP may include mapping various list of civic crowdfunding projects to "*CC strategy – IT trends*" mix.

In conclusion, to the best of the Authors' knowledge, this is the first attempt to provide a unified IT framework for civic crowdfunding studies. The taxonomy of CC strategies, as well as suggestions on ways in which various IT trends can be used to enhance civic crowdfunding via Mobile, are largely new ideas.

REFERENCES

Acharya, A., & Sinha, D. (2014). A concept map approach to supporting diagnostic and remedial learning activities. *Advanced Computing, Networking and Informatics*, *1*, 557–578.

AfrikStart. (n.d.). *Crowdfunding in Africa- Fundraising goes Digital in Africa: The Emergence of Africa-Based Crowdfunding Platforms*. Retrieved from https://afrikstart.com/report/

Ahmad, A. (2006). *Policies and Regulations for Expanding eUBanking to the Poor*. Academic Press.

Alampay, E. (2010). *Mobile Banking, Mobile Money and Telecommunication Regulations*. Academic Press. 10.2139/ssrn.1618166

Almerico, K. (2014, March 3). *Your Crowdfunding Campaign Is Doomed Without This*. Retrieved January 31, 2017, from Entrepreneur Middle East: https://www.entrepreneur.com/article/231882

Anonymous. (2012). CCK releases 2nd quarter ICT sector statistics for 2011/2012. Communications Commission of Kenya.

Anonymous. (2010). *About the Project*. Retrieved 04 01, 2017, from Yoza Project: https://m4lit.wordpress.com/about-the-project/

Anonymous. (2013). *Vodacom Tanzania reports five million M-PESA subs; transactions top USD823m*. Retrieved 04 06, 2017, from TeleGeography: https://www.telegeography.com/products/commsupdate/articles/2013/05/02/vodacom-tanzania-reports-five-million-m-pesa-subs-transactions-top-usd823m/

Anonymous. (2015). *Why does Kenya lead the world in mobile money?* Retrieved 02 03, 2017, from Economist: http://www.economist.com/blogs/economist-explains/2013/05/economist-explains-18

Anonymous. (n.d.). *Search Traffic: Mobile Friendly Test Tool*. Retrieved December 2016, from Search Console Help: https://support.google.com/webmasters/answer/6352293?hl=en

Bångens, D. L., & Söderberg, B. (2008). *Mobile Banking – Financial Services for the Unbanked? Report, The Swedish Program for ICT in Developing Regions*. SPIDER.

Barber, B. (2004). *Strong Democracy: Participatory Politics for a New Age*. University of California Press.

Barker, A., Krull, G., & Mallinson, B. (2005). Proposed theoretical model for m-learning adoption in developing countries. *mLearn 2005, 4th world conference on m-learning*.

Bruton, G., Khavul, S., Siegel, D., & Wright, M. (2014). New Financial Alternatives in Seeding Entrepreneurship: Microfinance, Crowdfunding, and Peer-to-Peer Innovations. *Entrepreneurship Theory and Practice*, 9–26.

Budiu, R. (2015, March 22). *The State of Mobile User Experience*. Retrieved January 26, 2017, from Nielsen Norman Group: https://www.nngroup.com/articles/mobile-usability-update/

Canada Media Fund. (n.d.). *Using social media effectively for your crowdfunding campaign*. Retrieved January 31, 2017, from Canada Meida Fund: http://crowdfunding.cmf-fmc.ca/best_practices/using-social-media-effectively-for-your-crowdfunding-campaign

Classy. (n.d.). *The Big Social Media Guide For Nonprofits*. Classy.

Davies, R. (2014). *Civic Crowdfunding: Participatory Communities, Entrepreneurs and the Political Economy of Place*. Center for Work, Technology and Organizations, MIT Center for Civic Media. 10.2139/ssrn.2434615

Davies, R. (2014b, May 9). *Civic Crowdfunding – Four Things We Know, Two Things We Don't*. Retrieved January 31, 2017, from RodrigoDavies.com: http://rodrigodavies.com/blog/2014/05/09/civic-crowdfunding-four-things-we-know-two-things-we-dont.html

Davies, R. (2014c, Oct. 21). *Three Provocations for Civic Crowdfunding*. Retrieved from https://rodrigodavies.com/three-provocations-for-civic-crowdfunding-fdff45dd4008

Davis, K. (1965). The urbanization of the human population. *Scientific American*, *13*(3), 41–53.

Debray, A., Kwon, H., & Gill, R. (2014). *Mobile Money opportunities for Mobile Operators*. White Paper, Huawei.

Endstrom, W. (n.d.). *Digital Persuasion: How Social Media Motivates Action and Drives Support for Causes*. Retrieved from Waggener Edstrom: http://waggeneredstrom.com/downloads/DSCA-Summary.pdf

Fleming, M. (2013, April 27). *UPDATE: Zach Braff's 'Wish I Was Here' Kickstarter Hits $2 Million Goal In 3 Days*. Retrieved April 09, 2017, from Deadline: http://deadline.com/2013/04/zach-braff-goes-kickstarter-route-for-wish-i-was-here-482485/

FORM 10-Q. (2016). *Quarterly Report Pursuant to Section 13 or 15(D) of the Securities Exchange Act of 1934:* LinkedIn Corporation.

Gallion, A. B., & Eisner, S. (1996). *The Urban Pattern*. Delhi, India: CBS Publishers.

Georgetown University & Waggener Edstrom. (2012). *Digital Persuation How Social Media Motivates Action and Drives Support for Causes*. Waggener Edstrom Worldwide and Georgetown University, School of Continuous studies, Center for Social Impact Communication.

Gregson, J., & Jordaan, D. (2009). Exploring the Challenges and Opportunities of M-learning, Within an International Distance Education Programme. Mobile Learning: Transforming the Delivery of Education and Training.

Hufner, A. (2016). *Motivation for Financial Backing of Reward Crowdfunding Campaigns- Based on Data from Germany and Norway (A multiple case study)* (MS Thesis). University of Agder.

Human Service Solutions. (n.d.). *Advantages of Mobile Website Optimization.* Retrieved January 26, 2017, from Human Service Solutions: https://www.hswsolutions.com/services/mobile-web-development/advantages/

Hutchinson, A. (2017, February 01). *Facebook Q4 Numbers – 1.86 Billion Active Users, 1.23 Billion Logging in Every Day.* Retrieved April 11, 2017, from Social Media Today: http://www.socialmediatoday.com/social-business/facebook-q4-numbers-186-billion-active-users-123-billion-logging-every-day

infoDev. (2013a). *Crowdfunding's Potential for the Developing World. World Bank, Finance and Private Sector Development Department.* Washington, DC: Information for Development Program (infoDev)/The World Bank.

infoDev. (2013b). *Crowdfunding's Potential for the Developing World. Finance and Private Sector Development Department.* Available at: http://www.infodev.org/infodev-files/wb_crowdfundingreport-v12.pdf

Instrgram. (2016, December 15). *600 Million and Counting.* Retrieved April 11, 2017, from Instagram: http://blog.instagram.com/post/154506585127/161215-600million

Jekins, K. (2014, December 17). *How to send a crowdfunding promotion email that works (includes templates).* Retrieved January 31, 2017, from Multitude: http://www.multitude.co.nz/mud/crowdfunding-promotion-email/

Kamau, M., & Donoghue, D. (2015). *Transforming our World: The 2030 Agenda for Global Action. (Final draft of the outcome document for the US summit to adopt the Post-2015 Development Agenda).* United Nations, Permanent Mission of the Republic of Kenya to the United Nations. Retrieved from https://www.uclg.org/sites/default/files/final_draft_outcome_document_un_sept_summit_july_8_1.pdf

Kumar, A., & Rai, A. K. (2014). Urbanization Process, Trend, Pattern and its Consequences in India. *Neo Geographia, 3*(4), 54–77.

Lake, R. (2015). *A Guide to Building a Portfolio with Crowdfunded Investments.* Retrieved 04 07, 2017, from Investopedia: http://www.investopedia.com/articles/personal-finance/120415/guide-building-portfolio-crowdfunded-investments.asp

Lewkowicz, K. (2016, May 10). *April Email Market Share: Mobile Rises To 56%, Its Highest Point Yet.* Retrieved April 11, 2017, from Litmus: https://litmus.com/blog/mobile-rises-to-56-market-share-longest-sustained-growth-in-2016

Lonavath, A. K. (2014). Structure of Family Size in Urban Areas: A study on Telangana, Coastal Andhra and Rayalaseema regions of Andhra Pradesh. *International Journal of Advanced Scientific and Technical Research, 1*(4), 1-9.

Luzar, C. (2013, January 21). *Effective Email Marketing For Crowdfunding Campaigns.* Retrieved January 31, 2017, from Crowdfund Insider: https://www.crowdfundinsider.com/2013/01/8555-email-marketing-crowdfunding/

Lyman, T., Pickens, M., & Porteous, D. (2008). *Regulating Transformational Branchless Banking: Mobile Phones and Other Technology to Increase Access to Finance.* Consultative Group to Assist the Poor (CGAP) Focus Note 43, Consultative Group to Assist the Poor (CGAP) Focus Note 43.

Macbeth, H., & Collinson, P. (2002). *Human Population Dynamics: CrossDisciplinary Perspectives.* Cambridge University Press. doi:10.1017/CBO9780511542480

Mutiga, M. (2014). *Kenya's Banking Revolution Lights a Fire.* Retrieved 04 06, 2017, from The New York Times: https://www.nytimes.com/2014/01/21/opinion/kenyas-banking-revolution-lights-a-fire.html

MXit. (n.d.). *The First Mobile Messenger.* Retrieved 03 30, 2017, from MXit: http://www.mxit.com/index.html

Novak, J., & Cañas, A. J. (2007). Theoretical Origins of Concept Map, How to construct them and their used in Education. *Reflecting Education*, *3*(1), 29–42.

Novak, J. D., & Cañas, A. J. (2006). The Origins of the Concept Mapping Tool and the Continuing Evolution of the Tool. *Information Visualization Journal*, *5*(3), 175–184. doi:10.1057/palgrave.ivs.9500126

Ochieng, L. (2016). *M-Pesa reports 27 pc jump in global users to 25 million.* Retrieved 04 06, 2017, from Daily Nation: http://www.nation.co.ke/business/M-Pesa-reports-27-pc-jump-in-global-users-to-25-million/996-3178018-5ykpjpz/index.html

Ordanini, A. (2009, March 23). Crowd funding: Customers as investors. *The Wall Street Journal.*

Ordanini, A., Miceli, L., Pizzetti, M., & Parasuraman, A. (2011). Crowd-funding: Transforming customers into investors through innovative service platforms. *Journal of Service Management*, *22*(4), 443–470. doi:10.1108/09564231111155079

Reuters. (2017, February 9). *Twitter Misses Fourth-Quarter Revenue, User Growth Expectations.* Retrieved April 11, 2017, from Fortune Tech: http://fortune.com/2017/02/09/twitter-q4-2016/

Riaga, O. (2016, July 4). *Kenya's e-Commerce deemed to explode and offer new opportunities for Kenyan entrepreneurs.* Retrieved December 13, 2016, from Kenya Tech News: Retrieved from http://www.kachwanya.com/2016/07/04/kenya-e-commerce-landscape-deemed-explode-offer-new-opportunities-kenyan-entrepreneurs/

Sarin, A. (2008). *Mobile phone banking in Africa* [Youtube Video]. Retrieved 04 06, 2017, from Department for International Development (DFID): https://www.youtube.com/watch?v=TNrDv4PQdCc

Schiller, B. (2014). *Pay For Your City: Crowdfunding For Civic Projects Is Unusually Successful.* Retrieved March 01, 2017, from Fast Company: https://www.fastcoexist.com/3031412/pay-for-your-city-crowdfunding-for-civic-projects-is-unusually-successful

Smith, C. (2017, March 22). *388 Amazing Twitter Statistics and Facts (February 2017).* Retrieved April 11, 2017, from DMR Stat | Gadgets: http://expandedramblings.com/index.php/march-2013-by-the-numbers-a-few-amazing-twitter-stats/

Statista. (2017, January). *Most famous social network sites worldwide as of January 2017, ranked by number of active users (in millions).* Retrieved April 11, 2017, from The statistics Portal (Statista): https://www.statista.com/statistics/272014/global-social-networks-ranked-by-number-of-users/

Statt, N. (2016, February 1). WhatsApp has grown to 1 billion users. More than doubling since Facebook acquired it. *The Verge*.

Strecker, E. (2013, March 13). *'Veronica Mars' reaches Kickstarter goal.* Retrieved April 09, 2017, from Entertainment: http://ew.com/article/2013/03/13/veronica-mars-movie-is-a-go-kickstarter/

Tilburg, D. A. (2015, October 22). *Civic Crowdfunding is Not About the Money.* Retrieved January 31, 2017, from VOOR JE BUURT: https://www.voorjebuurt.nl/civiccrowdfundingisnotaboutthemoney/

Tomei, L. (2004). *An Examination of Cognitivism: The Psychology of Knowledge and Strategies.* Retrieved 04 28, 2017, from Learning Theories -- A Primer Exercise: http://faculty.rmu.edu/~tomei/ed711psy/c_ausub.htm

Trucano, M. (2011, February 16). *Mobile learning in developing countries in 2011: What's new, what's next?* Retrieved November 16, 2016, from EDUTECH, The World Bank IBRD-IDA: http://blogs.worldbank.org/edutech/water/mlearning2011-whatsnew

Tshabalala, S. (2015). *Why South Africa's largest mobile network, Vodacom, failed to grow M-Pesa.* Retrieved 04 06, 2017, from Quartz Africa: https://qz.com/467887/why-south-africas-largest-mobile-network-vodacom-failed-to-grow-mpesa/

Venable, N. (n.d.). *Spike Lee's Kickstarter Campaign Was Mostly Funded By Rich People.* Retrieved April 09, 2017, from Cinema Blend: http://www.cinemablend.com/new/Spike-Lee-Kickstarter-Campaign-Was-Mostly-Funded-By-Rich-People-39104.html

Voor je buurt. (n.d.). *About Voor Je Buurt Civic Crowdfunding.* Last visited January 31, 2017. https://www.voorjebuurt.nl/about/

Vosloo, S. (2014). *BBC –Future – Future of education in Africa is mobile.* Retrieved 11 16, 2016, from BBC: http://www.bbc.com/future/story/20120823-what-africa-can-learn-from-phones

Wadhwa, K. (2013). *Wikipedia Zero Getting Wikipedia to the people who need it most.* Retrieved 03 30, 2017, from Blog.Wikimedia.org: https://blog.wikimedia.org/2013/02/22/getting-wikipedia-to-the-people-who-need-it-most/

Wang, D. (n.d.). *Optimizing Campaign Length.* Retrieved April 11, 2017, from Shopify: The Ultimate Guide to Crowdfunding: https://www.shopify.com/guides/crowdfunding

Wishart, N. (2006). *MicroUpayment systems and their application to mobile networks: Examples of Mobile enabled services in the Philippines.* Infodev.

Wu, R. (2015, August 10). *How to Use Social Media for Crowdfunding Campaigns.* Retrieved January 31, 2017, from Social Media Examiner: http://www.socialmediaexaminer.com/social-media-for-crowdfunding/

KEY TERMS AND DEFINITIONS

Campaign Backers: The group of people that are convinced about the campaign concept/idea and are willing to partake in such civic crowdfunding project in kind or in cash. Campaign backers help with the spread of the project through their social media pages and contacts.

CC Strategy-IT Trends Mix: The selection of a suitable civic crowdfunding strategy based on the nature of civic crowdfunding project and some IT trends to help in enhancing the success of the civic campaign.

Civic Project: Any project that will have a positive effect on the people in a local community, in which the project will take place. By local community the authors mean town, city, or local area.

Crowdfunding Platform: The online crowdfunding companies empowered by law of the land in which the project will take place to provide a platform for a campaigner to launch its civic crowdfunding project. Crowdfunding platforms are expected to have IT features that will support existing IT tools.

Feature Phone: A mobile phone that has limited capabilities mainly use for making a call and have access to the internet via custom browser only. Basically, the type of mobile phones that exist at the time when there were no smartphones.

ICT Trend: The general directions of the information technology inventions. It is interchangeable and the same with the term IT trend.

IT Tools: All existing IT technology tools such as Facebook, Twitter, live streaming, SMS tool, mobile friendly websites, etc.

Mobile: All mobile technologies which include devices with or without default call capability and can be used to access the internet or run social media/phone apps or both.

Chapter 3
Collaborative Consumption as a Tool for Agricultural Expansion in Developing Countries:
Enriching Farmers by Delivering Value to Consumers

Abubakar Benna
Durham University, UK

ABSTRACT

Collaborative consumption is a broader term encompassing emerging areas, such as crowdfunding and the sharing economy, which enhance consumer enablement through direct interaction. This chapter addresses opportunities and challenges of how to support small- and medium-scale farmers in developing countries. Traditional agriculture, as well as urban agriculture, is rising with the significant urbanization that is occurring in developing economies. There is currently limited research on the value of collaborative consumption as a catalyst for agricultural development. Consequently, the aim of this chapter is to provide an overview of how collaborative consumption in agriculture can be supported. The study is conducted based on the review of literature and case studies related to both agriculture and collaborative consumption. A few key observations are provided in order to assist with the formulation of strategies that increase producer and customer satisfaction, value addition, and engagement.

INTRODUCTION AND BACKGROUND

Collaborative consumption has rapidly grown since its introduction as a concept by Rachel Botsman and Roo Rogers in 2010 (Botsman & Rogers, 2010). The impact that cohesive relationships have on the management and growth of collaborative consumption based businesses is important in all contexts especially within the agricultural sector. The chapter aims to determine which aspects of interaction have the highest impact in agriculture within developing economies through the analysis of recent and historical trends. The particular relationship between crowdfunding and collaborative consumptions

DOI: 10.4018/978-1-5225-3952-0.ch003

impact on agriculture in the developing world is our primary focus. Collaborative consumption has been gaining popularity globally with new companies disrupting various sectors e.g. Uber and transportation; Airbnb and the hotel industry.

Collaborative consumption in the new sharing economy currently accounts for $15 billion in global revenues and is projected to increase to around $335 billion by 2025 (Vaughan & Hawksworth, 2014). These Peer to Peer businesses aim to streamline interactions between buyers and sellers by providing value addition through the removal of intermediaries. Collaborative consumption is divided into three distinct actors, namely the platforms which are the peer to peer facilitators of a marketplace for exchanging goods or services. The entrepreneurs are the suppliers of these goods and services and the consumers are purchasers who demand to buy or rent from the entrepreneur by means of a platform (Sundararajan, 2014).

The framework presented will examine agricultural produce that traditionally undergo the least amount of value addition along the supply chain from producer to consumer. Produce such as livestock and food staples are ideal candidates for collaborative consumption as there are efficiencies that could be gained by providing consumers a structured direct access to producers.

Farmers are considered entrepreneurs due to the inherent nature of farming as a business activity. A key problem of entrepreneurship in agricultural production and also in agribusiness is the lack of financial resources (Njegomir, Tepavac, & Ivanišević, 2017). In developing countries the major sources of financing are through government assistance and micro-credit, provided by microfinance institutions. Field research on microfinance in the rural farming communities in Remo Division of Ogun State, Nigeria, Nosiru (2010) found that micro-credits could have prospect in improving the productivity of farmers and contributing to uplifting the livelihoods of disadvantaged rural farming communities (Njegomir, Tepavac, & Ivanišević, 2017). Our study aims to review the application of collaborative consumption in ways that can improve on the achievements and shortcomings of what microfinance has done for rural agricultural expansion in developing countries.

Traditional supply chains in agriculture have posed challenges in food waste, distribution and rising costs due to multiple actors' involvement in the value chain. The aim of crowdfunding is to create a direct link between producers and consumers in an effort to reduce costs and risks to both parties.

We will explore the trends in the agricultural industry; in particular, how consumption and production is reflecting the major shifts in consumer demography and economics. This section will demonstrate how digital technology can increase the involvement of local consumers and producers as well as investors with financial resources to assist in creating sustainable value for all three parties.

The overall aim of this research is to investigate the impact of various forms of collaborative consumption factors on agricultural development. In order to achieve this, the research will explore current literature and gain insight into relevant academic theories. Additionally; a review of pre-existent, but related business models, will be conducted to aid in the understanding of the underlying principles that influence agricultural development. A comparison of these models with established microfinancing models that are prevalent in developing countries will assist in establishing a framework to provide a more suitable solution

The adoption of the sharing economy as an economic driver and a means of resource maximization has mainly occurred in the developed world. Recent evidence is showing the significant success and potential in emerging markets, with some developmental organizations seeing its potential to drive economic development and income generation (Cheney, 2017). Agriculture has been one of the sectors to lag behind in collaborative consumption technologies and initiatives, however it is the baseline of human existence and food in general is seen as the largest global industry, a sector that is growing at an astonishing pace (Murray, 2007).

All activities involved in agricultural production are predicated on the foundation of an entrepreneurial effort. There has even been the suggestion that without entrepreneurship local agricultural producers would be unable to survive (Njegomir, Tepavac, & Ivanisevic, 2017). Agribusiness can be classified into various sectors the majority of which are shown in Table 1.

The lack of financial resources in the agribusiness sector and in basic agricultural production has been particularly impactful on new entrepreneurs and farmers who have lower credit accessibility, especially in the developing world. There are a few alternative credit and financing facilities available to these individuals and these include microfinance, angel investment, venture capital and crowdfunding. The proliferation of most of these sources of finance in the developing world has been slow and mostly ineffective in creating any significant changes for small to medium agribusiness actors. Even in emerging economies such as Serbia, 70% of non-bank sources of financing in the agricultural sector are from government assistance, followed by microfinance(11.7%), assistance from friends and relatives (10%), business angels (5%) and venture capitalists(3.3%) (Njegomir, Tepavac, & Ivanisevic, 2017).

The reliance on government assistance has resulted in the inefficient use of resources where many regions are able to be self-subsistent in the production of food, however most rely on significant imports. Table 2 shows the amount of land still available for cultivation which, if mobilised properly could significantly increase economic growth, improve food security and create a more balanced income distribution.

A significant development that has assisted the agriculture and food sectors recently has been the proliferation of microfinance. We examine the applicability of Crowdfunding in the improvement of agricultural production with a comparative analysis of other existing financial models; especially mi-

Table 1. Agribusiness sub-categories

• Farms • Credit Institutions • Agricultural Corporations • Suppliers of Inputs • Manufacturing Companies	• Transportation Providers • Wholesalers • Marketers • Restaurants • Retailers

Table 2. Available uncultivated land globally

Potential Availability of Uncultivated Land in Different Regions		Share of Land With Travel Time to Market (%)	
Region	**Total Area (1,000 ha)**	**< 6 hours**	**> 6 hours**
Sub-Saharan Africa	201,546	47	53
Latin America and the Caribbean	123,342	76	24
Eastern Europe and Central Asia	52,387	83	17
East and South Asia	14,341	23	77
Middle East and North Africa	3,043	87	13
Rest of World	50,971	48	52
Total	**445,624**	**59**	**41**

Deininger & Byerlee, 2011.

crofinance. Field research on microfinance in rural farm communities in Ogun State, Nigeria found that microfinance has the ability to improve farm production efficiency and can also contribute to the improvement of the livelihoods of poor rural farming communities(Nosiru 2010 as cited in (Njegomir, Tepavac, & Ivanisevic, 2017). An analysis of relative historical influences draws parallels advancing the growth of the collaborative consumption sector.

AGRICULTURE IN THE DEVELOPING WORLD

The development of Agriculture is seen as one of the most important factors required for poverty reduction and improved food security. In Sub-Saharan Africa, agricultural productivity per capita has remained stagnant over the last 40 years. In most of Sub-Saharan Africa, South Asia and South East Asia agriculture is mostly an activity for the rural poor on small holder farm operations. Many of these farmers are very efficient users of the resources available to them; however they remain in poverty due to the lack of technical and economic empowerment available to them (Jama & Pizarro, June 2008).

The growing levels of food insecurity in the developing world has become more widespread in recent years due to drought and conflict, in 2017 the most affected countries being Nigeria, Somalia, Yemen and Sudan (UNDP, 2017). Jama & Pizzaro state that the Green revolution was successful in India due to major technological and institutional changes which led to lasting impacts on addressing food security. Similar short-lived initiatives were also seen in Zimbabwe after independence, in Kenya leading up to the 1970s and in Nigeria after import restrictions were imposed on rice and maize. In recent years the highest poverty rates are still seen in Africa where nearly half of the population are smallholder farmers. This shows the unsustainable nature of some of the initiatives employed mostly due to rapid population growth, misguided and unsupported institutions and government corruption. This is counterintuitive given that African farms produce staple crops such as yams, cassava, maize and other cereal crops which provide high caloric intake and are more suitable for storage.

Other factors attributing to the lack of improvement in agricultural practices include the following (Jama & Pizarro, June 2008):

1. **Soil Infertility:** The use of inorganic fertilizers and proper application of organic fertilizers is usually only performed by a small fraction of the farming populace and farmers who do use them utilize amounts that are inadequate. Outside Africa, the use of fertilizers led to a 50% to 75% increase in yields.
2. **Irrigation:** Drought has severely impacted production and the use of new technologies in water harvesting and reuse, conventional and drip irrigation is required to ensure adequate yields are achieved.
3. **Market Access:** Forming trust relationships and building connections to supply chains as well as dissemination of information on new technologies and farming techniques have impacted the ability of small holder farms to compete. Information is required to better understand methods of delivery, quality standards, products and processes.
4. **Improved Seed Genetics:** Addressing the yield shortfall requires the selective breeding of plant genetics to achieve the best results.

5. **Extension Services:** The ratio of agricultural officers to farmers is often insufficient and even where there is availability of technologies and techniques; it is often out of reach of rural smallholder farmers.
6. **Land Tenure Rights:** Informal land ownership and lack of government registration dis-incentivize farmers from improving soil quality and investing in water resources. Furthermore this restricts their access to credit facilities and reduces the marketability of land under existing communal tenure systems.
7. **Credit Access:** With most farmers being women, gender inequality limits their access to funding. The lack of collateral resources severely limits them from accessing any available sources of funds.

The largest contributor to the above factors is the lack of access to credit. The majority of agricultural credit is provided by NGOs and government organizations. Malawi, in 2005 started a universal fertilizer subsidy program which resulted in record harvests in that year and the following year. These initiatives form the foundation of a start towards poverty alleviation and food security in such nations, but a requirement still exists for more private sector initiatives that are built on entrepreneurship. This can also be achieved through Public-private partnerships to develop sustainable production and distribution systems. Such institutions could allow farmers to bridge the gap between the search for partners, distance to formal markets and contract formation (Ortmann & King, 2010). Vertical integration of the supply chain can increase market share through access to the end users, however this requires a scale that is not achievable by single or group small holder farmers. Collaborative consumption may provide a solution to help bridge this gap.

April Rinne, a sharing economy pioneer, stated that "If people can meet more and more of their needs through their phone, we don't require some kind of central intermediary to interact with. This unlocks all kinds of assets, all kinds of talents and skills, all kinds of opportunities." (Cheney, 2017). Rinne also stated that "At the intersection of smart cities and the sharing economy is the role of the individual and the role of the human relationship". She introduces the concept of sharing cities which could be more sustainable, smart and resilient.

DEFINITION OF COLLABORATIVE CONSUMPTION

The sharing economy builds a community around the sharing of resources that lead to the creation, production, distribution, trade and consumption of goods and services by different people (Matofska, 2014). The current model has worked well in developed countries for expensive, popular items such as cars and homes, which are commonly underutilised (The Economist, 2013). Two companies which have had great success in these sectors and also serve as the symbolic models for collaborative consumption are Airbnb (hotels) and Uber (transportation). Figure 1 shows a model of the sharing economy as proposed by Hamari et al (2015).

Crowdsourcing is the originating concept behind the sharing economy; it facilitates resource mobilization where products, services or ideas are harnessed through the collaboration of numerous people or organisations (Goodrich, 2013). The rapid adoption of these concepts has led to the development of Collaborative Consumption, a concept pioneered by Rachel Botsman and Roo Rogers. It is described as a way of creating value from sharing resources to balance personal self-interest with the benefit of the larger community (Rowan, 2011).

Figure 1. Conceptual mapping of the sharing economy
Hamari, Sjöklint, & Ukkonen, 2015.

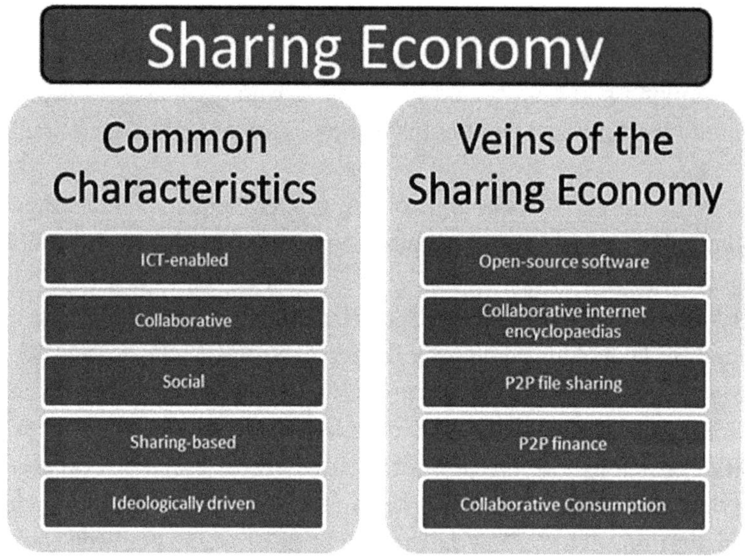

Numerous collaborative consumption based businesses have emerged in various sectors. Collaborative consumption facilitates the use of technology to maximize functional value through renting, lending, swapping, bartering, gifting and sharing products. These consist of various business models ranging from charitable, non-profit to for-profit enterprises.

Collaborative consumption has been spreading rapidly, due in part to rising debt levels and has been accelerated since the 2008 financial crises which caused people to rethink ownership, and overconsumption (Bassett, 2014). The four main drivers of this movement, as presented by Botsman (2013) are shown in Figure 2. The adoption of this model also is ideally situated to control the excesses of modern day consumerism which creates a significant amount of trash, pollution and wastes the world's limited resources (Botsman R., 2013).

There are traditional and informal models of Collaborative consumption, including second hand clothing exchanges, cooperatives, community gardens, and even the community library. The distinction of these from the recent movement is technology's ability to facilitate sharing in ways that have never

Figure 2. Drivers of collaborative consumption
Botsman R., 2013.

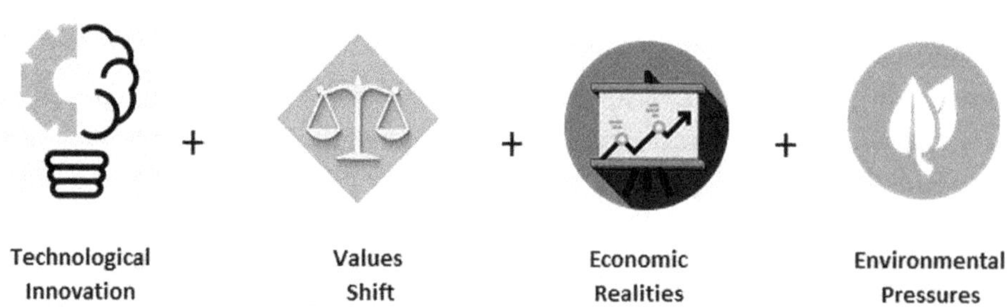

been possible before (John, 2013). Today's consumption is facilitated by technology that is growing at a rapid rate and increasing levels of efficiency that separates it from the traditional confines of the sharing economy (Botsman & Rogers, 2010). The application of collaborative consumption in conjunction with crowdfunding may present feasible actions for new agricultural entrepreneurs seeking to capitalise on the resources available through small holder farms with an underlying driver of a triple bottom line, which involves social, environmental and financial measures of business success.

FINANCIAL RESOURCES FOR THE AGRICULTURE SECTOR

Rising world food prices and population has resulted in a need for alternative sources of finance in agriculture, particularly in developing countries. The penetration of mobile telecom and the internet has greatly assisted other sectors in creating efficiencies never seen before. Access to banking and financial services has remained a challenge in the pursuit of financial inclusion particularly amongst rural small holder farmers. Financials services remain a major impediment to the growth of the agricultural sector which is predominantly located in rural areas. Lenders alleviate the need for screening applicants and the enforcement of loan obligations by charging high interest rates, requiring collateral, or only lending to borrowers with a repayment history or with alternate sources of consistent income (Meyer, 2015). Meyer identifies limitations to financial institutions in providing resources to the agricultural sector which include:

1. Risks to yield caused by weather, diseases and insects.
2. Price risks caused by the local and global market variations.
3. Uncertainties in timing due to repairs and reinvestments.
4. Illness, accidents and other lifecycle risks.
5. Liquidity risks caused by borrowers requiring funds simultaneously due to seasonality.
6. Differing yields amongst farms due to location and farm management practices.
7. Currency and inflationary risks.
8. Low levels of financial intermediation.
9. Requirement for substantial profitability.
10. Compromised court systems.
11. Disregard for contractual obligations.

These factors severely limit the interaction of financial institutions with small holder farms and cooperatives. There have been various financial models introduced to increase the security of investment and proffer financial inclusion for agricultural producers. In this section we will discuss the most prevalent non-traditional models and how they have performed.

Microfinance

Microfinance was introduced to increase financial inclusion to the marginalised communities in developing countries. Critics have objected to the disproportionate focus of credit alone to alleviate poverty (Meyer, 2015). It is expected that by 2019 market volume will increase to over $14 billion (Etzensperger, 2014). The system encourages group lending through a peer screening and guarantee arrangement to ensure repayment. An example is the Grameen Foundation which started in Bangladesh and has grown to become one of the largest MFIs with offices around the developing world. The successful application of (Micro Finance Institution) MFI loans require adaptive individual lending, accurate record keeping and the use of loan officers which increase the costs and risks. MFIs in Sub-Saharan Africa have higher operating costs of 19% in comparison to global rates of 14% with an internal rate of return of only 1% (Meyer, 2015). This is unacceptable for most financial institutions as an alternative investment vehicle and greatly reduces the survival and growth of this form of finance which has resulted in the slowing expansion of offerings in Africa.

To mitigate some risks, MFI's have provided credit scoring using mobile phones to allow smallholder farmers to establish a rating and review system. Cignifi in Brazil provides a mobile phone based scoring system by combining repayment information with credit card data. This strategy further enhances the elimination of an information gap that allows financial investment to individuals who have no history with conventional banking systems.

Social Investment Funds

Private investors and development agencies have targeted the value chain as opposed to providing financial resources. The growth of these funds has reached US$5 billion and almost all focus on agriculture (Meyer, 2015). The majority of these funds are based in the US and Europe which increases transactional costs. Many investors are unwilling to invest due to lack of legal protection and limited options for exit strategies. An example is Root Capital, a non-profit social investment fund that lends to business too large for MFIs and who are unable to access credit from commercial banks.

Crowdfunding

The increased significance of crowdfunding in developing countries as an alternative funding source has resulted in new methods of financial inclusion. The successful implementation depends on supportive government regulation, cultural suitability, modern technology and the creation of trust relationships. It is similar in nature to MFI's with the distinction that there is a direct relationship between the lenders and their borrowers where lenders choose who will receive finances. An example is Kiva.org which has lent to over a million borrowers and US$ 979 million to date (Kiva, 2017). Several crowdfunding platforms have emerged in various countries due to increase growth of the middle class and rapid adoption of technology. The main factors that affected the success of crowdfunding platforms include strong social media presence, availability of early stage ventures for funding, strong community networks and access to education (Meyer, 2015).

Member Owned Financial Institutions

Accumulating savings and credit associations (ASCA) as well as Rotating savings and credit associations (ROSCA) and Cooperatives have existed for decades and have millions of members in the developing world. An estimated 7% of the African population are members in some form of cooperatives. These organisations are dependent on the contribution of their members to provide a form of financial servicing to one another in an organized manner but are limited due to the amount of savings possible by members. They create a forced saving environment where funds are available based on need. Some of these cooperatives are successful and have grown into large organisations. Many of them face conflicts due to the fact that members are both owners and borrowers but they can be successful when they are well managed and regulated. Their sustainability is dependent on strong business models, cautious growth, low costs of services and a reliance on member networks rather than government or NGO services. An example is CARE International in Kenya which developed a mobile application to improve access and reduce transaction costs which was identified by members as a limitation on their ability to perform with current restrictions.

Warehouse Receipt Systems

These systems allow for the storage and classification of farm produce in a collateralised fashion to improve agricultural lending and marketability. Some systems operate at the village level to avoid issues with large scale warehousing; an example is a rice inventory product Grenier Commun Villageois in Madagascar which provides six month loans to allow producers to store their yield during harvest for subsequent marketing in the higher priced off-season.

COLLABORATIVE CONSUMPTION AS A MODEL FOR AGRICULTURE

Collaborative Consumption is widely viewed as a capitalist alternative to most traditional forms of financial inclusion. The intersection of this philosophy with crowdfunding provides a capitalistic solution to some of the issues discussed. Capitalism is an unmatched solution for addressing human development, increasing efficiency, job creation and increasing wealth (Porter & Kramer, 2011). Porter and Kramer state that the solution lies in creating shared value by increasing economic power for society through focusing on the needs and challenges, where businesses acting for profit and not as charitable donors, are the most powerful forces in fixing current issues. Redefining the purpose of a corporation to create a shared value, or win-win solution, will catalyse innovation, growth and productivity in a global economy.

The solution to developing economies has been relegated to governments and NGO's which have thus far been unable to break the cycle of poverty. Corporate social responsibility has arisen as a necessary cost due to external pressures and for the improvement of company images. By focusing on a shared value and a triple bottom line, companies can increase the overall pool of economic and social value. Porter and Kramer recount the Fair Trade movement which has served small holder farms, particularly in coffee production, by increasing the revenue they receive through equitable trade. Fair trade focuses on redistribution of income rather than increasing the overall value created in an economic system. By utilising a shared value approach the focus would be mostly on improving outreach to farms to enable improved yields, quality of produce and sustainable farm management. Studies of cocoa farmers in Ivory Coast show that fair trade methods increased incomes by 10% to 20% whereas shared value investment could raise incomes by 300% (Porter & Kramer, 2011).

The concept of shared value serves the same ethos as collaborative consumption and crowdfunding. It involves businesses acting towards the involvement of the community in order to achieve a shared objective with synergistic reciprocity. Working towards the success of the community leads to increased demand for businesses products in a community that requires successful business for job creation and economic stability. This concept of value creation increases the interdependence of economic and social development. The increased propagation of crowdfunding and collaborative consumption could be attributed to more consumers being focused on the impact the products they purchase have on the overall value chain. More people are becoming interested in how their consumption patterns are affecting the various actors involved in the movement of products through the supply chain. Businesses are also more effective at marketing and telling the story of their products than governments or NGOs, which increases market acceptance by consumers.

More business is evolving to cater to socially conscious consumers while providing social and economic value. An example is WaterHealth international, a for-profit enterprise which provides water purification and distribution of clean water at an affordable price to over one million consumers in India, Philippines and Ghana. Thomson Reuters has also developed a monthly service for farmers to provide weather and crop market price information as well as agricultural techniques to over 2 million rural farmers which has increased their incomes by over 60% (Porter & Kramer, 2011). Olam international, a cashew producer has opened local processing plants in Africa and created strategic relationships with local farmers which collectively provided 17,000 jobs to local people of which 95% were women in rural areas. These are all examples of how corporations are utilising local presence to enhance socio-economic development.

The application of collaborative consumption enables these practices to achieve even greater efficiency. By providing both the funding vehicle to enable rural farmers to improve production as well providing direct access to the consumers of their products, more economic value can be gained. Many supply chains are inefficient, particularly in developing nations and through the vertical integration of these chains; companies can greatly increase access, affordability and profitability to the various contributors and recipients. The promotion of local food systems is based on the improvement of sustainable practices and minimization of negative impacts to the people and businesses in the system. Connecting consumers with farmers who grow their food and the land on which it is grown, allows the creation of economic benefits for farmers, consumers, society and nature while providing the resources to build communities (Flörkemeier, 2012).

The direct application of both collaborative consumption and crowdfunding has been seen in Community Supported Agriculture (CSA) which is the direct partnership between the producers and consumers who share the risk and reward of production. These organizations traditionally are based on Subscription models where consumers receive a specific share of the yield based on their contributions. An alternate form is a Shareholder model where consumers form groups and hire farmers to produce for them, possibly after the purchase of land. In both models the CSA's will arrange for the distribution of the produce to their members either directly or through centralised distribution sites.

The main benefit for farmers is the shared risk of production as well as a reliable market source and a reduction of waste and food spoilage. Additionally, most CSA's will pay membership fees upfront which enables the farmers to have sufficient capital for inputs. For the consumers the main benefits include traceability of their food source, cheaper access to good produce and the ability to contribute to a sustainable system. The community benefits due to a focus on preserving income within the local economy. The use of collaborative consumption technology could further strengthen these networks by providing the ability to group local farmers as well as urban consumers to increase the economic value of production. By facilitating linkages to urban centers farmers are able to attract higher prices for their products and consumers are able to receive regionally grown products at cheaper prices. Further to this, technology could allow this aggregation to result in excess supply being sold to alternative markets which could then be distributed on a sharing ratio between the producer and members of the system. This stimulates more interaction into the system and could attract further membership which may lead to even greater economic value creation.

The issues identified with land access for producers could be alleviated if consumers become investors where they are able to pool together funds for the purchase of farmland. The increasing price of productive farmland could provide substantial equity to the system and allow consumers/investors to capitalise on their contribution. This would also increase the commitment of members, especially if the farmers can earn equity in the land and eventually purchase it from members through the increased economic value of their production and resultant higher incomes. This could provide a fully integrated financial system through crowdfunding as well as a market through collaborative consumption where efficiency is maximised. A system such as this also would provide urban consumers the opportunity to participate in micro investments in farmland where normally the costs of purchasing large tracts of land are out of reach of most individuals as it is controlled by mostly institutional funding or long established farming families.

The use of technology could also further increase producer and consumer involvement as the consumer being the landowner can request certain specifications on inputs and the types of produce. The vested interest of the consumers and farmers, who would eventually own the land, could result in better farm management practices and a willingness to invest in better farm technology and infrastructure. An additional income stream from this could be derived from eco-tourism where urban residents visit rural farms. The trajectory of various models coupled with the emergence and availability of technology in many rural areas as well as the increased consciousness of consumers in the food chain, may provide the necessary components to see such models arise in the near future.

A significant determinant of the success of such a model will be the trust relationships that can be fostered through the use of an intermediary. This provides a unique business opportunity for companies who could be the actors to provide a platform to facilitate these relationships and engage both the consumer and producer in a synergistic manner. This is a form of equity crowdfunding, an example of which has recently launched in South Africa called Livestock Wealth where investors can finance the purchase of cattle which are subsequently sold to market for a return on investment. Although this is not a fully vertically integrated platform, there is no access to land ownership or direct to consumer sales, it is a great sign of the possibilities that digital platforms provide for developing nations. This theoretical marriage of collaborative consumption and crowdfunding may lead to a new sector of the sharing economy. This new subset maintains the elements of vertical integration and collaborative consumption (collaborative integration) as well as equity crowdfunded production, much like the block chains have disrupted currencies with companies such as Bitcoin. We will refer to this new subset as Equity Crowdfund Integration (ECI)

There has been limited crowdfunding ventures in the agricultural space and those that exist are mostly in the developed world. In the US, a company called BarnRaiser has a mission of raising US$1Billion to provide capital for food innovation (Roocke, Oct 2015). It provides urban residents the ability to fund ideas and beliefs that are in line with their own. Some projects on the platform will provide rewards to backers if the project is eventually successful. Reward based model analysis has shown that the funding costs is usually higher than the market price of the main reward received (Yoo & Choe, 2014). This provides further merit for platforms in the agro-food sector as they can reward backers with produce or provide additional value added services such as farm to table restaurants.

The shared value objective in collaborative consumption would likely see more impact and growth in an equity based model rather than a charitable one, especially with the high rate of growth that is achievable in adequately managed systems in developing countries.

Some of the other factors that can contribute to a more efficient system include a strong active social network, a reliable payment system that eliminates cash transactions, a passionate audience and the appropriate regulatory framework. Research in Zimbabwe on the plausibility of crowdfunding shows a significant correlation between these factors and the success of platforms (Munyanyi & Mapfumo, 2016). The research also shows that the use of platforms as 'network technologies' improves the dissemination of product information and customer awareness as well as willingness of customers to purchase. These factors all contribute to the Total cost of ownership which is greatly impacted by transaction costs.

Peter Murrell proposes a few farming characteristics that are relevant to transaction cost analysis (Murrell, 2001).The first characteristic of a joint product is the belief that in producing output, farmers can change land quality. A collaborative ownership model of the land will ensure that these changes are beneficial to its value, as land use specification is often too complex to be fully covered in contractual relationships. Another issue is landlord authority and insecure tenure where short term contracts are used by landlords to enforce authority and increase their returns on rents.

The use of an equity based crowdfunded production approach would eliminate the need for such vested interest agreements and would work towards a longer term shared value solution. This is especially beneficial due to the long term payback period in land investments. A further factor explored by Murrell is the costly monitoring of land in conventional tenure relations; he argues that landlords will gain significantly if the tenant uses the land in the manner that is consistent with landlord specifications, which implies value addition methods of management. Land quality variation and non-measurability is another factor that impacts transactional costs and can lead to issues with conventional rental relationships.

The process by which investors work with farmers to purchase the land where the farmers earn equity, in the case of crowdfunded production could alleviate this concern due to both parties having an equity stake in the selection of the best possible land for both production and long term value upside potential. This also ensures that information is shared accurately and transparently between the farmers and investors\consumers in order to make the best decisions. The requirement that the land chosen can produce ample yields for the investor's consumption as well as provide extra income for the farmer to earn greater equity will ensure there is a constant balance in maintaining their best interest and sharing information. The final issue of tenant immobility suggests that in traditional rental agreements, farmers can be disadvantaged in the long run by the acquisition of equipment and farm specific knowledge which could lead to losses if their contracts are terminated. An equity based model ensures that this human and physical capital is theirs to lose through mismanagement and can be retained if they provide their best efforts towards the success of the partnership. The challenge for the digital economy is the facilitation and nurturing of these relationships.

A major factor in traditional rent models required for success is trust in equitable future treatments by both parties as well as the trust in the security of tenure. The introduction of new equity based participation models will also increase trust and the commitment of farmers when they compare their model with what other farmers are receiving. Sharing can initially show a reduction in transaction costs and an improvement in quality, however the long term effect is best summarized by Schelling who stated that "risk a small investment to create a tradition of trust" (Schelling, 1960). Masuku et al. (as cited in Ortmann & King, 2010) analysed sugarcane growers and millers in the Swaziland sugar supply chain. Their reasearch showed that higher levels of trust lead to greater cooperation and higher commitment levels to the business relationship. They found that relationships built on trust and mutual respect were more likely to succeed than those of convenience supported by legal contracts. Reciprocity creates a positive cycle of interactions and encourges social integration, inclusion and collaboration.

A long term shared value approach of ECI allows small holders to benefit from stable and long term trading relationships which facilitate active involvement of the wealthier more dedicated and connected actors (investors/consumers) to ensure that production can create excess and that the excess is marketable at optimal value. As a platform expands its services across cities and countries, it is able to exercise greater power in the purchase of inputs, quality standardization, marketing and sale of outputs, transportation and distribution systems as well as legal protection from unstable and corrupt governments.

Wynne and Lynne (as cited in Ortmann & King, 2010) anaylsed survey data from small and large poultry farms in rural KwaZulu-Natal and outlined the impact of commercial poultry production on the local economy. They outlined that the removal of various constraints from a large number of small enterprises would have a more positive effect than the encouragement of large enterprises to grow even larger. This was due in part to the improvement of eduction, infrastructure, technology and knowledge transfer as well as maintaining the revenues in the communities that are generating them. Ortmann and King indicate that meat, poultry and eggs are the most favorable produce for vertical integration, long term contracting and supply relationships. By building the capacity of small holder farms through ECI, linkages for the supply of excess produce can be created with supermarkets in urban areas which are becoming more popular in developing countries due to the high quality standards, food safety and consistency of supply. Such relationships would also increase the attractiveness for new investors in the system. Research in Botswana showed that herd productivity in ranches increased with greater investment in operating inputs and fixed improvements and was in correlation with the security of land tenure (Ortmann & King, 2010).

In urban areas where religious, ethnic or cultural affiliations create a demand for specific foods, preparation and ritual slaughter these foods may be unavailable in most super markets and the direct linkage with farmers for these growing segments of the population provides a unique niche market that could create added long term shared value in an ECI system.

COLLABORATIVE CONSUMPTION: COMPARISON TO MICROFINANCE.

With Collaborative consumption at such an early stage and some of the proposed solutions such as ECI primarily theoretical, a review of foundational predecessors can help in increasing our understanding of the interactions in such systems. The foundational elements of formal Collaborative Consumption and the sharing economy were pioneered by the microfinance sector.

Microfinance provides us a comparative analysis due to its similar reliance on the ability to borrow, the need for trust, social collateral, community and accountability. The main distinction between these systems and modern day collaborative consumption are: the use of technology, as well as the diversity and geographic distribution of online communities.

Muhammad Yunus pioneered microfinance as the founder of Bangladesh's Grameen Bank in 1983 (Dowla, 2006). The scheme depends on community participation for the borrowing of funds or purchase of shared assets, where community members participate as co-borrowers or guarantors.

Grameen setup its services with the provision of loans to groups of 5 socially knit members with pre-existing trust relationships and a willingness to guarantee each other's ability to repay. Two members initially received the loans, and with their suitable repayment history two more members became eligible for loans. A fifth person, was elected as the chairperson of the group, and would be the last to receive any funding. The use of these groups leveraged peer pressure to guarantee repayment. This encouraged members to create a support system, especially during times of difficulty (Dowla, 2006).

Rinne (2012) discusses important lessons that could be learnt from microfinance which are applicable in the world of Collaborative Consumption. These are discussed below:

1. **Empowerment:** Microfinance fosters empowerment by allowing people access to previously unattainable resources. Collaborative Consumption similarly empowers people to create economic value from underutilized assets or skills. In recent years more people are using collaborative consumption as a sole income source, which is a change from the initial periods where it was seen as a form of income supplementation. Gerstner (2014) identified an employee who left Goldman Sachs to work fulltime with the DogVacay platform as a dog sitter, walker and trainer. More options are now available for people who would otherwise have never had access to livelihoods they enjoy and are committed to.
2. **Trust, Reputation, and Social Collateral:** Rinne (2012) describes that in microfinance, a participant's reputation is equivalent to a bankable credit rating. The importance of social collateral in group lending ensures that members are responsible for each other upholding their repayment obligations. Innovative platforms have enabled the facilitation of social collateral through ranking systems and user feedback. Rowan (2011) describes a new era where physical wealth matters much less than reputation.
3. **Risks:** There is an innate risk of lending without any physical collateral to someone that may have no form of credit history or verifiable identity. The use of formal and informal systems (e.g. group education, support services, social capital, and identity verification) worked in microfinance to mitigate these risks, and these are applicable in the new sharing economy.
4. **The Importance of an Effective Enabling Environment:** Rinne (2012) defines an enabling environment as:

the legal and regulatory framework within which a business, sector, or idea is allowed to manifest and operate. It includes laws and policies that permit, encourage, and mainstream the creation of companies and supporting infrastructure, as well as promote good governance and foster a socially responsible community of customers and beneficiaries (Rinne, 2012, para. 14).

Dowla (2006) states that "group lending enables development of social relations/cohesion" (Dowla, 2006, p. 111). The evolution of collaborative consumption will enable actors in the system to develop their own regulatory frameworks. Contrary to this, the abuse by operators, of unregulated platforms could result in a decreased level of trust from the regulatory authorities and may lead to more stringent restrictions for activities in the sector.

5. **Diversity of Models:** There are various types of Microfinance Institutions (MFI's), all with different mandates to provide services ranging from credit, savings, cooperatives to non-profit (Rinne, 2012). This same diversity is increasing in collaborative consumption and will lead to more interesting models developed.

THE GROWTH OF COLLABORATIVE CONSUMPTION AND CROWDFUNDING

Rinne (2012) and Rowan (2011) believe that the sharing economy has been based on a trust facilitated by technology. Platforms providing the ability to view inventory, create schedules, accept deposits and online payments have facilitated the removal of barriers to the sharing of resources. The use of social media and technology has allowed the platforms to expand in a much faster fashion than was previously possible.

The increase in accountability through the use of profiles, rating systems and identity verification has resulted in participants feeling more secure about performing transactions which assist them in saving money or making money with dormant assets (Gerstner, 2014).

Freese & Schonber (2014), state that some segments of collaborative consumption are growing by as much as 30% annually. The factors that have been encouraging this growth are as follows:

1. **A New Consumption Culture:** The millennial generation of consumers are more comfortable with access to an asset rather than ownership of it.
2. **Scarce Resources:** Freese and Schonberg (2014) believe that the scarcity of raw materials and resources have led to higher product prices and a need for low cost alternatives. The recent economic crisis has also led to more people being conscious of how they spend and earn their money (Lee, Rabanal, & Sandri, 2010).
3. **Digitalisation:** Innovations in communications technology has increased access to customers and providers.
4. **Demographic Trends:** The movement of people into urban centers has resulted in a greater focus on environmental impact through the elimination of pollution and congestion. The increased life expectancy of residents coupled with the increase in single person households has led to greater requirements for targeted mobility offerings.

The factors discussed above can be viewed as additional drivers of collaborative consumption as well as crowdfunding based business models as identified by Freese & Schonber (2014) in line with the similar drivers identified by Botsman (2013).

The crowdfunding industry is predicted to raise over $1 Trillion by 2025. As discussed earlier, one of the pioneers of Crowdfunding in the developing world has been Kiva.org. Founded in 2005 its focus has been to facilitate loans to entrepreneurs in underserved and less privileged locations particularly those in the agricultural sector. Their platform acts a meeting point for borrowers and lenders. Kiva is currently active in 83 developing countries and has relationships with over 300 field partners who facilitate the loan process. Their current field partners include MFIs, social businesses, schools and non-profits. Kiva has experienced three main risks in loan repayment; firstly there is borrower risk, followed by the risk of working with field partners and finally currency risk. (Moleskis & Canela, 2016). Currency risk is mitigated by sharing liability or keeping funds in US dollars.

Moleskis & Canela (2016) conducted a detailed study of Kiva and showed that the largest proportion of lenders were based in the US and Canada. Interestingly the top lender categories were students at 15% followed by teachers at 8% of the overall reported occupations. These findings provide some insight for new participants on where the ideal sources of investment may originate from. Agriculture (22.93%)

combined with Food (24.18%) formed the two largest sectors represented in loan request on the Kiva platform. The greatest majority of borrowers were women with their proportion rising to 74% of overall loan recipients. Additionally, Africa (27.78%) and Asia (34.47%) were the regions with the greatest loan requests. These additional findings indicate to us where the demand for crowdfunding is greatest and also are encouraging signs that people in these regions and of such demographics have availed themselves of the resources to seek other avenues for securing financing and moving towards financial inclusion.

For companies evaluating the success of Kiva.org it is also encouraging to see that loan request expiration rates are about 3% on average. On the Kiva platform a loan is posted for 30 days and it will expire if the funding goal is not reach, at which point all funds are returned back to the lender. In addition to this, In Africa the expiration rate is 1.4% while in Asia it is only 1.7% even though the majority of loans originate in these regions. Default rates for loans on Kivas platform have been steadily decreasing where in 2014 only 134 out of 157,308 loans were in default. (Moleskis & Canela, 2016)

The success of both collaborative consumption as well as crowdfunding platforms evidence the likelihood for significant growth in the sector, rooted on the ability of platforms to address associated risks.

THE CHALLENGES OF COLLABORATIVE CONSUMPTION

Gerstner (2014) highlights two issues presented as risks to collaborative consumption within the sharing economy; these are specifically taxes and insurance. Gerstner (2014) reports that in the US only a few platforms issue a statement of income, therefore developing nations will likely be lagging far behind in reporting. This can result in the loss of tax revenue for income that is not reported to the government tax collector. Utilizing an ECI model would eliminate some of these shortfalls as the platform would be required to maintain accurate record keeping satisfying investors need for transparency.

Established sharing services provide insurance coverage for liability and damage caused by users. The risk of damage or liability is borne by the consumer who may be required to pay, or the provider who may experience lawsuits for damages. It is important that any platform, particularly in the agricultural sector provides adequate insurance coverage to ensure both the farmers and investors are adequately covered for loss of investments, equity and revenues. The lack of a centralised trust and verification system may mean that abusers may move from platform to platform unnoticed. The ECI model eliminates such dubious behavior as all participants in the system are looking for long term shared value.

The overall sector is still at its infancy; with the risks associated such as insurance, tax, and reputation as evidenced by the research from Malhorta and Van Allstyne (2014). It remains clear the sector offers many opportunities for the efficient use of underutilised assets, cost savings, environmental efficiency and the redistribution of wealth from corporations to individuals (Botsman R., 2013).

The growth of this sector particularly in the area of agriculture is impacted primarily by the concepts of trust and accountability. These form the basis for the transaction due to the collaborative nature, which brings together people with no prior interaction. Trust as a limiting factor in the growth of platforms is reliant on one party's willingness to be vulnerable to the others actions. (Mayer, 1995). Zucker's three central modes of trust production are: Characteristic based, institutional based, and process based trust (Zucker, 1986).

Characteristic based trust is held on the basis of harmonies between the interacting parties, where they identify with one another on the basis of ethnicity, sex or age. Son et al. (2006) suggest that this definition does not lend well to the electronic marketplace, due in part to a lack of demographic visibility.

Institutional based trust is dependent on societal structures where participants have a sense of commonality within which consistent interaction leads to the creation of trust in future transactions. Structural safeguards enhance the level of trust and protect participants against losses. These safeguards include "guarantees, regulations, promises, legal recourse or other procedures" (McKnight et al., 2002).

The final form of trust is process-based which relies on the experiences from interactions with one another, or the information available on various transactions. Trust mechanisms are built on a foundation of accountability and the reciprocity of transactions which serve as "reputation capital", described by Botsman as a form of implied currency in platforms (Botsman R., 2012).

FUTURE RESEARCH DIRECTIONS

The rapid adoption of collaborative consumption presents various research opportunities.

Lamberton (2015) suggests research could be conducted to examine how similarity and relatedness are assessed and the relation to their effects on collaborative consumption. This will further divulge the importance of trust in transactions whereby the importance of trust could decrease due to the efficiency of the collaboration.

Further research to overcome the limitations discussed could be continued to firstly examine the acceptability of collaboration by consumers and identifying specific limitations present. Additionally researchers should seek to understand more detailed lessons from the successes of microfinance which could be applied in collaborative consumption efforts. More research on the concept of ECI could shed light to new models that could be created to further enhance financial inclusion and poverty alleviation.

CONCLUSION

The expansion of collaborative consumption in recent years has changed the way some industries are viewed by the general public. Airbnb, for example has disrupted the hotel and vacation rental industry by allowing home owners and travelers globally with an alternate solution. These disruptions have the potential to impact agriculture in unprecedented ways if creative entrepreneurs are willing to accept the challenge and create options for consumers, investors and producers. The spread of mobile phone technology across the most remote rural areas of developing nations provides an inimitable opportunity to link rural producers with urban consumers as well as linkages to international investors who can help in the facilitation of investment and knowledge transfer. With the right platform there is an opportunity to create lasting value which leads more people to financial inclusion, improves food security and ultimately empowers the less privileged amongst us to make the best use of the resources available to them by providing collaborative objectives.

REFERENCES

Afuah, A., & Tucci, C. L. (2013). Value Capture and Crowdsourcing. *Academy of Management Review*, *38*(3), 457–460. doi:10.5465/amr.2012.0423

Barry, J. S. (2014, April). Crowdsourcing in the 21st Century. *The CPA Journal*, 5.

Bassett, K. (2014, March). Prepare to Share. *Managementtoday.com*, 35-38.

Botsman, R. (2013). *The Sharing Economy Lacks a Shared Definition*. Retrieved 02 12, 2015, from http://www.fastcoexist.com/3022028/the-sharing-economy-lacks-a-shared-definition

Botsman, R. (2014, September). Sharing's Not Just for Startups. *Harvard Business Review*, 23–25.

Botsman, R. (2012, August 20). *Welcome to the new reputation economy*. Retrieved 02 21, 2015, from http://www.wired.co.uk/magazine/archive/2012/09/features/welcome-to-the-new-reputation-economy?page=all

Botsman, R., & Rogers, R. (2010). *What's Mine Is Yours: The Rise of Collaborative Consumption*. New York: Harper Business.

Busarovs, A. (2011). Crowdsourcing as user-driven innovation,New business Philosophy's model. *Journal of Business and Management*, *4*, 53–60.

Cheney, C. (2017, March 9). *What can the sharing economy bring to emerging markets?* Retrieved 05 05, 2017, from https://www.devex.com/news/what-can-the-sharing-economy-bring-to-emerging-markets-89214

Cheney, C. (2017). *What can the sharing economy bring to emerging markets?* Retrieved May 12, 2017, from https://www.devex.com/news/what-can-the-sharing-economy-bring-to-emerging-markets-89214

Collaborative Consumption. (2015). Retrieved 02 10, 2015, from http://www.collaborativeconsumption.com/about/

Deininger, K., & Byerlee, D. (2011). *Rising Global Interestin Farmland: Can It Yield Sustainable and Equitable Benefits?* Washington, DC: The World Bank. doi:10.1596/978-0-8213-8591-3

Desai, S. (2014, August). Effects of latest trends on sharing economy. *Siliconindia*, 10.

Dowla, A. (2006). In credit we trust: Building social capital by Grameen Bank in Bangladesh. *Journal of Socio-Economics*, *35*(1), 102–122. doi:10.1016/j.socec.2005.12.006

Dubois, E., Schor, J., & Carfagna, L. (2014, Spring). Connected consumption a sharing economy takes hold. *Rotman Management*, 50-55.

Etzensperger, C. (2014). *Microfinance Market Outlook 2015*. Zurich: responsAbility Investments AG.

Finley, K. (2013). *Trust in the Sharing Economy: An Exploratory Study* (MA Thesis). University of Warwick.

Flörkemeier, T. (2012). *Local Food Systems and Community Supported Agriculture*. Freiburg: Albert-Ludwigs-Universität Freiburg.

Gallardo, J. (2001). *A Framework for Regulating Microfinance Institutions:The Experience in Ghana and the Philippines*. The World Bank.

Gerstner, L. (2014, July). Cash In on the Sharing Economy. Money, 58-61.

Goodrich, R. (2013, February 26). *What is Crowdsourcing?* Retrieved 1 18, 2015, from http://www.businessnewsdaily.com/4025-what-is-crowdsourcing.html

Hamari, J., Sjöklint, M., & Ukkonen, A. (2015). *The sharing economy: Why people participate in collaborative consumption*. Copenhagen: Social Science Research Network.

Jama, B., & Pizarro, G. (2008, June). Agriculture in Africa: Strategies to Improve and Sustain Smallholder Production Systems. *Annals of the New York Academy of Sciences*, *1136*(1), 218–232. doi:10.1196/annals.1425.034 PMID:18579884

John, N. A. (2013). Sharing, collaborative consumption and Web 2.0. London: Media@LSE, London School of Economics and Political Science ("LSE").

Kiva. (2017). *Kiva.org*. Retrieved 05 13, 2017, from www.kiva.org

Koch, C. (2014, May). Ready to join the sharing economy. *Director*, 66.

Lakhani, K. R. (2013). Using the Crowd as an Innovation Partner. *Harvard Business Review*, *91*(4), 60–69. PMID:23593768

Lamberton, C. (2015). Consumer Sharing: Collaborative Consumption, from Theoretical Roots to New Opportunities. Cambridge Handbook of Consumer Psychology, 0, 1-54.

Lee, J., Rabanal, P., & Sandri, D. (2010, January 15). U.*S. Consumption after the 2008 Crisis*. International Monetary Fund.

Matofska, B. (2014). *What is the Sharing Economy?* Retrieved 12 08, 2014, from http://www.thepeoplewhoshare.com/blog/what-is-the-sharing-economy/

Mayer, R. C. (1995). An Integrative Model of. *Academy of Management Review*, *20*(3), 709–734.

McAlpine, T. (2014, December). The Sharing Economy. *Credit Union Management*, 40-41.

Meyer, R. L. (2015). *Financing agriculture and rural areas in sub-Saharan Africa Progress, challenges and the way forward*. London: International Institute for Environment and Development.

Microfinance. (2014). In *Wikipedia*. Retrieved 12 08, 2014, from http://en.wikipedia.org/wiki/Microfinance

Moleskis, M., & Canela, M. Á. (2016). Crowdfunding success: The case of kiva.org. Barcelona: IESE Business School.

Munyanyi, W., & Mapfumo, A. (2016). Factors Influencing Crowdfunding Plausibility in Post Hyperinflationary Zimbabwe. *Journal of Entrepreneurship and Business Innovation*, *3*(1), 18–27. doi:10.5296/jebi.v3i1.9244

Murray, S. (2007). *The World's Biggest Industry*. Retrieved 05 05, 2017, from https://www.forbes.com/2007/11/11/growth-agriculture-business-forbeslife-food07-cx_sm_1113bigfood.html

Murrell, P. (2001). The Economics of Sharing: A Transactions Costs Analysis of Contractual Choice in Farming. *The Bell Journal of Economics*, *14*(1), 283–293. doi:10.2307/3003555

Nicole. (2010). *Collaborative Consumption Will Save Us*. Retrieved 12 8, 2014, from http://www.aviewfromtheedge.net/blog/2010/11/01/collaborative-consumption-will-save-us/

Njegomir, V., Tepavac, R., & Ivanisevic, N. (2017). Alternative Sources of Financing entrepreneurial undertakings in agriculture. *Economics of Agriculture*, *1*(64), 295–306.

Ortmann, G. F., & King, R. P. (2010). Research on agri-food supply chains in Southern Africa involving small-scale farmers: Current status and future possibilities. *Agrekon*, *49*(4), 397–417. doi:10.1080/03031853.2010.526428

Owyang, J., Samuel, A., & Grenville, A. (2014, Mar 02). *Are we becoming a collaborative economy? Possibly*. Retrieved 01 16, 2015, from http://www.slideshare.net/jeremiah_owyang/sharingnewbuying/1

Porter, M. E., & Kramer, M. (2011, January). Creating Shared Value: How to reinvent capitalism—and unleash a wave of innovation and growth. Harvard *Business Review*, 1–17.

Rinne, A. (2012). *Shareable*. Retrieved 12 08, 2014, from http://www.shareable.net/blog/lessons-from-microfinance-for-the-sharing-economy

Roocke, N. (2015). Crowdfunding - an option for projects in agriculture. *Australian Canegrower*, (26), 20.

Rowan, D. (2011). *Rentalship Is the New Ownership in the Networked Age*. Retrieved 12 8, 2014, from http://www.wired.com/2011/02/rentalship-the-new-ownership/

Saxton, G. D., Oh, O., & Kishore, R. (2013). Rules of Crowdsourcing Models, Issues, and Systems of Control. *Information Systems Management*, *30*(1), 2–20. doi:10.1080/10580530.2013.739883

Schelling, T. (1960). *The Strategy of Conflict*. Cambridge, MA: Harvard University Press.

Schulist, K. (2012). *Collaborative consumption: A new form of consumptionin a changing economy* (MBA Thesis). University of North Carolina.

Sundararajan, A. (2014). *Peer-to-Peer Businesses and the Sharing (Collaborative) Economy: Overview, Economic Effects and Regulatory Issues*. New York: NYU Stern School of Business.

The Economist. (2013, March 9). *The rise of the sharing economy*. Retrieved 01 10, 2015, from http://www.economist.com/news/leaders/21573104-internet-everything-hire-rise-sharing-economy

UNDP. (2017). *Averting Famine in Northeast Nigeria, Somalia, South Sudan and Yemen*. UN Development Programme.

Vaughan, R., & Hawksworth, J. (2014). *The sharing economy:how will it disrupt your business?* PWC.

Villano, M. (2014, December). The sharing economy 2.0. *Entrepreneur*, 56-58 .

Yoo, Y. G., & Choe, Y. C. (2014). Current Status of Korean Crowdfunding Industry and its Applicability to Agrifood Sector. *Advanced Science and Technology Letters*, *49*, 213–221. doi:10.14257/astl.2014.49.41

Zucker, L. (1986). Production of Trust: Institutional Sources of Economic. In B. M. Cummings (Ed.), *Research in Organization Behavior* (pp. 53–111). Greenwich, CT: JAI Press.

Zweig, J. (2013). *live.ca*. Retrieved 02 10, 2015, from http://www.liveca.ca/pay-no-tax-how-the-cra-knows-youre-cheating/

KEY TERMS AND DEFINITIONS

Collaborative Consumption: A system through which consumers are able to interact with other consumers and owners directly or through an intermediary to share resources.

Crowdfunding: A system where entrepreneurs are able to receive funding from investors with an aligned vision for new or existing ventures through the use of established platforms.

Crowdsourcing: The practice of amalgamating the knowledge and input of various individuals to arrive at innovative solutions.

Equity Crowdfunded Integration: The process through which investors can participate as consumers with producers to create a vertically integrated and jointly owned supply chain.

Shared Value: A process where the common goal is to increase the benefit of all members while increasing overall growth.

Sharing Economy: A system through which consumers, producers, and intermediaries utilize resource sharing to increase efficiency or reduce waste.

Smart City: A local environment facilitated by technology to achieve efficiency and access to information in a way that creates shared value.

Social Collateral: The value of a person or organizations reputation based on their interaction with others and the economy or market they participate in.

Chapter 4
From Informal to Inclusive Urbanization:
Options for Funding the Transformation in India

Manisha Jain
Leibniz Institute of Ecological Urban and Regional Development, Germany

N. Sridharan
BHOPAL, India

Artem Korzhenevych
Leibniz Institute of Ecological Urban and Regional Development, Germany & TU Dresden, Germany

ABSTRACT

The contemporary process of urbanization prevalent in the countries of the Global South, especially in Africa and Asia, is characterized by an unprecedented rise in urban populations, exceeding the capacity of local authorities to provide essential services. In particular, local authorities lack the funding required to build adequate infrastructure. One striking feature of contemporary urbanization is the growth in informal urbanized settlements, called "census towns" in India, "urban villages" in China, and "townships" in South Africa. Compared to India, China and South Africa have been able to turn around their cities and revamp them within 10 years. These countries present similarities and differences in managing and providing basic urban services. In this chapter, an attempt is made to analyze and compare the urbanization process in these countries and to identify some financial alternatives and policy implications to foster inclusive growth by integrating informal settlements into mainstream urbanization with focus on India.

DOI: 10.4018/978-1-5225-3952-0.ch004

INTRODUCTION

Contemporary process of urbanization is closely associated with the Global South, especially certain nations of Asia and Africa. The recently released, 'United Nations report on World Population Prospect-the 2017 revision' estimated that, in mid-2017, 77% of the world's population lived in Asia and Africa. Currently, these two continents are home to 4.5 and 1.3 billion people respectively (UN, 2017:1). The world's population is expected to rise by 2.2 billion between 2017 and 2050. During this period, Africa's population will grow by 1.3 billion and Asia's by 750 million (UN, 2017:3). Globally, Africa will experience the highest rate of population growth, followed by Asia, North America and Latin America. In contrast, Europe's population is forecasted to decrease by 2050.

The process of urbanization has been associated with development due to increase in economic opportunities. The traditional theories of urbanization such as 'modernization theory' postulate that technological developments release workers from agricultural activities, allowing them to take up industrial jobs in urban areas (Berliner, 1977; Bradshaw, 1987; Kasarda & Crenshaw, 1991; Dutt, 2001). The traditional urbanization as experienced in the Global North has been characterized by rural to urban migration. This 'modernization theory' explains the development in the Global North. Comparatively, the process of urbanization in the Global South has been different, which is due to not only rural to urban migration but also natural urban population growth as well as rural to urban reclassification (also called *in-situ urbanization*).

The theory of 'in-situ urbanization' proposes that rural activities are superseded by urban activities *without* rural to urban migration between settlements (for China see Zhu, 2004: for India see Pradhan, 2013). Rural land adjacent to urban areas is converted into urban usage due to low price of rural land. The annexation of the rural areas into urban areas increases the spatial extent of the services infrastructure provided by the urban government. Due to lack of resources, the majority of such developments are not connected or provided with basic infrastructure.

Urbanization process in the Global South is also characterized by a failure to generate sufficient formal jobs for unskilled rural-to-urban migrants, forcing them into informal employment. In India, for instance, economic development has not followed the traditional path from an agricultural-based economy to an industrialized economy and finally to a services-based economy. Due to the limited infrastructure for the supply of power and water needed by modern industries, as well as the lack of available developed land supply and environmental restrictions for industrial location in urban area, India has skipped the phase of industrialization to move directly to the service sector. As service jobs require skilled and educated workers, rural unskilled migrants are unable to find formal jobs and are pushed into informal employment, further restricting their access to formal housing and to urban amenities.

Informal settlements in the Global South have their own particular sets of characteristics. In South Africa, for instance, they are termed 'townships and informal settlements' and are located on the periphery of towns or cities. During the period of apartheid, these were residential areas for non-white residents (Writer, 2016). In China informal settlements are called 'urban villages' (Wang et al., 2009) whereas in India they are known as 'census towns' (Pradhan, 2013). Urban villages are also identified in India.

Pradhan (2013) has estimated that the number of India's census towns grew from 1,362 to 3,894 in the period 2001-2011 while the total population living in such census towns went up by 30%. Several studies have identified the growth of urban villages in China (refer Hao, 2012; Zheng et al, 2009). A recent World Bank report edited by Mahajan (2014) found that more than half of South Africa's urban population are living in townships and informal settlements.

Consequently, a large percentage of the urban population in countries such as South Africa, China and India reside in informal settlements. While informal settlements have also been a feature of development in countries of the Global North such as Britain, France and the USA, the magnitude of informal settlements was low and more resources were available to address the problem of informal growth compared to the Global South.

Informal settlements are developments that fall outside the purview of formal planning. Although such settlements house residents working in both the formal and informal economies, and hence contributing to the local GDP, they are deprived of urban services. Such a trend hinders the positive economic development associated with urbanization. Inclusive urbanization means incorporating informal settlements into mainstream process of urbanization by providing these with basic urban amenities. Expanding urban facilities to such settlements not only boosts economic growth but also reduces damage to the environment and to human health posed by such informal developments.

Initially, governments in South Africa, China and India attempted to hinder the development of informal settlements by implementing demolition measures. However, over time they have come to appreciate the potential role of informal settlements in the urban economy. While various attempts have been made to regularize such developments, a large percentage of the urban population still lives in informal settlements or slums.

This chapter elaborates on the work of Jain and Xie (2017). Here we undertake a comparative analysis not only of urbanization process but also institutional characteristics in countries of the Global South, specifically India, China and South Africa. These countries face similar problems with regard to informal settlements. While the process of urbanization began around the same time, only China and South Africa have begun to make headway in resolving some of the issues related to informal settlements. The main questions addressed here are: Which lessons can be learnt from the success of China and South Africa in improving urban governance and infrastructure delivery? Which mechanisms can be used to integrate informal settlements into mainstream urbanization? What are the potential innovative and traditional instruments for delivering urban amenities to informal settlements? Can crowdfunding be used to reduce the gap between informal and mainstream urbanization in the Global South?

The chapter is divided into five sections. This opening section is followed by an examination of the urban infrastructure delivery situation in India, China and South Africa. The third section looks at the alternatives for financing infrastructure to include informal settlements into formal urbanization process. The fourth concluding section offers some policy recommendations and financial alternatives for inclusive urbanization, and in the last section, some insights for future research are highlighted.

URBAN INFRASTRUCTURE DELIVERY: LESSONS LEARNED FROM CHINA AND SOUTH AFRICA

Planning Challenges

One of several reasons for the rise of informal settlements is poor spatial planning with little or no integrated provision of infrastructure (for South Africa see Todes (2008), for India see GoI (2011 a)). In most countries of the Global South, spatial planning is limited to physical plans indicating the future layout of cities as well as the density and intensity of land uses (Watson, 2009). Such spatial planning provides no integrated infrastructure development, implementation policies and instruments or public participation. The exception is China (e.g. Shanghai), where land use plans incorporate infrastructure plans.

In India, the primary focus at national level is economic planning, guided by the Five-Year Plans. These plans take the form of infrastructure investment plans for different sectors, which must be implemented by lower tier governments at the state and city level. In contrast, spatial plans are formulated at the regional and city levels, and are not integrated with the infrastructure investment plans. Urban development in India is the responsibility of state governments, and hence most infrastructural projects are planned and financed by state or local government. The central government is merely responsible for infrastructure related to power distribution, ports, railways, roads and airports. In addition, the central government has set up various schemes such as the Urban Infrastructure Development Scheme for Small and Medium Towns (UDISSMT), Smart Cities, Swachh Bharat (Clean India Mission) to support cities in financing infrastructure for water supply and sanitation.

The Government of India recognized the problems of unplanned urban growth and passed a 74th Constitutional Amendment Act (CAA), one of the clause of the act deals with the integrated urban and regional development. The act recommends establishment of lower tier of planning committees such as District and Metropolitan Planning Committees for integrated and coordinated planning of the urban and rural areas. However, states have been reluctant to establish these committees and where these have been established they are dysfunctional, and thus despite reforms the crisis continues.

Unlike India, spatial planning with integrated infrastructural development has evolved and been implemented in South Africa over the years. There exist various instruments to ensure infrastructure-integrated developments such as the National Spatial Development Planning Framework, Spatial Development Initiatives, Spatial Development Perspectives, the Regional Industrial Development Strategy and, more recently, the Green Paper on National Strategic Planning. These have undergone a number of reforms over the years with the aim of achieving integrated urban and infrastructure development (Oranje, 2010). In particular, the policy of offering free basic services such as water, electricity and sanitation in urban areas has been vitally important. This policy has succeeded through interdepartmental cooperation and a commitment by the nation government to allocate resources. However, there has been considerably less progress in the supply of free basic electricity and sanitation (Mosdell, 2006). Institutionally, there was an initial shift during a sixteen-year period of reform away from centralized to decentralized systems of planning, a trend that eventually gave way to a centralized planning system, whereby instructions for developments are dictated by the central government (Oranje, 2010).

Planning in China takes the form of Five Year Plans (similar to India), which are formulated by the national government. The main aim of these is to ensure economic and social development. The Plans encompass overall planning, specialized planning and regional planning, the latter consisting of economic as well as spatial plans (land-use plans) to be obeyed by lower tier governments (Wang and Shen, 2014; Zhou and Zhao, 2017). Unlike India, spatial planning in China takes place at national, provincial, prefectural and town levels (MLIT, 2016), thus providing a clear vision for spatial development, and integrating urban development with infrastructure provision at all tiers of government. China has been comparatively successful in achieving infrastructure-integrated development due to its centralized top-down government and devolution of powers to local authorities to exploit the sale of land and real estate for infrastructure funding. This policy has resulted in a massive investment in urban infrastructure, particularly in Shanghai and Beijing.

Urban Governance Challenges

Over the last few decades, India has seen rapid urban growth that has exceeded the institutional capacity to provide necessary infrastructure. A majority of the country's cities are crippled by these population pressures. Acknowledging the problems of unplanned growth, the 74th Constitution Amendment Act (CAA) of 1992, a landmark reform that decentralized governance in India, awarded constitutional status to municipalities.

The reform recommended the creation of a State Financial Commission (SFC), a District Planning Committee (DPC) as well as a Metropolitan Planning Committee (MPC) in each state in order to improve regional governance. The role of the SFC is to recommend the distribution of generated revenue between state and local bodies, to determine the taxes and fees that may be appropriated by local bodies, to determine the grants-in-aid from the state to local bodies as well as the measures needed to improve the financial position of local bodies. However, some states have made slow progress in creating SFCs whereas others have yet to make a start (Mathur & Peterson, 2006).

The 74th CAA also made a provision for DPCs and MPCs to consolidate and coordinate the plans prepared by panchayats and municipalities in order to address spatial planning for larger areas. This provision made clear that spatial planning encompassing both rural and urban areas must be coordinated at the district level by DPCs and at the metropolitan level by MPCs. However, not all states have established SFCs, DPCs and MPCs, and even where these have been set up, they are predominantly dysfunction (GoI, 2007). This gap in the administrative hierarchy merely exacerbates the problem of the poor integration of spatial planning and infrastructure development. Moreover, the states have been reluctant to empower their municipalities, thereby hindering the provision and maintenance of urban amenities.

With little planning to accommodate the rapid urban increase, especially as rural to urban unskilled migration, the informal settlements in India increase. Simply because the government fails to deliver sufficient affordable housing for the lower income group, and the municipalities with lack of financial resources are not able to cope with the pressure of infrastructure demand.

Compared to the situation in India, South Africa's cities have made major advances in the provision of basic services over the past twenty years due to sufficient capital investment, largely from the private sector. However, in the face of growing demand, the public sector will have to invest more strongly in new infrastructure (Karuri-Sebina, 2016). Various reforms over the years have strengthened city governance. For instance, Johannesburg's many independent municipalities were consolidated into a single metropolitan government under a mayor supported by a professional city manager. Furthermore, there is a clear separation between the role of the city government as policymaker and its role as service provider (Shanke et al., 2010).

In contrast to the approach of the India and South Africa governments, the Chinese government has prudently invested in its cities to meet prospective demand. The comparatively better managed process of urbanization in China can be attributed to specific urban policies and reforms. The national government has raised local urban bodies to provincial status under a powerful mayor, and has incentivized growth. The local authorities use the appreciation of land value to finance capital investment. Furthermore, they have the power to regulate land use and to tax new developments. Some of the value added through land development is used by the local authorities to finance urban infrastructure (Acoca et al., 2014; Dobbs & Sankhe, 2010).

Provision of Affordable Housing

Over a twenty-year span, national policy in India has shifted from upgrading slums to in-situ redevelopment, which promises better quality housing, faster construction and clearer identification of beneficiaries. The Pradhan Mantri Awas Yojana-Housing For All (HFA) mission was recently launched with the aim of constructing 20 million dwellings by 2022 (GoI, 2015 b). It departs from previous schemes in involving the private sector and exploiting real estate (e.g. increased floor area ratio/transfer development rights) as a financing tool. However, the focus of this mission is on statutory towns identified by the 2011 Census of India, and does not extend to so-called "census towns", i.e. informal settlements.

Moreover, following the 74th Constitution Amendment Act, which empowered local authorities to alleviate urban poverty, upgrade slums, provide housing and manage urban services, etc., there has been only slow devolution of financial resources, restricting the capacity of local authorities to fully realize their new responsibilities. As a result, in 2011 there was an estimated shortfall in the housing stock of 29 million dwellings in rural areas and 22 million dwellings in urban areas (Tiwari & Rao, 2016:10).

In contrast to India, access to housing is a constitutional right in South Africa. The government of South Africa provides free land for the building of housing for poor income groups. The national policy of removal of all slums by 2015 has led to a significant boom in government-led construction, supported by free land allocation and capital subsidies for lower income groups as well as subsidies to encourage private developers to build affordable housing. These dwellings are located close to transit and employment opportunities (Sankhe et al, 2010).

The unprecedented demand for affordable housing in India can only be compared to the situation in China, which until 1990 had a policy of state provision of housing, only later turning to the private sector for affordable housing. The affordable housing programme for lower and middle-income groups has ensured the construction of dwellings at only 50% to 75% of the standard market price. The government has offered multiple incentives for house construction, including free land allocation, the provision of basic infrastructure as well as tax exemptions; together, these have significantly reduced the cost of housing. The Chinese authorities have also pursued a policy of ensuring sufficient affordable rental accommodation for lower income groups (Sankhe et al, 2010).

Problems of Municipal Finance

Informal settlements are settlements, which are deprived of basic infrastructure provision. This is the case when due to urban activities the rural areas are transformed into urban without sufficient infrastructure. The rural authorities do not have sufficient fund to provide for urban population or urban activities. Also, due to the annexation of the rural into urban, the formal jurisdiction of the municipalities increases but there resources are limited, which further escalates the problem of informal urbanization.

Local governments should have sufficient funds to carry out their responsibilities while locally-generated revenues should be sufficient to finance services they provide to residents (Rao & Bird, 2010). Urban local authorities in most of India's states are empowered to derive their income from various sources such as taxes, charges, fines and penalties as well as remunerative enterprises. The most important source of funding at local level are the charges imposed on services. The main charges are for water supply and wastewater removal and treatment, electricity, garbage disposal, public transport and recreation. In addition, local bodies also depend upon grants and contributions, loans and some miscellaneous sources.

Under colonial rule Indians were exploited by the British, after independence government made the use of resources free. Since then in India the primary function of government is generally seen as providing urban infrastructure and services; indeed, basic services have traditionally been considered social goods to be provided at no charge or at nominal prices to users (Savage & Dasgupta, 2007). Now people are unwilling to pay for the basic services. The consequence is that measures like introduction of new or increase of existing service charges are very unpopular. Since the politicians fear losing elections because of increased user charges, the user charges are not increased. The local authorities have become more dependent and demand higher transfers from higher-order government.

In addition, there are a number of reasons for the poor tax revenue collection in Indian cities. The most significant of these is the poor coverage and collection efficiency of property tax. Poor coverage is due to (i) wide-ranging exemptions, (ii) deficient information systems and no up-to-date municipal cadaster of land and properties, (iii) many vacant properties, (iv) ambiguity in ownership and tenancy rights, and (v) an inability to adopt market-based valuation. All of these severely constrain local revenue generation (Rao, 2013). Other factors are corruption, a lack of personnel as well as poor official record-keeping. Together these lead to insufficient tax collection at the municipal level, hindering the delivery of adequate urban infrastructure. For instance, the 13th CFC report estimated that property tax made up only 0.16% to 0.24% of GDP while service charges contributed only 0.13% of GDP (GoI, 2009).

The existing municipal tax base is too narrow and predominantly limited to property tax. Furthermore, user charges for services are grossly underutilized (Garg, 2007; Nallathiga, 2008). Consequently, municipalities are dependent on the state and central governments to provide urban infrastructure. Despite the administrative changes of the 74th CAA, states have been reluctant to devolve powers to lower-tier governing bodies, a fact which seems to have constrained urban service delivery. The frequent under-funding of India's municipalities serves to constrain the potential role of cities in economic development (Mohanty et al, 2007; Ramanathan & Dasgupta, 2009; Bandyopadhyay & Rao, 2009).

According to a McKinsey report published in 2010, India's annual per capita expenditure on infrastructure is a mere $17, contrasting sharply with the $116 and $127 spent per capita in China and South Africa, respectively. Unlike India, 40 to 50% of infrastructural projects in South Africa's large cities and 60 to 70% in its small cities are publicly funded. Its cities are funded by property taxes and service charges as well as by grants from the central government for urban infrastructure projects. China has been able to invest in urban infrastructure ahead of demand, a remarkable achievement. For instance, half of the new infrastructure required for the provision of urban services in Shanghai was funded through taxes and user charges, with the rest financed through land monetization, bank loans and 30% by local taxes such as VAT (Sankhe et al, 2010).

Despite several attempts from the central and the state government in India, available resources for funding urban infrastructure are nowhere close to the demand. There is a need to look for alternative innovative measures to be able to fund urban infrastructure, more specifically for integrating informal settlements into formal urbanization. In the following section, an attempt is made to review the available options and underscore the alternatives that can be utilized for funding urban infrastructure.

FINANCING INSTRUMENTS FOR INFRASTRUCTURE DELIVERY

Government funding as well as innovative approaches are required to integrate informal settlements into mainstream urbanization. As Alm (2011) points out, there are many ways by which local authorities can mobilize resources for infrastructure provision and maintenance. These include: a) municipal borrowing from private capital markets by issuing bonds; b) municipal borrowing from specialized financial institutions/intermediaries; c) taxes; d) fees imposed on user services, land- and asset-based sources such as impact fees and development charges, betterment levies, the exploitation of municipal assets, tax increment financing; e) central government finance via intergovernmental transfers; and, f) international donors. From that of conventional tools of PPP for infrastructure financing (Annez, 2010), the New Urban Agenda aims to secure financing through land value capture, the appropriate pricing of infrastructure, as well as devolution and decentralization. Annez reiterates the importance of the focus on designing subsidies transfer and land value capture. Kim (2016) has identified five practical sources of innovative financing for infrastructure, specifically innovative value capture, user participation and the user-investor approach (crowdfunding), direct institutional investor engagement in a greenfield project, the multi-jurisdictional and pooled approach, as well as socially-responsible financing. Some of these, namely value capture, crowdfunding, and pooled finance, are already being employed in India's so-called metro cities. The alternative forms of infrastructural funding can be grouped into innovative (crowdfunding) and traditional instruments (decentralized infrastructure provision and land value capture or land monetization). This section discusses some of these approaches.

Traditional Instruments

Moving Towards Decentralized Infrastructure Provision

The rapid growth and outward expansion of urban areas increases the cost of centralized infrastructure provision and maintenance. As an alternative, decentralized infrastructure provision can help reduce the cost of ever longer pipelines in countries such as India.

Decentralized systems are a good example of integrating informal growth into the formal urbanization process. Some best practices from Latin America and South Africa confirm the potential of a decentralized system to serve informal settlements. Decentralization is a way of strengthening the role of local government and an effective means of addressing environmental and health concerns. The basic tenet is that *local* rather than *centralized* control will result in more accountable service providers and better services (Parkinson & Taylor, 2003).

The capital investment required for decentralized systems is less than centralized systems. Decentralized wastewater treatments systems can serve small communities, with byproducts in the form of bio-gas used as a source of energy and decontaminated water utilized for irrigation. Similarly, solar panels can be installed on residential and commercial buildings to generate electricity. Some social enterprises and NGOs in India have constructed decentralized water plants in informal urban housing settlements (Jain et al, 2016). These decentralized systems seem to be a good way to provide basic amenities to informal settlements while incorporating such settlements into mainstream process of urbanization, thereby exploiting the economic potential of urbanization.

This decentralized provision of infrastructure has already been implemented in the planned city "New Okhla Industrial Development Authority" (NOIDA) and Greater NOIDA adjacent to Delhi, where a decentralized water and sewer treatment system is provided at the zonal level within the city and user charges are levied by the Special Purpose Vehicle created for the development of the city.

Potential of Land Monetization

Peterson (2008) suggests three forms of land-based financing, namely developer exactions (including impact fee collections), value capture and land asset management. The government of India has laid out a detailed framework (2017) for land value capture (both area- and project-based), suggesting measures such as land value tax, land use change fees, betterment levies, development charges, transfer of development rights (TDR), a premium on relaxing rules or the floor space index (FSI)/ floor area ratio (FAR), vacant land tax, tax increment financing, land acquisition and development, as well as a land pooling system. While most of these value capture tools are utilized in various forms in India's metropolitan cities, they are not practiced in small- and medium-sized towns for infrastructure financing. For example, Mumbai and adjoining Municipal Corporations make use of TDRs, which allow a developer to build at a higher FAR/FSI on some other designated parcel of land in a zone where FAR is low. The Municipal Corporation provides public infrastructure on the zone thus vacated by the developer. Sending and receiving zones are earmarked in the Mumbai Development Plan. In fact, as land is always a scarce resource in Mumbai, TDRs are traded on the market as a kind of stock.

The newly formed Andhra Pradesh State followed the example of Gujarat and Maharashtra in making use of the land pooling tool to mobilize land and provide infrastructure development for its new capital Amaravati. It was able to accumulate more than 33,000 acres of land for development through the land pooling scheme. Furthermore, in 2014 the central government granted exemption from capital gains tax (Clause 37-A, Section 10) in order to encourage farmers and others to permit the development of the capital city on their land. In this way, the landowners could reap the benefits of increased land values. In India's recent history, the land pooling mechanism can be considered one of the most successful models for the provision of high quality infrastructure.

Innovative Instruments

Civic Crowdfunding

Infrastructure can also be funded by mobilizing household savings in the form of crowdfunding. This is a financing method whereby individuals contribute small sums to achieve some shared goal (Vadgama et al., 2015). Crowdfunding combines the key aspects of crowdsourcing with those of micro-financing (Kim, 2016). Crowdsourcing harnesses the creative solutions of a distributed network of individuals, whereas microfinancing, initially employed as a way to provide low interest loans to people on small incomes, is now used as a strategy to finance small initiatives. Together these two approaches can help mobilize a large base of financiers to fund different initiatives and ventures (Gasparro, 2015). Regarding local infrastructure projects in India, civic crowdfunding may prove to be a practical method of raising funds that cannot be obtained any other way.

The term 'civic crowdfunding' refers to a subcategory of crowdfunding whereby citizens, often in partnership with government, 'propose, fund and deliver projects that aim to provide a community service or deliver public value through a local-area-improvement project' (Griffiths, 2016). While civic crowdfunding may usefully supplement traditional sources of institutional funding, it is best suited to financing certain types of projects. In particular, it is ideal for projects with a social dimension, which have a clear and limited scale, and whose impacts can be realized quickly.

The experience of civic crowdfunding throughout the world suggests that one of the key factors for its success is in boosting feelings of ownership and responsibility amongst citizens. Such direct civic engagement tends to reduce skepticism towards government-led projects. Additionally, projects funded by crowdfunding generally tackle specific needs of the community and are therefore less prone to a misallocation of taxes (Muellerleile et al., 2014).

The four main crowdfunding models applicable to civic projects are (Griffiths, 2016):

1. Donation-based crowdfunding (no financial or material returns expected by the donor),
2. Reward-based crowdfunding (donors expect a tangible non-financial reward in the form of a product or some other benefit such as a handwritten letter by a celebrity),
3. Community shares (non-transferable shares are issued by, for example, a cooperative society; shareholders can withdraw their share capital subject to set terms and conditions),
4. Municipal bonds (lenders to the local government are guaranteed a stream of future interest payments over the period of the bond as well as the full return of the invested amount after the bond matures).

Municipal bonds are especially suited to funding large long-term projects such as infrastructure-related repairs, green space improvements, school upgrades and even the construction of new transport infrastructure. While municipal bonds are widely used in the USA, this approach is now starting to gain a foothold in cities elsewhere such as Ahmedabad and Bangalore in India or Johannesburg and Kigali in Africa (Kim, 2016).

Wider use of this instrument in India is limited by the fact that, under current governmental regulations, a permit is required for the issuance of municipal bonds. Permits are only provided on an ad-hoc project-by-project basis. Yet the wider introduction of tax-free municipal bonds could generate huge additional revenues for local urban bodies with tight budgets (Vadgama, 2015).

In India, donation-based, community-based and municipal bond-based crowdfunding is only found in metropolitan cities. For example, the Advanced Locality Management (ALM) as practiced in Mumbai (Baud & Navtej, 2008), the role of Resident Welfare Associations in delivering basic services (Mahadevia et. al., 2014), and Urban Decentralization (Mehra, 2013). These measures describe how the Resident Welfare Associations (which are people's housing cooperatives) are used to coproduce various urban services in Mumbai and Delhi. The services started as user charge based services such as solid waste management at the neighborhood level, were later scaled up to cover many more utilities and services.

Interestingly, many cities in India have started issuing municipal bonds. In fact, in the 1990s there was something of a race to assess bond credit ratings. Recently, Pune Municipal Corporation's issuance of an INR 200 Crores bond at a coupon rate of 7.59% was oversubscribed. This was intended to fund a water supply project worth around INR 2300 Crores. The Pooled Financing Mechanism has been popular in India since 2006 when the Indian government set up a scheme for Pooled Finance Development Fund with a focus on bankable urban infrastructure projects. Many state governments have established their own State Pooled Finance Entities to generate funding for infrastructure through bonds. The state of Tamil Nadu, for example, has successfully utilized this pooled method to finance infrastructure in small- and medium-sized towns (Kapur, 2009).

Milaap began as a crowdfunding platform for micro-loans for people in rural India, helping low-income borrowers with projects such as education, energy and water and sanitation. It has donors and lenders from over 120 countries for close to 50,000 projects, and has raised over USD $12.7 million (Milaap, 2017).

Equity-Based Crowdfunding

The equity-based forms of crowdfunding include real estate equity, social service equity and new towns equity. Real estate crowdfunding involves the pooling of funds by multiple investors in a real estate project. Investors make investments in commercial or residential properties and in exchange, they hold an equity stake in the property. Each investor shares in a portion of the rental income the property generates (Athwal, 2016). Although, crowdfunding sector is largely focused on commercial businesses, it can also work for charities and social enterprises. Many charities already partner with donations-based organizations to encourage fundraising for specific projects, and these donations can benefit from gift aid. Social enterprises can do the same (Roche-Saunders and Hunt, 2017). Finally, new town equity or community ownership is a kind of crowdfunding, where people pool in resources to invest in commercial or residential projects as well as cities and townships are being developed.

These forms of crowdfunding are prevalent in the west, and are slowly becoming popular in India. Some projects are already conceptualized based on crowdfunding (see EMBARQ Network, 2017; Pereira, 2017). "Homegrown cities", a concept by Pareira (2017), is an innovative solution of incorporating slums into main cities by using local knowledge, labor and investment. The project raised more than 10,000 euro by 92 investors. In China, crowdfunding has become very famous although government is still skeptical about it. Various forms of crowdfunding are used for restoring the Great Wall of China, developing organic farming within Beijing and integrating rural with urban by supporting entrepreneurial efforts of the rural population (Zhang et al., 2014).

An example of community ownership is the development of self-contained townships, an innovative example in Pune (India) is the Magarpatta township, which is based on the walk to work and walk to school principle. As Gupta et al (2012) rightly call it Farmers Direct Investment (FDI), it is a township development by a community of 120 farmers facilitated by the government with no land acquisition and no cost to public authority. The landowners are shareholders and entitles to profit-sharing. They receive sale precedes thus benefit from escalating land prices. Landowners have the opportunity to turn into entrepreneurs and not being displaced from their land.

Crowdfunding has a huge potential in India, however, it is not backed by the Indian government, as the Securities and Exchange Board of India (SEBI) claims the Indian public lacks adequate investment knowledge or experience and requires strict protection.

CONCLUSION AND POLICY RECOMMENDATIONS

In order to reap the benefits of urbanization processes underway in countries of the Global South, it is necessary to integrate informal settlements into mainstream urbanization as well as to ensure that city dwellers are adequately provided with urban services. This will require reforms in several areas. Such reforms need government funding as well as innovative (crowdfunding) tools to generate revenue for the delivery of urban services. These points are discussed below.

While there already exist various proposals to integrate spatial development with infrastructure delivery, these have generally taken the form of guidelines, and hence lack regulatory enforcement. In order to ensure integrated spatial and infrastructural development, the central government has to issue binding regulations to lower tier governments, combined with the devolution of funding to these lower tier administrations. A policy of integrated spatial and infrastructural planning needs to be established at the national level; subsequently, it needs to be enforced to lower tiers of government.

While the central government has recommended reforms to decentralize powers in favor of stronger local government, state governments have been reluctant to empower local authorities. To encourage such decentralization, it would be helpful to make central governmental funding to the states conditional on their adoption of reforms. Although this has been partially successful under JNNURM, there are still some deficiencies, in particular the rather dysfunctional SFCs, DPCs and MPCs. Stricter regulation and implementation of reforms is necessary to empower lower-tier authorities to streamline their functions.

Basic services are subsidized in India, hindering the revenue of the local government to provide for basic services. Clearly, it is important to appropriately charge users and to fine abusers. User charges and taxes to generate revenue should be revised as follows:

1. The delinking of user charges from providers (for example, water supply and sanitation are provided by state-level special purpose boards) and charges need to be linked to capital, and operation and maintenance costs;
2. Removing property tax from the municipal/local authority control (The total property tax that can be imposed is currently limited to 23% in most cases. Moreover, the property tax is a composite tax consisting of water, sanitation and, in some cases, education tax. These must be uncoupled.);
3. Annual revision of property tax valuation. While this is already done in many states based on the Unit Area Method, the practice should be more widely adopted;
4. Also, while the mechanism of pooled financing has been adopted in some states, it should be utilized for the funding of infrastructure projects, especially in India's small- and medium-sized towns

Crowdfunding is relatively new for the countries of the Global South but it has a potential of developing townships and delivering common infrastructure. Crowdfunding projects for development of townships and other infrastructure projects have been undertaken in India but these examples are scarce. There is a need of government support, so that large projects using civic and equity-based crowdfunding can be implemented. It will encourage citizens to collaborate with the government in funding urban infrastructure. Finally, decentralized infrastructure will reduce the cost of connecting informal settlements with the main trunk infrastructure; tools such as land value capture will help local governments generate revenue from land development to provide basic services.

FUTURE RESEARCH DIRECTIONS

This chapter is an attempt to illustrate the possibilities of incorporating informal settlements into mainstream urbanization by a mix of innovative and traditional fiscal instruments. It illustrates descriptive comparison of the struggle to deal with urbanization in an inclusive manner in the three large countries of the Global South. However, it lacks case-study based comparison of crowdfunding alternatives for inclusive urbanization. Crowdfunding is comparatively new in these countries and there is a need to develop research models and methodology, which address the issue of data and institutional complexities to undertake comparative research in the countries of Global South in order to learn from their best practices.

REFERENCES

Acoca, A., Chattaraj, S., & Wachter, S. (2014). *Urban governance and development of informality in China and India*. Social Science Research Network.

Alm, J. (2011). *Municipal Finance of Urban Infrastructure: Knowns and Unknowns*. Working Paper 1103. Department of Economics, Tulane University, New Orleans, LA.

Annez, P. (2010). *Financing Indian Cities: Opportunities and Constraints in an Nth Best World*. The World Bank. Policy Research Working Paper 5474.

Athwal, N. (2016). *A beginner's guide to real estate crowdfunding*. Available online: https://www.landlordology.com/real-estate-crowdfunding/

Bandyopadhyay, S., & Rao, M. (2009). *Fiscal Health of Selected Indian Cities*. Policy Research Working Paper No. 4863. Washington, DC: World Bank.

Baud, I., & Navtej, N. (2008). Negotiated spaces for representation in Mumbai: Ward committees, advanced locality management and the politics of middle-class activism. *Environment and Urbanization*, *20*(2), 483–499. doi:10.1177/0956247808096124

Berliner, J. (1977). Internal migration: A comparative disciplinary view. In A. Brown & E. Neuberger (Eds.), *Internal migration: A comparative perspective* (pp. 443–446). New York: Academic Press. doi:10.1016/B978-0-12-137350-4.50028-7

Bradshaw, Y. (1987). Urbanization and underdevelopment: A global study of modernization, urban bias, and economic dependency. *American Sociological Review*, *52*(2), 224–239. doi:10.2307/2095451

Dobbs, R., & Sankhe, S. (2010). *Comparing urbanization in China and India. McKinsey Quarterly*.

Dutt, A. (2001). *Global urbanization: Trends, form and density gradients*. Allahabad: Professor R. N. Dubey Foundation.

EMBARQ Network. (2017). *You too can build a sustainable city through crowdfunding*. Available online: http://www.smartcitiesdive.com/ex/sustainablecitiescollective/friday-fun-you-too-can-build-sustainable-city-through-crowdfunding/330406/

Garg, S. (2007). Overview of Urban Infrastructure Finance in India. In Financing Cities: Fiscal Responsibility and Urban Infrastructure in Brazil, China, India, Poland and South Africa (pp. 108-157). The World Bank.

Gasparro, K. (2015). *Funding Municipal Infrastructure: Integrating Project Finance and Crowdfunding*. National Science Foundation.

Government of India (GoI). (2007). *Local governance: An inspiring journey into the future*. Government of India, Second administrative reform commission, 6th report.

Government of India (GoI). (2011). *Working Group on Environmental Sustainability of Indian Cities for the formulation of the 12th Five Year Plan. Ministry of Housing and Urban Poverty Alleviation Government of India (GoI). 2009. Report of the 13th Finance Commission*. New Delhi: Finance Commission India.

Government of India (GoI). (2015). *Housing for all (urban): Scheme guidelines 2015*. Ministry of Housing & Urban Poverty Alleviation. Government of India.

Griffiths, H. (2016). *Civic Crowdfunding: A guidebook for local authorities*. Future Cities Catapult.

Gupta, A., Dalal, S., Basu, D., & Joseph, A. (2012). *Magarpatta City: Farmers direct investment (FDI)*. Working paper No 384. Indian Institute of Management Bangalore.

Hao, P. (2012). *Spatial evolution of urban villages in Shenzhen*. ITC dissertation number 205. ITC Printing Department.

Jain, M., & Xie, X. (2017). The rise of informal urbanization in the Global South: A breach of urban planning or bridging the gap of urban infrastructure supply? In N. Schlitz & J. Poerting (Eds.), *Aktuelle Forschungsbeiträge zu Südasien: 7. Jahrestagung des AK Südasien, 27./28. Januar 2017*. Augsburg.

Jain, V., Chennuri, S., & Karamchandani, A. (2016). *Informal Housing, Inadequate Property Rights Understanding the Needs of India's Informal Housing Dwellers*. FSG Reimagining Social Change.

Kapur, V. (2009). *Financing Urban Infrastructure in Small and Medium Towns- Pooled Bonds as an Instrument of Financial Inclusion*. Paper presented in a Seminar on Financing Urban Development, Chennai, India.

Karuri-Sebina, G. (2016). *The State of South African Cities Report. South African Cities Network (SACN)*. Johannesburg, South Africa: SACN.

Kasarda, J., & Crenshaw, E. (1991). Third World urbanization: Dimensions, theories and determinants. *Annual Review of Sociology*, *17*(1), 467–501. doi:10.1146/annurev.so.17.080191.002343 PMID:12285403

Kim, J. (2016). *Handbook on Urban Infrastructure Finance*. New Cities Foundation. Available from: http://bit.ly/NCFUrbanFinance

Mahadevia, D., Bhatia, N., & Bhatt, B. (2014). *Resident Welfare Associations (RWAs) in BSUP Sites of Ahmedabad: Experiences of Mahila Housing SEWA Trust (MHA). CUE working Paper 25, September 2014*. Ahmedabad, India: Center for Urban Equity, CEPT University.

Mahajan, S. (2014). *Economics of South African Townships: Special Focus on Diepsloot*. Washington, DC: The World Bank.

Mathur, O., & Peterson, G. (2006). *State Finance Commission and urban fiscal decentralization in India. India urban initiatives*. Washington, DC: The Urban Institute.

Mehra, D. (2013). What has urban decentralization meant? A case study of Delhi. *Pacific Affairs*, *86*(4), 813–833. doi:10.5509/2013864813

Milaap. (2017). *Crowdfunding for India: Raise funds online for yourself, loved ones, charities and more*. Available online: https://milaap.org/

Ministry of Land, Infrastructure, Transport and Tourism, Japan (MLIT). (2016). *An overview of spatial policy in Asian and European Countries: China*. Retrieved August 9, 2016, from http://www.mlit.go.jp/kokudokeikaku/international/spw/general/china/index_e.html

Mohanty, P., Misra, B., Goyal, R., & Jeromi, P. (2007). *Municipal Finance in India – An Assessment. Study No. 26*. Mumbai: Department of Economic Analysis and Policy, Reserve Bank of India.

Mosdell, T. (2006). Free basic services: The evolution and impact of free basic water policy in South Africa. In U. Pillay, R. Tomlinson, & J. Toit (Eds.), *Democracy and delivery: Urban policy in South Africa* (pp. 283–301). Cape Town: HSRC Press.

Müllerleile, T., Joenssen, D., & Müllerleile, A. (2014). Crisis, Co-Financing, and Crowdfunding: Igniting Regional Development. *Proceedings of International Conference for Entrepreneurship, Innovation and Regional Development*.

Nallathiga, R. (2008). Trends and Perspectives of Urban Public Finance in Select Countries and India. *ICFAI Journal of Urban Policy*, *3*(1), 16–32.

Oranje, M. (2010). Post-Apartheid National Spatial Development Planning in South Africa- A Brief History. *European Spatial Research and Policy*, *17*(2), 55–70. doi:10.2478/s10105-010-0010-8

Parkinson, J., & Taylor, K. (2003). Decentralized wastewater management in peri-urban areas in low-income countries. *Environment and Urbanization*, *15*(1), 75–89. doi:10.1177/095624780301500119

Pereira, A. (2017). *Homegrown Cities*. Available online: https://www.indiegogo.com/projects/homegrown-cities#/

Peterson, G. (2008). *Unlocking Land Values to Finance Urban Infrastructure: Land-Based Financing Options for Cities. Gridlines; No. 40*. World Bank.

Pradhan, K. (2013). Unacknowledged urbanization: The new census towns of India. *Economic and Political Weekly*, *48*(36), 43–51.

Ramanathan, R., & Dasgupta, S. (2009). *Estimates of Urban Infrastructure Financing Requirements in India, 2006-2031*. Available from: http://www.cprindia.org/sites/default/files/working_papers/HPEC%20REPORT.pdf

Rao, G., & Bird, R. (2010). *Urban Governance and Finance in India*. Rotman School of Management Working Paper No. 1568858.

Rao, M. (2013). *Property Tax System in India: Problems and Prospects of Reform*. Working Paper No. 2013-114, National Institute of Public Finance and Policy.

Roche-Saunders, G., & Hunt, O. (2017). *Crowdfunding for charities and social enterprises: Crowdfunding has created new opportunities for raising funds from the public.* Crowdfunding focus. Charity and Social Enterprise Update, Summer 2017.

Sankhe, S., Vittal, I., Dobbs, R., Mohan, A., Gulati, A., Ablett, J., & Sethy, G. et al. (2010). *India's urban awakening: Building inclusive cities, sustaining economic growth.* McKinsey Global Institute.

Savage, D., & Dasgupta, S. (2007). *Governance framework for delivery of urban services.* India Infrastructure Report 2006.

Tiwari & Rao. (2016). *Housing Markets and Housing Policies in India.* Asian Development Bank Institute. No. 565.

Todes, A. (2008). Rethinking spatial planning. *SSB/TRP/MDM, 2008*(53), 10-14.

United Nations (UN). (2017). *World urbanization prospects: The 2017 revision.* New York: Department of Economic and Social Affairs.

Vadgama, C., Khutwad, A., Damle, M., & Patil, S. (2015). Smart Funding Options for Developing Smart Cities: A Proposal for India. *Indian Journal of Science and Technology, 8*(34). doi:10.17485/ijst/2015/v8i34/85418

Wang, L., & Shen, J. (2014). Changing spatial planning in China's five-year planning system. *Urban Design and Planning, 167*(5DP5), 189–195. doi:10.1680/udap.14.00008

Wang, Y., Wang, Y., & Wu, J. (2009). Urbanization and informal development in China: Urban villages in Shenzhen. *International Journal of Urban and Regional Research, 33*(4), 957–973. doi:10.1111/j.1468-2427.2009.00891.x

Watson, V. (2009). 'The planned city sweeps the poor away. . .'. Urban planning and 21st century urbanization. *Progress in Planning, 72*(3), 151–193. doi:10.1016/j.progress.2009.06.002

Writer, S. (2016). *These are the biggest townships in South Africa.* Available online: https://businesstech.co.za/news/general/132269/these-are-the-biggest-townships-in-south-africa/

Zhang, T., Yip, C., Wang, G., & Zhang, Q. (2014). *China crowdfunding report: How to leverage crowdfunding to support China's social and environmental SGB's.* China Impact Fund.

Zheng, S., Long, F., Fan, C., & Gu, Y. (2009). Urban Villages in China: A 2008 Survey of Migrant Settlements in Beijing. *Eurasian Geography and Economics, 50*(4), 425–446. doi:10.2747/1539-7216.50.4.425

Zhou, X., & Zhao, M. (2017). Comparison of Territorial Spatial Planning System between China and Japan and Its Enlightenment. *Journal of Service Science and Management, 10*(01), 54–71. doi:10.4236/jssm.2017.101005

Zu, Yu. (2004). Changing urbanization processes and in-situ rural-urban transformation: reflections on China's settlement definitions. In T. Champion & G. Hugo (Eds.), *New forms of urbanization: Beyond the urban-rural dichotomy* (pp. 207–228). Aldershot, UK: Ashgate Publishing Limited.

KEY TERMS AND DEFINITIONS

Basic Services: Basic services encompass all public services from education and health to transportation, power, sanitation, housing, and water supply.

Global South: The term used to designate those relatively poor, emerging nations such as China, India, and South Africa whose economies are not yet fully developed.

Inclusive Urbanization: A process of including informal developments or settlements into mainstream urbanization by providing basic services.

Informal Settlements: Settlements that develop outside the jurisdiction of formal planning authorities.

Urban Governance: Exercising administrative authority to manage urban affairs from the provision of basic and social amenities to economic matters and law and order.

Urbanization: A process characterized by the concentration of population in large or main cities.

Chapter 5
Applications of Crowdsourcing in Sustainable Urban Development Planning in Developing Countries

Ismaila Rimi Abubakar
University of Dammam, Saudi Arabia

ABSTRACT

To efficiently manage growth and changes arising from rapidly increasing population and urbanization trends, developing countries need to employ appropriate tools to analyze the key issues involved. Globally, crowdsourcing is increasingly being applied to facilitate sustainable urban development (SUD) planning process. Crowdsourcing has already proved capable of generating new models for urban planning and governance that source and mobilize diverse social actors working toward sustainable and innovation-oriented urban space. However, few studies have explored crowdsourcing applications in SUD planning in developing countries. Therefore, based on desktop study, this chapter examines applications of crowdsourcing in SUD planning in developing countries. The chapter reviews the conceptual and historical foundation of crowdsourcing, and highlights some exemplary applications of crowdsourcing in SUD planning worldwide. It then discusses the challenges and potentials of crowdsourcing as a tool in planning for SUD in developing countries and concludes with future research directions.

1. INTRODUCTION

Urban areas around the world are growing at a rate never experienced before. The most important driving force behind urban growth is population increase. Over the past three decades, the number of urban residents in the developing countries has more than doubled (Soltész, 2010). The UN projected that by 2030 Asia and Africa alone would be home to additional 2.5 billion urban dwellers or about 90% of global urban population growth, and that 37% of the increase in global urban population by 2050 is expected to happen in China, India and Nigeria alone (UN, 2015). High birth rates, explosive rural-urban migration,

DOI: 10.4018/978-1-5225-3952-0.ch005

extreme poverty, high unemployment rates, social exclusion and inequality, increasing crime, inadequate social services, dilapidated infrastructure, and unfavorable business climates are the characteristics of urbanization in several developing countries (Abubakar & Dano, 2018). Developing countries are nations with lower living standard, human development index and degree of industrialization compared to the developed countries. In many of these countries, cities suffer from widespread environmental deterioration, including water and air pollution and soil contamination, and health conditions are often far below decent standards (Abubakar, 2011; Soltész, 2010).

Nonetheless, cities are the global economic avenues for production, innovation and trade, and they will continue to substantially influence the economic, sociocultural, and environmental sustainability of our societies (Abubakar et al., 2016; Stratigea et al., 2015). Urbanization can only be sustainable in developing countries if there is the political will to empower residents to solve their own problems in partnership with local authorities and to actively participate in decision-making processes affecting their lives (Abubakar & Aina, 2016; Benna & Garba, 2016). In the twenty-first century, if cities are not only to survive and prosper but also to be lively and inclusive they must undergo a major transformation, which cannot be effectively achieved without innovative tools and commitments. This requires finding ideas and answers to urban problems from stakeholders that are outside the boundaries of planning agencies (Seltzer and Mahmoudi, 2012). One of the innovative tools that is progressively being applied in planning for sustainable urban development (SUD) throughout the world is crowdsourcing (Certoma et al., 2015; Mirbabaie et al., 2016; Misra et al., 2014).

Crowdsourcing as one of the major techniques for open innovation involves handing out a challenge or a problem to a sizeable and diverse group of people, hoping to arrive at novel solutions more robust than those found within an agency or organization (Brabham, 2009; Howe, 2006). Through crowdsourcing, citizens can contribute in SUD process in several ways. Many planning objectives and tasks can be achieved when essential ideas, content or services are obtained from a large group of people. Crowdsourcing can also help overcome some challenges of SUD process, including lack of or restricted access to data, limited financial, technical and managerial resources and challenges in urban governance (Abubakar & Aina, 2006). However, there are few studies that explored crowdsourcing applications in developing countries (Ingwe, 2017; Papadopoulou & Giaoutzi, 2014; Roth et al., 2013). In a review of 346 articles on crowdsourcing published from 2006-2012, Hossain and Kauranen (2015, p. 6), found that more than three quarters are from developed countries and that only three developing countries (China, Brazil and South Korea) are among the top 20 countries in terms of authorship of the articles. Even among the few studies on crowdsourcing in developing countries, very few have explored its application in SUD planning. This chapter, therefore, address this research gap by analyzing the potentials and challenges of utilizing crowdsourcing in planning for SUD with emphasis on developing countries.

Based on desktop study, data were collected from secondary sources such as journal articles, textbooks, official reports and website contents. Data analysis involves qualitative content analysis where themes related to the objectives of the paper were generated from the reviewed documents and then synthesized. This chapter is presented in six sections. Section two reviews the concept of and lays the historical foundation of crowdsourcing. Section three highlights some exemplary applications of crowdsourcing for SUD planning. This is followed by underscoring the challenges of applying crowdsourcing in planning for SUD in developing countries in section four. Section five discusses some potentials for utilizing crowdsourcing as a tool in planning for SUD in developing countries. The paper concludes with future research direction in section six.

2. CONCEPTUAL AND HISTORICAL FOUNDATION OF CROWDSOURCING

This section reviews the concept of crowdsourcing and key terminologies related to the phenomenon. It also reviews the historical foundation of the term. This is to provide a context for better understanding of the various applications of crowdsourcing as well as the challenges and potentials of its utilization in SUD planning in developing countries.

2.1 The Concept of Crowdsourcing

According to Howe (2006) crowdsourcing is the process of outsourcing a task usually done by employees of an organization/company to an indeterminate, predominantly large group of people through an online open call. Similarly, Brabham (2009) describes crowdsourcing as a valid, complex model for solving problems that tap into the combined intelligence of the community to accomplish a task. Recently, Estelles-Arolas and Gonzalez-Ladron-de-Guevara (2012) have analyzed 209 related articles and found 40 existing definitions of crowdsourcing and its eight common features: a task with a clear goal, clearly defined crowd, a well-defined compensation for the crowd, known problem owner, outlined benefits for the problem owner, open call, online process, and internet usage. They subsequently incorporate these features and produce a comprehensive definition of crowdsourcing as:

... an online strategy, in which an organization proposes defined task(s) to the members of the crowd via a flexible open call. By undertaking the task(s), the members contribute their work, knowledge, skills and/or experience and receive reward, including economic reward, social recognition, self-esteem, or the development of individual skills. The organization will obtain these contributions and utilize the results for the defined goals.

There are many terms and concepts related to crowdsourcing that emerged from various scholars and practitioners. These terms, arranged in alphabetical order, include: 'collaborative intelligence/systems', 'community systems', 'crowd wisdom', 'human computation', 'mass collaboration', 'peer production', 'smart mobs', 'social search/systems', 'user-generated content', and user-powered systems (Doan et al., 2011; Pedersen et al., 2013). Such variants are expected, because of the budding nature of the concept and its applications. However, crowdsourcing has been the dominant term in the literature (Pedersen et al., 2013). The four main components of crowdsourcing: the problem or task, the problem owner, the crowd and the platform are explained below:

- **The Problem/Task:** The problem or task is an account of the original condition and the preferred ending condition. The problem may be simple or complex, short-term or long-term and of different geographical scale, and it is at the heart of crowdsourcing (Pedersen et al., 2013). In urban development for instance, simpler tasks include mapping projects or surveys. Complex problems include infrastructure improvement process, which needs to be broken into smaller tasks.
- **Problem Owner:** This refers to the entity be it individual, organization, company or planning agency that needs a problem solved or a task done. The problem owner initiates the crowdsourcing process by asking a crowd to solve a problem. It is the owner's responsibility to clearly define the problem/task, specify the requirements of the needed solution, determine and manage the crowdsourcing activity, and to evaluate and select the submissions that meet the specified requirements.

- **The Crowd:** This is the enthusiastically established collection of persons who partake in solving a crowdsourcing problem. These crowdsourcing participants or actors are often called the knowledge networks. These persons interrelate with the problem owner with a defined workflow and work individually or in collaboration with other members of the crowd to accomplish a given task (Pedersen et al., 2013).
- **The Platform:** This is usually a website or an application on the internet or smartphone which participants can utilize in making their contributions. A crowdsourcing platform is developed either by the problem owner to provide solutions to specific problems or by a third party for solving diverse problems (see Table 1 for examples). Notable example of third party platforms that can be used for diverse crowdsourcing tasks include Amazon Mechanical Turk (MTurk), as well as social media like Facebook, Twitter, WhatsApp and YouTube.

When an organization such as a planning agency has tasks to be accomplished through crowdsourcing, it first selects a platform (developed in-house or by a third party) which it uses to create an open call and hand the tasks off to the crowd. Contingent upon the type of task, the crowd can be exclusive to a community or open to anybody ready to carry out the task. In a crowdsourcing process, many solutions are typically produced and then systemically sifted. After completing the tasks collaboratively or individually, the crowd members afterward submit the solutions back to the problem owner. For complex problems, single task is broken down into simpler ones and the output is combined to complete the initial task. Finally, if the organization is satisfied with the output the participants are paid or given some incentives (Thuan et al., 2016).

2.2 Historical Foundation of Crowdsourcing

Although the concept behind crowdsourcing, which is basically getting a crowd to perform a task, has been existing for a long time, the term ''crowdsourcing'' was conned and defined by Jeffrey Howe about a decade ago in Wired magazine (Howe, 2006). In the publication, the author sparked interest in the term by chronicling the development of a process he believed counteracts the growing outsourcing of problem-solving to Chinese and Indian companies. This process, he argued, taps into the unexploited talents and wisdom of people on a global scale. The author reported how four different problems were addressed by separate individuals through this process that he named, 'crowdsourcing' by blending the word 'crowd' with 'outsourcing'. The concept literally refers to obtaining what you require from persons loosely affiliated through the Internet rather than from within or from traditional vendors. It is such a promising strategy that depends on the crowd to get specific tasks accomplished. Howe (2006) opined that the term crowdsourcing is embedded in a basically egalitarian belief that every individual has some talent or knowledge that will be valuable to other persons.

Crowdsourcing is considered as one of the major techniques for open innovation, which is an idea that originates from the innovation and business literatures. According to Seltzer and Mahmoudi (2012, p. 1), "open innovation refers to the conscious effort by firms to incorporate ideas originating outside the firm in innovation processes within the firm, or to send internally created ideas outside of the firm for commercial application". However, Zhao and Zhu (2012), differentiated crowdsourcing from open innovation, arguing that crowdsourcing is not ''open,'' because it relies on specific and independent work. Another distinction the authors made is that unlike in open innovation, in crowdsourcing the problem owner lacks control over the crowd. Seltzer and Mahmoudi (2012) noted that how the concept is defined and operationalized is continuously being debated, especially in associations with other terms such as open innovation, user innovation and co-creation.

According to Prpic and Shukla (2016, p. 4366), crowdsourcing applications can be compared along seven common features: the cost of crowdsourcing process; reliability of the crowdsourcing technique; scale of crowd size; anonymity of the crowd; type of crowdsourcing platform; duration of the crowdsourcing process; and size of the problem/task. In general, these characteristics allow practitioners and researchers to compare and recognize the relative variations among various methods of crowdsourcing, so that they can vividly display the essential trade-offs that an organization faces when considering which methods to pursue (Prpic and Shukla, 2016). Crowdsourcing has given birth to many concepts such as crowdvoting which refers to an online process of assembling opinions and judgments of a large group of people on a certain issue or topic, crowdsolving which is a collaborative approach of completely solving a specific problem, and crowdfunding which is a process that allows numerous people to fund a project by contributing tiny amounts to reach a definite monetary target.

3. CROWDSOURCING APPLICATIONS IN SUD PLANNING

Sustainable urban development (SUD) can be defined as a process of physical concentration of people, land uses and economic activities within an urban area in a manner that ensures a balance among environmental, economic and social objectives. As mentioned earlier, crowdsourcing can be an effective tool in complementing SUD process. Although SUD process consists of several stages, the following are the planning activities in which crowdsourcing has been widely applied: planning goal and objective settings, data collection, plan implementation, environmental monitoring, and urban governance (Table 1).

3.1 Planning Goals and Objectives Setting

Sustainable urban development refers to planning and management process that fosters mixed-use development, organized greens areas, multi-modal transportation system and social inclusion. While planning goals are broad statements about what urban plan intends to achieve for the future of a community, objectives on the other hand are more specific statements that address a specified outcome of the plan. Goals and objectives setting is an important stage of SUD planning that needs citizen's input, given that the future of a city is tremendously impacted at this stage. Crowdsourcing provides many opportunities for planners to take suggestions about public interest and to see what goals and objectives are particularly important to citizens. Using websites and social media such as Tweeter, Facebook and WhatsApp, communities are increasingly being involved in setting goals and objectives for SUD plan and in getting their feedback that is useful in re-examining contentious or unpopular goals and objectives. For example, Misra et al. (2014) have developed a crowdsourcing mechanism for involving a sizable group of stakeholders in the planning and operating of transportation system in the USA. The mechanism allowed for gathering sparse data on facilities such as bike routes as well as for soliciting feedback on the quality of transit service.

Similarly, crowdsourced contributions nowadays help to monitor, analyze, and model city form and functions. For example, Crooks et al (2014) established an innovative approach of studying urban morphology by focusing on information gathered from volunteered datasets such as trajectory and OpenStreetMap as well as social media. This new bottom-up method of studying, planning and manag-

Table 1. Summary of major crowdsourcing applications in SUD planning

Applications	Initiatives	References	Examples of Crowdsourcing Platforms
Planning goals and objectives setting	Serving public interest	Crooks et al. (2015), Papadopoulou and Giaoutzi (2014)	Shareabout, social media such as Facebook, Twitter, WhatsApp
Data collection	Citizen science	Keating et al. (2013), McCormick et al. (2017), Prpic and Shukla (2016)	Amazon Mechanical Turk (MTurk), social media like Twitter, Facebook
	Online survey	Behrend et al. (2011), Bosha (2015), Edgar et al. (2016),	SurveyMonkey, SurveyPlanet, Google Forms, TryMyUI,
	Crowdmapping	Chilton (2009), Gonzalez et al. (2013), Karam and Melchiori (2013)	Geo-Wiki, Google Map Maker, OpenStreetMap, Wikimapia. Web-GIS
	Content sharing	Doan et al. (2011),	Ask Ville, Google Earth, Wikipedia YouTube, Yahoo Answers, blogs, ResearchGate.
Plan implementation	Civic crowdfunding	Afrikstart (2016), Correia de Freitas & Amado (2013), Davies (2014).	Crowdfunder, Crowdrise, Citizinvestor, GoFundMe, Indiegogo, Invested. in, Kickstarter, Neighbourly, Quirky, RocketHub, Spacehive.
Environmental monitoring	Pollution detection	Maisonneuve et al. (2010), Stevens, and D'Hondt (2010)	Crowdflower, NoiseTube, Tongal
	Environmental activism	Massung et al. (2013)	eYeka, Kickstarter, Innocentive
	Disaster response	Goodchild and Glennon (2010), Mirbabaie et al. (2016),	Twitter, Facebook, WhatsApp
Urban governance	Public participation	Brabham (2009), Stratigea et al. (2015), Seltzer and Mahmoudi (2012), Kleinhans et al. (2015), Williamson and Parolin (2012)	eGov, Yelp, Quirky, Social media such as Facebook, Twitter and MySpace
	Urban management	Certoma et al. (2015), Misra et al. (2014), Gellers (2016).	Social media apps such as Facebook, Twitter, WhatsApp

ing cities supplements traditional urban studies by providing new lens for the study of urban activities. These crowd contributed data offer a direct narrative of urban forms and functions from the communities that through their activities shape urban spaces. Crowdsourcing thus promotes the advent of a new paradigm in urban morphology, with a significant shift from conventional to crowd-harvested content (Crooks et al., 2014).

3.2 Data Collection

Planning process involves collection of huge amount of data, which is analyzed to arrive at alternative course of actions towards achieving specific planning objectives. The advent of information and computer technology has revolutionized data collection process in many professions including urban planning. Through crowd science, online surveys, crowdmapping and content sharing, large volume of planning intelligence can be collected from a large study area and within a brief period and at low cost. That is why crowdsourcing has recently gain popularity in data collection to the extent that some researchers consider it as a distinct "research method" (Edgar et al., 2016 p. 2).

Citizen Science

Citizen or crowd science is a collaborative research conducted wholly or partially by nonprofessional or amateur scientists. It is a form of crowdsourcing where a crowd undertakes a study to solve real-world problem. Through this method, planning agencies obtain insights and views from a large group of distinct persons, and request them to voluntarily perform a task or provide some feedback (Certoma et al. 2015; Prpic and Shukla, 2016). This approach rallies the community to contribute in a scientific process towards addressing some of the contemporary global challenges such as poverty, social exclusion and climate change. Crowd science has been applied in ways that include the identification of research questions, data collection and analyses, interpretation of research results, development of applications and technologies, making new discoveries, and providing solutions to complex problems. It is generally utilized for improving science, providing solutions to social problems or creating modern technologies.

Online Surveys and Interviews

An online survey is a questionnaire which the target audience can complete over the internet. It can help produce accurate data for a wide range of uses, quickly and cost-effectively. Free online survey platforms including SurveyMonkey, SurveyGizmo, SurveyPlanet and Google Forms are increasingly being utilized in collecting socioeconomic data. Similarly, social media, such as Facebook and Twitter provide motivating opportunities for social science and public health research. These new communication platforms, according to McCormick et al. (2017) offer the ability to examine social data consisting of vast amounts of digital traces of human behavior on a diversity of topics, on a huge scale, and over short periods of time. Through this ability to collect information from a wider range of participants, researchers can achieve more representative samples, and strengthen study results and recommendations (Behrend et al., 2011; Edgar et al., 2016).

Surveys done through crowdsourcing have been deemed as viable as other techniques of data collection in social sciences and humanities. Edgar et al. (2016) compared self-administered data collection method with three different crowdsourcing platforms and found that crowdsourcing is indeed a viable way to collect survey information, as respondents have duly completed the tasks and provided useful information. However, they recommend that complex tasks may require the skills of an interviewer to administer unscripted probes. Similarly, some researchers argue that data produced online parallel more well-researched data collection methods such as surveys, ethnography and structured observation (McCormick et al., 2017). They added that, "social media data allow researchers to collect reports of behaviors that are unsolicited and unprompted by the researcher" (McCormick et al., 2017, p. 392)

Crowdmapping

This is a process where organizations or planning agencies submit an open call for geographic information from volunteers to collaboratively produce maps or update existing ones. Several community mapping projects rely on user-generated spatial content. As cities in developing countries are rapidly growing, maps become obsolete without updating. Crowdmapping thus allows sharing of skills, resources, and experience towards projects for updating and annotating maps. Crowdmapping allows users to add and edit non-movable and permanent features such as buildings, parks and roads. Using platforms such as

Geo-Wiki, OpenStreetMap, Wikimapia, the quality of global land cover maps is improved with the help of network of volunteers from across the globe.

For example, in the USA the office of research and development of Environmental Protection Agency and science and decisions center of U.S. Geological Survey sponsor community mapping projects across the country using smartphone and tablet technology (<https://www.digitalgov.gov/communities/federal-crowdsourcing-and-citizen-science/> accessed: June 03, 2017). Similarly, Gonzalez et al. (2013) developed a map-based annotation system where people shared structured data of places and incidents. Crowd can collaboratively geo-tagged any information on the map. Through this map updating system, attributes, names and tags are attached to a geographical coordinate on a map. Thus, planning agencies and cities in developing countries can utilize the crowd to create several data layers regarding the spatial structure and functioning of a city, the infrastructures, as well as the natural and sociocultural resources (Stratigea et al., 2015).

Content Sharing

There is a growing online source of urban data. Secondary data such as maps, statistics, books, technical reports, journal articles needed in planning process are freely shared online. Similarly, key information and case studies about sustainable development practices, challenges and ways forward in developing countries is being shared by the crowd via several popular online information sharing systems. These include *Wikipedia* which is an online encyclopedia with entries contributed by crowds, *YouTube* which is a video sharing site where crowd upload and download content and *Yahoo Answers* which is a general question-answering forum that provides a collection of human reviewed information. Additional way of content sharing is online brainstorming that brings more ideas into the mix. Innovative ideas are developed out of a pool of existing parts and recombining what is already known, thus, crowd knowledge and expertise is highly valuable.

3.3 Plan Implementation

Plan implementation is the process of transforming plans into actions, which involve executing the proposals contained in the plan. It is an essential part of SUD process that follows the plan making stage. However, in developing countries, because of limited financial and technical resources for implementing SUD plans the much-needed urban infrastructure and basic urban services cannot be provided. Thus, several SUD plan documents end up on planning agency shelves and as research and teaching documents at higher education institutions. However, sustainable funding for important urban development projects is nowadays possible through civic crowdfunding. Urban development projects can be executed through online donations, cash transfers using mobile phones or offering of services. As such, crowdfunding offers an opportunity for cities in developing countries to overcome the triple challenges of resource limitation, the need to contain rapid urbanization and improve the quality of life of urban dwellers.

In developed countries, strategic use of crowdfunding by the public sector in urban development process is an emerging collaborative venture that utilizes the web to promote the urban sharing economy. Capitals for urban development activities ranging from community park development to neighborhood upgrading are being raised through this evolving collaborative funding. Examples of SUD projects implemented using civic crowdfunding include building new multi-purpose community center in the town of Glyncoch, UK where £792.021 was raised from various funders (Correia de Freitas and Amado,

2013). The well landscaped center is energy-efficient and it is used for hosting workshops, community groups and local business conferences. A similar, but smaller, project is the upgrading of Stevenson square in Manchester City, UK, through planting of edible plants and improved landscaping. This project raised the required amount of £39,354 from funders as well as volunteer services and contribution of tree seedlings, hanging baskets and materials for pavements (Correia de Freitas and Amado, 2013). Successful implementation of these two projects indicate that both larger and smaller projects that aim to enhance the urban environment can be financed through civic crowdfunding.

There are usually two models for crowdfunding as an innovative method of procuring capital, using social networking, from large groups of small investors that contribute low sums. Either a city use it as an innovative way to solicit capital to implement plans for improving the urban environment or the citizens propose specific projects they would like to be implemented and look for financing via crowdfunding. If urban planning agencies in developing countries adopt this approach to urban planning, it will turn out to be a better interlink of the destiny of urban projects and developments. It will help provide public goods to underserved communities and will increase participation and improve a sense community ownership of the projects. However, some observers pointed out that crowdfunding opportunities are heavily concentrated in major cities and are skewed towards projects related to the environment such as urban greening, renovation of schools, and heritage conservation (Davies, 2014).

3.4 Environmental Monitoring

Sustainable development planning involves environmental monitoring for characterizing the quality of the environment to minimize the risks of harmful effects of human activities on plants, animals, lands, air and water bodies. Using crowdsourcing for instance, a noise pollution monitoring system called NoiseTube enables citizens to measure and map urban noise pollution using smartphones (Maisonneuve et al., 2010). This low-cost solution allows people to measure their own exposure to noise in their surroundings by using GPS-equipped cellphones as noise sensors. The crowd-generated and geo-localized data are then automatically sent and shared online with citizens who contribute to produce a collective noise map of their city. Another example is in the USA, where the Environmental Protection Agency coordinates voluntary air and water monitor projects at the state and local levels where trained volunteers monitoring the condition of their local waters by collecting water quality data over time to assess the health of local streams, lakes, estuaries and wetlands. The agency together with the crowd help build community awareness about pollution problems, help identify and restore problem sites, become advocates for their watersheds and increase the amount of needed water quality information. (<https://archive.epa.gov/water/archive/web/html/index-18.html>, accessed: May 09, 2017). Crowdsourcing thus facilitates assessing and monitoring the quality of environmental resources: air, land, water, and vegetation.

In environmental activism, crowdsourcing contributes to raising publics' consciousness of ecological issues at hand (Matthias and D'Hondt, 2010). It allows the status of environmental resources to be verified by the citizens who are directly confronted with environmental pollution. Another important application of crowdsourcing is in disaster management, which refers to organizing and managing resources and responsibilities to lessen the impact of disasters. During disasters, such as earthquakes hurricanes and floods, people volunteered with geographic information about the area or the situation on the ground that helps the affected ones and support emergency service agencies to react faster and more efficient during such dangerous events (Mirbabaic et al. 2016). The crowdsourced information is then used to create disaster mitigation maps. Twitter for example has been used as additional communication tool during bushfires in Australia. Similarly, VGI has been utilized in disaster response during the four wildfires that stuck Santa Barbara area in the USA from 2007 to 2009 (Goodchild and Glennon, 2010).

3.5 Urban Governance

Urban governance is concerned about political, administrative, and socioeconomic decisions-making processes through which societies manage and govern their cities. Elements of governance are institutional efficiency, accountability, transparency and democracy/involvement. Participatory governance promotes inclusive and lively cities, which are platforms for democracy, diversity and cultural dialogue and where policies are formulated and implemented to drive more effectual resource management (Stratigea et al., 2015). Crowdsourcing by its nature has inherent potential of promoting these elements of governance. According to Certoma et al. (2015), crowdsourcing offers both context and process for gathering crowds around issues of common concern through tentative explorations of spontaneous bottom-up smart processes of socio-technological networks that can produce non-planned smart transition and empower citizens. The following are the two major applications of crowdsourcing in urban governance:

Public Participation in Planning Process

Public participation refers to the involvement in decision-making and knowledge production of the people affected by, concerned about, knowledgeable of, or having relevant experience/expertise on the issues at stake (Stratigea et al., 2015). Involving the public in plan making is a keystone for good planning practice. From a normative perspective, the people affected by plans ought to be engaged in making them. Citizen participation, according to Lane (2005), "is a variety of approaches and practices associated with key decisions and judgments entered from the moment that a planning problem is conceived". Since the publication of ''A Ladder of Citizen Participation'' about half a century ago, there has been upsurge in the institutional and systematic incorporation of public involvement in urban planning throughout the world (Seltzer & Mahmoudi, 2012). Local, regional, and state planning agencies have recognized public participation as an essential feature of the planning process and are therefore utilizing crowdsourcing in meeting public interest and fulfilling important sustainable development objectives. This is based on recognizing the political nature of planning, the advent of a pluralistic view of society and the notion that planning ought to be communicative by involving a wide range of stakeholders: decision-makers, professionals and citizens.

Planning for SUD cannot succeed without a core focus on the community directly affected. Crowdsourcing system facilitates gathering of stakeholder opinions, and harnessing their extensive 'genius' (Brabham, 2009). It increases the number of participants in the planning system, at the same time increasing community understanding of planning system. Web-based using social media such as Facebook and Twitter are easy and cost-effective approach to involvement. Other platforms are planning agencies websites designed to take input and feedback communications. For example, many local governments in Australia offer citizens with the opportunity to provide online feedback or input into their planning process (Williamson and Parolin, 2012). Specifically, 63% of metropolitan and 30% of non-metropolitan councils in Australia accept comments submitted online to plans that are on public exhibition (Williamson and Parolin, 2012, p.54). Given that opinions are subjective preferences that emerge from the interaction of stakeholders, planner should ensure a two-way knowledge exchange, involving interaction and negotiation among various actors.

Urban Management With the Crowd

Crowdsourcing is nowadays an important urban management tool, especially in the delivery of urban services, utilities and infrastructure. In many developed countries, cities and planning agencies develop blogs and platforms on their websites where they post urban management issues and get a rapid response from the community, which creates an atmosphere where all voices are equally heard. For instance, in Boston (Massachusetts, USA) a mobile application called Street Bump was developed to detect potholes and other street hazards using the accelerometer of smartphones. As citizens drive around the metropolis, the geo-located data on street quality is collected via crowdsourcing and automatically uploaded and integrated with the city's system for locating and fixing roads and pavements quality problems (Misra et al., 2014). In Australia for instance, 12% of metropolitan council host discussion forums on local planning issues, and 5% host blogs on local planning issues on their websites. Alternatively, third-party forums and blogs as well as social media offer an opportunity for planning agencies and city councils to engage with the public without significant modification to their current websites. In Australia, social media such as Twitter and Facebook are being used by 21% of metropolitan council websites, while third-party discussion forums and blogs were respectively observed on 12% and 5% of the councils (Williamson and Parolin, 2012). Other instances specified the way government agencies have used crowdsourcing in exposing ideas and providing improved accountability and transparency in urban management.

4. CROWDSOURCING CHALLENGES IN PLANNING FOR SUD IN DEVELOPING COUNTRIES

Remarkable progress has been made in the field of crowdsourcing as well as the use of digital tools and technologies in several walks of life such as engineering, commerce and information and computer technology (ICT). However, utilizing crowdsourcing as a tool in urban development planning in developing countries is challenged by a myriad of factors. This section, therefore, discuses four of the possible challenges: limited awareness, institutional barriers, lack of incentives and low quality of outsourced product/service.

4.1 Limited Awareness About Crowdsourcing

Notwithstanding that we are in a global village where information is highly diffused via telecommunication channels such as the internet, mobile phones, satellite television and radio, as well as other online and print media, there is limited awareness about crowdsourcing and its potentials in developing countries. Some of these limitations are highlighted below:

- In many developing countries, the applications of ICTs in general and crowdsourcing platforms especially their potential benefits in urban development planning are not fully appreciated (Chuene and Mtsweni, 2015). Plan making is still done using the traditional method of contracting out to consultants or carried out inhouse using the employees of planning agencies.
- Communities in the developing world rarely utilize the opportunities obtainable on the internet for crowdsourcing. For example, in 2015 about USD $32.3 million was generated by crowdfunding platforms based in Africa, which is less than 0.1% of the global crowdfunding market, estimated at

over USD $34.4 billion in the same year (Afrikstart, 2016). In addition, language differences make public participation in crowdsourcing activities very challenging (Stanley et al., 2013).

- Another challenge is that, even in the few existing crowdsourcing activities, tasks/problems are not well-defined and their context not clearly described so that the crowd can fully understand them. In some cases, technical concepts are not fully defined or are assumed to be known to the crowd, which consists of non-experts (Brabham, 2009).
- There is also limited understanding of the benefits of utilizing crowdsourcing in urban planning and management by both the crowd and problem owners (planning agencies) who are often not clear about what they need or don't need (Misra et al, 2014).

4.2 Institutional Barriers

Crowdsourcing is an emerging and yet to be established field of inquiry. In developing countries, although the importance of seeking crowd input in SUD planning is clear, institutional barriers make planners and planning agencies resistant to utilizing the opportunity afforded by crowdsourcing. Some of the major barriers are:

- Resistance from national governments, especially in sub-Saharan Africa where corruption is endemic and democratic government is not sufficiently institutionalized beyond holding elections, to 'open governance' and public involvement in development planning (Ingwe, 2017).
- Although substantial number of people in developing countries have mobile phones, there is limited access to high speed internet and/or smartphones, especially broadband network. Most crowdsourcing platforms are only in the form of applications that can only be used on smartphones. Similarly, crowdsourcing is difficult because internet speed is low as connections are mostly based on 3G network.
- Many planning agencies are reluctant to deploy crowdsourcing because their employees do not know how to design a crowdsourcing initiative and how to utilize and integrate it with planning process (Chuene and Mtsweni, 2015). Also, few agencies officials are comfortable with or have access to the internet.
- Complex projects such as urban planning need a more devoted crowd governance strategy. Managing the crowd and huge data is a challenge which if not carefully managed could lead to loss of control. As such, concerted efforts are needed to successfully manage the crowd and direct them towards the desired solution (Pedersen et al., 2013).
- There is also the challenge of funding the crowdsourcing activity. Even in some high-income countries, some studies reported that budgetary and operational obstacles such as lack of technical expertise prevent many planning agencies and local governments from employing and operating crowdsourcing platforms on their own websites

4.3 Disincentives and Lack of Motivation

An incentive is something that encourages a person to perform an action. Getting people to participate in crowdsourcing is a challenge, especially in developing countries. Lack of education and unfamiliarity with the use of internet or web-based technology, especially in rural areas, are major disincentives for crowdsourcing in developing countries (Stanley et al., 2013). Many studies have identified monetary prize as the main motivation factors for the public to participate in crowdsourcing. As such, because of extreme poverty levels in many developing countries (Abubakar & Dano, 2018, Ingwe, 2017), lack of financial incentives is one of the major challenges of getting the public to participate in crowdsourcing for SUD planning, particularly in tasks where the crowd members are required to interact more than once. In some instances, volunteers stop participating along the way, thereby stagnating the crowdsourcing activities.

Additional challenge of crowdsourcing in developing countries is that that several home-developed crowdsourcing platforms eventually become inactive (Chuene and Mtsweni, 2015). Indeed, crowdsourcing needs a strong, active, motivated crowd and a great deal of transparency on the part of the problem owner. But, public participation in urban planning is most often considered as leisure-time activity that competes with a range of other life necessities. Therefore, getting citizens to spend their time in crowdsourcing is difficult given that financial rewards are almost never possible. Even for the planning practitioners, and others engaged in developing public policy, defining problems for others to solve is challenging. Effective crowdsourcing needs money, time, and other commitments (Thuan et al., 2016).

4.4 Quality of Crowdsourced Product/Service

Another challenge is that with crowdsourcing, it is not clear who is contributing given that a task is thrown out to untested crowds. Can the crowd collect useful information or produce trustworthy solution/ task? Many studies have indicated that data collected and tasks accomplished without financial reward are often of inferior quality (Yuen et al, 2011; Zhao and Han, 2016). Thus, the issue of quality of the crowdsourced solution is very imperative (Goodchild and Glennon, 2010). In a systematic review of 23 articles on the use of volunteered geographic information (VGI) for disaster management, Mirbabaic et al. (2016) found that accuracy (52%), consistency (48%), and completeness (31%), are the most frequently used criteria for assessing VGI quality. In contrast, trustworthiness was mentioned the least (17%).

Another issue is that of uncertainty about the quality of crowdsourced data. As the volume of data obtainable from crowdsourcing is constantly growing, evaluating its quality is becoming a challenging task (Karam and Melchiori, 2013). Another challenge is that the locational, demographic and socioeconomic characteristics of the crowd members (such as age, gender, educational level, income) are self-reported, so the accuracy of the crowd composition depends on their honesty. Edgar et al. (2016) reported that in one crowdsourcing project, participants misrepresented themselves to meet the project's requirements. Sometime malicious content can be introduced to the crowdfunding system or platform. However, the issue of low quality of crowdsourced solution is not always the case as Goodchild and Glennon (2010) believe that that the quality of VGI can approach and even exceed that of authoritative sources.

5. POTENTIALS OF USING CROWDSOURCING IN SUD PLANNING IN DEVELOPING COUNTRIES

The development of crowdsourcing capabilities could have important implications for solving even the most enigmatic problems humanity face. Despite the challenges discussed above, the following are some of the opportunities to utilize crowdsourcing as a promising tool in SUD process in developing countries.

5.1 Internet Penetration and Mobile Phones

The emergence of Web 2.0 and its explosive growth has ushered in numerous exciting and never-existing possible crowdsourcing opportunities. The internet which rendered all kinds of communication easier and faster is an infrastructure of the contemporary service economy, and it is at present a hard-fact of community development. With increasing access to internet and mobile communication devices in developing countries, there are many potentials for participation in crowdsourcing, even in rural areas. The online social media are increasing the strategic importance of crowdsourcing, not only in SUD planning but as a means of income generation (Hossain and Kauranen, 2015). There are many crowdsourcing websites that display a list of available tasks, associated with reward and period that the crowd are expected to compete and complete the tasks. In addition to monetary reward, a worker gains credibility when his task is accepted or in some cases, the motivation is altruism (Yuen et al, 2011). Mobile crowdsourcing is currently presenting an innovative way for community development and employment creation in both rural to urban Africa (Stanley et al, 2013).

Another potential for crowdsourcing in the emerging economies is the astronomical growth in mobile phone diffusion and subscription. For example, in Sub-Saharan Africa total mobile subscription penetration has grown from 50% in 2010 to about 80% in 2015 and it is projected to reach 100% by 2021 (Ericson, 2015). In developing countries, even the low-income people are increasingly getting access to the Internet with their mobile phones. Mobile devices nowadays can be used as nodes in a sensor network for gathering, analyzing and sharing of local knowledge Using their mobile phones, communities in developing countries can monitor their surroundings and share their individual mobility patterns and socioeconomic activities which can then be aggregated to document an entire urban environment. Similarly, by turning smartphones into measurement tools, the barrier to environmental measurement technology has been strongly lowered towards achieving a democratization of environmental monitoring process (Matthias & D'Hondt, 2010). In Nairobi Kenya for example, crowdsourcing was used by university students to map informal public transportation using their cellphones (Ingwe, 2017).

5.2 Online Crowdsourcing Platforms

Crowdsourcing platforms bring a broad range of people to brainstorm, conceive and evaluate ideas towards solving a problem or accomplishing a task. The proliferation of online platforms such as MTurk, Geo-Wiki, Google Map Maker, OpenStreetMap, Wikimapia, Web-GIS, SurveyMonkey, in addition to social media like Facebook, Twitter, Youtube, WhatsApp, Instagram, has made it more accessible and simpler for people to become involved in diverse types of crowdsourced initiatives. New virtual platforms, such as NoiseTube, txteagle and mClerk, are used for crowdsourcing via mobile devices with Internet access (Matthias and D'Hondt, 2010; Hossain and Kauranen, 2015). These applications are mostly free to download and use. They are being used to connect intellectual and financial capital towards socio-economic and community development.

Some of the platforms specifically developed for developing countries include the Ushahidi project from Kenya where data is collected from the crowd and presents it in a well visualized format (bar charts, list, maps, or timeline) for the public agencies to make informed decisions (Ushahidi, n.d.). This open-source software is also a useful tool for environmental mapping and election monitoring. Another initiative by the water sector regulatory agency in Kenya is MajiVoice, which is a website that enables

Kenyans to conveniently and easily reach their water company using mobile phone or the Internet and get feedback via text message or from the website (http://majivoice.com/, accessed August 02, 2017). In south Africa, Mobilitate, an online crowdsourcing platform, enables citizens to report any service delivery problem to government (Chuene and Mtsweni, 2015). According to Afrikstart (2016) there were 57 active crowdfunding platforms located and operating in Africa in 2015, focusing mainly on social causes and charity, especially community development projects. Brabham (2009), demonstrates that social media are potential platforms for public participation in urban planning processes that developing countries can harness. In the developed countries, even if cities and planning agencies do not utilize the technology to engage their citizenry, the publics do utilize it to engage the planners.

5.3 Altruism and Social Network

Given that altruism is one of the key motivators for crowdsourcing, planning agencies can save cost by utilizing the crowd to get tasks done voluntarily or at a very low cost. The social network of friends, families and neighbors in developing countries can contribute their talents and skills towards SUD process. The abundance of this large, diverse network can provide their wealth of ideas, services, solutions towards planning and developing sustainable urban areas. With rising expenditure and shrinking revenue, planning agencies can utilize the sheer number and diversity of crowd that come together to tackle an issue, regardless of education, age and other factors as another potential of crowdsourcing in aiding SUD planning process.

The vast number of educated and enthusiastic youth in developing countries is yet another potential for crowdsourcing activities, given proper enlightenment and skills. Seltzer and Mahmoudi (2012) concurred that people are willing to engage in crowdsourcing because of their love of and commitment to their communities, opportunities for skills development, the challenge in the tasks involved, as well as for doing something when bored. Another opportunity for public engagement through crowdsourcing in developing countries is the abundance of civil societies in the form of workers' unions and non-governmental organizations (NGOs). Ingwe (2017) argued that citizen engagement via crowdsourcing in sub-Saharan Africa could be better promoted by international organizations and NGOs because they are known to encourage public engagement and not to stifle it. The organizations can also help create public awareness about the benefits of crowdsourcing.

6. CONCLUSION AND FUTURE RESEARCH DIRECTIONS

In developing countries where the rate of urbanization is very high, institutions are weak and financial, technical and managerial resources are scarce, urban planning and governance must incorporate some innovative techniques for urban development to be sustainable. This chapter has highlighted how crowdsourcing can facilitate SUD planning process by better serving of public interest, improved access to data, financing the implementation of development project, environmental monitoring and in fostering governance and citizen participation. Crowdsourcing draws on the wisdom of the crowd where solutions to a problem can emerge from heterogeneous, dispersed and independent crowds, consisting of acknowledged experts together with those without formal expertise. This can bring in newer perspectives and ideas to the planning problem at hand.

However, utilizing crowdsourcing in developing countries to achieve these benefits is challenged by a myriad of issues, including limited awareness about crowdsourcing, institutional barriers, disincentives and lack of motivation of the crowd and low quality of crowdsourced product/service. To effectively utilize crowdsourcing for SUD process urban planners and decision makers must also work in collaboration with other city stakeholders to overcome the identified challenges. Some opportunities of overcoming the challenges include rapid growth in access to internet and mobile phones, proliferation of online crowdsourcing platforms and altruism and social network that is abundant in developing countries. Brabham (2009) concludes that even though crowdsourcing is a very useful tool, it must not be used as a complete substitute for other types of innovations or public engagement. This is more especially on the part of government, because as representation cannot be guaranteed, a planning or development activity can be easily co-opted by elites having better access to their favor at the expense of the wider public.

As crowdsourcing activities in developing countries are at infancy, there is very limited data about crowdsourcing applications in SUD planning to be able to comprehensively assess existing challenges. Hence, future research through comparative case studies is needed to gain in-depth understanding of how each of the analyzed applications of crowdsourcing is being implemented in different regions of the global South. For example, it will be interesting to compare Latin America with Asia or Africa, or compare Asia with Africa with regards to how crowdsourcing is being utilized to aid SUD process. Future studies are also needed to investigate the obstacles and potentials of utilizing crowdsourcing in urban planning at country levels, more especially in Africa.

REFERENCES

Abubakar, I., & Aina, Y. A. (2006). GIS and Space Syntax: An analysis of accessibility to urban green areas in Doha district of Dammam metropolitan area, Saudi Arabia. *Proceedings of Map Middle East conference*, 1-8.

Abubakar, I. R. (2011). Distributional patterns of urban services in a modernist city of developing countries: A case study of Abuja, Nigeria. *Association of the Collegiate Schools of Planning 52nd Annual Conference.*

Abubakar, I. R., & Aina, Y. A. (2016). Achieving Sustainable Cities in Saudi Arabia: Juggling the Competing Urbanization Challenges. In Population Growth and Rapid Urbanization in the Developing World (pp. 42-63). Hershey, PA: IGI Global.

Abubakar, I. R., Al-Shihri, F. S., & Ahmed, S. M. (2016). Students' assessment of campus sustainability at the University of Dammam, Saudi Arabia. *Sustainability*, *8*(1), 59. doi:10.3390/su8010059

Abubakar, I. R., & Dano, U. L. (2018). Socioeconomic Challenges and Opportunities of Urbanization in Nigeria. In Urbanization and Its Impact on Socio-Economic Growth in Developing Regions (pp. 219-240). Hershey, PA: IGI Global. doi:10.4018/978-1-5225-2659-9.ch011

Afrikstart. (2016*). Crowdfunding in Africa. Fundraising goes Digital in Africa: The emergence of Africa-Based Crowdfunding Platforms*. Retrieved from http://afrikstart.com/report/wp-content/uploads/2016/09/Afrikstart-Crowdfunding-In-Africa-Report.pdf

Behrend, T. S., Sharek, D. J., Meade, A. W., & Wiebe, E. N. (2011). The viability of crowdsourcing for survey research. *Behavior Research Methods, 43*(3), 800–813. doi:10.3758/s13428-011-0081-0 PMID:21437749

Benna, U. G., & Garba, S. B. (Eds.). (2016). *Population Growth and Rapid Urbanization in the Developing World.* IGI Global. doi:10.4018/978-1-5225-0187-9

Bosha, E. (2015). *Factors influencing continuous data collection for a public safety crowdsourcing smart city project* (Doctoral dissertation). University of Fort Hare, South Africa.

Brabham, D. C. (2009). Crowdsourcing the public participation process for planning projects. *Planning Theory, 8*(3), 242–262. doi:10.1177/1473095209104824

Certoma, C., Corsini, F., & Rizzi, F. (2015). Crowdsourcing urban sustainability. Data, people and technologies in participatory governance. *Futures, 74*, 93–106. doi:10.1016/j.futures.2014.11.006

Chilton, S. (2009, November). Crowdsourcing is radically changing the geodata landscape: case study of OpenStreetMap. *Proceedings of the UK 24th International Cartography Conference.*

Chuene, D., & Mtsweni, J. (2015, May). The adoption of crowdsourcing platforms in South Africa. In *IST-Africa Conference, 2015* (pp. 1–9). IEEE. doi:10.1109/ISTAFRICA.2015.7190561

Correia de Freitas, J., & Amado, M. (2013, July). Crowdfunding in urban planning: Opportunities and Obstacles. *RC43 Annual Conference,* 10-12.

Crooks, A., Pfoser, D., Jenkins, A., Croitoru, A., Stefanidis, A., Smith, D., & Lamprianidis, G. et al. (2015). Crowdsourcing urban form and function. *International Journal of Geographical Information Science, 29*(5), 720–741. doi:10.1080/13658816.2014.977905

Davies, R. (2014). Civic crowdfunding as a marketplace for participation in urban development. Center for Work, Technology and Organizations, Stanford University.

Doan, A., Ramakrishnan, R., & Halevy, A. Y. (2011). Crowdsourcing systems on the World-Wide Web. *Communications of the ACM, 54*(4), 86–96. doi:10.1145/1924421.1924442

Edgar, J., Murphy, J., & Keating, M. (2016). Comparing Traditional and Crowdsourcing Methods for Pretesting Survey Questions. *SAGE Open, 6*(4), 2158244016671770. doi:10.1177/2158244016671770

Ericson. (2015). *Sub-Saharan Africa Ericsson Mobility Report. Market Overview.* Retrieved from www.ericsson.com/res/docs/2015/mobility-report/emr-nov-2015-regional-report-sub-saharan-africa.pdf

Estelles-Arolas, E., & Gonzalez-Ladron-De-Guevara, F. (2012). Towards an integrated crowdsourcing definition. *Journal of Information Science, 38*(2), 189–200. doi:10.1177/0165551512437638

Gellers, J. C. (2016). Crowdsourcing global governance: Sustainable development goals, civil society, and the pursuit of democratic legitimacy. *International Environmental Agreement: Politics, Law and Economics, 16*(3), 415–432. doi:10.1007/s10784-016-9322-0

Gonzalez, A. L., Izidoro, D., Willrich, R., & Santos, C. A. (2013, October). OurMap: Representing Crowdsourced Annotations on Geospatial Coordinates as Linked Open Data. CRIWG, 77-93.

Goodchild, M. F., & Glennon, J. A. (2010). Crowdsourcing geographic information for disaster response: A research frontier. *International Journal of Digital Earth*, *3*(3), 231–241. doi:10.1080/17538941003759255

Hossain, M., & Kauranen, I. (2015). Crowdsourcing: A comprehensive literature review. *Strategic Outsourcing*, *8*(1), 2–22. doi:10.1108/SO-12-2014-0029

Howe, J. (2006). The rise of crowdsourcing. *Wired Magazine*. Retrieved from http://www.wired.com/wired/archive/14.06/crowds_pr.html

Ingwe, R. (2017). Crowdsourcing-Based Geoinformation, Disadvantaged Urbanisation Challenges, Subsaharan Africa: Theoretical Perspectives and Notes. *Quaestiones Geographicae*, *36*(1), 5–14. doi:10.1515/quageo-2017-0001

Karam, R., & Melchiori, M. (2013, October). A crowdsourcing-based framework for improving geo-spatial open data. In *Systems, Man, and Cybernetics (SMC), 2013 IEEE International Conference on* (pp. 468-473). IEEE. doi:10.1109/SMC.2013.85

Keating, M., Rhodes, B., & Richards, A. (2013). Crowdsourcing: a flexible method for innovation, data collection, and analysis in social science research. *Social media, sociality, and survey research*, 179-201.

Kleinhans, R., van Ham, M., & Evans-Cowley, J. (2015). Using Social Media and Mobile Technologies to Foster Engagement and Self-organisation in Participatory Urban Planning and Neighbourhood Governance. *Planning Practice and Research*, *30*(3), 237–247. doi:10.1080/02697459.2015.1051320

Lane, M. B. (2005). Public Participation in Planning: An Intellectual History. *The Australian Geographer*, *36*(3), 283–299. doi:10.1080/00049180500325694

Maisonneuve, N., Stevens, M., & Ochab, B. (2010). Participatory noise pollution monitoring using mobile phones. *Information Polity*, *15*(1-2), 51-71.

Massung, E., Coyle, D., Cater, K. F., Jay, M., & Preist, C. (2013, April). Using crowdsourcing to support pro-environmental community activism. In *Proceedings of the SIGCHI Conference on Human Factors in Computing Systems* (pp. 371-380). ACM. doi:10.1145/2470654.2470708

McCormick, T. H., Lee, H., Cesare, N., Shojaie, A., & Spiro, E. S. (2017). Using Twitter for demographic and social science research: Tools for data collection and processing. *Sociological Methods & Research*, *46*(3), 390–421. doi:10.1177/0049124115605339

Mirbabaic, M., Stieglitz, S., & Volkeri, S. (2016, January). Volunteered Geographic Information and Its Implications for Disaster Management. In *System Sciences (HICSS), 2016 49th Hawaii International Conference on* (pp. 207-216). IEEE.

Misra, A., Gooze, A., Watkins, K., Asad, M., & Le Dantec, C. (2014). Crowdsourcing and its application to transportation data collection and management. *Transportation Research Record: Journal of the Transportation Research Board*, *2414*, 1–8. doi:10.3141/2414-01

Papadopoulou, C. A., & Giaoutzi, M. (2014). Crowdsourcing as a tool for knowledge acquisition in spatial planning. *Future Internet*, *6*(1), 109–125. doi:10.3390/fi6010109

Pedersen, J., Kocsis, D., Tripathi, A., Tarrell, A., & de Vreede, G. J. (2013, January). Conceptual foundations of crowdsourcing: A review of IS research. In *System Sciences (HICSS), 2013 46th Hawaii International Conference on* (pp. 579-588). IEEE.

Prpic, J., & Shukla, P. (2016, January). Crowd science: Measurements, models, and methods. In *System Sciences (HICSS), 2016 49th Hawaii International Conference on* (pp. 4365-4374). IEEE.

Roth, S., Kaivo-Oja, J., & Hirschmann, T. (2013). Smart regions: Two cases of crowdsourcing for regional development. *International Journal of Entrepreneurship and Small Business*, *20*(3), 272–285. doi:10.1504/IJESB.2013.056890

Seltzer, E., & Mahmoudi, D. (2012). Citizen participation, open innovation, and crowdsourcing: Challenges and opportunities for planning. *CPL Bibliography, 28*(1), 3-18.

Soltész, K. (2010). Sustainable urban development and developing countries. *Curentul Juridic, The Juridical Current. Le Courant Juridique*, *43*, 144–152.

Stanley, C., Winschiers-Theophilus, H., Onwordi, M., & Kapuire, G. K. (2013, December). Rural communities crowdsource technology development: a Namibian expedition. In *Proceedings of the Sixth International Conference on Information and Communications Technologies and Development: Notes-Volume 2* (pp. 155-158). ACM. doi:10.1145/2517899.2517930

Stevens, M., & D'Hondt, E. (2010, September). Crowdsourcing of pollution data using smartphones. *Workshop on Ubiquitous Crowdsourcing.*

Stratigea, A., Papadopoulou, C. A., & Panagiotopoulou, M. (2015). Tools and Technologies for Planning the Development of Smart Cities. *Journal of Urban Technology*, *22*(2), 43–62. doi:10.1080/10630732.2015.1018725

Thuan, N. H., Antunes, P., & Johnstone, D. (2016). Factors influencing the decision to crowdsource: A systematic literature review. *Information Systems Frontiers*, *18*(1), 47–68. doi:10.1007/s10796-015-9578-x

UN. (2015). *World Population Prospects: The 2015 revision. Key findings and advance tables.* New York: Department of Economic and Social Affairs, Population Division, United Nation.

Ushahidi. (n.d.). Retrieved from https://www.ushahidi.com/support/ushahidi-overview

Williamson, W., & Parolin, B. (2012). Review of web-based communications for town planning in local government. *Journal of Urban Technology*, *19*(1), 43–63. doi:10.1080/10630732.2012.626702

Yuen, M. C., King, I., & Leung, K. S. (2011, October). A survey of crowdsourcing systems. In *Privacy, Security, Risk and Trust (PASSAT) and 2011 IEEE Third International Conference on Social Computing*, 766-773. doi:10.1109/PASSAT/SocialCom.2011.203

Zhao, Y., & Han, Q. (2016). Spatial crowdsourcing: Current state and future directions. *IEEE Communications Magazine*, *54*(7), 102–107. doi:10.1109/MCOM.2016.7509386

Zhao, Y., & Zhu, Q. (2014). Evaluation on crowdsourcing research: Current status and future direction. *Information Systems Frontiers*, *16*(3), 417–434. doi:10.1007/s10796-012-9350-4

KEY TERMS AND DEFINITIONS

Crowdsourcing: A sourcing system in which organizations and agencies use largely advanced internet technologies to harness the efforts of a crowd to perform specific tasks or solve problems.

Developing Countries: Are nations with less-developed industrial base and a low human development index (HDI) relative to developed countries.

Innovation: Is the creation of novel ideas and solutions and their application to facilitate new business outcome (product/services) or meet new requirements.

Planning Process: Is a process of thoughts and actions for organizing the activities required to achieve a desired goal. It involves the making and maintaining a plan.

Urban Development: Is a process of physical concentration of people, land uses, and economic activity within an urban area.

Urban Sustainability: Seeking the management of urban functions in a way that a balance is maintained among environmental, social, and economic objectives.

Urbanization: Is a process that involves continuous rise in the number of people living in urban areas as well as the manners in which the society responds to the change.

Section 2

Opportunities and Challenges in Crowdfunding Markets

Chapter 6
A Comparative Analysis of Online Crowdfunding Platforms in Africa and the Middle East

Muhammad Aliyu Sulaiman
King Fahd University of Petroleum and Minerals, Saudi Arabia

ABSTRACT

This chapter seeks to fill a gap in the regional analysis of online crowdfunding platforms and projects by examining selected platforms in Africa and in the Middle East. The authors considered the quantity and quality of the actors: fundraisers, funders, and other stakeholders; analyzed characteristics, quality, fees, and general value for money; and evaluated the capacity of the platforms in terms of system interface, projects, and customer crowds aiming to enhance their overall capacity to become nodes of local and regional crowdfunding activities. These are connected to other district and urban centers that would serve as a springboard to organize and network with overseas centers for the growth and development of the regional centers.

INTRODUCTION

Many developing countries, including those in Africa and the Middle East, are faced with the complex problems of high population growth and rapid urbanization (UNDESA, 2014; Benna & Garba, 2015) with dwindling development resources to tackle them. The volume of development funds needed to reduce these problems to a manageable scale seems beyond the capacity of the traditional banking sources to provide, especially at the time some of them are struggling to stay afloat. The conditionality for obtaining development finance by local entrepreneurs, sub-national or by national governments from the traditional financial institutions are cumbersome, time-consuming and regulations too inflexible for loan seekers to meet (Belleflamme et al., 2013; Mollick, 2013; Vachelard et al., 2016).

The emergence of Alternative Finance options offers these development actors wonderful opportunities to try something new. These new projects funding options are particularly attractive as they are less costly in terms of time, less intrusive and cost of compliance (Mollick, 2013; World Bank, 2015). In addition,

DOI: 10.4018/978-1-5225-3952-0.ch006

their approach is more democratic, decentralized, poor empowering, and thus potentially disruptive to the established older (Ordanini et al., 2011; Belleflamme & Lambert, 2014; Berndt, 2016; CCAF, 2017).

There are important gaps in crowdfunding research that need to be filled. As an online-based project finance mobilizing activity, crowdfunding reaches out to all networked communities worldwide, not just the immediate area in which the platform is located. This global reach, significantly opens the opportunities for broad-based global participation, even though the rules guiding the crowdfunding activities many may be local or regional. Thus, research on the tension created by locally controlled funding activities that are open to global participants is a currently neglected area. Secondly, there seems to be lack of a proper place for alternative finance markets and projects in the current research agenda. Thirdly, there is inadequate attention given to cross-cultural studies among the community of scholars, and the approach has been generally neglected, although they hold the promise of providing a useful guide to the future in this rapidly growing field. Fourthly, there seems to be lack of appreciation that Africa and the Middle East are not only among the fastest growing regions of the world complex financial needs in the midst of local plenty; they are also the oldest inhabited regions of the world. These historic regions that are connected by legacies of cross-border flows of people, goods, services and ideas religion, city building experiences and many innovative ideas. This study seeks to draw attention to these neglected issues.

This chapter is structured as follows: after an introductory section, the background section seeks to explain the significance of studying Africa and the Middle East regions, provides a brief review of the literature on crowdfunding and then sketch out the backdrop against which the future development of the two regions and the role crowdfunding should be seen. Section three sets out the research agenda, namely the purpose, the methodology, and the processes of data collection and analysis. Section four reports the results, the discussions of which are taken up in section five. The issues of future research directions and the conclusions to draw from the research are discussed in section six.

BACKGROUND

Why Study Africa and the Middle East?

Africa and the Middle East are among the fastest growing regions in the world and their future growth will likely influence world events. This influence will just be a continuation of the historical legacies in trade, knowledge development, city building and innovations in civic life.

Africa and the Middle East are generally considered the oldest regions inhabited by human beings and the areas of the earliest growth of civilization. Although they may be lagging in online trade and investments, the two regions had for centuries used the trans-Saharan trade routes to ensure the flow of pilgrims, goods, and finance between Africa & Middle East (DAAOA, n.d.). For example, the famous Hajj journey by Emperor Mansa Musa during which he displayed so much wealth along the route that affected gold value not only in the Middle East but also in the rising states capitals of Europe (Nehemia, 1963). Beside the trans-Saharan route, there was another route between the two regions across the sea linking Zanzibar and Oman. Both the Saharan and the Zanzibar-Oman sea routes began to decline with the increased impact of sea route linking Europe with the Far East via the Cape of Good Hope.

In addition to trade exchanges, Africa and the Middle East have a long history in religious and cultural lies. It is significant that Islam first turned to Africa to seek refuge when the persecution of early Muslims in Arabia became unbearable (Hijazi, 2014). As Islam is essentially in the urban region the building of "knowledge cities" became a common feature linking network of scholars and libraries between the Muslim part of Africa and the Middle East from about the thirteenth century. This network boosted the growth and development of the then "knowledge cities" like Madina, Bagdad, Kairouan, Damascus, Cairo (Berkey, 1992), Timbuktu (Saad, 1983; Benna, 2013).

After Mecca, Medina and Jerusalem in the Middle East, Kairouan in Africa is considered the fourth holiest site in Islam. As Rabbat (n.d.) has pointed out, inside the walled city of Kairouan lies one of the oldest mosques in the Islamic world, the 7th-century Mosque of Uqba. The mosque in most Islamic cities has the remained the hub of daily religious, learning, social and commercial activities. In many cases, mosques architecture are non-domestic and are generally stand-alone surrounded by considerable open space. It may be noted that both the mosque and the city walls of the medieval cities were built through non-cash and non-digital voluntary "crowdfunding" contributions. Also noteworthy is the fact that the religious appeal of the old Middle East cities to the African elites seems to have been transformed by the digital technology and trade appeal cities like Dubai and Jeddah have to the current African elite.

The Influence of Urbanization and Digital Technology

This chapter seeks to compare crowdfunding markets in Africa with those in the Middle East as major tools for decentralized economic growth engines that empower citizens to mobilize adequate resources lift himself out of poverty. Africa and the Middle East have so much in common as noted above. Although there are deep historic cultural interactions, the important issue to this chapter is the rise of the "crowd" as a source of empowerment as reflected in population size, level of urbanization, level of human capital development resources needed to advance future growth.

Table 1 shows some of the key growth determinant variables for both Africa and the Middle East. Africa is the second-largest and second-most populous continent on earth, with an estimated population in 2017 of 1,246 billion people and the Middle East with 250 million, has about one-fifth Africa's population in the same year. Although Africa has relatively stronger international political relations due to its 54 sovereign states and countries, about a third of UN members, The Middle East states have a stronger economic and financial influence due to their dominance of the global oil market.

Crowdfunding is largely a technology-driven market. Table 1 reflects the influence of technology in daily activities of the citizens, as it shows that in the percentage of Internet users, Internet penetration (as also shown in Figure 1) and the number of Facebook users, Middle East is consistently better than Africa. Therefore, it is expected that the Middle East should have a higher level of crowdfunding activities and hence comparatively higher of in terms its decentralization and empowering effects than Africa.

Table 1. Internet users and 2017 population statistics for Africa and the Middle East

	Population (2017 Est.) in Millions	Population of World (%)	Internet Users, (31-Mar-2017) in Millions	Penetration (% Population)	Internet % Global Users	Facebook 30-Jun-2016 in Million
Total for Africa	1,246.5	16.6%	353.1	28.3%	9.4%	146.6 (11.8%)
Total for the Middle East	250.3	3.3%	141.9	56.7%	3.8%	76.0 (30.4%)
World Total	7,519.0	100.0%	3,739.7	49.7%	100%	1,679.4

Source: Internet World Stats.

Figure 1. Internet penetration in Africa and the Middle East, March 2017

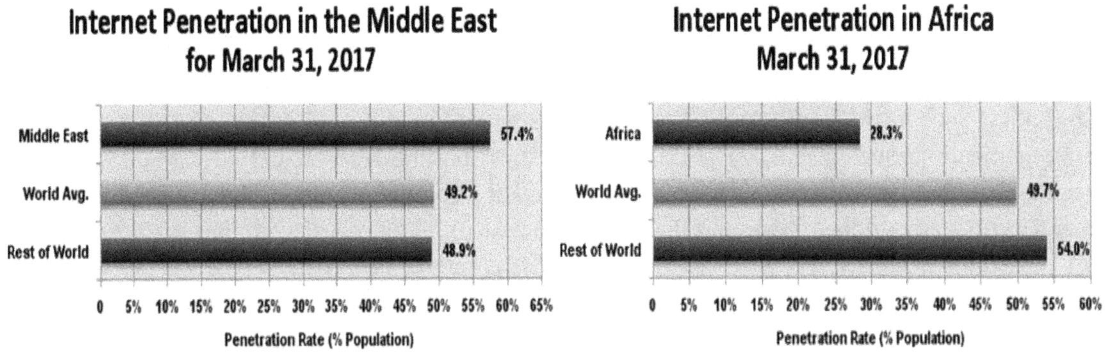

Source: Internet World Stats, 2017

LITERATURE REVIEW

The rapid rise of crowdfunding has raised awareness of and interest in its potential. Moreover, it has attracted the attention of scholars in diverse academic fields finance, economics and management, environment, social enterprise, design and urban development. These scholars have conducted studies in areas of broadening crowdfunding interests: initially on startups in films, music, and artists, but now extending to social enterprise, civic projects of various scales and engaging diverse private, public and social sector actors that operate both offline and online. In this section, we shall review the characteristics of research from the institutions of the Global North, primarily from North America and Europe before exploring the recent rise of crowdfunding research efforts in Africa and the Middle East.

Studies From the Global North

The literature on crowdfunding in North America and Europe is still in its infancy, but rapidly evolving (Belleflamme et al., 2012; Larralde & Schwienbacher, 2012). Most leading articles and empirical studies on crowdfunding are focused on the basic principles such as the various funding models, and the behavior of the entrepreneurial actors within the crowdfunding processes (Mollick, 2013; Belleflamme et al., 2013; Cummings et al., 2014). Other significant crowdfunding actors, such as the public sector managers, the social sector entrepreneurs have so far been of little interest. Furthermore, most of the studies are on social projects such industries as music or film or ventures from many domains (Hemer, 2011; Ordanini et al., 2011; Larralde & Schwienbacher, 2012; Belleflamme & Lambert, 2014).

At the community level, there have been attempts to view crowdfunding on how communities of creators and supporters interact with each other to accomplish crowdfunding goals to better support the tools and systems (Hui et al, 2014). Others explored how do offline communities engage online across civic crowdfunding projects (Stiver et al., 2015). Social enterprise researcher first reviews extant literature on financing social ventures and crowdfunding. Based upon the findings, creates an applicable model (Lehner, 2013), and a study by Daucettee (2015) goes beyond financial resources to include knowledge gathering, community participation, and organizational capacity building as well as how public official view crowds as providers of municipal public goods such as gardens, parks, bike lanes, and other infrastructure.

The Rise of Crowdfunding Research in Africa and the Middle East

The growing number of African and Middle East research reports has emerged within the last five years and most of it through the initiatives of foreign institutions like the World Bank (2013 and 2014), Research Centers such as the Cambridge Centre for Alternative Finance and Jönköping University, and by private organizations such as Afrikstart (2016) and Crowdfunding Hub (2017).

Approach to research by these agencies seems aimed at providing a comprehensive picture to crowdfunding activities at regional levels and then at national levels. The regional studies Africa (Afrikstart, 2016.), the Middle East (CCAF, 2016; World Bank, 2015) on East Africa (CCAF, 2017) and the national studies have been selective in Rwanda (Berndt & Mbassana, 2016) and Nigeria (Crowdfunding Hub, 2017). Subject area studies have so far been selective; dealing with the regulatory framework (CCAF, 2017), or with the beliefs of entrepreneurs (Berndt & Mbassana, 2016). The market platforms and their performances have been evaluated by firms such as Afrikstart (2016) to assess Africa-based platforms operations in Africa, foreign-based platforms serving Africa and then African platforms with cross-border attractions.

Looking at the date of these research shows that much has been achieved within a short time, however, much more need to be done. There are very few comparative studies of the regions (CCAF, 2016; World Bank, 2015). There are so for local-based research centers dedicated to the explosive field of crowdfunding, although Marmore Research (2015) has started with a focus on activities in the Gulf Region. Lacking in large numbers are studies of crowdfunding models as evolving over time and how the appeal to local or regional norms and culture (Mehra, 2015). A new organization Fsdafrica.org (2016) has conducted a survey of East African Landscape to explore ways of reducing poverty through financial sector development.

Crowdfunding Models, Their Contributions, and Returns

Crowdfunding simplifies the mobilization of capital for diverse development purposes by the entrepreneurs, public officials, and social groups, using numerous variations of the model. Table 2 shows the types crowdfunding market operations, the related forms of contribution and return as well as the motivation of the funder. As an evolving alternative form of funding projects, crowdfunding has many hybrid types which are too many or yet undefined to be listed here. Also omitted from the Table are some platforms define themselves in a sectoral vertical form, not by the type of investment they provide. The relative percentages each model for Africa in 2015 (Afrikstart, 2016) is shown in the second column.

The Contributions of Crowdfunding to Development

Crowdfunding contributions to development by enabling the mobilization of project finance in small amounts from many funders to allow entrepreneur realize their dreams, avoid the long process and often-futile quest for bank loans. At the same time, it seeks to fill missing elements of the emerging Knowledge Economy by people with creative minds and with the right set of skills to plan and deliver on their project proposals.

Table 2. Crowdfunding models with their related types of contributions, return and funders' motivations

Crowdfunding Model	Form of Contribution	Form of Return	Motivation of Funder
Donation Crowdfunding	Donation Africa(2015)-37%	Intangible benefits	Intrinsic and social Crowdfunding motivation
Reward Crowdfunding	Donation/Pre–purchase Africa(2015)-23%	Rewards but also intangible benefits.	Combination of intrinsic and social motivation and desire for reward.
Crowdfunded lending	Loan Africa(2015)-3.5%	Repayment of a loan with interest. Some socially motivated lending is interest-free	Combination of intrinsic social and financial motivation
Equity Crowdfunding	Investment Africa(2015)-33%	Return on investment in time if the business does well. Rewards also offered sometimes. Intangible benefits another factor for many investors	Combination of intrinsic social and financial motivation

Source: Nesta (2012) and Afrikstart (2016).

- **Contributing to an Emerging Worldview:** To ensure that their pet projects are executed, more and more people worldwide are pledging large and small funds thereby creating new funding channels for various social and sustainable development causes. These channels, according to Smith (2012), became known as crowdfunding. Thus local project initiative should be seen as part of this global enterprise. Furthermore, as growing global activity, crowdfunding has experienced – and is still experiencing- a rapid growth in size, spread, and complexity. Current data from Statista-the digital statistics portal- shown in Table 3 indicates the relative sizes of crowdfunding elements for the world, South Africa (representing Africa) and Saudi Arabia (representing the Middle East). While the transaction value of South Africa in 2017 is almost double that of Saudi Arabia, its projected growth rate is about half and both of these countries lag far behind the world's level. This result supports the findings of CCAF (2017) research that has found Africa and Middle East regions have among the slowest growth of the regions they have studied. It is therefore not surprising that the projected transaction values for the study regions do not look as good as the global trend; suggesting that much more efforts need to be exerted in both regions to use crowdfunding and other alternative finance channels to empower their citizens and governments the more.
- **Crowdfunding as Employment Generator:** The process of crowdfunding projects formulation and implementation are activities involving to social networking and collaboration where consumers actively participate in online –and offline - communities to share information, knowledge, skills, and suggestions about the evolving initiative. In this process, crowdfunding goes beyond the normal social-network contribution as it integrates the more proactive roles for consumers, including for example the selection of new initiatives to support and contribute monetary and social backing for them. Involvement in these processes by others may turn up to be job training for them and possibly as a job-creating tool.

Although sharing some features of traditional resource-pooling and social-networking phenomena, crowdfunding has some additional unique elements related to creating service platforms through which individual consumers can pool monetary resources to support and sustain new projects initiated by

Table 3. Comparison of crowdfunding elements for the world, South Africa, and Saudi Arabia, 2017

Crowdfunding Elements		World	South Africa	Saudi Arabia
Transaction Value in the "Crowdfunding" in 2017		US$194,815m	US$1,302m	US$721m
Transaction Value growth rate (CAGR 2017-2021):				
	Projected Annual Rate (Average)	27.87%	9.50%	17.10%
	Projected Amount in 2021	US$565,187	US$2,117m	US$1,465m
The average funding per campaign in 2017		US$ 43,028	US$14,721.0	US$57,820
Compared to the highest activity value in China (in 2017)		US$ 52,321	US$52,321m	US$52,321.30

Source: Statista data retrieved September 2, 2017.

others. These processes of customer participation are relevant to crowdfunding as well. The customers involved in crowdfunding are not only integrated into the service delivery stage, but also contribute to the design and set up the entire crowdfunding offering (Edvardsson & Olsson, 1996).

- **Other Benefits of Crowdfunding to Development Efforts:** The additional potential benefits to development efforts are many. First, it helps to reduce the systemic biases that are inherent in financial services system. Second, it helps establish a new way of doing business with speed, regard for the customer needs and with more convenience. Third, it is assisting in establishing a higher standard with lower cost and better speed of capital deployment. Fourthly, it greatly assists in the diversification of portfolios. Fifthly, crowdfunding activity helps to widen the pool of available capital for new innovative projects, and sixthly it increases competition among the types of development projects seeking capital (CCAF, 2017).

The Potentials and Challenges for Crowdfunding in Africa and the Meast

While the traditional offline type of crowdfunding has a long history (Vachelard et al., 2016), the Internet-based crowdfunding has a relatively short history and, despite is growing social impact, was for a while neglected by researchers. The literature on crowdfunding is still in its nascent phase, and to many academic researchers, it has remained insignificant to warrant serious study (Ordanini et al., 2011; Belleflamme et al., 2013; Mollick, 2013; Vachelard et al., 2016). The wake-up call came from researchers like Mollick (2013) who warned that the concept of crowdfunding needed and deserved far more academic attention than it had received up until the time of his writing. Clearly, the growing interest in crowdfunding activities shown in the public sphere has to be taken more seriously, mainly because it is gradually changing the paradigm on traditional funding sources, i.e. business angles, venture capital, and bank loans (Lawton & Marom, 2010). Perhaps it is the growing widespread interest across the social structure and the large amounts of funds it is yielding and has the potential to mobilize; that forced several academics to draw attention the opportunities, crowdfunding has, as a new way of financing (Ordanini et al., 2011; Belleflamme et al., 2013; Mollick, 2013, Vachelard et al., 2016). Thus, it is against this general global background that we briefly investigate the crowdfunding research and activities in Africa and the Middle East.

The Rise of Crowdfunding Markets in Africa and the Middle East

Online Crowdfunding is a relatively new business phenomenon in Africa and the Middle East and has been envisaged as likely a major transformative concept that could resolve the problem of unequal access to capital for small and medium scale enterprises and serves as an important lead to resolving economic inequality and political instability in both regions.

CCAF (2017) released a report of alternative finance benchmarking on Africa and the Middle East, in the report it was stated that a total of $242m in online alternative finance funds was raised across both Africa and the Middle East in 2015, out of which Africa registered $83.2m and the Middle East $158.8m. The report identified Israel, Kenya, and South Africa as the market leaders in the region, where Israel alone account for $124.3m out of the Middle East $158.8m raised in 2015, while Kenya and South Africa raised $16.7m and $15m respectively out of the Africa subtotal of $83.2m raised in 2015. Another interesting figure in the report was that 90% of online alternative finance platforms in Africa were originated from platforms headquartered outside of the continent and compare to the Middle East, 92.6% of the online funding are home-grown platforms headquartered within the region. And there are relatively low levels of peer-to-peer consumer and business lending activities exist in both continents.

Report by AfrikStart (2016) highlighted that pooling funds from a large number of people to support various initiatives was actually not new in Africa however, what is new is translating the process online, in its actual form of online crowdfunding on the Internet or on mobile phones. World Bank estimated that by the year 2025, the overall market potential of the crowdfunding market in Sub-Saharan Africa is $2.5 billion, while the overall amount raised through crowdfunding market for Africa-based platforms was $ 32.3 million in 2015, which is less than 0.1% of the global crowdfunding activity (AfrikStart, 2016). The story is almost the same for the Middle East and North Africa (MENA) region, with the overall amount raised via crowdfunding market for MENA-based platforms was $23.1m in 2015 despite the enormous potential for growth (Saqlain, 2016).

With this background, this study intends to make analyses of online crowdfunding platforms in these regions for the following purposes: (1) Cross-cultural comparison of Africa & the Middle East Crowdfunding activities. (2) Regional, cross-regional interactions, and region-global interactions as fundamental for future growth, (3) There is increasing pressure on the current pattern of globalization, largely because the gain from it in the West is diminishing. Eventually what is likely to happen is "regional globalization" (emerging regions trade among themselves – both online and offline) or "Surgical globalization" (where Sub-Sahara Africans and Arabs interact with their Diaspora Communities worldwide), (4). ICT and crowdfunding platforms are standardized devices, which work the same anywhere at anytime. However, their applications are culture-driven, that may be the Mobile banking developed first and fastest in Africa. So the same argument may be extended to crowdfunding behavior, where some regions put more emphasis on social projects over profit-making types. Here, the culture value-laden need considerations.

METHOD OF DATA COLLECTION AND ANALYSIS

As a conceptual empirical study, this chapter intends to: (1) develop an in-depth knowledge about the nature of crowdfunding platforms and projects in these two regions (Africa & the Middle East), as well as their role in social entrepreneurship. (2) provide insight on the nature of opportunities to foster crowdfunding across these regions. (3) to be more critical of the nature of the online crowdfunding platforms and projects, as well as the quantity and quality of the actors such as the fundraisers, funders/backers, and other stakeholders.

This chapter evaluates the capacity of the platforms in terms of the system interface, mode of operation, projects and customer crowds' types a conceptual framework was developed as a basis for the comparative analysis of online crowdfunding platforms in these regions. It uses some indicators such as the distribution of project size or volume, success and failure rates across regions based on the geographical locations. In this conceptual framework, six platforms were selected from the regions as case studies: two top platforms from Africa and the Middle East; one of which from each region have a local activity and the other one with regional outreach thereby making a total of four platforms. In addition to that, each region should have one platform with global outreach. Figure 2 presented the complete conceptual framework created using CMap tools.

Selected Crowdfunding Platforms

Overview of some existing crowdfunding platforms in both Africa and the Middle East reveal that there is low online crowdfunding platforms presence in both regions. Despite that many online resources indicated the sprang up of a large number of Africa-based and Middle East-based crowdfunding platforms between 2012 to 2015 (Afrikstart, 2016); CCAF, 2017), many of them have remained in an idea or a pilot stage and only very few of them have grown passed the early stage.

The six crowdfunding platforms selected as case study reflect the three major crowdfunding models; namely Charity (donation based), Reward (donation based) and Equity based models. The online crowdfunding platforms are M-Changa (from changa.co.ke), Thundafund (from blog.thundafund.com), Yomken (from yomken.com), Zoomaal (zoomaal.com) Afkarmena (from afkarmena.com) and Eureeca (from eureeca.com). The first three are from Africa and the last three are from the Middle East region. Below is the brief description of each of the platforms.

- **Yomken:** Is an open-innovation crowdfunding platform based in Egypt, it was launched in October 2013 with seed funding from the World Bank's Youth Innovation Funding (Parmar, 2013). Yomken offers services that target micro and small enterprises project from market space. Market Actors mainly the funders (the Crowd, NGOs, Corporate& Government Organizations) from the market space present project in the form of challenges and the crowd intelligence mainly fundraisers (student activities, Engineers & scientists, academic research and product design) as potential problem solvers are linked to the challenges so as to present ideas and skill to solve the challenges for a financial (or moral/financial) reward. Finally, Yomken charges 10% of the monetary value of reward from either the solution seeker or the sponsor of the challenge with advanced half payment and balanced upon finding a solution. Yomken is not based on "All or nothing" operation mode, this is because of the nature of its crowdfunding, which they often called Crowd Solving, and each challenge has a deadline, but it is not clear how long it takes to evaluate solutions submitted by crowd intelligence. For example, there are cases where a challenge remains in evaluating stage for more than five months from solution submission deadline.
- **Zoomaal:** Is regional crowdfunding platform based in Lebanon and was launched in February 2012 to supports innovative projects in the Arab world. Innovative and creative Arabs submit their projects based on the Zoomaal policies and the platform collect funds from supporters. Zoomaal charges 5% in an "all or nothing" method; that is if the campaign is successful, Zoomaal charges

5% otherwise, the contribution is returned to backers (Zoomaal, n.d.). Zoomaal is purely reward based donation model. Campaign on Zoomaal runs flexible for 60 days.

- **Eureeca:** Is global online crowdfunding platform based in Dubai and was officially launched in May 2013 to provide an opportunity to its investor network to buy equity in lucrative potential SME and at the same time enables viable businesses to efficiently raise capital from the crowd for its growth. Equity-based crowdfunding differs from charity or reward-based crowdfunding in the sense that, equity-based crowds are investors who effectively become co-owner of the business (Eureeca, n.d.). Eureeca charges application fee which is refundable in case the fundraiser project failed to pass Eureeca assessment. After a campaign is successful, Eureeca charges 7.25% of the amount raised. On Eureeca a campaign can run for 90 days. However, Eureeca has a flexible campaign period, for instance, a campaign can be closed before the 90 days' period if the funding target is reached or raise more funds in *Overfunding* status. Eureeca reported that 67% of proposals are overfunded. Optionally, a campaign that failed to reach its targeted amount in 90 days may be extended with a status of *Extra time.*
- **M-Changa:** Is a crowdfunding platform based in Kenya and was launched in August 2012 to serve as a fundraising platform for projects ranging from Health to community needs causes. M-Changa provides both online donation and mobile phone donation. Its mobile phone fundraiser platform is limited to some selected mobile service providers in Kenya who are known to operate mobile money transactions. M-Changa operates an "open-ended" mode which means that fundraiser can remain open for a very long period of time or indefinitely as follows; for its mobile phone fundraising platform, a fundraiser can remain open indefinitely provided that donation or withdrawal is made once fortnightly. However, on the online platform, a fundraiser can specify the length of the duration for which the fundraising will run (M-Changa, n.d.). M-Changa charges 4.25% of the total amount raised and it is mainly charity based donation model and rarely donation/rewards based.
- **Thundafund:** Is a South Africa leading crowdfunding platform and was launched in June 2013 to support creative and innovative ventures. Thundafund allows fundraiser to define two milestones each with a targeted goal amount. A campaign is run within the overall period of 30-90 days. Thundafund operates "all or nothing" model, it charges 7% of the total amount raised for regular projects and 5% for registered NGOs if a tipping point (milestone 1) is reached before the campaign period ends. Thundafund is purely reward based donation model.
- **Afkarmena:** Is an online crowdfunding platform that is based in Jordan and was launched in 2014 to support creative ideas in the Middle East. It is reward-based crowdfunding platform opened to the Middle East and North Africa (MENA) countries, but currently with projects domiciled in Jordan and Palestine. Afkarmena charges 5% of the total amount raised for successful regular projects. However, Afkarmena charges an NGO only 4% of the amount raised if the project is successful and have the opportunity to keep any money raised regardless if the project is successful or not (Afkarmena, (n.d.)). Afkarmena operates "all or nothing" model and campaign are run for 60 days' maximum.

This study uses data from the inception of each of the platforms as reported above, but since some of the platforms have fewer activities and relatively newer than others and the goal of the study is not to present a report on each platform, rather to analyzes the patterns and nature of crowdfunding in Africa and the Middle East. Thus, the study was done on samples of projects randomly selected to represents

Figure 2. Conceptual frameworks for regional analysis of online crowdfunding platforms

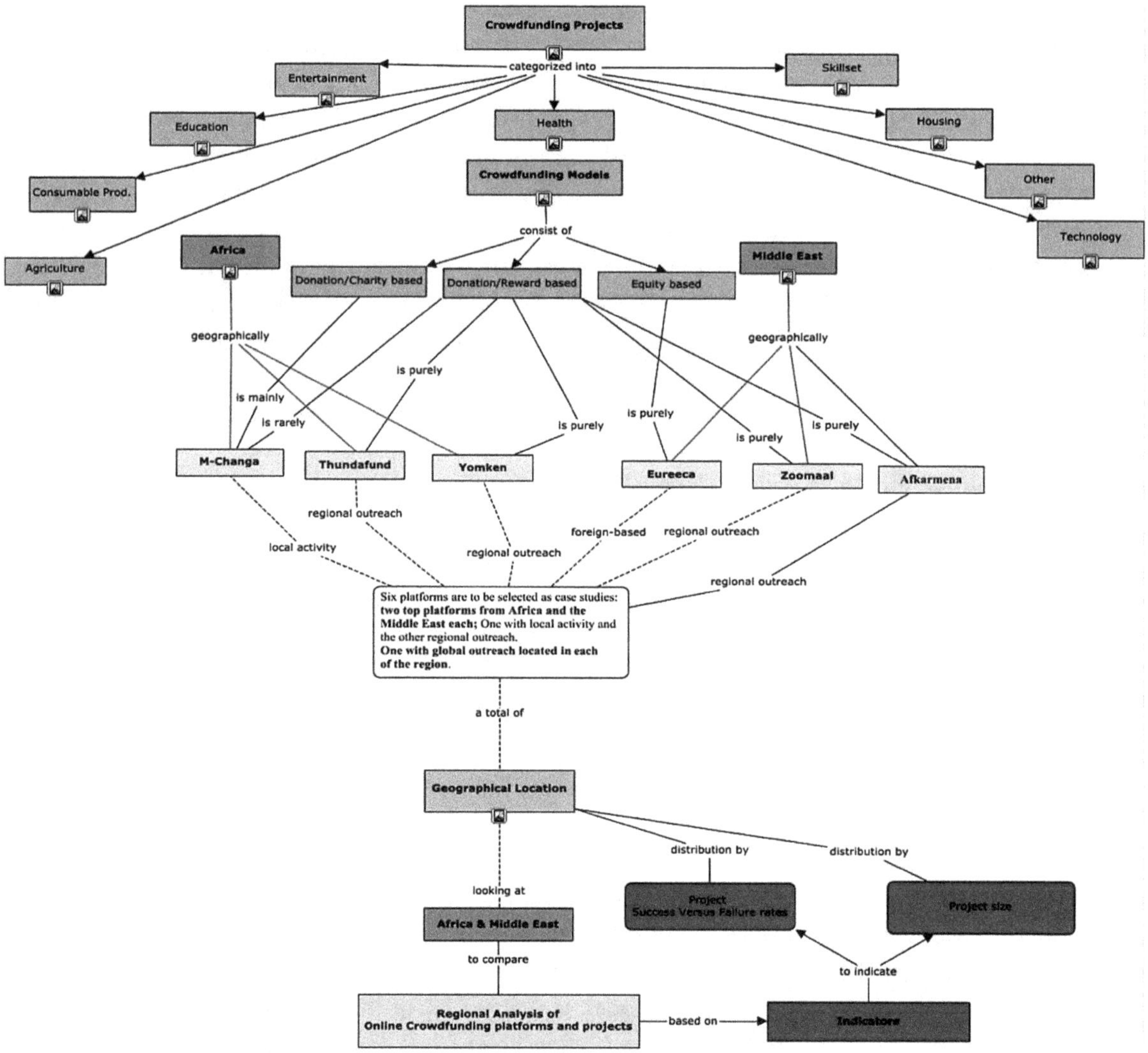

and reflects the general projects on those platforms, and where a platform has fewer projects, all available projects at the time of data gathering were used. Table 4 presents the number of projects available on the platforms at the time of this study and the total number of projects considered for this study.

The study limited the samples of some platforms to 40 mainly to avoid dominant of one platform above other and for unbiased comparison. Summaries of the data analysis based on platforms are presented in Table 4. It is obvious that the statistical summary published by some platforms based on the full population may have some gaps when compared with our sample data. For instance, Yomken publishes that it has 1500 innovators; 41 challenges, 132 solutions posted, 82% success rate and $112,800 money awards. Thundafund publishes that it has 12874 supporters; raised $1,108,402 and 248 successfully funded projects. Lastly, Eureeca publishes that it has 14,840 active investors; with an average investment size of $5,800, spread over 36 countries and with 67% proposal overfunded. This study believed that even though the coefficient may differ from the full population, the sample data used in this study

Table 4. Number of sample projects selected from each platform

SN	Online Crowdfunding Platform	No. of Selected Projects	Total Projects Available
1	Yomken	35	36
2	Zoomaal	44	179
3	Eureeca	21	21
4	M-Changa	40	2104
5	Thundafund	40	Above 430
6	Afkarmena	23	23

represents the general nature of the data in those platforms, hence the significance of the variables shouldn't be affected.

Variables

This section discusses some of the variables of interest in this study and presented in Table 5 and Table 6.

- **Project Goal:** It refers to the amount a project initiator wishes to rise through the platform. Since Yomken has a different model from the rest of the crowdfunding platforms studied, this study presents the money award for each project as its project goal. Among other factors, this study finding shows a positive correlation between project goals and success of a project. The Very high goal may lead to project not funded and very small goal result in a project to deliver. Hence, the need for realistic project goal.
- **Funding Level:** Refers to the actual amount raised during the crowdfunding campaign for a project. Projects are considered successfully funded when the amount raised is at least equal to the goal within the campaign period. There is a positive correlation between project goal and the funding level, but more importantly between "Pledge per baker" and funding level.
- **Backers:** Refer to the number of an individual that support a crowdfunding project. Backers play different roles ranging from financial support to a project to help in spread the awareness of the project to potential funders. Crowdfunding principle supports having a large number of backers for a project rather than the few number of backers, this help to reduce a potential influence a baker may have on the project. Hence, the higher the number of bakers the better for project funding.
- **Pledge/Baker:** Refers to an average pledge made by each baker. It is the mean pledge per backer, that is the funding level divided by the number of bakers. It is positively correlated with funding level.
- **Update:** Fundraisers are encouraged to post a regular update about their project campaign. Their study data have shown a positive correlation between successfully funded projects and available update.
- **Networks:** Refers to the available social media plug-in presents on a platform. Social media has been the key player for a successful campaign.

- **Days Left**: Refers to the number days left to end a project campaign on a platform. Projects that met its set goals is flagged successful or successfully funded project, otherwise, a project is flagged unsuccessful or failed project when they failed to meet up with the set project goal. An ongoing project is tagged live or open.
- **Connections:** Refers to the fundraiser and funders engagements via a platform feature refers to a comment. Comments allow bakers to express their view about a project and provides means through which project initiator can respond to some of the questions potential bakers have about the project. The connection is the number of times such communication takes place between fundraiser and funders. Analyzed data for this study reveals a positive correlated between connection and the success of a project.

RESULTS

This section presents an empirical description of crowdfunding and analysis of factors that lead to success or failure of projects based on the six online crowdfunding platforms selected for this study. Figure 3 presents the distribution of success, failure, and live projects rate in percentage across the countries in the Middle East and Africa. The result seems to suggest that there are more successfully executed projects from countries in the Middle East and part of North Africa. Countries that indicated 100% success or failure rates are usually the extreme case (outliers), they often contain a single project in the collected data.

Table 5. Summary statistics

Variables	All	Funded	Yomken	M-Changa	Zoomaal	Afkarmena	Thundafund	Eureeca
Funded	0.819 (0.425)		1.055 (0.573)	0.918 (0.306)	0.663 (0.367)	0.925 (0.402)	0.458 (0.092)	0.896 (0.810)
Goal	1399 (9921)	2560 (17106)	529 (595)	7766 (29084)	1301 (9995)	8206 (14609)	4003 (28905)	67037 (203616)
Funded %	0.740 (4.672)	1.141 (5.489)	**	1.118 (3.354)	1.122 (6.731)	1.151 (5.755)	1.134 (4.534)	1.179 (7.073)
Backers	101.24 (9229)	340.68 (6825.5)	5.92 (87)	1759.7 (36519)	41.969 (1055)	51.85 (474)	148.95 (2175)	35.75 (643)
Pledge/Backer	6111.4 (25191)	8024.5 (18149)	**	762.36 (2178.93)	345.52 (1444.78)	18661.61 (30648.42)	14486.55 (38947.75)	6463.48 (17525.7)
Updates	4.361 (29.667)	3.525 (17.167)	7.6 (38)	4.333 (13)	4.167 (25)	0.8 (4)	1.25 (5)	3 (18)
Networks	7.167 (217.5)	7.123 (111.67)	6 (30)	6 (78)	16 (416)	8 (40)	2 (16)	4.737 (90)
Days Left	83.708 (301)	15.714 (110)	0	0	0	0	0	0
Connections	640.83 (3855.5)	471.93 (2814.7)	0	0	2608.5 (15651)	0	50.75 (203)	172.33 (1034)

** Data not applicable or not available.

Table 6. Correlations

	Success	Goal	Funded %	Backers	Pledge/Backer	Updates	Networks	Days Left	Connections
Success									
Goal	0.4721								
Funded %	-0.0908	0.2962							
Backers	-0.7982	-0.1135	0.2303						
Pledge/Backer	-0.0428	0.0403	0.4323	-0.3159					
Updates	0.0758	-0.1976	-0.8100	0.0910	-0.8628				
Networks	0.3893	-0.2687	0.0941	-0.1441	-0.3686	0.1805			
Days Left	-0.0763	-0.2148	-0.1713	-0.1398	-0.0314	0.1376	0.0038		
Connections	0.4173	-0.2029	0.1814	-0.2370	-0.3908	0.1213	0.8960	0.0660	

Kenya and South Africa have the largest share of project volume in Africa, while in the Middle East region, UAE and Jordan are with the largest volume of projects as shown in Figure 4. However, the overall analysis of project size as shown in Figure 5, indicated that the Middle East generate more crowdfunding funds with 59% project volume from our data when compared with 41% project volume from Africa platforms.

Furthermore, analyzing result based on operational model type, and project distribution cross the regional platforms will provide concrete or informed pattern description of online crowdfunding activities in the Middle East and Africa.

Figure 3. Distribution of success, failure and on-going project rate across countries in the Middle East and Africa

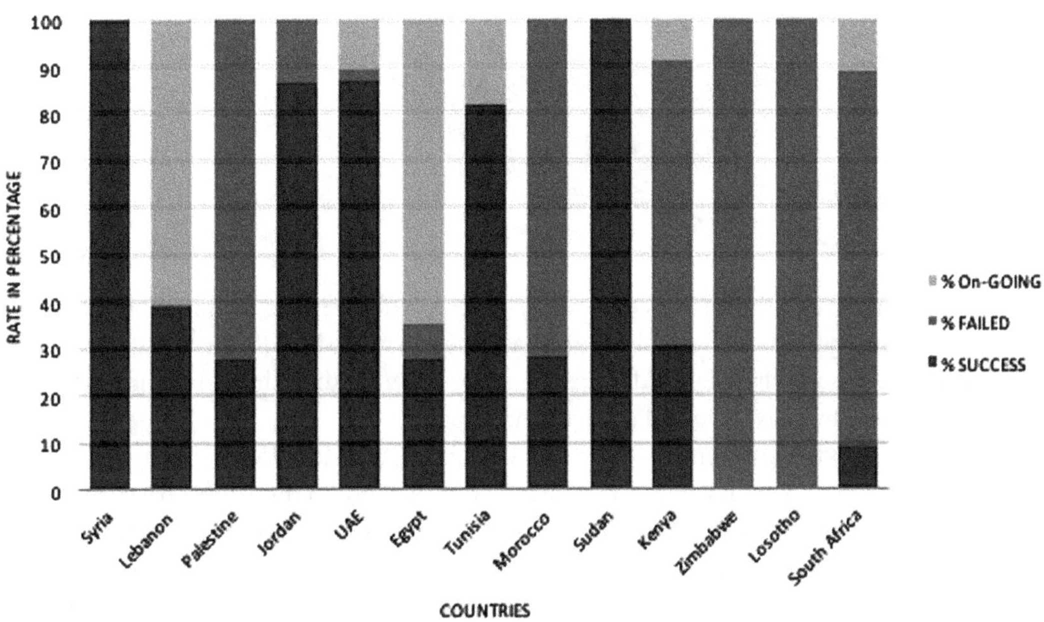

Figure 4. Projects volume (in dollars) across countries

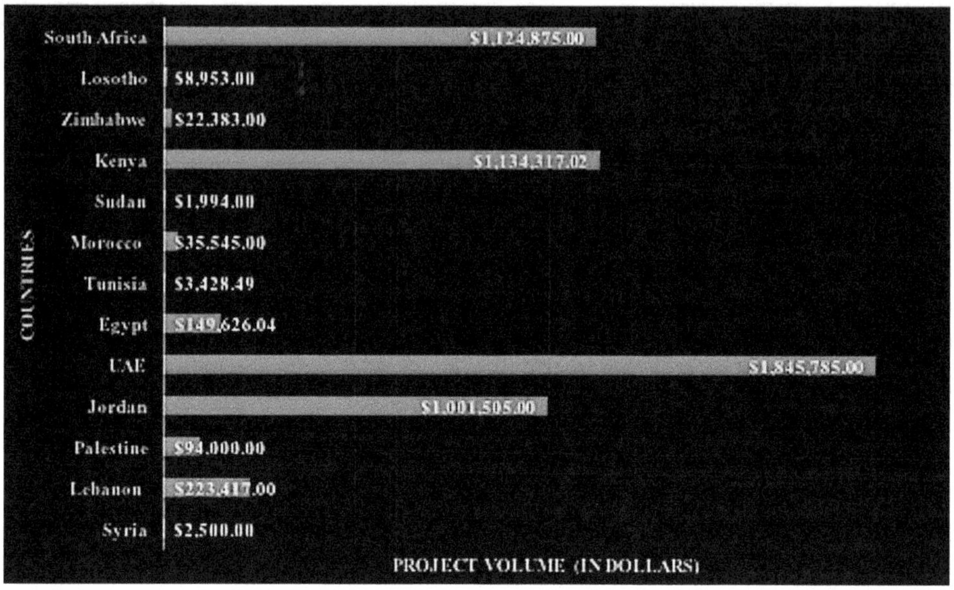

Figure 5. Comparing Africa and the Middle East online platforms in terms of fund raising volume

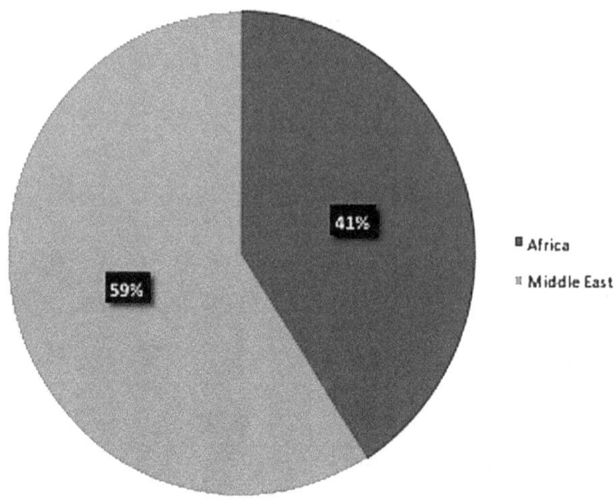

Figure 6 clearly indicated the influence of equity-based platform in generating more funding in the Middle East, since the equity-based model in our data comes from the Middle East platform only. Hence indicates part of the reason why the Middle East generate more funding through online crowdfunding platforms compare to Africa as indicated in Figure 5.

Three operational models are identified in these two regions; Charity (donation) based are popular in Africa crowdfunding, dominant in Kenya M-Changa platform. Reward (donation) based are popular in the Middle East and equally found in Africa. Thundafund, a South Africa leading crowdfunding platform is reward based, Yomken in Egypt is reward based, and both Zoomaal (in Lebanon) and Afkarmena (in Jordan) in the Middle East are purely reward based. Lastly, the Equity-based platform is available

Figure 6. Project volume (in %) distribution across the model type

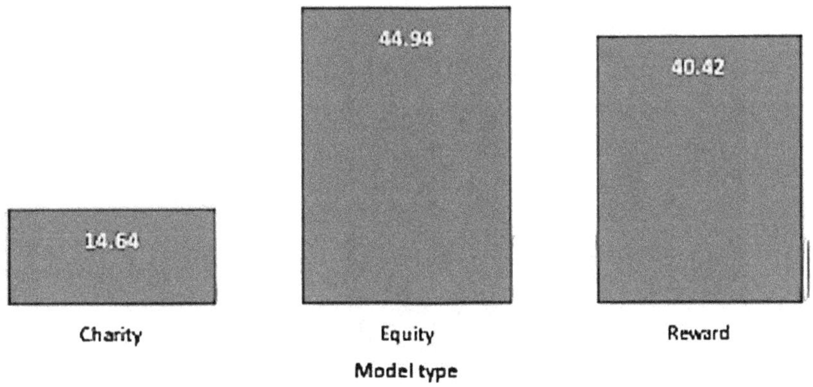

in both regions, but we were unable to include PitchOffice platform from Africa because the platform lacks adequate required information for this study, so only a leading equity-based platform in UAE was studied in this chapter; Eureeca is pure equity-based leading online crowdfunding platform in the Middle East. Figure 7 provides Success-Failure rates distribution based on the model types; Success rate is 62% across all platform and model type while the failure is 38%. However, Figure 8 gives a clearer picture of the pattern of the operational models across both regions. The analyzed result has shown that there are more project failure rates in both regions in terms of the donation-based model, and 100% success rate in terms of the equity-based model, which further validated the earlier results.

Based on the sample data analyzed, Africa and the Middle East projects are distributed into 9 categories namely; Agriculture, Consumable products, Entertainments, Education, Health, Housing, Skillset, Technology and other miscellaneous projects that do not fall into any of the eight mentioned categories. Figure 9 has indicated that projects that are based on Technology category are more prominent in both regions; projects ranging from renewable energy and Information Technology were more visible. Housing category was unpopular based on the cases studied. Education projects are the second popular projects,

Figure 7. Success-failure rate distribution across all model type

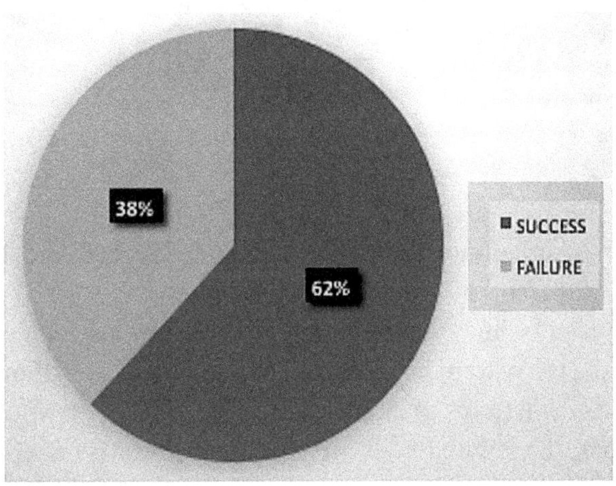

Figure 8. Model-based success-failure distribution

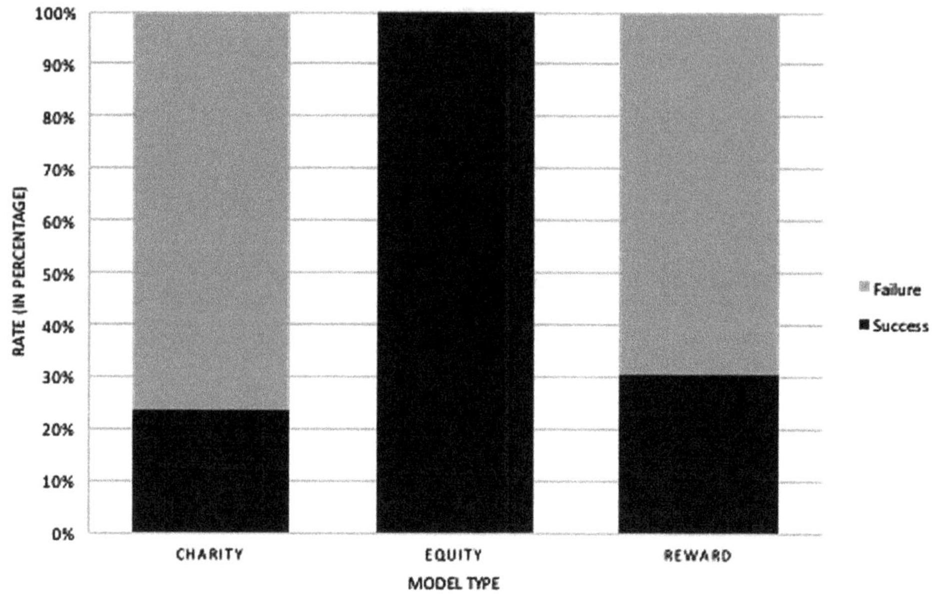

Figure 9. Project categories distribution across platforms in both regions

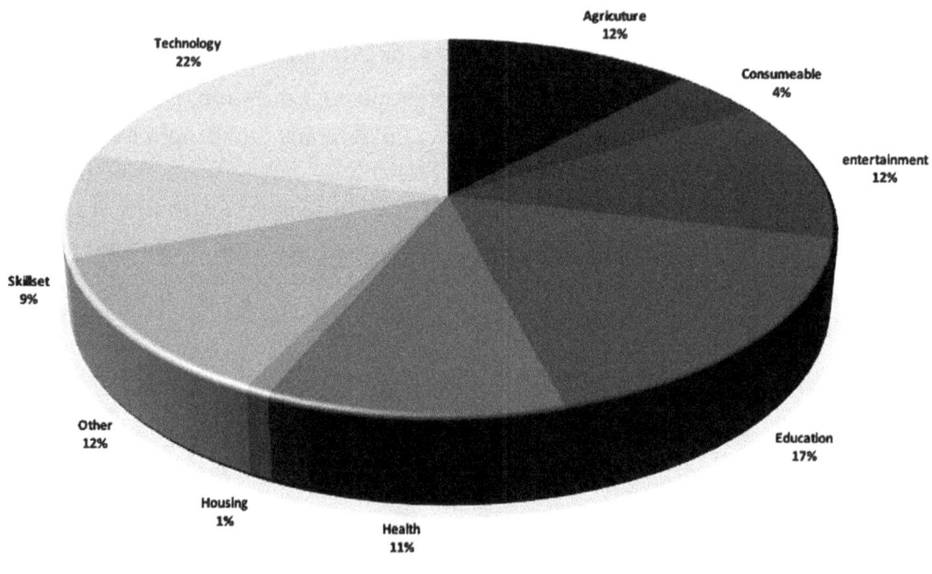

followed by Entertainments, Agriculture, and others category. Table 7 and Table 8 give details of the project categories and their distribution across platforms

Finally, this study analyzed online crowdfunding specifically for each region separately but in a contrasting manner. In Africa the pattern has shown that the online crowdfunding platforms have more failure rate than success in general terms as indicated in Figure 10, this result is further details in Figure 11 wherein both model types, the failure rate is higher than the success rate.

Table 7. Projects categories distribution across platforms

Crowdfunding Platform	Agriculture	Technology	Education	Health	Entertainment
Yomken	6	16	0	1	0
Zoomaal	0	11	11	4	10
Eureeca	0	9	0	2	0
M-Changa	6	7	2	15	2
Thundafund	1	1	16	0	10
Afkarmena	0	2	10	1	4
Total	13	46	37	23	26

Table 8. Projects categories distribution across platforms

Crowdfunding Platform	Skillset	Consumable Prod.	Housing	Others
Yomken	7	1	1	3
Zoomaal	2	0	0	6
Eureeca	0	4	0	0
M-Changa	1	1	1	5
Thundafund	3	3	0	6
Afkarmena	6	0	0	6
Total	19	9	2	26

Figure 10. Success failure rate distribution for Africa crowdfunding platforms

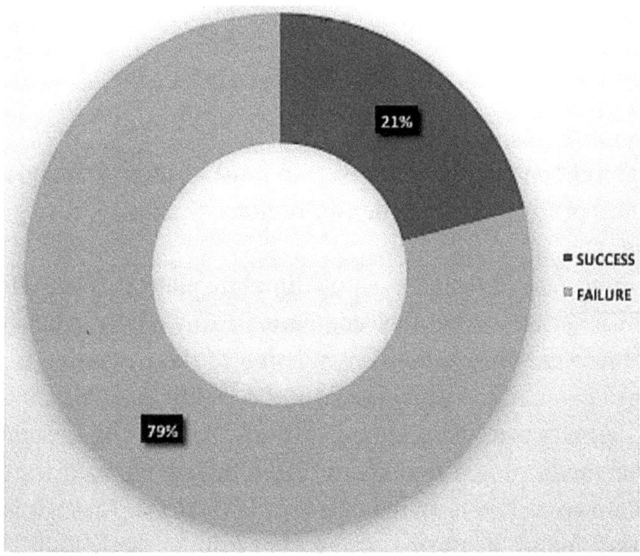

Figure 11. Model-based success-failure rate in Africa crowdfunding platforms

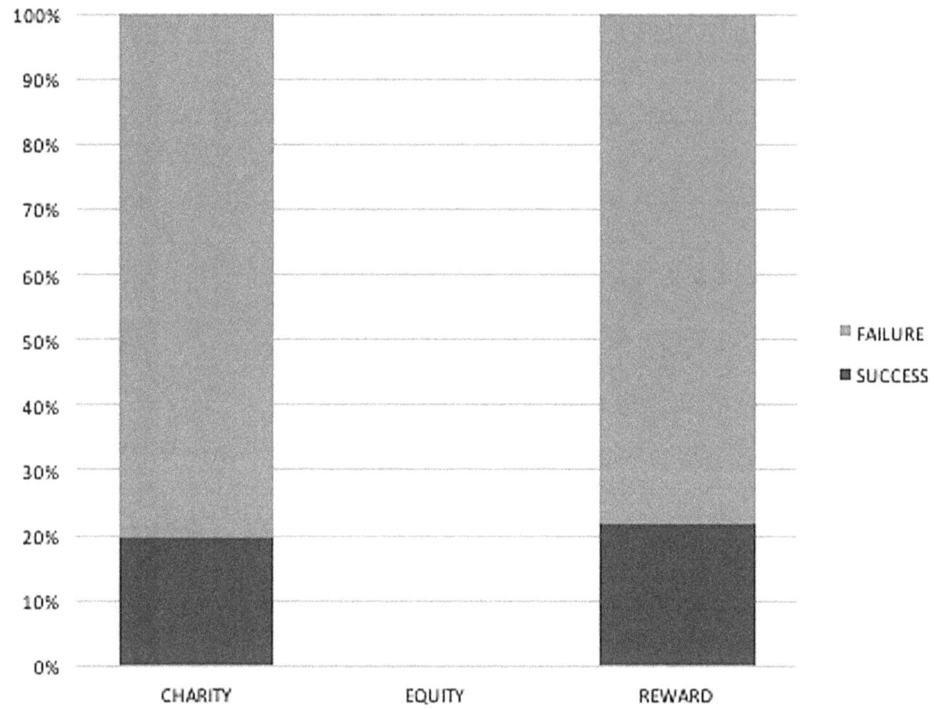

In contrast to the Africa platforms, the Middle East online crowdfunding platforms are more successful. Figure 12 indicates that 90% of the online crowdfunding projects are successful in the Middle East, the details based on platforms can be seen in Figure 13.

DISCUSSIONS

This section provides highlight on many of the observed issues that may directly or indirectly be associated with success or failure of the project in the two regions, the prospect to grow and challenges that need to be addressed.

Starting with the user interface of the online crowdfunding platforms in both regions. Almost all the platforms have standard user-friendly interface containing many of the standard features of the online crowdfunding portals. However, what is missing in some of the platforms is lack of encouraging or enforcing the fundraiser to communicate their project effectively in a text, picture, and videos. This is seen mostly in many of the Africa crowdfunding platforms. Another observation among the platforms is that it appears the social media plugin are underutilized. In general, many of the portals are not interactive enough like well-known platforms in the developed countries. Another issue is that unlike many Sub-Saharan Africa crowdfunding platforms, many platforms in the Middle East are multi-language

Figure 12. Success failure rate distribution for Middle East crowdfunding platforms

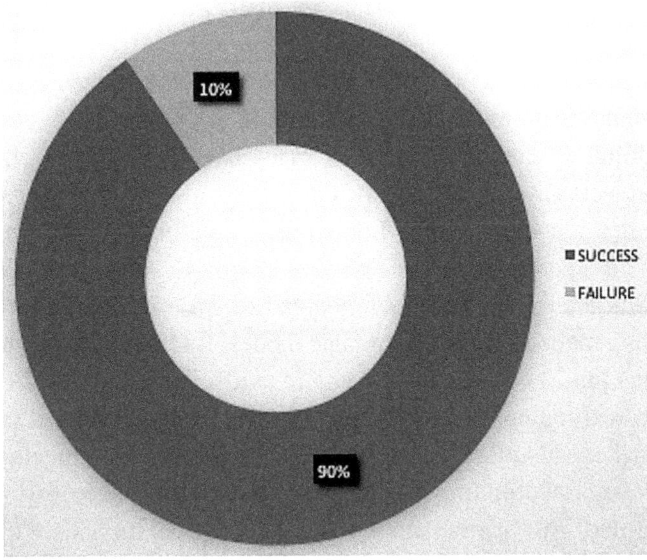

Figure 13. Model-based success-failure rate in Middle East crowdfunding platforms

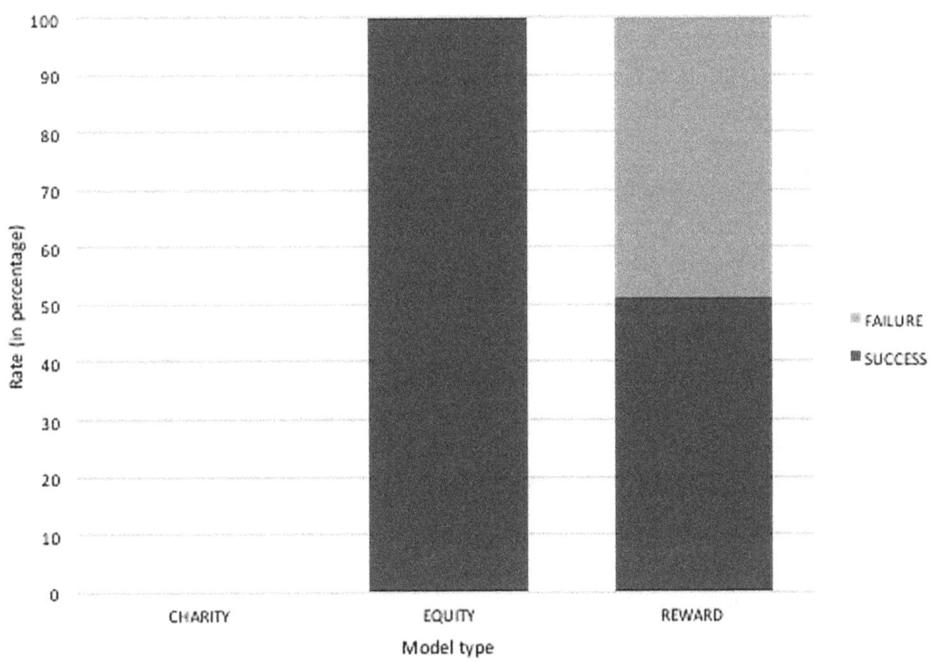

portals in both English and Arabic, this is missing in Africa, Africa crowdfunding platforms are not in the native languages of the community, the portals are mainly in English or French pending on which is the official language of the host country. Since the majority of Africa population speak their native language instead of official languages, what this means is that some significant number of a population have been excluded from participating in the crowdfunding of projects.

The beauty of crowdfunding campaign is to have many backers for a project, but in both Africa and the Middle East, most projects have fewer backers. On average a successful project has 100 plus backers in Africa, while the number of backers in the Middle East crowdfunding platforms is always lower, they are in the range of 20 to 50 on an average.

Both Africa and the Middle East operate mainly donation-based crowdfunding models. While many of the Africa crowdfunding models remains patronage model (charity) which is the most traditional form of crowdfunding in which funders do not receive any rewards. However, Middle East platforms mostly operate reward-based crowdfunding model in which funders receive a reward for donation in the form of postcard greetings, stickers and other forms of a gift. But usually not monetary.

Africa and Middle East crowdfunding platforms are facing the issue of trust. In many developing countries crowdfunding platforms operate in an unregulated space, this raises the issue of trust among crowd and investors in the case of equity-based platforms. It is obvious that for a successful crowdfunding, both crowd and investors need the adequate protection of their contribution towards a project. Currently, no existing law that empowered crowdfunding platforms to hold fundraiser accountable if they failed to fulfill their project campaign promises and objectives, the highest they could do is to blacklist a defaulter for the future launch of a campaign on their platform. However, almost all the platforms in Africa and the Middle East do not provide a page that will enable backers to report fundraiser that failed to comply with its obligation.

Lack of legislation has made most crowdfunding platforms in the developing countries to have unclear legal status. Currently, many crowdfunding platforms in Africa and the Middle East rely on existing money laundering and fraud legislation in their host countries. Without a deliberate effort by the government to legislate laws that will cover the activities of crowdfunding, many potential project backers will find it unsaved or unlawful to fund projects through online crowdfunding. Most of the online crowdfunding in developing countries are actually not licensed as a financial services organization, for that reason, it creates concerns among crowds of either being defrauded or breaking the law of the host country. Addressing this issue will unlock the full potential to grow for many Africa and the Middle East platforms.

Looking at the average number of backers and pledge per backer indices in this study, it is enough to draw an opinion that Africa and Middle East crowdfunding activities lack awareness. many young entrepreneurs or civil society in developing countries are unaware of how the of crowdfunding operates, and many others lack the skills and knowledge on what to do to invites potential backers to their campaign. This is seen in most of the platforms in Africa, some of the campaign pages poorly described the campaign aimed and objectives, a situation that will make it very difficult to convince a potential funder. Online crowdfunding is only popular among a fewer population with technical know-how or elite class this is because the majority of the populace, particularly in Africa, do not speak the adopted official language in their country. Lack of requisite financial capacity by the online crowdfunding founders, to aggressively engage communities to patronize the platforms, instead they relied on fewer individuals who have awareness of their platforms to invites many others to launch a campaign or limited their awareness campaign on social media and among their network of friends. And the reason for this is that many founders are either members of a civil society or a start-up entrepreneur.

Another issue with the online crowdfunding platforms in the developing countries is a lack of transparency; a standard online crowdfunding platform operates "all or nothing" mode with a campaign period in the range of 30 to 90 days. This means if the amount raised reaches the set campaign goal before the deadline specified by the fundraiser, the campaign is successfully funded, otherwise, the money is returned to the funders. Many crowdfunding platforms in developing countries do not strictly follow the standard mode, in some platform, a campaign can still be opened for funding long after the specified period by fundraiser has elapsed. There need to make the modus operandi clearer to potential crowds so that to encourage patronage.

FUTURE RESEARCH DIRECTIONS

This study has provided a comparative analysis of online crowdfunding platforms in Africa and the Middle East. As all signs have indicated that in the coming years more and more people in Africa and the Middle East will start to trust and patronizes online crowdfunding due to the government engagements and emergence of online crowdfunding organization, for instance Dubai has recently launches regulatory framework for crowdfunding platforms (Augustine, 2017) and South Africa Financial Service Board (FSB) proclamation to rule on crowdfunding by June 30 this year (Timm, 2017a) as a result of persistent call by African Crowdfunding Association asking FSB to craft a specific regulatory framework on crowdfunding. Even though the June 30 deadline was not met by FSB (Timm, 2017b), this can be seen as a positive attempt to resolve the regulatory issues that becomes a legal bottleneck to crowdfunding in developing countries. Thus, the future research direction is to scale up the investigation on crowdfunding activities in Africa and the Middle East so as to access the possible emergence of regional globalization where regions trade among themselves and surgical globalization which allowed Sub-Saharan Africans and Arabs interact with their diaspora communities worldwide.

CONCLUSION

This study was able to observe that projects are more successful when launched in platforms that are domiciled within the same countries. Multiple factors serve as motivation among backers supporting projects in both Africa and the Middle East; close affiliation to fundraiser based on strong family ties, elements of patriotism to the nation or locality where a civic-like project is to be executed, need for incentives in the form of social recognition as reward for funding, generosity for a good causes and financial gains.

This study observed that a significant percentage of equity-based platforms are overfunded in the Middle East data that was used in this study, an indication that there is a dire need for an alternative way of investment among the populace in the developing countries. Hence, we inferred that equity-based crowdfunding has a potential of becoming a global crowdfunding in developing countries through which the regional and surgical globalizations are a possibility. However, it requires an active legislation and deliberate government efforts to embrace the model for sustainable growth; through which what appears to be the core objectives of the equity crowdfunding is realized; i.e. facilitates easy access to alternative means of financing equity projects and capital gains.

Lastly, this study concluded that the volume of the funds raised for projects is high in equity-based crowdfunding compared to donation (reward or charity) models. Goal per project of the equity-based platforms is lower than the other two. Africa and the Middle East crowdfunding platforms need to set up upper limit for a project goal to discourage fundraiser setting up goals that are not feasible, a situation that makes it difficult to hit a campaign goal within the campaign time. Donation based models are still highly needed in Africa and the Middle East, but projects that will have social and economic values to the entire community should be encouraged (e.g. support for civic and SME startups projects) rather than projects that are individualistic in nature (e.g. personal causes).

REFERENCES

ACFA. (n.d.). *Africa Crowdfunding Association Purpose.* Retrieved from http://africancrowd.org/about/acfa-purpose/

Afkarmena. (n.d.), *Fees & Special features.* Retrieved from https://www.afkarmena.com/en/page/fees-special-features/

AfrikStart. (2016). *Crowdfunding in Africa- Fundraising goes Digital in Africa: The Emergence of Africa-Based Crowdfunding Platforms.* Retrieved 5 8, 2017, from The AfrikStart Crowdfunding Africa:https://afrikstart.com/report/

Agrawal, A., Catalini, C., & Goldfarb, A. (2011). *Offline Relationships, Distance, and the Internet: The Geography of Crowdfunding.* Cambridge, MA: National Bureau of Economic Research. doi:10.3386/w16820

Babu Das Augustine. (2017, August 1). *Dubai launches a regulatory framework for crowdfunding platforms.* Retrieved from http://gulfnews.com/business/sectors/banking/dubai-launches-regulatory-framework-for-crowdfunding-platforms-1.2067534

Belleflamme, P., Lambert, T., & Schwienbacher, A. (2010). *Crowdfunding: An Industrial Organization Perspective.* Prepared for the workshop Digital Business Models: Understanding Strategies, Paris, France.

Belleflamme, P., Lambert, T., & Schwienbacher, A. (2012). *Crowdfunding: Tapping the Right Crowd.* Retrieved from http://innovation-regulation2.telecom-paristech.fr/wp-content/uploads/2012/10/Belleflamme-CROWD-2012-06-20_SMJ.pdf

Belleflamme, P., Lambert, T., & Schwienbacher, A. (2013). Crowdfunding: Tapping the right crowd. *Journal of Business Venturing.*

Belleflamme, P., Lambert, T., & Schwienbacher, A. (2014). Crowdfunding: Tapping the right crowd. *Journal of Business Venturing, 29*(5), 585–609. doi:10.1016/j.jbusvent.2013.07.003

Benna, U. G. (2013). Timbuktu, the African Medieval Knowledge City: The Role of Knowledge Development Actors. *Journal of Information & Knowledge Management, 12*(3).

Benna & Garba. (2015). Population Growth and Rapid Urbanization in Developing World. IGI Global. doi:10.4018/978-1-5225-0187-9.ch014

Berkey, J. P. (1992). *The transmission of Knowledge in Medieval Cairo: A Social History of Islamic Education*. Princeton University Press. doi:10.1515/9781400862580

Berndt, A., & Mbassana, M. (2016). Crowdfunding: the beliefs of Rwandan entrepreneurs. *East Africa Research Papers in Business, Entrepreneurship and Management*. Available at: http://ju.se/download/18.b50f80815532427699617f/1465522955791/EARP-BEM+2016-05+Adele.pdf

Burtch, G., Ghose, A., & Wattal, S. (2013). An empirical examination of the antecedents and consequences of contribution patterns in crowd-funded markets. *Information Systems Research*, *24*(3), 499–519. doi:10.1287/isre.1120.0468

CCAF. (2016). Financial Statements for the year ended March 31, 2016. Cambridge Centre for Alternative.

CCAF. (2017). *The Africa and the Middle East - Alternative Finance Benchmarking Report. Cambridge Centre for Alternative Finance, University of Cambridge Judge Business School*. Cambridge Centre for Alternative Finance.

Crowdfunding Center. (n.d.). *AFKARMENA*. Retrieved from http://www.thecrowdfundingcenter.com/?page=platform&domain=afkarmena.com

Crowdfuning hub. (2017). *Current State of Crowdfunding in Europe. An overview of the Crowdfunding Industry in 27 Countries: Trends, Volumes, and Regulations*. Retrieved from http://www.crowdfundinghub.eu/

Cummings, S., Maile Petty, M., & Walker, B. (2014). Innovation is not the only thing. In C. Bilton & S. Cummings (Eds.), *Handbook of management and creativity* (pp. 97–127). Cheltenham, UK: Edward Elgar.

DAAOA. (n.d.). The Trans-Saharan Gold Trade (Seventh–Fourteenth Centuries). In *Heilbrunn Timeline of Art History*. New York: The Metropolitan Museum of Art. Retrieved from http://www.metmuseum.org/toah/hd/gold/hd_gold.htm

Daucettee, J. (2015). *Crowdfunding for Public Goods and Philanthropy*. Retrieved from https://medium.com/the-digital-civil-society-lab/crowdfunding-for-public-goods-and-philanthropy-c7c7c5976898

Edvardsson, B., & Olsson, J. (1996, April). The key concept for new service development. *Service Industries Journal, 16*(2), 2. doi:10.1080/02642069600000019

Eureeca. (n.d.). Retrieved from https://eureeca.com/Crowd-funding-pages/FrontEnd/home/FAQ/Investor/English

Fsdafrica.org. (2016). *East Africa Crowdfunding Landscape Study: Reducing Poverty Through Financial Sector Development*. Retrieved from https://www.fsdafrica.org/wp-content/uploads/2016/10/16-11-07-Crowdfunding_Report-final-1.pdf

Gerber, E. M., & Hui, J. S. (2012). *Crowdfunding: Motivations and Deterrents for Participation*. Retrieved from http://www.segal.northwestern.edu/media/pdf/2012/May /29/segal_report_12-02.pdf

Gerber, E. M., Hui, J. S., & Kuo, P.-Y. (2012a). *Crowdfunding: Why People are Motivated to Participate*. Retrieved from http://www.segal.northwestern.edu/media/pdf/2012/May /29/segal_report_12-02.pdf

Hemer, J. (2011). *A Snapshot on Crowdfunding*. Fraunhofer ISI Working Paper. Retrieved from http://www.legalefiscale.it/wp-content/uploads/2016/09/StudioCrowdfundig.pdf

Hijazi, A. T. (2014). *Islam in Perspective. Najashi: The King who supported Muslim emigrants*. Retrieved from http://www.arabnews.com/news/546951

Hufner, A. (2016). *Motivation for Financial Backing of Reward Crowdfunding Campaigns- Based on Data from Germany and Norway (A multiple case study)* (MS Thesis Report). University of Agder.

Hui, J. S., Greenberg, M. D., & Gerber, E. M. (2014). *Understanding the role of Community in Crowdfunding Work*. Retrieved from https://egerber.mech.northwestern.edu/wp-content/uploads/2012/11/Gerber_UnderstandingtheRoleofCommunityinCrowdfundingWork.pdf

Krätli, G., & Ghislaine, L. (2011). *The Trans-Saharan Book Trade: Manuscript Culture, Arabic Literacy and Intellectual History in Muslim Africa*. London: Brill.

Larralde, B., & Schwienbacher, A. (2012). Crowdfunding of Small Entrepreneurial Ventures. In D. Cumming (Ed.), *The Oxford Handbook of Entrepreneurial Finance* (Vol. 369). New York: Oxford University Press.

Lawton, K., & Marom, D. (2010). *The Crowdfunding Revolution: Social Networking Meets Venture Financing*. Academic Press.

Lehner, O. M. (2013). Crowdfunding social ventures: a model and research agenda. *Venture Capital: An International Journal of Entrepreneurial Finance*, 289-311. DOI:10.1080/13691066.2013.782624

Lydon, G. (2009). *On Trans-Saharan Trails: Islamic Law, Trade Networks, and Cross-Cultural Exchange in Nineteenth-Century Western Africa*. Cambridge University Press. doi:10.1017/CBO9780511575457

M-Changa. (n.d.). Retrieved from http://changa.co.ke/faq/

Marmore Research. (2015). *Marmore Company Reports. Ooredoo (Qatar Telecommunications Company)*. Retrieved from https://www.e-marmore.com/MarMore/media/TOCDownloadPDF/Ooredoo-Executive-summary.pdf

Mehra, V. (2015). *Crowdfunding in Arab Region*. Retrieved from https://www.linkedin.com/pulse/crowdfunding-arab-region-vinod-kumar-mehra

Mollick, E. (2014). The dynamics of crowdfunding: An exploratory study. *Journal of Business Venturing*, *29*(1), 1–16. doi:10.1016/j.jbusvent.2013.06.005

Muller, M., Soule, T., Daniel, S., Geyer, W., & Cheng, L.-T. (2013). Crowdfunding Inside the Enterprise: Employee Initiatives for Innovation and Collaboration. *Proceedings of the SIGCHI Conference on Human Factors in Computing Systems*. doi:10.1145/2470654.2470727

Nehemia, L. (1963). The Thirteenth- and Fourteenth-Century Kings of Mali. *Journal of African History, 4*(3), 341-353.

Nesta. (2012). *An Introduction to Crowdfunding*. Retrieved from http://www.ema.eu/fileadmin/content/REALISE_IT_2/REALISE_IT_3/IntroToCrowdfunding.pdf

Ordanini, A., Miceli, L., Pizzetti, M., & Parasuraman, A. (2011). Crowd-funding: Transforming customers into investors through innovative service platforms. *Journal of Service Management*, *22*(4), 443–470. doi:10.1108/09564231111155079

Parmar, N. (2013). *Today $249 for clay pots - tomorrow the region*. Retrieved from http://www.thenational.ae/business/industry-insights/finance/today-249-for-clay-pots-tomorrow-the-region

Rabbat, N. (n.d.). *The Islamic City: Historicity and Abstraction*. Retrieved from https://archnet.org/system/publications/contents/10625/original/DTP103010.pdf?1468397437

Saad, E. N. (1983). *The Social History of Timbuktu: The Role of Muslim Scholars and Notables 1400 - 1900*. Cambridge, UK: Cambridge University Press.

Saqlain, S. (2016). *Developing Crowdfunding Ecosystems in the Middle East*. Retrieved 5 8, 2017, from Entrepreneur- Middle East: https://www.entrepreneur.com/article/278955

Smith, T. (2012). *Crowdfunding: A new source of finance for sustainability and renewable energy*. Retrieved August 16, 2017, from http://www.climatechangenews.com/2012/07/31/crowdfunding-anew-source-of-finance-for-sustainability-and-renewable-energy/

Stiver, A., Barroca, L., Minocha, S., Richards, M., & Roberts, D. (2014). *Civic crowdfunding research: Challenges, opportunities, and future agenda. In New media & society* (pp. 1–23). The Open University. Retrieved from http://oro.open.ac.uk/41478/1/CivicCrowdfunding_NMS_December2014.pdf

Thundafund. (n.d.). Retrieved from https://blog.thundafund.com/how-does-thundafund-work/faqs/

Timm. (2016, April 13). *South Africa's FSB to rule on Crowdfunding by June 30*. News, Venturebun.

UN DESA. (2014). *World Urbanization Prospects: The 2014 Revision, Highlights*. New York: United Nations, Department of Economic and Social Affairs, Population Division.

Vachelard, J., Gambarra-Soares, T., Augustini, G., Riul, P., & Maracaja-Coutinho, V. (2016). *A Guide to Scientific Crowdfunding*. Retrieved from http://journals.plos.org/plosbiology/article?id=10.1371/journal.pbio.1002373

Ward, C., & Ramachandran, V. (2010). *Crowdfunding the next hit: Microfunding online experience goods*. Workshop on Computational Social Science and the Wisdom of Crowds, Whistler, Canada.

World Bank. (2013). *Annual Report 2013*. Author.

World Bank. (2014). *Annual Report 2014*. Author.

World Bank. (2015). *Annual Report 2015*. Author.

Yomken. (n.d.). Retrieved from https://www.yomken.com/about#faq

Zoomaal. (n.d.). Retrieved from https://zoomaal.com/help/how

KEY TERMS AND DEFINITIONS

Campaign Backers: The group of people that are convinced about the campaign concept/idea and are willing to fund or support a campaign by spreading the project through their social media pages and contacts.

Campaign Period: Every crowdfunding campaign is expected to specify a period through which the campaign will start and end. A typical campaign period ranges between 30 to 90 days. However, some platforms allowed flexible campaign period that exceeded this range.

Closed/Ended Campaign: A campaign project that is inactive because it has passed its campaign period. Donate button for ended campaign project is disabled or deactivated.

Crowdfunding Platforms: Are the online portals developed based on content management system (CMS) framework to allow fundraisers create campaign page and manage the fundraising project by interacting with funders and other campaign backers under the overall control of the platform founder(s).

Failed Project: A failed project is the crowdfunding project that failed to meet up with its goal within the campaign period.

Funding Level: The total amount of money realized during the campaign and after the campaign ends.

Open/Live Campaign: A campaign project that is actively open for fundraising within the campaign period. During this period, the donate button is still enabled or activated.

Overfunded Projects: Projects with funding level much higher than the project goal at the end of a campaign.

Project Goal: The amount of money set up by the fundraiser or campaign initiator, enough to execute the campaigned project after deducting the charges fee by the crowdfunding platform based on their charges policy.

Successfully Funded: Crowdfunding campaign that reaches its project goal within the specified campaign period is tagged as a successfully funded project.

Chapter 7
Africa and Indian Crowdfunding Markets:
A Cross-Cultural Comparative Analysis

Umar Lawal Dano
University of Dammam, Saudi Arabia

Umar Garba Benna
Benna Associates, Nigeria

ABSTRACT

Developing countries will account for 90% of the new 2.5 billion urban population inflow projected by 2050. To provide decent urban environment new non-traditional financial sources such as crowdfunding are needed. In developing these sources, mutual learning experiences are the key to success but cross-cultural studies among cultures remain limited; this chapter seeks to address this issue. Africa and India are likely the key beneficiaries of future urban growth and most likely users of alternative finance tools to fund their growth. Both are slow starters in rapid urbanization and the use of crowdfunding but are making rapid progress.

INTRODUCTION

Developing nations, in their attempts to find adequate funds to finance their many huge projects to upgrade the quality of life of their youthful populations, have to depend less on the traditional funding sources thus turning to the emerging "alternative finance"(Cambridge Centre for Alternative Finance CCAF, 2017). They seem to be betting the development of alternative internal financial instruments and channels. In 2015, more than one hundred and forty-five billion dollars (US $145) was raised and it is still scaling up and spreading worldwide CCFI (2017). Crowdfunding is such an application which depends on the contributions of many to fund charity, social or business projects (Kirby and Worden 2014, Afrikstart 2016). It offers a cheap and effective alternative to traditional funding opportunities for innovative entrepreneurs, both social and private. Civic crowdfunding may be expanded to include the

DOI: 10.4018/978-1-5225-3952-0.ch007

mobilizing of none-monetary assets –skills, labor, ideas etc. towards completion of municipal projects. Majumdar (2015) suggests that in the aftermath of the 2008 worldwide financial crisis, small entrepreneurs found it increasingly tough to raise funds. As a response, equity crowdfunding emerged as a viable option for mobilizing capital to support innovative, entrepreneurial ideas and ventures. Equity crowdfunding model merges the complexity of public funding, with the systemic risks of venture capital financing.

Out of all the developing world, Africa and India governments are likely to mobilize more resources in order to lift their citizens out of poverty, provide hard and soft urban development infrastructure and put their citizens on the path to prosperity. Their selection, which is based on development finance needs consideration, may be explained thus: out of the 2.5 billion people to be added to global urban population by 2050, about 90 per cent of this increase will be concentrated in Asia and Africa (UN-DESA, 2014). The same projection shows that India (404 million), China (292 million) and Nigeria (212 million) will account for about 37 per cent of the increased urban population. Africa's urban population is expected to triple by 2050 and so will be its slam population unless adequate measures are taken to avert the rise (UNDESA 2014. Thus, both India and Africa need massive urban development finance in order to move their rural majority to an urban majority as expected by 2050.

Despite the popularity of crowdfunding in academy and practice, there is a lack of cross-cultural studies. To fill this gap, this research explored similarities and differences in the background of the two studied areas. The research evaluates the performance of both the local and foreign-based platforms and discusses the possibility of tapping into the diaspora markets by local platforms. The chapter reviews the key crowdfunding guidance instruments as they evolve with particular emphasis on regulatory instruments.

The chapter is divided into five main parts. After the introduction in the first part, the second section sets out the general determinants of the crowdfunding market growth in Africa and India on a comparative basis. Section three evaluates the performance of the home- and foreign-based crowdfunding platforms while section four analyzes the markets development regulatory approaches in Africa and India. The final section proposes future research direction and conclusion.

CONTEXTS OF THE AFRICAN AND INDIAN CROWDFUNDING MARKETS

Factors Binding the African and Indian Crowdfunding Markets

This chapter is not about the comparison of a continent and a country. It is about comparing their crowdfunding (CF) markets as instruments for decentralized economic growth that empowers citizens to mobilize adequate resources in order to lift themselves and their families out of poverty towards living a successful life. The idea is not to compare a bunch of grapes and an apple. it is to examine that which serves the farmer's interest the more even though it is clear that as fruits, they are similar and dissimilar in many respects.

Africa and India have so much in common than either of them wish to accept. Although there are deep historic cultural interactions, what matter most in this chapter are the emergence of the crowd as source of empowerment as reflected in population size, level of urbanization, and level of human capital development resources needed to advance future growth. As Table 1 shows, there is a remarkable level of similarities on these issues.

Table 1. Key crowdfunding growth determinants variables for Africa and India, 2017

	Population (2017 Est.)	Internet Users (Year 2000)	Internet Users 31-Mar-2017	Net Penetration (% Population)	Facebook Users 30-Jun-2016
India	1,342,512,706	5,000,000	462,124,989	34.4%	157,000,000
Africa	1,246,504,865	16.6% of world	345,676,501	27.7%	146,637,000

Source: Internet World Stats 2017

Table 1 shows some of the key growth determinant variables for both Africa and India. Africa is the second-largest and second-most populous continent on earth, with an estimated population of 1.17 billion people in 2015 and India 1.311 billion in the same year. These figures tend to influence international political relations where Africa is home to 54 sovereign states and countries, about a third of UN members. The political situation interplays with economic dynamics, in which both Africa and India are growing fast. The projected GDP of Africa in 2050 is $29 trillion, placing it in the same range as India's GDP in the same year.

Crowdfunding market is largely technology driven market. The Table also reflects influence of technology in daily cultural activities as it shows that in the number of Internet users, Internet penetration and the number of Facebook users, India is consistently better than Africa. Therefore, it is expected that India does have higher level of crowdfunding activities, and hence have comparatively higher decentralization and empowering effects than Africa.

- **Global Economic Growth Engine:** Africa is being tipped as the global economic growth engine of the coming decades. Its vast natural wealth and favorable demographic profile are expected to turn the continent as a whole into a growth engine that is expected to run faster than any of the world's current economic powerhouses, including China, Brazil and India. The International Monetary Fund forecast that six of the 10 highest growing economies between 2012 and 2017 will be Africa. India has appeared to be under the shadow of its neighbor China, but has shown remarkable economic resilience thereby proving to be a match to China but currently ahead of Africa.
- **The Rising Middle Class in Africa and India:** The rapid urbanization, rising disposable income and connectivity have triggered unprecedented economic activity and growth in the two regions, and have made them the new engines of global growth, along with a somewhat fading China. The implications are, partly, that the rapidly growing industries in India need Africa's commodities and its vast African market to pay for them as well as the 54 African states for global political influence.
- **Common Crowdfunding Market Traits:** To both Africa and India, crowdfunding is not a new concept. As it can be seen in Table 1, both regions have similar figures in most indicators, such as size of internet users and Facebook users, that underpin the growth of crowdfunding market. Both cultures have been building city walls, mosques and temples by crowdsourcing funds and/or labor from urban residents. It is common to collect funds from neighbors, friends and relatives for weddings or to celebrate festivals. The modern avatar of such collections is to digitize the concept. It is no longer the neighborhood or the city; it is global. The project backers could be anyone, anywhere. They could be relatives and friends, but they could also be complete strangers who believe in your idea. Internet and crowdfunding platforms are the enablers.

Historically, humankind is generally believed to have originated in Africa, but cross to other parts of the world through Arabia and India (Njoh, 2000). The common colonial heritage and the anti-colonial struggles that bind most Africans and Indians provide lasting common experiences of European colonialism, as it has left on them its imprint in terms of thought, action, language, law, tradition and commerce. These experiences create a relationship between colonial heritage and human development but not between colonial heritage and the ability to translate economic gains into improved condition, according to Njoh (2000). The concept of Africa–India relations refers to the political, economic, military, and the continuing cultural connections between the Indian and the African continent. Since 2008, an annual African-Indian summit seeks to strengthen these cultural ties and to initiate new areas regarding information and communication technology (ICT), trade (including e-commerce), good governance and people-centered approach to development (Afrikstart; 2016).

As indicated, there are areas of differences that directly or tangentially affect crowdfunding market behavior. First, considering the physical area size, Africa is 30 million Km^2 and India is 3.3 million Km^2. Second, Africa's symmetry on axis of the equator enables it to have balanced climatic and vegetation zones while India is in Northern Hemisphere. Third, on governance, Africa has 54 governments of various ideological shades ranging from democracies, dictatorships to monarchies; India has one federal form of government, with a stable democracy. Fourth, Africa is culturally more diverse and deeply rooted in all the Abrahamic religions –Islam, Christianity and Judaism- while India is predominantly Hindu with a large Muslim minority. Fifth, in terms of languages Africa has about six official and about 2,000 non-official languages.

Literature Review

Crowdfunding Research

The general literature on crowdfunding suggests potential for continuous and sustained gains in terms of funds, channel to share information with a wider public, upsurge of understanding of projects and products, ways to improve them, and maximize their marketability (Berndt, 2016). Other areas concern enhancing ability to mobilize, manage and allocate finance using digital technologies to develop specific projects in exchange for service delivery. The culture-related crowdfunding studies are emerging from Africa with Berndt (2016) survey of activities in the continent (Afrikstart, 2016) and Berndt & Mbassana (2016) focusing on Rwandan cultural context. Indian research focuses on establishing an effective crowdfunding market with Mollick (2014) exploring suitable legal framework conducive to business environment (Sharma 2016).

Crowdfunding Actors and Processes

The crowdfunding actors gain, apart from funds, recognition and vital information about their projects and their societal impacts (Belleflamme et al. 2011). The campaign process forges a new affiliation with crowdfunders (Gerber and Hui, 2013; Giudici et al., 2012) who may also serve as brand ambassadors. Three elements are vital to this process: decision to use crowdfunding, a campaign brief and the marketing tools (Barnett, 2015). There are signs for emerging crowdfunding actors and evolving processes from within and from outside Africa (Afrikstart, 2016), with a strong upsurge from East Africa (CCAF

2017). Similarly, the actors and the processes of crowdfunding in India are emerging (Nejak 2016, AlliedCrowds 2016a).

Crowdfunding Potential and Challenges Research-Crowdlending

Opportunities created by the growth of crowdfunding activities are many and growing. For example, research suggests that every successful crowdfunding campaign generates additional 2,2 jobs and that the impact of funds raised through crowdfunding is immediate (Best, at el. 2014). In Africa and India, which are new crowdfunding markets the employment generation (Aidid 2017, Kirby & Worner 2014) and the community impact of crowdfunding funds are instantaneous (Appsafrica 2016). The challenges facing the emerging African and Indian markets relate to developing suitable regulations and using them to nurture vibrant crowdfunding ecosystems (CCAF 2017, Majumdar 2015)

Crowdfunding Market Actors and Models

Crowdfunding market actors are extremely important in the transformations envisaged in the emerging alternative finance system. They are important to the changing global system, even more important to the African and Indian "global growth poles", where funds have to be mobilized to lift billions of people out of poverty.

Crowdfunding may be viewed as a complex ecosystem, which may vary substantially in function depending on the specific model under consideration. This market ecosystem is assumed to be made up of three main components: the platform, the demand side, and the supply side.

The platform is the nerve system of the ecosystem, as it is the technologically created solutions to allow the seamless digital matching demand with supply. The demand side consists of individuals and variety of entities seeking funds for various purposes. Depending on the specific crowdfunding model under consideration, this category of actors may be called "beneficiaries (donations, or reward-based crowdfunding), borrowers (debt), or issuers (equity), who can range from individuals to micro, small and medium enterprises (MSMEs), nongovernmental organizations (NGOs), non-profit entities (for example, charities), start-ups, and financial businesses" (GPFI, 2016:3). With respect to the supply side, the market actors may comprise of "donors (donation), backers (reward), lenders (debt), and investors (debt, equity). Investors range from private individuals to angel investors and venture capitalists, businesses, and large financial institutions. Besides the platform, the borrower and the crowd of investors, there are entities necessary for the crowdfunding ecosystem to work (the enablers), including payments" (GPFI, 2016:3).

The above analysis of the crowdfunding market actors, in terms of current social units at the urban and sub-national levels, can greatly help Africa and India to test and use the market. However, given their urgent need to lift hundreds of millions out of poverty and chart a prosperous path for billions in the decade ahead, there is need to broaden the discussion. The size of the ecosystem should be scaled up to the continental level, and the donors, backers, lenders, and investors should be of vastly greater scale.

It is also important to remember that much of the existing traditional financial management structure and practices in Africa and India has been built over many decades with cumulative experiences spanning colonial, post-colonial nationalist fervor, civil wars and post-war management but without real retooling to fit the current adventure into digital technology penetrating environment. Thus the public finance managers at the various institutions at supra-national, national and sub-national are new to the applications of digital technologies let alone how to manage them. The private sector and the social sectors are a bit better due to the influence of globalization and their roles in it. All of them need to be prepared for disruptive changes triggered by innovations in the "Alternative Finance" system and the changes in the traditional financial system itself. In any case, the changes needed in the future financial architecture at the various levels have to start immediately.

Types of Market Models

The literature generally lists four main models of crowdfunding: donation, reward, peer-to-peer lending and equity crowdfunding (SEBI, 2014, Majumdar 2015). The donation/social lending and the reward models are collectively called community crowdfunding, while Peer-to-Peer lending and equity are known as "financial return crowd-funding"(Kirby &Worner, 2014). To these arch-types, new categories are sometimes added to fit the situation. For example, in its 2015 report, the Afrikstart (2016) has created a "hybrid model", which signifies the temporary nature of the category, while Kirby & Worner (2014) listed three main business models in their financial return crowdfunding models: the client segregated account, the notary, and the equity crowd-funding. The general structure of the models is shown in Figure 1.

How Do These Models Work?

The crowdfunding models are designed to provide maximum benefits to all market actors, however, market imperfection always set in. Below is a brief explanation of how the market models are expected to work (Kirby &Worner 2014).

1. **Donation Crowdfunding:** In this model, the funds are transferred from contributors/donors without any expectation or liability for returns on such transferred funds. Usually, donation crowdfunding is undertaken for charitable causes to promote the common good, without any reward or expectation.
2. **Reward Crowdfunding:** Here the funds are transferred from contributors with an agreement, tacit or otherwise, that fund-raisers would reward contributors in many ways. These ways include pre-payment of a future product, free merchandise, and many other forms of favors.

Figure 1. Types of crowdfunding market models

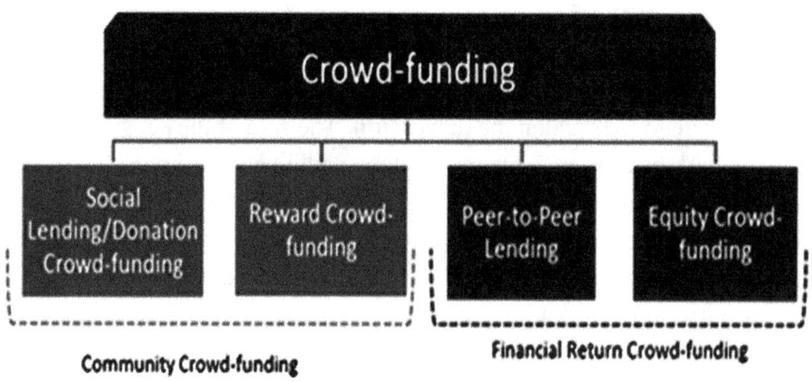

3. **Peer-to-Peer Lending:** In this case, individual lenders and borrowers are matched using software of an online Platform. The small funds inflows are aggregated by the platform and the loan is originated and released to the borrower. In the case of a bulk loan, requirements are covered by the individual bulk lenders who may choose to provide funds for part of the requirement.
4. **Equity Crowdfunding:** Here an equity stake in the company raising funds is offered in proportionate to the quantum invested. The contributors then assume the risks and liabilities of shareholders in the company.

Benefits and Costs of the Crowdfunding Markets

As Africa and India are on the verge of rapid growth regarding crowdfunding markets, it is important to explore the markets' potential benefits and costs so as to take them into account in developing relevant policies and regulatory framework.

- **Important Benefits:** A number of researchers (Afrikstart 2016, Majumdar 2015, Kirby and Worner 2014) have identified the potential benefits to crowdfunding markets in Africa and India they include but not limited to the following:
  - For the African and Indian investors, a key advantage so far has been lack of regulations, the compliance of which would cost time and money.
  - The use of the Internet in the crowdfunding marketplace means that an entrepreneur can directly trade an idea that is viable and profitable.
  - The main benefit of crowdfunding to entrepreneurs is the ability to mobilize capital for a project by giving up minimal equity interest.
  - Since individuals make up the majority of the crowdfunding investors, the risk is spread out and the requests usually filled.
  - An important benefit is the lower cost of capital and higher returns to most investors in crowdfunding market.
  - In urban or regional development situations, crowdfunding can help economic recovery of an area by financing small and medium enterprises (SMEs), which are generally recognized as the real engine of economic growth.
  - In addition to the above, other non-financial gains are also important. They include boosting the reputation of the project initiators, the project marketing process, which often results in positive feedback, the audience engagement by initiators, which is good for social networking in the community instant access to good market testing, and feedback, which can be gained at pre-release access events.
- **Main Risks:** The above potential benefits must, however, be balanced against potential risks in the crowdfunding markets of Africa and India as warned by Afrikstart (2016), Kirby and Worner (2014), and Majundar (2014). Most common issues faces by the market include those of the investment management, privacy concerns, intellectual property and ways to protect and to nurture the start-ups. The following risks are related more to the operational issues of the crowdfunding markets.
  - **Risk of Taking Things Easy:** There is tendency to increase business risk when there is low cost of capital and the relative ease of access and engagement on the crowdfunding portals.

- Apart from the increased risk due to ineffective control, it is generally recognized that startup enterprises have an inherent risk of failure.
- Danger of default is generally recognized, especially in equity crowdfunding due to its high default/investment ration.
- Risk of platform closure/failure is also high despite the short life of crowdfunding, as evidenced by cases in poorly regulated markets.
- Risk of fraud is high especially in the peer-to-peer lending and equity crowdfunding markets, heightened by the online interactions aspect of these industries.
- As an online activity, crowdfunding is naturally open to the risk of cyber-attack and many of the markets in Africa and India are unprepared to guard against such attacks.
- The inability of investors to sell their investments in secondary markets in Africa and India creates illiquidity risk.
- As unregulated and poorly monitored markets, there is opaqueness in the marketing process in Africa and India thereby leading to high disclosure of risks to markets in both regions.

Market Growth Potentials and Hurdles

The growth of crowdfunding markets and other elements of alternative financial markets are of great importance to Africa and India. To avoid costly mistakes and delays, it is also important to identify the potential hurdles that might have to be crossed in the process of developing the markets.

Growth Drivers and Hurdles for Crowdfunding Growth in Africa and India

Drivers of crowdfunding growth in Africa include, but not limited to, the following factors: the real market need of alternative source of financing, the expansion of mobile technology, the use of online social media, platforms, and networks, the rise of a middle class, and the active contribution of the African Diaspora.

- **The Real Market Need of Alternative Source of Financing:** The growth in crowdfunding markets can result in poverty reduction in Africa and India by efficiently mobilizing and channeling savings towards growing sectors that can help people improve themselves, by reducing the vulnerability of people through linking citizens requiring finance with investors or donors. The markets provide much-needed and new forms of financing for those in need of them, either groups or individuals, such as startups, SMEs, charities, social enterprises and various community-based projects, or individuals who need to fund children education, medical treatment, and similar social purposes. As the CCAF (2017) pointed out, there is a great deal of potential for these new forms of finance to provide access to funding which would promote economic development and financial inclusion in developing emerging and developed countries alike. Africa and India may be poor probably due to the huge unused or underdeveloped capital or alternative resource for mobilizing markets like crowdfunding.

Crowdfunding growth is driven by the widespread adoption of ICT (Information and Communication Technology) among the people thereby leading to an increase in mobile phone usage across Africa. About 67% of Africans had a mobile phone in 2015, from a total population of 1.13 billion. As hinted in Table 1, there were about 722.5 million mobile phones on the continent, with 127.5 million being smartphones, as estimated by ITU in 2017and by 2015 StarTimes Group report on "Content Building in the Digital Era". By leveraging mobile technology, crowdfunding platforms have used innovative ways to create and to promote the crowdfunding projects via SMS, and have allowed the use of mobile money to fund the crowdfunding projects.

- **Online Social Media, Platforms, and Networks Are Also Key Drivers of the Rise of Crowdfunding in Africa:** As crowdfunding is firstly based on peer-to-peer funding, it requires an active community engagement and extensive online social interactions between the crowdfunding project creator and the potential project funders and backers. Therefore, Facebook, Twitter, and other social media platforms have played a vital role to foster the emergence of crowdfunding in Africa. In November 2015, it was estimated that about 125 million Africans were on Facebook, according to Internet World Stats (IWS, 2017). In some African countries, such as South Africa, Nigeria, Kenya, Uganda and Ghana, connecting to Facebook was the most common usage of the mobile phone, even before sending text messages. A survey of 3,500 mobile users from these countries conducted by GeoPoll and World Wide Worx in 2015 revealed that 48% of the mobile phone owners used primarily their mobile phone to connect to Facebook. Sending SMS only came second in terms of phone activity with 42% (IWS, 2017).

The rise of the African middle class, estimated at 350 million people by the African Development Bank, also contributes through channel funding to the crowdfunding campaigns launched in the existing Africa-based crowdfunding platforms. Furthermore, the African Diaspora made their financial contributions by sending back home $35.2 billion in remittances in 2015 (World Bank 2015).

The Indian middle class will most likely dominate global crowdfunding market activities because of its sheer size, economic power and its agility in crowdfunding market activities. The WEF (2016) suggests that the middle class is already half of the total population and has doubled in size over an eight-year period from 300 million in 2004 to 600 million in 2012. At the same time, its spending power has increased to cover all people spending between $2 and $10 per capita per day, but the highest rise is the group spending between $4 and $6 per day (WEF 2016). With this trend, the middle class includes such unexpected groups as mechanics, carpenters, decorators, drivers and indeed street vendors. With the household disposable income rising twenty-fold since 1990, a larger Indian crowd will have even more to invest in the various models of the crowdfunding market.

The African Diaspora can sometimes bring up to one-third of the money needed to fund the projects in some Africa-based crowdfunding portals (World Bank 2013). Another critical factor that influences the amount of money raised by the crowdfunding platforms of each country is the level of involvement of the Diaspora to fund local projects in Africa. In Kenya for instance, about 35% of the funds received by the crowdfunding platform M-Changa are from the members of the Kenyan Diaspora from 50 countries (World Bank 2013). Tunisian and Moroccan crowdfunding platforms also receive a great deal of funding of the projects from the Diaspora based in France, The distribution showed nearly130 million African Diaspora in North America.

AlliedCrowds (2016a) report on diaspora crowdfunding demonstrates the significant role of Diaspora communities in promoting crowdfunding: a positive correlation exists between crowdfunding and remittances. If well planned, and managed by the governments of the developing nations, the personal remittances of the Diaspora can be channeled to finance local initiatives in their home countries directly via crowdfunding portals.

According to the World Bank (2013), in 2012, migrants sent an estimated $60 billion home to African countries, with some agents charging up to 12% for the transfer service. However, the African Institute of Remittances aims to leverage those remittances for Africa's development. Another institution conducting research to investigate the willingness and the barriers to investing and/or donating back home is the Diaspora Investment Alliance. It is hoped that African governments will use the findings to develop suitable policies to attract investments into African ventures.

Although the amount of $32.3 million raised by Africa-based crowdfunding platforms is an encouraging figure, Africa-based crowdfunding platforms account for less than 0.1% of the global crowdfunding activity. It estimated the global crowdfunding market at $34.4 billion in 2015. In comparison with global figures and trends, crowdfunding in Africa is at a relatively nascent phase (Massolution Research 2015).

Hurdles to Crowdfunding Platform Growth

Due to the hurdles being faced by the crowdfunding growth in Africa (to its market potential of $2.5 billion) and to a lesser extent in India as well, there is a need to scale up over the current situation faced by the market. In particular, the following areas need careful considerations: low Information Technologies penetration, low level of social media usage, low level of financial flows, low level of financial regulatory activities, and low level of awareness of crowdfunding.

CROWDFUNDING MARKETS PERFORMANCE ANALYSIS

The above is a comparative analysis of the contexts and performance of crowdfunding markets in Africa and India. In order to draw attention to increasing Internet focus of economic and to some extent social activities, the local-based and foreign-based platforms undertaking the financing of cross-border projects are identified. Thus, the analysis of the African and Indian crowdfunding markets performances are considered by using two data sets: one is comprehensive portal data that allows us to compare South Africa and India, and the second is a set of data that enables us to highlight the way the Internet is nudging towards more and more global online activities.

Analysis of Crowdfunding for South Africa and India in 2017, and the Projected 2017-2021

South Africa is the hub of African crowdfunding activities, and it has the longest experience and broadest of all other African countries. Probably from that hub, the crowdfunding platforms began to spread to East Africa and North Africa and now are extended to West Africa. Thus, South Africa seems to be the best representative of African crowdfunding activities and data comprehensiveness, comparable to India. A comprehensive data set is digitally collected, managed and marketed by *The Statistical Portal*. This portal manages global digital data on a wide array of activities and services that include digital media, digital advertising, e-commerce, and e-services. Of interest to this chapter is the e-commerce sub-set that deals with data on smart home, FinTech, eHealth and eTravel. The FinTech category stores data on digital payments, business finance and personal finance. The crowdfunding data is in the business finance category, which consists of crowdfunding (reward-based model and the pre-financing of products, art, music, films, software or scientific research), the equity-based crowdfunding (named Crowdinvesting), and lending-based crowdfunding (called Crowdlending). The analysis of the data on these three types is used in Table 2 to compare South Africa and India.

The data show that except for the projected annual growth, South Africa has better performance. For example, in the 2017 transaction value it has 1.5 times the performance of India; in the 2021projected value it is 1.4 times and it is three times better in the average funding per campaign in 2017. Thus despite India higher projected rate of growth, South Africa has a higher performance with respect to the listed activities both now and the projected future. This suggests that as other African nations begin to take an active part in crowdfunding market, the signs are that Africa's future is bright in internally mobilizing local resources for development.

- **Local and Cross-Border Crowdfunding Activities:** The second set of analysis, which seeks to assess crowdfunding activities by local platforms serving their localities, local platforms serving foreign communities and foreign-based platforms serving African and Indian communities are as follows:
  - Top Funded Crowdfunding Project Categories In Africa and India In 2015
  - Africa- and Indian-Based Crowdfunding Platforms Funding Projects Abroad
  - Foreign Crowdfunding Platforms Funding Projects In Africa and India

Top Funded Crowdfunding Project Categories in Africa and India in 2015

- **African Case:** These are useful indicators of the values of the actors as voluntary change agents. Each individual participant acts as an agent for the offering, selecting and promoting of the projects in which they believe. The list of the projects is a clear indication of the values held by the individual participants as well as collaborating group or groups. The higher among the invested may reflect the ranking of the substance of the social activities or facilities. The ranking reflects the value preferences not of the users but of the facility or service development actors. Thus ranking business and entrepreneurship higher than arts and entrainments, in this case, reflects the value of the foreign crowdfunding actors, not that of the Africa beneficiaries.

Table 2. Comparison of crowdfunding elements for South Africa and India, 2017

Crowdfunding Elements		S. Africa	India
Transaction Value in the "Crowdfunding" in 2017		US$1,302m	US$91m
Transaction Value growth rate (CAGR 2017-2021):			
	Projected Annual Rate (Average)	9.5%	60%
	Projected Amount in 2021	US$2,117m	US$1,533m
The average funding per campaign in 2017		US$14,721.0	US$4,792.2
Compared to the highest activity value in China (in 2017)		US$52,321m	US$52,321m

Source: Statista (2017).

Crowdfunding activity is said to be a form of voting activity (CPFI 2016). To this end, the relative funds raised for the different grouping areas would tend to reflect the relative values attached to each project type. Thus based on the funded project categories in Africa in 2015, the business and entrepreneurship category is the most preferred and the least is Arts and Entertainment. On this basis, Table 3 reflects the relative values of this emerging voting system and the indicative motives represented in the process.

- **Indian Case:** The global crowdfunding businesses generated about $34.4 billion in 2015 (Nejak, 2016). There is no reliable figure available on how much was raised in India, although it was a small percent of the global amount, which is unlikely to reflect the proliferation of the local crowdfunding sites. Part of the explanation may be that the local crowdfunding is limited to giving donations and loans. Another clarification offered by the Securities and Exchange Board of India (SEBI) suggests that at this stage, the Indian public lacks adequate investment knowledge or experience and so requires strict protection in order to put the whole activity in a legal limbo (SEBI 2014), something similar to the situation in Africa (CCAF, 2017). This suggests the need for an intensive awareness campaign and training of potential investors.

As part of the analysis of crowdfunding activities of the local platforms with foreign operations and the foreign-based with local operations, Table 4 presents details of the top Indian crowdfunding platforms with local and global operations. Nejak (2016) reported the judgment about India's top 10 platforms in 2015.

- **Comments:** The Table shows there are two Peer-to-Peer platforms: Rang De and Faircent, and six donations platforms, namely Ketto, Wishberry, FuelAdream, Catapoolt, Bitgiving and crowdera. The top hybrid donations/loans platforms are Milaap and impact-Guru. All of these, according to Nejak (2016) operate in a number of places across India. In addition to local operations, Impact-Guru has offices in 6 countries, Wishberry has presence in 60 countries, Milaap operates in over 120 countries, and Crowdera specifies that it is a completely free global crowdfunding platform.

Africa- and Indian-Based Crowdfunding Platforms Funding Projects Abroad

Although many would claim that crowdfunding is still mainly a developed-world phenomenon, it seems clear to many entrepreneurs in Africa that its potential to stimulate innovation and create jobs in the

Table 3. Top funded crowdfunding project categories in Africa in 2015

Categories	Amount Raised	Types of Indicative Motives
Business & Entrepreneurship	$17.8 M	(profit-motive, Innovation-motive & services)
Real Estate	$13.6 M	(developer motive)
Travel	$ 319,434	(exploration motive)
Social Causes	$ 307,860	(social change agent, social entrepreneur)
Creative & Innovative Projects	$-219130	(creative – motive, innovative -motive
Arts & Entertainment	$43,641	(creative art)

Source: Afrikstart, 2016.

Table 4. Top Indian crowdfunding platforms with local and global operations, 2015

Name and Date Established	Type of Model	Main Characteristics
Rang De 2008,	P2P Lending	Attracted 9,699 social investors and disburse 50,008 loans. 93% to women. Raised USD 7 million and paid USD 5 million. Has 25 field partners in 16 states of India
Faircent 2013	P2P Lending	It has over 6,000 potential lenders and 26,000 potential borrowers on its platform, and has disbursed about USD 973,000 in 2 years.
Ketto2012	Donations	Supports fundraisers in community/social projects, creative arts, and personal development. Has raised USD 6 million through more than 100,000 backers to fund over 10,000 projects
Wishberry2010	Donations	Dedicated to funding creative projects – music, stand-up comedy, film production, art, dance, design, photography, publishing, and theatre. Completed 325 projects, and raised USD 1.3 million from over 11,000 backers in 60 countries.
FuelADream 2015	Top donations	Started with 14 projects in creative arts, social causes and charities, and it is capable of hosting 20 new projects monthly.
Catapooolt2013	Top donations	Supports projects in creative, sports, political and social enterprises, and business startups. It funded 40 projects, and raised USD 150,000 from 2,000 contributors. Offers access to 300,000 retail outlets.
Bitgiving2013	Top donations	Funds entrepreneurial, creative and social projects. Handled over 650 projects.
Crowdera2014	Top donations	Has raised over USD 537,000 helping several prestigious nonprofits, individuals, and organizations.
Milaap2011	Donations/loans	Helped projects in education, energy and water &sanitation. Accepts donations and micro-lending for emergencies, neighborhood projects, etc. Operates in over 120 countries, handles about 50,000 projects, and raised over USD $12.7 million
Impact Guru 2014	Donations/loans	It helps individuals, non-profits, social enterprises, startups, corporations. It raised about $8.5 million, and works with 100 causes and agencies from 6 countries

Source: Nekaj(2016).

developing world has been noticed and some of them have taken steps to take a claim in the global marketplace. To illustrate this point, Wealth Migrate of South Africa offers real estate services to clients in Shanghai, Singapore, the U.S., the U.K. and Australia shall be examined. Next is Pitch, Office of Nigeria that has projects from the Diaspora communities in North America, Europe, and the Middle East; it also includes Islamic Relief of South African-based faith-based crowdfunding dealing with social causes in stress-ridden areas such as Somalia, Ethiopia, Yemen and Syria (Afristart 2016).

Similarly, some Indian platforms have operations abroad in countries where there are large Indian Diaspora communities. KettoKetto, Wishberry, and Fuel Adream platforms, for example, have operations in the UK and other areas where there are large Indian communities (Jain 2015). With support from the local institutions and multinational development agencies, these pioneers could make crowdfunding become a powerful development tool in the developing world as well.

Foreign Crowdfunding Platforms Funding Projects in Africa

Africa needs all the home-based as well as the foreign-based crowdfunding markets it can mobilize in order to equip its youthful population with skills and jobs in the coming Fourth Industrial Revolution. According to a report by World Economic Forum (WEF, 2016), Sub-Saharan Africa has more than 60% of its population under the age of 25, making the region the world's youngest region currently, and by

2030, it will be home to more than one-quarter of the world's under-25 population. Luckily, this situation presents Africa with a golden demographic opportunity as this young population enters the world of work, because it is the best prepared, best-educated and globally integrated the continent has had. However, for Africa to leverage this opportunity, it needs to unlock the latent of its young people and prepare them for the future work at home and abroad. In effect, Africa will be presented with the opportunities that India now has- as discussed elsewhere in this chapter-- that is resulting in rising middle class, rising personal and national income, and hiking in global influence.

While there are indications that a number of African economies are relatively under-exposed to labor market disruptions at present, this picture is changing rapidly. The African governments and leaders to prepare for tomorrow's job market must use this favorable market condition. Thus, this section seeks to explore characteristics and opportunities offered by foreign-based platforms in Africa, and it also highlights the need to interact with the crowdfunding markets in many African Diaspora communities worldwide.

The current level and the potential of foreign crowdfunding platforms in Africa can be judged from the fact that they were able to raise a total of US$94.6 million in 2015, but a year later the amount rose to US$190 million, Based on this increment, Afrikstart (2016) projects that this could climb up to US$ 2.6 billion for Sub-Saharan Africa alone.

Many foreign crowdfunding platforms are finding their ways into Africa markets; it is always useful for policy-makers to take stocks of the top foreign platforms operating in Africa so as to guide future decisions. In 2015, the top three foreign platforms were Kiva raising 35.9 million, Better place and Gofundme. The others who raised between one and five million in 2015 were the Globalgiving, Youcaring, Givengain, Razoo and Justgiving as shown in Table 5

Relative to their home based operations, the range of projects categories and models used in Africa might be considered to be signs of more hopeful future in Africa. Most funded crowdfunding projects from foreign platforms in 2015 were for the benefits of children, a category in which US$ 14 million were raised, followed by the area of education (13.5 million), women and girls ($10.8million), health services ($9.6million) and then disaster and recovery ($8.2 million). With respect to the types of models, data from Afrikstart (2016) show that the four active foreign crowdfunding models operating in Africa, in 2015, raised cash ranging from Equity model's $1.7 million to Donations model's $ 48 million. The Loans model and the Reward model raised $42.2 million and $2.8 million respectively.

Table 5. The top foreign crowdfunding platforms operating in Africa in 2015

Foreign Platform	Amount Raised
Kiva	$35.9 M
Betterplace	$9.9 M
Gofundme	$9.1 M
Globalgiving	$4.6 M
Youcaring	$4.5 M
Givengain	$4.3 M
Razoo	$3.4 M
Justgiving	$1.6 M

Source: AlliedCrowds Open Analytics 2017 /Afrikstart 2016.

Emerging Trends in Evolution of Crowdfunding Platforms

A few researchers have identified emerging trends in the evolution of crowdfunding platforms (CPFI 2016, Afrikstart 2016). The main trends are moving in three main directions: a) hybridization, (b) institutionalization and complexity, and (c) consolidation. Some platforms are specializing in any of these but usually, there is no clear-cut platform type preferred. The transaction areas and the pattern of transactions also are changing. The categories of platforms are also changing with some of the operations. Many platforms are strategically putting themselves in a situation where they can take advantage of new developments.

CROWDFUNDING MARKETS DEVELOPMENT REGULATIONS

In the section above, e comparative analysis of the investment by the private sectors in both Africa and India has been provided; it was largely free from interference from the public sector. Public sector involvement came much earlier at the stage of the development of ICT infrastructure. Now, as the tempo of activities in the crowdfunding market is picking up, the government seeks to come back to regulate the behavior of the market in the public's interest. This section analyzes the approach of the two cases understudy. At this stage, the focus is on the approach, as there is no substantive regulation on the ground. Before the explanation of the approach, there is need to have more discussion on why regulation is necessary.

The crowdfunding market is part of the increasingly important digital economy. It comprises markets that are based on digital technologies that drive the marketing of products and services through e-commerce. The growth of the digital sector has triggered economic development recently, and the drive towards a digital world has profound impacts on humanity that reaches outside the context of digital technology alone.

Digital markets, including crowdfunding platforms, are imperfect due to the characteristic information asymmetry, barriers to entry and exit of actors, and differentiated products. Hence, there is a need for government's intervention in order to rectify these situations. Such intervention is supposed to involve strategic decision making on the part of individual firms to invest with a risk factor (Mankiw 2009). Also, a perfectly-functioning market should, in theory, maximize value for consumers, but in practice, this is not usually the case. Thus, government's regulation of markets, including the emerging crowdfunding markets in Africa and India, becomes necessary. It is therefore important to identify the rationales for regulation and some of the tools used. Table 6 shows the types of reasons for government intervention in normal societal activities and examples of suitable intervention that might be used by the governments in Africa and India to generate trust and confidence in the regulations guiding crowdfunding behaviors by all relevant parties.

African Approach to Markets Development Regulations

The Cambridge Centre for Alternative Finance (CCAF, 2017a) led other institutions to carry out a study of different crowdfunding models and their regulatory approaches in the East African countries, such as Kenya, Tanzania, Uganda and Rwanda. Also in this report, there is a brief review of the relevant regulations with respect to South Africa. A similar study has been conducted by the same institution in North Africa and the Middle East (CCAF, 2017b). There is no known study on this topic on West Africa or

Table 6. Government intervention rationale and example of regulation

Intervention Reason	Examples of Regulation
Weak Competition	• The Competition Commission investigates mergers that may impact competition. • Regulators may set prices for some services which might otherwise be priced too high
Externalities	• Externalities can be positive or negative: positive types are benefits that are infeasible tax to provide; while negative externalities are costs that are infeasible to tax to not provide. • Negative externalities can be reduced by taxing goods when their production generates spillover costs so that the taxation effectively increases the cost of producing such goods.
Lack of information and/or difficulty making informed decisions	• The Financial Services Authority mandates certain types of information disclosure when selling financial products • The Food Standards Agency enforces food safety rules
Social objectives	• In some cases, social objectives are achieved through state funding. In other cases, they are achieved by placing regulatory obligations on firms • Public goods such as defense or free Wi-Fi connection are provided by the state.

Central Africa, so it is assumed that East Africa is Africa's incubator for Africa's crowdfunding – and indeed alternative finance- development guidance instruments.

The CCAF (2017a) study shows that crowdfunding market activities are growing fast across East Africa, with the fastest being the non-financial return based types, like rewards and donations models. While these are scaling up, the equity and loan-based markets are just going to emerge. Given these two speed growth, it is important that the whole system is given a very careful attention by the financial regulators in East Africa and indeed Africa, so as to identify and apply for the possible economic and social benefits, and at the same time turning various risks and problems into opportunities.

Drawing on the lessons and experiences from the UK, the USA, Malaysia, New Zealand and India, the CCAF (2017a) report makes some insightful recommendation on priority regulatory and policy areas deemed necessary for crowdfunding market development in the studied East Africa countries.

Presented below are first the key findings, then a summary of the main recommendations and an action plan proposed by the research team.

- **Findings:** The following are some of the main findings of the team:
  - There is no modified or specific crowdfunding regulation in East Africa or South Africa.
  - Non-financial return-based models- rewards and donations- dominate market activity in East Africa.
  - Financial return-based loan and equity models are at the very earliest stages of development.
  - Loan- and equity-based models dominate total global activity, and account for the majority of market activity in global markets, while donation- and rewards account for a small percentage of total market activity.
- **Recommendations:** The study does not recommend new crowdfunding regulations in East Africa at this time. Some other regulator-led, market development initiatives to be considered should include the following:
  - "A living database of all, existing, regulator-acknowledged platforms in East Africa.
  - Regulator engagement opportunities - to bring together the East African crowdfunding industry, practitioners, experts, potential funders and fundraisers.

    - Develop a regional regulatory laboratory or 'Sandbox' to guide crowdfunding businesses through the relevant regulatory processes and requirements.
    - Regulators should encourage the East African crowdfunding platforms to build a regionally-focused industry association to undertake self-regulation and institute guidelines and principles to foster innovation while protecting investors."
- **Action Plan:** The study proposed a three-phased set of policy and regulatory action plan, which is designed to encourage the growth and development of crowdfunding models in East Africa. The plan is intended to provide the necessary precautionary and monitoring measures to protect all stakeholders, especially retail customers. In the first phase of the three parts, the plan is focused on mapping, education and engagement, and its time frame ranges from short-term to medium-term with ongoing activities. The second phase activities consist of developing the crowdfunding Ecosystem and Trust-inducing Initiatives and consists of four parts, with a medium-term framework of activities. The third phase is targeting government support and endorsement in which there are three phases, within the timeframe of medium to long-term.

Indian Crowdfunding Regulatory Approach

The Securities and Exchange Board of India (SEBI) released a consultation paper in June 2014 on crowdfunding in India. It was an attempt to seek responses on key issues raised regarding benefits and risks of crowdfunding and the best approach to regulate its market activities in the public interest. It also set out suggested principles on which crowdfunding regulations in the future may be based. These principles are outlined below:

1. Access to Markets and Eligibility for Fundraisers
2. Accreditation of Investors and Investment Limits
3. Regulation of Portals, Recognized Stock Exchanges, Technology Business Incubators (TBIs), and Associations and Networks of PE or Angel Investors
4. Procedures include;
    a. Application;
    b. Undergo screening and due diligence;
    c. Public approval.

One of the contributors to the discussion was Majumdar (2015) and KPMG (2016) whose contribution could help African regulators as well. The first issue he pointed out is that the SEBI proposal was silent on Peer-to-Peer lending that involves a borrower seeking funds on a debt basis, a set of creditors who agree to lend funds to the borrower and an intermediary. The second aspect missing from the proposed SEBI regulations, according to him, is that of cross-border crowdfunding- African and Indian investors can function within and across borders, and so foreign firms can cross into Africa and India. The cross-border investment and fundraising market activities and the global nature of digital networks and application of social media and particularly the uncertainty regarding contract law application in different jurisdictions, as Kirby and Worner (2014) argue, are issues needing further research and clarification (.

Comment on the African and India Approaches

Both the African and the Indian approaches are commendable. The Africa approach seeks a gradual, phased-out approach that enables the regulation learn about the systems' response to any intervention. The Indian approach seeks the opinions and suggestions of stakeholders before formal regulations are enacted. In introducing innovation, sometimes, the new models tend to gain enough traction to the extent that they disrupt the incumbent system. People often point to how the worldwide success of Uber and other ridesharing platforms have triggered debate around the regulation of rideshare platforms. On the other hand, there are arguments that the rise of certain crowd-based and collaborative models covers the symptom of failing economy (Guardian 2014), especially if such models facilitate the use of informal labor or encourage tax avoidance.

In any case, there is no ready or easy answer, that is why the African gradual approach has many advantages. It seeks to map and to make sense of the challenge as the first step towards proactively understanding it and responding to it This should be viewed as a pro-type approach, in which an innovative initiative and its societal impact need to be identified and addressed. Among these are issues of land use and planning, taxation, insurance, licensing and others. In many of these cases, the local communities might have already considered them so as to provide some insightful lessons which can establish the socially acceptable solutions.

FUTURE RESEARCH DIRECTION

This chapter provides a basis for further research work in order to explore in detail areas where crowdfunding may be of the highest relevance to financial inclusion at the global, supra-national, national and sub-national levels. It also provides general background by defining crowdfunding, outlining its evolution and ecosystem, detailing the basic categories of crowdfunding, citing their main financial and non-financial benefits and risks for two of the future most populous global growth poles so as to advocate the use of crowdfunding for broadening and deepening of financial inclusion.

Further work could focus on the following issues:

- A more in-depth political-economic analysis of the potential of crowdfunding to serve excluded and underserved customers (supra-nationals, nationals and sub-nationals).
- The impact of crowdfunding on improved access to credit and other financial products of unserved and underserved customers (supra-nationals, nationals and sub-nationals).
- Ways of establishing effective legal and regulatory framework to address the risks faced by fundraisers and funders
- Ways of enhancing level of customer awareness concerning the risks and benefits of crowdfunding

CONCLUSION

This chapter is a comparative study of the emerging crowdfunding markets in Africa and India. However, the real issue is larger; it is about how to use technologies for the service of a fairer and more inclusive global system. We have seen how crowdfunding started as a tiny phenomenon and how it quickly grow into a major global industry which opens up huge opportunities for financial inclusion for small start-ups as well as multinationals. The interest of this chapter is on how it could do the same at the global level for nations and communities with limited or no options to get a financial return on their savings.

This chapter hopes that the global policy community can help create crowdfunding industry that will deliver its promise to promote financial inclusion with sound and enabling legal regulations. Policy makers at different levels need to find ways to regulate crowdfunding so that it can achieve its market-building potential, while appropriately managing the risks that come with it. Platforms need to be subjected to an appropriate regulatory regime that is adequately tailored to crowdfunding and adequately protects both funders and fundraisers. As indicated in the previous section, further research should focus on relating planning and policies to making crowdfunding markets contribute to the issue of financial inclusion based on needs at the global, national, sub-nationals and within social groups.

REFERENCES

Afrikstart. (2016). *Afrikstart Crowdfunding in Africa Report*. Retrieved from http://afrikstart.com/report/wp-content/uploads/2016/09/Afrikstart-Crowdfunding-In-Africa-Report.pdf

Aidid, A. (2017). *Crowdfunding in Africa: Opportunities and Challenges*. Retrieved from https://www.covafrica.com/2017/02/crowdfunding-in-africa-opportunities-and-challenges/

AlliedCrowds. (2015). *Developing World Crowdfunding-Sustainability through Crowdfunding*. Author.

AlliedCrowds. (2016b). *Crowdfunding Annual Report January 2016*. Retrieved from http://alliedcrowds.com/reports

AlliedCrowds. (2016a). *Developing World Crowdfunding Prosperity through Crowdfunding*. Author.

Appsafrica. (2016). *Crowdfunding in Africa is gaining momentum*. Available at: https://www.appsafrica.com/crowdfunding-in-africa-is-gaining-momentum/

Barnett, C. (2015). Trends Show Crowdfunding To Surpass VC In 2016. *Forbes*.

Belleflamme, P., Lambert, T., & Schwienbacher, A. (2011) Crowdfunding: tapping the right crowd. Center for Operations Research and Econometrics (CORE).

Berndt, A. (2016). Crowdfunding in the African Context: A New Way to Fund Ventures. In Entrepreneurship and SME Management Across Africa (pp. 31-49). Academic Press.

Berndt, A., & Mbassana, M. (2016). *Crowdfunding: The Beliefs of Rwandan Entrepreneurs*. Retrieved from https://www.researchgate.net/publication/310597267_Crowdfunding_The_Beliefs_of_Rwandan_Entrepreneurs

Best, J., Neiss, S., Swart, R., Lambkin, A., & Raymond, S. (2013). *Crowdfunding's potential for the developing world*. InfoDev. Retrieved from http://documents.worldbank.org/curated/en/409841468327411701/Crowdfundings-potential-for-the-developing-world

Cambridge Centre for Alternative Finance (CCAF). (2017a). *Alternative Finance*. Retrieved from http://Jbs.cam.ac.uk

Cambridge Centre for Alternative Finance (CCAF). (2017b). *Africa and Middle East Alternative Finance Benchmarking Report*. Retrieved from https://www.jbs.cam.ac.uk/faculty-research/centres/alternative-finance/publications/africa-middle-east/#.Wbr9cbIjGT8

Gerber, E. M., & Julie, H. (2013). *Crowdfunding: Motivations and deterrents for participation*. Retrieved from https://www.scholars.northwestern.edu/en/publications/crowdfunding-motivations-and-deterrents-for-participation

Giudici, G., Nava, R., Lamastra, C., & Vereco, C. (2012). *Crowdfunding: The New Frontier for Financing entrepreneurships?* Available at SSRN: http:// ssrn.com/abstract=2157429

GPFI (Global Partnership for Financial Inclusion). (2016). *2016 Progress Report to G20 Leaders*. Retrieved from http://www.g20.utoronto.ca/2016/gpfi-progress-report.pdf

Guardian. (2014). *Crowdfunding: Essential advice for charities*. Retrieved from https://www.theguardian.com/voluntary-sector- network/2014/sep/17/crowdfunding-charities-essential-advice-fundraising

Internetworldstats. (2017). *Internet Usage Statistics For Africa*. Available at:http://www.internetworldstats.com/stats1.htm

Jain, J. K. (2015). *Crowd-Funding in Microfinance in India: Issues, Challenges and Opportunities. UK Government's Department for International Development (DFID) and Small Industries Development Bank of India*. SIDBI.

Kirby, E., & Worner, S. (2014). *Crowdfunding: An Infant Industry Growing Fast*. Retrieved from http://www.iosco.org/ research/pdf/swp/Crowd-funding-An-Infant-Industry-Growing-Fast.pdf

Kirby, E., & Worner, S. (2014). *Crowd-funding: an Infant Industry Growing Fast*. Madrid, Spain: International Organization of Securities Commissions. Retrieved from https://www.iosco.org/library/pubdocs/pdf/IOSCOPD459.pdf

KPMG. (2016). *Fintech in India A global growth story*. Retrieved from https://assets.kpmg.com/content/dam/kpmg/pdf/2016/06/FinTech-new.pdf

Mankiw, N. G. (2009). *Macroeconomics* (7th ed.). New York: Worth Publishers.

Massolution. (2015). *The Crowdfunding Industry Report*. Available at:http://www.crowdsourcing.org/editorial/global-crowdfunding-market-to-reach-344b-in-2015- predictsmassolutions-2015cf-industry-report/45376

Mollick, E. (2014). The dynamics of crowdfunding: An exploratory study. *Journal of Business Venturing*, *29*(1), 1–16. doi:10.1016/j.jbusvent.2013.06.005

Nejak, E. L. (2016). *Top Indian Crowdfunding Platforms With local and Global Operations*. Retrieved from http://crowdsourcingweek.com/blog/indias-top-ten-crowdfunding-platforms/

Njoh, A. J. (2000). *The Impact of Colonial Heritage on Development in Sub-Saharan Africa.* Retrieved from www.msu.ac.zw/.../1299832433impact%20of%20colonial%20heritage%20on%20dvt

SEBI (Securities and Exchange Board of India). (2014). *Consultation Paper on Crowdfunding in India.* Retrieved from http://www.aibi.org.in/PR%20- %20Consultation%20Paper%20on%20Crowdfunding%20 in%20India.pdf

Sharma, A. M. (2016). Crowd Funding: An online Financing option. International Journal in Multidisciplinary and Academic Research, 5(3).

Statista. (2017). *The Statistics Portal: FinTech.* Retrieved from https://www.statista.com/outlook/377/112/ crowdinvesting/south-africa#

UNDESA. (2014). *World Urbanization Prospects.* Retrieved from https://esa.un.org/unpd/wup/publications/files/wup2014-highlights.Pdf

World Bank. (2013). *Diaspora Remittances Must Open the Door to Financial Inclusion.* Retrieved from http://www.worldbank.org/en/news/feature/2013/10/10/diaspora-remittances-must-open-the-door-to-financial-inclusion

World Bank. (2015). *Crowdfunding in Emerging Markets: Lessons from East African Startups.* Retrieved from https://www.infodev.org/infodev-files/crowdfunding-in-east-africa.pdf

World Economic Forum (WEF). (2016). *The Future of Jobs and Skills in Africa: Preparing the Region for the Fourth Industrial Revolution.* https://www.weforum.org/reports/the-future-of-jobs-and- skills-in-africa-preparing-the-region-for-the-fourth-industrial-revolution

KEY TERMS AND DEFINITIONS

Cross-Cultural Study: A specialization analysis that uses various data from many societies to examine the scope of human behavior related to specified fields.

Crowdfunding: The use of small amounts of funds from a large number of individuals or organizations in order to raise funds for a project, business/personal loan, or other financing needs through an online web-based platform.

Crowdfunding Market: A regulated system of using web-based platforms to enable the funding a projects or ventures by raising numerous small amounts of cash from a large number of people.

Crowdfunding Models: As the model matured, more crowdfunding sites started to appear on the web such reward-based, equity, donation, and many forms of hybrids.

Equity Crowdfunding: The process whereby people (i.e., the crowd) invest in the new unlisted firm in return for shares in that company, and as a shareholder, one has partial ownership of and the profit from the company.

Market Benefits: An investor, entrepreneur to acquire required funds to start a project quickly, cheaply, and with the help of an engaged community. The non-profits also access beneficiaries with ease, quickly with community support.

Market Risks: No assurance of reaching target, intellectual property goes to public, undervaluing real costs, legal requirements, faulty platform technology.

Platform: The crowdfunding websites created and maintained by entrepreneurs in which transactions take place. Examples in Africa are Afrikstart and Miva Funding, and Indian examples are Faircent, Wishberry, and Catapooolt.

Chapter 8
A Comparative Analysis of Africa and Chinese Crowdfunding Markets

Innocent Chirisa
University of Zimbabwe, Zimbabwe

Liaison Mukarwi
Uinversity of Zimbabwe, Zimbabwe

ABSTRACT

This chapter compares the African and Chinese crowdfunding markets with a view to draw lessons from the two markets. China has a longer experience than Africa in the crowdfunding activities; crowdfunding processes in the country may not be directly applicable to the African states, but there are lessons that can be learnt by individual or group of African or Asian governments. These differing experiences identified can serve as a practical guide for urban development actors longing for sustainable funding for important urban development projects. In order to gather this data, the authors conducted a desktop review of literature, both grey and published being work on crowdfunding in Africa and China. Data collected were analysed using thematic content analysis. The chapter argues that the low adoption of crowdfunding by Africa can be attributed to a number of factors, including national regulatory environments that are not conducive for crowdfunding of equity and debt, and unconducive technological environments where e-commerce is not widely utilised.

INTRODUCTION

The future growth of Africa is not so dissimilar from that of Asia, especially China (Koch and Siering, 2015; Arvanitis, 2015). The urbanization of China represents the greatest demographic change witnessed in late 20th and early 21st century. Similarly, Africa's urbanization will be the largest shifts for the rest of this 21st century (Arvanitis, 2015). Given that Chinese context resemble the African context, there are a lot of lessons that can be drawn from China's growth initiatives to map Africa's growth trajectory. The potential for a demographic dividend is clear as witnessed from China. By 2050, the greater population

DOI: 10.4018/978-1-5225-3952-0.ch008

of Africa will be in urban areas and will be having greater share of the world's labor force (World Bank, 2015). This creates the potential for a rapid increase in the per capita incomes which is the demographic dividend given that both worker productivity and the share of the population that is employed increase. In the interest of a modesty growth in Africa, there is need for a deliberate investment in sustainable infrastructure, both soft and hard (ibid). However, funding is a challenge especially in development projects. Crowdfunding has been named to be an innovative funding mechanism that can assist most jurisdictions to harness the demographic dividend (Mollick, 2014). Crowdfunding involves the soliciting funds, in all amounts, from many people essentially via the internet. Wicks (2013:5) describes crowdfunding as an act where many people (crowd) support, financially, a development project through contributing small amounts of money either in return for a reward, equity or as a donation. This provides the much needed alternative to the traditional forms of finance required build sustainable infrastructure for sustainable urban development (ibid). It relies on social networking and uses the internet, through online platforms, to spread the word about a project or product that needs funding (ibid). In the past decade, crowdfunding has evolved into a billion dollar market. It is growing around 300 percent per year and is concentrated in North America and Europe, and rapidly rising in the Asian countries (The World Bank, 2015). The total crowdfunding market is composed of various subtypes, including lending (debt), equity, and royalty-based models, as well as non-securitised types, such as charitable donations and rewards crowdfunding (ibid).

Although the Chinese crowdfunding market is still small as compared to Europe or America, it is able to attract huge sums of funds through its various crowdfunding platforms. However, its growth is being slowed by the concerns of negativity and suspicion by the authorities in China fearing issues of illegal fundraising and foreign capital monitoring (China Impact Fund, 2014:2). In the world, Africa is the lowest performing crowdfunding markets. Despite this slow adoption, crowdfunding has been heralded as an opportunity to expand access to capital for projects. It has the potential to reach about 2.5 billion by 2025 (World Bank, 2015; Hui et al, 2014:1). In Africa, this challenge is compounded by several issues which are both political as well as the lack of breadth and depth of financial markets. Within this framework, crowdfunding comes as a new opportunity that can facilitate the transfer of funds from those who are looking to donate or invest to those in need of the capital (Pazowski and Czudec, 2014). It is understood that community-based financial solidarity and fundraising are an integral part of the African culture and traditions, pooling resources through crowdfunding seems viable. The pooling of funds in most African communities is customary where kinships through cultural ties support various social and economic projects in their local families and communities. This therefore makes it just a matter of time for Africans to take the opportunity to translate the traditional fundraising processes to online crowdfunding platforms (ibid). In this sense, it can be argued that crowdfunding is a viable alternative source of funding for development projects in the African continent.

This present chapter compares the African and Chinese crowdfunding markets with a view to drawing lessons from the two markets. Though the jurisdiction seems to be similar, the crowdfunding processes in China are not directly applicable to the African states and vice-versa but there are lessons that can be learnt by individual or group of African or Asian governments. This chapter is structured to include the following headings, Introduction, Literature Review, Methodology, Results and Discussion and, Conclusion and Recommendations.

LITERATURE REVIEW

The rapid growth of crowdfunding globally has led some in the development sector to see the crowd as a potential solution to the funding challenges faced by development agents when they try to serve the 'bottom of the pyramid (Cambridge Centre for Alternative Finance, 2017:5). To this end, there has been a global increase in the number of crowdfunding platforms because of the high demand for capital, the surge in mobile penetration, and the growing middle class (ibid).

Crowdfunding: An Overview

Crowdfunding originated from the word crowdsourcing (China Impact Fund, 2014:7). Crowdsourcing, as described by Howe (2003), is the process of taking a task traditionally performed by a designated internal agent or employee and give it to an undefined outside person or agent, in the form of an open call. In the above sense, crowdfunding is an open call to people to provide or contribute small amounts of money either in exchange for a reward or as a donation. In this way, those seeking funds appeal directly to the crowd for financing and investment, through the internet, thus sidestepping traditional financing systems like banks (China Impact Fund, 2014:7; Wicks, 2013:6). According to Freedman and Nutting (2015:1), in agreement with the above, crowdfunding is a way of collecting many small contributions from the crowd, through the use of online funding platforms, to finance projects or enterprises. In the United States of America, crowdfunding gained momentum in 2003 when a musician solicited funds for music digital recording. Crowdfunding started as a website where musicians sought donations from their fans to produce digital recordings. This method of fundraising evolved into a platform for financing films or video productions and photography as well as music.

Crowdfunding platforms sprung up making it possible for fund seekers to campaign or call-out to the people (crowd) appealing for funding detailing the incentives or rewards offered if it lending, reward or equity-based, and the needs if it is donation based. The platforms allow those seeking funds to pitch on the website charting how much money is needed, what it is needed for and what, if anything, one can get as a return for contributing (Pazowski and Czudec, 2014). The potential contributes (funders) can then browse the pitches/campaigns presented on the crowdfunding platform and get in touch with those looking for finance and other potential funders for decision making on whether or not they want to back the campaign (ibid). Upon being satisfied with the information got from the interaction, the potential funder then makes a decision on the same. According to China Impact Fund (2014), many of the crowdfunding platforms operate on an "All–or–Nothing" model. This model stipulates that if the targeted amount for each campaign is not realized within the targeted timeframe, the contributions made are then returned to the respective contributors and the financing process stops. The crowdfunding platforms are categorized into four types though there are variations that may exist for example hybrid models and those platforms that define themselves in a sectorial vertical not barely by the finance they provide (Wicks, 2013:6; Pazowski and Czudec, 2014). The categorization was precisely put by Pazowski and Czudec (2014:2) as shown on Table 1.

A brief description of the above-mentioned crowdfunding models is provided in the ensuing paragraphs.

Table 1. Models of crowdfunding

Type	Form of Contribution	Form of Return	Motivation of Funder
Donation Based Crowdfunding	Donation	Intangible benefits	Intrinsic and social motivation
Reward Based Crowdfunding	Donation / Pre-purchase	Rewards but also intangible benefits	Combination of intrinsic and social motivation and desire for reward
Crowdfunded Lending	Loan	Repayment of the loan with interest. Some socially motivated lending is interest-free	Combination of instinct social and financial motivation
Equity-Based Crowdfunding	Investment	Return on investment in time if the business does well. Rewards also offered sometimes intangible benefits another factor for many investors.	Combination of intrinsic, social and financial motivation

Source: Pazowski and Czudec (2014:2).

Donation Based Crowdfunding

The donation model of crowdfunding is a way of raising money for social or charitable projects from an online community appealed to donate to such projects (Pazowski and Czudec, 2014, 2012:3; Steinberg, 2012). This type of crowdfunding involves accumulations of donations of varying sums of money meant to support a specific cause or project for example drought relief, or fight against diseases like ebola, cholera or HIV. Sometimes, the funders will receive a "thank you" or a special mention or even a physical item such as a postcard in return of the donation. It is appreciated that the pledges made under this type of crowdfunding are donations and nothing is expected in return (Steinberg, 2012:3). Established charity organization usually mobilize these funds through their own websites. In most countries, donation-based crowdfunding is a critical pillar as it forms an alternative source of finance in cases of disasters, for example, the donations for fighting Ebola in Western Africa. In 2014, GlobalGiving, a non-profit donation-based crowdfunding platform, launched an Ebola Epidemic Relief Fund to court donors to voluntarily contribute directly to the Ebola relief efforts in West Africa (Crowdfund Insider, 2014). In this way, donors were afforded a chance to directly contribute their money to a project which they feel strongly that they can create an impact.

Reward Based Crowdfunding Model

Rewards-based crowdfunding is an attractive fundraising option for many small businesses or creative social and entrepreneurial projects (Steinberg, 2012). The model allows people to contribute to projects getting non–financial rewards as a return. The model operates in a tiered system that correlate rewards to the contributions; the more one donates the better the reward received (ibid). The model can be described as a reward costing the fundraiser little or a donation because the contribution far exceeds the monetary value of the reward (Pazowski and Czudec, 2014, 2012:3). In some instances, this is a presale agreement where the project owners crowdfund the cost of their project or product, and give the funders/donors a chance to be the first recipients of the product when the project is complete (ibid). The person or the company behind the crowdfunding campaign, set the donation amounts after determining the total amount of money needed for the successful implementation of the project. The donation amount, however, will come with the specific reward or incentive attached to it (Hui et al, 2014). After setting the above mentioned, the person behind scheme then pitches the project in need of funding on a crowdfunding platform clearly stipulating the amounts needed and the deadline for the donations. When the project has been pitched on the crowdfunding platform, the interested backers then donate to the project using the stipulated ways and sharing their views, activities, and progress on social media networks. The popular platforms that are operating the reward model include the Kickstarter and Indiegogo in USA and Peoplefund it in the UK.

Lending Based Crowdfunding Model

Crowdfunding platforms can offer lending possibilities to entrepreneurs and investors in those countries that allow it (Sosense, 2015). Lending Based crowdfunding is largely an evolution of the peer–to–peer lending model which was started by individual firms for example firm like Lending Club and Zopa (Pazowski and Czudec, 2014, 2012). Crowdfunded lending, unlike the traditional lending agreements, it cuts the institutional middle men with the effect of allowing the lenders an opportunity to choose the investments they want themselves. This also allows entrepreneurs to benefit from lower interest rates as compared to traditional loans given by banks (ibid). In this crowdfunding model, those people seeking debt appeal to the public through the crowdfunding platform by uploading their pitch which details the amount needed, the rewards to be earned and the deadline. Upon this being available on the platform, each of the interested member of the crowd takes a small chunk of the overall loan. It must be noted that some crowdfunding platforms focus on social causes and thus offer interest–free loans; a social lending model. In the social lending model, there are minimal or no interest at all. It can also be a forgivable loan where contributors can receive their money back only if the project has become profitable (Hui et al, 2014). On the other side, some crowdfunding investors operate the platforms as an investment, where the interest rates are decided by either those seeking the loan or the market interest rates. However, the downside of lending based crowdfunding is that the crowdfunding loans are not contract-based and thus there are no legal guarantees for either party in the process (ibid).

Investment-Based Crowdfunding Model

This model entails the use crowdfunding to invest in equity or profit share in businesses or projects (Hui et al, 2014; Sosense, 2015; Pazowski and Czudec, 2014). However, this model has been the slowest to grow because of regulatory restrictions. Crowd investment creates a platform for interested parties to receive profit share (equity) from the companies they support. The investors, using this model, can choose a project to fund based on potential. Essentially, the contributors buy shares that give them some form of control in the project (Pazowski and Czudec, 2014). In most instances, the investors contribute to the project through a purchase of a share of the profit to be realized. In this case, contributors do not have ownership rights but instead receive a financial reward in cases that the projects realize profits. However, it is a requirement that those behind the projects to be funded under this model craft a solid business plan since the crowd investor require the same. Also, the project initiators or owners must give the funders some decision-making power so that they can influence the decisions made by their shareholders (CCAF, 2017:5). The popular sites offering equity-based crowdfunding include Crowd Cube in UK and Symbid in Netherlands. Platforms like Quirky offer a revenue or profit–sharing model that allows the investor to capitalize on the success of the projects that he/she supports (ibid).

Challenges in Crowdfunding Markets

The crowdfunding markets have risks that can lead to the project founders or funders lose out. These risks form the challenges faced in crowdfunding markets. According to Kirby and Worner (20114:4), the key risk involved in crowdfunding markets include the following risk of default, risk of platform closure/failure, risk of fraud, risk of illiquidity (there is no secondary market thus investors can sell their participation), risk of cyber-attack and lack of transparency and disclosure of risks. There is a concern that insufficient scrutiny of the market would allow confusion and fraud in the crowdfunding market (ibid). In such markets, there is the danger of cross-jurisdictions which may affect the regulation of the activities. Some crowdfunding platforms are international, open to the world, thus introducing cross-border complexities on crowdfunding activities. The problems that may arise include the contract law enforcement which is complex to enforce across jurisdictions. This would require an understanding of the legal implications of cross-border operations before entering into the crowdfunding market (CCAF, 2017:5). Crowdfunding markets are also threatened by the risk of default and fraud. The risk of default/ investment failure in equity crowdfunding is projected to be around 50% (Mollick, 2014; Cheung et al, 2008). The anonymity that is created by the online aspect in the processes of equity crowd-funding increase the risk of fraud, for example, funds can be put to different use than what was is initially disclosed. In other cases, those behind the scheme 9creators of crowdfunding pitch) may also portray an idea that he/she doesn't own thus misleading the funders. Malicious crowdfunding platform creators use this process to gain access to a funder's personal and financial records, for example banking and credit card information, and use this information to defraud the sponsor (Cheung et al, 2008). Due to these possibilities, the crowdfunders are encouraged to do due diligence before giving their money. It is disheartening that a lot of times, the funders don't practice due diligence in the exercise. Moreso, because that there are no guarantees in the crowdfunding platforms, there are limited or no follow-up mechanisms where the crowdfunders can ask how their money was used or demand their promised rewards if the project owners choose to dishonor their promises (ibid).

The crowdfunding platforms have no protection of intellectual property that is if one pitches up information on an online crowdfunding platform which is patented he/she may lose the opportunity to patent it and the idea is open to being stolen by others (Nead, 2017). However, many of the creators or founders of projects who would be soliciting funds through the crowdfunding mechanism have no such knowledge thus they end up losing the rights to their proprietary information. The issue of ownership of ideas is not clear given that a project owner can use an idea put up by someone commenting on a certain product or service. Under these circumstances, the project owner does not acknowledge the commenter for the idea (ibid). The danger associated with this is that it could lead to a public relations meltdown that can spill into courts as it can create legal battles. The crowdfunding markets require efficient and effective regulation to curtail the above-mentioned risks (Mollick, 2014; Nead, 2017). However, there is the dilemma in regulating crowdfunding. Governments are caught in the midst because there danger that excessive regulation many ends up killing innovation and development that could benefit from this wild funding but also leaving it open creates other problems. In this sense, the funders or project creators must be aware of the risks involved in crowdfunding regardless of whether the governments are regulating it or not (Bijkerk, 2014:2). The regulatory frameworks can be in three forms, namely; prohibition, no prohibition but with high regulatory barriers to market entry inhibiting market growth and regulation can allow crowdfunding markets to grow but with stringent rules on who can invest, number of investors (backer or creator) allowed to invest, and the credibility and size of the creator or founder of the project (ibid).

Benefits of Crowdfunding

Crowdfunding involves financing of a project or venture by raising the required sum through small contributions from a lot of people (Hui et al, 2014). This act allows entrepreneurs, innovators, development actors, and business owners to use their social networks to mobilize capital for various activities and projects (ibid). Also, crowdfunding can be an efficient way of gathering important insights on any project idea. In some instances, the insights from the people around the world assist the project owners to refine their ideas and strategies with the aim of coming up with solutions that the community is looking for; sharing an idea online generates expert guidance on how ideas can improve it (World Bank, 2013:26). It can be taken as free, crowdsourced brainstorming. Crowdfunding is also another way of testing the public opinions on the project founder's idea. In this view, if people invest in that project this becomes a good sign that the idea has public acceptance and works well in the community (ibid). For entrepreneurs, crowdfunding promotes network marketing. The crowdfunded are the ambassadors of the project thus they help in marketing and promoting it through their own connections (Mollick, 2014).

Also, most importantly, crowdfunding gives access to easy capital of finance. It is understood that any idea requires financial resources to be a reality. Traditionally, urban development actors (including the public sector, semi-public, the private sector, citizens, households, NGOs, and other social groups) faced a long and difficult road to secure funding (Hui et al, 2014; Mollick, 2014; Cheung et al, 2008). The funding options included bank loans, development grants, borrowing from family members and friends and savings. However, the advent of crowdfunding provided an alternative source of funds to implement development or investment project basing on the support of the engaged community. It's more efficient than traditional fundraising (World Bank, 2013:27). The setting of crowdfunding campaigns is efficient and effective in getting the message to the right people as compared to loan finance or accredited investors. With the right platform, one can attract fast capital which could not be easily raised through the traditional means (ibid). On social return, crowdfunding allows sustainable funding of creative activities that achieve common purposes, for example, infrastructure development. Donation based approaches tend to target community-based project and relief projects, for example, the fund's mobilization fight hunger, diseases and or support war victims (Crowdfund Insider, 2014). This benefits the community socially by equipping the disadvantaged members of the community to rebuild their capacity in this world (ibid). Crowdfunding also proffers financial returns that encompass the return that accrues to those funders, for example, those invested in equity or loan based crowdfunding expect a positive financial return.

The Opportunities and Challenges of Crowdfunding in Africa and China

Crowdfunding has been a significant force for creative development in the United States of America and Europe. In this view, crowdfunding can also become an equally powerful force in propelling development in Africa. Crowdinvesting is a cost-efficient and less risky way of getting African projects successful through sustainable funding (Nead, 2017; Zhang et al, 2014; Aidid, 2017). Many of the diasporas perceive that there are fewer barriers in involving themselves in funding local projects than it is foreign land and thus they have an important role to play in promoting international investments in their locales for example in Africa or China (Aidid, 2017). The diasporas acknowledge that crowdinvesting in foreign projects require a greater leap of faith than investing at home. Crowdfunding, therefore, creates more ways of accessing capital to bankroll projects. Traditionally, urban actors would either borrow at fixed rates from banks or seek investment from established business communities (ibid). However, in Africa, access to credit is constrained due to various liquidity challenges. Banks are highly risk-averse thus the would-be borrowers often fail to meet the requirements to qualify for bank loans. This is also the case in China. According to Shira and Associates (2017), in China, start-ups and entrepreneurs have several difficulties in accessing loans finance, both from commercial banks and institutional investors. This is also increased by the fact that banks allocate a low percentage towards small entrepreneurs. The above-mentioned predicaments, therefore, create opportunities for the expansion of crowdfunding in these jurisdictions. Crowdfunding in these circumstances, therefore, enables those who want funding/ capital to appeal directly to supporters or potential customers without burdensome inquiries into their creditworthiness or incomes.

Recently, in China, there have been many new entries into the crowdfunding market. This is not only because of the massive potential of Chinese crowdfunding markets, but because of the high prevalence of smartphone use in China (Li, 2016; Ardeman, 2016). There are 650 million internet users in China, and of this total, 86% are accessing the internet through smartphones. Furthermore, there is also a marked increase in the use of electronic money, for example, Alipay has 350 million users, with WeChat Wallet, and Baidu Wallet among others vying for the same market share (Shira and Associates, 2017). Also, this the case in Africa. Given that crowdfunding is a digital mechanism, it is assumed that African crowdfunding can leverage on the increased use of mobile networks to transact (Aidid, 2017). The rapid expansion in African mobile technology penetration cannot be overemphasized but is a well-known fact. Indeed the people in Africa are using mobile phones for transactions that range from common purchases to peer-to-peer micro-lending (ibid). In Africa, even though there is less familiarity (and in certain cases, trust) on online fundraising as a capital-raising tool, the high prevalence of mobile phones presents an opportunity for modest increases in crowdfunding activities.

However, despite positive momentum within the crowdfunding markets, the markets in China have been rocked by serious allegations of fraud (Shira and Associates, 2017). Examples include the Ezubao case. Ezubao is an online finance company that offered fake investment products to nearly one million investors and pilfered over US$7.6 billion. In 2015, the online finance company was investigated, shut down, and discredited by local officials as a large Ponzi scheme (ibid). In this view, cases like the Ezubao highlight the need for oversight in what may one day be the world's largest crowdfunding market. This also gives a negative dent to the African crowdfunding market. In most African countries, crowdfunding is operating in an unregulated space (Aidid, 2017). The absence of regulation means an absence of adequate investor protections. This also gives rise to abuse, for example, MMM in Zimbabwe that fleeced many people of their hard earned money with no trace of those creators. Without the laws that protect privacy, mandate disclosures and ensure that contributors have room for legal redress, the crowdinvestors may not sufficiently trust the project owner for them to fund his or her venture. In the United States of America, for example, Title III of the JOBS Act in regulating equity crowdfunding, it permits companies to issue securities through crowdfunding platforms (ibid). Similar laws rules in African nations would enable the investors to make informed decisions and thus improve the crowd investor confidence. This can also mitigate the concerns about money laundering and fraud (Aidid, 2017; Shira and Associates, 2017; Nead, 2017). In this sense, African and Asian governments must enact clear laws on crowdfunding so that investors can have clarity on how to make their contributions legally (Aidid, 2017). In China, the regulations place higher requirements for prospective investors, it stipulates that investors must be accredited and the accreditation is highly burdensome (Shira and Associates, 2017).

METHODOLOGY

This study was a comparative study which sought to unravel the similarities and differences in two crowdfunding markets, one giant market (China) and a small but growing market (Africa), with the aim of deducing lessons for both markets. The study hypothesized that the first in the field may not be the best thus there would be a mutual learning experience. This inquiry was a desktop study which relied heavily on secondary data. The secondary data were collected from literature, both grey and published, and public documents. The study reviewed text books, journal articles, research thesis (published and unpublished) and conference papers to get insights of other researchers on crowdfunding in general and in China and Africa in particular. It also reviewed several websites of the organization or institutions in crowdfunding operating on a global scale or solely in the two jurisdictions under study. This was to get data on the experiences of these institutions in either providing crowdfunding services or regulating the practice. The two major sources gave deep insights crowdfunding experiences in China and in various African states. The data sought, which were mainly qualitative, were analyzed using discourse analysis and presented as texts and tables. These were packaged in themes under several headings and subheadings. The study undertook an extensive review of the crowdfunding sector in the two jurisdictions, Africa and China.

RESULTS AND DISCUSSION

The study sought to compare the crowdfunding markets in Africa and China with the aim of deducing learning points that can improve the African crowdfunding markets. This section presents the Chinese and African case and provides an abridged discussion noting the similarities, differences and areas of deficiency in policy or otherwise.

Crowdfunding: Case of China

Notwithstanding its relatively new presence, crowdfunding industry in China is already sizable and maintains exponential growth (Li, 2016:62). China is the world's second-largest regional market (after the US) for a financial return on crowdfunding (ibid). The crowdfunding markets in China are mobilizing a huge amount of money through the loans-based, rewards donations-based, and equity-based crowdfunding platforms (Zhang et al, 2014:2). However, the Chinese government viewed crowdfunding with negativity and suspicion due to concerns of illegal fundraising and a need for careful monitoring of foreign capital. This eased in recent years. Consequently, China witnessed an unprecedented growth in internet banking and or financing spanning to include online money transfers, equity crowd funding, peer-to-peer lending (loan-based crowdfunding), and online wealth management (Cheung et al, 2008:5). In 2011, after some years of rapid development, the first crowdfunding platform appeared in China. Since then, there was a tremendous increase in the number of various crowdfunding platforms in China that shot to 332 by the end of April 2016. Consequent to this rise in crowdfunding platforms in China, RMB 11.424 billion (about $101.69 billion) was successfully raised by crowdfunding platforms in 2015; a 305.1% growth from RMB 2.82 billion realized in 2014 (Li, 2016). This alternative finance market expanded from USD $5.56 billion in 2013 to $101.7 billion in 2015. While equity crowdfunding has a comparatively small market value than the other three major crowdfunding types (lending, donation-based, and reward-based) on a global scale, it is rather the mainstream crowdfunding practice in China through which the campaigners are often able to raise a larger amount of funds than other crowdfunding models. Equity-based crowdfunding is favored by capital in China.

The Chinese government acknowledges the strategic importance of providing access to capital for their economy and that internet finance is the way forward. The fast-paced atmosphere in crowdfunding and internet finance created a chaotic environment that had seen headlines have been peppered with acts of fraud and blatant incompetence by less respectable internet finance companies (Koch, 2015). Ezubao, is one of the widely known debacle, collapsed having fleeced billions from investors (Arvanitis, 2015). Allegedly 95% of the offers were considered fake (ibid). In this this light, the Chinese Government through it various agents that include the People's Bank of China (PBOC), the China Insurance Regulatory Commission (CIRC), the China Banking Regulatory Commission (CBRC), and the China Internet Information Technology Office (CIITO) jointly produced what they termed the "Guiding Opinions" with the aim of promoting a healthy development of internet or online finance (Zhang et al, 2014). This was the first step towards a more comprehensive regulation that was issued by the Chinese government to supervise internet finance and crowdfunding. The "Guiding Opinions" stipulated the general rules and governmental policy commitments, and specific measures that regulate internet finance including internet payment, online insurance services, online lending, equity crowd funding, internet fund sales and internet consumer finance (Nead, 2017; World Bank, 2015; Li, 2016).

These regulations, on equity crowdfunding, defined the role of a crowdfunding platform. They also stipulated the responsibilities of the crowdfunding platform regarding the investors and the creators. Most importantly, the regulation stated that a new platform should register with the Securities Association of China (SAC). In this way, the new platform becomes a member of the securities association. The set requirements for one to qualify as an accredited investor included investing at least RMB 1 million in a single project, having net assets of RMB 10 million or net assets of RMB 3 million and an average annual income of RMB 500,000 for the previous three years (Li, 2016). The key issue in regulations is the fact that an equity crowdfunding platform must be a legal Chinese company or a partnership enterprise with a bona fide Chinese company. In addition, it is also charged that the platform must have a minimum net assets of RMB 5 million (approximately £500,000) and have a specialist in equity crowdfunding. It is required, according to the regulations in China that the platforms must have at least two senior management staff who have at least three years of work experience in finance or IT. Furthermore, the platform should have a real-name authentication and must perform due diligence on both the entrepreneur and the investors. It is also a legal requirement that an equity-based crowdfunding platform cannot offer online lending service (ibid).

The growth of crowdfunding in China is largely attributed to technological advancement. Technology makes crowd-funding viable (Wei and Paul, 2014). China has the largest internet user base (ibid). This can be seen by the fact that crowdfunding has grown rapidly responding to the widespread use of mobile technology that promoted internet access. Crowdfunding platforms only started to grow substantively after the technological innovation of the web 2.0 applications that made use and access more easy and available to the general populace (Shen, 2016). The web 2.0 represents technological change and innovation that allowed internet users to the creation of content that can be hosted on websites (ibid). The technology allowed one to capture the "wisdom of the crowds" in website design and software development; all this assisted in coming up with crowdfunding platforms palatable to the users. This leap in technology created the means to promote online peer-to-peer lending and or equity crowdfunding websites. This made crowdfunding viable by reducing the cost and time of transactions involved in crowdfunding (Li, 2016). This website architecture stimulated user participation by enabling the borrowers to create profiles which they can upload pictures and descriptions of how they will use the money raised from each crowdfunding pitch made (ibid). The technological advancement provided the capacity to online platforms to create a social-networking environment where the borrower or issuers voluntarily provide information to potential investor or lenders in a socially interactive way. This also cut the cost and time involved in raising finance for projects; online platforms are convenient for both the issuer and the funder. In addition to increasing the potential to reach many people on using the platforms, it provides both investment opportunity seeking and capital raising facilities.

Crowdfunding: The African Context

The developing countries of Africa are the lowest performing crowdfunding markets globally (World Bank, 2015:1). In 2015, crowdfunding market in the African was projected to have totaled about $70 million, constituting about less than half a percent of the crowdfunding activity globally (ibid). Although crowdfunding is still at its nascent stage in Africa, it can be seen that it is on the rise. To date, Africa hosts over 57 active crowdfunding platforms with targeted to raise more than $126.9 million in 2015 (AppsAfrica, 2016). The African region has the donation-based crowdfunding activity topping the list and equity-based crowdfunding platforms still in the development phase as seen in countries like Kenya, Ghana, and South Africa (World Bank, 2013:19). South Africa is leading country in the African crowdfunding hosting about 21 active platforms. Nigeria follows up with a total of 9 operational platforms (Afrikstart, 2016:9). Africa-based crowdfunding platforms managed to raise money estimated at US$32.3 million in 2015 despite operating in an environment marred by low internet use, poor social media use, and limited funds transfer and or payment solutions (AppsAfrica, 2016). The funds mobilized were mainly directed to business start-ups and SMEs (about $17.7 million), real estate projects (about US$13.6 million), travel trips (about US$319,434), and donations to social and charity projects (about US$307,860) (ibid). It can be seen that Africa-based crowdfunding platforms mainly specialize in promoting crowdfunding campaigns related to social causes (31.5% of the total platforms), business and entrepreneurship projects (21%), and then creative and innovative projects (17.5%) (Afrikstart, 2016:1).

In Africa alone, over $250 million was raised via various alternative finance channels in the period 2013-15, and East Africa was the largest alternative finance regional market across Africa in the same period. It seems there is a material and fast-growing market opportunity for East African economies to engage in crowdfunding. A case can be seen from the Kenya as is presented in Box 1.

As can be noted from Box 1, for crowdfunding to gain momentum across Africa, and to reach its market potential, it must be relieved from its current technological, cultural, and regulatory constraints and barriers (World Bank, 2013; 2015; Cheung et al, 2008). Africa has low internet penetration which its usage stood at 29% across Africa in 2015 (Afrikstart, 2016:20). For one to access the crowdfunding platforms, he/she must have internet access thus this low internet penetration affects negatively the expansion of crowdfunding markets in Africa. The crowdfunding platforms operating in Africa need to increase their websites traffic to get greater exposure to their crowdfunding projects, and to drive potential

Box 1. Crowdfunding in Kenya

In 2015, around $22 million was raised in Kenya, with an additional $8.5 million raised in the first quarter of 2016. This suggests the market is rapidly growing (at a rate of well over 50% year-on-year), albeit from a low base point. Donation-based crowdfunding accounts for around two-thirds of market activity, with the rest provided by non-financial return-based lending models, such as Kiva. It is likely that most funding comes from funders outside of Kenya, given the location of platforms providing funding. Peer-to-peer business and consumer lending and equity-based crowdfunding are seemingly non-existent, or at least only, just beginning to emerge at present. This is despite the fact that both debt and equity-based crowdfunding account for the largest proportion globally. Given Kenya's track record with innovative financial services, such as with mobile money and payments, and various microfinance models, we anticipate that Kenya, and East Africa more broadly, will be a hot bed of innovative alternative financial services.

Currently, no existing legislation that regulates donation, rewards, loan or equity-based crowdfunding in Kenya. The crowdfunding is regulated by laws or policies meant for various other facets of the economic not specifically meant for crowdfunding. Platforms offering crowdfunding services by sending information over communication systems through short-code services will need to be licensed as Communication Services Providers (CSPs) by the Communications Authority of Kenya. If a platform offering crowdfunding services provides notifications and alerts in connection with the crowdfunding products that it offers, the platform will need to be licensed as an Applications Service Provider (ASP). If the platform will not operate a communications infrastructure in Kenya but has servers located outside of Kenya, and if the platform is web-based and does not provide any alerts or notifications, it may be arguable that the platform will not require either a CSP or an ASP license. If the platform is deposit-taking, the provisions of the Microfinance Act (MA) Act will apply to it. If the platform is defined as a 'specified' non-deposit-taking microfinance institution, it is unclear whether it would require a license under the MA Act, as the relevant regulation has yet to be implemented in Kenya. Under the proposals set out in the Public Fundraising Appeals Bill (2014), a license will be required prior to collecting money through a fundraising system. The Public Fundraising Appeals Bill (2014) establishes elaborate licensing procedures to adequately vet fundraising appeals before being made public. Although not explicitly set out in legislation, the various policies of Kenya have the ability to endorse new crowdfunding models in the absence of strict governing legislation.

Adapted from Cambridge Centre for Alternative Finance (CCAF) (2017:29-31)

project backers to come to their website to fund these projects (World Bank, 2013; 2015). The above said is only possible through increased internet usage in Africa, alongside great digital marketing strategies from crowdfunding platforms. Hopefully, mobile broadband internet in Africa is set to increase as the coverage of 3G or 4G networks expands across Africa, more local content is created, and a range of new apps are being developed; all this will promote growth in crowdfunding as the project founders would reach a wider range of funders (Afrikstart, 2016:22). The low internet penetration also translates to the low social media usage. Since crowdfunding requires building strong online social media presence for projects to be funded, increased social media penetration across Africa is a prerequisite for crowdfunding to succeed in Africa and currently, it is very low (ibid).

Payment systems impact platform choice. Limited funds transfer and payments solutions are affecting the growth of the crowdfunding markets. For example, the credit cards transactions cannot be used in all African countries, and Paypal is only available in 40 countries in Africa hence the African crowdfunding platforms have a small local pool of potential contributors (World Bank, 2015:2). Besides, many Africans are not used to make online payments. Hence, processing payments online comes as a real challenge for many crowdfunding platforms. Payments via mobile phones have come as a relief for some platforms. Other crowdfunding portals circumvent the problem by allowing the crowdfunding project creator to process offline payments through in-country wire transfer, by check or cash exchange, in order make it easier for people in Africa to back projects. There is poor regulation in African crowdfunding market. There is currently no legal and regulatory framework, similar to the JOBS Act that was enacted in the USA, which sets the crowdfunding rules in any African country (Afrikstart, 2016:20). Most crowdfunding platforms are currently operating out of any crowdfunding regulation, unless they opted for a license as a financial services or a registered credit provider. The absence of regulation limits the expansion of equity-based or debt-based crowdfunding platforms in Africa, as it deters potential investors to pool their money in platforms in which they have no basic investors' protection rights and clear exit strategies (World Bank, 2015). The African Crowdfunding Association (ACfA) was founded in 2015 to lobby actively on creating a legal framework (Afrikstart, 2016:22).

There is serious lack of awareness about crowdfunding. Although fundraising among local communities and families is deeply entrenched in the African culture, translating the process online is still a novelty for many Africans (World Bank, 2013; 2015). For crowdfunding to expand in Africa, it requires promotion, education, and addressing mistrust from the general public. Many Africans lack of awareness about this alternative source of funding that has potential to democratize access to capital. Furthermore, some Internet-based solutions that involve online money payments are sometimes viewed as fraud or scams. Thus, building trust around online fundraising is paramount (World Bank, 2015). It can easily be achieved as crowdfunding is a relatively transparent process where all projects are displayed online, the project creator profile is verified, and funders can be identified when they back a project, as long as they opt to do so. Educating and mentoring crowdfunding project creators to craft compelling crowdfunding campaigns -with great videos, storytelling, and marketing- are also key success drivers for crowdfunding to take a strong foothold in Africa (ibid). Finally, the level of financial literacy among Africans will drive or slow the adoption of equity-based or debt-based crowdfunding platforms in Africa.

Synthesis of the Results

The Chinese and African markets, by virtue of their differences in economic growth, they resemble grave differences. However, it must not be construed that these markets are different or can be different, they are following the same path but only are at different stages of developments. As countries are growing economically, they are on the verge of trying new innovative financing models powered by technology. The noted differences can be summarized on Table 2.

Table 2. A cross-examination of the Chinese and African crowdfunding markets

Issue	Chinese Crowdfunding Market	African Crowdfunding Markets
Main Crowdfunding Model	Equity-Based Crowdfunding	Donation and Reward Based Crowdfunding
Regulation	Fairly regulated (has regulations in place specifically for crowdfunding)	Not adequately legislated (regulated by allied acts and policies which act as a disincentive to its growth)
Crowdfunding Platforms	Many local crowdfunding platforms	Few crowdfunding platforms and of those few, many are hosted outside Africa
Payment systems	Effective mobile banking, internet banking, PayPal and Credit Card systems	• Mobile Banking • Low internet banking, PayPal and Credit Card systems
Investment Security	• High securitization of investment through Securities Association of China (SAC) • Active anti cyber-attack initiatives, laws and detection technologies	• Growing securitization of investment through Financial Market laws • Growing anti-cyber initiatives, enacting laws and acquiring cyber-attack detection technologies
Awareness	High awareness of crowdfunding	Low awareness of crowdfunding
Internet Access as a tool for effective crowdfunding	• High internet use base • High social media user base	• High internet use base • High social media user base
Government Policy	Supportive through regulation	Mostly not supportive, no deliberate policies to promote nor regulate in many African countries

Source: Authors (2017).

As shown on table 2, it can be appreciated that Africa is still a long way to go to boost crowdfunding as an alternative financing source. This is from a view that Africa is still lagging in terms of technology use in general and internet in particular. Regulation for internet banking has not been enacted neither had confidence bestowed in the crowd that it is a viable financing model as compared to the traditional a funding channel (like banks or trust). As for China, the measures instituted are overly cautious and very difficult to enforce. It has been postulated by Li (2016) that the regulators or rather the governments must focus on promoting effective disclosure and securities from the project initiators or crowdfunding founders so as to give full and better information for effective crowdfunding decisions. It has also been charged that, China has high entry thresholds for one to qualify as a crowdfunding platform, crowdfunding measures like these are essentially analogy to private equity funds (ibid). This is an indication that the authorities are failing to acknowledge equity crowdfunding as an innovative financing model. As such, the regulators must carefully review the crowdfunding founder qualifications and promote crowds to participate through their contributions to promote rapid growth of equity crowdfunding as a true new alternative for fundraising for development initiatives.

Overall, in the two markets, it can be seen that crowdfunding has the potential of funding huge urban development needs. Crowdfunding can assist in the funding of the development of infrastructure like roads, sewer and water reticulation and even social housing schemes in the growing economies, which today are facing serious economic challenges that have led to dilapidation and inadequacy of the same. This is noble considering that international development finance has dwindled. Before crowdfunding urban development actors depended on loan, searching for grants, pitching venture capitalists or tapping into their savings. Crowdfunding, however, provides a method to obtain the funds needed to launch an idea quickly and with the support of an engaged community. It's more efficient than traditional fundraising (World Bank, 2013:27). With the right platform, one can attract fast capital which could not be easily raised through the traditional means (ibid). In Africa, this also presents a good opportunity for supporting urban development given a crop of populist governments in the same. Populist governments have squandered resources meant for meaningful development at the expense of pleasing the electorate, for example, in Zimbabwe, the scraping of all municipal bills owed by residents to the council through a ministerial directive towards the 2013 harmonized elections. This affected the smooth operation of municipalities up to now.

FUTURE RESEARCH DIRECTIONS

This chapter revealed that crowdfunding is a necessary tool in spearheading urban development thus there is a need for policy changes by governments to promote greater acceptance of this particular form of funding among laypeople. This promises massive returns for the African community. The need for facilitation of the African crowdfunding market development cannot be overemphasized. Capacity building involving boosting the crowdfunding regulator capacity, enhancing technological prowess of Africans and awareness building among the urban development actors is critical. The crowdfunding trust-building initiatives that involve the creation of regulations that regulate and supervise the market to avoid abuse of the funds are equally important. Research and development in crowdfunding is an important tool to advance sustainable practice (of crowdfunding) in urban development. In this interest, it is crucial for both markets, China and Africa, to interrogate how technology can spearhead or hinder this noble cause, understanding issues of cyber-attacks and how accountability can be promoted especially on donation-based crowdfunding. It is understood that, though Africa is rapidly urbanizing, it is mostly rural thus there is a need to analyze how the rural people and communities can be embraced and benefit from crowdfunding, removing the urban bias in the process. The rural-urban divide promotes digital divide thus there is a need for innovative ways of eradicating these disparities. There is a need for an analysis of how the youth can be mainstreamed in this noble cause; equity-based programming and policies for youths will help determine whether African youths can transform the continent and break vicious cycles of poverty and inequality.

CONCLUSION AND RECOMMENDATIONS

There are two forces that promote crowdfunding. The widespread use of information and communication technology (ICT) as it provides the infrastructure to appeal to millions of investors locally and abroad, and the social acceptance of technology-enabled social networks that allow investors to interact with people online and build trust among people with whom they may have few traditional connections. Combined, these two forces can push crowdfunding to grow as successful funding mechanism for economic, physical and social development projects. The study revealed that the experiences in China and African contexts are in the same direction but at different levels of maturity or growth. The African context is still growing to be a giant market as is in China. China is taking a lead in crowdfunding owing to the rampant growth in technologies which is a key to crowdfunding. Africa is still growing technologically hence the low adoption of crowdfunding. Countries like Zimbabwe are still to craft cyber-laws which is one pointer to the low but growing use of the internet. Overall, the study recommends the facilitation of the African crowdfunding markets through the capacity building that involves boosting crowdfunding regulatory frameworks, enhancing the technological prowess of Africans and awareness building among the urban development actors. There is a need for creation of regulations that regulate and supervision the market to avoid abuse of the funds; this builds trust and confidence in the market. The governments are key in supporting or endorsing the crowdfunding schemes. This can be through a transparent regulatory processes. There is a need for research and development in crowdfunding as an important tool to advance sustainable practice (of crowdfunding) in urban development.

Specific strategies to drive crowdfunding can be categorized into four, including economic, technological, social and cultural. Economically, the government can craft securities regulations that allow easy registration for equity offerings, strategically tie crowdfunding to patriotic and cultural messages, and form a crowdfunding market alliance. Socially, there is need to harness top social media experts or bloggers to communicate with local and diaspora audiences, hold media and educational events to build awareness and understanding and hold regular crowdfunding events with trusted third parties to teach successful techniques. This builds the capacity of the funders (crowd). Technologically, where appropriate, the African countries must apply lessons learned from the developed world, considering the buy, build or white label to determine gaps in existing technology for online financial transactions. The people must be technologically able to transact or understand risks associated with online transactions. This is reinforced by an effective cyber regulation to protect the funders and founders. Culturally, there is need to leverage existing incubator/accelerator/structured co-working spaces as hubs for innovation in funding, foster professional investor and consumer confidence in crowdfunding through education and communication and encouraging the participation of women and girls.

REFERENCES

Afrikstat. (2016). *Fundraising goes Digital in Africa: The emergence of Africa-Based Crowdfunding Platforms*. London: Afrikstart.

Aidid, A. (2017). *Crowdfunding in Africa: Opportunities and Challenges.* Accessed 08/07/17 from https://www.natlawreview.com/article/crowdfunding-africa-opportunities-and-challenges

Appsafrica. (2016). *Crowdfunding in Africa is gaining momentum.* Accessed 20/05/17 at https://www.appsafrica.com/crowdfunding-in-africa-is-gaining-momentum/

Ardeman, D. (2016). *Why Chinese equity crowdfunding is taking its lead from the UK – and what challenges the sector faces.* Accessed 20/05/17 at http://www.cityam.com/money/crowdfunding

Arvanitis, Y. (2015). Financing for innovation: What can be done for African SMEs? *AEB*, *6*(6), 1–8.

Bijkerk, W. (2014). *Risks and Benefits of Crowd-funding*. Tokyo: International Organisation of Securities Commissions.

Cambridge Centre for Alternative Finance (CCAF). (2017). *Crowdfunding in East Africa: Regulation and Policy for Market Development: Reducing poverty through financial sector development.* London: Cambridge Centre for Alternative Finance.

Cambridge Centre for Alternative Finance (CCAF). (2017). *The Africa and Middle East Alternative Finance Benchmarking Report.* London: Cambridge Centre for Alternative Finance.

Cheung, C. M., Lee, M. K., & Rabjohn, N. (2008). The impact of electronic word-of-mouth. *Internet Research*, *18*(3), 229–247. doi:10.1108/10662240810883290

Insider, C. (2014). *GlobalGiving is Raising Funds for Ebola Epidemic Relief.* Accessed 17/05/17 from https://www.crowdfundinsider.com/2014/08/47495-globalgiving-raising-funds-ebola-epidemic-relief/

Koch, J., & Siering, M. (2015). Crowdfunding Success Factors: The Characteristics of Successfully Funded Projects on Crowdfunding Platforms. *ECIS 2015 Completed Research Papers,* Paper 106.

Li, J. (2016). Equity Crowdfunding in China: Current Practice and Important Legal Issues. *The Asian Business Lawyer*, (18). Accessed 20/05/17 at https://ssrn.com/abstract=2842752

Mollick, E. (2014). The dynamics of crowdfunding: An exploratory study. *Journal of Business Venturing*, *29*(1), 1–16. doi:10.1016/j.jbusvent.2013.06.005

Nead, N. (2017). *Nine Risks Associated with Crowdfunding.* Accessed 17/05/17 from http://crowdfund.co/nine-risks-associated-with-crowdfunding/

Pazowski, P., & Czudec, W. (2014). *Economic Prospects and Conditions of Crowdfunding.* Paper presented to the Management, Knowledge and Learning International Conferences, Portoroz, Slovenia.

Shen, E. (2016). *China Equity Crowdfunding Market Research Report 2016 is issued; —Equity-for-Feel Model is Popular among Platforms.* Accessed 21/05/17 at http://en.pedaily.cn/Item.aspx?id=220799

Shira & Associates. (2017). *The Growing Potential of Crowdfunding in China.* Accessed 08/07/17 from https://www.eastwestbank.com/ReachFurther/News/Article/The-Growing-Potential-of-Crowdfunding-in-China

Sosense. (2015). *5 Crowdfunding models you should know*. Accessed 17/05/17 from https://www.sosense.org/5-crowdfunding-models-know/

Steinberg, S. (2012). *The Crowdfunding Bible: How to Raise Money for any Start-up, Video Game, Or Project*. New York: Overload Entertainment, LLC.

Wei, L., & Paul, M. (2014). China's Central Bank Leads Effort to Regulate Internet Finance. *WSJ*. Accessed 21/05/17 at http://online.wsj.com/news/articles/SB10001424052702303874504579376111028523376

Wicks, M. (2013). *Crowdfunding: An introduction*. Victoria: Blue Beetle Books Inc.

World Bank. (2013). *Doing Business 2014: Smarter Regulations for Small and Medium-Size Enterprises*. Washington, DC: World Bank Group.

World Bank. (2013). *Crowdfunding's Potential for the Developing World*. Washington, DC: World Bank.

World Bank. (2015). *Crowdfunding in Emerging Markets: Lessons from East African Startups*. Washington, DC: World Bank.

Zhang, T., Yip, C., Wang, G., & Zhang, Q. (2014). *China Crowdfunding Report: How to Leverage Crowdfunding to Support China's Social and Environmental SGBs*. Beijing: China Impact Fund.

KEY TERMS AND DEFINITIONS

Africa: The world's second-largest and second-most-populous continent.

China: A populous nation in East Asia whose vast landscape encompasses grassland, desert, mountains, lakes, rivers. It is the second largest economy in the world.

Crowdfunder: A member of the crowd or public who contributes towards a crowdfunding project.

Crowdfunding: A practice of generating capital investments or funds for a project, cause, or enterprise by acquiring funds from many individuals.

Crowdfunding Market: A medium that allows crowdfunding entrepreneurs and funders to interact in order to facilitate an exchange of the funds.

Crowdfunding Platform: A website created for the purpose of advertising a crowdfunding project.

Internet: Means of connecting a computer to other computers anywhere in the world via dedicated routers and servers.

Regulation: A rule of order having the force of law, prescribed by a superior or competent authority, relating to the actions of those under the authority's control.

Regulatory Capacity: The ability of a responsible authority to make rules and enforce the rules relating to the actions of those under that authority's control.

Social Media: Includes websites and applications that enable users to create and share content or to participate in social networking.

Technology: The branch of knowledge that deals with the creation and use of technical means and their interrelation with life, society, and the environment drawing upon such subjects as industrial arts, engineering, applied science, and pure science.

Urban Development: The positive change or improvement in the socio-economic, environmental, and physical facets of an urban area.

Chapter 9
Crowdsourcing as a Tool for Improving Learning in Tertiary Institutions in Developing Countries

Indo Benna
Mohammed AlMana College of Health Sciences, Saudi Arabia

ABSTRACT

Higher education in many developing countries faces the triple challenges of inadequate funding, need to improve quality of learning outcomes, and the pressure to increase quality of graduates. Crowdsourcing offers opportunity for institutions to face these problems with little resource expenditure. The chapter describes/analyzes how crowdsourcing can be applied in curriculum and teaching material development activities through collaborative efforts of higher education institutions from different parts of the world to develop suitable curriculum for teaching English for specific purpose. The chapter analyzes the process and the evaluates the outcome of the crowdsourcing tool and suggests that its application can keep higher education institutions in developing countries in forefront of education and research innovation, and prepares members in these institutions for innovative problem solving and for the challenges of the online world.

1. INTRODUCTION

There are many issues facing higher education, among them are the need to improve quality with increased intake, but with dwindling means for internal resources mobilization and for tapping from the global community of educators. The key challenge is the design and implementation of collaborative educational programs that integrate the students' culture and background as well as the anticipated future workplace demands. The discussion on how higher education is using or can use the emerging new tools such as crowdsourcing to achieve its broadening objectives with limited resources through collaboration seems to be muted and needs exposure to a wider community involved in the various sectors of higher

DOI: 10.4018/978-1-5225-3952-0.ch009

education, whose resources and opinions can be tapped relatively quickly and inexpensively (Sharma 2011). Additionally, while crowdsourcing is frequently discussed in terms of the power of a massive and anonymous public (Estellés-Arolas 2012), however its techniques are also being applied to smaller, more specialized audiences. This application to more specialized or more specific audiences seems to be a gap in academic research that needs to be highlighted.

Careful exploitation of the opportunities offered by these two types of crowds, a crowdsourcing project can be used to create culturally suitable English for Specific Purpose (ESP) curriculum for higher education. In practice, however, there are many other benefits as well. For example, many communities or institutions have used it as a strategy for numerous new digital projects that aim to create or strengthen community spirit around and through crowdsourcing projects. Well-designed crowdsourcing tools endeavor to point out the value added to the project by each participant to the project as a whole.

This chapter seeks to explore how crowdsourcing can be used to develop and implement educational program that integrates the students' culture and background as well as their projected workplace demands. Progressively narrowing the scope of the study, its background is focused on the review of the growth and development of ESP in the Middle East, as good example of active regions of the developing world.

The chapter is divided into five main sections. After this introductory part, the next section explores the growth and development of ESP and crowdsourcing in the Middle East context. The third section explains the process of ESP curriculum development based on the Middle East using both theory and practice to produce curriculum components. In the fourth section, the evaluation and application processes of the developed curriculum are discussed. Finally, the direction of future research and the conclusion drawn from the experience are presented.

2. GROWTH OF ESP AND CROWDSOURCING IN THE MIDDLE EAST

English for Specific Purposes (ESP) and crowdsourcing are emerging strategies that are increasingly being used to achieve desired policy goals, including higher education. Higher education is a knowledge-based industry that needs an inflow of ideas and innovative ways of doing things - including those provided by ESP and crowdsourcing- in order to increase its own efficiency and productivity. In this section, we shall discuss the growth of ESP first and then explore the role of crowdsourcing on higher education in the Middle East.

- **ESP and Its Growth:** By way of providing a background to the growth of ESP, this section briefly explores its form, approach and rationale using the available literature and then identifies the major growth factors.

The primary focus of ESP focuses on language context rather than on teaching syntax and language structures (Lorenzo, 2005). In this sense, ESP is considered different from English language teaching in that it focuses on outcome rather than language syntax (Dudley-Evans and St. John 1998). Because of the diversity of global socio-economic activities Belcher (2004) observes that ESP increasingly encompasses a diversifying and expanding range of purposes. Regarding its teaching method, ESP bases all decisions with respect to content and method on the learner's reason for learning (Hutchinson and Waters 1987).

However, a definition of ESP, as Dudley-Evans (1998) maintains, 'requires much more than an acknowledgment of the importance of needs analysis.' This suggests that there are additional features or characteristics that are central to ESP. In his extended definition of ESP, Dudley-Evans and St John (1998) proposed a definition of ESP with characteristics grouped into absolute and variable types as presented in Table 1.

- **ESP Growth Factors:** The growth of ESP may be attributable to a combination of a number of important factors, some of which are the following:

First, as Table 2 shows, English is important due to its emergence as the global lingua franca (Chan, 2017) triggered by the growing influence of globalization. In a recent study, it constituently was first in geographic spread, in application in the areas of economy, communication, knowledge, media and diplomacy. While languages with colonial spread –such as English, French and Spanish- benefited from the historic adventure, the rise of Mandarin may be associated with the recent performance of China in the areas of the economy, communication, as well as in knowledge and media.

Most of the development of ESP was influenced by the old style globalization, which is gradually giving place to a new form. The emerging form of the globalization is affected by geopolitical and technological transformations which are reshaping the economic, business, and political models of the old form of globalization, creating a completely different system with the following new features that are bound to influence changes in ESP programs.

- **The New Economic System:** Instead of the unipolar world, the global economy is growing more multipolar, with growing number of regional economic growth poles. The emerging growth centers are becoming important centers of diverse activities including cultural and language development.
- **The New Business System:** Growing protectionism, changing production costs around the world, emerging new industries are slowing growth in trade and international investment. These factors are dispersing worldwide supply chains, while on the rise in digital systems are integrating regional businesses and activities. The global decentralization and regional integration of businesses are bound to have the impact of ESP use and learning.
- **The New Political System:** Global economic transformations are triggering political changes whereby national political interests are over riding global political concerns. However, international and regional political issues such as digital security, terrorism and money laundering are forcing nations toward collaborative actions, which may influence the future development of ESP.

Table 1. Absolute and variable ESP characteristics

ESP Characteristics	
Absolute Characteristics	**Variable Characteristics**
• Defined to meet specific needs of the learner • Related to or designed for specific disciplines • Makes use of the underlying methodology and activities of the discipline it serves • Centered on the language (grammar, lexis), skills, discourse and genres appropriate to these activities.	• Uses, in specific teaching situations, a different methodology from that of General English • Designed for adult learners, either at a tertiary level institution or in a professional work situation, and could also be for learners at secondary school level • Generally designed for intermediate or advanced students; • Assumes some basic knowledge of the language system, but it can be used with beginners.

Source: Dudley-Evans & St John (1998: 4-5).

Table 2. Ranking of global languages efficacy based on five domains

RANK	SCORE	LANGUAGE	NATIVE (MM)	GEOGRAPHY	ECONOMY	COMMUNI-CATION	KNOWLEDGE & MEDIA	DIPLOMACY
1	0.889	English	446.0	1	1	1	1	1
2	0.411	Mandarin*	960.0	6	2	2	3	6
3	0.337	French	80.0	2	6	5	5	1
4	0.329	Spanish	470.0	3	5	3	7	3
5	0.273	Arabic	295.0	4	9	6	18	4
6	0.244	Russian	150.0	5	12	10	9	5
7	0.191	German	92.5	8	3	7	4	8
8	0.133	Japanese	125.0	27	4	22	6	7
9	0.119	Portuguese	215.0	7	19	13	12	9
10	0.117	Hindi*	310.0	13	16	8	2	10

If all Chinese dialects/languages (Mandarin being the largest) are considered as one it would not change the rank ordering. However, if Urdu and Hindi – and all the Hindi dialects – are taken as one it would vault it past Portuguese and Japanese.

Source: Chan, 2017

Second, the tremendous development in all scientific, technical and economic activities on an international level required an international language that meets the needs of both the experts and the learners.

Third, in language institutes, a revolution in linguistics has helped to redirect the focus, the form and mechanics of the language to its actual use in daily communication in ways that the language curriculum can be designed to meet different and specific contexts.

Fourth, it appears that emerging developments in the field of educational psychology has influenced the growth of ESP by stressing the vital role of learners, their inspirations and needs so that curricula for the language courses consider them.

These factors created a new generation of learners of English language, learners who not only wanted to learn but were more significantly aware of why and how they would use it in their daily activities in such fields as commerce, economy, medicine, finance and engineering. Through this emerged English for Specific Purposes (ESP). Because of its global situation in the areas of crude oil sales and related financial flows, international commerce, huge spending in education, the Middle East has become an important global region in ESP growth and development.

- **ESP Research in the Middle East With a Focus on Saudi Arabia:** Arabic is the official language of most countries in the Middle East, although in most technology-oriented higher institutions this rule is relaxed to allow the official use of English as the medium. While relatively elevated at the university level, however, English teaching and learning has been given limited importance at the other levels of the educational system both by the authorities and students, who seem to study it only in order to go through examinations.

There are signs that there is a renewed interest in the region as the example of Saudi Arabia shows. According to Rahman & Alhaisoni (2013), the importance of English language has risen rapidly due to the increased worldwide demand for English and its recognition as the language of 'science and technology, business and commerce' as well as its global spread. The authors suggest that English is accepted as one of the important subjects in the school system of the Kingdom and is afforded that official recognition.

This point seems to be supported by the growing crop of literature on a range of ESP issues expressed in the last five years. Just to illustrate some of these issues, Ahmed (2012) has set out a theoretical framework on the growing demand for ESP in Saudi Arabian higher education. Saleh &Elyas (2015) focuses on ESP for linguistic analysis of Qur'anic Surah to help recent convert to Islam and Javid discusses the unusual role of students, teachers and teaching methods in response to the needs of growing ESP programs. While Koci (2016) emphasizes that students' needs analysis are vitally important in the development of ESP, Alsamani (2016) provides a conceptual framework for incorporating computer students' project assignment into ESP program, and Younes & Albalawi (2016) identifies ESP speaking needs for business students. More recently Fadel & Rajab (2017) study the English language needs of the female students in Computing and Information Technology.

The key findings of other similar studies may be summarized as follows: First, on the communicative needs of health professionals Alharby (2005) finds that the curriculum of English language course at the college level was not adequately defined in terms of the medical students' future occupational needs. The context of the medical field requires a high level of English communicative skills since these professionals deal with patients' lives. Communication skills literally have "life or death" consequences.

Second, regarding the effectiveness of ESP course for business administration by Liton (2012) reveals that the existing ESP Course syllabus is not tailored appropriately according to the students' needs in the workplace. It, therefore, suggests that ESP course should be redesigned in assimilating the learners' real needs in the job field and teacher-centered traditional ESP classes need to be replaced by the learner-centered task-based language teaching (TBLT) and communicative approach as a teaching technique.

Third, on the suitability of courses to students' needs and attitudes, Abdalla (2013) shows that the majority of respondents indicated that their needs for studying ESP course rest with the four language skills of listening, speaking, reading and writing together with grammar and vocabulary. Fourth, about the evaluation of the effectiveness of using ESP course for Preparatory Year Program (PYP) students by Al Fraidan (2012), referring to the two books they were using finds that both books would be appropriate if they are merged and additional materials included to form suitable ESP teaching material. Fifth, on the effectiveness of using ESP course for PYP students, Younes& Albalawi (2016) reveals that the existing ESP Course syllabus is custom-made to properly fit the students' needs in the workplace. It recommends that ESP courses should be re-structured to integrate the learners' culture and background.

Crowdsourcing and the Social Networking

Many researchers date the growth of crowdsourcing in the Middle East to the time when an informal trader called Mohamed Bouazizi, set himself on fire on December 17th, 2010 in protest of harassment and humiliation by Tunisian policeman. Bouazizi's protest led to a chain of events, assisted by Al Jazeera, got the video from nawaat.org and broadcast it back to Tunisia informing Tunisians of the unfolding story. Bouazizi's protest, assisted by Al Jazeera TV, snowballed into a full-blown revolution that engulfed not only Tunisia but also the Middle East. Most importantly it redefined the role of the "crowd" of largely students of higher education using networked smart-phones to provide the international news agency with live pictures of events and reactions to them from various streets, in different cities and in multiple countries. Thus, the Arab Spring - as this the Middle East revolutions came to be called- has shown the power of the social media and the young people who used it to trigger social and political change, thereby underlined the significance of crowdsourcing in a global political context.

Most of the media outside the Middle East as well as local Middle East media attribute the growth of crowdsourcing to the work of Jeff Howe (2006), who described crowdsourcing as "the act of a company or institution taking a function once performed by employees and outsourcing it to an undefined (and generally large) network of people in the form of an open call." However, crowdsourcing has long non-digital and non-cash history. For example, In 1714, according to McGonigal (2011), the British Government established a commission offering 20000 pounds (roughly 12 million dollars) to anyone who could invent a way to determine 'longitude' on a sailing vessel and the prize went not, to an Oxford don, but to John Harrison, an uneducated cabinet-maker from Yorkshire. Firms turned to crowdsourcing tool; Netflix too sought help from the crowd to solve a non-recurring challenge and awarded a 'Netflix Prize' to the team that came up with a solution. Such open innovation or crowdsourcing initiatives help companies gain a competitive edge over others.

Digitalization and globalization converge to create fertile ground for the emergence and growth of crowdsourcing, which many believe to be a potent problem-solving tool that combines knowledge, energy, and creativity of the worldwide online community to great effect. Internet-based companies with global reach such as Google, Amazon, Facebook, and eBay and MySpace have lucrative businesses that are dependent on the contributions of their users from across the world, both internal and external to their organizations. Howe (2008), on the original exponent of crowdsourcing, pointed out that it is not a single strategy but four. He explains its robustness by highlighting the four strategies derived from crowdsourcing based on the type or resources it uses in each case. The models include (a). Crowd Wisdom, that uses crowd's knowledge for specific themes, (b) Crowd Creation, which uses crowd's creative energy to develop plotlines and concepts; (c) Crowd Voting, the model using crowd's judgment to organize vast quantities of information; and (d) Crowdfunding, that which uses crowd's collective funds for projects development. The strategy functions as a distributed problem-solving and production process, which operate by sourcing tasks to generally undefined, large group of people or communities through an open call (Li & Hongjuan, 2011). These large individual participants or groups form the "crowd". Many authors have suggested that in the development of his crowdsourcing ideas, Howe was to a large extent inspired by Surowiecki (2004) who through an extensive research concluded that in most given situations the judgment of the group is smarter than that of the smartest among them; and this idea he defined as the "wisdom of crowds".

- **Educational Activities and Crowdsourcing:** Crowdsourcing may be used to enhance the activities in higher education in many ways. For example, a recent trend of crowd creation project in higher education is the rise of student-generated guide to colleges and universities through the appraisal by students-based "crowd." One such project is called Unigo, which is mainly student-generated that provides a useful guide to North American colleges for all interested parties including potential applicants. As described by Dee (2008), the project initially featured less than 300 colleges but it quickly grew to include over 100,000 institutions. At the same time its contents in terms of number and material-types, as well as the number of its users grew rapidly.

Other important examples are that the strategy can be applied to produce crowdsourced college textbook, create new and more relevant curricula as well as courses or class teaching materials. Solemon, et al, (2013) use the four crowdsourcing strategies identified by Howe (2008) to illustrate examples of projects that were developed in the USA. Table 3 summarizes examples of a few of the crowdsourcing projects for creating crowdsourced content in the USA. According to the authors, the Online Textbook

Table 3. Summary of crowdsourcing projects for creation of crowdsourced content

Project Name	Institution	Volunteers	Project	Source
Online Textbook	Brigham Young University, USA	682 students of Project Management class	Textbook – Project Management for Instructional Designers	(Wiley, 2011)
Crowdsourcing Textbooks	North Carolina State University, USA	120 students	Textbooks - Object Oriented Design, Architecture of Parallel Computers	(Gehringer, 2011)
Management Through Collaboration Book Project	St John's University, USA	Almost 1000 management educators and researchers in about 90 nations	Textbook – Management through Collaboration: Teaming in a Networked World	(Wankel, 2009)
The SOS Classroom	University of Southern California, USA	Teachers, parents, and students	Course materials for K-8 students – ESL (English as a second language), language arts, math, music, and science	http://sosclassroom.org/

Source: Solemon, et al, (2013). A Review Of The Uses Of Crowdsourcing In Higher Education http://www.aessweb.com/pdf-files/ijass-si-3(9)-2066-2073.pdf

project initiative of the Brigham Young University, USA sourced the contributions from over 680 students of Project Management course in order to produce an electronic textbook (Wiley, 2011).

Applications of Crowdsourcing in Translation and Language Learning

Due to the increased globalization and cross-cultural activities, the demand for translation and language learning is on the rise. The translations may be of textbooks, trade literature or culture related texts. The languages benefiting from the translated material are those associated with the global rise of their economies, such as Mandarin and Hindi.

It is increasingly being realized that the best people to help translate the content materials related to product or service are the relevant customers themselves. As indicated, above crowdsourcing is becoming a tried and tested strategy of increasing the global reach for multinational businesses, including higher educational institutions, and engaging local clienteles directly in their native languages. This strategy often opens up many other opportunities. First, it enables the tapping into the knowledge and resources of the local customers, enthusiasts, and brand advocates. Secondly, it affords high levels of scalability and flexibility, which are very important but usually not easy to achieve by other means. Thirdly, it provides an opportunity for a snowballing of closer interactions with the local customers and allowing them to shape the development of products and services in accordance with the preferences and culture of the local markets.

- **Engaging the Multilingual Crowd:** In the multilingual crowdsourcing solutions, some companies such as Moravia (2017) are able to get the best of the crowdsourced model by integrating it effectively with other translation processes and similar work activities. In other cases, the best approach seemed to be one that only manages, develops, and uses clients' current crowds. In yet other cases it is imperative to build client-specific crowds from the firm's large and global resource pool. There are many ways followed by different firms, however, for Moravia (2017) the most typical scenarios for crowdsourced solutions include the following steps:

- First, translation of select types of the client- and user-generated content.
- Second, the aggregation and analysis of reviews or user comments, e.g., from blogs, Twitter feeds, and onsite reviews
- Third, product evaluation and testing, whether prior to an official release or as part of incremental updates
- Fourth, keyword testing, which includes getting the most relevant local terms that are to be used to optimize the concise summary of the global strategies and online campaigns
- Fifth, consists of suitable terminology and style advance and administration
- Sixth, the language quality reviews and assessment

- **Crowdsourcing Language Learning:** Recently language learning is being crowdsourced. Doulingo (2017) for example is a new platform that consists of a language-learning website and application, as well as a digital language proficiency assessment. The platform provides all its language courses free at no cost to the users. It is a scalable system, which by the end of November 2016, offered "68 different language courses across 23 countries, with 22 additional courses in development" Doulingo (2017). It is a versatile application that is available on iOS, Android and Windows 8 and 10 platforms with about 150 million registered users across the world.

Its language courses components offer not only written lessons and dictation but also speaking preparation for the more mature learners. It has a scalable skill tree, which allows users to progress through according to the ability of the users. In addition, there is vocabulary section where learned words can be put into practice. In the process, users accumulate experience points when lessons are completed and skills are regarded gained when all lessons associated with the skill are completed.

- **Creating a Crowdsourcing Culture:** To better understand the different crowdsourcing capabilities, it is first important to appreciate the layers of actors involved in the process. 1. The client layer – a firm or person that has a task that needs to be fulfilled, and is occasionally called "the seeker." 2. The crowd layer – consisting of persons who are eager and able to undertake the required task as specified by the client company or persons, and 3. The platform layer – that is an online marketplace through which projects are announced to the crowd (Nylund, Mats, Gopalkrishnan, Asha 2014).

Thus, it is this collaborative effort between a news organization, its audience, that crowdsourcing culture is created, and through which the roles of citizen contributors are plainly well defined in ways to ensure generation of a new crowdsourcing culture. Philips (2012) defined this type of collaboration as open innovation and often uses both by business corporate companies and media firms in various combinations, as categorized hereunder with relevant examples:

1. **Suggestive/Participative:** This format encourages anyone with an idea to submit it, review and rank from others. For example, the company Yle Svenska (July, 2016) regularly welcomes varied ideas or pitches for shows to be telecasted on the channel.
2. **Suggestive/Invitational:** This (usually) event or campaign based initiative invites specific individuals or teams to submit ideas of their choice (on chosen topics). An example is when the Al Jazeera

news media invites documentary filmmakers to submit stories or films focusing on certain themes (environment, activism etc.) IBM's IdeaJam periodically invites chosen people to submit ideas and this list of chosen individuals keeps getting updated (Philips 2012).

3. **Directed/Invitational:** In this case, the firm builds a web of selected individuals/partners to participate in innovation. For example Procter & Gamble's Connect + Develop program allows firms to partner with Proctor & Gamble in innovation activities.
4. **Directed/Participative:** A sponsor directs a group to address a specific topic/problem or opportunity. For example, many journalists from media companies- such as BBC, CNN or Al-Jazeera- tend to use social media to connect with the crowd and crowdsource news either on a continuing basis or targeted to a particular happening/event.
5. **The Opportunities and Challenges of Crowdsourcing:** The benefits of crowdsourcing are immediately understandable: it is highly scalable; the workforce is available instantly, and one can get as many or as few resources as one requires. Revolutionize information collection and processing systems are emerging and are enabling in-depth, large-scale, and cost-effective information gathering, more accurate techniques for information extraction from data.

In the current business environment where goods and services are sent to open, international markets, many businesses demand that highly qualified individuals with extreme product knowledge translate the accompanying product instructions over ever-tighter production schedules. Some of the affected companies claim that over eighty percent of the crowdsourced projects have deadlines shorter than 24 hours. Admittedly, crowdsourcing has its challenges, too. Experience has shown, for example, that the larger the crowd, the more complex are its management activities. According to Philips (2012), some of these activities include:

- Recruiting and engaging the right in-country talent
- Creating a community where that talent can share their expertise
- Managing that community to ensure that business requirements are met

These changing and challenging situations suggest that it is also important to manage carefully the crowdsourcing process so that when volunteers are not available, professionals can step in and make sure that deadlines and quality standards are kept.

3. ESP CURRICULUM DEVELOPMENT: WITH MIDDLE EAST FOCUS

The development of ESP curriculum is an important component of higher education in many non-English speaking developing countries. The Middle East is emerging as an important global region of growing ESP activities. This may be due to its increasing importance to the stability of the global economy, especially in view of the rising flows of people, finance, information and trade between it and the rest of both developed and developing worlds. In this section we analyze the experiences and importance of crowdsourcing curriculum development both in general terms and as it relates to ESP.

Crowdsourcing Curriculum Development

A wide variety of new options and opportunities are created by the rapid increase of access to free high quality digital educational material and the growth of online workers, both of which are probably triggered by the expansion in Information Technologies. One of these opportunities is crowdsourcing that offers all development actors, including higher educational institutions to harness the time, knowledge and resources of large crowds of online users at any time and space. To the ESP departments and teachers, crowdsourcing offers the opportunities to use the wisdom of the billions of online crowd as well as the offline crowd to develop and run new curriculum to meet the changing societal needs. Worldwide, crowdsourcing is a rapidly growing activity that is embedded in large and small organizations such that it is estimated by 2018 (Deloitte 2016), with crowdsourcing about seventy-five percent of all high performers, including educational institutions, will perform better, faster and produce goods and services at lower costs.

Other important benefits of crowdsourcing for businesses as identified by Deloitte (2016) are worth highlighting, as they may prove useful to higher educational institutions. Besides faster design and quick prototype production ability, is has proved capable of achieving these abilities with higher quality and more elasticity, besides its demonstrated capability to accomplish tedious tasks. In the area of talent identification and use, crowdsourcing has shown the capacity to open up new external talent pools and has the means of efficient management and retention of internal talent. Any team given the responsibility to develop new education curriculum, will find these emerging qualities of crowdsourcing as useful guides to draw up its action plans.

The diversity of backgrounds, knowledge, skills, and abilities within the global crowd is already helping ESP teams to develop new curricula proposed by Maggio et al. (2016), and Helps and Grant (2013). These crowdsourcing platforms are intended to promote issues of "openness" (open education, open access, open source, open science, open data, etc.) among the communities of educators across developing countries.

Maggio et al. (2016) created an online system that crowdsourced the curriculum for their massive, open, online course (MOOC) that was intended as a personalized learning experience. With the help of other instructors, the team led a 13-week course for over 12,000 learners from 178 nations. The instructors offered the participants the chance to "increase their understanding of the foundations of open knowledge creation, use, dissemination, and evaluation; collaborate with learners from other cultures and disciplines; work effectively in rapidly changing knowledge environments; and develop as independent, self-directed, lifelong learners." The result showed that personalized learning can be promoted through networked technology but allows learners to create their own learning involvement, that many students were unprepared for the flexible approach and preferred clear direction. Other observations were that personalized learning needs a balance between student autonomy and teachers' strong direction and between content openness and licensing and that effective personalized learning needs a blend of pedagogies with new technologies.

Helps and Grant (2013) proposed a system to house curriculum and teaching material on diverse fields and act as quality assured crowdsourcing platform. It will be flexible and open to all global community of educators to contribute and use to design quality curricula and support material suited to them, but which will be published and distributed worldwide for use by educators from the developing countries.

From the literature review, it is clear that there are few types of research on the use of crowdsourcing for the development of ESP curriculum in the Middle East which seems to be lagging behind other regions of the developing world. The application of crowdsourcing in ESP curriculum development is a potentially rich area for academic research which should be explored not only in the Middle Eastern countries, but also other developing countries.

ESP Curriculum Development Process

Many researchers have used or proposed ESP curriculum development process around the world and in the Middle East. Smith (2000) suggests four ways of approaching curriculum theory and practice, which is applied for ESP, as a body of knowledge to be *transmitted*, an attempt to achieve certain ends in students – *product*, as *process* and as *praxis*. While viewing curriculum in these terms, it is important to stress that curriculum development must respond to the spirit of the time, by using emerging ideas and the digital technologies to maximize the effectiveness of the ESP curriculum. Hence, the author advocates the crowdsourcing of tasks, ideas, influence, and support.

As discussed above, crowdsourcing offers tremendous opportunities to mobilize diverse resources and support from the "crowd" to achieve an effective outcome. In the present case, the crowd may consist of people and organization internal and external to the institution and the mode of interaction with them may be online or offline. The internal crowd may include curriculum developers, other faculty, learners, administrative & technical staff, and other stakeholders for personnel, commercial resources, and political support. The external crowd may include public agencies, allied institutions, granting agencies or others who have supported the curriculum, professional societies, existing and potential consumers of ESP graduates, donors for funding, political support, researchers and authors, and curricular development institutions at the local, national and international levels.

The online exchange uses virtual or cyberspace that implies the use of the wired and wireless network often using free online collaborative tools such as Dropbox, Google Docs, Slack, Skype, Google Hangouts, Trello, and Asana (Flowerdew 2012), The offline is reality (i.e., real life) physical, face to face interactions based on the mechanisms of meetings, syllabus materials, reports, site visits.

Framework for ESP Curriculum Development

After a careful analysis of the ideas of these authors, the following six steps are accepted for use to guide the development of ESP curriculum in developing countries with emphasis on the Middle East. Figure 1 shows a framework for ESP curriculum development- based on the proposal by Lynn (2011) that forms the basis of discussion in this section. In each stage in the framework, main purpose, the process, and the key resources are identified, but these should be seen as part of a broader context of crowdsourcing with a wider reach in time and space. There is need to also emphasize that these stages reflect the fact that ESP is capable of self-renewal (Flowerdew, 2012) and is continually evolving in the process of which is widening and deepening its scope.

Stage 1: ESP Problem Identification/Needs Assessment

- **Purpose:** To identify the ESP problems related to the field that is to be addressed by the curriculum and to make a general needs assessment related to the relevant field, for example, business, health sciences, or engineering sciences.

Figure 1. Framework for ESP curriculum development
Source: Developed by the author based on the proposal by Lynn (2011).

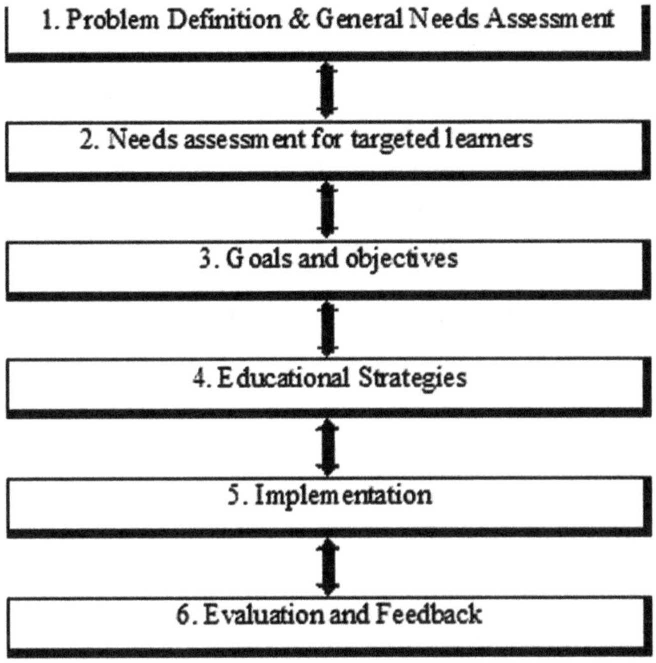

- **Process:** Identify and analyze ESP needs & related problems; "what" and the "how" of a course, impact on clients, stakeholders, and society; define how it is currently being addressed; suggest how it should be addressed by stating an ideal approach.
- **Resources:** Some of the researchers on this topic include Lynn (2011), Flowerdew (2012), and Smith (2000). Smith (2000) in particular suggests that there is a clear link between curriculum as a theoretical concept (Syllabus), which influences practical elements (process & praxis), which in turn affects the productive outcome (product). Douglas (2012) explores the theory and practice of assessment in ESP, then reviews specific areas of learning.

Stage 2: ESP Needs of Targeted Learners

- **Purpose:** To define, in operational terms, the target ESP learners' needs that should be met by the proposed curriculum.
- **Process:** A number of online and offline activities by the curriculum development team are to be carried out if the ESP objectives are to be achieved. The first activity is to identify the differences between the ideal and actual characteristics of the ESP targeted learner group and their environment. Second, the team needs to identify ESP targeted learners and define the appropriate educational intervention needed. Third, assessments are needed in the following areas: the existing and planned training; existing and perceived proficiencies, existing deficiencies and future needs; define learning styles and strategies, identify barriers, enabling and reinforcing factors; inventory existing recourses: crowdsourcing information, teachers, IT, and other factors.

Methods for target learners' needs assessment may include the use as appropriate the following: Informal discussions /formal interviews, focus group discussions, questionnaires, direct observation of skills, examinations, audits of current performance, and strategic planning session.

- **Resources:** Lynn (2011) provides a categorized list of the desired information about learners and suggests methods for learners' needs assessment. Toister (2014) provides good insight on adult learning theory, understanding the four stages of learning, comparing active vs. passive learning, ways of overcoming learning barriers, and methods of turning theory into practice. Crowdsourcing of language skills is suggested by Paltridge & Starfield eds. (2012) while resources on the following skill areas are provided by the authors as follows: speaking skill by Feak (2012), listening by Goh (2012), reading by Hirvela (2012), writing by Hyland (2012), and the skill of vocabulary by Coxhead (2012).

Stage 3: ESP Goals and Objectives

- **Purpose:** To set the goals and objectives of the ESP curriculum, the curriculum development team has to define the general and the specific ESP educational and quantifiable targets covering all activities of the curriculum.
- **Process:** The ESP learners' needs analysis should lead to the definition of goals and objectives of the curriculum. They should guide the sequential choices of curriculum contents and assignments, suggest effective learning and evaluation methods, and inform on expected curriculum outcome.
- **Resources**: Talbot (2017) highlights the importance of long-term, goal-oriented, big-picture-driven professional practice, and how these could be incorporated in the process for designing and developing ESP curriculum using four objective-based questions. Lynn (2011) lists the functions of goals and objectives, suggests how to write goals and objectives, identifies the types and outcome of objectives including knowledge, skill, and attitudinal.

Stage 4: ESP Curriculum Educational Strategies

- **Purpose:** To generate suitable educational strategies that meet the needs of the learners in terms of material content and methods.
- **Process:** Define the ESP educational strategies that should have clear contents and methods based on quantifiable cognitive, affective and psychomotor objectives; preferably using multiple methods to meet varying learning styles and motivations of the learners. Then develop suitable methods for meeting cognitive needs, the choice of educational tools, skills learning, self-directed learning, and for promoting teamwork.
- **Resources:** Lynn (2011) provides useful strategies for selecting educational methods, plans for the choice of educational tools, methods for meeting cognitive objectives, approaches to advance self-directed learning, and identifies educational strategies for stimulating teamwork. Ilarde (2014) summarizes key elements of ESP course design, skills and strategies plan and its application in the developing world.

Stage 5: ESP Curriculum Implementation

- **Purpose:** To identify resources needed for the full implementation of the curriculum in terms of personnel (faculty and support staff), time (available from faculty, support staff, and learners), facilities (space, equipment, and utilities) and funds (direct, indirect and opportunity costs).
- **Process:** The implementation of the ESP curriculum needs adequate resources (personnel, time, facilities and funds) and support (internal and external, see crowdsourcing). Next, it needs an effective management structure that can deal with barriers and hurdles of financial shortage or resistance from people & institutions. Finally, there should be an effective execution plan (piloting, adjustments, phasing of full implementation).
- **Resources:** Ahmed (2014) identifies key issues in ESP teaching -such as able to design teaching materials, develop effective teaching methodology, apply various technologies in ESP class and review teaching objectives. In addition, managing the curriculum requires careful consideration of instructors' teaching skills and learners' changing needs. While these are generally under control of the teaching faculty, there are issues beyond their control. For example, Storey (2007), Lynn (2011) and Flowerdew (2012) highlight the issue of mobilization of resources - including monetary support- for curriculum implementation in which intra- and inter-organizational management skills are crucial for support from senior administrators. Such support can be very important in assisting new opportunities or in helping to overcome challenges.

Stage 6: ESP Curriculum Evaluation and Feedback

- **Purpose:** To complete fully the curriculum development cycle by providing guidelines on how to enhance the curriculum, attract support for it, assess progress and satisfy external institutional and marketing demands.
- **Process:** This consists of the evaluation of the ESP curriculum after some years of application to provide a feedback for possible revision of the curriculum. The evaluation results may be used to mobilize support for the ESP curriculum, evaluate individual learner's achievement, fulfill external demands, and to serve as a basis for presentations and publications. The feedback normally defines the users, resources used in the curriculum to determine if it meets its goals and objectives. It consists of the evaluation questions carefully structured and their responses, includes explanations of how the ethical concerns are addressed, reports data collection and analysis; and includes a report on the methodology of data collection and analysis.
- **Resources:** The issues of evaluation and feedback have been highlighted by Smith (2000), Lynn (2011), Kelly (2009) and Bruner who is reported by Clark (2010) the leading advocate of the spiral curriculum that seek to revisit basic ideas, building on them until the student has grasped the full formal concept. A similar concept being promoted is the constructivist approach, which proposes that learning is best via pro-active engagement with the educational environment. These spiral and constructivist approaches to learning have democratizing tendencies and are supported and promoted by the application of online interaction and crowdsourcing activities.

4. DRAFTING ESP CURRICULUM

From the general staged ESP curriculum development description, the focus is now on the crowd to produce a draft ESP curriculum that will become much more instrumental and more relevant to local and regional needs, and therefore much more practical. To this end, this section will discuss the form and content of the following four action instruments that will guide the learners and the instructors in their daily activities:

- Course Information
- Course Syllabus
- Course Plan
- Student Learning Outcomes Alignment With Assessment

Course Information

The course information is a document that concisely describes the intended learning outcomes and it is the means by which these outcomes are accomplished. This section sets out the theoretical background against which the skills and knowledge contents must be seen. Thus, after a brief discussion on the theoretical approaches to course information, its main components are discussed as follows: general course information, learning outcomes and assessments, and the main learning resources.

Approaches to Course Design

Hutchinson and Waters (1987) identify three main types of approaches to course design: language centered, skills-centered, and learning-centered.

- **Language Centered Course Design:** The basic idea behind the language-centered approach is to create direct correlations between the language taught in the classroom and the language of the subject area as it is used in the real world. This approach is essentially the oldest type of course design in the ESP teaching method. Out of the many problems associated with the language-centered approach, is that it lacks depth and some researchers criticize as "just a surface level approach" (Hutchinson and Waters 1987, p. 66).
- **Skill-Centered Course Design:** This approach seeks to guide learners in developing skills and strategies that will continue even after the ESP course by making learners better processors of information. This approach tries unlocking the processes that would enable the learner to perform better, to apply the processes to the ESP course. The approach, according to Hutchinson and Waters (1987), is based on two fundamental principles: the theoretical and the pragmatic: In the theoretical basis, the underlying language behaviors are certain skills and strategies, which the learner uses. The pragmatic principle is based on the distinction between goal-oriented courses and process-oriented courses. Needs analysis plays two roles in a skill-centered approach: first, it provides a basis for discovering the essential competence that enables people to perform in the target situation, it enables the course designer to discover the potential knowledge and abilities that the learners bring to the ESP course.

- **Learning-Centered Approach:** This approach is based on the principle that the learner determines the learning process. While teachers can influence what is taught, likewise the learners themselves determine what to learn. In this approach, Hutchinson and Waters (1987) remind us, learning is seen as a process in which the learners use what knowledge or skills they have in order to make sense of the flow of new information. Thus, learning is not just a mental process; it is a process of negotiation between individuals and society.

To sum up, it is clear that language-centered approach concentrates on performance, while the skills-centered approach concentrates on competence, and the learning-centered approach focuses on how to get competence.

General Course Information

The general course information normally includes the name of the institution, department, course code and title, credit hours, core and pre-requisite if any, mode of instruction (e.g. lecture, blended, e-learning, etc.), basic instructor information (name, phone number, email, office hours). Under this part, is also the course objectives which state the main purpose of the course, the course description gives a general description of the course and what it offers to the students as well any plans for developing and improving the course that are being implemented.

Detailed course content may also be presented in this part. It shows the topics to be covered and the number of weeks it will take to cover the topics, contact hours and the weeks in which summative assessments are to take place.

- **Learning Outcomes and Assessments:** The second part of the course information deals with the learning outcomes and assessments. In this section, the course learning outcomes (categorized under different learning domain- knowledge, cognitive skills, interpersonal skills and responsibilities and psychomotor) should be spelled out and assessment methods and teaching strategies pointed out.
- **Student Academic Counseling and Support:** The third part of the course information may be on student academic counseling and support where the institutional requirements for availability of instructors for individual student consultations and academic advice are stated (the amount of time instructors are expected to be available each week to support students).
- **Learning Resources:** The last part of the course information may include the list of required and recommended textbooks for the course, reference materials, electronic materials (such as websites, supplemental readings, etc.) as well as the facilities that are required for the successful execution of the course.

There should also be a section which shows how the course will be evaluated and what the improvement processes are. The evaluation process depends on what individual institutions follow, for example, peer observation/evaluation, departmental surveys, etc. Whatever method is followed, there should be a clearly stated plan for improvement of the course based on the results of the evaluation.

Course Syllabus

The syllabus is an academic document that communicates course information and defines expectations and responsibilities (Storey 2007). It is descriptive (unlike the prescriptive or specific curriculum) and ensures that students have easy access to the course syllabus by either handing out hard copies on the first day of class or by posting a digital copy on the institutional website.

The course syllabus should contain the following minimum information: course title, time, required texts and other materials; course topics; major assignments and exams; course policies on grading, academic integrity, attendance rules and contact information of the instructor. The structure of the syllabus should consist of at least the following topics.

Course Profile

1. **General Course Information:** Title, time, course code and number, instructor's contact, etc.
2. Course Description
3. Course Objectives
4. Course Learning Outcomes
5. Course Contents (Topics to be covered)

Course Guidance

6. Teaching Methodology
7. Assessment Tools
8. General Rules
9. Recommended Books, References & Teaching Materials

Course Plan and Aligning Student Learning Outcomes With Assessment

The Course Plan provides details instructional guidelines for plan units of teaching, select materials, and learning activities, set up working groups, arrange the teaching-learning environment and seek to move students forward towards learning outcomes.

- **Define Course Goals:** The purpose is to determine what the students are to learn and accomplish. The goals should specify the content, cognitive development, and personal development.
- **Theoretical Background:** Establish sequence in order of succession, the content materials have to be organized to show what should be the sequence of topic/units. Ensure cumulative learning by reinforcement and integration of materials. In selecting an approach, consider the preferences of other instructors, while providing variety in the mode of learning (Ilarde 2014). With respect to the course material selection, select the main topics and arrange them is a sequence and where possible use the latest textbooks or the current literature. At the same time, use the desired content to refine the course goals.

- **Alignment of Student Learning Outcomes with Assessment:** An important curricula document that guide instructors on assessment (both formative and summative) is the alignment of the student-learning outcome to appropriate assessment procedures. For example, in an ESP course, to assess a speaking skill, a role play or simulation may be used with the help of a rubric. It is very important that each learning outcome under the four English language skill including vocabulary is carefully aligned to particular assessment modes.

Draft Curriculum Implementation: Piloting and Survey of Effectiveness

Review how other institutions have piloted new curricula as well as the evaluation of its effectiveness.

Process

1. Draft to be given to all members of the crowd within and external to the institutions for their comments and suggestions.
2. The feedbacks to be used to improve the curricula documents and get them approved by institutional policy-making body. The curricula will then be piloted for at least one semester.
3. After a semester of piloting, conduct a survey to assess the effectiveness of the curricula including opportunities & challenges encountered. Survey data should be collected from the learners and the ESP course instructors.
4. Make adjustment and improvement on the curriculum and get approval for final adoption
5. Review the curricula every three years or as deemed necessary by the policy-making body of the institution at the recommendation of the relevant departments.

5. DIRECTION OF FUTURE RESEARCH

The general worldwide trend in ESP research includes such topics as genre, corpus studies, English as a lingua franca, advanced academic literacies, identity, and ethnographic approaches to researching specific purposes of language use (Paltridge 2015). Of increasing importance are such topics as the need to develop courses that meet learners' needs and how to balance qualitative and quantitative types of research in ESP as well as the growing argument that teachers need to learn more about their learners' imagined communities and how this can be achieved.

In the Middle East, recent ESP research efforts include an investigation in the communicative needs of health professionals by Alharby (2005), a study on the effectiveness of ESP course for business administration by Liton (2012). Other studies related to crowdsourcing include the exploration of the suitability of courses to students' needs and attitudes by Abdalla (2013), the external and internal evaluation of ESP courses, and an evaluation of the effectiveness of using ESP course for PYP students by Al-Fraidan (2012). Also, Younes & Albalawi (2016) investigates the effectiveness of using ESP course for PYP students at Tabuk University from the teachers' perspectives. However, there is still need for research in the application of crowdsourcing in the development of ESP curriculum in the Middle East as well as other regions of the developing world.

With respect to future research direction, Gollin-Kies (2014) propose more studies applying mixed quantitative and qualitative techniques and more of the collaborative and larger scale types that are conducted across institutions as well as across nations and regions thereby encouraging multi-disciplinary approach. This will foster greater collaboration among faculty, students and institutions in ways that can spill over into other academic areas.

In addition to the importance of collaboration between institutions, there is also the need for members of these institutions to continue research engagement in the following areas:

First, studies that seek to identify current issues and future directions in their learners' professional areas

Second, enhance the management and development of research to eliminate, reduce or deflect issues in their learners' disciplines.

Third, researchers should seek to deal with the following Research Questions and/or Research Areas

1. Increase the effectiveness and equity or inclusion concerns in their learners so as to ensure a positive impact on the society.
2. Ensure greater efficiency and cost-effectiveness of their research on their students, in ways that have impact on the society.
3. Create the optimal combination of ESP teaching tools so as to enhance goals achievements.

6. CONCLUSION

The key challenge of this chapter demonstrates how crowdsourcing can be used to improve higher education through the design and implementation of collaborative educational programs that integrate the students' needs, culture and background as well as the anticipated future workplace demands. The ideas, experiences and materials from the offline and online digital crowds are used as key resources to design and implement ESP programs by constantly drawing resources from the crowds located across continents.

To strengthen the learner-centered approach, efforts should be on drawing authentic materials from worldwide experiences leaving the participating faculty to initially sieve these materials using local values and judgments. It is in the application and evaluation of the draft curriculum that the learners' understanding and judgments are fully employed and reflected in the final revised document before it is fully implemented as a program that meets learners' culture and background.

ESP is an offspring of globalization that was defined by specific types of economic, business, and political models prevalent in the last few decades, but these models have been affected by the profound structural shifts in the global socio-economic system, which have been triggered by digitalization (BCG 2017). These transformations in the political economy and network technologies are redefining the economic, business, and political models of the old largely non-digital globalization system, thereby creating quite a different paradigm. It is therefore very important for the institutions to be aware of this changing direction and the needs of paradigms, without this fundamental understanding, a mere review and replacing curriculum is like putting new wine in an old bottle! [or like watering a desert plant with a sieve]!

REFERENCES

Abdalla, H. (2012). The Needs And Attitudes Of Science Students To ESP: A Case Study Of Taif University In Khurma, Saudi Arabia. *English Teaching*, *4*(8).

Ahmad, A. N. (2010). Is twitter a useful tool for journalists? *Journal of Media Practice, 11*(2), 145-155.

Ahmed, J. (2012). *Theoretical Framework & Growing Demand of ESP in Saudi Arabia.* Retrieved from https://www.kau.edu.sa/Files/0053226/Researches/65162_36509.pdf

Ahmed, M. K. (2014). The ESP Teacher: Issues, Tasks and Challenges, *English for Specific Purposes World, 42*(14). Retrieved from http://www.esp-world.info/Articles_42/Documents/Ahmed.pdf

Alfehaid, A. F. T. (2011). *Developing An ESP Curriculum For Students Of Health Sciences Through Needs Analysis And Course Evaluation In Saudi Arabia.* Retrieved from https://lra.le.ac.uk/bitstream/2381/10289/1/2011alfehaidaftphd.pdf

Alharby, M. (2005). *ESP Target Situation Needs Analysis: The English Language Communicative Needs As Perceived By Health Professionals In The Riyadh Area.* Retrieved from http://faculty.ksu.edu.sa/majed/Documents/alharby_majid_200505_phd.pdf

Alsamani, A. S., & Daif-Allah, A. S. (2016). Introducing Project-based Instruction in the Saudi ESP Classroom: A Study in Qassim University. *English Language Teaching*, *9*(1), 2016.

Belcher, D. D. (2004). Trends in teaching English for specific purposes. *Annual Review of Applied Linguistics*, *24*, 165–186. doi:10.1017/S026719050400008X

Boston Consulting Group (BCG). (2017). *Going Beyond The Rhetoric.* Retrieved from https://www.bcg.com/publications/2017/new-globalization-going-beyond-rhetoric.aspx

Chan, K. L. (2017). *The World's Most Powerful Languages.* Retrieved from https://knowledge.insead.edu/leadership-organisations/the-worlds-most-powerful-languages-6156

Clark, S. (2010). *Jerome Bruner: Teaching, Learning and the Spiral Curriculum.* Retrieved from https://sheldonclark.files.wordpress.com/2011/07/jerome-bruner-teaching-learning-and-the- spiral-curriculum2.pdf

Coxhead, A. (2012). ESP and Vocabulary. In The Handbook of English for Specific Purposes. John Wiley.

Deloitte. (2016). *Using the crowd in enterprise.* Retrieved from https://www2.deloitte.com/content/.../deloitte-uk-crowsourcing-using-the-crowd.pdf

Douglas, D. (2012). ESP and Assessment. In The Handbook of English for Specific Purposes. John Wiley.

Doulingo.com. (2017). *Duolingo.com Traffic Statistics.* Retrieved from http://www.alexa.com/siteinfo/duolingo.com

Dudley-Evans, T., & St. John, M. J. (1998). *Developments in English for Specific Purposes: A Multidisciplinary Approach.* Cambridge, UK: Cambridge University Press.

Estellés-Arolas, E., & González-Ladrón-de-Guevara, F. (2012). Towards an Integrated Crowdsourcing Definition. *Journal of Information Science*, *38*(2), 189–200.

Fadel, S., & Rajab, H. (2017). *Investigating the English Language Needs of the Female Students at the Faculty of Computing and Information Technology at King Abdulaziz University in Saudi Arabia*. Retrieved from http://www.ccsenet.org/journal/index.php/elt/issue/view/1813

Feak, C. B. (2012). ESP and Speaking. In The Handbook of English for Specific Purposes. John Wiley.

Flowerdew, L. (2012). Needs Analysis and Curriculum Development in ESP. In The Handbook of English for Specific Purposes. John Wiley.

Al Fraidan, A. (2012). Evaluation of Two ESP Courses. *Journal of Language Teaching and Research, 2*(5).

Goh, C. M. (2012). ESP and Listening. In The Handbook of English for Specific Purposes. John Wiley.

Gollin-Kies, S. (2014). Methods reported in ESP research articles: A comparative survey of two leading journals. *English for Specific Purposes*, *36*, 27–34. doi:10.1016/j.esp.2014.04.001

Helps, W. I., & Grant, E. S. (2013). *Crowdsourcing Curriculum Design*. Retrieved from http://micsymposium.org/mics_2013_Proceedings/submissions/mics20130_submission_23.pdf

Hirvela, A. (2012). ESP and Reading. In The Handbook of English for Specific Purposes. John Wiley.

Howe, J. (2006). The Rise of Crowdsourcing. *Wired Magazine, 14*(6), 1-4.

Howe, J. (2008). *Crowdsourcing - How the Power of the Crowd is Driving the Future of Business*. Random House Business.

Hutchinson, T., & Waters, A. (1987). English for specific purposes: A learning-centered approach. Cambridge: Cambridge University Press. *Journal of Education and Practice*, *3*(6), 2012.

Hyland, K. (2012). ESP and Writing. In The Handbook of English for Specific Purposes. John Wiley.

Ilarde, M. J. (2014). *ESP Course Design and skills and strategies*. Retrieved from https://www.slideshare.net/jaysonilarde/esp-course-design-and-skills-and-strategies

Kelly, J. (2009). *Challenges - Red Kayaks and Hidden Gold: The Rise, Challenges and 11 Value of Citizen Journalism*. Oxford, UK: Reuters Institute for the Study of Journalism. Retrieved from http://reutersinstitute.politics.ox.ac.uk/fileadmin/documents/Publications/Red_Kayaks_Hidden_Gold.pdf

Koci, A. (2016). *ESP courses in Kosovo Higher Education System*. Retrieved from https://aab-edu.net/assets/uploads/2017/01/ICLLC2016_Book-of-Abstracts.pdf

Liton, H. A. (2012). Developing EFL teaching and learning practices in Saudi colleges: A review. *International Journal of Instruction*, *5*(2), 129–152.

Lorenzo, F. (2005). *How is English for Specific Purposes (ESP) different from English as a Second Language (ESL), also known as general English?* Retrieved from www.usingenglish.com

Lynn, J. (2011). *Curriculum Development in Six Steps for Med-Ed*. Retrieved from https://medicine.osu.edu/education/Documents/curriculum_design_2010.pdf

Maggio, Saltarelli, & Stranack. (2016). *Crowdsourcing the Curriculum: A MOOC for Personalized, Connected Learning*. Retrieved from http://er.educause.edu/articles/2016/3/crowdsourcing-the-curriculum-a-mooc-for-personalized-connected-learning

McGonigal, J. (2011). *Reality is broken: Why games make us better and how they can change the world.* New York: Penguin Press.

Moravia. (2017). *Translation services for a digital world.* Retrieved from https://www.moravia.com/

Nylund, M., & Gopalkrishnan, A. (2014). *Crowdsourcing in Media.* Retrieved from http://dspace.arcada.fi:8080/xmlui/handle/10478/64

Paltridge, B. (2015). *Keynote: Developments in English for Specific Purposes Research.* Retrieved from http://jaltcue.org/files/OnCUE/OCJ9.2/OCJ9.2_pp73-85_Paltridge.pdf

Paltridge, B., & Starfield, S. (Eds.). (2012). *The Handbook of English for Specific Purposes.* Wiley-Blackwell. doi:10.1002/9781118339855

Philips, J. (2012). Open Innovation Typology. In P. Sloane (Ed.), *A Guide to Open Innovation and Crowdsourcing: Advice from Leading Experts* (pp. 22–36). Kogan Page.

Sharma, P. (2011). *Crowdsourcing in Higher Education IT.* Retrieved from http://er.educause.edu/articles/2011/9/crowdsourcing-in-higher-education-it

Smith, M. K. (2000). Curriculum theory and practice. In *The encyclopaedia of informal education.* Retrieved from www.infed.org/biblio/b-curric.htm

Solemon, B. (2013). *A review of the uses of crowdsourcing in higher education.* Retrieved from http://www.aessweb.com/pdf-files/ijass-si-3(9)-2066-2073.pdf

Storey, C. W. (2007). *Insights into Language Curriculum Development.* Retrieved from http://e-flt.nus.edu.sg/v4n12007/storey.pdf

Surowiecki, J. (2004). *The Wisdom of Crowds.* Anchor Books.

Talbot, P. (2017). *English for Specific Purposes (ESP): An Objectives-Oriented Approach.* Retrieved from https://www.linkedin.com/pulse/english-specific-purposes-esp-objectives-oriented-approach-talbot

Toister, J. (2014). *Instructional Design: Adult Learners.* Retrieved from https://www.lynda.com/Higher-Education-tutorials/Instructional-Design-Essentials-Adult-Learners

Wankel, C. (2009). Management education using social media. *Organizational Management Journal, 6*(4), 251–262. doi:10.1057/omj.2009.34

Wiley, D. (2011). *Project Management for Instructional Designers. Iterating Towards Openess.* Retrieved Jan 10, 2013, from http://opencontent.org/blog/archives/2119

Yle's Strategy for 2016–2020. (2016). Retrieved from https://yle.fi/aihe/artikkeli/2016/01/13/yles-strategy-2016-2020

Younes & Fatimah. (2016). *Investigating the Factors Leading to Speaking Difficulties: Both Perspectives of EFL Saudi Learners and Their Teachers.* Retrieved from https://papers.ssrn.com/sol3/papers.cfm?abstract_id=2814824

KEY TERMS AND DEFINITIONS

Collaboration: Cooperate and work with other people to produce teaching materials, for example, a curriculum and teaching resources.

Crowdsourcing: Individuals with diverse opinions or contributions relevant to a subject who are able to make a contribution both online and offline.

Curriculum: An educational program of study outlining course information, goals, objectives, plan, and assessment procedures.

Developing Countries: Countries that have relatively low GDP (gross domestic product), low level of health facilities, lower standard of living and life expectancy.

English for Specific Purpose: A learner-centered approach to teaching the English language which focuses on developing communicative ability in a specific discipline such as business, IT, health sciences, and engineering.

Globalization: The interaction of people across the world through the flow of money, ideas, and culture.

Higher Education: An education which is attained at a post-secondary institution with experience in research, teaching, and community service relevant to the English language.

Middle East: A geographical and cultural region located between Asia and Europe consisting of the Gulf States, Iraq, Iran, Jordan, etc.

Section 3
Evolving Crowdfunding in Emerging Economies

Chapter 10
Volunteerism in Urban Development the Case of Non-Cash, Non-Digital Crowdfunding Growth in Nigeria

Rabiu Bena Abdullahi
Waziri Umaru Federal Polytechnic, Nigeria

ABSTRACT

Crowdfunding is a digital-based tool for mobilizing cash for various projects contributing to urban development. This chapter argues that for societies with low digital penetration and less cash but with huge human resources and high physical interaction, crowdfunding should be used as tool for mobilizing human capital for urban development. In this sense, volunteering is a form of crowdfunding. This chapter explores the influence of volunteers in developing and maintaining their urban communities. As an activity aimed at promoting the welfare of other individuals or groups through services or cash transfers, volunteerism is a useful tool for emerging economies to fill the gap between their development resource demand and availability. Review of few relevant concepts and experiences reveal the potential contributions of paid and unpaid volunteers in Africa with a focus on the efforts to shift the Nigerian economy from an oil-based to an urban-based.

INTRODUCTION

Crowdfunding is a digital-based tool for mobilizing cash for various projects contributing to urban development. This chapter argues that for societies with low digital penetration and less cash but with huge human resources and high physical interaction, crowdfunding should be used as tool for mobilizing human capital for urban development. In this sense, volunteering is a form of crowdfunding. The focus in this chapter is to review the concepts of volunteerism, volunteering, volunteer, urban based activities,

DOI: 10.4018/978-1-5225-3952-0.ch010

urban based economy and oil based economy to facilitate their usage. Volunteerism is the art of doing a willy-nilly work or rendering services to an individual or community by the volunteer. While volunteering is about giving ones time to a good cause, voluntarism could be the concept of volunteering activity. In this case, one don't get paid, but gets the chance to use ones talents, develop new skills, and experience the pleasure that comes from making a real difference to other people's lives, as well as ones' own'(www.volunteerbristol.org.uk; 2017). In the United States, for example, volunteerism is neither a new concept nor an un-common activity, in 1851 the first Youth Movement Christian Association was started where women volunteered their time to sew supplies for the soldiers. Barton founded the American Red Cross in 1881 and began mobilizing volunteers for disaster relief operations, including relief for victims of the Johnstown Flood in 1889 (www.encyclopaedia, 2017).

Moreover, volunteerism could mean the policy or practice of volunteering one's time or talents for charitable, educational, or other worthwhile activities, especially in one's community. Contextually, therefore, concept of volunteerism is used to mean; The principle of donating time and energy for the benefit of other people in the community as a social responsibility rather than for any financial reward" (Collins English Dictionary - 2012 Digital Edition).

In another view, volunteerism is a situation where an individual or group provides services for no financial gain to benefit another person, group or organization. Volunteering is also renowned for skill development and is often intended to promote goodness or to improve human quality of life. Volunteerism also helps to improve the way people are governed. Therefore, from the local level to the global level, volunteerism is an extremely common activity.

The definition of volunteerism may vary between people, time-periods, situations, cultures and countries as indicated above. However, in most cases, volunteerism is understood as: 'an expression of self-motivation and interest to get involved in social causes which benefit both volunteers and those for whom the action was taken'. In this chapter, therefore, volunteerism is seen as a situation where an individual or group provides services for no financial gain to benefit another person, group or organization. This definition is in line with Kidd (2013) but contradicts the radical ideas of Okeke (2017). As used in this chapter, volunteering is an activity related to skill development in the course of offering free service that is intended to promote goodness or to improve human quality of life.

This chapter, therefore, seeks to explore the volunteering models that are capable of promoting urban development in Africa. That is, to use the literature to explore a few relevant concepts and identity one for use in the analysis of the potential contributions of paid and unpaid volunteers in African countries, focusing on the potential role of paid volunteers in shifting the Nigeria economy from oil-based to an urban-based. This aim will be achieved through desktop review of literature and database analysis.

BACKGROUND

Generally, the history of volunteering may dated back to early 1700s when the missionary volunteer corps started to flourish. According to Wikipedia (2017), the verb was first recorded in 1755. It was derived from the noun volunteer in 1600 to mean one who offers himself for military service, from the Middle French voluntaire. One early incidence of non-digital crowdfunding can be seen in one of the world's most famous landmarks. In 1885 the Statue of Liberty in United States of America was partially financed by the crowd. This was after it became clear that the American Committee of the Statue of Liberty could not raise all the funds needed for monumental base for the Statue of Liberty, a local newspaper-led campaign attracted small donations such that within half a year the sum of $101,091from more than 160,000 donors of various ages, calling and nationalities (Putzier 2015).

The modern internet-based crowdfunding, according to Agrawal et el., (2014), first gained popular and mainstream use in the arts and music communities. The first noteworthy instance of online crowdfunding in the music industry was in 1997, when music fans collectively raised US$60,000 to finance the entire U.S. tour for the British rock band called Marillion. They subsequently used this method to fund their studio albums.

On the growth of non-cash and non-digital volunteers, this goes back to during the Great Depression when several volunteer groups emerged to target the specific need of the community. This trend continued up to 1960 after the revolutionary war in Cuba ended; Ernesto Che Guevara (created the concept of 'volunteering work', according to Wikipedia (2017, www.en.wikipedia/volunteering/note_2). This was created with the intention that workers across the country volunteer a few hours of work on the centers. Another dimension of voluntarism is the principle that individuals are free to choose goals and how to achieve them within the bounds of certain societal and cultural constraints. The concept has more recent usage coinciding with the phrase community service, which is rendered free or are given regular pay, and this non-cash, non-digital type is the dominant sense in which it is generally used in this chapter.

The Need for Volunteers for Urban Development

The essence here is to review literature on the concepts of volunteering and voluntarism and relate it to African setting and the need for volunteers for urban development.

Susan J. Ellis (2017:3) differentiates between "voluntarism" and "volunteerism"; accordingly, she defined "Voluntarism" (the older term) to refer to everything voluntary. In the United States this includes religion. It certainly encompasses the entire "voluntary sector," but "voluntary" in the "voluntarism" context means not mandated by law (as government is). Many voluntary sector (non-profit) agencies have a volunteer board because that is a legal requirement, but may not utilize volunteers in direct service in any way. There are subjects within "voluntarism" that have nothing to do with volunteers, such as Unrelated Business Income Tax legislation, proposal writing, and compensation law.

Voluntarism is also used to describe non-coercive methods of recruiting soldiers, from participants in European and American military service to youthful combatants in civil war in Sierra Leone, Liberia, DRC, Rwanda and South Sudan:

- Skills-based volunteering
- Virtual Volunteering
- Micro-Volunteering
- Corporate
- Community
- Social volunteering
- Peace corps volunteering
- South –south volunteering
- Diaspora volunteering
- National volunteering
- Community-led volunteering
- Celebrity volunteering

Voluntarism has been a phrase used in labour relations. In Britain, it means the state refrains from directly intervening in industrial relations. In the early American labour movement it meant trade unions should focus on "pure and simple" gains in wages and working conditions and not independent labour politics and industrial unionism. The concept of volunteering as part of corporate philanthropic practices was started in Nepal in the 'Licchavi' period, (400 – 750 A.D.), in the form of social and religious contributions, including constructing temples, water taps, foot trails and public shelters. Most of the volunteer work in society was carried out in the name of 'religion', with many forms of the practices still existing today. As a result, the number of temples, foot trails, water taps and public shelters has dramatically increased within the trading areas of the country (http://www.volunteeraidnepal.org/ 2012vol's profile).Moreover, volunteering has always been a large part of Nepalese culture. Many traditional 'mutual-help' social organization are still in existence and delivering their services in society through volunteers. Throughout time, Nepalese communities have evolved from primitive religious societies to the commercial societies that exist today. Within these commercial societies, competition is high, opportunities are wide, and the spirit of volunteerism is at an all time high (ibid).

As stated earlier, volunteerism is seen as 'altruistic' activity where an individual or group provides services for no financial gain to benefit another person, group or organization. Moreso volunteerism implies rendering of selfless service or kind to the needy of such without a commensurate return to the volunteer. In the same vein, volunteers contribute to the overall health and well-being of communities around the world. Organizations rely on volunteers because they almost never have sufficient resources to hire enough staff to support their programs. A robust volunteer program also adds legitimacy to an organization and demonstrates community support for their work. The review made above implies that the term 'volunteering' connotes more than one exact meaning; each usage is determined by the context and interpretations. Some examples of volunteer work include:

1. Delivering meals to homebound seniors, manning the phone lines at domestic violence centres and serving in the volunteer fire department.
2. Keeping neighborhood parks and waterways clean and safe for everyone.
3. Tutoring or mentoring youth on everything from homework to soccer skills.
4. Walking dogs, cleaning cages and helping with adoptions and feedings at animal shelters.
5. Responding to natural disasters.
6. Ensuring that museums and cultural festivals run smoothly by taking tickets, leading tours and staffing information booths.
7. Provision of urban services and maintaining urban infrastructure facilities.
8. Provide access to internet communication network to urban communities.
9. Volunteering in the delivery of public services.

Volunteering provides many benefits to both mental and physical health. Volunteering helps counteract the effects of stress, anger and anxiety. The social contact aspect of helping and working with others can have a profound effect on the overall psychological well-being of the volunteer and by extension the community. While there is practical benefits derived by the volunteer, some researches also indicates that age does not matter much when it comes to volunteering.

There is no age limit as to who volunteer is, as such it cut across young and old, active and retired as noted in the literature ...volunteers are no longer predominantly middle-aged, middle-class white women.

Instead, they embrace a much wider segment of the community, including males, youth, seniors, people of colour, and so forth (www.CNCS, 2006).

Nigerian Volunteering Programmes

In Nigeria, "Youth unemployment" is one of the biggest economic problems. Youth Empowerment and Development Initiative developed a program "Urban Achievers" aimed at engaging, encouraging and providing necessary skills needed for the job market. Urban Achievers program is a well-rounded program that creates a platform for graduates, undergraduates, skilled and unskilled unemployed youths to acquire skills to achieve success in their lives. There are various volunteering groups and youth corps in Nigeria that is established to render voluntary services and kinds to the communities as complimentary efforts to what government does. Such groups include as contained in Table 1.

The program adapted the highly effective football for development model piloted by YEDI's international NGO partner; *Grassroots Soccer* for Nigeria. Therefore, adoption of the sport model is effective in using volunteering to solve some developmental needs of the community. Provision of city amenities and infrastructure using community development volunteers like ELI intern & volunteer group partner with local organizations to provide basic health facilities, orphanage, planting of trees and provision of safe drinking water and good roads across Africa. In the same vein, the existence of Nigerian Non- government organisations (www.nnngo.org) is also serving complimentary purposes. The organization have initiated programs that were specifically focused on the growth of our sector and in creating an enabling environment for the work with a view to positively impact pro-people development in communities throughout Nigeria. An increasingly popular form of volunteering among young people, particularly gap year students and graduates, is to travel to communities in the developing world to work on projects

Table 1. Volunteers in Nigeria for urban development

Name of Group	Main Aims	Collaborators
Youth Empowerment and Development Initiative YEDI Established June 2011	Use innovative, volunteer-based models to overcome challenges of unemployment, equip them with skills for community development and entrepreneurship development	NGO Partner, Grassroots Soccer for Nigeria, ELI Intern & volunteer group
The Nigeria Network of Non Governmental Organisations Established. 2004	Aim to promote interconnectivity at grassroots, provide opportunities for CSOs/NGOs/CBOs and PVOs to contribute through developmental activities with a view to positively impact on urban development of communities throughout Nigeria	NNNGO is in affiliation with Civil Society Pillar, Community Democrats, International Council for Social Welfare, National Council for Voluntary Organizations, People in Aid, REPAOC and International Forum of National NGO Platforms
National Peace Corps Established: March 2013	Promote social and economic development, Empower and pre-occupy Nigerian Youths through job creation	Peace Corps Volunteers, Youth Organization,
Technical Aid Corps Established: Oct 2004	Sharing Nigeria's know-how and expertise with other African, Caribbean and Pacific (ACP) countries. Promote understanding	Assistance in law Engineering, Agriculture, Medical Lab, Technology, and Sport, Architecture, Radiology, Accountancy, Insurance, Metrology, Lecturing, Coaching and Artisanship
African Union –Youth Volunteer Corps: Established Dec. 2010	Promote volunteering to build a more integrated continent by bringing youths together to share skills, knowledge, creativity and learning.	ICT, Cyber Security, TELECOMMUNICATIONS, Pan African e-Network, e-Governance, IVOs.

Source: Composed by the author from various sources, 2017.

with local organizations. A typical example is the Nigerian Technical Aid Corp scheme where professional volunteers are posted/sent to some countries to render voluntary services either ad teachers or medical doctors and lawyers.

Other organizations operating as volunteer groups in Nigeria include the following that are saddled with the responsibility or are interested in the following areas:

- **Notre Dame Mission Volunteer Program in Nigeria:** The newest site is in Nigeria in West Africa. Volunteers live with the Sisters of Notre Dame in the city of Enugu and serve as Volunteers for Peace (VFP).
- **Volunteer Abroad in Nigeria:** Volunteers for Peace are a non-profit organization, founded in 1982, that offers placement in over 3000 voluntary service projects.
- **Get Involved With Hands at Work in Nigeria:** Volunteers serving with Hands at Work are able to encourage and support our local communities by their very presence.
- **VIP Volunteers in Nigeria:** Volunteers for International Partnership (VIP): This program provides people with hands-on experience and helps them to see, experience and understand life in Nigeria.
- **Volunteer to Teach in Nigeria at TWB CTLCs (Teachers Without Borders):** We are an organization comprised of teachers and volunteers, supported by all those who believe in education as a passport to human resource development.
- **Business Development Internship in Nigerian Startup- Wecyclers:** The general purpose intern at Wecyclers will work directly with the CEO of the company, Bilikiss Adebiyi-Abiola.
- **Orphanage Care Volunteer Placement:** There are many children who have no one to look after them after the death of their parents.
- **Healthcare:** Although Nigeria has a relatively strong economy, the state and local governments in rural areas are absent. There are few hospitals and under-staffed clinics. Administering basic vaccines and assisting clinics is a rewarding volunteer activity.
- **Community Development:** Income inequality, AIDS education, child-care, and other issues hinder community development. Working in small community projects or small-scale industries to build and support a community is a difficult but rewarding and worthwhile experience.
- **Youth Development and Education:** Youth support through education is crucial to prevent the poor from falling into the black hole of poverty. Tutoring or teaching in small, elementary schools is but one way to help promote education.

Despite the above run down programmes there is inadequate information specifically addressing urban development issues in Nigeria. The projects that are mainly reconstruction of houses, schools, clinics, and provision of water are done directly by respective state governments. Volunteering often plays a pivotal role in the recovery effort following natural disasters, such as tsunamis, floods, droughts, hurricanes, and earthquakes. For example, the 2010 Boko Haram killings in the North eastern States of Borno, Yobe and Adamawa in particular attracted a large number of volunteers worldwide, deployed by non-governmental organizations, government agencies, and the United Nations. It is an example of mutualism at work, pooling resources and assistance and leveraging social media. However, it is worth to mention that, the effort of redeveloping the war ravaged areas in the North-east has no private sector involvement either as partners or volunteer groups.

Nigeria's cities, as elsewhere in Sub-Saharan Africa, lack adequate infrastructure for housing, sanitation, water, and open space amenities. Much of this is due to the absence of land planning statutes that encompass the evolving functions and responsibilities of urban areas, as numerous Nigerian research studies have documented, (www.msuweb.montclair.edu CERAFM002 Taylor 1988.pdf)

Suitable Volunteering Models for Urban Development

Review of literature has shown that in volunteering sport model is adopted in urban development process. This study will adopt three models of hybrid, volunteer process, stages & transition used in sports (Berit Skirstad, 2012) within the context of volunteerism in urban development with specific attention on non-digital based building, management and maintenance of cities. In other words, this study focuses on 3 types of youth volunteer corps and its role in promoting the process of building, management and maintenance of cities using sports volunteer-based models (hybrid, process and stages and transition) which are not only non-digital but also non-cash based.

It is against these challenges that proposal is made in this chapter, that third model of transition through program of inclusiveness and sustainability be established by engaging community, volunteer group and the government in the provision and maintenance of development projects across African Countries The Berit Skirstad model of sport is the one chosen for urban developments derive in Nigeria. Nigeria as a continental development program recruits and works with youth volunteers, to work in all 54 countries across the African Union. AU-YVC promotes volunteering to deepen the status of young people in Africa as key participants in the delivery of Africa's human development targets and goals. It brings people together to share skills, knowledge, creativity and learning to build a more integrated continent and by implication strengthen Africa's relevance in the globalized world. Involvement of IVOs (International Volunteering Organizations) and Volunteering for Development (VfD) helped in no small measure towards speedy development and accountability of the budgetary funds allocated to the projects that are indeed directly connected to community needs. Adoption of these models of volunteering in sports is underpinned by the spirit of sportsmanship where enthusiasm, cooperation and common goal attainment are demonstrated and upheld by each player as a team member.

Crowdfunding and Volunteering are activities by crowds for the public good. Crowdfunding is part of "alternative finance" strategy through which projects of various sizes may be funded or venture established by raising monetary contributions of different amounts from a large number of people. Generally, two broad types of funds are collected: the Financial Return that are directed towards profit making ventures of increasingly complex types, and the Non-financial Return (community services) types that are for social good (CCAF, 2017).

In addition to the online financial schemes, recently there has emerge E-volunteering which consists of two types; off-site and onsite. It should be noted that E-volunteering has many elements in common with traditional methods of volunteering. As normally understood, the onsite volunteering is a formal or informal activity freely undertaken for the common good on behalf of non-governmental organizations or local communities. Through physical interactions, the participants get to know, appreciate and give back to a community, gaining new skills, and making new connections, as explained by Kacprowicz, & Borowiecka (2014).

Similarly, the off-site or online volunteering is non-paid tasks for social good but undertaken online, using wired or wireless networks. The benefits of online volunteering include flexible schedule for both, blended service options by combining online and onsite work to suit circumstances, allow wider range of expertise to contribute together or sequentially, offers opportunity for working on creative project, it offers opportunity to engage more diverse and large volunteer groups from worldwide (World Bank 2010,Cuso International 2016)

Thus, from theoretical perspective, Nigeria has the opportunity to use many tools of growing styles volunteering from financial return to non-financial, from onsite to offsite e-volunteers.

Lessons From the Public-Spirited History

The current efforts by various Nigerian authorities to mobilize resources for the much needed urban development may have some lessons to learn from their own history. The traditional method of finance and saving system in Nigeria began at a time immemorial. It is one of the most predominant types of informal finance, it is called Adashe in Hausaland (Northern Nigeria), Esusu in Yorubaland (Western Nigeria), in Igboland (Eastern Nigeria) it is called "Isusu" or "Utu", while the Ibibio call it "Etibe" and the Kalahari call it "Oku" Ojo, I.F. (2014).

Moreover, Ojo (ibid) opined that, "literally, Asusu, Esusu or Utu means saving container or account. The money being conserved or saved or kept for certain period of time before it is withdrawn by the owner". The modus operandi of the volunteering cash crowdsourcing is that, certain number of people voluntarily come together to reach a concrete agreement before its operation can be effective. Accordingly, the leader(s) of the group shall be unanimously appointed among the gathering interested members. It consists of such small groups of about 5 – 20 members or more, who usually came from a similar economic background usually artisans, market women, and petty-traders in the society. The amount generated is given to each contributor in rotational basis thus empowering one another to create wealth and thus trigger growth in the local economy. Similarly, the traditional fundraising institutions such as Esusu Cooperatives in South-West Nigeria and the Harambee system in Kenya as noted by Adeokun et al (2014) have been a vital source of capital formation for low income earners.

The non-cash volunteering called 'Gayya' in Northern Nigeria is practiced where members in a community come together to form a group or club where energy is gnarred to execute community project or help the needy member of the community especially with the sole aim of empower such individuals, or solve a problem faced by the community.

From historical perspective also, Nigeria has many lessons that can be polished and reset for use currently and in the future. Using volunteers for urban development in Nigeria it has precedence especially in the Southwest and the Northern parts, where large-scale urban development was mainly constructed and maintained by volunteer force. This legacy stem from pre-colonial invasion, and even before Islamic system. In most cities in the north of Nigeria has three major public works:

- **The City Wall:** Used for defensive purposes in large cities with socio-econ resources especially in the Hausa States like Kano, Katsina, Zaria and Sokoto and their secondary towns. and in the South West of Nigeria, like Benin and Oyo. Figure 1 and Figure 2 show examples city walls built through volunteers in different times of Nigeria's history. Figures 1 show remnant of the historic Kano city wall that was built between 1095 through 1134 and completed in the middle of the 14th century, of about 15 meters high, and has been described as "'the most impressive monument in West Africa", according to World Heritage Sites (2017). Figure 2 shows part of ancient Benin City wall, which Wesler (1998) described as the world's largest man-made earth structure. A better description was offered by Fred Pearce of the New Scientist (1999) and he described it as:

Figure 1. Volunteer built Kano City massive wall
Source: African Legacy (2000).

Figure 2. Volunteer built Benin City wall
Source InformAfrica.com,(2015).

They extend for some 9,900 miles (16,000 kilometers) in all, in a mosaic of more than 500 interconnected settlement boundaries. They cover 2,510 sq. miles (6,500 square kilometers) and were all dug by the Edo people. In all, they are four times longer than the Great Wall of China, and consumed a hundred times more material than the Great Pyramid of Cheops. They took an estimated 150 million hours of digging to construct, and are perhaps the largest single archaeological phenomenon on the planet.

In addition to city walls, some cities have established regional defensive settlements – or *ribat*- as "early warning centers" against attackers with the role to slow down the enemy armies and also to alert the city of impending attack (Salau, 2011). All these defensive activities- from the city wall building, its maintenance, defensive roles in case of attach, *ribat* service- were carried out on volunteer basis.

- **The Marketplace:** As local and regional commercial focus of activities, markets were important to urban community as centers of commerce and exchange of goods and services. They also served as production and distribution of goods for local consumption and for regional trade. In addition, they serve other services such as social networking, social meeting places, entertainments, and many other. They are therefore large and complex public facilities, the building and upkeep of which used to be shared volunteer community activities. As Benna (2014), using Timbuktu example, explained the main tasks used to be shared among youth cohorts from different neighborhoods.

Kurmi Market in Kano city, according to UNESCO (2017) is one of the oldest and largest local markets in Africa. Its economic and cultural influences went beyond local and region, but extend to serve as an international market where North African and some European goods were traded for local goods through trans-Saharan trade. The market was well-organized and well laid out of human scale, and built of much block by local volunteers. Each lane contains of many traders, who trade in identical good, e.g. leatherwork, textiles, iron and brass work, spices etc.

- **The Mosques and Other Public Buildings:** In most parts of Nigeria, urban places of worship and common community use were built and maintained using volunteer force. The contributions come in various forms and affordability. Some used or contribute their skills, labour, foods, drinks and drumming. The elders would supervise, the youth supply the labour and the build craftsmen would direct what to put where. The activity would be repeated daily until the project is completed.

An Example of a large-scale public works built by volunteers in ancient cities was the Emir's Palace. In Kano, Muhammadu Rumfa who ruled Kano from 1463 to 1499 built thc Emir's Palace. The palace has 3 gates namely Kofar Kwaru, Kofar Fatalawa and Kofar Kudu. According to UNESCO (2017), the palace is divided into 3 sections. At the south are the Administrative buildings with rooms (Soran Zauna Lafiya, Soron Giwa and Soron Bello and Rumfar Kasa). The central part consists of members of the emir's family and at the northern parts are the stables and the servants' rooms

Replicating the Lessons

The World Bank (2016), after exhaustive study is of the view that the current urbanization model in Nigeria is unsustainable, largely because the number of jobs created is low, productivity growth is sluggish, and poverty rate is high. These problems, however, are type that a transformative urbanization model should solve for Nigeria.

The World Bank (2016) identified limited employment creation and productivity growth, and few gains in living conditions in cities as the twin urban challenges, along with their underlying causes as the hurdles to Nigeria's growth. These two key issues are outlined in Table 2 in which urban challenges are identified as, first, the limited employment creation and productivity growth (due to poor business environment and market fragmentation); second, few gains in living conditions in urban settlements (due to limited access to basic services and long distance to jobs and services). The underlying causes of each of these elements are highlighted.

Table 2. Nigeria's key urban challenges and their underlying causes

Urban challenge	*Underlying causes*
Limited employment creation and productivity growth	
Poor business environment	Weak land tenure and poor land management
	High costs of registration
	Poor infrastructure
	Heavy urban congestion
	High levels of corruption and poor judiciary
Market fragmentation	Lack of regional transport infrastructure
	Administrative/institutional inconsistencies
Few gains in living conditions in urban settlements	
Limited access to basic services	Poor land management and urban planning
	Lack of interjurisdictional coordination
	Insufficient infrastructure investment
	Inadequate local revenue sources
	Poorly designed intergovernmental expenditure responsibilities
Distance from jobs and services	Poor intra-urban connectivity
	Expensive public transport

Source: World Bank (2016).

These two important urban development issues, the World Bank (2016) report suggests, can be solved through the efficient restructuring of the country's institutions, infrastructure, and interventions. Each of these proposed policy instruments is briefly discussed below.

- **On Institutions:** The World Bank (2016) suggests focusing on those related to the development of land, service provision, and finance. It argues that constrained job growth is a function of messy business environment, which stems from institutional deficiencies in urban land management and uncoordinated institutional responsibilities for urban planning, rules for basic service provision, and inadequate urban finance. People are likely to respond to clear land rights and management systems, by making short- and long-term investment and trade decisions and municipal authorities can prepare future growth plans, investments, tax regimes and general urban development guidance system with confidence. The guidance system can trigger economic activities among all social sectors in ways that with uplift most people out of poverty and enhance urban quality of life for the majority.
- **On Infrastructure:** The World Bank (2016) suggests massive investments in hard and soft infrastructure and urban services, both with and between cities. The implementation of regional and urban plans should be comprehensive, dealing fairly with all areas including informal slum areas.
- **On Interventions:** The World Bank (2016) suggests going beyond institutional reforms and greater infrastructure investment interventions that target improve living conditions in slums within cities and at the regional level, the lagging regions, especially those affected by Boko Haram insurgency in the North-east and in the North-west.

The following development resources need to be explored:

1. All alternative finance sources, especially crowdfunding markets (Afrikstart 2015, CCAF 2017)
2. E-Volunteering (Kacprowicz, & Borowiecka 2014; Koerten & van den Besselaar 2015, Cuso International 2016)
3. Volunteer Technology Communities (World Bank, 2010)

The World Bank (2016) study suggests that the weak economic growth in Nigeria was mainly due to the following interconnected causes. First, the sectoral distribution of jobs shows that the labour-intensive sectors are low in productivity and slow in growth, while the fast-growers are capital intensive with minimal labor use. Second, the dominant informal firms are incapable of enhancing their productivity to capture urban economies of scale and specialization. Third, the business environment of poor power supply, transport network, financial system and ineffective bureaucracy make planned growth difficult. Fourth, the fragmented market of disjointed cities raises production costs and reduces the agglomeration and localization effects.

To overcome some of these problems and to help Nigeria catch-up and transform its urban economy, we propose the application of the following programs using alternative finance strategies, encouraging the growth of start-up ecosystem, the used of diverse types of online and onsite volunteers, enlarging volunteers to include retiring senior citizens and encouraging interactions between local and Diaspora sister communities:

1. Comprehensive Area Upgrading with Digital Networks
2. Redevelopment Areas of Decaying Zones into "Smart" Communities
3. Creation of Industrial Park(s) in every Local Government
4. At least Science and Technology Parks built by every Federal, State and Private University
5. Proto-type Innovation Districts in all state capitals and Abuja

The seed money for the initial take-off of these ventures will come from the following sources:

1. All looted funds and resources realized from the efforts of EFCC and other agencies,
2. Fifty percent cut of salaries and allowances of the 2019 members of National Assembly,
3. All Nigerian Banks, Governments (Federal, State, and Local) should surrender 5% of their statutory allocations or profits.

The Programs: Recruitment and Management

Volunteer programs many be viewed as the non-financial channel and instruments of the emerging alternative finance system. Both volunteerism and alternative finance seek to encourage local development resource mobilization by operating outside the traditional finance system dominated by banks and capital markets. Tables 1 and 2 shows the current state of the main volunteer programs in Nigeria designed for socio-economic development.

It seems imperative that recruitment into these programs should be clear, voluntary and online similar to the approach used in the N-Power program. In addition, the sound recruitment practices, it is important to ensure that the programs are effectively managed, and the achievements fully explained to the public. Each program need to need to fully evaluated and, if needed, revised at regular interval so as to bring it at par with prevailing best practice in the field.

Boosting volunteer programs makes sense. First, because the triple impact of the decreasing oil prices, low levels of non-oil-based internally generated revenues (IGR), and a rising infrastructure deficit are combining to create and urgent investment challenge for Nigeria. Second, the rising demand for urban development investment triggered by the huge and growing urban population and the growing middle class, seem far beyond the capacities of the traditional financial system to provide. To this end, the following new programs are proposed;

1. N-Senior Citizen Volunteer Corp
2. N-Diaspora Volunteer Corp

N-Senior Citizen Volunteer Corp

Retired persons have a unique set of skills and knowledge to offer as volunteers, especially as mentors and tutors to younger generations, in giving career guidance, and in offering companionship and care. The offered service benefits the giver and the community due to its mental and physical health gains, fosters positive social and family ties, and enhances the image of seniors as active and vital community members (Stevenson 2014, Wu 2011). Thus, borrowing from the lessons of history, we recommend that Nigerian Senior Volunteer Corp should be established and its deep experience and far-sightedness be mobilized for urban and national development. The membership should be open to professional and non-professionals of retired age, whether from the public sector (civil service, universities, parastatals), from the private sectors (managers and technical in the local and multi-national firms), and from the community (renown leaders and organizers). Senior citizens add the much needed reliability and maturity to the system.

Table 3. Main Nigerian volunteer programs, 2017

Program Data	Main Aims and Areas	Components	Achievements
N-Power Scheme Established June 2016	assist to improve the inadequacies in our public services in education, health and civic education	N-Power Agro, N-Power Health, N-Power Teach, N-Power Community Education	1.Teachers - 500,000 2.Knowledge – 25,000 3.Build- 75,000
National Youth Service Scheme. Established. May 1973	inculcate discipline, raise moral tone, shared national experience	As job creators, they should work with the National Directorate of Employment and Entrepreneurship incubation centres	Graduated hundreds of thousands, some find in their place of posting
National Peace Corps Established: March 2013	Promote social and economic development, Empower and pre-occupy Nigerian Youths through job creation	Permanent Staff Officers, Peace Corps Volunteers, Student Membership	Affiliated to many global agencies, e.g. UNESCO, Green Economy regional office in Kenya
Technical Aid Corps Established: Oct 2004	Sharing Nigeria's know-how and expertise with other African, Caribbean and Pacific (ACP) countries. Promote understanding	Assistance in law Engineering, Agriculture, Medical Lab, Technology, and Sport, Architecture, Radiology, Accountancy, Insurance, Metrology, Lecturing, Coaching and Artisanship	Received commendation from UNDP, United Nations Volunteers Service, the commonwealth and other relevant international development agencies.

Source: Composed by the author from various sources, 2017.

N-Diaspora Volunteer Corp

Diaspora contributions can significantly transform economies, is best demonstrated by China, Korea and India (World Bank 2016, AfDB, ND).Their strategies were built on shared development objectives between the government and the Diaspora, and supported comprehensive policies, governance structures and incentives to generate sound enabling environment for mobilizing Diaspora capitals (expertise, investments, entrepreneurship and corporate affiliations) targeting critical growth areas. Nigeria should seek to improve on these strategies, using the combination of the emerging alternative finance and e-volunteering concepts (Chikezie 2011, Wapmuk 2014). This group can be mobilized not only to channels its diverse capitals toward urban development projected like Industrial Parks, Science and Technology Parks, and Innovation Districts in various part of Nigeria. The group can also engage in knowledge generating and training, in policy and advocacy activities, and in networking with other volunteer groups.

Areas of National Urban Development Needs

According to UNDESA (2014) world's urban population is projected to receive additional 2.5 billion people by 2050 and nearly 90 per cent of the increase will be in Asia and Africa. India, China and Nigeria combined are projected to account for 37 per cent of this increase. While India will add 404 million urban citizens, China 292 million and, which seems insufficiently prepared for this urban transformation will add Nigeria 212 million.

Insufficiently prepared because even the current level Nigeria's rapid urban expansion has not yet found sufficient financing for its urban development needs. This is largely because the triple impact of a long-term drop in oil prices, low levels of non-oil-based internally generated revenues (IGR), and a growing infrastructure deficit pose a serious investment challenge. It must be admitted that the future of the oil price is looking better and the level of production is on the up-swing and the government has taken some prudent measures to improve infrastructure delivery system- as evidenced by the Abuja Airport runway reconstruction and the concrete highway built by Dangote. If in addition the Alternative Finance and E-Volunteering toots are made to work effectively, then the recommended urban development programs will include the following:

- Reconstruction of urban centers in B-Haram affected areas,
- Upgrading City Centers at least one in each state,
- Major Development Corridors.

Reconstruction of Urban Centers

Reconstruction of urban centres in Boko Haram affected Areas: Boko Haram insurgency has greatly disrupted urban socio-economic activities, destroyed hard and soft infrastructure facilities in the North-eastern parts of Nigeria. As shown in Figure 3, Borno State is epic-center of their activities and it is followed by the immediate neighboring states. All cities and towns in these states need varying levels of reconstruction activities. The state capitals and local government headquarters need to be assessed as to the exact level of work needed within urban centers with respect to redevelopment in physical infrastructure (utilities, roads, transport, etc.) and social infrastructure (educational, health, commercial, employment, security and other facilities). The safe and smooth connections between towns need to be

Figure 3. Nigeria states affected by the Boko Haram's activities
Source: #BringBackOurGirls, 2017.

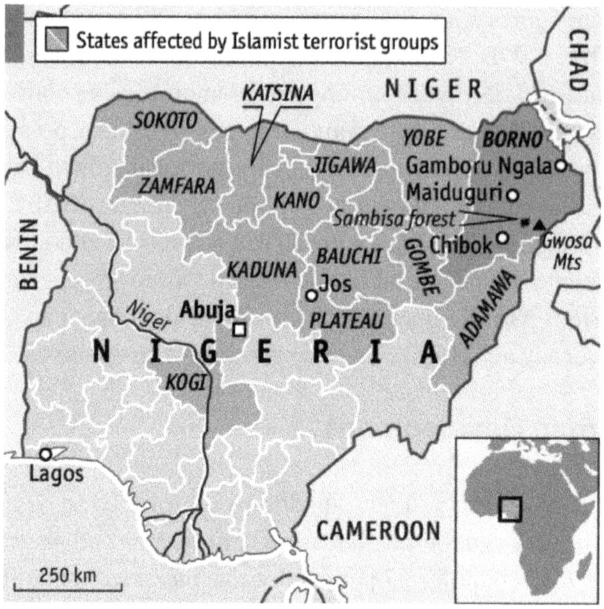

restored. After meeting the deficit, it is vital that the needs of the growing urban population to, say 2050, are carefully planned and resources for the implementation is mobilized. Job creations and production facilities, such industrial parks (UNIDO, 2016), innovation districts (Katz & Wagner, 2014), and science and technology parks (RS 2009) need to be established in association with universities and polytechnics, as described elsewhere in this chapter.

Upgrading City Centers

Upgrading city centres at least one in each state: Many state governments have executed a number of urban development projects in preparations for the last election campaign season. Most of these projects were impressionists and intended to attract temporary political support. Projects capable of real urban transformation in terms of job creation, reduction of poverty and enhancing urban quality of life are the type recommended here, including but not limited to: redevelopment areas of decaying zones into "smart" communities, industrial parks(UNIDO, 2016), innovation districts(Katz & Wagner, 2014), and science and technology parks (RS 2009). Every stage in the development of these projects creates useful jobs, if well organized. From the planning and design, to the construction and commissioning, and to its upkeep can provide well-paying jobs to many young people. Those who work in them generate products that will be circulated in the marketplace, thus creating more jobs down the line.

Major Development Corridors

Nigeria can generate many types of corridor development based of transport network, railway network, or river systems. These can then be used as the basis of structuring economic activities across the nation.

A good example is the so-called LAgos-KAno-JIbiya (LAKAJI). As shown in Figure 4, this Corridor is a 1,225 km transport route that runs from the port of Lagos in the Southern part of Nigeria, through the commercial center of Kano, and ending in Jibiya at the border with Niger (USAID, 2015). It has strategic significance for national, regional and international trade, as it is the main route for moving imported goods to northern Nigeria, and exports to southern port, using both road and rail systems. By connecting Lagos to Kano, the proposed corridor connects Nigeria's largest and most important commercial centers and feeds many local and regional markets. This corridor has the potential of using multiple industrial parks, innovation districts (Katz & Wagner, 2014), and science and technology parks (RS 2009) to grow in to the largest one of its kind in Africa.

To sum up, urban development in many parts of Nigeria has a long history of volunteer contribution. With the convergence of deep ICT penetration and the emergence of alternative finance solutions, this chapter advocates the revival of volunteerism for urban development, supported by local and Diaspora communities worldwide.

IMPLICATIONS OF THE REVIEW OF THEORETICAL FRAMEWORKS

The digital cash-based crowdfunding is a platform that brings the benefits and security of mobile commerce and payments to volunteers, community and government at all levels. For example, as *Business Wire* reported, in Kenya it provides a digital platform that connects smallholder farmers, agents, buyers and banks in East African countries such as Kenya, Uganda and Tanzania. 2KUZE, which in Swahili

Figure 4. The proposed LAKAJI development corridor in Nigeria
Source: LAKAJI (USAID NEXTT) 2013.

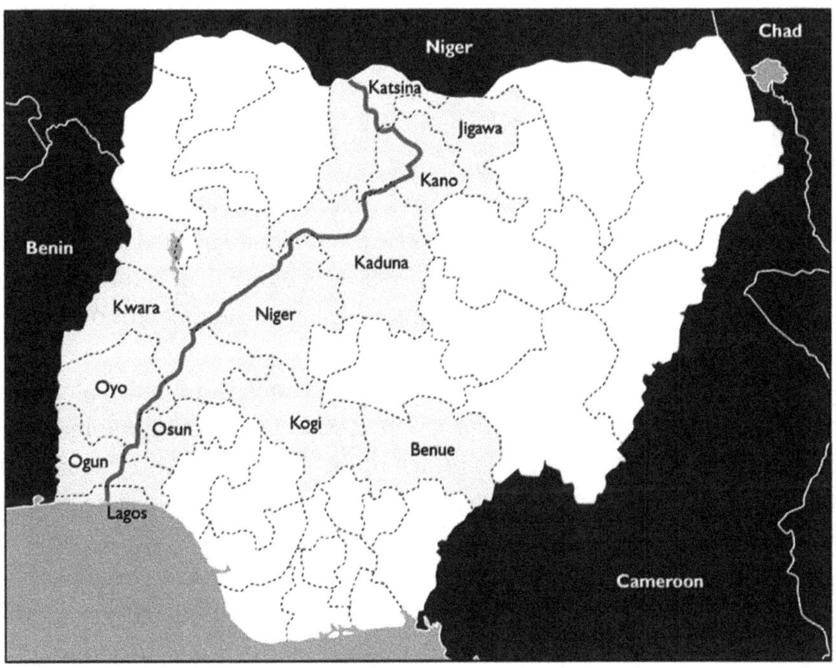

means "Let's grow together", enables farmers to buy, sell and receive payments for agricultural goods via their feature phones.

It is believed that by using mobile, a technology that is so ubiquitous among farmers in Africa, can improve financial access, bring in operational efficiency and facilitate faster payments. The digital cash based collaboration between the facilitators and farmers in the market helped to deliver a solution that can be implemented and make an impact without any major changes to the day-to-day. According to Business Wire (2017) In early 2017, some 2,000 small-scale farmers in Nandi Hills, Kenya are currently using the solution to sell their produce and working with farmer-friendly agents to ensure they reach the right buyers for the best price. 2KUZE is one of several broad-based collaborations on which the Mastercard Lab for Financial Inclusion is working. The Lab was established in Africa to contribute to the company's global commitment to connect 500 million people to formal financial services through the use of public-private partnerships with governments, the private sector and non-governmental organizations.

Similarly in Nigeria more than 2million farmers were registered and had timely access to fertilizers and improved seeds at moderate prices which boost production of rice and maize in the country in the year 2016 as aspect of crowdfunding in the country. The different models have been of help in locating issues that have not been explored enough previously and to discover new approaches and insights. Firstly the definition of volunteering was made according to its many nuances and meanings, and that was much needed. Previously many researchers used the term as if it had only one exact meaning. The different theoretical frameworks were of value in order to see what needed to be added as components to the existing knowledge as e.g. the life-cycle of volunteering and how volunteering changes the volunteers. It helped to illumine what was missing in the process the volunteers went through.

There were differences between newcomers, volunteers and veteran volunteers and those who have left the organization after burnout or other reasons. By and large, the reviewed above have shown that volunteering covers a wide spectrum of activities in which the volunteers' time is given to benefit another person, group or cause (Cheung, 2006). Without volunteers, many activities and services offered by these organizations simply could not operate. This is especially true for sports and leisure sector. Moreover volunteers help to satisfy various social and community needs, contribute to build social capital and improve the quality of life of the people (ibid:2).

In recent times in Africa, volunteers are becoming central element in community survival. They play important role in delivering services across range of diverse areas from social welfare, sports (Joanna, Cheung, 2006), and infrastructure facilities. Municipal governments internationally are struggling with decrease funding; some relied on volunteers to provide resources and needed facilities. The willingness of community members to volunteer is critical for the success of urban development projects. As mentioned somewhere in this write, there are varied reasons why people volunteer in community development projects and the motives for such volunteering

Therefore, this write up presents an overview of leading concepts in both volunteerism and offers recommendations for social workers to select appropriate approaches to manage volunteers professionally across different contexts. Especially as a consequence of the pressure on budgets under prevailing economic conditions, the general retreat of the governmentally financed welfare state, the growing demand for social services, and changes in the availability of volunteers, social workers across all policy fields and organizational contexts and cultures will feel pressured to involve more volunteers in urban development programs. It is imperative to recommend the application of volunteering sport model concept in the provision of urban development projects such as good housing, infrastructure, markets, abattoirs and health facilities in all the 774 local government headquarters across the country.

FRAMEWORK FOR IMPACT ANALYSIS OF CONTRIBUTION OF NIGERIAN VOLUNTEER PROGRAM TO THE NATIONAL DEVELOPMENT

The test of the effectiveness of the Volunteer Program is in its contributions to solving the immediate urban problems of the North East Region, the decaying, poverty stricken urban centers and its contributions to the long-term sustainable future growth of Nigeria is outlined below. We will suggest a framework for the analyses of the contributions of each volunteer program in terms of its physical, social and economic impact in each of the projects targeting national problem areas.

This set out the basic framework only, the details have to be worked based on time and place the decision and action have to be taken. It may also be possible that the framework has to be fine-tuned at that time.

Table 4 is the proposed framework to assess the impact of the Nigerian Volunteer Program at the national level with respect to urban development problems facing the Boko-Haram affected north-east region. This problem is expected to last from immediate to medium term period of five years. The criteria for achievement in terms of physical, social and economic development should be defined and applied by each component of the volunteer program. These are then used to assess progress within cities and towns in the region, as well as between zones of the regions.

Table 5 is the proposed framework to assess the impact of the Nigerian Volunteer Program at the national level with respect to urban development problems facing the decaying city centers of Nigeria, which are the hub urban poverty. These areas are generally socially strong but economically weak. With adequate funding and good management the keys physical, social and economic development issues could be solved. Every year, it is expected that each component of the volunteer program should identify its achievement in solving physical infrastructure, social facilities upgraded and new economic activities generated and new jobs created.

Table 6 is designed to evaluate the progress achieved the each component of the volunteer program in meeting the future growth needs of Nigeria. All the participants should eventually face this long-term program. The evaluation in this case should go beyond quantities of physical, social and economic contributions and be extended to include issues of transformative achievement. With respect to the volunteer components, in this case, the role of Senior Volunteer Corp and the Diaspora Corp will be very important, and so would the evaluation of their impact.

Table 4. National development problem A: Boko-Haram affected region

Projects Targeting National Problem Areas	Contributions of Volunteer Schemes in Physical, Social and Economic Terms				
	N-Power	NYSC	NPC	TAC	Others
1. Comprehensive Area Upgrading with Digital Networks					
2. Redevelopment Areas of Decaying Zones into "Smart" Communities					
3. Creation of Industrial Park(s) in every Local Government					
4. At least Science and Technology Parks built by every University					
5. Proto-type Innovation Districts in all state capitals and Abuja					

1. N-Power Scheme, 2. National Youth Service, 3. National Peace Corps, 4. Technical Aid Corps, 5. Others

Table 5. National problem Area B: Decaying urban centers

Projects Targeting National Problem Areas	Contributions of Volunteer Schemes in Physical, Social and Economic Terms				
	N-Power	NYSC	NPC	TAC	Others
1.Comprehensive Area Upgrading with Digital Networks					
2. Redevelopment Areas of Decaying Zones into "Smart" Communities					
3. Creation of Industrial Park(s) in every Local Government					
4. At least Science and Technology Parks built by every University					
5. Proto-type Innovation Districts in all state capitals and Abuja					

1. N-Power Scheme, 2 National Youth Service, 3. National Peace Corps, 4. Technical Aid Corps, 5. Others

Table 6. National problem Area C: Meeting future urban growth needs

Projects Targeting National Problem Areas	Contributions of Volunteer Schemes in Physical, Social and Economic terms				
	N-Power	NYSC	NPC	TAC	Others
1. Comprehensive Area Upgrading with Digital Networks					
2. Redevelopment Areas of Decaying Zones into "Smart" Communities					
3. Creation of Industrial Park(s) in every Local Government					
4. At least Science and Technology Parks built by every University					
5. Proto-type Innovation Districts in all state capitals and Abuja					

1. N-Power Scheme, 2 National Youth Service, 3. National Peace Corps, 4. Technical Aid Corps, 5. Others

In terms of timeframe, the activities in this section are expected to peak and become more complex towards 2050, when Nigeria will have more than 400 million people and the third most populous nation on earth. There will be huge technological, socio-economic and political changes affecting urban worldwide. It is against this background and we as national and sub-national changes that adjustments to the impact assessment framework needs to be made. Also the increased tempo of online activities and the greater contributions of alternative finance system suggest an expansion of the framework for impact analysis.

FUTURE RESEARCH AND CONCLUSION

Future Research

The study of volunteerism has generated multiple conceptual frameworks yet no integrated theory has emerged. This article identifies three major challenges, or layers of complexity, that a unified theory of volunteering faces. First, volunteering is a complex phenomenon that has permeable boundaries and spans a wide variety of activities, organizations, and sectors. Second, different disciplines attribute different meanings and functions to volunteering. Third, existing theoretical models did not specify area of applicability.

Furthermore, in various cultures there are no terms such as volunteers. In India, the term is social work and in Russia no specific word is used to denote volunteers. Also, historically the term volunteer changed dramatically from considering volunteering as soldiers who join wars without being forced to do so to our current understanding of volunteering as the underpinnings of civil society (Ellis & Noyes, 1990).

Moreover, living in some urban areas is deteriorating; poor performance of urban governance and several plans and programmes never yielded any affirmative results like the case of Kathmandu (Nepal). Aside from adding financial value, the labor of volunteers also has the potential to increase human, social, and physical capital. Yet, having demonstrated the importance and value of volunteer work, it is also important to consider another question: how can volunteerism be sustainable? Furthermore, the ownership and participation of community members in the development project is fundamental for both the success and sustainability of the project. Volunteerism should establish people-centered models of development that privilege the marginalized and are informed by local knowledge and experience. Notably, volunteer programs are most effective when participants are aware of the local and national power structures in which their work takes place. Evidently, sustainability is important in terms of volunteer placement (i.e., matching volunteers' skills to the project's needs), project monitoring, and capacity-building. However, Brown finds that true sustainability comes from the lasting, positive changes that shape the ideas and thoughts of individuals as a result of their time as volunteers.

An example of sustainability here is Profugo. At Profugo (www.profugo.org, 2017), this exact form of sustainability is evident in the reflections of former field fellows, interns, and volunteers. Profugo also encourages community participation and ownership of its development projects by valuing local knowledge and experience and transferring project control to community members. For example, although the wells constructed during the Water for Life project community project in Wayanad, India were built using funds and expertise from Profugo, they are now controlled and maintained by community members.

CONCLUSION

All said and done, volunteering is shredded with controversies surrounding its meaning, applications, benefits and problems. There is no unified modus operandi either internal or internationally. The vision of volunteering is to create a world where brighter futures are possible because all communities have equal access to a better quality of life. There should be Center of Development using sport model as a channel in which the volunteers work alongside a community to generate social change that is sustainable, cost efficient, and long lasting. The essence is to use the model / approach to foster positive community development that focuses on infrastructure, health, human and social development. In conclusion, volunteering has been a cultural practice among communities in Nigeria since time immemorial. Development projects such as roads, defense city walls, town halls and such facilities were provided through volunteering efforts of community members. However, with new urbanized cities and population increase, the need for government to partake in such projects delivery efforts by volunteerism is paramount.

REFERENCES

Adeokun. (2014). *Reworking Traditional Fund Raising Institutions for Affordable Housing Provisions: A Review of Nigeria and Kenya Case Studies*. Retrieved from www.eprints-convenantuniversity.edu.ng/2683/1/

African Legacy. (2000). *Hausaland Walled Cities & Towns - remote sensing studies*. Retrieved from https://csweb.bournemouth.ac.uk/africanlegacy/kano_walls.htm

African Media Agency. (2017). *Digitising East Africa's agricultural sector*. Retrieved from www.biz-community.com /sendToFriend.aspt/156413pdf

Afrikstart. (2015). *Crowdfunding Africa*. Retrieved from http://afrikstart.com/report/wp-content/uploads /2016/09/ Afrikstart-Crowdfunding-In-Africa-Report.pdf

Agrawal, A., Catalini, C., & Goldfarb, A. (2014). Some Simple Economics of Crowdfunding. National Bureau of Economic Research, (2014), 63-97.

BringBackOurGirls. (2017). *Map showing location of Chibok, Borno, etc*. Retrieved from https://www.pinterest.com/pin/433541901601586039/

Business Wire. (2017). *Mastercard Launches Mobile Marketplace to Digitize East Africa's Agricultural Sector*. Retrieved from http://www.businesswire.com/news/home/20170116005049/en/Mastercard-Launches-Mobile-Marketplace-Digitize-East-Africa%E2%80%99

Cambridge Centre for Alternative Finance (CCAF). (2017). *Crowdfunding in East Africa*. Retrieved from https:// www.jbs.cam.ac.uk/faculty-research/centres/alternative-finance/ publications/crowdfunding-in-east-africa/#.WRc4_9wlFY0

Clark, B. (2011). *The History & Evolution of Crowdfunding*. Retrieved from http://mashable.com/2011/09/15/crowdfunding-history/#0u8WF.phe8qf

Clark, B. (2011). *The History & Evolution of Crowdfunding*. Retrieved from http://mashable.com/2011/09/15/crowdfunding-history/#0u8WF.phe8qf

Clarkson, N. (2015). *A brief History of Crowdfunding*. Retrieved from https://www.virgin.com/entre-preneur/brief-history-crowdfunding

Cnaan, R. A., Handy, F., & Wadsworth, M. (1996). Defining who is a volunteer; Conceptual and empirical considerations. *Nonprofit and Voluntary Sector Quarterly*, *25*(3), 364–383. doi:10.1177/0899764096253006

Cuso International. (2016). *E-Connect: Cuso International's E-Volunteering Guide*. Retrieved from http://www. cusointernational.org/docs/default-source/publications/Training-Resources/e-volunteering-toolkit.pdf?sfvrsn=4

Erian, P. (2015). Social innovation. Seismic: shake up your city! Seismic. In The Civic Economy Opportunities and challenges for European cities. Academic Press.

Haski-Leventhal, D., & Bargal, D. (2008). The volunteer stages and transitions model: Organizational socialization of volunteers. *Human Relations*, *61*(1), 67–102. doi:10.1177/0018726707085946

Hustinx, L., Cnaan, R. A., & Handy, F. (2010). Navigating Theories of Volunteering: A Hybri Map for a Complex Phenomenon. *Journal for the Theory of Social Behaviour*, *40*(4), 410–434. doi:10.1111/j.1468-5914.2010.00439.x

InformAfrica.com. (2015). *African History: Facts about the Great Walls of Benin*. Retrieved from http://www.informafrica.com/african-history/african-history-facts-about-the-great-walls-of-benin/

Kacprowicz, M., & Borowiecka, B. (2014). *E-Volunteering Handbook*. Retrieved from http://e-volunteering.eu/wp-content/uploads/2014/11/evolunteering-handbook.pdf

Katz & Wagner. (2014). *The Rise of Innovation Districts: A New Geography of Innovation in America*. Academic Press.

Koerten, H., & van den Besselaar, P. (2015). Crowdsourcing and Citizen Science in biodiversity research http://www.synthesys.info/wp-content/uploads/2014/01/NA3-Del.-3.4-Crowdsourcing-report-Phase-1.pdf

Lakaji. (2013). *Agricultural Growth Corridor Summit (AGCIS) Schematics*. Retrieved from http://www.nigerianextt.org/?page_id=334

Lee, B. (2006). *A New Challenge Model of a Volunteer Program*. Retrieved from www.volunteerprogramme

Mansour, E. Z. (2017). *Role of NGOs in development*. Retrieved from https://www.slideshare.net/MansourEsmaeilZaei/role-of-ngos-in-development

Ojo, I. F. (2014). Article. *European Journal of Business Management, 2*(1). Retrieved from http://www.ejobm.org

Omotosho, O. A., & Snyder, M. (2002). Considerations of Community: The context and Process of Volunteerism. *The American Behavioral Scientist*, *45*(5), 846–867. doi:10.1177/0002764202045005007

Pearce, F. (1999). African Queen. *New Scientist*, (2203). Retrieved from http://www.yorku.ca/nhp/seminars/2004_05/Ribat.pdf

Profugo.org. (2017). Retrieved from www.profugo.org/cite

Putzier, K. (2015). Crowdfunding: A short history. *Tapping small-time investors is nothing new — it's older than the Statue of Liberty.* Retrieved from https://therealdeal.com/issues_articles/crowdfunding-a-short-history/

Report of a Symposium (RS). (2009). *Understanding Research, Science and Technology Parks: Global Best Practice*. Retrieved from http://www.nap.edu/catalog.php?record_id=12546

Rogers, K. (2017). *"Ubuntu": What Does It Mean?* Retrieved from www.africanimpact.com/VolunteerinAfrica

Salau, M. B. (2011). *Ribats and the Development of Plantations in the Sokoto Caliphate: a Case Study of Fanisau*. Retrieved from www.yorku.ca/nhp/seminars/2004_05/Ribat.pdf

Sutton, R. I., & Straw, B. M. (1995). What theory is not. *Administrative Science Quarterly*, *40*(3), 371–38. doi:10.2307/2393788

UNESCO. (2017). *Ancient Kano City Walls and Associated Sties*. Retrieved from http://whc.unesco.org/en/tentativelists/5171/

UNIDO. (2016). *Ecoindustrial Parks In Developing And Emerging Countries*. Retrieved from https://www.unido.org/fileadmin/user_media_upgrade/Resources/Publications/Envionment/2016

Urban Development Corporation (UDC) Detroit. (2017). *Volunteer*. Retrieved from http://urbandevelopmentcorp.org/volunteers/

USAID Nigeria. (2015). *LAKAJI Corridor*. Retrieved from http://www.nigerianextt.org/?pageid=334

WeslerKit, W. (1998). Historical Archaeology in Nigeria. Africa World Press.

Wilson, J. (2017). *Volunteerism Research: A Review Essay*. Retrieved from www.//journals.sagepub.com

World Bank. (2010). *Volunteer Technology Communities: The World Bank Open Development*. Retrieved from https://www.gfdrr.org/sites/gfdrr/files/publication/Volunteer%20Technology%20Communities%20-%20Open%20Development_0.pdf

World Bank. (2016). *From oil to cities: Nigeria's next transformation*. Retrieved from http://documents.worldbank.org/curated/en/711661468010811972/pdf/106150-PUB-ADD-DOI-ISBN-SERIES-OUO-9.pdf

KEY TERMS AND DEFINITIONS

Decaying Urban Centers: Many urban centers in Nigeria have attracted rural migrants, but they lack employment opportunities and have inadequate urban infrastructure to meet the needs of immigrants.

Future Urban Growth: The urban areas in Nigeria are facing tremendous growth pressure due to waves of rural-urban migration and natural population growth, requiring additional social and physical infrastructure.

National Development Problem: Urban development problems that have regional and national significance. In this case, the North-Eastern region of Nigeria has experienced decline due to the activities of Boko Haram terrorists and also the gradual drying up of Lake Chad, on which farmers and fishermen depended for their livelihood.

Non-Oil-Based Economy: The country whose major source of revenue is from other sources such as agriculture, tourism, mining instead of oil.

Oil-Based Economy: The country whose major source of income comes from based activities that are tied to natural resources, mainly oil.

Urban Activities: Activities in urban setting in which land uses are dominated in the city.

Urban Volunteer Research: Facts finding group of individuals who are interested in urban matters as its affects the society.

Volunteer Corps: An organized group of people who render themselves to the service of humanity at a fixed pay, typical example here are the National Youth Service Corp.

Volunteerism: A willy-nilly offer of service or gift to the needy without expectation in reciprocal form.

Chapter 11
Prospects and Options for Sustainable and Inclusive Crowdfunding in African Cities

Innocent Chirisa
University of Zimbabwe, Zimbabwe

Liaison Mukarwi
University of Zimbabwe, Zimbabwe

Abraham Rajab Matamanda
University of the Free State, South Africa

ABSTRACT

The utility of crowdfunding in promoting sustainable development is beyond doubt due to its popularity in the Global North. The application of this concept in the Global South, especially in Africa, is ill-understood and questionable considering the high levels of corruption, poverty, and poor governance. Applying the concept of crowdfunding in Africa then becomes problematic. The chapter aims to undertake a critical analysis of the concept of crowdfunding and its sustainability in advancing the success of urban-based projects in African cities. What can (or should) be the defining pillars for sustainable and inclusive crowdfunding? What are the known (or even unknown) limits and prospects to initiatives like crowdfunding? What are the answers to the colonial legacy derived scepticisms about self-worth and context? What options do the African cities have? The chapter engages a mix of methodologies including literature review, document review, and case studies. Thematic content analysis is applied in building up the discourse. From the study, five critical observations emerge.

INTRODUCTION AND BACKGROUND

The utility of crowdfunding in promoting sustainable development is beyond doubt due to its popularity in the Global North, where it is highly touted and deemed as a genial option for sustainable urban development, among other policy programmes and projects (CrowdfundingHub, 2016; European Com-

DOI: 10.4018/978-1-5225-3952-0.ch011

mission, 2014). The application of this concept in the Global South, especially in Africa is ill-understood and questionable considering the high levels of corruption, poverty and poor governance (World Bank, 2013). Applying the concept of crowdfunding in Africa then becomes problematic. The foregoing has led to urban areas in Africa being centres of problems emanating from shortage of social services and facilities (UN-HABITAT, 2010). According to Wetlake, Baeck and Bone (2016, traditionally, crowdfunding has been reserved to the realms of arts and music, but recently it has been developed to be used as a tool to fundraise a plethora of projects. Crowdfunding is gaining popularity in all facets of everyday life as it offers a platform where citizens from different areas can pool resources for a common cause (World Bank, 2013). A recent research by Nesta estimated that crowdfunding facilitated £3.2 billion worth of loans, investments and donations in the UK in 2015 (Wetlake, Baeck and Bone, 2016). Civic crowdfunding represents a further development of the tool, as individuals and organizations begin to raise funds through online platforms for local urban development projects, as opposed to applying for traditional governmental or charity grant funding, or leaving urban development to local governments or developers (Nesta, 2012).

In African urban centers, infrastructure decay and a shortage of public utilities and services are rampant (UN-HABITAT, 2014). The shortage and filthy state of the same are attributed to financial challenges bedeviling most local authorities for example the Kampala municipality blames financial challenges on the water and sanitation services challenges they face (World Bank, 2011). Among the challenges leading to financial problems include corruption, poor corporate governance, thieving and abuse of public funds, poor revenue collection as well as poor cost recovery measures (UN-HABITAT, 2010; Maathai, 2009; Lawal, 2007). In this context which is marred by this myriad of anomalies and ills, it then becomes very difficult for Africans to consider or even imagine entrusting their funds into the hands of the government. Most importantly, the dominant question among the urban crowds, as it were, is about the dividend that accrues to each one of them after investing their few resources which build up into a pool of financial resources ultimately. With this background, African cities have not taken advantage of crowdfunding to support its sustainable urban development initiatives. However, there seems to be an increasing trend towards the use of crowdfunding in Africa (Boum, 2016). Following the definition by Gaziulusoy and Twomey (2014:13), defining crowdfunding (also known as crowd financing and crowd investing) as the process of a party requesting and acquiring financial or other resources from many individuals with the purpose of realising a specific project; this presents great opportunities for African municipalities to bankroll their development initiatives from the public. The same issues leading to financial shortages in most local authorities in Africa are also affecting the use of crowdfunding as a tool for funding urban development. Applying the concept of crowdfunding in Africa under the obtaining environment and situation is problematic and questionable to a great extent; the lack of transparency and accountability affects crowdfunding. In this view, the purpose of this chapter is to undertake a critical analysis of the concept of crowdfunding and its sustainability in advancing the success of urban-based projects in African cities. The study sought to gather and present information on pillars for sustainable and inclusive crowdfunding, the limits and prospects of crowdfunding; options available for the African cities have. In this quest, the study engaged a mix of methodologies including literature review, document review and case studies. Thematic content analysis is applied in building up the discourse. The chapter is organised to include a literature review; conceptual framework; results, discussion, and synthesis; policy options and practical implications; conclusion and definition of key terms.

LITERATURE REVIEW

Crowdfunding

According to Gaziulusoy and Twomey (2014:13), crowdfunding is increasingly popular, both as a source of venture capital and an investment opportunity. Crowdfunding is not only an alternative financing approach, but it also has broader implications for the generation of business models (Herman, 2013). Crowdfunding is also becoming popular among communities and local governments as a way of financing major public projects when government policy or funding fails to deliver what citizens desire. Of utmost importance are the two often-cited examples of successful crowdfunding efforts in the United States of America which include the Hurricane Katrina disaster relief fundraising campaign and President Barrack Obama's first term election campaign in 2008 (Nordicity, 2012: 5). As a result, crowdfunding also signals a potential in facilitating institutional change in which power becomes more distributed, decisions on public spending become more democratized and participatory, and local governments develop their own 'business models' for increased self-reliance rather than relying on central government funding. Marchand (2015:22) posits that launching a crowdfunding is not charity fundraising, the majority of the crowd expects something in return for their investment (Magala and Rubagumya, 2005). It is necessary to use incentives to lure potential backers. It is therefore critical to consider how crowdfunding initiatives may be undertaken so as to increase the success of the projects as well as accrue the full benefits of the process. To fully understand the concept of crowdfunding it is thus critical to focus on the four crowdfunding models which are explicitly explained in the forthcoming section.

Four Crowdfunding Models

Four different types of crowdfunding are found in the literature: donation-based (patronage model), reward-based, lending-based and equity-based (Marchand, 2015). With very different terms and requirements, it is necessary to understand the nuances involved with each branch of crowdfunding so as to choose the path most relevant to the goals and needs of such effort. The categories, according to Marchand (2015) are shown in the following section:

Rewards Crowdfunding

Rewards-based crowdfunding is the most common type of crowdfunding option available. This type involves setting varying levels of rewards that correspond to pledge amounts. A standard rewards campaign offers at least three levels of pledges/rewards. Rewards campaigns tend to work well for client-facing, tangible products who require less than $100,000 in funding and typically last for 1-3 months (Marchand, 2015). Belleflamme et al (2015) argues that fundraisers on reward-based crowdfunding do not offer a stake in the project or a monetary payment, but offer other rewards to funders. According to Nesta (2012) this model offers rewards as well as intangible benefits that are a combination of intrinsic and social motivation. It is succinctly presented that rewards and benefits are personal and it is up to the fundraiser to define those benefits.

Equity Crowdfunding

Equity crowdfunding is the exchange of actual shares in a private company for capital (Marchand, 2015). This is an investment type of crowdfunding that is associated with a return on investment if the business or investment pays off well in the long run (Nesta, 2012). In this form of crowdfunding, entrepreneurs can set investor caps, minimum pledge amounts, etc. as well as approve or deny investors who wish to view their business documents. Equity campaigns are typically several months or longer in length and fit well with start-ups seeking $100,000 or more in funding.

Donation Crowdfunding (Patronage Model)

Donation crowdfunding is exactly what it sounds like; the campaigns amass donations without being required to provide anything of value in return. This type of campaign serves social causes and charities best. The Donation model has its roots in philanthropy and is basically derived from the online donation model used by charities around the world. Nordicity (2012) observe that the key with this model is that although contributors may receive recognition or rewards for their contributions, they do not receive any rights or equity in the project which means that the donations are just meant to alleviate society and help for particular causes. Thus Nesta (2012) argue that the donation model is associated with intangible benefits as the motive of the contributors is intrinsic and socially grounded. Donation campaigns are often 1-3 months in length and work well for amounts under $10,000.

Lending Crowdfunding

Lending-based crowdfunding is just similar to any typical lending scenario, where individuals lend money to a project or company with the hope and expectation that it will be repaid at an agreed date, usually with interest (Herman, 2013). Furthermore, lending based crowdfunding allows entrepreneurs to raise funds in the form of loans that they will pay back to the lenders over a pre-determined timeline with a set interest rate. However, Nesta (2012) argues that some platforms focus more on social causes and as a result, they offer interest-free loans, a good example being Kiva – the micro-lending site. Lending campaigns tend to take place over a shorter time span of around five weeks and works well for entrepreneurs who don't want to give up equity in their start-up immediately.

Sustainable Urban Development

Freund (2007: vii) has observed, "Urbanisation is one of the most important social processes observed and written about over time". Muchadenyika and Williams (2016) also assert that urbanization is an essential determinant of social change though the process has to be premised on good governance. From a variety of beginnings, cities have evolved into sites where more and more complex activities take place (Morris, 1994; Mumford, 1961). At a certain point historically, the city may look parasitic on the productive countryside, where the balance between human beings and nature is so much better sustained (Howard, 1902). However, further along the line the city itself becomes the logical home for multitudes of social and economic activities that are fundamental to the material life of mankind (Kostof, 1991).

In this era and beyond, the goals of development have shifted form just mere development to sustainable development. With this motif, cities have to look into the future wherein their development initiatives today must not jeopardize the ability of the future generations to do the same (Sustainable Cities International, 2012). Therefore, this calls for the conscious use of natural resources; the focus of development now must consider the social, economic and environmental aspects with the aim of balancing them for a better today and tomorrow (Campbell, 1996). In the drive to sustainability, there has been growing literature and advocacy on smart cities and or smart growth. Schuringa (2013:20), states the objectives of smart growth as including the mix of land uses, promotion of compact building design, creating a range of housing opportunities and choices; creating walkable neighbourhoods, fostering distinctive, attractive communities with a strong sense of place; preservation of open space, farmland, natural beauty, and critical environmental areas; strengthening and directing development towards existing communities; provision of a variety of transportation choices; making development decisions predictable, fair and cost-effective and community engagement in development decisions. These objectives require a great deal of finance and financial discipline, technology and innovation, collaboration and participation, and inspiring leadership (good governance) among others. Yet, local authorities are usually financially constrained which makes the realization of these smart cities just a pipeline dream which is never fully achieved.

According to Saunders and Baeck, on technologies, (2015:11), "…successful smart cities of the future will combine the best aspects of technology infrastructure while making the most of the growing potential of 'collaborative technologies', and above all the citizens who power them…" These sentiments point to the need of investing in the human factor whereby capacitating the technological prowess of the people will enable cities to effectively harness the power of citizens through digital technologies (Schuringa, 2013; Saunders and Baeck, 2015). Drawing on examples from all around the world, there are four emerging methods which are helping city governments to harness the collaborative power of citizens, powered by the growing ubiquity of smart phones, the increasing preference for online transactions, combined with the emergence of low–cost hardware and peer–to–peer technologies. Saunders and Baeck (2015:11), mention the four methods that include:

- **The Collaborative Economy:** Connecting distributed groups of people, using the internet and digital technologies, to make better use of goods, skills, and space. This is important in cities where resources, particularly space, are limited.
- **Crowdsourcing Data:** People can use low–cost sensors to measure and create crowdsourced maps of their environments; city governments can crowdsource data from social media sites and sensors in mobile phones, as a supplement to city–wide Internet of Things networks.
- **Collective Intelligence:** Decision making and problem-solving are usually left to experts, yet citizens know a huge amount about their cities. New digital tools make it easier for people to get involved in policymaking, planning and budgeting, and this could help cities make smarter and more democratic decisions.
- **Crowdfunding:** People can connect with each other online to collaboratively fund community projects and city governments can use crowdfunding to make spending decisions that more accurately reflect the needs and wishes of citizens.

Important to crowdfunding is technology because the former usually use technological platforms like the internet to reach out to people. Crowdfunding internet platforms have sprung up, allowing fund seekers to "call out" or campaign to the "crowd" for their projects by funding incentives offered: lending, rewards / donations, and equity (Zhang *et al*, 2014). Through these platforms, people worldwide have recognized and capitalized on this opportunity, transforming crowdfunding from a small idea into a global phenomenon (*ibid*). Moreso, the other pillars to sustainable and inclusive crowdfunding include effective financial public management (transparency), good governance (trust), political stability, and social capital. These together with technologically connected societies; crowdfunding can be a resource to mobilize not only financial resources but ideas, business and partnerships for urban-based projects; all in line to promote sustainable urban development (Schuringa, 2013).

CONCEPTUAL FRAMEWORK

Thus, this can be a tool to sustainable urban development amid key enablers and threats as is shown on Figure 1.

Crowdfunding is a complex phenomenon which is represented in Figure 1 as nested in an intrinsic web that has key enablers, key threats which all facilitate or stifle sustainable urban development. The key enablers are the set of variables that promote the success of crowdfunding. Such variables include innovation, public participation, efficient public financial management and good corporate. Each one of the variable helps to promote trust and accountability within municipalities which will give the impetus for citizens to invest their funds in municipality urban development projects (Chaligha, 2014; Magala and Rubagumya, 2005). Through these key enablers, people worldwide have recognized the utility of crowdfunding. With over 500 active crowdfunding platforms around the world in 2012, estimated funds raised through crowdfunding platforms increased from USD 1.5 billion in 2011 to USD 5 billion in 2013, a 240% rise in just two years. With its growth and increasing global recognition, crowdfunding opens new options not only for SGBs, but also for impact investing – to intentionally promote SE benefits through investment (World Bank, 2013).

Figure 1. Conceptual framework
Source: Authors.

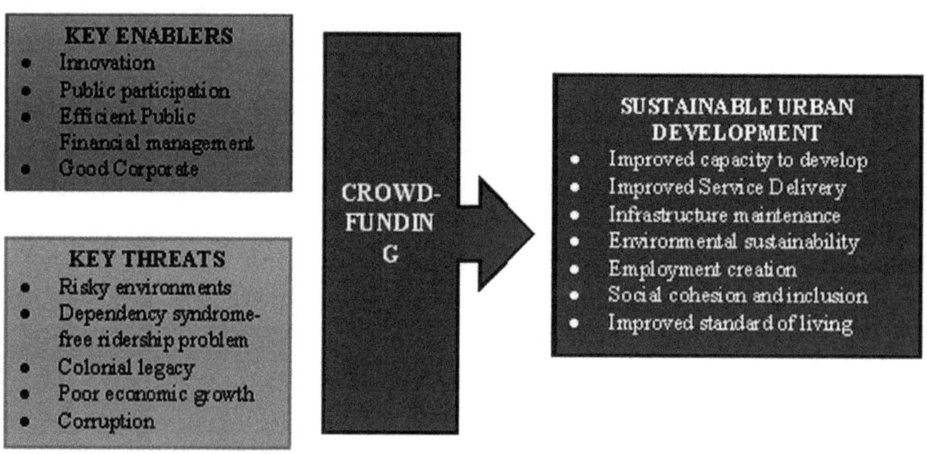

In as much as there are multiple key enablers, there are also some key threats which limit prospects of crowdfunding and ultimately compromises the sustainability of urban development projects. Variables such as risky environments, dependency syndrome-free ridership problem, colonial legacy, poor economic growth, and corruption are the key detriments to the success of crowdfunding initiatives. Each one of these key threats negatively impacts on crowdfunding and those who have the ability to invest in urban development are always discouraged when these key threats are multifaceted. Hence, governments are always grappling with these key threats as they seek to maximise on the key enablers and create environments that facilitate crowdfunding. So in environments where there is limited trust between the public institutions and the public, crowdfunding is problematic.

Once the crowdfunding initiatives are effected, then municipalities are better positioned to engage in sustainable urban development. It is through sustainable and inclusive funding mechanisms (like crowdfunding) that municipal capacity to propel development can be boosted. Most municipalities and town councils in Africa are capacity strapped due to limited finances to bankroll infrastructure projects among others (Madlongwa, 2014; Zhou and Chilunjika, 2013). A well-resourced and capacitated municipality can promote positive sustainable urban development evidenced by improved service delivery, routine and timeous infrastructure maintenance and expansion, economic opportunities creation (employment among others) and a general increase in the standards of living. The foregoing statement is supported by UN-HABITAT (2009: 10) which argues that the challenge for local government is to keep cities economically viable by delivering a high level of services and, at the same time, keeping taxes sufficiently low so as to discourage individuals and businesses from locating in their jurisdiction. Again, the development scores registered also assist in mobilizing funds through crowdfunding; a progressive municipality which is showing positive signs of growth attracts more funders than a rundown municipality. The sense here is a successful municipality exhibit excellence in public financial management than a rundown municipality.

Perspectives and Theories

Social Capital Theory as Coined by Coleman (1988)

Coleman (1988:98) defines social capital to consists of some aspect of social structure, and facilitates certain actions of actors, whether persons or corporate actors, within the structure. He adopts a middle line between two theoretical traditions which are, first, a functionalist view of social action which is conditioned by social structure and, second, a rational theory which suggests that actors' goals are determined by utility-maximizing pursuit of his/her self-interest (*ibid*). He, Coleman, views social capital as productive meaning that actors use it to achieve particular ends that would have been impossible without it. According to Andriani (2013), social capital has the utility of relationships which breed a sense of trust, cooperation and reciprocity thus have a positive impact on the wealth of the society by reducing transaction costs, facilitating collective actions and lowering opportunistic behavior. Coleman also defines social capital as a collective resource utilized by actors who are goal-oriented signaling the need for an element of embeddedness in a social structure. This is a notion that sees social capital as essentially residing in the social structure of relationships among people. This dimension sets it apart from both financial and human capital.Social capital, despite its less tangible character, according to Coleman (1988), shares with financial capital an ease of making the micro-macro transition. Social capital infuses with value those aspects of social structure that become resources, which become utilizable for goal-seeking actors.

Global Trends, Realities, and Direction

Bafana (2016:5) posits that "…cities growing horizontally are struggling to deal with increasing urban populations and are not likely to be sustainable over the long term because of challenges with congestion, infrastructure, pollution and social disaggregation…" The rapid urbanization emanating from the accelerated rural to urban migration can exacerbate poverty and inequality as people pour into the cities in search of jobs and opportunities, straining available services such as water, transportation and waste management (Mugumbate *et al*, 2013; Feresu, 2010). Urbanisation, particularly in the developing world, has been accompanied by increased levels of crime, violence, and lawlessness (Chirisa et al, 2016). Global studies show that 60% of all urban residents in developing countries have been victims of crime at least once over the past five years, 70% of them in Latin America and Africa," says UN-Habitat's website (Bafana, 2016). Women and children are often the most affected, especially when fear hinders their access to basic services in the city. Crime and insecurity in the city restrict urban social and economic development, and often jeopardize opportunities and policies that support the poor in urban areas.

Among other innovative urban financing mechanisms globally, crowdfunding emerged to be the most trending today. The financing mechanisms have been instrumental in bankrolling projects ranging from real estate, physical infrastructure development, ICTs, and housing. As an example, Marchand (2015) cites an enormous growth of real estate crowdfunding in the United States of America. However, Europe is lagging behind in the utilization of crowdfunding as financial resource making the US to take a lead in the application of crowdfunding as a financial resource for real estate development and investing. Countries like the Netherlands, Germany and United Kingdom have explored this alternative financing source though it is still of practical relevance to learning these conditions and requirements in order to assist crowdfunding in their respective contexts (*ibid*). Zhang *et al* (2014:39) also point out that while crowdfunding is growing in popularity, its growth remains small in China's financial market. During the first half of 2014, Chinese crowdfunding platforms have raised a total of CNY 188 million (USD 31million), much lower than the CNY 500 million (USD 81.5 million), the amount raised through Alipay, an online money market fund, during their first quarter of 2014. A possible reason for crowdfunding's limited presence may be a lack of trust between Chinese internet users. By its nature, crowdfunding requires trust and social participation. Therefore, Chinese crowdfunding platforms may have to provide oversight and supervision to protect project investors and foster greater trust among the internet population (*ibid*).

Crowdfunding emerged to be effective and lucrative in places where there is effective public participation in decision making. Also important to note, the touted participatory budgeting need the assistance of other financing mechanism like crowdfunding. Correia de Freitas and Amado (2013:13), charge that most participatory budgets, where citizens propose their own projects, can only fund a small percentage of the proposed projects but by using crowdfunding the municipality could boost available funding and increase a number of funded projects. Municipalities could also run their own crowdfunding platforms continuously instead of integrating them into seasonal budget actions. These platforms would increase the visibility of public participation in urban planning and could generate, besides funding, increased awareness and interest in the urban environment. Also, social capital is an important ingredient in crowdfunding and or collaborative urban development. However, Claridge (2004:39) observe that existing studies of social capital that highlight differences in rich and poor communities are a key issue in instituting successful collaborative funding mechanism like crowdfunding. This is because key productive assets of asocial network lie within the actors in the network. However, the wealthy actors generally have access to higher quality information and generally have greater power of influence than the poor hence rich communities have 'more' social capital. The role of poverty in societies affects social capital making such initiatives like crowdfunding less common in poverty-stricken societies. Poverty can greatly limit participation, limiting social capital benefits, and further disadvantaging these groups (Kamete, 2002).

Governance systems also affect the rate of economic growth which, in turn, seems to suggest also growth in attendant services and utilities in urban areas. Rosen (2002:1) has argued that under a decentralized system, individuals with similar tastes for public goods group together, so communities are more likely to provide the types and quantities of public goods desired by their inhabitants. A decentralized governance system is the one that put citizens in charge of their local affairs and vocal in the means and way of production of public services and utilities. Another advantage is that decentralized systems foster intergovernmental competition. If citizens can choose among communities, then substantial government mismanagement may cause citizens to choose to live elsewhere. This threat may create incentives to government managers to produce more efficiently and be more responsive to their residents (*ibid*). Finally, a decentralized system may enhance experimentation and innovation in locally provided goods and services. For many policy questions, no one is certain what the right answer is, or even whether there is a single solution that is best in all situations. One way to find out is to let each community choose its own way, and then compare the results. If the innovations are successful, other jurisdictions can imitate them. If not, the costs to the country as a whole are small. This discussion makes it clear that a purely decentralized system cannot be expected to maximize social welfare. Most African governments are still centralized with theoretical decentralization structures not effectively empowered to deliver under a decentralized setup (UN-HABITAT, 2010).

Dabán and Hélis (2009:4) charge that, "...if well-managed, resource revenues could represent a big economic opportunity for resource producing countries. However, the management of resource revenues poses significant challenges in the form of the so-called "resource curse" - a complex phenomenon through which an abundance of resource revenues can translate into stagnation, waste, corruption and conflict..." Some of the challenges derive from the macroeconomic and budgetary difficulties of managing large and volatile funds. Yet other challenges derive from the way in which resource revenues are generated. Because they derive from depleting an exhaustible asset and can, in some occasions, be generated without the scrutiny of taxpayers, donors, and lenders, resource revenues may pose important intergenerational, political economy and governance challenges. To overcome these challenges, the existing large body of literature on the resource curse recommends the implementation of prudent macroeconomic policies and the strengthening of the institutional framework, and in particular, of the Public Financial Management (PFM) system (*ibid*).

RESULTS, DISCUSSION, AND SYNTHESIS

Freund (2007: viii) argues that Africa is also a good place to study cities because African cities are so varied. This continent has one-industry towns, diverse urban economies, fragile and nascent urban development traceable from the historical record and the work of archaeologists as well as some of the Third World metropolises that rightly exercise the minds of development experts. In light of crowdfunding, Africa has not yet made considerable inroads in capitalizing benefits therefrom despite its desperate need to match urban population growth with the attendant services, infrastructure and utilities.

Regional Trends, Realities, and Direction: A Focus on Africa

Africa is rapidly urbanizing and it only comes second to Asia. Projections are that the population growth in Africa will double from 1 billion in 2010 to approximately 2 billion by 2040 and this figure is expected to reach 3 billion by 2070 (UNECA, 2014: 2). The rate of urbanization for Africa is estimated to be 4% per year (Bafana, 2016). Figure 2 and Figure 3 give a clear indication of the projections of the urbanization rates in Africa and the urban population from 1950-2050 and it is clear that the rates for Africa are escalating at unprecedented rates. This rapid urbanization in Africa is attributed mainly to rural-urban migration resulting from rural poverty which compels people to go to urban areas in search of greener pastures, natural population increase and spatial reclassification of urban areas (Kamete, 2002; Mugumbate *et al.*, 2013; Chirisa *et al.* 2016). Ironically, urbanization in Africa is occurring without commensurate economic development. Hence, Chenal (2016) argues that despite this rapid growth it is estimated that even by 2050 sub-Saharan Africa will still be the least urbanized region in the world. Bafana (2016:5) has argued that with an annual economic growth rate of about 5% over the last decade, driven mainly by the commodities boom. Moreover, municipalities in most African countries serve for those in North Africa and South Africa lack legal and administrative frameworks which are prerequisite for efficient service delivery and urban management or urban planning, land tenure and finance (UNECA, 2014).

Subsequently, there has been a myriad of socio-economic challenges characterized with the urbanization is Africa where for example 63% of Africa's urban population in sub-Saharan Africa live in slums that are synonymous with overcrowding, inadequate housing and lack access to water and sanitation (UN-Habitat, 2013). Unemployment, lack of industries and municipalities which are confronted with a

Figure 2. A graph showing world urbanisation for different world areas from 1950-2050
Source: https://uwcm-geog.wikispaces.com/Urban+Environments

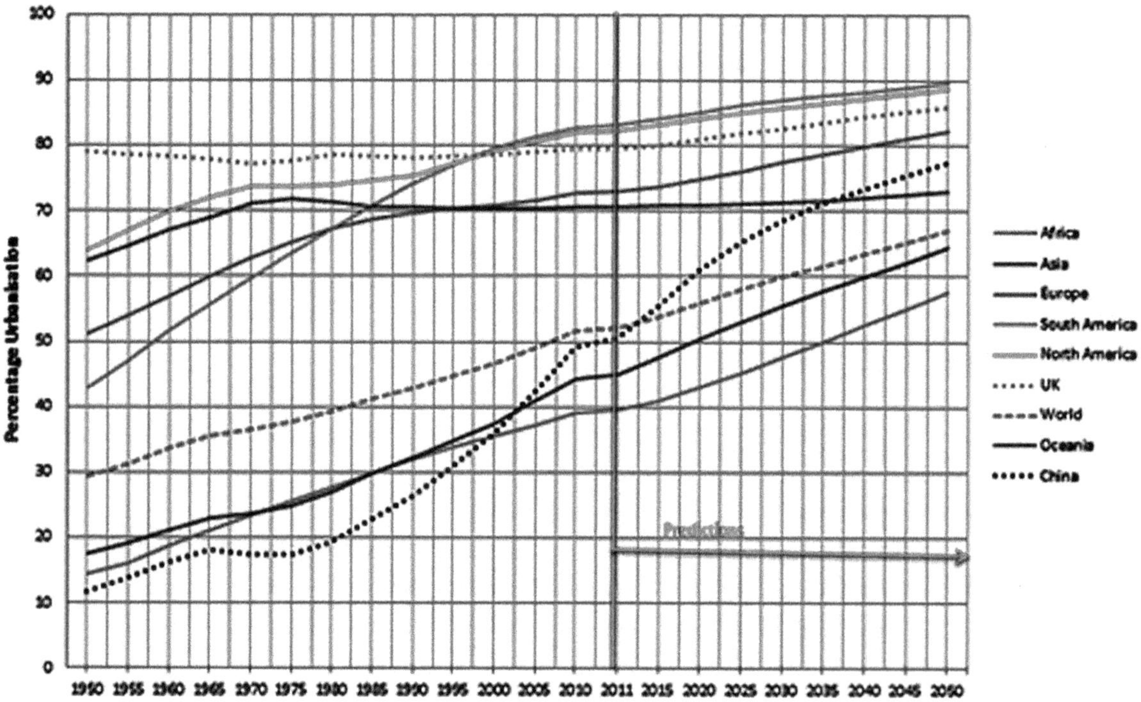

For a more accurate representation see the electronic version.

myriad of challenges ranging from financial to human factor capacity tend to exacerbate the challenges emanating from urbanization in Africa. Thus, urbanization in the Africa of today is an untapped tool for development and economic growth. Around 50% of Africa remains at incomes belowUS$1,25 per day with a mere 4% receiving more than US$10 per day i.e. the middle class (APR, 2012: 17). This is a clear indication that the majority of Africans do not have the funds which are the life blood of urban development projects. However, Swilling (2010) suggest that by 2020, 128 million households in Africa will have transited to middle class a move which is expected to boost consumption and spending potentials. If this will be realized it means that households will have more disposable incomes hence they will be better positioned to engage in crowdfunding mainly in lending and reward-based funding.

Upon their independence, African nations embraced a variety of imported development models but it is now evident that all these models have failed to achieve the set goals (UN-Habitat, 2014:7). Unsurprisingly, since these development concepts were derived from conditions prevalent outside Africa and were conceived at a time and under conditions that were vastly different from today's African realities, they failed to stimulate or unleash strong economic growth. Likewise, the urban development models of post-independence Africa were based on concepts, philosophies, and conditions that prevailed in the advanced economies during the mid-20th century (Lushaba, 2009; Matunhu, 2011). It is now clear that these approaches are of limited use to Africa, given today's very rapid urbanisation, limited urban-based industries, high fossil fuel costs, rapidly diminishing resource bases, fiercely competitive global economic and financial environments, as well as the increasingly-felt threats and impacts of environmental and climate change (Sihlongonyane, 2015). This can be attributed to colonial legacy. Hensel, Allison and Khanani (2008:10), define colonial legacy as involving post-independence relations between a former colony and its former colonial ruler. Because colonial rule inevitably involves close (if unequal) political and economic ties between the ruler and its colonies (Herbst, 2000), it is true that many postcolonial states maintain relatively close ties with the ruler after decolonization signified by a retain of political and economic institutions that are colonial which serve a minimalistic approach to achieving sustainable urban development in Africa (Sihlongonyane, 2015; Obeng-Odoom, 2015).

Figure 3. Percentage of population residing in urban areas by region, 1950-2050
Source: UNDESA (2012).

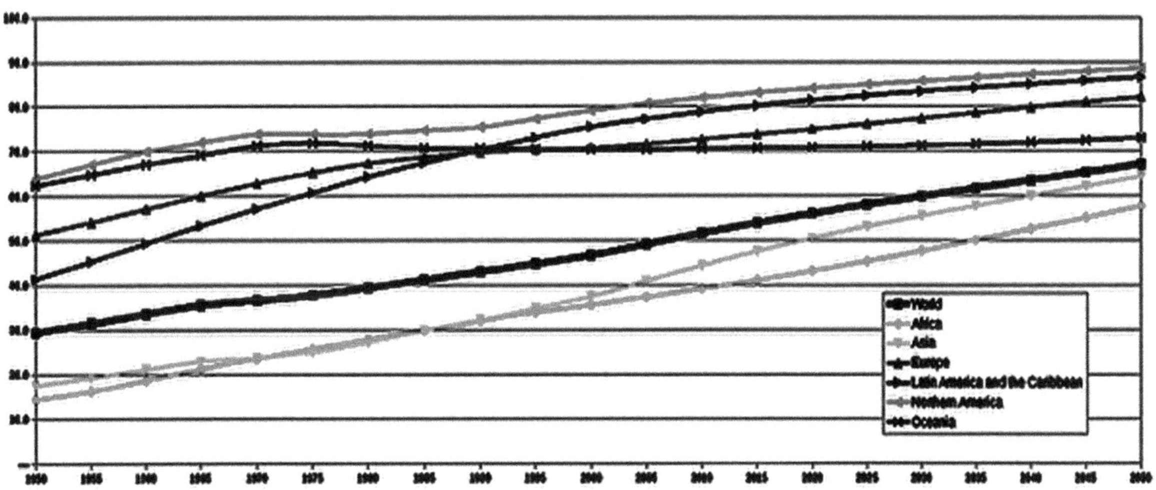

**For a more accurate representation see the electronic version.*

Governance has been a contentious issue in the region (Matovu *et al.*, 2015). Citizen power and participation, though increasingly getting on the map, the progress is still limited across the region, with only a few cases like South Africa having registered tremendous headways. With respect to participatory budgeting in sub-Saharan Africa, citizens have opportunities to provide input, but in many instances their input is limited and the allocation of resources is still determined largely by local officials and councilors (Shall, 2007: 222). Moreover, citizen input is solicited only with regard to the capital budget, which represents only a small proportion of the total budget (Atkinson, 2015). Despite these problems, civic participation has increased the number and range of projects implemented by local authorities that have a direct impact on communities involved in the participation process. Participation has also improved relations between citizens and local authorities, as citizens feel that local authorities have become more transparent and trustworthy.

Among the problems bedeviling the region is poor public financial management marred with corruption and misappropriation of public funds (UN-HABITAT, 2014). Records of public funds mismanagement are also a bottleneck factor in Africa (Pwiti and Ndoro, 1999:143; Mdolongwa, 2014). Besides, there are various skepticisms derived from the colonial legacy which seems to point that Africa cannot do anything meaningful without external support (Lushaba, 2009: Matunhu, 2011). Unfortunately, that argument is evidenced in the manner in which the regional bodies bespeaking of African freedoms – the African Union (AU), AfDB, the Southern African Development Corporation (SADC), for example, are financed externally hence remain as appendages of the European Union, the International Monetary Fund (IMF) and the World Bank. This seems to point to the fact that as long as funds are outsourced, the internal mechanisms to fund development will always remain in a sorry state. The main reason is that the financial aid comes with conditions attached to it which in most cases stifle sustainable development in Africa a good example being the structural adjustment programmes that were popular in the 1990s.

According to Dabán and Hélis (2009:8), regarding resource revenues' (Dutch disease) challenges, African states are struggling to map how to avoid the resource curse, a complex phenomenon in which, through several economic, institutional and political economy transmission mechanisms which translate into stagnation, waste, and conflict. The high trade deficit facing Africa as a region or rather African states as an individual has a negative impact on capital investment. This, trade deficit, led to shifting of capital and labour into the production of non-traded goods and an erosion of the competitiveness ofthe non-resource economy. Two very illustrative cases of Dutch disease are Equatorial Guinea, where cocoa and coffee production declined from approximately 60 percent of Gross Domestic Product (GDP) in 1991 to less than 9 percent of GDP in 2001, and Nigeria, where, between 1970 and 2000, oil exports led to the rapid collapse of agriculture exports (Toto Same, 2008; Otaha, 2012). This has led to depleted resource base to institute sustainable urban development marked with proper urban planning, decent housing, adequate water and sanitation services, high-quality health services, and positive economic growth. To date, according to UN-Habitat (2014:241), informality and lack of planning are rampant in Africa hence municipalities struggle to levy land and housing rates; to finance its development. This affects the ability of municipalities to respond to current and future developmental challenges, thereby undermining urban sustainability (Bird, 2010). Increases in rate collection for land and housing have unfolded over recent years but overall revenue collection still remains weak in the sub-region. Fjeldstad *et al* (2014) indicate that the local revenue potential in sub-Saharan Africa are often low and collection costs high. Improved institutional systems may have contributed to this increase (*ibid*).

Prospects and Limitations for Inclusive and Sustainable Crowdfunding in Africa

It has been pointed out that trust, capacity, and spirituality are three fundamental pillars for crowdfunding (Marchand, 2015: 22). Most governments in Africa lack trust due to their conduct which include corruption, abuse of public funds, and imposition of policies on people. An example being high rates of corruption registered in countries like Nigeria, Zimbabwe and Kenya (Matthew and Idowu, 2012; Sithole, 2013). In Nigeria, corruption compromises service delivery, causes the endemic problem of power supply, the collapse of infrastructure and ultimately poverty in the country (ActionAid, 2014). Sithole (2013) cites Student Activity Fee Allocation Community (SAFAC) (2002) who illustrates that approximately 62% of Zimbabweans believed that all or most of their public officials were involved in corruption. The Anti-Corruption Trust of Southern Africa (ACT-Southern Africa) (2013) gives a detailed account of the corruption cases that occurred in Zimbabwe, yet the perpetrators of such ills were never brought to trial. Under these conditions, people in Africa ask about the dividend that accrues to each one of them after investing their few resources which build up into a pool of financial resources ultimately and the assurance that they will get the dividend. The failure by the municipalities or institution to convince people of an assurance that their money is safe creates challenges in incentivizing potential backers by offering goods or services in return for their contributions is therefore a necessity. As said by Marchand (2015), launching a crowdfunding is not charity fundraising, the majority of the crowd expects something in return for their investment. Therefore, lending and reward crowdfunding mechanisms are more appropriate in Africa.

Iannaccone and Klick (2003:2), a charge that spirituality sidesteps the negative images frequently associated with institutionalized religion, and especially conservative Protestant religion, in both academic and media culture. The term is sufficiently elastic and popular that it can be applied to all traditional religions, all new religions, and a wide range of non-religious activities deemed virtuous or therapeutic (*ibid*). Moreso, Finke (2003:3) adds that, in Africa, religious activities such as prayers, rituals, miracles, and mystical experiences, build up over a lifetime, not only increasing confidence in the truth of a religion but strengthening emotional ties to a specific religion. Together these emotional attachments and the mastering of a religion become investments that build up over time and constitute religious capital for example in Nigeria, several religious organization that harbors many congregants contributing to building big churches, improving the lives of their needy members and charitable activities (Anozie, 2013). This capital helps to explain the religious activity and satisfaction of individuals. Spirituality helps in building social capital. Organization for Economic Cooperation and Development (OECD) (n.d.: 103), defines social capital as networks together with shared norms, values and understandings that facilitate co-operation within or among groups.

With an increasing spirituality in African cities, it becomes an important point where the municipal authorities can appeal to the readily available religious capital. In Zimbabwe, religious ministries like Prophetic Healing and Deliverance (PHD) has been involved in various urban projects for example housing schemes, construction of a hotel and several guest houses for religious tourism (Chibango, 2016). Recently, it has been in the clean-up campaign in Harare Central Business District (CBD), an initiative that greatly helps to restore sanity in Harare (ZBC, 03 December 2016). Also, in the crowdfunding spirit, like any other fundraising venture would require friend-raising. This friend-raising is a form of social capital that is espoused by Coleman (1988). The prospects of having huge numbers of contributors of funds lie in the capacity of the organization to convert the citizens into meaningful contributors.

However, crowdfunding is merely limited to reward and donation based as the fundraisers are motivated by different personal and intrinsic motives. This also presupposes branding of the project and making it attractive and worth of investing in (Nesta, 2012). The capacity also extends to the ability of the authorities to take advantage of the technological innovations to harness the collective power, financial and technical, to propel sustainable urban development. This capacity in Africa seems to be low signified by the limited use of technology; most municipalities in Africa (serve for a few in South Africa) rarely have internet platforms to amass citizen views and contributions, a sign of limited capacity if one considers the technological era we are living in at the present moment.

The limits to all these also include politicisation of the process, contrasting ideology among contributors as well as mistrust of the financial managers. Uncertainty, in the general milieu of fundraising, including the national policies is also a cause of concern for example in Zimbabwe where policy inconsistence had been a major blow to meaningful foreign direct investment (Nyamwanza *et al.*, 2015; Herbst, 2008). With reference to countries in Latin America, but a situation that also applies cogently in Africa Max-Neef (1991: 20) has observed, “Over and above the economic consequences of daily devaluation (financial speculation, a chronic decrease in productive investments and a systematic deterioration of real wages), constant inflation, with annual rates of three or even four digits, erodes a people’s faith in their country and gives rise to a deep uncertainty about the future. Concern for the “health” of a currency generates collective feelings of growing pessimism in relation to the country, the state and the future of each individual. This acute deterioration in confidence, along with a sense of uncertainty and skepticism creates a phenomenon which is difficult to reverse and an environment where innovative alternatives.”

POLICY OPTIONS AND PRACTICAL IMPLICATIONS

In the knowledge of the many options of crowdfunding, African states must embrace this innovative financing mechanism which has the potential to draw the municipalities in the sustainable pathways. The limitations as had been indicated in the previous sections, an improvement in those highlight areas will improve the regions’ predicament in instituting crowdfunding as a tool to improve not only the lives of the people but promote sustainable development. In this light, also taking from Shah (2007:1), public participation is a direct-democracy approach which can improve the standing of African states in taking advantage of sustainable crowdfunding. This enhances transparency and accountability public resource management which in the end reduce government inefficiency and curb clientelism, patronage, and corruption. These named rots affect trust, a necessity in crowdfunding hence removing these trust eroding agents will present opportunities for the African urban centers in promoting crowdfunding. Participation strengthens inclusive governance by giving marginalized and excluded groups the opportunity to have their voices heard and to influence public decision making vital to their interests. Done right, it has the potential to make governments more responsive to citizens’ needs and preferences and more accountable to them for performance in resource allocation and service delivery.

It is also recommended, in the auspices of social capital (spirituality), a pillar of sustainable and inclusive crowdfunding, that African cities must embrace social capital in all forms. According to the OECD (n.d.: 103), one fairly straightforward approach divides social capital into three main categories including; bonds - links among people based on a sense of common identity such as family, close friends and people who share our culture or ethnicity; bridges -the links that stretch beyond a shared sense of identity, for example to distant friends, colleagues and associates; and linkages - links to people or groups further up or lower down the social ladder. Most importantly, it has been seen that spirituality is an important pillar which happen to be growing in Africa. In this light, it is of importance that local authorities invest in building social capital, religious capital included, to amass many resources to be used in sustainable urban development. Matunhu (2011:72) states that the African renaissance approach to development underscores the importance of social movements whose mandate is to engage people to face issues of justice, inequality, and sustainability from a collective or communal approach. The African renaissance theory, unlike its predecessors, advocates for local solutions, pluralism, community-based solutions and reliance on local resources; giving much relevance to social capital. Therefore the critical issue is the 'transformation' of institutions, technology, values and behavior consistent with ecological and social realities in Africa. Embracing social capital requires reforms in institutions technologically, organisationally, technically and or otherwise so as to enhance social ties and harness the benefits therefrom to propel development.

Considering the rampant corruption and abuse of official power that is prevalent in municipalities in Africa, there is need to create and sustain more solid and flexible institutions and human factor through capacity building. This is because corruption is one major element that limits the prospects to initiatives like crowdfunding in Africa. Enhancing the capacity of municipalities in Africa may be effected through changes in organizational structures, skills development, and human factor development, making sure that mandates and responsibilities are streamlined and finally making efforts to improve resource allocation among different sectors. Interestingly, these reforms and improvements are nothing new as various cities in Africa have reconfigured their municipalities yet there has been an insignificant improvement in the degree of civic participation which remains a fallacy due to the complexity of implementing it. Hence, this is one critical aspect that has to be considered if corruption is to be minimised in African cities as the systems remain top-down and vulnerable to corruption.

In the abstract, we raised the question: What are the answers to the colonial legacy derived skepticisms about self-worth and context? The major implication of colonization in Africa is the urban divide which also seems to be exacerbated by the colonial policies and ideologies through urban governance that perpetuate segregation at various levels (Watson, 2009). Hence, of utmost importance in Africa are efforts to close the existing urban inequality gaps which in most instances results in the perpetuation of poverty and classism in cities. Most African cities are still haunted by inequalities with regards spatial development as well as income distribution. Therefore if sustainability is to be realized as well as benefit from crowdfunding, municipalities must redress the urban inequalities so that those who are currently marginalized feel as part of the whole. This may be achieved through the adoption of instruments and urban planning approaches that promote inclusiveness, prosperity and sustainability. In this regard, urban planning and development projects must be inclusive and integrate the concerns of all groups in society. Of particular interest is the focus on improving the means of livelihoods as well as creating employment opportunities so as to harness the opportunities associated with urbanization. This may be achieved through improvements in the urban designs, slum upgrading programmes as well as urban governance which by all means must be inclusive and participatory.

Overall, it is now time to adopt transformative national urban policies that emphasize the utility of urbanization as a transformative process that needs to be capitalized on. Such policies have to be proactive and recognize that urbanization is associated with multiple opportunities that can spearhead not only local economic development but it can contribute to national economic growth. Furthermore, urbanization can contribute to poverty reduction especially urban poverty which seems to so rampant in most cities in Africa amid the rapid rate of urbanization that is currently being experienced. The urban policy will have to be mandated by the central governments so that the policies facilitate better direction and course of action to support urban development that is hinged on creativity, productivity, and inclusivity. UNECA (2014) suggest that such an urban policy will have to be premised on the notion of optimising endogenous development through nurturing and utilization of local assets, mostly human capital, management of local potentials and maximising on local opportunities.

The success of urban development projects as well as the efforts to stifle the limits to initiatives like crowdfunding in Africa may be enhanced through collaboration and coordination. The utility of collaboration cannot be underestimated as it is increasingly becoming a tool that is used to facilitate the sustainability of urban development projects (Healey, 2010). Mason (2007) has demonstrated how collaborations have been using to facilitate urban development in Vancouver, while the same tool has been used in Guatemala for a social housing project (Morales, 2013). The rationale is to create conditions where different levels of government work together in policy development, programme implementation and service delivery with a view to promoting the efficiency of service delivery. Such collaboration may also encompass all the stakeholders such that there is the consensus with regards the projects that are undertaken in urban areas. Furthermore, collaboration and coordination also promote the success of the urban projects because it cuts across departments and sections thus enabling an integrated approach to the urban development process.

CONCLUSION

There is a huge scope for improving urban environments by engaging in crowdfunded many urban development projects in African cities. Prudent, thus, is an analysis of the factors raised in this study and to champion context-based strategies. Much of the raised concerns are surrounding governance that affects trust and capacity to pursue sustainable crowdfunding. Governance describes the way a Council or government manages its affairs in pursuing its strategic and corporate objectives and ensuring appropriate high levels of accountability. It comprises the policies and practices by which a Council meets its responsibility to the community to achieve long-term financial sustainability. It is critical that governance policies and practices are efficient, effective and transparent. Good financial governance enhances public confidence in Local Government and helps to ensure that a Council is in a position to make decisions that are properly responsive to the interests of its community.

REFERENCES

ACT-Southern Africa. (2013). *Zimbabwe: Corruption Cases: Lest we Forget: Bad Leadership Examples for Accountability, Transparency, and Integrity in Zimbabwe*. Available at: https://actsouthernafrica.wordpress.com/2013/03/14/zimbabwe-corruption-cases-lest-we-forget-bad-leadership-examples-for-accountability-transparency-and-integrity-in-zimbabwe/

ActionAid. (2014). *Corruption and Poverty in Nigeria: A Report*. Abuja: Action Nigeria.

AfDB. (2011). *Africa Infrastructure Country Diagnostic 2011. Africa's Infrastructure: A Time for Transformation*. AfDB.

Andriani, L. (2013). *Social Capital: A Road map of Theoretical Frameworks and Empirical Limitations.* Working Papers in Management. Birkbeck University of London.

Anozie, C. E. E. (2013). Christian Church: A Catalyst for Economic Development in Nigeria. *African Research Review, 7*(4), 274–287. doi:10.4314/afrrev.v7i4.17

Atkinson, A. B. (2015). *The colonial legacy: Income inequality in former British African colonies.* Research Brief based on the WIDER Working Paper 2014/45.

Bafana, B. (2016). Africa's Cities of the Future: Proper Planning Key to Sustainable Cities. *Africa Renewal, 30*(April), 4–5. doi:10.18356/59905b7c-en

Belleflamme, P., Omrani, N., & Peitz, M. (2015). *The Economics of Crowdfunding Platforms.* Core Discussion Paper 2015/15, CORE, Voice du Roman Pays.

Bird, R. M. (1999). *Rethinking Subnational Taxes: A new Look at Tax Assignment.* IMF Working Paper WP99/165. IMF, Washington, DC.

Boum, E. (2016). *Crowdfunding in Africa: Fundraising goes Digital in Africa: The Emergence of Africa-Based Crowdfunding Platforms.* Johannesburg: Afrikstart.

Buhr, W. (2003). *What is infrastructure?VolkswirtschaftlicheDiskussionsbeiträge 107-03.* Universität Siegen, FakultätWirtschaftswissenschaften, Wirtschaftsinformatik und Wirtschaftsre.

Campbell, S. (1996). Green Cities, Growing Cities, Just Cities? Urban Planning and the Contradictions of Sustainable Development. *Journal of the American Planning Association, 62*(3), 296–312. doi:10.1080/01944369608975696

Chaligha, A. E. (2014). *Transparency and Accountability in Local Governance in Tanzania. Repoa Brief 45(2014).* Dar es Salaam: Repoa.

Chenal, J. (2016). *Capitalizing on Urbanization: The Importance of Planning Infrastructure, and Finance for Africa's Growing Cities.* Available from https://www.brookings.edu/wp-content/uploads/2016/05/foresightafrica2016_ch4-1.pdf

Chibango, C. (2016). Prosperity Gospel, a Pathway out of a Socioeconomic Crisis? The Case of PHD Ministries of Walter Magaya, Zimbabwe. *Modern Research Studies, 3*(1), 55–82.

Chirisa, I., Bobo, T., & Matamanda, A. (2016). Policies and strategies to Manage Urban insecurity: Focus on selected African Cities. *Journal of Public Policy in Africa, 3*(2), 93–106.

Coleman, J. S. (1988). Social capital and the creation of human capital. *American Journal of Sociology, 94*, 95–120. doi:10.1086/228943

Correia de Freitas, J., & Amado, M. (2013). *Crowdfunding in urban planning: Opportunities and Obstacles.* Conference Paper 2013.

CrowdfundingHub. (2016). *Current State of Crowdfunding in Europe: An Overview of the Crowdfunding Industry in more than 25 Countries: Trends, Volumes and Regulations.* CrowdfundingHub, Armsterdam.

Dabán, T., & Hélis, J. (2009). *A Public Financial Management Framework for Resource-Producing Countries*. IMF Working Paper, WP/10/72. International Monetary Fund.

Feresu, S. B. (Ed.). (2010). *Zimbabwe Environmental Outlook: Our Environment, Everybody's Responsibility. Executive Summary. The government of the Republic of Zimbabwe*. Harare: The Ministry Of Environment and Natural Resources Management.

Finke, R. (2003). *Spiritual Capital: Definitions, Applications, and New Frontiers*. Prepared for the *Spiritual Capital Planning Meeting*.

Fjeldstad, O., Chambas, G., & Brun, J. (2014). *Local Government Taxation in sub-Saharan Africa: A Review and an Agenda for Research*. CMI Working Paper 2014:2. CMI.

Freund, B. (2007). *The African City: A History*. Cambridge, UK: Cambridge University Press. doi:10.1017/CBO9780511618307

Healey, P. (2010). *Making Better Places: The Planning Project in the Twenty-First Century*. Hampshire, UK: Palgrave Macmillan. doi:10.1007/978-1-137-01379-8

Hensel, P. R., Allison, M. E., & Khanani, A. (2008). *Colonial Legacies and Territorial Claims*. Paper presented at the conference National Territory and Sovereignty: Sixty Years since the Founding of the Nation, Seoul, South Korea.

Herbst, J. (2008). *Government and Politics in Zimbabwe*. Harare: University of Zimbabwe Publications.

Herman, D. (2013). *Crowdfunding: Catalysing Growth, Investment and Access to Capital*. Toronto: Deepcentre.

Howard, E. (1902). *Garden Cities of Tomorrow*. London: Faber and Faber.

Iannaccone, L. R., & Klick, J. (2003). *Spiritual Capital: An Introduction and Literature Review. Preliminary draft*. Paper prepared for the Spiritual Capital Planning Meeting.

Kamete, A. Y. (2002). Governance for sustainability? Balancing social and environmental concern in Harare. Chr. Michelsen Institute, Development Studies and Human Rights, Bergen.

Kostof, S. (1991). *The City Shaped: Urban Patterns and Meanings Through History*. London: Thames and Hudson.

Lawal, G. (2007). Corruption and Development in Africa: Challenges for Political and Economic Change. *Humanities and Social Sciences Journal*, *2*(1), 1–7.

Levišauskait, K. (2010). *Investment Analysis and Portfolio Management*. Vytautas Magnus University Kaunas. Retrieved from http://www.bcci.bg/projects/latvia/pdf/8_IAPM_final.pdf

Lushaba, L. S. (2009). *Development as Modernity, Modernity as Development*. Dakar: CODESRIA.

Maathai, W. (2009). *The Challenges for Africa*. New York: Pantheon Books.

Magala, C., & Rubagumya, A. (2005). *Why Pay? Motivators for Payments of Local Market Dues in Rwanda and Uganda*. Amsterdam: SNV.

Marchand, F. (2015). Equity-based Crowdfunding Real Estate Markets: An institutional Comparison of Crowdfunding Real Estate Markets and Their Employment as Alternative Financing Tool for Real Estate between the Netherlands and the US. Unpublished P2 Report, Delft University of Technology.

Mason, R. J. (2007). *Collaborative Land use Management: The Quieter Revolution in Place-Based Planning*. Rowan and Littlefield Publishers.

Matovu, G., Chirisa, I., & Matamanda, A. (2015). Local Development and Governance in Anglophone and Lusophone Africa and Its Relevance to the EU Agenda: Continuity with Change. *Journal of Public Policy in Africa*, *3*(1), 20–36.

Matthew, E. E., & Idowu, C. A. (2012). *Political corruption and national development in Nigeria*. Paper presented at the International Conference on Democracy, Governance and Curbing Corruption in sub-Saharan Africa, Cheyney University of Pennsylvania.

Matunhu, J. (2011). A Critique of Modernization and Dependency Theories in Africa: Critical Assessment. *African Journal of History and Culture*, *3*(5), 65–72.

Max-Neef, M. A. (1991). *Human Scale Development: Conception, Application and Further Reflections, Dag Hammarskjöld Foundation*. New York: The Apex Press.

Mdlongwa, E. T. (2014). *Local government at the heart of poor service delivery*. Available at: http://www.psam.org.za/research/1460540011.pdf

Morales, J. A. (2013). *Sustainable Development By Means of a Collaborative Planning Framework. The Case of Municipal Housing in Guatemala City* (MSc Thesis). University of Twante.

Morris, A. E. J. (Ed.). (1994). History of Urban Form: Before the Industrial Revolution. London: Prentice Hall.

Muchadenyika, D., & Williams, J. J. (2016). Social Change: Urban Governance and Urbanization in Zimbabwe. *Urban Forum, 2016*(27), 253-274.

Mugumbate,, J., & Maushe,, F., & Nyoni. (2013). Ruralisation of Urban Areas: Reversing Development in Zimbabwe. *International Journal of Advanced Research in Management and Social Sciences*, *2*(7), 13–30.

Mumford, L. (1961). *The City in History*. New York: Harcourt Brace Javanovich.

Nesta. (2012). *An Introduction to Crowdfunding*. Nesta.

Nordicity. (2012). *Crowdfunding in a Canadian Context: Exploring the Potential of Crowdfunding in the Creative Content Industries*. Nordicity.

Nyamwanza, L., Paketh, L., Mhaka, C., Makaza, F., & Moyo, N. (2015). An Evaluation of the Policies Instituted by the Government of Zimbabwe in Promoting Survival and Growth of SMEs: The Case of Glenview Area 8 SMEs. *International Journal of Novel Research in Marketing Management and Economics*, *2*(2), 35–44.

Obeng-Odoom, F. (2015). The Social Spatial, and Economic Roots of Urban Inequality in Africa: Contextualizing Jane Jacobs and Henry George. *American Journal of Economics and Sociology*, *74*(3), 550–586. doi:10.1111/ajes.12101

OECD. (n.d.). *What is social capital? OECD Insights: Human Capital*. OECD.

Otah, J. I. (2012). Dutch Disease and Nigeria oil Economy. *African Research Review*, *6*(1), 82–90.

Pwiti, G., & Ndoro, W. (1999). The Legacy of Colonialism: Perceptions of the Cultural Heritage in Southern Africa, with Special Reference to Zimbabwe. *African Archaeological Review*, *16*(3), 143–153. doi:10.1023/A:1021624632398

Africa Progress Report (APR). (2012). *Africa Progress Report. Jobs, Justice and Equity. Seizing Opportunities in Times of Global Change*. Africa Progress Panel.

Rosen, H. S. (2002). *Public Finance: Essay for the Encyclopedia of Public Choice*. CEPS Working Paper No. 80.

Saunders, T., & Baeck, P. (2015). *Rethinking Smart Cities from the Ground Up*. London: Nesta.

Schuringa, T. (2013). *How Social Entrepreneurs and Civic Innovation Can Affect Smart Growth in New Jersey*. New Jersey Future.

Shah, A. (Ed.). (2007). *Public Sector Governance and Accountability Series - Participatory Budgeting*. Washington, DC: The World Bank.

Sihlongonyane, M. F. (2015). The Challenges of Theorising about the Global South: A View from and African Perspective. *Africa Insight*, *45*(2), 59–74.

Sithole, A. (2013). Corruption in Zimbabwe Urban Local Authorities: A Case of Gweru City Council. Asia. *Journal of Social Sciences and Humanities*, *2*(3), 2–33.

Sustainable Cities International. (2012). *Indicators for Sustainability: How Cities are Monitoring and Evaluating their Success*. Vancouver, Canada: SCI.

Swilling, M. (2010). *Africa 2050: Growth, resource productivity and decoupling*. Policy Brief for the 7th meeting of the International Panel for Sustainable Resource Management of the United Nations Environment Programme.

Toto Same, A. (2008). *Mineral-Rich Countries and Dutch Disease: Understanding the Macroeconomic Implications of Windfalls and the Private Prospects: The Case of Equatorial Guinea*. Washington, DC: The World Bank.

UN-Habitat. (2009). *Guide to Municipal Finance*. Nairobi: UN-Habitat.

UN-HABITAT. (2010). *State of African Cities 2010*. Nairobi: UN-HABITAT.

UN-HABITAT. (2013). State of The World's Cities 2012/2013: Prosperity of Cities. UN-Habitat.

UN-Habitat. (2014). *The State of African Cities 2014 - Re-imagining sustainable urban transitions*. Nairobi: UN-Habitat.

UNDESA. (2012). *World Urbanization Prospects: The 2011 Revision.* New York: UNDESA.

UNECA. (2014). *Contribution to the 2014 United Nations Economic and Social Council (ECOSOC) Integration Segment.* Nairobi: ECOSOC.

Westlake, S., Baeck, P., & Bone, J. (2016). *Another Year of Growth For P2P Lending and Crowdfunding in the UK.* Nesta.

World Bank. (2011). *Water Supply and Sanitation in Uganda: Turning Finance into Services for 2015 and Beyond.* Nairobi: World Bank.

World Bank. (2013). *Crowdfunding's Potential for the Developing World.* Washington, DC: World Bank.

ZBC. (2016). *PhD Ministries conduct clean-up campaign.* Available at: http://www.ZBC.co.zw/index.php/news-categories/local-news/71738-phd-ministries-conducts-clean-up-campaign-

Zhang, T., Yip, C., Wang, G., & Zhang, Q. (2014). *China Crowdfunding Report: How to leverage Crowdfunding to support China's Social and Environmental SGBs.* Dao Ventures & China Impact Fund.

Zhou, G., & Chilunjika, A. (2013). The Challenges of Self-Financing Local Authorities: The Case of Zimbabwe. *International Journal of Humanities and Social Science*, *3*(11), 233–245.

KEY TERMS AND DEFINITIONS

Colonial Legacy: The post-independence relations between a former colony and its former colonial ruler.

Crowdfunding: The practice of funding a project or venture by raising many small amounts of money from a large number of people, typically via the internet.

Financial Governance: The way a corporate or an authority manages its financial affairs in pursuing its strategic and corporate objectives and ensuring appropriate high levels of accountability.

Infrastructure: The material development of systems which provide necessary urban services.

Participatory Budgeting: A decision-making process through which citizens deliberate and negotiate over the distribution of public resources.

Public Finance Management: The mobilization of revenue; the allocation of these funds to various activities; expenditure; and accounting for spent funds.

Real Estate: Property comprised of land and the buildings on it as well as the natural resources of the land including uncultivated flora and fauna, farmed crops and livestock, water and minerals.

Social Capital: Networks together with shared norms, values, and understandings that facilitate cooperation within or among groups.

Spirituality: A sense of connection to something bigger than ourselves, and it typically involves a search for meaning in life.

Urban Development: The social, cultural, economic, and physical expansion and growth of cities, as well as the underlying causes of these processes.

Chapter 12
Crowdfunding:
Can It Support Urban Local Bodies in India?

Jyoti Chandiramani
Symbiosis International University, India

Gargi Patil
Symbiosis International University, India

ABSTRACT

The chapter studies and attempts to understand the idea of crowdfunding and the possibility of it being adopted and adapted within the urban Indian framework. It explores the potential of crowdfunding – the civic variety, which can supplement a small but meaningful percentage of financial resources required to provide urban services in Indian cities. The objective of using the crowdfunding platform is to create sustainable and livable cities. While the delivery of basic urban services is the responsibility of the urban local bodies, it is observed that the available financial resources at their disposal poses an impediment in service delivery. With the process of urbanization gaining momentum, India will require billions of dollars to build the much-needed urban infrastructure and provide basic urban services. It is envisaged that civic crowdfunding, which addresses the varied requirements of urban citizens, may be the appropriate solution to the problem.

INTRODUCTION

Crowdfunding, is an alternate method of raising capital, which has evolved and been found to be very popular in USA and UK having seen a meteoric rise in its global value from $ 880 million in 2010, to $ 34.4 billion of capital, by 2015-16 (Massolution Report, 2015). Crowdfunding gained momentum in USA post the subprime mortgage crises in 2008, resulting in the failure of a number of banks. The compelling situation thus shifted the focus of banks' away from lending to small business, resulting in a market gap and the genesis of an alternative channel of capital financing, referred to as 'crowdfunding', with an inherent potential to enhance market efficiency. While North America in 2015, accounted for 50% ($17.25 billion) of the market, it was followed by Asia with 30.5% ($10.5 billion) and Europe at 18.7% ($6.48 billion) (Bhatia, 2016). Given the universality of online banking, cheaper smartphones

DOI: 10.4018/978-1-5225-3952-0.ch012

and smarter technology, these factors have provided an enabling environment resulting in limitless possibilities and opportunities for crowdfunding.

In the Indian context, there is a view that crowdfunding has been a practice followed over the years for building temples and collecting funds for important festival celebrations. In the present digital age, crowdfunding is relatively new, is being explored and envisaged to be one of the biggest financial changes in history, having the potential to revolutionize the way money is exchanged (Prabhu, 2016).

The chapter is a study attempting to understand the idea of crowdfunding, particularly civic crowdfunding and its inherent features that have the potential for being adopted and adapted within the urban Indian framework. It is motivated by the growing urbanization process in India, wherein the urban population at 439.8 million in 2017 (Worldometers, 2017) is poised to increase to 590 million by 2030 (McKinsey Global Institute (MGI) Report, 2010). This will compel the constitutionally empowered Urban Local Bodies (ULBs) or city administrators to facilitate planned development, provide amenities and services to urban settlements. It requires raising revenues through taxations and user charges and earmarking expenditure, in order to build the urban infrastructure and services for Indian cities. Additionally, with the future making of cities guided by the United Nations (UN) - Sustainable Development Goals (SDG-11), the functions and responsibilities of the ULBs are widened to ensure livable, inclusive, safe, resilient and sustainable cities. This poses additional challenges for ULBs, which have been resource constrained as discussed by (Pethe, Nallathiga, Gandhi, & Tandel, 2014), (Bandyopadhyay, 2014) and (The World Bank Group, 2015). Given the existing situation, it is felt that crowdfunding platforms have the potential to provide opportunities for being explored and utilized at the city level to achieve the above-mentioned outcomes. The authors hence pose the question:

Given the critically low levels of financial resource available with the ULBs in India, coupled with the challenges to raise further resources, can crowdfunding platform be the appropriate platform, to provide meaningful financial resources, required for ensuring and enhancing quality of urban services to the citizens of a developing and emerging economy like India?

To address the above question, the schematic framework of the chapter begins with the introduction, followed by the background of crowdfunding, which discusses the concept, models and issues of crowdfunding. It is also supported by a sub-segment that throws light on the various cases of crowdfunding in India and its emerging potential to fund social or civic projects. The ensuing section throws light on the ULBs and the quality of urban services provided. It also puts forth the schedule XII of the Indian Constitution which defines the various functions of the ULBs and links it with the targets highlighted in the SDG (11), 'Sustainable Cities and Communities' discussing the financial provisions required for the delivery of the same. The succeeding part highlights the scope of civic crowdfunding and its potential to address the future concerns of urban development. This is further supported in the subsequent segment wherein the authors present three designed hypothetical case studies, with respect to select wards in Pune city, governed by Pune Municipal Corporation (PMC). The chapter ends by discussing the future research direction and the pertinent conclusions.

CROWDFUNDING: A BACKGROUND

Crowdfunding is a method of seeking or soliciting funds (small amount) from multiple investors through a web-based platform or social networking site for a specific project, business venture or social cause (SEBI, 2017). While crowdfunding is an umbrella term that describes the use of small amounts of money, obtained from a large number of individuals or organizations, to fund a project, a business or personal loan, and other needs essentially through an online web-based platform (Kirby & Worner, 2014), civic crowdfunding, on the other hand is the practice of raising monetary contributions for public interest projects from a large pool of donors through crowdfunding platforms. It provides an opportunity to citizens to contribute towards city development projects and also empower them to collectively participate and increase their well-being and solve societal issues. This practice has seen some success as it has helped to finance a wide range of civic initiatives, from social innovation to urban commons (World Urban Campaign, 2014).

There are several advantages associated with civic crowdfunding, which includes, giving the citizens an idea to have much more power to design the city they are living in and participate in the future of the city they aspire. They can realize or complete various local area projects by raising capital through crowdfunding platform. The project can also be tested democratically whether it is supported by citizens and this form of crowdfunding is considered to be much more efficient since it does not need to pass through the long governmental procedures (Hung-Yi1, n.d.).

Civic crowdfunding projects, campaigns and movements are project specific, wherein fundraisers clearly define how much funding is required and how it will be spent on (specific targets) as compared to traditional funding strategies. This brings with it transparency that are lacking in government agencies. It involves a diverse range of funders – small as well as large – hence promoting community participation. Most civic crowdfunding platforms, set limitations on the duration of campaigns – ranging between 30 to 90 days, thereby creating a sense of urgency and also addressing the problem of time lag, which is often associated with governmental bodies. The civic crowdfunding method thus allows funds to be collected more cheaply than through lengthy grant application processes or more traditional fund-raising methods (Keane & Griffiths, 2017).

There are numerous forms or models of crowdfunding (Reserve Bank of India, 2016) (Refer Table 1), some are charitable donations that provide intangible benefits but no financial returns; on the other hand, equity crowdfunding provides financial returns (Kirby & Worner, 2014).

The reward-based (RbC) type is the largest crowdfunding platform in terms of numbers growing at a Compound Annual Growth Rate (CAGR) of 79%, while the equity-based (EbC) category shows the highest growth rate in value terms at 114% CAGR globally. Donation-Based (DbC) and RbC generally attract fewer finances per project as compared to lending-based (LbC) and EbC (Crowdsourcing, LLC, 2012). In the Indian context, empirical evidence reveals both, the RbC and the civic crowdfunding or project based platform are picking up with more signs of such activities being widely observed (Vadgama, Khutwad, Damle, & Patil, 2015).

Crowdfunding experienced significant growth in 2014 attributing this to the rise of Asia as a major crowdfunding region, which grew by 320% in volume, raising $3.4 billion, thereby placing the region slightly ahead of Europe which raised $3.2 billion. North America continued to lead the world in crowdfunding volumes, growing by 145% and raising a total of $9.46 billion (Jain, 2015) - Refer Table 2.

The crowdfunding platform has its share of complexities, which varies from country to country depending on the financial regulations prevalent (Kirby & Worner, 2014), and the fact that crowdfunding essentially takes place over an online portal. This may therefore be associated with risk of fraud, lack of transparency, money laundering, cyber-attacks, misuse of funds, poor management decisions, and other issues. Equity and peer-to-peer lending have been associated with 50% and 30% risk of defaulters or investment failure respectively (Prinsha K, 2016). For crowdfunding to be successful, a supportive ecosystems and factors like forward thinking regulations, effective technological solutions, strong social

Table 1. Various models of crowdfunding

Sr. No.	Types of Crowdfunding	Sub-Types of Crowdfunding	Description
1	Community Crowdfunding	a) Donation Crowdfunding	Citizens donate small amounts to meet the larger funding aim of a specific charitable project while receiving no financial or material return in exchange
		b) Reward Crowdfunding	Individuals donate towards a specific project with the expectation of receiving a tangible (but not financial) reward or a product at a later stage
2	Financial Return Crowdfunding	a) Peer-to-Peer Consumer Lending	Individuals using an online platform to borrow from a number of individual lenders each lending a small amount
		b) Equity Crowdfunding	Sale of a stake in a business to a number of investors in return for investment, mostly used by early stage firms
3	Debt Based	a) Peer-to-Peer Business Lending	Debt based transactions between individual and existing businesses with are mostly SMEs with the many individuals contribution as one loan
		b) Debt Based Securities	Lenders receive a non-collateralized debt obligation typically paid back in an extended period of time, similar to purchasing a bond but with different obligations and rights
4	Civic Crowdfunding		It is a practice of raising monetary contributions for public interest projects from a large pool of donors through crowdfunding platforms

Source: (Kirby & Worner, 2014) and (Partridge, 2015).

Table 2. Growth structure of crowdfunding globally

Sr. No	Growth Rates by Region in 2014	Growth Rates By Models in 2014	Most Active Categories in 2014
1	North America: Volume grew by 145% to $9.46 billion	Lending-based Crowdfunding grew 223% to $11.08 billion	Business and Entrepreneurship at 41.3% / $6.7bn
2	Asia: Volume grew by 320% to $3.4 billion	Equity-based Crowdfunding grew 182% to $1.1 billion	Social Causes at 18.9% / $3.06bn
3	Europe: Volume grew by 141% to $3.2 billion	Hybrid-based Crowdfunding grew 290% to $487 million	Films & Performing Arts at 12.13% / $1.97bn
4	South America: Volume grew by 167%	Royalty-based Crowdfunding grew 336% to $273 million	Real Estate at 6.25% / $1.01bn
5	Africa: Volume grew by 101%	Reward-based Crowdfunding grew 84%	Not Available
6	Oceania: Volume grew by 59%	Donation-based Crowdfunding grew 45%	Music and Recording Arts at 4.54% / $736m

Source: (Jain, 2015).

media, market penetration, internet usage and cultures that adapt to this new type of investment mechanism are required (World Bank Document, 2013).

To promote, educate and establish crowdfunding in India, the National Crowdfunding Association (NCFA) was launched in January 2013, providing its members with opportunities to shape the industry, learn the details of the marketplace, and stay informed and ahead in an ever-evolving economy. The association opened membership to the general public including interested parties such as entrepreneurs, investors, lawyers, technologists, financial advisors, regulators, students and media professionals whether donation based or equity based (Nagalakshmi & Cecilia, 2014).

In order to regulate and set up a framework for crowdfunding in India, the Securities and Exchange Board of India (SEBI) – the regulator of the securities market, rolled out a "Consultation Paper on Crowdfunding in India" in 2014. The paper received large responses and discussed the possibility to provide fresh avenues for startups and Small and Medium Enterprises (SMEs), set up by young entrepreneurs and technology professionals to raise early stage funding through internet based platforms, potentially more efficient and cost effective than through public issue or private placement offering. EbC and DbC are primarily based in the private placement route as defined under Section 42, Companies Act 2013. The RbC route is primarily modeled on SEBI's Alternative Investment Fund (AIF) Regulations, 2012 (SEBI, 2017). The guidelines highlighted the following:

1. Companies can raise up to Rs.10 core in a year through entities under this route
2. Only 'accredited investor' would be allowed to participate in crowdfunding activities
3. The investors would include High Net Worth Individuals (HNIs) with a minimum net worth of Rs. 2 crores
4. It also includes companies with a minimum net worth of minimum Rs.20 crore, Eligible Retail Investors (ERIs) and Qualified Institutional Buyers (QIBs) as defined by SEBI (SEBI, 2017).

While in 2014, the NCFA in India lacked clarity with respect to its position on crowdfunding, it was only in March 2017, SEBI suggested additional disclosure norms to make investors aware of the risks associated with crowdfunding systems. The SEBI Chairman also pointed out that the present household savings in the capital market were very low and there existed a potential for the crowdfunding market to be tapped (The Hindu, 2017). It also pointed out that crowdfunding has the potential to raise funds at a lower cost of capital, without undergoing rigorous processes associated with the Banks in India, and while this may be risky, it is an option providing returns and can be used to diversify new investment avenues even for infrastructure facilities (SEBI, 2017). Vadgama, Khutwad, Damle and Patil (2015) in their paper, suggests that there exists substantial evidence to support the argument that crowdfunding platforms are experimenting with different formats suitable within the Indian framework. With respect to the value of crowdfunding in India in 2016, it ranged between Rs. 350-Rs. 450 crores in a span of 18 months (Menon, 2016). However, the data may not be accurate, as there are no specific data sources available giving the actual quantum of investments accrued from crowdfunding platforms. Further, given the prevailing socio-economic conditions of India which includes - constrained level of profitability, technology, education, socially evolved systems and infrastructure facilities in terms of computers, websites, and technological know-how, this may pose may pose a challenge and thus India may not be able to replicate international crowdfunding models on a scale at which it has progressed in the developed nations.

Having discussed the genesis and growth of crowdfunding, the various models and the issues crowdfunding has had to face with respect to the regulators, the ensuing segment throws light on the relevant crowdfunding platforms and various initiatives thereby helping prepare a favorable case for this platform to be encouraged to address some major concerns of urban India.

CASES OF CROWDFUNDING IN INDIA

The ten large scale and popular crowdfunding platforms and many more such small initiatives in India seems few (Refer Table 3), as against 344 such platforms in US and 87 in UK - (Prinsha K, 2016). A Bloomberg survey, further reiterates the issue that crowdfunding has no reliable data sources available for India, yet local crowdfunding sites are proliferating and drawing attention from supporters, with the added advantage that India presently has the second-largest internet market globally having more than 342 million mobile users and online payment options. Thus making it easy to fund such initiatives (Nekaj, 2016).

A few known cases of crowdfunding in India have been highlighted in the present segment to give an idea of the vast scope of opportunities that prevail.

While India has seen successful crowdfunding initiative in the 1970s–wherein the Reliance Industries' textile business was crowdfunded by communities across the state of Gujarat, in the present day context, India with its large market and human capital has become a popular destination for global business and investment opportunities (Nagalakshmi & Cecilia, 2014).

The crowdfunding platform Milaap has been able to garner resources from 120 countries across the world, contributing over Rs. 90 crores spread across more than 49,000 projects. Milaap began in 2010 as a microfinance platform (in the form of loans) for rural poor. By 2014, Milaap broadened its functional horizon addressing various personal and social causes (Bloomberg Technologies, 2017).

Table 3. Popular crowdfunding platforms in India

Sr. No.	Type	Website	Description
1	Fund for Unity	www.fundforunity.com	Working on civic projects such as building a blood bank, providing nutrition, education and healthcare
2	Milaap	www.milaap.com	They raise money for victims of accidents and natural disasters & have projects about education and environment
3	Catapoolt	http://crowdfundinsider.com	Popular among youth and start-ups for providing attractive funding ideas to private business
4	Ignite Intent	http://igniteintent.com	Reward Based Platform which caters mostly to youth, entrepreneurs and start-ups for small scale business activities
5	Ketto	http://ketto.org	Popular for projects about child welfare, education, health and women empowerment
6	Pick A Venture	http://signup.pikaventure.com	Provides funds for new business ideas
7	Start 51	http://www.start51.com	The bulk of the site caters to design, film, music and arts
8	Wishberry	https://www.wishberry.in	Deals with design, arts, photography, dance and film
9	Bit Giving	https://www.bitgiving.com/	Specifically caters for social causes targeting non-profits, societies and trusts
10	Fund Dreams India	www.funddreamsindia.com	This platform supports by generating funds for victims of acid attacks

Source: (Prinsha K, 2016) and (Padmanabhan, 2016).

Aurad Shahajani a village in Latur district of Maharashtra state, India - experienced success with crowdfunding, wherein the villagers battling against water scarcity resorted to a crowdfunding platform 'Digital Rural Connect' (DRC), to overcome the challenge. A young resident from the village, who had migrated out, helped the villagers to connect with the outside world, with the objective of getting funds to address the water supply woes. The project was an outcome of public participation of resident and non-resident villagers, who joined hands and came up with a crowdfunding effort without availing of any funds from the government (Times of India, 2017).

Suryoday Parivar, an Indore-based NGO introduced the concept of crowdfunding to farmers in the Marathwada & Vidarbha region of Maharashtra. The project was started in Horti, a small village in the Osmanabad district of Maharashtra, with the objective to re-build an 8 kms long canal within 15 days, with a project cost of Rs. 6 lakhs. The collaborative effort saw 700 farmers contributing 50% of the total cost of the project (Varma, 2017). The remaining amount was collected from fueladream crowdfunding platform (Fuel a Dream, 2017).

In another case in the city of Indore located in Central India, crowdfunding has been used to provide lodging and schooling facilities for 31 children orphaned by farmers' suicide (Bloomberg Technologies, 2017).

An organization - vChalk, founded in 2014 by Daniela Gheorghe, has raised $2400 to offer remedial English and Math classes for the children of street vendors and factory workers in Bangalore in Karnataka state of India (Bloomberg Technologies, 2017).

The state of Maharashtra, India, digitized their classrooms using Liquid-Crystal Display (LCD) projectors and laptops worth Rs. 78,000, in a Marathi-medium government school at Dhekusim, in Ambaner Taluka in Jalgoan District. The villagers came together to improve the conditions of the school and collected funds through crowdfunding of about Rs. 5.5 lakhs. This was also with an objective to encourage students to go to government school. The Maharashtra State Council of Education Research and Training (MSCERT) has another noteworthy crowdfunding case, wherein between July 2015 and December 2016, school teachers in the state managed to raise about Rs. 216 crore. The funds collected, have been utilized for revamping classrooms, building new toilets and digital initiatives, among others. According to the MSCERT data, Ahmednagar district has ensured the maximum public participation, having raised over Rs. 30 crore, followed by Pune (Rs. 19.82 crore), Solapur (Rs. 19.03 crore), Aurangabad (Rs. 15.59 crore) and Nashik (Rs. 14.80 crore) (Khan, 2017).

A team of students from the city of Mumbai and Pune, came up with an initiative 'One village one library' to address the absence of libraries in villages, in the state of Maharashtra. Based on their survey they believed that crowdfunding platforms would be the right means to help them address the issue and in May 2017, they identified select districts of Amravati, Pune, and Yavatmal for this initiative (Sawant, 2017).

Fund for Unity adopted by the Government of Gujarat, is a digital initiative and civic crowdfunding platform, which aims to utilize funds contributed by the people to supplement government investment in backward regions of Gujarat. The platform seeks individual public and private philanthropic funds for enhancing the social and physical infrastructure, and consequentially the HDI, in backward regions of Gujarat (Fund for Unity, 2017).

The process of creating a new capital city - Amaravati, for the newly created state of Andhra Pradesh, witnessed the State Government launch crowdfunding initiative 'My Brick, My Amaravati' in October 2015. The initiative allows an individual to buy a digital brick for Rs.10 and his/her name is engraved on it and is kept in a repository. In a span of eight months the project saw 2.25 lakh donors with a total of 54.89 lakh bricks collected. The total estimated investment requirements for the creation of the new city capital amounts to Rs. one lakh crore (Sridhar, 2015).

With the relevant cases discussed above, the subsequent segment of the chapter discusses urbanization in India, highlighting the functions of the ULBs, along with the recent inclusion of achieving the targets as laid down by the United Nations (UN) - SDGs to be adopted by cities in India. It describes the state of urban services and the financial constraints that pose tremendous challenges, for the efficient and timely urban service delivery provided by the ULBs. The study proceeds to explore if the project based or civic crowdfunding platform, can address the urban concerns.

URBAN LOCAL BODIES AND URBAN SERVICE DELIVERY IN INDIA

Urbanization in India in 2015 increased to 33% from 31.2% as per the 2011 Census, revealing a much slower pace of urbanization compared to major emerging economies like Brazil (85.7%), Russia (74%), China (55.6%) and South Africa (61.6%). Also for the first time, in the 2011 Census, the absolute growth in numbers of urban population at 91 million, was greater than the rural population at 90 million, with 64.82% of the urban population concentrated in the 468 cities (Mohan, 2016), having a population of over one lakh and this number is likely to increase to 71% by 2031 (MOUD, 2015).

To cater to the increasing needs of a growing urban population, there is an urgent requirement to make provision for additional infrastructure and urban services like roads, transport, traffic support, street lighting, water supply, sewerage, storm water drains and solid waste management (HPEC Report and Recommendations, 2011). The responsibility of urban service delivery in India is under the purview of ULBs, and they are required to administer and govern the nearly 8000 urban centers (IIHS, nd).

India follows the local self-governance model in a manner of decentralized democracy, wherein layers of local governments, which are closest to the people, are required to address and provide for 18 functions as defined under the 12th Schedule of the Indian Constitution – post the 74th Constitution Amendment Act (CAA) (Refer Table 4). In addition, ULBs presently are also required to address the various targets and indicators as spelt out in the 11th SDG, adopted by UN, with the objective to make cities and human settlements inclusive, safe, and resilient. India along with 193 nations adopted the 17 SDGs, in September 2015. (United Nations, 2015).

The 74th CAA (1992) was revised, with the rationale to ensure decentralized power and responsibility through the provision of constitutional status, granting recognition to local government and putting the relationship between the States and the ULBs on a firmer footing. However, 25 years later, in 2016 it has been clearly observed that the real decentralization of power remains an unfinished agenda, with respect to the real devolution of funds, functions and functionaries as envisaged in the amendment. This is because only 26% of urban India is governed by ULBs (Tandel, Hiranandani, & Kapoor, 2016). While the Ministry of Urban Development (MOUD), directed the state governments to convert Census Towns to ULBs, which would facilitate planned development and efficient service (Press Information Bureau, 2016), this decision lies in the domain of the State government. Its implementation therefore depends on the second tier of governance to act in a timely manner to strengthen the administrative framework. Further, Tandel, Hiranandani, & Kapoor, (2016) point out that while the census towns are governed by panchayats but are recognized by the census of India as being urban, this mismatch results in misallocation of resources leading to unsafe development of densely populated clusters. This results in absence or poorly managed and delivered urban services to a large segment of urban population.

Table 4. List of 18 functions of the Urban Local Bodies under the 12th Schedule of the Indian Constitution and select targets of 11th Sustainable Development Goals

Sr. No.	List of Functions of the ULB	11th SDG: Sustainable Cities and Communities
1	Urban planning including town planning	
2	Regulation of land-use and construction of buildings	11.3) Population and land use - sustainable human settlement planning which is participatory and integrated
3	Planning for economic and social development	11.8) Support positive economic, social and environmental links between urban, peri-urban and rural areas
4	Roads and bridges	
5	Water supply for domestic, industrial and commercial purposes	11.1) Basic Services
6	Public health, sanitation conservancy and solid waste management.	11.1) Basic Services
7	Provision of fire services	11.1) Basic Services
8	Urban forestry, protection of the environment and promotion of ecological aspects	11.6) Reducing air pollution - reduce the adverse per capita environmental impact of cities
9	Safeguarding the interests of weaker sections of society including the handicapped and mentally retarded	11.5) Protecting the poor and people in vulnerable situations
10	Slum improvement and up-gradation	11.1) Safe and affordable housing and basic services and upgrade slums
11	Urban poverty alleviation	11.9) Implementing integrated policies and plans towards inclusion
12	Provision of urban amenities and facilities such as parks, gardens and playgrounds	11.7) Access to safe, inclusive and accessible, green and public spaces / areas
13	Promotion of cultural, educational and aesthetic aspects	11.4) Strengthen efforts to protect and safeguard the world's cultural and natural heritage
14	Burials and burial grounds, cremations, cremation grounds and electric crematoriums	11.1) Basic Services
15	Cattle pounds; prevention of cruelty to animals	
16	Vital statistics including registration of births and deaths	
17	Public amenities including street lighting, parking lots, bus stops and public conveniences	11.2) Improving public transit – sustainable mobility
18	Regulation of slaughter-houses and tanneries	

Source: 12th Schedule of the Indian Constitution and United Nations (UN)-SDGs (UNDP, 2015).

A study by McKinsey Global Institute (MGI) Report in 2010, reviewed the urban service delivery in India, and a snap shot has been highlighted in (Figure 1). The study revealed that according to the 2001 Census, India's urban services were woefully inadequate with respect to water supply, public transportation, parks and open spaces, sewage treatment and solid waste management, among others when compared with the best in class of the basic services standard that ULBs are required to provide.

To address the issues pertaining to India's urban infrastructure and other functions and to understand what are the issues and challenges, the MOUD further set up a High Powered Expert Committee (HPEC) in 2008, which presented its report in 2011 highlighting the following service delivery standards:

Figure 1. Key indicators of quality of life for benchmarking of urban service delivery
Source: (McKinsey Global Institute (MGI) Report, 2010).

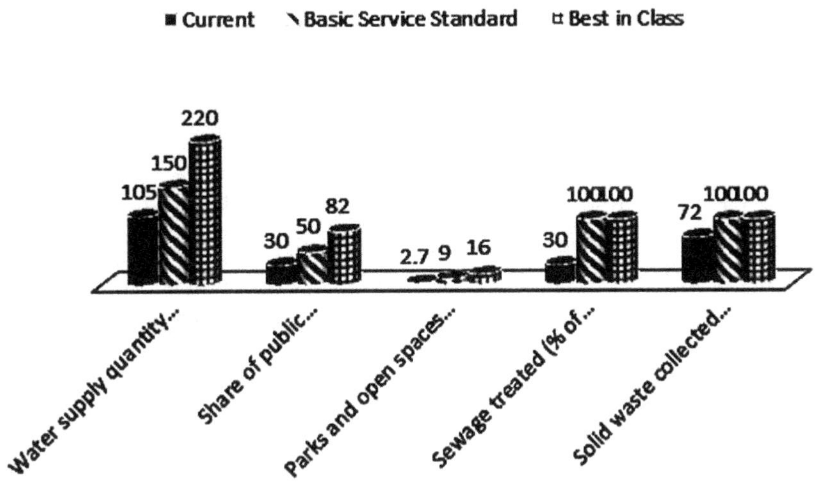

1. **Water Supply:** 100% piped water, 24x7 flow, and 135 lpcd consumption per capita
2. **Sewerage:** 100% collection, transportation and treatment 11% area for cities
3. **Solid Waste:** 100% collection, transportation and treatment
4. **Urban Roads:**
   a. **Area Under Roads:** 11% area for cities and 7% for towns
   b. **Road Density (km per sq. km.):** 12.25 km per sq. km. for cities and 7 km per sq. km. for towns
5. **Storm Water Drains:** Network covering 100% road length on both sides of the road
6. **Urban Transport:** Rail-based and road-based Mass Rapid Transit System for cities with population 1million and above, city bus service for smaller cities and towns
7. **Street Lighting:** IL luminance: 35 Lux for all cities and towns; 40 m spacing for major roads, 45 m for collector roads, and 50 m for access road spaces
8. **Traffic Support Infrastructure:** Details by city size in the Committee's Report

The Annual Survey of India's City-System (ASICS) Report of 2016, also highlighted that Indian cities score poorly, with an overall 4.4 on a scale of 10 compared with leading global cities like London and New York's with their respective scores being 9.3 and 9.8 and are known for their excellent infrastructure and sound urban policies.

Given this backdrop, there is a need to arm the ULBs to be able to provide the required urban infrastructure and services that will help the citizens to negotiate the city comfortably. However, what is observed is that India's ULBs are highly constrained with inadequate financial resources. With urban areas becoming increasingly important in policy making not only in terms of population share but also in terms of economic wealth, the finances of ULBs have been assuming great importance (Nallathiga, 2008).

According to the HPEC Report of 2011, around $1.2 trillion capital investments is necessary to meet demands of Indian cities by 2030, to enable India to maintain and accelerate economic growth and provide basic urban services. The investment required for the eight major sectors of urban infrastructure which includes: roads, transport, traffic support, street lighting, water supply, sewerage, storm water drains and solid waste management has been estimated at $506.3 billion (HPEC Report and Recommendations, 2011). Additionally, the MGI 2010 Report, estimates $134 per capita per annum, as the capital expenditure requirement over the next 20 years from 2010 to 2030, to address the urban issues (Refer Figure 2).

The 2016, ASICS Report analyzed that Indian cities generate an average of just 37% of the expenditure that they are required to spend every year, making them heavily dependent on State Governments. With a stagnant revenue base which is further constrained by the established fees and tax rates, as well as by narrow tax bases, this poses serious resource challenges for the ULBs, resulting in poor urban services provided, and a low livability index. (Ellis & Roberts, 2016). While large cities such as Delhi, Hyderabad, Mumbai and Pune are able to generate more than 50% of the resources required, the rest of the cities generate only between 17% and 47%. This adversely affects their ability to invest in improving quality of life for citizens, with the per capita spending on an average being Rs. 2364 per annum across 21 cities and ranges from Rs. 418 in Patna to Rs. 8886 in Mumbai.

It is estimated that by 2030, Indian cities will contribute to about 70% to India's GDP from 63% in 2011 (HPEC Report and Recommendations, 2011). In order to ensure fiscal responsibility and adequate decentralization, a well-defined fiscal framework is needed, which can include crowdfunding as a source of revenue generation. Indian cities lack in both; a formal platforms of participation that give its people a sense of ownership over the city, and democratizing information which facilitates interested and informed participation by enabling its people to get a true image of what ails their city (ASICS, 2016).

Given the vast amount of financial resources required and its ensuing challenges, to fund India's urban infrastructure and urban service delivery, to ensure quality of life or a decent livability index, for its increasing population, as highlighted in the present segment, compels the authors to pose a question

Figure 2. Financial required for Indian cities for better service delivery
Source: (McKinsey Global Institute (MGI) Report, 2010).

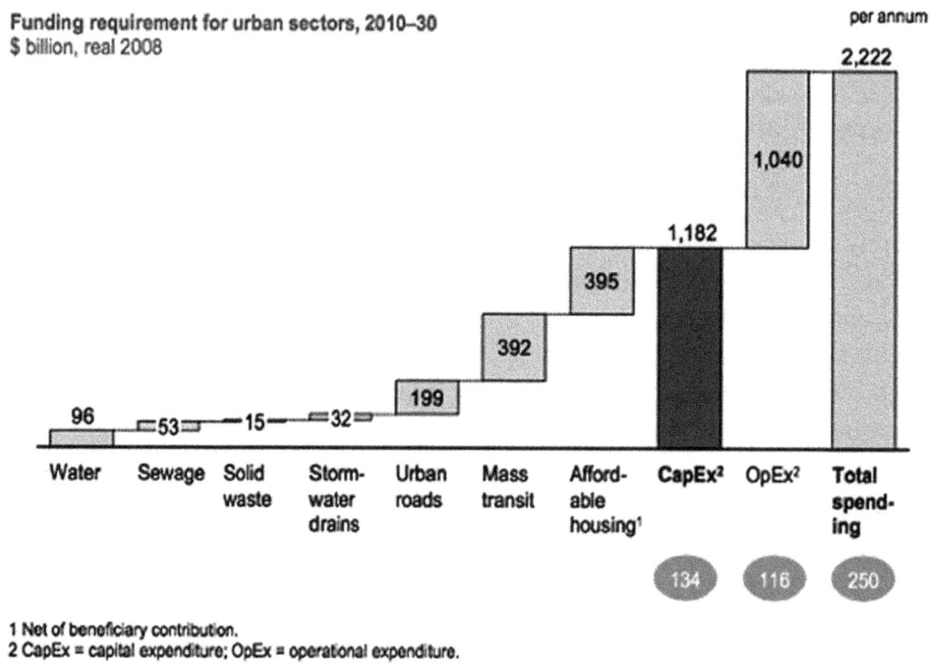

- whether civic crowdfunding can complement ULBs to ensure enhanced urban service delivery to the urban population? The following segment of the chapter attempts to address this question.

CIVIC CROWDFUNDING AND URBAN DEVELOPMENT

As an economy moves from lower middle income (with a GNI per capita between $1,006 and $3,955) to higher-middle income group (with a GNI per capita between $3,956 and $12,235) – according to World Bank Data (2016), it is observed that the cities or urban centers not only contribute to the growth but are also responsible for generation of pollution, waste, energy consumption and carbon emission, thereby creating and posing various environmental and ecological constraints. Thus, apart from providing urban services, the ULBs are also required to devise strategies and policies which will require them to build greener buildings, cities and address the ecological and environmental concerns towards creating sustainable cities (Cohen & Muñoz, 2016).

A recent, 2017 assessment of ULBs revealed that, 94 cities from 14 states in India, received credit ratings for issuing municipal bonds, to enable them to raise funds for their urban infrastructure requirements (at 2009-10 prices), wherein an investment of Rs. 39 trillion was estimated. It was observed that 55 of these cities got "investment grade" ratings, while 39 received credit ratings below the investment grade (BBB-), implying that the ULBs were required to undertake necessary interventions to improve their ratings for obtaining positive response to the municipal bonds to be issued. However, urban India goes beyond the 94 cities to nearly 8000 urban centers with much larger investment requirements (IIHS, nd). To add to the above, is the fact that in the last 20 years, a meager amount of Rs. 1,500 crore has been raised by 25 ULBs (Bhaskar, 2017). While on a global scale, for the global cities, the World Bank has estimated that to address the infrastructure gap in developing cities alone requires $1 trillion per year, with Official Development Aid (ODA) to emerging economics being only $135 billion; it is therefore imperative that all possible funding opportunities need to be explored for the future of urban development. It is therefore envisaged, that the civic crowdfunding variety will help fill up some of the resource gaps in the city finances (Partridge, 2015).

According to EMBARQ Network, more than 170 cities across the world have already signed up to use citizinvestor.com, which is a crowdfunding platform that raises money for public projects. The main areas of potential of crowdfunding for Indian cities according to Partridge (2015) include:

1. The potential to unlock access to finance barriers for young businesses and start-ups, thereby helping cities to grow jobs and increase competitiveness.
2. To help communities to collaborate and invest in their own spaces (local areas) and places, which is likely to improve the civic and ecological environment.
3. The ULBs can develop a specific crowdfunding platform at the city level or at the geographical level bringing together different funders and city stakeholders to create a dedicated platform tailored to the local urban context and try to match funding requirements.

The civic crowdfunding projects and platforms, seeks to crowd fund public services and/or functions of the ULBs. These projects are by far the most numerous but have attracted less attention than large-scale endeavors (Davies, 2014). Further most of the civic crowdfunding projects belong to a specific category of public goods called 'urban commons'. Civic crowdfunding allows citizens and civil society to rethink their neighborhood and potentially produce or renew urban commons. While such an exercise could provoke challenges and concerns in a democratic country like India, since these projects are driven by civil society and/or citizens instead of elected public authorities, but such initiatives provides opportunities, flexibility, better coordination, reducing the financial costs and thereby creating a new model of co-production, wherein the sub-national governments have a key role to play by facilitating citizens' initiatives (World Urban Campaign, 2014). Although civic crowdfunding is of recent origin, there are very few studies in this regard, that provides quantitative empirical evidences. It appears that civic crowdfunding projects have mostly tackled neighborhood issues and the emerging typical project tend to be "a small-scale garden or park project in a large city that produces a public good for an underserved community" (World Urban Campaign, 2014).

Civic crowdfunding allows citizens unprecedented access into infrastructure management through initial financing and decision-making. When civic projects compete for crowdfunding, success inherently relies on popularity, appeal and saleability. Conceivably, a municipality could be swept away by the crowdfunding wave, resulting in under-service for lower income areas without the means to pre-finance public improvements. Crowdfunding civic infrastructure thus assumes significant municipal cooperation and support, as the local government carries long-term operation and maintenance expenses and is liable for safety in the public realm (Harriman, 2017).

To support the argument in favor of civic crowdfunding, an instance has been highlighted, wherein the Mayor of London, in 2014 for the first time, resorted to the use of the Spacehive civic crowdfunding platform. Later the initiative was expanded to 57 such campaigns across London. The programme encouraged members of the public (or crowd) to propose local-area-improvement project ideas and enabled the Mayor and other members of the crowd to make financial donations towards these projects. The idea to fund local civic improvement projects, thus signals a changing tide for regeneration and planning engagement (Keane & Griffiths, 2017).

With this backdrop on civic crowdfunding, the authors further highlight three hypothetical case studies to explore the possibility of civic crowdfunding in city of Pune, Maharashtra State, India. The cases will act as references trying to explore different functions carried out by the ULBs – that can be addressed through the civic crowdfunding platforms.

CASES WITH SOLUTIONS

Hypothetical Case 1: A Study of Open Spaces – Maintenance of a Public Garden

The authors carried out a study of open spaces, which highlights:

- **Function-12:** Provision of urban amenities and facilities such as parks, gardens and playgrounds of the 12th Schedule and;
- **UN-SDG-11.7:** Access to safe, inclusive and accessible, green and public spaces / areas (Refer Table 4).

A study of the Joggers Park an open space, in an upmarket location in Pune (Kalyani Nagar – Refer to Map/ Figure 3).

Figure 3. Map of Kalyani Nagar Area in Pune City
Source: Maps of India.

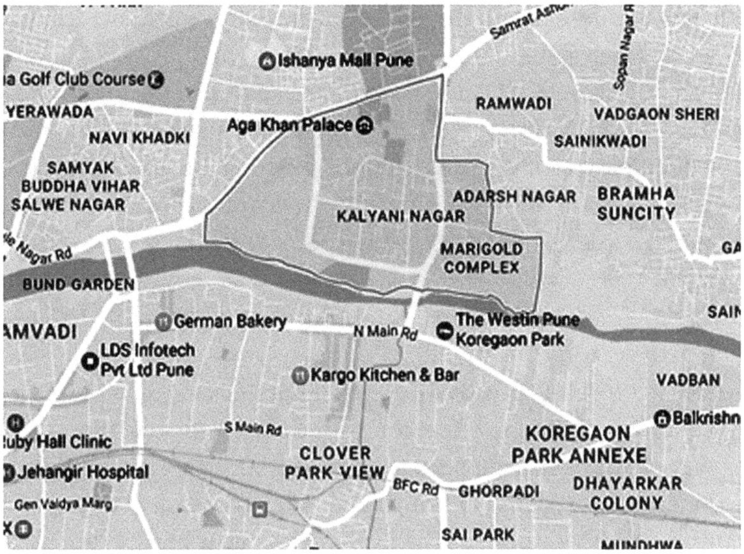

Figure 4. Map of Joggers Park in Kalyani Nagar Area, which was surveyed
Source: Maps of India.

- **Objective:** Assessment of the cleanliness of the toilets in the garden – keeping in mind recommendations for the Clean India Campaign – Swachh Bharat Abhiyan.
- **Findings:** A detailed discussion with the garden inspector revealed that while the Pune Municipal Corporation (PMC), which is the ULB, had constructed and provided community toilets separately for Ladies and Gents (not all gardens and open spaces in the city of Pune have such facilities) and while the Health Department of PMC had appointed two persons to clean the toilets, who are permanent employees and are paid in the range of Rs. 30,000-35,000 per month by the PMC, it was observed that the common toilets were not well maintained, while all other amenities provided in the public garden were above the satisfactory mark.

About Joggers Park:

- Located in an upmarket locality in Kalyani Nagar, Pune.
- An open space – public park of nearly 6 acres, with a 500 meters circular walking track, adequate benches for seating, play area for children, an open gymnasium – encouraging fitness for the citizens, adequate flora (approximately 300 small and 500 large plants / trees), community hall, yoga room, waste collection bins, water storage tank, drinking water facility, waste collection bins, good aesthetics and adequate manpower to maintain the garden and a ticket collector.
- Enjoys a daily footfall of nearly 850-900 on weekdays and 1000-1200 on weekends (Saturday and Sunday).
- **Entry Fees:** Re.1 per person or monthly pass of Rs.20, following the principles of not for profit motive (therefore low entry fee) and inclusion.
- The electricity bill of the garden is paid directly by the PMC to the state electricity department - Maharashtra State Electricity Board (MSEB).
- **Solution:** The authors therefore proposed civic crowdfunding, which could take the form of public subscription / donations as a solution to address this anomaly. A ballpark figure was calculated for manpower and cleaning material at Rs. 30,000 a month amounting to Rs.3.6 lakhs per annum. A detailed discussion with various stakeholders (citizens, ULB, Civil Society Organizations - CSOs and the private sector) revealed that such an amount could very successfully be raised through civic crowdfunding.

It was concluded that the civic crowdfunding platform includes civic participation in pool funding – a voluntary and participatory format, wherein stakeholder would get a sense of ownership and also ensures better service delivery by better planning, implementing and monitoring the cleanliness in the garden. It would create responsible communities, creating user groups and galvanizing local support for an idea. This type of an attitude needs to be nurtured and motivated and is very much the need of the hour in India. It is important to develop a class of responsible citizens who can take ownership of a small but important aspect of service delivery.

A similar yet differentiated success story can be seen in the form of Public Private Partnership (PPP) model adopted by the Ahmedabad Urban Development Authority (AUDA) which had tied up with AMUL (Anand Milk Federation Union Limited) – a dairy cooperative since 2001. In the city of Ahmedabad in Gujarat State of India, through the PPP model, AMUL maintains 126 out of 214 gardens, and in return AUDA allows AMUL to put up a retail shop in the AUDA gardens (Bagchi, 2014). Since maintaining these gardens cost the government a huge sum of money and a lot of effort is needed to deal with different contractors and addressing people complains – this was a good initiative on part of AMUL (Tiwari, 2009), relieving the ULB from one of their various functions. In the Pune case study, it was envisaged that civic crowdfunding could play a similar role as played by AMUL with respect to gardens in Ahmedabad City. The authors therefore foresee that the civic crowdfunding model can be replicated in the nearly 160 gardens and landscape in Pune city.

Hypothetical Case 2: Maintenance of Burial Places or Crematories

The researchers carried out a study of Pune Tamil Samaj Crematory - a burial and crematorium site, adjoining the Mula Mutha River, in Koregaon Park area which highlights:

- **Function-14:** Maintenance of burials and burial grounds, cremations, cremation grounds and electric crematoriums of the 12th Schedule (Refer Table 4).
- **Objective:** To assess the amenities provided for people who invariably need to visit the burial or crematoriums under distressed condition to bid farewell to their near and dear ones.
- **Background:** It has been observed over the years by the researchers that an unfortunate situation takes citizens / people to a burial / crematorium site. Often the environment in such open spaces have not been maintained, the colour paint on the walls are flaking, there is no place to sit for senior citizens, the toilets are filthy and there maybe occasions when one is required to wait for a couple of hours till the turn comes for cremation or burial. It is at this point when the citizens may find difficulty in getting drinking / bottled water, or some tea/coffee or biscuits, which may be a necessary short-term stimulant required in the given situation.
- **Findings:** It was marked that the state of the toilets were far below the satisfactory level, the service of running tap water was unavailable 24x7, and tap and wash basin fittings required to be replaced or repaired.
- **Area of the Burial or Crematorium:** Approximately 1-acre land area.
- **Physical Infrastructure:** Separate toilet for females and males, sitting area (benches), waste disposal (dustbins), with 3 facilities of - burial, fire cremation and electrical cremation, parking area, drinking water, and a temple.
- The above facilities or services along with the wages for manpower employed to maintain the site are provided and maintained by PMC.
- The cost of wooden planks is to be borne by the user while the electric crematorium and burial facility was provided without a charge. Therefore, zero revenue was generated at the site.
- The crematory in charge is paid Rs. 7,000 to 8,000 per month (on contract basis), and toilet cleaner is paid Rs. 30,000 monthly (who is a permanent employee).
- **Solution:** The authors after conducting focused group discussions with various stakeholder, therefore proposed civic crowdfunding as a solution to address the upkeep and maintenance of the site by adopting the following courses: i) keeping a donation box – clearly indicating that the proceeds of the same would take care of the maintenance of the site. ii) Using a civic crowdfunding platform, with an objective to specifically maintain such a site to experience a favorable well maintained environment, which has the urban commons provided for citizens at distressed times.

Hypothetical Case 3: Local Area Transport

A field study was undertaken in the Kalyani Nagar Prabhag / Ward no. (17) of Pune city that is governed by the PMC, which highlights:

- **Function-17:** To provide for public amenities including street lighting, parking lots, bus stops and public conveniences of the 12th Schedule and;
- **UN-SDG 11.2:** Improving public transit – sustainable mobility.
- **Objective:** To assess the existing public transport facility in the said area and its adequacy to cater to the needs of the local citizens providing last mile connectivity.
- **Findings:** The Kalyani Nagar area which is a part of Prabhag / Ward no.17, has adopted a mixed land use which has resulted in the local area including: residential and housing societies, offices, commercial areas, retail shops, restaurants, hawkers, schools, temples, a theater, garden, public toilets, banks, ATM's and others, whereby posing a large constrain to commuters as the roads are narrow, strained by traffic congestion and a plethora of private vehicles and public transport like cars, two-wheelers, buses, auto rickshaws, cyclists and tempos are being used, besides a lot of traffic which passes through this area as it connects two prominent areas - Nagar Road and Koregaon Park.

It was observed that on week days the area faces traffic congestion, making it difficult for the residents in the area to even negotiate the streets for their daily chores.

- **Solution:** After a thorough study conducted by the authors, it is proposed that through the civic crowdfunding model, to introduce a 4 km 'round trip' mini bus service in the area. This would entail acquiring two mini busses (seating capacity of 30 persons), along with hiring of three drivers and bus conductors each (an additional driver and bus conductor) to provide service for 365 days for 18-19 hours a day. This would facilitate easy mobility for the residence for their local shopping, other basic requirements and would also provide last mile connectivity to access the operational Bus Rapid Transit System (BRTS), which can connect the commuters to different parts of the city. Further, the bus service will be convenient once the proposed metro between Ramwadi and Vanaz, covering a distance of 14.9 kms, will be operational in due course of time.

The proposed funding requirement for the 'round trip' bus service project would bring together the participation of various stakeholders, including resident citizens, corporate and local government, to discuss, deliberate and design the pilot project and contributing towards creating a workable framework – involving ward level planning of urban transport, which if successful over a period of time can be replicated to other areas/ wards in the future.

FUTURE RESEARCH DIRECTION

The successful crowdfunding cases discussed in the earlier section of the chapter are mostly private initiatives with limited role of the government. It is therefore suggested that future research should be directed towards the study of civic crowdfunding with ULBs as an important stakeholder. One of the limitations of the present study is the absence of extensive research carried out on this subject matter in India and therefore only few official sources and news articles can be the grounds of the present study undertaken. This may also be attributed to the fact that crowdfunding is of recent origin. Further, to ensure the success of the civic crowdfunding models, it is necessary to prepare well defined and detailed prototypes with comprehensive Standard Operating Procedures (SOP), which the authors feel will help exploit the potential civic crowdfunding, resulting in the cities being awarded with report cards for better delivery of services, thereby enhancing the 'livability index".

CONCLUSION

With the process urbanization in India inching upwards, it is evident that the nearly 8000 urban centers are financially constrained, posing a major challenge for the ULBs to successfully build the urban infrastructure required along with timely and efficient delivery of urban services. The relevant cases discussed in the chapter bring forth the point that crowdfunding in India is an idea whose time has come. An argument in favor of crowdfunding – the civic variety emerges, since such platforms are known to provide opportunities to entrepreneurs, government, social change makers and various stakeholders in cities. This is also supported by the fact that cities are inherently characterized with the advantage of scale economies or agglomerations, with respect to income, education, technology and all that can be accrued, when compared to rural. It is envisaged that civic crowdfunding also brings with it a much desired transparency and involvement of stakeholder's participation in governance and a sense of ownership of the city. It is thus concluded that, crowdfunding as well as civic crowdfunding, can positively support development initiatives of a city as is a practice followed in many countries. This can further provide pooled finance by stakeholders, improving the access to capital, helping manage supply and demand of urban services, which are largely driven by innovation and efficiency. Cooperation can thus be struck between the development sector and specific crowdfunding platforms for co-funding strategies that are aligned with the SDGs.

REFERENCES

ASICS. (2016). Annual Survey of India's City-Systems 2016: Shaping India's Urban Agenda. ASICS.

Bagchi, D. S. (2014, June 24). *Public Garden Maintainance Through PPP - A case of Ahemdabad.* Retrieved from https://dhwanishahbagchi.wordpress.com

Bandyopadhyay, S. (2014, May). *Municipal Finance in India: Some Critical Issues.* Retrieved from International Center for Public Policy (Working Paper 14-21): http://scholarworks.gsu.edu/cgi/viewcontent.cgi?article=1010&context=icepp

Bhaskar, U. (2017, May 15). *94 cities get rated as urban local bodies prepare for municipal bonds.* Retrieved May 21, 2017, from Livemint: http://www.livemint.com/Politics/KjJbJIc7eENNMAqTonjqcN/94-cities-get-Crisil-ratings-as-urban-local-bodies-prepare-f.html

Bhatia, S. (2016, December 16). *The Genesis and Rise of Crowdfunding.* Retrieved July 16, 2017, from Linkedin: https://www.linkedin.com/pulse/genesis-rise-crowdfunding-shobhit-bhatia-msc

Census of India. (2011). Primary Census Abstract for Slum. Author.

Cohen, B., & Muñoz, P. (2016). *The Emergence of the Urban Entrepreneur.* Retrieved from https://books.google.co.in/books?id=tBYsDAAAQBAJ&pg=PA161&lpg=PA161&dq=World+Bank+Urban+Crowd+Funding&source=bl&ots=cpOt-2N89y&sig=fB3Pr86ywtrRP6-6AJRle-5_x4U&hl=en&sa=X&ved=0ahUKEwiwl_nqqvnTAhWIPY8KHWozCaYQ6AEIRDAF#v=onepage&q=World%20Bank%20Urban%20Crowd%20Funding&f=false

Crowdsourcing, LLC. (2012, May). *Crowd Funding Industry Report.* Research Report - Abridged Version. Author.

Davies, R. (2014, September 1). *Civic crowdfunding as a marketplace for participation in urban development*. Stanford.

Ellis, P., & Roberts, M. (2016). *Leveraging Urbanization in South Asia - Global Economic Prospects, 2016*. World Bank.

Fuel a Dream. (2017). *Fuel a Dream - Suryoday Parivar Case-Study.* Retrieved July 15, 2017, from Lets Make a 8KM Canal for 700 Drought-Hit Farmers in 15 Days: https://www.fueladream.com/home/campaign/216

Fund for Unity. (2017). *Fund for Unity Crowd Funding Platform.* Retrieved from http://fundforunity.statueofunity.in/

Griffiths, H., Madden, P., & Howe, C. (2016). *Civic Crowdfunding - A guidebook for local authorities.* Retrieved September 6, 2017, from Catapult - Future Cities: http://about.spacehive.com/wp-content/uploads/2017/03/Civic-Crowdfunding_A-Guide-for-Local-Authorities.pdf

Gupta, D. (2009, November 18). *JNNURM: Community participation fund.* Retrieved July 18, 2017, from India Water Portal: http://www.indiawaterportal.org/opportunities/jnnurm-community-participation-fund

Harriman. (2017, May 2). *Crowd Funding Municipal Projects; A Look at the Impact of CrowdFunded Infrastructure in Rotterdam.* Retrieved from http://harriman.com/inspirations/crowdfunding-municipal-projects-look-impact-crowdfunded-infrastructure-rotterdam/

Hung-Yi, C. (n.d.). *Crowdfunding and its Interaction with Urban Development.* Nagoya University.

IIHS. (n.d.). *Urban Transport in India - Challenges and Recommendations.* Retrieved from www.iihs.co.in

Jain, J. K. (2015). *Crowd-Funding in Microfinance in India: Issues, Challenges and Opportunities. UK Government's Department for International Development (DFID) and Small Industries Development Bank of India (SIDBI).* DFID and SIDBI.

JNNURM Document. (2013, November 22). *Jawaharlal Nehru National Urban Renewal Mission (JNNURM).* Retrieved from https://www.gktoday.in/jawaharlal-nehru-national-urban-renewal_06/

Keane, A. O., & Griffiths, H. (2017, March 20). *Civic Crowdfunding – A Guidebook for Local Authorities.* Retrieved July 23, 2017, from Spacelive - Catapult - Future Cities: https://about.spacehive.com/civic-crowdfunding-a-guidebook-for-local-authorities/

Khan, A. (2017, April 18). *Maharashtra schools raise Rs 216 crore via crowdfunding*. Retrieved from http://indianexpress.com/article/india/maharashtra-schools-raise-rs-216-crore-via-crowd-funding-4617328/

Kirby, E., & Worner, S. (2014). *Crowd-funding: An Infant Industry Growing Fast*. Academic Press.

McKinsey Global Institute (MGI) Report. (2010). *India's Urban Awakening: Building Inclusive Cities and Sustainable Economic Growth*. Author.

Menon, S. (2016, September 9). *Crowd control: Sebi warning turns off crowdfunding tap for startups*. Retrieved July 17, 2017, from ET Rise by Economics Times: http://economictimes.indiatimes.com/small-biz/money/crowd-control-sebi-warning-turns-off-crowdfunding-tap-for-startups/articleshow/54202702.cms

MHRD. (2017, September). *Constitutional Provision*. Retrieved September 12, 2017, from Ministry of Human Resource Development (MHRD) under Government of India (GOI): http://mhrd.gov.in/article-243w

Ministry of Housing & Urban Affairs. (2016, May 17). *States asked to convert 3,784 urban areas into statutory Urban Local Bodies*. Retrieved from http://pib.nic.in/newsite/PrintRelease.aspx?relid=145405

Mohan, M. (2016). Geospatial Information from Satellite Imagery for Geovisualisation of Smart Cities in India. *ISPRS - International Archives of the Photogrammetry. Remote Sensing and Spatial Information Sciences, 41*, *B8*, 979–985.

MOUD. (2015, April). *The Future of Urban Development and Services: Urban Development Recommendations for Government of India*. Retrieved July 19, 2017, from World Economics Forum: http://www3.weforum.org/docs/WEF_IU_FUDS_Urban_Development_Recommendations_Government_India_Report_2015.pdf

Nagalakshmi, S., & Cecilia, G. U. (2014). Crowd Funding – An Emerging Trend in India. *International Journal of Scientific Research*, *3*(4), 71–73. doi:10.15373/22778179/APR2014/206

Nallathiga, R. (2008). Trends and prespectives of urban public finance in select countries. *ICFAI Journal of Urban Policy*, 16-32.

Nekaj, E. L. (2016, August 18). *India's Top 10 Crowdfunding Platforms*. Retrieved from Crowd Source Week: http://crowdsourcingweek.com/blog/indias-top-ten-crowdfunding-platforms/

Padmanabhan, A. (2016, March 27). *Crowdfunding Platforms in India for Tech Start-Ups*. Retrieved July 15, 2017, from Indian Engineering Design Forum: https://www.iedf.in/index.php/blog/item/crowdfunding-platforms-in-india-for-tech-start-ups

Partridge, A. (2015, July 1). *Crowdfunding City Futures?* URBACT in Ireland.

Pethe, A., Nallathiga, R., Gandhi, S., & Tandel, V. (2014, February 15). *Re-thinking urban planning in India: Learning from the wedge between the de jure and de facto development in Mumbai*. Academic Press.

Prabhu, D. (2016, October 28). *Is Crowdfunding Legal in India? SEBI Regulations & It's Implications*. Retrieved July 16, 2017, from Linkedin: https://www.linkedin.com/pulse/crowdfunding-legal-india-sebi-regulations-its-deepak-prabhu

Press Information Bureau. (2016, May 17). *States asked to convert 3,784 urban areas into statutory Urban Local Bodies.* Retrieved from http://pib.nic.in/newsite/PrintRelease.aspx?relid=145405

Prinsha K. (2016). A Study on Crowd Funding and its Implications in India. *Indian Journal of Research - Paripex, 5*(1), 233-235.

RBI Executive Summary, . (2011). *Municipal Finance in India – An Assessment. Executive Summary on Performance of ULB's in India.* Retrieved from Reserve Bank of India: http://www.rbi.org.in/scripts/bs_viewcontent.aspx?Id=1157

HPEC Report and Recommendations. (2011, September 29). *Urbanization in India - HPEC Report and Recommendations.* Isher Judge Ahluwalia.

Report, M. (2015, March 31). *Massolution Posts Research Findings: Crowdfunding Market Grows 167% in 2014, Crowdfunding Platforms Raise $16.2 Billion.* Retrieved July 16, 2017, from Massolution - Crowd Powered Business: https://www.crowdfundinsider.com/2015/03/65302-massolution-posts-research-findings-crowdfunding-market-grows-167-in-2014-crowdfunding-platforms-raise-16-2-billion/

Reserve Bank of India. (2016, April). *Consultation Paper on Peer to Peer Lending.* Retrieved July 17, 2017, from Reserve Bank of India (RBI) - Database: https://www.rbi.org.in/scripts/bs_viewcontent.aspx?Id=3164

Sahasranaman, A. (2014, June 6). *Financing Metropolitan Governments in Developing Countries.* Retrieved from IFMR Finance Foundation: http://financingcities.ifmr.co.in/blog/category/municipal-finance/

Sawant, A. (2017, May 2). *College students to crowdfund library project in rural Maharashtra.* Retrieved from http://www.dnaindia.com/india/report-college-students-to-crowdfund-library-project-in-rural-maharashtra-2424422

SEBI. (2017, March 11). *Consultation Paper on Crowdfunding in India.* Consultation Paper on Crowdfunding in India. SEBI.

Sridhar, G. (2015, April 14). *Crowd funding gaining pace for Amaravati project.* Retrieved from http://www.thehindubusinessline.com/news/national/crowd-funding-gaining-pace-for-amaravati-project/article8476414.ece

Srivastava, M., M, K. J., & Sagar, M. (2014). An Insight into Crowd Funding in India. *International Journal of Management and Social Science Research Review, 1*(6), 56–62.

Tandel, V., Hiranandani, K., & Kapoor, M. (2016, July 28). *What's In A Definition? A Study on Implications and Suitability of Urban Definitions in India through its Employment Guarantee Programme.* Retrieved May 18, 2017, from IDFC: http://www.idfcinstitute.org/site/assets/files/9615/tandel_et_al_28th_july_whats_in_a_definition.pdf

Technologies, B. (2017, June 7). *Parched Indian Villages Uses Crowd Funding to Build Canal.* Retrieved July 14, 2017, from Bloomberg Technologies: https://www.bloomberg.com/news/articles/2016-08-08/parched-india-village-uses-crowdfunding-to-build-canal

The Hindu. (2017, February 10). *SEBI to form panel to facilitate crowdfunding*. Retrieved July 16, 2017, from The Hindu: http://www.thehindu.com/todays-paper/tp-business/SEBI-to-form-panel-to-facilitate-crowdfunding/article17280456.ece

The World Bank Group. (2014). *UN World Urbanization Prospects (WUP), 2014 - Final Report*. Department of Economic and Social Affairs, Population Division.

The World Bank Group. (2015, September 24). *Leveraging Urbanization in India*. Retrieved September 13, 2017, from Leveraging Urbanization in India: http://www.worldbank.org/en/country/india/brief/leveraging-urbanization-india

Times of India. (2017, May 27). *Crowdfunding helps Latur youths get internet connectivity to home village*. Retrieved from http://timesofindia.indiatimes.com/city/pune/crowdfunding-helps-latur-youths-get-internet-connectivity-to-home-village/articleshow/58866158.cms

Tiwari, K. (2009, May 7). *Amul watering AMC, Auda parks*. Retrieved May 19, 2017, from Amul watering AMC, Auda parks: http://www.dnaindia.com/india/report-amul-watering-amc-auda-parks-1253682

UN Habitat. (2016). Urbanization and Development: Emerging Futures. World Cities Report 2016. Author.

UNDP. (2015). *United Nations - 17 Sustainable Development Goals (SDGs)*. Retrieved May 5, 2017, from Goal 11: Make cities inclusive, safe, resilient and sustainable: http://www.un.org/sustainabledevelopment/cities/

United Nations. (2015, September 25). *Sustainable Developmwnt Goals (SDGs)*. Retrieved November 8, 2016, from 17 Sustainable Developmwnt Goals (SGDs) to Transform Our World: http://www.un.org/sustainabledevelopment/sustainable-development-goals/

Vadgama, C., Khutwad, A., Damle, M., & Patil, S. (2015). Smart Funding Options for Developing Smart Cities: A Proposal for India. *Indian Journal of Science and Technology*, *8*(34), 1–12. doi:10.17485/ijst/2015/v8i1/85418

Varma, V. (2017, June 7). *Can crowdfunding help build a canal? A village in parched Marathwada thinks so!* Retrieved July 14, 2017, from The Indian Express: http://indianexpress.com/article/india/india-news-india/crowdfunding-in-india-marathwada-drought-canal-farmers-2838988/

World Bank Data. (2016). *Gross national income per capita 2016, Atlas method and PPP*. Retrieved from http://databank.worldbank.org/data/download/GNIPC.pdf

World Bank Document. (2013). *Crowdfunding's Potential for the Developing World*. Washington, DC: World Bank.

World Urban Campaign. (2014). *Crowd Funding – A collective option for urban sustainable development*. Retrieved from http://www.worldurbancampaign.org/civic-crowdfunding-collective-option-urban-sustainable-development

Worldometers. (2017, July). *India Population (LIVE) 1,343,205*. Retrieved from http://www.worldometers.info/world-population/india-population/

KEY TERMS AND DEFINITIONS

Basic Urban Services: Facilities provided by the government/urban local bodies to the citizens and are also referred to as public goods, comprising of water, sanitation, waste management, energy, mobility, public health, education, affordable housing, security of tenure, etc.

Civic Crowdfunding: The practice of raising monetary contributions for public interest projects from a large pool of donors through various crowdfunding platforms that may or may not give financial returns.

Crowdfunding: A means of raising funds/capital (small amount) from multiple investors through a web-based platform or social networking site for a specific project, business venture, or social cause.

Sustainable Cities: A city designed to use ecology, economy, and equity and has the ability to provide clean and healthy environment, economically self-reliant, self-renewing, and provide equal opportunities for all members of the society. It also considers the environmental impact, inhabited by people dedicated towards minimization of required inputs of energy, water, and food.

Urban Local Bodies (ULBs): Urban local bodies are the lowest level administrative units that govern cities or urban areas. In India these generally take the form of a municipal corporation or a municipality.

Chapter 13
Improving Quality of Urban Life Through Enhanced Energy Policy in Africa

Ibrahim Umar Benna
Oxford Brookes University, UK

ABSTRACT

Neither urban quality of life research nor effective urban energy policy research is new in Africa, but funding the future needs in these two areas requires exploring the new options, such as the emerging crowdfunding market. It is projected that by 2100 Africans will account for 40% of global population and majority urban residents, with huge workforce, a growing middle class, experiencing hyper-globalization, and increased innovation, all of which will enhance quality of urban life. For Africa to meet its large-scale energy-deficit and expected huge future demand triggered by rapid and massive urbanization, alternative renewable sources are considered in the supply policy options. Similarly, alternative visions of how energy can contribute to inclusive economic growth in Africa are examined and ways to fund them explored. To leap-frog Africa's development while the traditional funding mechanism helps, sustainable option lies in innovative alternative finance, especially crowdfunding markets in Africa and in diaspora.

INTRODUCTION

United Nation study (UNDESA, 2014) has indicated that the rise in population growth and urbanization is projected to increase the global urban majority by 2.5 billion people by the year 2050, with 90 per cent of that growth concentrated in Asia and Africa. Africa, led by Nigeria's projected 212 million people will need massive investment in energy to power the expected growth, expand the essential infrastructure, and help meet the accompanying rising demand for energy to service lighting, heating and cooling. These are great demand in the intense urban residential, industrial, commercial and social activities in the future to sustain current growth, create new and better-paying jobs, as well as lift millions of people out of poverty and slums (WEF, 2016; Jarrett 2017).

DOI: 10.4018/978-1-5225-3952-0.ch013

Added to this massive huge demand is a huge energy deficit in most African countries where two-thirds of the people – an estimated 620 million - have no direct access to electricity (WEF, 2016). Such energy deficits in Africa tend to reinforce high rates of poverty, especially for women and the urban poor in the slums. Unfortunately, the poor urban communities of Africa are driven to pay among the world's most expensive unit prices for energy. Many communities are not only paying unreasonable prices, they are forced to pay in humanitarian terms, such as the inability to eliminate avoidable child deaths, unable to achieve universal secondary education, and in their failure to achieve more inclusive growth, a sustainable mix of land-use and even gender parity.

The current energy deficit and the projected huge demand in the future add up to create African energy crisis that is indeed the continent's growth and urban quality of life crises. Solving these would require such energy efficiency can offer practical and cost-effective solutions to budget constrained governments and citizens to meet their energy needs without sacrificing their development priorities. Thus, for Africa to leap-frog its development, improve the quality of life of its urban development actors (public, private and people) it must craft an effective green energy policies and can be funded using a mix of traditional and innovative alternative funding instruments.

The next section of the chapter discusses how urban development actors use innovations in energy and information technologies to promote innovative solutions in the key quality of life areas of health, education, and commerce. This is followed by a review innovations energy reform, its efficient use in urban activities and ways of applying it at the various spatial levels. The funding mechanisms for achieving these energy reforms are discussed the fourth section. The fifth section examines future research directions in these areas, with a conclusion section.

IMPROVING QUALITY OF URBAN LIFE IN AFRICA

It is expected that the global urban population will increase by about 2.7 billion by 2050. Africa is racing against time and dwindling resources to uplift the quality of life of its increasing urban majority population. An essential part of this task is determining how to meet the immense demands for urban infrastructures, development of new and improvement of existing housing infrastructure within the limited available funds (UNDESA 2014). The planning and design of these new developments will be used to reshape existing or create new urban landscapes with major implications for infrastructure costs, energy consumption as well as the livability and social and economic resilience of cities. As Table 1 shows Africa had a low-level in the 1950s will have the highest percentage by 2050.

Improving Quality of Life Through Urban Design

The quality of urban life can be enhanced greatly by means of careful urban design, which is achievable with high-energy efficiency using the traditional spatial tools that include selection of compact design, and urban management process that includes directed public participation.

- **Quality of Life and Energy Efficiency:** To sustain a livable and energy efficient future, major developments within cities is the key. Achieving a city's maximum potential requires the modernization of urban spatial development, on the principle of human-scale solutions, such as maximizing the accessibility to jobs, commercial stores and shops, social services and environmental

Table 1. Annual percentage of population at mid-year residing in urban areas

Global Region	1950	1975	2010	2035	2050	%
Africa	14	24.7	38.3	49.3	55.9	299.3
Asia	17.5	25	44.8	58.4	64.2	266.9
Europe	51.5	65.4	72.7	78.3	82	29.2
Lat Am & Carib	41.3	60.7	78.4	83.9	86.2	106.2
North America	63.9	73.8	80.8	85.1	87.4	36.7
Oceania	62.4	71.9	70.7	71.7	73.5	17.8

Source: UNDESA 2014.

amenities accessible to the population by walking, cycling, and public transportation. The development of urban spaces within cities has implications in terms of its strong 'lock-in' effects: what that means is that as cities expand and grow, once urban forms are defined, it is very costly to overhaul. The following sections will explain how urban form significantly impacts energy usage, infrastructure costs along with the social and economic resilience of a city.

- **Dynamics of Urban Form:** Primarily political economy, transportation technologies, land markets, and urban development policies influence the transformation of urban forms. Urban form refers to the design of a metropolitan area, town or city, spatial extension and physical layout. Very good examples exist in many old cities of the Islamic world, the basic form of which has been replicated in many new cities worldwide.

Political economy refers to the dynamics and interactions of the various players and rules involved in any urban development decision-making processes, which influence the pattern of land usage (e.g., conversion of rural areas versus increasing density of existing urban built-ups).

Key drivers of urban transformation include transportation technologies. According to Wortmann (1985), the extension of urban areas in a city has a direct link to the average distance that can be travelled within an hour. Therefore, improving quality of roads would leave to improved traffic speed which in turn may encourage urban sprawl. Latest technologies lead to improved transportation infrastructures which may significantly change how space is distributed and population densities are controlled within the city.

Land value is a driving factor for the rate at which rural land is being converted for urban use. The cheaper rural land has become more accessible with improved transport technologies and road infrastructures. Having access to more rural land increases the availability of are for urbanization. Having no land value controls naturally forces markets to send cities to head for an urban extension.

Urban development policies are responsible for determining uses of urban lands, how city blocks are sized, how plots are subdivided, street patterns, the structure and hierarchy of road networks and the how social services and environmental amenities are spread out.

Urban form is impacted by growth management issues like urban sprawl, growth patterns and phasing of developments. Controlling the Floor Area Ratio (FAR) is one of the key policy tools for urban planning –this refers to the ratio of the floor area over the building footprint area, leading to controlled population density. FAR is commonly used as a delegate for population and job densities and its regulations heavily impact land prices and built densities.

- **Spatial Dimension and Spatial Energy Efficiencies:** Urban planners, city managers and indeed all urban development actors in Africa need to be aware of the relationships between spatial dimension and spatial energy efficiencies in shaping the quality of urban life. Sometimes short-term gains tend to becloud judgements on how to achieve long-term goals of livable and sustainable cities.
    - **Spatial Dimension:** Energy efficiency is strongly impacted by the structure and distribution of land use and the way urban plots and street networks are formed, sized, and scaled. Optimizing these aspects of urban form can reduce energy needs by a factor of two to four (Salat and Bourdic 2011; 2013). It is evident in many historic global city centers that energy efficient urban forms are displayed in a balance of street sizes and functions: few very large streets, an average number of medium-sized streets and many narrow streets to encourage walking. A good example is Paris, where 60 percent of its streets (the historical street network) is less than 12 meters wide and accommodate low-speed traffic (Bourdic and Salat 2012). It has a high density of narrow streets with close intersections and continuous sidewalks to create a lively, safe and walkable urban landscape. Walking distances tend to be shorter and the system of close intersections provides convenience to pedestrians, allowing them to easily change directions, enabling and encouraging non-motorized travel options such as walking and cycling for daily short trips.
    - **Spatial Energy Efficiencies:** Which has a strong impact on the quality of life, is affected mainly by the following factors:
        - The spatial dimension of urban areas, whereby beyond a certain level the quality of life begins to decline;
        - The coordination of resident and job densities, with inadequate coordination quality of life suffers;
        - The accessibility of jobs, services, and amenities by walking, cycling, and public transportation; and
        - The extent to which the built environment adapts to local climate conditions.

The first three factors directly influence the demand for motorized transportation while the last affects the buildings operational demand for energy.

- **Quality of Life and Urban Form:** Studies of cities (Newman & Kenworthy 2996, Mizokami & Maroyama 2013) around the world indicate that a city's livability standards and its level of energy consumption are closely linked to its physical structure. Elements that define a city's shape include the spatial distribution and dimensions of buildings, streets and parks, as well as the spatial coordination of residences, jobs, social services and environmental amenities. The following characteristics are often exhibited in the most energy efficient and livable cities:
    - **Compact Built-Up Areas:** The residential, commercial, institutional areas have their building in very close proximity. Thus, the densities of urban activities in terms of residential, commercial, entertainment, manufacturing and other job-creating services may be strategically spread throughout transit corridors and matched with social and environmental services and amenities.
    - **Dense and Variety of Street Sizes:** Street networks of diverse types and hierarchies are planned in dense and interconnected manner. Not only does the traffic flow smoothly, it al-

lows for varied sizes of traffic load and considers efficiency in functions fulfilling the needs all users, particularly pedestrians, cyclists and transit users.

- ◦ **Community Responsive Transport:** Public transport modalities correlate to population and job densities, providing access in walking distance.
- ◦ **Walkable Community Facilities:** Social services and environmental amenities such as schools, hospitals, parks and green spaces are designed to maximize accessibility by walking.
- ◦ **Human Scale Defines Design Concept:** Urban blocks are small sized and buildings are aligned along streets to create various street fronts and vibrant sidewalks.
- ◦ **Mixed-Use Concept:** Multi-functional (or mixed) uses are ingrained in neighborhoods, blocks and even individual buildings.
- ◦ **Design With Climate:** Design and layout of buildings and streets are adapted to local climatic conditions.

- **Participatory Planning and Design:** Sustainable urban planning and design that meets the needs of the residents, must be inclusive, participatory and open to the diverse development actors of the community or city. The normally the development actors consist of three broad categories: public officials whose daily decisions and actions shape the city's form and development: the private sector consisting of firms of assorted sizes that produce goods and services, market and transport them; and the consuming community- or the "crowd"- which is increasingly becoming active in invest production as well (Surowiecki 2004).

Historically in most Africa urban planning, design and development was the sole responsibility of the public sector, which was initially the colonial government and after independence the national government (Benevolo 1967). At that time the government planned, designed and directly –through the Public Works Department, which built all the major physical infrastructure including transport, utilities and associated service. They also planned, designed and built social infrastructure, including facilities for educational, health, social facilities and sports. It had a strong control on the development commercial and banking. Only in recent decades has the private sector started taking an active part in the planning, design and development of cities as contractors, consultants, and private developers of the industrial, residential and sports/entertainment facilities (Njoh 1999). So far, the third sector – the community sector- has been largely a spectator rather than real activities participant in urban development. The type of peripheral role it has played has been in "community development/improvement" and in the role of the NGOs in seeking the greater participation of the households and citizens in the urban development.

With the increased penetration and use of Information Technology devices, the time has come for greater and possibly a lead in the planning, design and development of local areas and indeed cities. The sharing or collaborative economy, and the emergence of alternative finance that put the "crowd" at the center of the societal initiative are providing a roadmap to new directions. Thus, the new roles each sector of urban development actors are going to play is in the evolving and African countries and city governments should seek to play an important part in this process.

Transforming Urban Quality of Life Through E-Learning

To leap-frog its development to the level that clear the backlog of its deficit in education and bridge the gap between the demand and supply for educational opportunities, Africa must include e-learning as an important part of its policy tools. It is not surprising; therefore, that E-learning is catching on quite fast in most part of Africa. Governments across the continent have started numerous initiatives that will allow students to gain access to education in a way that was never considered impossible. The African e-learning market was estimated to reach US$513 million by 2016 year-end (Ambient Insights 2016), linking more schools to the national electricity grid, broadening internet services to educational institutions and allowing foreign e-learning companies seeking opportunities to thrive in Africa. An example is Positivo BGH, an Argentinean educational device manufacturer that has multiple on-going projects in Rwanda and Kenya to produce devices. Other companies such as Samsung, Intel and Microsoft are also expanding their services into the education sector in Africa.

Most African countries have initiatives to expand the scope of digital learning to enhance the quality of life of their people. The governments of Nigeria, Tunisia, and Angola have programs that provide easy, cheap and quick access to education. Each with its own approach, there may be a need to learn from each other on implementation strategies and best practices. Table 2 shows some of the activities of government in Eastern and Southern Africa as possible lessons to learn from.

Contributions of Energy Through E-Health to Urban Quality of Life

Many African Health systems focus their efforts on communicable diseases while reducing their attention on non-communicable diseases that has been growing and currently accounts for 22% of the disease burden. To address those challenges, African countries are developing healthcare services and are strengthening their health strategies by developing e-Health potential (Africa 4Tech org. 2016).

Table 2. Selected e-learning Initiatives of some governments in eastern and southern Africa

Country	E-Learning Initiatives
Botswana	• 2015 - Botswana took the e-learning approach seriously and implemented various programmes to push this agenda • Investments of US$3 million were made start a digital studio, enabling the education sector to produce high-quality courses accessible on radio and television • 2016 - saw the launch of Botswana College of Distance and Open Learning (BOCODOL), a fully online learning system that can enroll students with internet connectivity from anywhere.
Kenya	• 2013- Kenya Digital Literacy Programme created to develop e-learning tablets • Kenya Institute for Curriculum Development (KICD) is doing what it can in terms of aggregating digital books to create one portal for education content. • 2016 - the learning tablets are provided to all schools that are connected to electricity and by next year the real impact of the new system should be felt.
Rwanda	• 2007 - Rwanda introduced digital learning through their One Laptop Per Child programme. The initiative aimed to provide 2.5 million children in primary school with learning devices • ICT master plan - deployed over 26 innovations with half of it in the ICT field within the last three years • National internet coverage through Liquid Telecom, boasting that the whole country is covered with its fiber optic
South Africa	• South Africa is hailed to be the biggest e-learning market in Africa according to a new study [PDF] by Ambient Research • Gauteng Govt- distributed 88,000 Huawei tablets to 2,200 schools in the province starting in January 2014 • Private tuition-"As an example, the M-Ubuntu programme in South Africa offers pupils in the partner schools a tutorial service in reading and writing, conducted by specialists resident in the United States, the United Kingdom, Sweden and Italy," a report by UNESCO [PDF] in 2015 observed. • Ambient Research (2016) "The University of South Africa (UNISA) UNISA is a pan-regional virtual university with over 310,000 students (3,500 come from outside Africa.) Over half of all UNISA students take at least one online course a year."
Uganda	• Created computer classes in over 1,000 secondary schools and currently all universities have computer learning centers. • Establishing investing in digital learning through mobile phones

There are at least five ways access and use of energy has contributed health component or urban quality of life. Most examples are from North and West Africa and cover a wide area of health services such as prevention, diagnostic, treatment, patience follow-up, and professional development.

- **African eHealth Contribution at Awareness (Prevention) Level:** Various social media tools have been used as an early warning to prevent the spread of communicable diseases – for example Ebola and various flu types- by informing the population about the disease risks and how to handle them. The African eHealth ecosystem addresses the issue by using SMS, WhatsApp and other mobile and Internet applications to alert, prevent and inform the population. An example is OPISMS, which aims to increase coverage via SMS reminders of vaccination dates and spreading awareness about to the importance of this medical procedure (Africa 4Tech org. 2016).
- **African eHealth Contribution at Diagnostic Level:** In this case, the key is to identify and track the patients especially in cases of infectious diseases. Moreover, accessing to reliable databases and providing remote diagnostic in isolated areas is an important challenge. Among recent African eHealth initiative DOCTOCLINIC allows patients to get treated by a healthcare professional without the need to travel and to pick up at the nearest pharmacy for their prescription without having to queue (Arinola & Obiako, 2017),
- **African eHealth Contribution at Treatment Level:** If treatment requires receiving pharmacovigilance follow-up, checking the efficiency of the prescription, or controlling the authenticity of drugs, ICTs can help by allowing electronic tracking of drugs or optimizing the patients' treatment. African eHealth initiative such as Mpedigree (promoted by YAI Eugene Boadu, Marketing Director of Mpedigree, Ghana) addresses this issue by providing a mean to fight against drugs counterfeiting (Arinola & Obiako, 2017),
- **African eHealth Contribution at Patient Follow-Up Level:** To follow up changes in pregnant women and mothers of under-5, or to follow the progress of the patients on their recovery process or to assist a patient suffering from chronic diseases, African eHealth initiative has developed several alternative systems. A good example is the **e-room**-- promoted by Saad-Eddine Said, Co-Director of NGO Terre Sans Frontière, Morocco (Africa 4Tech org. 2016) -- which uses open source technology to connect people in remote areas with a professional team of volunteers to either assist during emergency situations or to set-up classes for the children of the community (Arinola & Obiako, 2017),
- **African eHealth Contribution at Improvement and Learning Level:** Improving Africa Health systems requires also forming health workers, improves inter-professional exchanges and connecting isolated medical centers with better-equipped urban hospitals. African eHealth ecosystem addresses this issue by developing innovation such as Chartler is a software that improves the efficiency of health systems, facilitating collaboration between practitioners and access to medical information and clinical quality standards. Chartler is a product promoted by YAI Omasirichukwu Udeinya, CEO of Novadge (Arinola & Obiako, 2017),

E-Commerce Africa

The growth of e-commerce in Africa was triggered by two main factors: the rapid penetration of information technology and rapid economic growth. The tremendous increase in the growth of Information technologies ownership and use in virtually all parts of Africa enabled the consumer to look beyond the local market for desirable goods. This occurred at a time when many African economies experienced a rapid rise in economic activities tied to high demand in commodities in the beginning of the 2000s (Krogman & Khumalo 2016, Mohammed 2016, UNCTAD 2015). This increased prosperous triggered a rise in the quality of life of the average African citizen, however, as the commodity boom burst, many economies and their consumer started to reduce e-commerce activities.

Most African consumers and manufacturers are constrained by the friction of distance between the actors in the production – distribution chain, added to which is the problem inadequate and inefficient infrastructure. This geographic separation tends to limit competition, which unfavorably affects price, variety, and greatly affects innovative potential. All these issues combine to limit economic activities within and among African economies.

The emergence of e-commerce has proved to the effective answer to all these constraining factors. It offers the chance to market, buy and sell goods over the internet, which offers consumers not only, convenience: more variety of goods and services but also at cheaper prices, along with retrievable information. For the suppliers, e-commerce offers better market reach, both in terms of spatial distance and is accessible at any time and many business activities are automated.

The tendency of e-commerce to promote social equity makes it even more appealing to the emerging African economies. As e-commerce enables equal access to markets and many opportunities, its benefits will be equally shared to all members of the society. Its redistributive effects enable people with no access to capital to pursue greater opportunities using such tools crowdfunding and crowdsourcing. Farmer and women in remote villages, for example, can also gain huge benefits through wireless Internet not only to trade, but also to get life-saving information on medicines and healthcare, agro-base information and new innovative ways of doing things.

Internationally, e-commerce has been transforming the conduct of trans-border trade via the explosion in consumer choices. The UNCTAD (2015) estimates the number of online traders in six global regions showing changes between 2013 and projected 2018 that give a clear indication where growth is expected. Table 3 shows that by far the largest estimated growth in online buyers is projected for the Middle East and Africa, with a predicted 82% increase from 2013 to 2018.

Table 3. Estimated number of online buyers worldwide, by region, 2013–2018

Region	Total Users (Million)		Growth (%) 2013–2018
	2013	2018*	
Asia and Oceania	460.3	782.4	70
Western Europe	182.3	210.2	15
North America	172.3	203.8	18
The Middle East and Africa	93.6	170.6	82
Latin America	84.7	139.3	64
Central and Eastern Europe	86.4	117.4	36
World	1 079.6	623.7	50

Source: UNCTAD, 'The Information Economy Report 2015: Unlocking the Potential of E-Commerce for Developing Countries', 2015, http://unctad.org/en/PublicationsLibrary/ier2015_en.pdf, retrieved 4 July 2017

With respect to the role middle class is expected to play in boosting the e-commerce in Africa, Mohammed (2016) suggests that as Africa's middle class rises and spends more money online, a new wave of online entrepreneurs is bound to emerge, thereby triggering a new lifestyle. For example, the estimates show that roughly a third of the continent spends between $4 to $20 a day - this group is expected to grow to 42% by 2060, amounting to more than a billion high-level consumers.

In summary, it seems there are two competing stories emerging in Africa: one of the vibrant domestic digital businesses, and the other of feeble but strengthening international e-commerce. Many domestic e-commerce activities in bigger African economies (such as Nigeria, Kenya and South Africa) are growing strong, even though no such development is observable in the smaller countries. Against the backdrop of these strong poles of domestic African markets, is the slow flow of international online commerce.

ENHANCED ENERGY POLICY IN AFRICA

This section reviews innovations energy policy reform, the purpose of which is to improve the quality of life of the population. The paradoxical situation is examined whereby energy poor African are living in an energy-rich continent, with grave impact on quality of life. Then follows an examination of scenarios for African Energy Infrastructure and their potential quality of life impacts. The discussion then focuses on renewable energy technologies and their quality of life impacts, which sets the stage the discussion on suitable Renewable Energy Policies for Africa and how best to manage them.

Africans Are Energy Poor Living in an Energy-Rich Continent, With Grave Impact on Quality of Life

Africans are energy poor- with generating capacity less than Germany (REN21 2015)- in a continent that is known to be energy-rich but poorly developed. The level of development varies regionally. In the Sub-Saharan Africa, most people face severe energy poverty, and low availability of energy services that constrain general economic activity. In the North African, countries and South Africa there are significantly higher levels of electric power and overall energy consumption in support of higher socio-economic development.

All over Africa, meeting current and future energy need is a major challenge. Generally, biomass energy source is the most widely used for cooking across the continent. Fossil energy is preferred in electricity generation and in the transport sector. Renewable sources are used in the electricity sector and have seen a significant expansion in recent years, though – except for hydro – from a very low base. South Africa leads the continent in both installed capacity and investments (IASS 2016). Studies have shown that most of the renewable energy capacity is grid-connected and off-grid uses have been on the upswing in recent years (REN21 2015, IEA 2014). The majority of African governments have developed active renewable energy policies and programs, which show the strong application in the electricity sector. It is noticeable that the total primary energy demand in Africa grew by almost 50 per cent between 2000 and 2012 (IASS 2016). Predictably, bioenergy took the largest share of this growth, followed by oil and gas sources.

While the continent is a major producer of fossil fuel, many African countries are reliant on fossil fuel imports. For example, in 2009, 38 out of the 54 African countries were net oil-importing countries (AfDB 2009). The import dependency has many down sides: it creates the net outflow of foreign exchange, raises the vulnerability to supply disruptions and increases price volatility. Despite the high electricity tariffs in Sub-Saharan Africa, pricing frequently fails to reflect supply costs. This price gap creates a major obstacle to the financial sustainability for many of the Sub-Saharan power utilities - that is in addition to the negative impact on the much-needed foreign direct investment in the sector (IEA 2014). All these challenges may be attributable to corruption, weak institutions and poor transparency in the public domain

Scenarios for African Energy Infrastructure and Their Potential Quality of Life Impacts

Many African and global institutions are alarmed by the current low-level of access to energy by most Africa publics and the prospects of its continuation into the future in the face of the high population growth and the rapid urbanization. Thus, there have been many initiatives to plan for a more effective energy delivery system and three of them are briefly presented.

First, in 2014 Africa-EU Energy Partnership (AEEP) produced a report in which it evaluates the likelihood of the Partnership reaching its target of 18 GW based on the existing project pipeline (AEEP 2014). The report concludes that if 50 per cent of the project pipeline is implemented, then the AEEP target is achievable and can help lift the quality of life considerably. However, if only 25 percent of the project pipeline is implemented, Africa will fall short of meeting the AEEP target without making any significant impact on the quality of life for the African majority.

The second effort is the International Energy Agency (IEA) plan that describes a probable pathway for the African electricity sector in its "New Policies Scenario" which assumes the extension of policies currently in play and the implementation of political commitments announced by mid-2014 (IEA 2014: 70). The IEA adopts that the total installed capacity of renewable energy will amount to 50 GW by the end of 2020. In the more ambitious "African Century Case" scenario, the installed capacity will reach 52 GW. An additional capacity of 25 GW and 27 GW was built into the scenarios. Though the sizes of conventional power plants are also likely to increase strongly till 2020, electricity production by using renewable energy is expected to reach 23 per cent by then. Table 4 provides an overview of the scenarios discussed above.

The third study was the combined efforts of McKinsey, the World Energy Council and industry associations like the Global Wind Energy Council (GWEC) that produced scenarios for Africa energy development (McKinsey 2015, WEC 2013, GWEC 2014). The scenarios initiated by McKinsey and the World Energy Council project a modest increase of the installed renewable energy capacity in the years ahead. However, the "medium scenario" developed by the GWEC, that uses the current project pipeline and national targets, significantly exceeds the AEEP and IEA scenarios. It projects a total capacity of 19 GW by the year 2020 – a rise of 17 GW above the 2014 figure. (GWEC 2014).

Table 5 shows the cumulative capacity target of the selected countries and is quite close to the expected capacity additions by the IEA (12-14 GW). Algeria's program in bioenergy tops all other African countries and has strong plans in the development of hydro, wind and solar. Egypt has the most ambitious target in wind power and second in hydropower. Ethiopia has the strongest program in hydropower target (22 GW by 2030), although environmental considerations and cross-border issues with Kenya

Table 4. Scenarios for renewable energy in Africa by 2020 (in Gw)

	IRENA	AEEP	AEEP	IEA	IEA
	Current	25% Scenario	50% Scenario	New Policies	Century Case
Year	2014	2020	2020	2020	
Hydro	29	34	40	41	43
Biomass	1	-	-	2	2
PV	1	1*	2*	7	7
GSP	0	-	-	-	-
Ocean	0	-	-	-	-
Wind Geothermal	2	2	3	-	-
Not Specified	-	2	3	9	0
Total renewable energy capacity	34	39	48	59	61
Additional renewable energy capacity		5	14	25	27

Source: Author's own graph based IRENA (2015b), AEEP (2014), IEA (2014), GWEC et al. (2014).
* The AEEP report provides an aggregate value for PV and CSP capacity

Table 5. Technology specific targets for additional renewable energy capacity of selected African countries for the year 2020

	Wind Power	Hydropower	PV	CSP	Geothermal	Bioenergy
Algeria	1,881**	5,064**	766**		6**	375**
Egypt	7,200		220	,100		
Ethiopian	770	9,481**			379**	
Kenya	635*		423*		2,250**	
Morocco	2,000	2,000	2,000			
Rwanda		382*			310*	300*
South Africa	2,700		2,700			
Tunisia	797**		566**	188**		113**
Uganda		1,285*			45*	
Libya	600		344**			
Nigeria	23**	1,114**	273**			
Sudan	240**		235**	18**		
Total	16,846	14,262	11,825	2,071	2,990	788

Source: IASS-Potsdam (2016).
* The target must be fulfilled before the year 2020. There is no specific target for the year 2020 or beyond.
** The target refers to a year after 2020 (e.g. 2030). We assume a constant increase in renewable capacity till 2020

create challenges (Vidal 2015). Kenya dominates in the geothermal development and Morocco plans a balanced investment in the development of wind, hydro and solar power resources. South Africa leads in solar and has a strong wind power program. According to the national targets, the largest capacity additions until 2020 may come from wind power.

According to IASS (2016), it is estimated that the total final energy used in sub-Saharan Africa will increase by 70% to reach 722Mtoe in 2040 - that is equal to half the level used by the United States in 2016. Bioenergy remains to be the largest fuel source in the projected target requirement, which is about 380Mtoe by the year 2040 (IASS 2016) - but its portion of the total drops from around 70% to just over half.

Renewable Energy Technologies and Quality of Life

- **Renewable Energy Technologies:** like hydropower make up a large portion of the total power supply in Africa, with potentials to expand and grow with the deployment of a wider range of technologies. Many countries are actively developing or considering the development of their renewable energy resource potential. Using Renewables can improve energy security by reducing the dependence on imported fuels and help branch out the power mix. Deployment can be in a decentralized manner, enabling them to be deployed faster than centralized power plants (however small-scale projects can prove to be costly in terms of the lack administrative skills) and can provide local employment for deployment and maintenance. Development of renewable technologies can also help provide remote communities enhanced the quality of living through availability of more and better-paying jobs, increased access to good education, health and better mobility.
    - **Bioenergy:** In sub-Saharan Africa, this is the main energy source – with solid biomass traditionally in the residential sector and its modern use in the form of solid biomass and biogas for power generation and heat contribute to only as a small portion. Given that nearly one-third of sub-Saharan Africa is covered by forest and thus residues from the forest and agricultural constitute a significant percentage of the available biomass resources to improve quality of life. The plan targets with generate more job opportunities and better access to services
    - **Hydro-Technologies:** This is not only the most important but also the most used of African energy systems. Its attractiveness stems from large-scale development potential and cost-effectiveness lower technology requirement. Technically, the hydropower potential in Africa is estimated to be 283 GW and can generate at least 1,200TWh per year – contributing as 8% of the global technical potential, according to IASS (2016), which suggests that this amount of electricity exceeds triple the current electricity consumed within sub-Saharan Africa. With these developments will come greater opportunities to move up the socio-economic ladder.
- **Solar Technologies:** Have had little to no impact on the power sector in Africa in the past but have recently started to gain potential in many countries. The potential for solar energy in the continent is enormous especially since most of the continent enjoys bright sunlight 320 days of the year on average, providing irradiance levels of almost 2 000kWh per square metre (kWh/m2) annually (European Commission JRC, 2011). This will enlarge the range of opportunities for individuals, start-ups, the SME and even larger firms, resulting in reduced poverty, reduce crime and eliminate slums
- **Wind Power Technology:** Generates only 190 MW in all sub-Saharan Africa due to its limited application compared to other methods like hydropower. With increased technology innovation, Sub-Saharan Africa's wind energy generation is set to rise and is projected at around 1 300GW (Mandelli, et al, 2014), making a significant contribution to enhance the quality of life of many off-grid communities, thereby creating new jobs and better quality of life.

- **Geothermal Technologies:** Contribute only a small fraction of Africa's power supply but provide an appealing alternative where there are resources. East African Rift Valley has a large deposit of this resource and is considered one of the most exciting potentials in the world for geothermal development. It is estimated to provide energy generation between 10GW and 15GW (IASS 2016) – that is more than the current East Africa's total power generation capacity. This technology seems to be concentrated in specific regions in Africa and so will positive and negative effects be concentrated,
    - **Coal:** An estimate of 120 billion tonnes of coal deposits are spread throughout southern parts of the Africa. This amounts to less than 1% of the global coal resources – a small number reflecting lack of serious exploration efforts. South Africa has 90% of the Africa's coal industry amounting to 36billion tonnes of proven reserves (IASS 2016). Other countries will join South Africa with improved technologies for exploration, mining and use of this resource. While this technology can lift a large portion of communities out of poverty, great care is needed in dealing with the unintended consequences – such environmental pollution and global warming-- arising from its application.

Renewable Energy Policy for Africa and It Management

- **Strategies and Policies for Renewable Energy Deployment in Africa:** Many African countries already support grid-connected renewables via feed-in tariffs, auctions, net metering and investment incentives. The South African auction program has been especially successful in deploying renewables. While most renewable energy deployments was grid-connected in the past two decades, several countries have adopted policies for decentralized approaches for rural electrification based on renewable energy. Finally, the establishment of regional power pools and renewable energy transmission corridors is an important building block for the future expansion of renewable energy.

The long-term development aspirations of Africa, as well as the economic growth achieved to date, are expected to create lifestyle changes and consumer shopping habit that result in more demand for energy. In this respect, increased growth from household demand will be triggered using electricity to power household appliances like lights, refrigerators, stoves, washing machines, and air conditioners. Outside the home, increased demand will come from the transport sector, both the public and the private mode of transport. Changes in lifestyle will not only increase citizen's demand for fuel but also affect choices of its type and quality. Modern renewable energy will provide an important alternative to support the growing African population as it strives for improved living standards, more comfort, and quality health services and better inconveniences. The demand for these services by the rapidly growing youthful urban population could easily triple the renewable energy demand in Africa (IRENA 2015)

Studies have shown that along with economic gains, many benefits arise from innovations and local value creation use of renewable energy in various global regions (IRENA 2015c). For example, due to their higher labor intensity, most renewable energy technologies create more jobs opportunities than fossil-based energy. (Jacob et al. 2015). With the declining technology costs and the growth in local innovations, there will be a rise in the share of local value creation in proportion to the total project cost. To take advantage of this growth potential, many African countries including Rwanda and South Africa have introduced policies that encourage the manufacturing of components locally. Countries also seek to attract investment in the manufacturing of components.

- **Regional Power System Integration and Planning:** Africa is a vast and complex continent that consists of 54 states. The planning and development of its energy infrastructure to lift the quality of life of its people is a complex undertaking. However, technological innovations have enabled the achievement of regional power system integration, which allows the enhanced integration of large shares of renewable energy sources. The regional integration system consists of regional energy pools and their connecting corridors. This regional integration approach could save more than US$40 billion in capital spending (McKinsey 2015) but has allowed for the establishment of a few regional power pools in many regions of Africa. Among these regional pools are the Maghreb Electricity Committee (Comelec), the West African Power Pool (WAPP), the Central African Power Pool (CAPP), the Eastern African Power Pool (EAPP) and the Southern African Power Pool (SAPP) (AEEP 2014, IRENA 2014a). Several corridors are planned to connect these regional pools and are the responsibility a continental agency called Programme for Infrastructure Development in Africa (PIDA), whose Priority Action Plan is planned for completion by 2020. Like the legendary Cape to Cairo railway, PIDA's strategic goal is to establish an Africa Clean Energy Corridor reaching from South Africa (Cape Town) to Egypt (Cairo).

MIXED FUNDING STRATEGY WITH FOCUS ON CROWDFUNDING

Funding sources for African energy infrastructure (AEI) consist of domestic African governments' investments and external funding from multilateral institutions (such as the African Development Bank, the World Bank, and other traditional donors), including private participation in infrastructure (PPI), and Chinese investments. According to the Amadou Sy & Copley (2017), the estimated amount required to meet AEI needs in 2013 was about US$63billion, but only $8 billion was mobilized from the domestic and external sources. Thus in 2013 the AEI bill had a gap of $55Billion and probably the gap has since widened.

Using Domestic and International Funding Sources

- **Domestic Finance:** This is mostly through public budget allocation and forms the largest source of AEI funding (IMF 2014). The funding trend has shown that African governments see the value and thus have increased investments in AEI within the last few years (Amadou Sy & Copley (2017). The enthusiasm of investing in general energy infrastructure seems to match the rising interest in expanding the scale and scope of renewable energy component. A survey of policy tools to promote renewable energy growth in Africa shows the use of a wide variety of mechanisms.

The current policies, as shown in Table 7, include fiscal incentives such as capital subsidy, grant or rebate; The second type is investment or production tax credits; and the third type are reductions in sales, energy, CO2, VAT or other taxes. Production payment is also common and lastly the tools of investment, loans, or grants are often used. However, the survey shows that tool applied by most African governments is the one focusing on reductions in sales, energy, CO2, VAT or other taxes.

Access to affordable funds at various stages of development is vital to the sustainability of any off-grid project. Because energy projects are different in their scale and risk-return profile, it is logical that conventional approaches to funding them need careful considerations. Drawing from the long experiences with off-grid renewable energy schemes has led to the creation of workable business models and funding resolutions that eliminate many of the current challenges. The key to promoting the AEI sector is tackling associated risks and to capitalize on growing financing commitments to the sector in Africa. In this regard, IRENA (2015) draws to attention how the Tanzania Energy Development and Access Project direct funds into subsidies, special collateral funding, preferential interest rates and technical assistance for off-grid projects.

- **External Finance:** The private participation in infrastructure (PPI), the official development finance (ODF), and Chinese investment are the three main sources of external financing for AEI. These sources account for 97 percent of all such external investments Amadou Sy & Copley (2017). Generally, the external funding for AEI across the three major external sources has tripled between 2004 and 2012. During this period, the levels of ODF investment increased but its dominance of infrastructure funding declined due to an up surge in private investment to over 50 percent of external financing and, as a result, China became a major bilateral source.

A study by IEA (2016) reveals the level of Chinese commitments as it shows that Chinese companies acting as the main contractors during the period between 2010 and 2015 were responsible for about 30 percent of new capacity additions in sub-Saharan Africa. The study further demonstrates that during the same period, the Chinese funding amounted to about $13 billion that is about one-fifth of all investments in the region's power sector (IEA, 2016). With respect to Chinese contribution to output in the renewable energy growth, it accounted for 56 percent of the total 17 gigawatts of generation capacity. This is corresponding to 10 percent of prevailing installed capacity in the region planned for in 2010-2020 and its contribution in the hydropower amounted to 49 percent of the total (IEA, 2016).

Shift in Funding Actors and Their Behavior

The above discussion has shown a few emerging trends. The first trend is the emergence of renewable energy type and its increasing importance relative to other energy sources. The second trend is the relative rise of China and the relative decline of the traditional Western actors in this development field, both in terms of their traditional developers and external sources. The instability of these sources, suggest that future efforts should be exerted to develop local energy private sector funding which has so far played an insignificant role in the development of energy either off- or on-grid.

It is clear that more countries in Africa need to invest more of their rich renewable energy asset base, especially in solar and wind power, and especially at the time of rapidly falling prices of low-carbon technologies. Countries need to do more to generate more resources by expanding their tax-base to allocate toward energy infrastructure. The ratio of tax revenues to GDP in 2013 ranged from 25 percent in South Africa to 2.8 percent in the Democratic Republic of the Congo (Amadou Sy & Copley (2017). Clearly, countries with smaller tax-to-GDP ratios need to scale-up their revenue sources to fund their energy infrastructure investment gaps. Given the rate of rapid urbanization and the number of competing demands, suggest that while this strategy would help, it will not solve the huge funding challenge. Additional new innovative sources must be identified and exploited.

Table 7. Fiscal incentives and public financing policies used in Africa

	Capital Subsidy, Grant, or Rebate	Investment or Production Tax Credits	Reductions in Sales, Energy, CO2, VAT, or Other Taxes	Production Payment	Investment, Loans, or Grants
Algeria		•			
Angola					•
Benin			•		
Botswana	•		•		
Burkina Faso		•	•	•	
Cape Verde			•	•	
Cameroon			•		
Côte d'Ivoire			•		
Egypt	•		•		
Ethiopia			•		•
Gambia			•		
Ghana	•		•		•
Guinea			•		
Kenya			•	•	•
Lesotho					•
Libya			•		
Madagascar			•		
Malawi			•		
Mali			•		•
Mauritius	•				
Morocco					•
Mozambique					•
Niger			•		
Rwanda			•		•
Senegal			•		
South Africa	•		•		•
Sudan					
Tanzania			•		
Togo			•		
Tunisia	•		•		•
Uganda	•		•		•
Zambia	•		•		
Zimbabwe					

Source: Adapted from REN21 (2015).

The recent emergence of alternative finance mechanism that offers significant opportunity to develop and harness renewable energy infrastructure by the "African crowd" should be given adequate attention. Many of the renewable energy projects are in a connected-decentralized form to enable business and community investors to make significant contribution to fill the AEI investment gap. Renewable, low-carbon technologies have the potential to rapidly expand energy access throughout the continent. As Amadou Sy & Copley (2017) noted, Africa has a vast renewable energy asset base, particularly in solar and wind power, and its added advantage is that the prices of low-carbon technologies are increasingly falling rapidly. Several challenges within the sector and along the need for entire power value chain need to be addressed for a renewable revolution to occur.

Crowdfunding Market as a Tool for Energy Infrastructure Funding in Africa

Crowdfunding is increasingly gaining acceptance in Africa in recent years. It uses online platforms as a base to raise funds for business ventures by collecting small sums of money from a large pool of investors (or the crowd). The size of African crowdfunding market in 2015 was estimated at about $70 million, which amounted to less than one percent of the global total. However, the potential for growth of this investment tool was projected to rise to $96 billion by 2025 based on a growth rate of 300% per year (World Bank 2013). The number of crowdfunding platforms has also been growing at a rapid pace and five models have emerged: Donations, Peer-to-Peer Lending, Hybrid, Equity-Based, and the Rewards-Based. As shown in Figure 1, the early growth of the models shows that the Donations and Equity-Based Models are the fasted growing (Afrikstart, 2015).

Opportunities created by crowdfunding to African entrepreneurs are three. The first is that crowdfunding creates more channels for businesses to access much-needed capital. Instead of the challenges faced when borrowing from the banks, this mechanism appeals directly to idea supporters or potential customers without tedious inquiries into business histories or financial standings. The second is leveraging the increased use of mobile networks in which Africa is rising to become a global leader. The third allows entrepreneurs to use crowdfunding platforms by subsidizing the costs of marketing and promotion for free.

Against these wonderful opportunities, Aidid (2017) draws our attention to the challenges facing the crowdfunding market in Africa. The absence of regulation means an absence of proper investor protections, ensuring legal protection and enhanced business trust is the first. Also, lack of transparency about the legal status of these crowdfunding organizations creates a risk to foreign investors. These two challenges will be solved as the market drive towards maturity to include all urban development actors as its participants, investing in the grid and off-grid renewable energy networks within African countries and across the continent.

Crowdfunding Market Actors and Space of Activities

Two broad categories of crowdfunding operators have emerged and both focusing their activities in the African market. The first is the Africa-based crowdfunding platform that is managed from and services African market and the second is the foreign-based platform operated from abroad but services Africa, in some cases other global markets as well.

- **The Africa-Based Crowdfunding Platforms:** A recent study has shown 57 active crowdfunding platforms based and operating in Africa in 2015 (Afrikstart, 2015). Out of these 21 were South Africa-based, and 9 based in Nigeria. In terms of their operating models, 21 Donations, 19 Equity, 13 rewards-based portals, 2 peer-to-peer lending platforms, and 2 hybrid platforms. In terms of their projects specialization, the study shows the dominance of social causes (31.5% of the total platforms), business and entrepreneurship projects (21%), and then creative and innovative projects (17.5%). Most African countries are yet to give legal backing for Crowdfunding activities, despite this, the platforms in South Africa raised some $30.8 million, in Egypt $842,000, and in Nigeria $314,445 in 2015. Regarding how the funds raised by Africa-based crowdfunding portals were used, substantial part was directed to fund startups and SMEs ($17.7 million), real estate crowd funded projects ($13.6 million), followed by travel crowdfunded trips ($319,434), and $307,860 was donated to social causes and charity projects.
- **Foreign-Based Crowdfunding in Africa:** Foreign-based Crowdfunding portals raised $94.6 million in 2015 to fund various projects in Africa, mostly donations ($48 million) and loans ($42.2 million) according to Afrikstart (2015). These development actors seemed keener to fund social-impact projects, which aimed to help children ($14 million), to promote education ($13.5 million), and to uplift women and girls ($10.8 million). According to Afrikstart (2015) at least 14 platforms operating from Europe are serving Africa only to the exclusion of other global Crowdfunding markets. Although there may be few Africa-based Crowdfunding platforms serving global crowdfunding space, there seems to be none that target the many and sizeable Africa Diaspora communities around the world, especially in Europe, North America and the Caribbean. This is a potentially huge source of projects funding source.
- **The Contributions of Islamic Finance to African Development:** Although the potential has long been recognized, only recently has activities of the African Islamic finance industry started in full swing after overcoming the geopolitical barriers, civil unrest and regulatory hurdles. According to Hussain & Lawrence (2013) in 2015, for example, the Africa Finance Corporation accepted a US$50 million from the Islamic Development Bank (IDB) for investments in projects across many African countries. The projects will focus on infrastructure and agriculture in ways to promote the economic and social development of the communities concerned. To date the ICD has granted US$2.2 billion of approvals, including 18 new projects and eight capital raises in 2012 alone, of which six were in Africa (Hussain & Lawrence, 2013). In about half of the African countries, the IDB is becoming a regular participant in a few PPP projects designed to reduce poverty, promote the growth of jobs and socio-economic development of the continent. Thus, it can be an important partner in the innovative energy development projects promoted by the public, private and the community sectors.

FUTURE RESEARCH DIRECTION AND CONCLUSION

Future Research Directions

Future research should continue to investigate ways of improving quality of urban life in Africa, enhancing energy policy, and of developing a funding strategy centered on crowdfunding

- **Improving Quality of Urban Life in Africa:** It seems bridging the demand-supply gap to improve the quality of urban life in Africa would need the support digital transformation on a large scale. This would require innovative ways of working, not just latest technologies, which include the Internet of things, Sensors, and 3D printing. Urban centers must be organized so that they are capable of crafting policies and programs that can make efficient use of the emerging technologies so as seize new opportunities and overcome challenges at least costs. There is need to encourage innovative enterprises that create many taxable jobs and develop the needed hard and soft infrastructure.

Accelerating digital transformation must be a key priority for all African governments at the urban, national and regional levels. They all have important roles in improving quality of life through urban design and development, e-Learning, e-health, e-commerce and through contributions to effective energy policy. Thus, the focus of future research in these areas need not be on tools or structures even though important, but more process: plans, leadership and new strategies of efficiently managing cities into qualitative, safe, productive environment that is efficient and socially inclusive

- **Enhancing Energy Policy in Africa:** Africans are energy poor but living in an energy-rich continent, with grave impact on quality of life. To improve the quality of urban life and efficiency of the urban economy, a number of scenarios for African energy infrastructure and their potential impact on the Quality of life are explored. Renewable energy technologies are showing encouraging results around the continent and many of them are cost-effective with decentralizing tendencies, which makes widespread power generation and distribution efficiently managed. Given that urban areas produce a high percentage of global energy-related CO2 emissions, it is crucial to understand the relationship between urban activities and the resulting carbon emissions. Therefore, future research should investigate ways to minimize the environmental impacts of power generation and distribution in urban residents.
- **Mixed Funding Strategy With Focus on Crowdfunding:** The funding of large-scale urban development projects has depended on domestic and international banking systems. However, both systems have depended on public bailed-out, suffering from past bad lending policies and practices. Hence, alternative development financial sources should be explored and utilized by all African governments. Future research should, therefore, explore alternative urban development financing sources, especially the promising crowdfunding market. Among the areas for investigations are how to put the system on a sound legal footing, strengthening its operations and reliability and explore ways and means of its expansion and acceptability by potential funders in both Africa and Africans in Diaspora.

CONCLUSION

Cities have proved to the engines of economic growth around the world, however for Africa, achieving a high quality of urban life is an insurance for sustained growth needed by its growing youthful urban population. The gains of the superior quality of urban life encourage higher densities, more knowledge and greater economies of scale, the combination of which could trigger rising investment, more creativity, skilled labor, and better earnings. Failure is bound to recall the images of the growth of slums in Asia and Latin America and their consequences to the political stability of those regions and to their socio-economic order over almost half a century. More recently, the evidence of Arab spring is clear and its impact is fresh and is still being felt in the Middle East

As suggested in the chapter, the overarching issues in transforming African cities and hence their quality of life, including ways to put urban development issues on a sharp focus, ways to sustain development financing, ways to manage the giant economic transformation, and ways to create an effective urban agenda. These issues pose a gradual roadblock that most African policymakers tent to ignore as it requires long-term planning and multi-year expenditures, coordination among the different levels of government, engagement with the private sector, and major improvements in governance. Not all these seem to be part of the characteristics of African politicians, but which they have to acquire lest the bomb drop on their laps!

REFERENCES

AfDB. (2009). *Oil and Gas in Africa*. New York: Oxford University Press Inc.

Africa 4Tech org. (2016). *eHealth in Africa*. Retrieved from http://africa4tech.org/wp- content/themes/afourtech/papers/A4T%20-%20EHEALTH%20-%20Single.pdf

Afrikstart. (2015). *Crowdfunding in Africa*. Retrieved from http://afrikstart.com/report/wp-content/.../Afrikstart-Crowdfunding-In-Africa-Report.pdf

Aidid, A. (2017). *Crowdfunding in Africa: Opportunities and Challenges*. Retrieved from https://www.covafrica.com/2017/02/crowdfunding-in-africa-opportunities-and-challenges/

Arinola, O., & Obiako, N. (2017). *eHealth Africa (eHA) is collaborating with the World Health Organization (WHO), Bill and Melinda Gates Foundation (BMGF), AEEP (2014): Status Report Africa-EU Energy Partnership. Progress, achievements and future perspectives*. Retrieved from http://www.iass-potsdam.de/sites/default/files/files/study_march_2016 _the_future_of_africas_energy_supply.pdf

Benevolo, L. (1967). *Origins of Modern Town Planning*. Cambridge, MA: MIT Press.

Bright, J. (2015). *Why Africa may be on the verge of an Internet boom*. Retrieved from http://fortune.com/2015/02/16/nigeria- internet-startups/

GWEC. (2014). *Global Wind Energy Outlook 2014*. Greenpeace.

Hussain, A., & Lawrence, J. (2013). *The Islamic Development Bank Assisting Private Sector Growth in Africa*. Retrieved from http://www.klgates.com/the-islamic-development-bank-assisting-private-sector-growth-in-africa-11-05-2013/

IEA. (2014). *Africa Energy Outlook. A Focus on Energy Prospects in Sub-Saharan Africa*. IEA.

Institute for Advanced Sustainability Studies (IASS). (2016). *The Future of Africa's Energy Supply*. Retrieved from http://www.iass- potsdam.de/sites/default/files/files/study_march_2016_the_future_of_africas_energy_supply.pdf

IRENA. (2014). *RE-thinking Energy: Towards a new power system*. IRENA.

IRENA. (2015). *Renewable Energy Capacity Statistics 2015.* IRENA.

Jacob, K., Quitzow, R., & Bär, H. (2015). *Green Jobs: Impacts of a Green Economy on Employment. BMZ/GIZ.* Bonn: Eschborn.

Krogman, H., & Khumalo, N. (2016). *Plugging Africa into e-commerce.* Retrieved from https://www.afdb.org/en/blogs/industrialisation-and-trade-corner/post/plugging-africa-into-e- commerce-16592/

Mandelli, S., Barbieri, J., Mattarolo, L., & Colombo, E. (2014). Sustainable Energy in Africa: A Comprehensive Data and Policy Review. *Renewable & Sustainable Energy Reviews, 37*, 656–686. doi:10.1016/j.rser.2014.05.069

McKinsey. (2015). Brighter Africa — The Growth Potential of the Sub-Saharan Electricity Sector. McKinsey & Company.

MohammedO. (2016). *The New Online Shoppers.* Retrieved from https://qz.com/478714/africas-emerging-consumer-class-is-a-boon-for-the-continents-online-retailers/

Njoh, A. J. (1999). *Urban Planning, Housing, and Spatial Structures in Sub-Saharan Africa.* Ashgate.

Ojabo, D. (2016). *eHealth Africa Providing Technical Support to Help Curb Nigeria's Meningitis Outbreak.* Retrieved from https://www.ehealthafrica.org/latest/2017/5/8/ehealth-africa-providing-technical-support-to-help-curb-nigerias-meningitis-outbreak

Okpala, R. (2009). Regional Overview of the Status of Urban Planning and Planning Practice in Anglophone (Sub-Saharan) African Countries. In *UN Habitats* (p. 10). United Nations.

REN21. (2015). *Renewables 2015. Global Status Report.* Paris: Renewable Energy Network for the 21st Century.

Salat, S., & Bourdic, L. (2011). Factor 10: Multiplying by 10 Resource Productivity in the Urban World. *Proceedings of the World Sustainable Conference.*

Salat, S., & Bourdic, L. (2013). Urban Complexity, Efficiency and Resilience. In Z. Morvaj (Ed.), Energy Efficiency— A Bridge to Low Carbon Economy. Academic Press.

Surowiecki, J. (2005). *The Wisdom of Crowds.* Anchor Books. Retrieved from https://www.ehealthafrica.org/latest/2017/3/30/ehealth-africa-transforms-disease-surveillance-and-response-in-sierra-leone

Sy & Copley. (2017). *Closing The Financing Gap For African Energy Infrastructure: Trends, Challenges, And Opportunities.* Brookings Institute Report.

UNCTAD. (2015). *The Information Economy Report 2015: Unlocking the Potential of E-Commerce for Developing Countries.* Retrieved from http://unctad.org/en/PublicationsLibrary/ier2015_en.pdf

UNDESA. Population Division. (2014). World Urbanization Prospects. New York: United Nations Department of Economic and Social Affairs, Population Division.

Vidal, J. (2015). *Ethiopia dam will turn Lake Turkana into 'endless battlefield', locals warn.* Available at: http://www.theguardian.com/ global-development/2015/jan/13/ethiopiagibe-iii-dam-kenya

WEC. (2013). World Energy Scenarios — Composing Energy. World Energy Council.

WEF. (2016). *Africa's energy poverty is keeping its people poor*. Retrieved from https://www.weforum.org/agenda/2016/09/africa-s-energy-poverty-is-keeping-its-people-poor

World Bank. (2011). *World Bank and Energy in Africa. The World Bank, 2011. Web. 20 Sept. 2012 2012*. World Bank Fact Sheet.

World Bank. (2013). *Crowdfunding's Potential for the Developing World*. Retrieved from http://documents.worldbank.org/curated/en/409841468327411701/pdf/840000WP0Box380cr owdfunding0study00.pdf

KEY TERMS AND DEFINITIONS

Africa: Geopolitical continent of 54 nations.
Alternative Finance: Digitally delivered funds through internet and mobile phones.
Crowdfunding: Raising funds from a large number of people using digital technology.
Energy Policy: Choices in energy type generation, distribution, and pricing.
Quality of Life: Quality of socio-economic relations.
Renewable Energy: Energy from sunlight, wind, rain, tides, waves, and geothermal heat.
Urban Design: Shaping the socio-physical setting for urban life.

Chapter 14
Exploring the Crowdfunding of Nigerian Volunteer Corps' Efforts in Urban Development

Rabiu Bena Abdullahi
Waziri Umaru Federal Polytechnic, Nigeria

ABSTRACT

In another chapter in this volume the author highlighted the potential role the various volunteer programs are expected to play in promoting urban development in Nigeria. This chapter, advocating urban development alternative to oil as driver of growth, carries the analysis further in three important ways: Firstly, by sharpening the ideas on the ways in which volunteerism enhance governance as the leading component of urban development, the poor state of which intensifies the many challenges. Secondly, the potential impacts of volunteer corps in social, economic, and knowledge development in selected key sub-national and national development problem areas. Thirdly, funding the huge volunteer programs that meets the speed and scale of expected urban development is considered to be beyond the traditional public finance mechanism and need the support of the emerging "alternative finance," which include but are not limited to crowdfunding to deal with the emerging and persistent development challenges.

INTRODUCTION

Since the oil boom of 1970s most Nigerian cities have experienced quantitative onward and upward growth in terms of spatial expansion but without real qualitative development of new technology, new ideas and new ways of doing things. The very few places, like Lagos, that introduced qualitative development- in terms of industrial parks, active innovative startup ecosystem, and high quality real estate project- are clearly reaping the benefits, as their internally generated revenues are the envy of other cities. While Lagos is attracting large numbers of people daily, there are the resources, the job opportunities and expanding utilities to come with the inflow. On the other hand, most other cities have not only large population growth, subserviced significant urban expansion, and lack resources to deal with the persistent high urban poverty, inequality, and rising crime. Thus while these cities' growth was heavily based on the consumption of oil revenues, Lagos ensured local production for internal development.

DOI: 10.4018/978-1-5225-3952-0.ch014

The Nigerian Volunteer Scheme, if well managed, can help use the Lagos type solution to urban development to uplift the country's urban system in stages. First, changing perception in consumption-based cities have arisen because of oil wealth, but unlike cities around the world have been the engine of development, these cities have been incapable of improved economic productivity, provide well-paying jobs, lift their citizens out of poverty or ensure a constant supply of essential services. Second, it is hoped that they will help propagate the Lagos type of urbanization model that with well-designed reform, urbanization can be transformative force leading to sustainable economic growth, inclusive social progress, poverty reduction in high environment quality. These can be achieved by, first, by tackling areas of urgent national development needs that are remedial in nature, and, second, by focusing on issues of longer-term development requirement of the nation. Using these measures and with the contributions of the volunteer corps, Nigeria will be able to achieve the type of transformation suggested by the World Bank (2016) in its report: *From oil to cities: Nigeria's next transformation.*

This chapter seeks to carry out deeper analysis on the potential role of the various volunteer programs are expected to play in promoting urban development in Nigeria. First, it aims to sharpen the ideas on the ways in which volunteerism enhance governance as the leading component of urban development, the poor state of which intensifies the many challenges. Second, it analyzes the potential impacts of volunteer corps in social, economic, and knowledge development in selected key sub-national and national development problem areas. Third, it advocates that funding the huge volunteer programs that meets the speed and scale of expected urban development is considered to be beyond the traditional public finance mechanism and need the support of the emerging "alternative finance", which include but not limited to crowdfunding to deal with the emerging and persistent development challenges.

The chapter is structured such that Section 2 discusses volunteerism and national development considering its broad range of components. Section 3 explores the potential impacts of volunteerism at the different levels of Nigerian administrative system. The funding issues are explored in Section 4. Section 5 discusses future research directions, while Section 6 provides some concluding remarks.

VOLUNTEERISM AND NATIONAL DEVELOPMENT

Role of Volunteers in the Areas of National Urban Development Needs

According to UNDESA (2014) world's urban population is projected to receive additional 2.5 billion people by 2050 and nearly 90 per cent of the increase will be in Asia and Africa. The UNDESA projection shows that India, China and Nigeria combined are expected to account for 37 per cent of this global increase by 2050. Further breakdown shows that India will add 404 million urban citizens, China 292 million and, Nigeria, which seems insufficiently prepared for this urban transformation will add 212 million urban residents (World Bank 2016).

To meet the emerging urban development challenges, especially the physical and social infrastructure needs new urban households, as well as the cumulative backlog of the present urban population living in slums, inadequate housing the role of volunteers need to be broadly defined. The lack of effective and accountable governance, for example, can be a barrier to progress, undermining national and local efforts to improve lives and the prospects of communities. For the sustainable development agenda to succeed, improving governance, tackling inequalities, and expanding voice and participation need to be addressed simultaneously. Volunteerism can help by giving voice to the diverse types of stakeholders and by mobilizing people and civil society organizations to contribute to solutions. In order to realize the full potential of volunteerism at the national and local levels, the volunteer corps can help mobilize all major urban development actors. These actors should include the local, state and federal public sector agencies; the private sector –local and foreign firms; as well as the social sector comprising of civil society organizations, bilateral and multilateral development organizations, and other stakeholders.

Within the framework of the following selected areas of National Urban Development Needs, as discussed by the author in another chapter of this volume, we would like to elaborate in details the possible roles of volunteer corps with respect to the following:

- Reconstruction of urban centers in Boko-Haram affected areas,
- Upgrading City Centers at least one in each state,
- Major Development Corridors.

Volunteer Corps in the Reconstruction of Urban Centers in Boko-Haram Affected Region

It seems clear that the ability of volunteers to support development progress depends on the willingness of national governments to ensure that the space and supportive environments, which encourage their participation and initiatives, are available. The lessons from worldwide experiences suggest that volunteerism can help to produce social trust, promote social inclusion, advance basic services, and increase human development. Furthermore, research by UNV (2015) also shows that volunteers and volunteerism carry the greatest benefits where empowering circumstances like freedom of speech and association and an atmosphere of active political participation are commonly available. Table 1 shows the potential contributions of the Nigerian Volunteer Corp to governance with respect to the elements of participation, accountability and responsiveness.

The contributions made by N-power supersede that of other volunteer corps as indicated in Table 1. The N-power has the most significant contributions to governance by providing employment to over 1.7 million people over the years and contributed more than a million community projects ranging from

Table 1. Contribution of volunteers to reconstruction of Boko-Haram affected region

Projects Targeting National Problem Areas	Potential Contributions of Volunteer Corps to Governance With Respect to: Participation, Accountability, Responsiveness (H M L))				
	N-Power	NYSC	NPC	TAC	Others
1. Comprehensive Area Upgrading with Digital Networks	H	M	H	L	M
2. Redevelopment Areas of Decaying Zones into "Smart" Communities	H	M	H	L	M
3. Creation of Industrial Park(s) in every Local Government	H	L	H	H	L
4. At least Science and Technology Parks built by every University	H	L	H	H	M
5. Proto-type Innovation Districts in all state capitals and Abuja	H	L	H	H	H

1. N-Power Scheme, 2.National Youth Service, 3.National Peace Corps, 4.Technical Aid Corps, 5. Others
Rating of Volunteer Corps contribution to governances H = High, M = Medium, L = Low

roads, culverts, water supply, health, electricity distribution, agriculture and sanitation to other vital services (*Daily Trust* 2017).

Similarly, to encourage investment in the region, the USAID provides $2 million to new and existing Nigerian businesses up to $125,000 to catalyze private investment in agribusiness and transport of a minimum value of $300,000. Furthermore, following the resuscitation of five uniformed voluntary organisations 200,000 graduates were hired for volunteering services (Vanguard 2017). This is likely to go a long way to reduce the communication gap between the government and the communities across the length and breadth of the country.

Next to NPC in the size of contribution is TAC whose impacts is coming from outside the region, the growing need to extend skilled manpower services to needy communities become imperative this tends to trigger start-up businesses in the various communities, thereby providing white collar jobs, thus helping to create future middle class consumers in the region. The Information Technology in particular has brought about new job opportunities, and hence not only is this helping to build economic turn-around in the area but also sowing the seeds of new information driven economy.

The NYSC ranked next by virtue of its youthful engagement and enthusiasm expressed by the participants. The National Information Technology Development Agency (NITDA) provided an ICT center at the orientation camps for training of corps members (Naija247News 2017). In appreciation of the impact IT as mentioned above, the National Youth Service Corps (NYSC) has urged the Federal Government to make its Skills Acquisition and Entrepreneurship Development (SAED) compulsory for all corps members in the country (*Thisdayonline* 2017). This effort would not bridge the knowledge gap of the IDP; it would also help to support the efforts of the Presidential Committee on Northeast Initiative (PCNI) at rebuilding the Northeast (NITDA 2017).

Accordingly as complimentary effort, the National Information Technology Development Agency (NITDA), has set up a multi-million naira Digital Capacity Building Centre for the training of Internally Displaced Persons (IDPs) from all parts of Nigeria, especially from the North-east region at the Praxis Catholic e-School for IDPs in Abuja (*Daily Trust* 2017b). It will also assist other Nigerians interested in acquiring knowledge in all areas of information and communication technology to boost the quality of education for national development. Of importance also, the USAID in collaboration with the Federal Ministry of Communication and Technology recently launched two important initiatives called the #smartwomanNigeria and which seek to provide training for 1000 girls in collaboration with #Huawei as part of Government's #GWIN programme (Nigeria Annext www.nigeriannext.org)

From the above discussion, it seems obvious that, while all the volunteer corps has made significant contributions, the problems of the region are so diverse and so huge that there is the need for the government to emphatically embark on poverty alleviation programs with the support of the volunteer groups, that will impact positively on the lives of the people. The improved physical, social, and psychological quality of life of a society and its members, both in a domestic setting and within the larger regional setting, will give the citizens a deeper sense of patriotism.

- **Remarks:** Since urban environmental problems are complex, cross sectoral and inter-organizational approach suffices (hence the high impacts by N-power, NPC and NYSC and TAC) because of inter-governmental collaborations are necessary. UNDP Nigeria is investing resources in interventions aimed at rebuilding North-East Nigeria through strengthening of community resilience, livelihood support and reconstruction. The case of sustainable Ibadan Project II (1995) readily comes to mind. Given the current realities and cash position of the Nigerian government, developing Nigeria's infrastructure (as pre-requisite for diversifying the economy) will require significant private sector funding, strong collaborations between the government and the private sector(Adekalu,2016). Also required is significant foreign investment, hence the high impact scored by N-power, TAC and to an extent others as shown in Table 1 in all the problem areas. Ideas are not new but the use of ICT: These initiatives are not all "new". As already stated in the introduction, the social economy has a long tradition in Europe. However, it receives new inputs from technological, social and political developments in Africa. The decreased consumer trust in the corporate world in the aftermath of the financial and economic crisis, the retreating welfare state, governments advocating "the active citizen" has gone a long way to accept volunteerism in urban development efforts, hence the use of N-power and TAC in the ICT drive. Many of the programmes are co-ordinated under African Union for example PIDA(programme infrastructure development for Africa), Internet Exchange Point (IXP), E-Post, e-Network for e-Governance, e-commerce, etc are established to help in upgrading decaying urban centers in Nigeria and indeed other African countries.

Volunteer Corps in the Upgrading City Centers at Least One in Each State

United Nations Report on Volunteers (2015) suggests that volunteerism can progressively be a vehicle for members of excluded and/or marginalized enclaves to be involved in their governance. It also provides the access to local services, resources, and chances they need to progress their living conditions. Often the volunteers form coalitions with the local officials as well as with people with similar interests as important strategy to provide support to the excluded groups. This helps them not only to access new information and strengthen their capabilities, but also to enhance their chances of holding local officials to account. Many groups worldwide have used this strategy with considerable success and some of the Nigerian volunteer corps has used it effectively. Table 2 shows as assessment of the potential contribution of the Nigerian Volunteer Corps to governance with respect to participation, accountability, and responsiveness

Harnessing the Potential to Develop Nigerian Cities is exerting pressures on local government as noted by Ojendal and Sedara (2007) in Brown, E (2008,P17), there is no doubt that relationships are evolving between local authorities and grassroots initiatives are greatly contributing to institutional social capital. As it is shown in Table 2, local volunteer groups are associations and volunteer-led initiatives are making impact on urban governance through developmental programs. The Federal and State government leaders are overwhelmingly supportive of including volunteers in development efforts in cities in the states .Each state government has worked extensively with networks and mass mobilization of volunteers in its recent history hence the recognition of youth corps scheme as national programmes. Volunteers are still perceived to be an essential part of reaching national development goals, particularly in the health sector, education, community projects, security and infrastructure. Government officials at all levels in this research were very open to working with grass-roots volunteers. Involvement of youth in all the volunteer groups both local and international indicates that Nigerian youth are agents of development. N-power, youth corps, and Peace Corps partner with government to execute development projects. In what turns out to be a sort of specialization, the N-power provides free manpower, while NYSC render free training and capacity building to other stakeholders hence the high score in the rating as shown in the Table.

Table 2. Volunteer Corps potential contributions to governance in upgrading decaying urban centers

Projects Targeting National Problem Areas	Potential Contributions of Volunteer Corps to Governance With Respect to: Participation, Accountability, Responsiveness (H M L)				
	N-Power	NYSC	NPC	TAC	Others
1. Comprehensive Area Upgrading with Digital Networks	H	H	H	M	M
2. Redevelopment Areas of Decaying Zones into "Smart" Communities	H	H	L	M	L
3. Creation of Industrial Park(s) in every Local Government	H	M	L	L	L
4. At least Science and Technology Parks built by every University	H	H	L	H	M
5. Proto-type Innovation Districts in all state capitals and Abuja	M	H	M	M	L

1. N-Power Scheme,2 National Youth Service, 3. National Peace Corps, 4. Technical Aid Corps, 5. Others
Rating of Volunteer Corps contribution to governances H = High, M = Medium, L = Low

- **Discussion of the Overall Results:** The various volunteering youth corps in Nigeria as contained in Table 2 is established to render voluntary services and kinds to the communities as complimentary efforts to what government does. The relevance of involvement of IVOs (International Volunteering Organizations) and Volunteering for Development (VfD) helped in no small measure towards speedy development of respective areas and enhance the accountability of the budgetary funds allocated to the projects that are indeed directly connected to community needs. The community development volunteer programs seek to empower individuals and groups of people by providing them with the skills they need to affect change in their own communities (TAC, NYSC). In Nigeria, the volunteering Corps works with local NGO's and the local communities towards the upliftment of the society based on the criteria contained in Table 2. All types of volunteers are provided with opportunities to help in building eco-friendly homes or alternatively work with local village communities in the war-torn North-East Nigeria and help in the rebuilding of education, construction and medical projects in both internally displaced communities and respective local permanent communities.

Volunteer Corps in the National Major Development Corridors

At the national or cross-border level, a number of social groups in collaboration with volunteers are using technology to build alliances that are designed to advance volunteerism and connect development actors. The rapid penetration of mobile phone and similar devices is expanding the reach and scope of volunteerism. It enables motivated and engaged people and groups in Kano, Maiduguri and Calabar to collaborate, learn from each other, and discover new opportunities and resources. In these days of effective social media the excluded groups remain so for a only a short while, because they somehow find ways of actively participation within border or across border active engagement, in ways that could have positive impacts on their communities and on themselves.

Table 3 shows the potential contributions of volunteer corps to physical development and governance in the National Major Development Corridor In the Table, each of the volunteering corps is rated by the author based on their contributions to physical development of the communities, as collected from official report and newspaper articles.. According to this qualitative rating, N-power has most significant impacts on the 5 projects targeting National Problem Areas as contained in the table, while the remaining Volunteer Corps contribute significantly at medium or low impact level.

POTENTIAL IMPACTS OF NIGERIAN VOLUTEERS

In this section, we discuss the potential impacts of all the volunteer corps in the social, economic, and knowledge development in selected key sub-national and national development problem areas.

Volunteer Corps Impacts in the Reconstruction of Urban Centers in Boko-Haram Affected Region

The North- Eastern states of Nigeria are the area's most affected by the Boko Haram insurgency. The volunteer corps assigned to that area has joined forces with the local development communities to effect changes on the ground with respect to social, economic, infrastructure and knowledge development of those areas. The combined impacts of these volunteers on the ground are assessed in Table 4 with respect to improvement in each of these areas. Table 4 show an assessment of the impact of all Volunteer Corps in the development of the reconstruction of Boko-Haram Affected Region in Nigeria.

Among the volunteer corps participating directly in development projects in the North-East region are those working with UNDP. As general development leader in the region, UNDP visits Beneshiek and speaks with a community in need. UNDP Nigeria is on the ground in three most affected states; Yobe, Borno, and Adamawa. With the establishment of our sub-office in Maiduguri, the UNDP have scaled up development work to build upon successes and pilot interventions from 2016, including immediate livelihood support, infrastructure reconstruction and rehabilitation, and de-radicalization and prevention of violent extremism (UNDP 2017).

Table 3. Volunteer Corps potential contributions to governance in national major development corridor

Projects Targeting National Problem Areas	Potential Contributions of Volunteer Corps to Governance With Respect to: Participation, Accountability, Responsiveness (H M L)				
	N-Power	NYSC	NPC	TAC	Others
1.Comprehensive Area Upgrading with Digital Networks	M	L	L	H	M
2.Redevelopment Areas of Decaying Zones into "Smart" Communities	H	L	H	M	L
3.Creation of Industrial Park(s) in every Local Government	H	M	M	L	M
4.At least Science and Technology Parks built by every University	M	M	H	H	L
5.Proto-type Innovation Districts in all state capitals and Abuja	H	L	H	M	L

1. N-Power Scheme, 2 National Youth Service, 3. National Peace Corps, 4.Technical Aid Corps, 5. Others
Rating of Volunteer Corps contribution to governances H = High, M = Medium, L = Low

The potential impact of all volunteer corps in the development of the reconstruction of Boko-Haram affected region in Nigeria is shown in Table 4. It shows the qualitative assessment with respect to five main areas of development activities. These areas include Comprehensive Area Upgrading with digital networks, creation of industrial parks in every local government area, initiate at least a science and technology parks in collaboration with every university, and promote a proto-type Innovation districts in all state capitals and Abuja

It is evident that the projects executed by these Corps in North- Eastern states of Borno, Yobe and Adamawa are many and of diverse types.. In this region both World Bank, UNDP, Federal and Borno state governments contributed significantly in restoring peace, stability and provision of shelter in the affected communities. With the establishment of the UNDP sub-office and other international donor and volunteering organizations in Maiduguri, they have scaled up the volunteering work to build upon successes and pilot interventions from 2016, including immediate livelihood support, infrastructure reconstruction and rehabilitation, and de-radicalization and prevention of violent extremism (Wikipedia1, 2017). An Integrated Community Stabilization Program, which is aimed at helping both internally, displaced people and host communities to better withstand the crisis and to pave the way towards a peaceful, sustainable future.

Specifically, UNDP in conjunction with the volunteer corps have made positive contributions to the integrated development programs in at least 50 communities in five LGAs where close to 350,000 most vulnerable conflict-affected people benefited. Among the integrated growth intervention are the generous cash grants of over 80,000 most weak conflict-affected people; provided cash-for-work to 4,000 diverse civic employees; supported over 3,400 farmers with agricultural inputs, farm tools and funds to restart agricultural activities. Other interventions included rebuilding some 11 schools, clinics and civic buildings. In addition, it provided grants to 3,200 small business owners, equipped and trained community for new economy and skills. Most of the citizens are participation in radio publicity program. The intervention targeted 4.2 million people with radio public service announcements and dramas on peace-building and gender-based violence prevention messages throughout the north eastern region UNDP (2017). The multinational Oil company, Total, has donated 200 health facility vehicles to Borno State Government

Table 4. Potential impact of all volunteer corps in the development of the reconstruction of Boko-Haram affected region in Nigeria, redevelopment areas of decaying zones into "smart" communities

Projects Targeting National Problem Areas	Potential Impact of All Volunteer Corps in the Following Development Areas (H M L)			
	Social	Economic	Infrastructure	Knowledge
1. Comprehensive Area Upgrading with Digital Networks	H	M	H	H
2. Redevelopment Areas of Decaying Zones into "Smart" Communities	M	H	H	M
3. Creation of Industrial Park(s) in every Local Government	M	M	H	M
4. At least Science and Technology Parks built by every University	H	M	H	H
5. Promote Proto-type Innovation Districts in all state capitals and Abuja	M	H	H	H

1. N-Power Scheme, 2.National Youth Service, 3.National Peace Corps, 4.Technical Aid Corps, 5. Others
Rating of Volunteer Corps contribution to governances H = High, M = Medium, L = Low

as its contribution towards the reconstruction of the health sector in the state as reported by the Nigerian Television Authority (NTA News 9.00pm of 12/7/17).

Volunteer Corps in the Upgrading City Centers at Least One in Each State

Many Nigerian cities have large areas that show signs of decay of physical conditions of buildings and infrastructure services as well as glaring evidence social decay, with evidence of crime, drug abuse and delinquency. These areas are usually inhibited by first or second generation of poor people, carrying out informal or outright illegal activities. The combined efforts of volunteer corps can successfully turn such areas around using targeted and scaled up investments in social, economic, infrastructure and knowledge development. Table 5 potential Impact of the combined efforts of the Volunteer Corps in fostering social, economic, infrastructure and knowledge development in upgrading decaying Nigerian urban centers. It shows their potential contributions in the social, economic, infrastructure and knowledge development in five projects targeting national problem areas.

The state capitals and local government headquarters need to be assessed as to the exact level of work needed within urban centers with respect to redevelopment in physical infrastructure (utilities, roads, transport, etc.) and social infrastructure (educational, health, commercial, employment, security and other facilities). The safe and smooth connections between towns need to be restored. After meeting the deficit, it is vital that the needs of the growing urban population to, say 2050, are carefully planned and resources for the implementation is mobilized. Job creations and production facilities, such industrial parks (UNIDO, 2016), innovation districts (Katz & Wagner, 2014), and science and technology parks (RS 2009) need to be established in association with universities and polytechnics, as described elsewhere in this chapter.

Volunteer Corps in the National Major Development Corridors

There are many potential corridor development areas, the growth that can trigger waves of socio-economic development activities to meet the present and future needs of Nigeria's huge urban growth potential.

Table 5. Potential impact of all volunteer corps in upgrading decaying urban centers

Projects Targeting National Problem Areas	Potential Impact of All Volunteer Corps in the Following Development Areas (H M L)			
	Social	Economic	Infrastructure	Knowledge
1. Comprehensive Area Upgrading with Digital Networks	H	H	H	H
2. Redevelopment Areas of Decaying Zones into "Smart" Communities	L	H	H	L
3. Creation of Industrial Park(s) in every Local Government	H	M	H	M
4. At least Science and Technology Parks built by every University	H	M	L	M
5. Proto-type Innovation Districts in all state capitals and Abuja	H	H	M	L

1. N-Power Scheme, 2.National Youth Service, 3.National Peace Corps, 4.Technical Aid Corps, 5. Others
Rating of Volunteer Corps contribution to governances H = High, M = Medium, L = Low

The combined efforts of the volunteer corps alone cannot generate development of such magnitude, but they can contribute to a substantial part of it. The volunteers' diverse background in social development, economic development, infrastructure development and knowledge development can make appreciable impacts. Figure 1 shows the proposed LAKAJI (Lagos-Kano-Jibiya regional Development Corridor) development corridor that can form the first part and backbone of such development corridors. Table 6 show an assessment of the potential impact of all Volunteer Corps in the development of LAKAJI corridor.

LAKAJE has strategic significance for national, regional and international trade, as it is the main route for moving imported goods to northern Nigeria, and exports to southern port, using both road and rail systems. By connecting Lagos to Kano, the proposed corridor connects Nigeria's largest and most important commercial centers and feeds many local and regional markets. This corridor has the potential of using multiple industrial parks, innovation districts, and science and technology parks along the spine road that connects major cities and projects to enable Nigeria to grow in to the largest developed country of its kind in Africa. The impact of such projects cannot be over emphasized. It brings about frog-jump development in all the settlements that are located along the corridor as shown in Table 6.

The following were achieved so far with the establishment of the Lakaji project.

1. Supported exporting firms obtain $9 million in new investment and generate $1.9 million in new exports
2. Facilitated the creation of four new agribusinesses along the LAKAJI Corridor
3. Operationalization of LAKAJI Corridor Management LTD/GTE as a Public Private Partnership advocacy platform for the improvement of the Corridor's competitiveness
4. Established a *Project Development Facility* to stimulate early stage agribusiness investment; current pipeline of investment proposals worth $46 million
5. Provided technical assistance and training to more than 100 exporting firms
6. Helped the Nigerian Export Promotion Council (NEPC) and the Kwara State government create national and state cashew export strategies
7. Supported the establishment of the National Food Safety and Management Committee (NFSMC) and provided technical assistance and training to some of its members

Table 6. Potential impact of all volunteer corps in the LAKAJI national major development corridor

Projects Targeting National Problem Areas	Potential Impact of All Volunteer Corps in the Following Development Areas (H M L)			
	Social	Economic	Infrastructure	Knowledge
1. Comprehensive Area Upgrading with Digital Networks	H	H	H	M
2. Redevelopment Areas of Decaying Zones into "Smart" Communities	H	H	M	M
3. Creation of Industrial Park(s) in every Local Government	M	H	M	L
4. At least Science and Technology Parks built by every University	H	H	M	M
5. Proto-type Innovation Districts in all state capitals and Abuja	H	L	H	H

1. N-Power Scheme, 2.National Youth Service, 3.National Peace Corps, 4.Technical Aid Corps, 5. Others
Rating of Volunteer Corps contribution to governances H = High, M = Medium, L = Low

8. Assisted Nigerian cashew factory to obtain the African Cashew Alliance (ACA) Seal
9. Helped the Government of Nigeria revise its national Food Safety Policy and Implementation Strategy
10. Trained and provided technical assistance to Nigerian government representatives to participate in a WTO Ministerial and to implement improved trade policy, trade strategy and tariff analysis. (NigeriaNextt, 2017)

Above are the impacts of corridor in the economic and physical development of Nigeria. There is need for government to protect such investments along the corridor and ensure security along the international trade centers along the corridor between Nigeria and Niger republic.

FUNDING VOLUNTEERISM IN NIGERIA

The funding of the Nigerian Volunteer Corps projects of the national, regional and local significances has be based on a variety "crowdfunding". In this case, the crowd would be assumed to be at the local, regional, national and international levels, making contributions to the development in monetary and non-monetary terms, some of them are motivated by social giving other many be interested in make investments for profits.

In Table 7, the main relevant projects targeting national problem areas are listed against the elements related to the funding of the Volunteer Corps developments activities with respect to project design development costs. Other cost components are physical infrastructure development, Social and startup Businesses development, and the costs associated with virtual, offsite, development activities of some of the Volunteers who may choose to work online. The startup business development is seen as important and innovative component of the whole program due its tremendous jobs generating and later local revenue generating potentials.

Against each project and volunteer activity-types are inserted numbers that correspond to potential crowdfunding elements, which are described in details later. It is considered unnecessary to include the Nigerian funding public institutions, such as local, state and the federal governments as part of the crowd, this is because they are central to it. Whether the listed contributing members of the crowd succeed or fail in funding the projects, the public funding will be available to provide the minimal needed support.

*Table 7. Crowdfunding recommendation**

Crowdfunding of Volunteerism				
Projects Targeting National Problem Areas	**Project Design Development**	**Physical Development**	**Social/Biz Development**	**Virtual Development**
Reconstruction of urban centers in Boko-Haram areas	1, 2, 3 4 5 8 9	1, 2 3 4 7 8 9 10	1, 2 3 4 7 8 9	ITU, MasterCard 7 8 9
Upgrading City Centers at least one in each state	1, 3, 5	7 6 8 9	7 6 8 9	7 8
Major Development Corridors	1, 2, 5	1 2 3 4 6 7 8 9 10	1, 2 3 4 6 7 8 9 10	7 8 9

*Figures in the table are obtained in the text below.

Recommended Crowdfunding Sources

The Crowd, in this case, will consists of diverse International, multinational, regional and national organizations, as well as specialized institutions, NGOs, the Private section, Diaspora individuals and organizations. The numbers in Table 7 correspond to the numbers of the recommended crowdfunding source as shown in this list. The detailed description of the crowdfunding actors are given in the next section.

1. International organizations (United Nations or government linked)
2. Official government development cooperation
3. NGOs, charity organizations, trust funds
4. Development cooperation at the level of higher education
5. Research funding organizations
6. Organizations with a regional scope
7. Equity Crowdfunding
8. Private organizations
9. African Diaspora Funding Development
10. Islamic Development Finance Institution

DETAILED DESCRIPTION OF THE CROWDFUNDING SOURCES

International Organizations (United Nations or Government Linked)

The Nigerian Volunteer Corps can expect wide-ranging financial and other material supports from many agencies of the United Nations. Identified below are just few of the main agencies that are approachable with planned and well-reasoned requests.

- **The UN-Habitat:** Is the United Nations program with many decades of global experience working towards a better urban future. It seeks to advance the development of socially and environmentally sustainable settlements and to achieve adequate housing for all. (See https://unhabitat.org/un-habitat-at-a-glance/#).
- **FAO (Food and Agricultural Organization of the United Nations) (www.fao.org):** Is suitable agency to support balanced regional development. It supports beekeeping projects in developing countries like Nigeria. Applications for projects with budgets over $US10,000 must be submitted through your government ministry or specific agency (so-called Technical Cooperation Program at http://www.fao.org/tc/tcp/). For projects with budgets under $US10,000, beekeepers' groups and associations may apply for small project funding from the TeleFood Special Fund (http://www.fao.org/food/english/index.html).
- **IFAD (International Fund for Agricultural Development):** Is dedicated to eradicating rural poverty in developing countries through agriculture developmental programmes at rural level (www.ifad.org).
- Other UN agencies relevant to the Nigerian development are UNDP (United Nations Development Programme) (www.undp.org); UNIDO, UNICEF (United Nations Children's Fund) (www.unicef.

org) that supports development of children; and WHO (World Health Organization) (www.who.org) that supports health-related projected.

- **The World Bank (www.worldbank.org):** Collaborated with public and NGOs to support development at the levels of the community, urban, regional and national. The local Nigerian office has a long history of collaboration with governments at urban, state and national levels.
- **International Telecommunications Union (ITU http://www.itu.int/en/about/Pages/overview.aspx):** This is a United Nations specialized agency for information and communication technologies – ICTs responsible for the allocation of global radio spectrum and satellite orbits, create the technical standards that ensure networks and technologies seamlessly interconnect, and strive to improve access to ICTs to underserved communities worldwide. Within Nigeria, internet service providers such as MTN, EcoNet, and others provide services to consumers such as the Nigerian Volunteer Corps members who select to provide services online. The ITU policies and actions, through the local providers, can affect the Volunteers cost levels and the quality of services.

Official Foreign Governments' Development Cooperation

The NGO or local Volunteer Corps with specific defined projects in any city or state can approach suitable any official donor government aid office for project support, either in cash or in kind, as part of the bilateral cooperation programs. The following list of official government aid departments is just few examples that can be approached for information on what is available and how to go about getting the desired support funding. More information about other potential support can be found from the Internet. Detailed information regarding Official government aid, inclusive of specific bilateral cooperation programs information can be found on the respective websites, or in the local embassies in your country.

List of Nigerian regular development partners includes:

- **British Council:** www.britishcouncil.org
- **UK:** DFID (www.dfid.gov.uk)
- **Canada:** CIDA (www.acdi-cida.gc.ca)
- **Germany:** GTZ (www.gtz.de)
- **United States:** USAID (www.usaid.org)
- **Netherlands:** (www.minbuza.nl)
- **Japan:** JICA (www.jica.go.jp)
- **Europe Aid Cooperation Office:** http://ec.europa.eu/comm/europeaid/index_en.htm

NGOs, Charity Organizations, Trust Funds

There are thousands of large and small NGOs that are eagerly looking for new opportunities and projects, which are promising in terms of impact on development at the local or regional levels. The Nigerian Volunteer Corps will find that some of them are interested collaborating to improve the physical facilities or social programs with lasting community-wide impacts. Some would collaborate on profit making initiatives targeting vulnerable target groups such as AIDS orphans, women, disabled or elderly among other social groups.

It is helpful to propose different scenarios for your project funding (in cash or kind) requirements after giving a clear indication the Corps' share. For instance a minimal cost, medium cost and high cost scenario, leading to different outcomes. This leaves the NGO a choice, and gives an impression of a thoroughly thought out project.

The following is just selected few examples. The Volunteer Corps with specific fundable projects need to use the internet to search for partners that are more suitable:

- **ADRA (Adventist Development and Relief Agency International - www.adra.org):** This agency seeks to make impact around the world through a range of programs and initiatives in nine key impact areas. The areas are related to social justice, disaster response, economic growth, children, gender equity, water, community health, sanitation &hygiene, hunger &nutrition, livelihoods & agriculture.
- **Christian Aid (www.christian-aid.org.uk):** Christian Aid is an agency of the churches in the UK and Ireland. We work wherever the need is greatest – irrespective of religion or race- suitable for early stage impact in the Boko Haram affected areas.
- **Rockefeller Organization (ww.rockfound.org):** This is committed to fostering knowledge and innovation to enrich and sustain the lives and livelihoods of poor and excluded people throughout the world. It could help in reviving education in all the educationally challenged areas.
- **Ford Foundation (www.fordfound.org):** Strengthen democratic values, reduce poverty and injustice, promote international cooperation and advance human achievement. This could help in urban upgrading and slums redevelopment.
- **CARE International (www.careinternational.org):** This is one of the world's largest independent relief and development organizations, working in more than 70 countries and benefiting over 45 million poor and marginalized people.
- **ActionAid International (www.actionaid.org):** Is an international development agency whose aim is to fight poverty and support Volunteer Corps efforts in the North-east and in the slums of cities.
- **Doctors Without Borders:** (Medicine Ces Frontiers).

Development Cooperation at the Level of Tertiary Education

The development of tertiary educational institutions is clearly one of the greatest needs of the Boko Haram affected areas, due to the large-scale destruction of educational infrastructure generally and the tertiary sector in particular. The chief complaint of the terror group is rapid expansion of this type of education and the result of the group activities has turned the area into an educational lagging region. Key to its revival is the development tertiary sector that would provide local teachers to secondary and primary sector. Thus, the need to emphasize the development cooperation at the level of tertiary education with interested government and organizations.

1. Dutch organization for international cooperation in higher education (NUFFIC) (www.nuffic.nl)
2. German service for academic exchange (DAAD) (www.daad.de)
3. The British Council may also have opportunities(www.britcoun.org/education)

4. UN/DESA – Office of Human Resources for International Cooperation – United Nations Department of Economic and Social Affairs (http://www.un.org/esa/desa/)
5. USAID- The United States of America International Development (https://www.usaid.gov/)

Research and Research Funding Organizations

Many of the Nigerian urban problems require immediate and medium solutions but require sound understanding of the factors shaping them. Thus, they require policy-oriented research approach that requires support of local and international centers of excellence. Given below are just a few of such centers, and the Nigerian Volunteer Corps need a clear research and training development plan with which to approach these and other institutions for support.

- **The Academy of Sciences for the Developing World (TWAS):** Supports research by means of awards and scholarships, but the main activity of interest is the provision of research grants and the support of research units in least developed countries. http://www.twas.org.
- **International Foundation of Science (IFS):** Supports scientists in developing countries by awarding research grants. Applicants must be citizens of, and carry out research in, a developing country, at the start of their research career and work at a developing country university or national research institution (www.ifs.se).
- **The Third World Organization for Women in Science:** Offers postgraduate training fellowships (www.twows.org).

Additional research opportunities are in other development organizations, such as the organizations focused on higher education or several NGO's or trust funds (e.g. Rockefeller Organization).

Organizations With a Regional Scope

Many African regional organizations offer development assistance in cash or kind that could prove useful to the Nigerian Volunteer Corps in their efforts to uplift the general development of the nations' cities, regions and the national spatial structure. A selection of these agencies is presented below, but thousands more exist and would have to be searched as the need arises.

- **Africa Development Interchange Network (ADIN):** Use development facilities in potentially rich African regions to produce needed resources in other African regions (potentially poor), through the following programs: Agriculture, Healthcare, Education, Trade, etc. E-mail: adin_apd@yahoo.com
- **Africa Infrastructures Foundation:** The aim of the organization is to provide first-class services to the African community and African and international development organizations to sustain Africa's infrastructures with the purpose of improving the quality of the environment and enhancing socio-economic development through the principles of sustainable development. http://africaprosperity.com/index.php/region/west-africa/nigeria/region/items/view/Africa-Infrastructures-Foundation

- **African Centre for Empowerment, Gender and Advocacy, the (AC-EGA):** Purpose: AC-EGA is a regional NGO working on projects on gender, capacity development, research and policy advocacy specializing in women's health, governance and competence in decision-making. E-mail: acega@insightkenya.com
- **African Association of Remote Sensing of the Environment (AARSE)**: This professional association encourages the development and practice of remote sensing and geographic information systems (GIS) as well as products of these geo-information technologies in their respective areas of operation. http://www.africanremotesensing.org/
- **African Development Information Services (AfDevInfo):** AfDevInfo tracks the mechanics of political and economic development across Sub Saharan Africa. This commercial, not-for-profit enterprise draws together a diverse range of publicly available data and presents it as an accessible and ever expanding online database. http://www.afri-dev.info/about-us-2/
- Development banks work through the governments; they may anyway have some budget lines available. African Development Bank Group (www.afdb.org)

Equity Crowdfunding

Despite its' relatively rent development, crowdfunding is growing into a big business. Crowdfunding enables people with projects or needs to the Internet masses to appeal for contributions to cover a wide variety personal to community needs. Worldwide, the crowdfunding industry annually raises higher than US$34 billion annually, and this projected to nearly triple to about US$93 billion by 2025 (Theim 2017). Social giving crowdfunding enables donors target money to specific, personal or community charitable appeals. Estimates put the number of social giving platforms to more than 3,500, according to consultancy NextGen Crowdfunding (2017).

The rise of charitable niche is in response to the unraveling of the social safety net and as a 21st century replacement for the fundraiser in the church or mosque, and other means of community help mobilization of the past. This new social giving allows people greatly expand their universe of potential givers beyond their immediate specialized or social circles. Thus, well-conceived community projects in Maiduguri, Kaduna, or Jos can expect donations from a wide range of individuals and community of donors, with 'communities' very broadly defined, including Cape Town, New York or London.

- **Crowdfunding Models:** The five main crowdfunding models in use in Africa as identified by Afrikstart (2015) are Donations, Peer-to-Peer Lending, Hybrid, Equity-Based, and Rewards-Base. Of these models, the most popular in 2014 were rewards-based platforms but in 2015, the donations-based and equity-based platforms became more popular. At the same time, six new donations-based platforms that fundraise for social causes and community projects were launched in 2015. Four new equity-based crowdfunding platforms were also created that year.

With regard to the type of activities, Afrikstart (2015) survey shows that in 2015, 31.5% of Africa-based crowdfunding platforms focused in endorsing projects related to social causes. The second type of activity was business and entrepreneurship (21%), which was followed by creative and innovative projects (17.5%). In 2015 new types of activities included renewable energy, healthcare, and education and thus the Volunteer Corps can expect funding in these projects type and well-conceived innovative types.

Commercial and Other Organizations

Start-up ecosystems are emerging as key growth centers in urban areas round the world. Many technology-based start-ups are not seeking large funds in hardware or office space. Rather, they seek access to growth-giving environment such as professional networks, mentors, diverse learning-community, and varied talent. Cities are best suited to meet their needs, as they provide diversity and allow for constant interaction and collaboration. The Nigerian urban centers are suited for this innovation ecosystem, which the Nigerian Volunteer Corps can nurture and use as key urban regeneration and development tool.

The following list shows some of the emerging seeds along these lines. The list includes collaborative ventures funded by established firms, institutions, startups and global model can be applied in cities in both developed and developing countries. The same trends are driving the urbanization of organic innovation ecosystems in New York City, London, Stockholm, Mumbai, Buenos Aires and Nairobi. This presents a great opportunity for developing countries to build innovation ecosystems in cities and create communities of entrepreneurs to support the creation of new sectors and businesses.

- **The Abuja-Based Ventures Platform:** A seed-stage fund and accelerator that actively finds, funds and supports innovative companies solving real problems. http://www.venturesplatform.com/#about
- **Microsoft's Affordable Access Initiative:** Grant program has for the second year in a row made a number of grants to individuals and organizations… https://www.microsoft.com/en-us/affordable-access-initiative/home
- **The Legatum Centre for Development and Entrepreneurship:** At the Massachusetts Institute of Technology has partnered the Mastercard Foundation. http://legatum.mit.edu/what-we-do/
- **Village Capital:** Already very active in Africa, Village Capital looks set to scale up its activities after announcing the close of a US$17.7 million fund by its investment arm VilCap Investments. http://vilcap.com/
- **Social Innovation Fund:** Nigerian incubator Co-Creation Hub (CcHub) partnered Venture Garden Group, Omidyar Network and the Bank of Industry to launch the NGN1 billion (US$5 million) Social Innovation Fund, which will back young entrepreneurs with solutions to local problems. http://cchubnigeria.com/contact-us/
- **UNICEF:** An unusual one, but UNICEF has launched a US$9 million Innovation Fund for start-ups in emerging markets developing solutions with the potential to improve the lives of the world's most vulnerable children. It will invest in open source technologies for children. https://www.unicef.org/where-we-work

African Diaspora Funding Development

Throughout Nigeria, innovative grassroots organizations work actively to transform their towns, cities and communities for the better. They do not always get the recognition and support they need. The Nigerian Volunteer Corps has the opportunities to turn this situation round. With well-planned projects and the support of their local communities, they can approach agencies like the Africans in the Diaspora (Aid), an organization that is changing the way the world looks at philanthropy in Africa.

Africans in the Diaspora (Aid)- http://www.africansinthediaspora.org/- can be a game changer in African development. Compared to the US$255 m US foundations spent in Africa in 2010 and to the £89m UK aid to Africa in the same year, the sum of US$40bn that Diaspora Africans sent home in remittances in 2010 clearly uplift African economies many fold (Levy 2014). The size of the remittance had risen to US$60bn a year and grown further since that time, exceeding the combined funding from private foundations, bilateral and multilateral aid agencies.

The key lesson is that Nigerian Diaspora has important role to play the country's development at all levels. These matters to the potential role the Volunteer Corps can play and ensuring that the remittances are put to productive use to grow the economy, generating millions of creative startup, solve pressing urban and regional development issues. They need to formulate sound investable plans, provide the confidence that projects will be wisely and efficiently implemented with visible impacts and at the same time collaborate with local NGOs, startups and communities to demonstrate what can be achieved in uplifting decaying city centers, pulling up lagging regions and in integrating national spatial structure.

Islamic Development Finance

In the past, most governments in Africa have depended on traditional financiers such as export credit agencies, multilateral agencies, development financial institutions, commercial banks and private sector participants for most of their development funding requirements. Since the financial crises of 2008, however, these traditional sources of finance have weakened at a time of rising development funding needs. These needs were largely triggered by Africa's massive infrastructure gap due to high population increases and rapid urbanization. These situations led to search for alternative funding sources. In the previous section the African Diaspora remittances has been highlighted as one option. In this section we propose Islamic Development Finance as an additional option. There are strong ties among Africa's significant Muslim population, and the considerable historic financial links between Africa and the Middle East since Mansa Musa's impact on the financial market of the region when he undertook pilgrimage in the 14th Century.

In recent years, according to Latham &Watkins (2016) there are cases of debut *sukuk* issuances from Senegal (100 billion CFA francs ($208 million) in June 2014) and South Africa ($500 million issue in September 2014). In addition, and in spite of the effects of the recent downturn in oil prices, many of the Gulf Cooperation Council states have sovereign wealth funds that, over the years, have amassed significant wealth, which may also be deployed through either conventional financial products or shariah-compliant instruments.

Potentially Africa is likely to be an important market for Islamic financial instruments. Although proportionately less than that of Senegal, the size of Nigeria's Muslim population and its ever-widening infrastructure gap also suggest that the *sukuk* market could be an ideal funding solution for the continent's largest economy. Nigeria also has introduced several legal and regulatory reforms to prepare a framework conducive to Islamic financing requirements. Several other African countries have established, or are in the process of establishing, a framework to gain access to investors seeking to use *Shariah* compliant. In practical terms some countries have already benefitting from the Islamic Finance while others are geared up their legislation. For example *sukuk* based legislative reforms were enacted in Nigeria in 2013 and Osun State benefitted from it, in Senegal in 2014, in South Africa in 2014. The following countries are establishing legislation to issue sukuk and/or introduce shariah-compliant instruments: Egypt, Ivory Coast, Kenya, Mauritius, Morocco, Nigeria, Tanzania, Tunisia, and Uganda (Latham & Watkins 2016).

For the future effective use of Islamic financial instruments, it is important that the new frameworks are developed by countries wishing to enter the *sukuk* market are consistent with current global market practice. The expectation is that such frameworks should accept and reflect the standards and practices in those countries where *sukuk* were issued successfully. On the other hand Africa's broader Islamic banking infrastructure is lagging far behind especially given the size of the continent's Muslim population.

FUTURE RESEARCH DIRECTION

The size and youthful nature Nigeria's population and the transformative potential of its urbanization are such that these two forces can comfortably replace oil as the engine of its future growth and development. With the oil price down and traditional lending banks in crisis, this chapter advocates drawing on Nigeria's huge human capital by supporting and expanding the country's various forms of volunteer corps and channeling their creative energies toward urban development. It suggests deploying the corps in the following areas: (1) Reconstruction of urban centers in Boko-Haram areas, (2) Upgrading City Centers at least one in each state, (3) Major National Development Corridors, and (4) Recommended Crowdfunding Sources. Future research need to be directed towards assessing level of and improving the contributions of the volunteer corps in opening up urban areas for investments and job-creation growths at the urban level and at the national level the focus need to be on lagging regions, besides those already identified, to determine the opportunities and challenges they pose to national development. The effectiveness of the urban management tools applied by the volunteer corps need to be evaluated with the view to sharpening them and strengthening the links between the corps and urban authorities.

The chapter suggests that the fund these programs should not rely only on the traditional aid-giving multinational and national governments, their NGOs and development agencies and African development institutions, but should explore sources of alternative finances, such as crowdfunding models, especially equity and civic types. Other new sources are private technology finance organizations interested in funding startup ecosystems, African Diaspora groups that have been remitting huge funds annually, and Islamic finance institutions backed by resourceful sovereign funds from the Middle East. Crowdfunding and other sources may be used to fund material for direct use in the projects. Future funding research should explore other evolving alternative urban development financing sources, pointing out the opportunities and challenges the present to the volunteer corps model. Further investigations are needed to determine how strengthen all the existing and the evolving funding channels and put them on a sound legal footing, strengthening their operations and reliability in achieving efficient urban system that replaces oil as the engine of Nigeria's growth and development.

Program evaluation research should be conducted at regular interval of, say five years, to determine the level of goals achievements, to identify the challenges and opportunities arising from the management of the program, and to make recommendations.

CONCLUSION

Nations with limited development finance but rich in human resources need to organize their socio-economic growth strategies in ways that make the most effective and innovative use human capital stock in the planning and implementing their national urban development. As Goldin (2014) points out that human capital encompasses the knowledge, customs, social, creativity and other character attributes in the people's ability to perform work to produce economic value. Nigerians are blessed with these collective traits in abundance, as can be witnessed in their talents, skills, abilities, experience, intelligence, training, and their judgment, which admittedly has not always put to the best use. Despite these human failings, this chapter advocates the use of these diverse forms of wealth to accomplish the goals of the sustainable and equitable national urban development through the volunteer corps.

In order to promote synergy and sustainable development of human capital and urban development in Nigeria, much more work needs by the government. Firstly, strengthen and deepen the national talent mix by encouraging the volunteers to continue working together as teams beyond their agreed service periods by encouraging them to form nationally networked cooperatives for promoting the sustainable development of human capital. Secondly, initiate a Diaspora Policy to encourage the contribution of their knowledge, skills and funds urban investment, and establish an Urban Synergy Policy designed to attract the worldwide high-tech enterprises, build a series of industry corridors across the nation, and create an attractive environment for investment. Finally, sustain and reinvigorate these policies through annual conferences and exhibitions aimed at expanding and scaling up of the achievements of the "Human Capital and Urban Capital Synergies" project.

REFERENCES

African Union Youth Volunteer Corps (AU-YVC). (2017). *Continental development program that promotes youth volunteerism in Africa*. Retrieved from www.neuvoo.com.ng/jobs/volunteering-jobs-in-Abj

Afrikstart. (2015). *Crowdfunding in Africa: Fundraising goes Digital in Africa: The emergence of Africa-Based Crowdfunding Platforms*. Retrieved from http://afrikstart.com/report/wp-content/uploads/2016/09/Afrikstart-Crowdfunding-In-Africa-Report.pdf

Balogun, A. (2016). *Infrastructure development in Nigeria: Better late than never*. Retrieved from http://www.lexology.com/1166035/author/Adekalu_Balogun/

Daily Trust. (2017). *FG to engage 200,000 community health volunteers*. Retrieved from www.dailytrust.com.ng/news/

Goldin, C. (2014). *Human Capital. Department of Economics Harvard University and National Bureau of Economic Research.*

Katz, B., & Wagner, J. (2014). *The Rise of Innovation Districts: A New Geography of Innovation in America*. Retrieved from https://www.brookings.edu/wp-content/uploads/2016/07/InnovationDistricts1.pdf

Latham & Watkins. (2016). *Africa's funding alternative. The continent accounts for less than one percent of global sukuk issuance. This may be about to change.* Academic Press.

Naija247News. (2017). *NPAC/TAC-Transformation of Nigeria's oil.* Retrieved from http://naija247news.com

Newshandle. (2017). *Federal Government Partners WTO, CNN to boost development.* Retrieved from www.newshandle.com/nigeria-vanguard

NextGen Crowdfunding. (2017). *Explore a New Ear of Crowdfunding.* Retrieved from https://www.nextgencrowdfunding.com/companies/title-iii-crowdfunding-reg-cf-541/

Nigerianextt. (2017). *Nigeria Expanded Trade and Transport Project.* Retrieved from www.nigerianextt.org

Nigeriannext. (2013). *Don't miss these women initiatives in Nigeria!* Retrieved from www.nigeriannext.org

NITDA. (2017). *NITDA set up multi-million naira training centre for IDPs in Abuja.* Retrieved from http://www.herald.ng/nitda-set-up-multi-million-naira-training-centre-for-idps-inabuja/#leTddyJd1XUwK4ac.99

UN-Habitat. (n.d.). Retrieved from https://unhabitat.org/un-habitat-at-a-glance/#

UNDESA. (2014). *World Urbanization Prospects.* Retrieved from https://esa.un.org/unpd/wup/publications/files/wup2014-highlights.Pdf

UNDP. (2017). *Rebuilding North-East Nigeria.* Retrieved from http://www.ng.undp.org/content/nigeria/en/home/ourwork/crisispreventionandrecovery.html

United Nations Volunteers (UNV) programme. (2015). *Delivering at Grassroots.* Retrieved from https://www.unv.org/annual-report-2015/

USAID Nigeria. (2015). *LAKAJI Corridor.* Retrieved from http://www.nigerianextt.org/?pageid=334

Vanguard. (2017). Retrieved from www.vanguardngr.com

Wesler, K. W. (1998). *Historical archaeology in Nigeria.* Africa World Press. Retrieved from https://www.lw.com/thoughtLeadership/africas-funding-alternative

Wikipedia. (2017). *Violent Extremism.* Retrieved from https://en.wikipedia.org/wiki/Violent_extremism retrieved 20/04/17

Wilson, J. (2017). *Volunteerism Research: A Review Essay.* Retrieved from www.http://www.journals.sagepub.com

World Bank. (2016). *From oil to cities: Nigeria's next transformation. Directions in Development.* Washington, DC: World Bank Group. Retrieved from http://documents.worldbank.org/curated/en/711661468010811972/From-oil-to-cities-Nigeria-s-next-transformation

KEY TERMS AND DEFINITIONS

Alternative Finance Mechanisms: The non-conventional sources of funds, which shifts from conventional banking system to the emerging financial-technology-based sources, to mobilize development resources to execute a given project in a community through modern system.

Non-Oil-Based Economy: An economy whose activities are diversify into non-oil areas such as agriculture, tourism, mining instead of oil. In Nigeria, the idea to shift emphasis from oil- to urban-based activities.

Oil-Based Economy: A country whose economy depends for major source of its income is derived from activities that are tied to natural resources mainly oil. Nigerian economy is a good example; for many decades, its major source of revenue has been from the export of crude oil.

Urban Activities: The basic idea is that the diverse social, cultural and economic production, transportation, and consumption activities in urban setting help shape the tempo and direction of urban growth through their impacts on land uses and the environment.

Urban Volunteer Research: An investigation on how the many types of online, offline, onsite, offsite volunteers contribute to urban growth and development.

Volunteer Corps: An organized group of people who render themselves to the service of humanity at a fixed pay, typical example here are the National Youth Service Corp.

Volunteerism: A willy-nilly offer of service or gift to the needy without expectation in reciprocal form. This offer and acceptance, as well as the services, can take place online or offline, and at home or abroad, via wired or wireless devices.

Compilation of References

Abdalla, H. (2012). The Needs And Attitudes Of Science Students To ESP: A Case Study Of Taif University In Khurma, Saudi Arabia. *English Teaching*, *4*(8).

Abubakar, I. R. (2011). Distributional patterns of urban services in a modernist city of developing countries: A case study of Abuja, Nigeria. *Association of the Collegiate Schools of Planning 52nd Annual Conference.*

Abubakar, I. R., & Aina, Y. A. (2016). Achieving Sustainable Cities in Saudi Arabia: Juggling the Competing Urbanization Challenges. In Population Growth and Rapid Urbanization in the Developing World (pp. 42-63). Hershey, PA: IGI Global.

Abubakar, I. R., & Dano, U. L. (2018). Socioeconomic Challenges and Opportunities of Urbanization in Nigeria. In Urbanization and Its Impact on Socio-Economic Growth in Developing Regions (pp. 219-240). Hershey, PA: IGI Global. doi:10.4018/978-1-5225-2659-9.ch011

Abubakar, I., & Aina, Y. A. (2006). GIS and Space Syntax: An analysis of accessibility to urban green areas in Doha district of Dammam metropolitan area, Saudi Arabia. *Proceedings of Map Middle East conference*, 1-8.

Abubakar, I. R., Al-Shihri, F. S., & Ahmed, S. M. (2016). Students' assessment of campus sustainability at the University of Dammam, Saudi Arabia. *Sustainability*, *8*(1), 59. doi:10.3390/su8010059

ACFA. (n.d.). *Africa Crowdfunding Association Purpose.* Retrieved from http://africancrowd.org/about/acfa-purpose/

Acharya, A., & Sinha, D. (2014). A concept map approach to supporting diagnostic and remedial learning activities. *Advanced Computing, Networking and Informatics*, *1*, 557–578.

Acoca, A., Chattaraj, S., & Wachter, S. (2014). *Urban governance and development of informality in China and India.* Social Science Research Network.

ActionAid. (2014). *Corruption and Poverty in Nigeria: A Report.* Abuja: Action Nigeria.

ACT-Southern Africa. (2013). *Zimbabwe: Corruption Cases: Lest we Forget: Bad Leadership Examples for Accountability, Transparency, and Integrity in Zimbabwe.* Available at: https://actsouthernafrica.wordpress.com/2013/03/14/zimbabwe-corruption-cases-lest-we-forget-bad-leadership-examples-for-accountability-transparency-and-integrity-in-zimbabwe/

Adeokun. (2014). *Reworking Traditional Fund Raising Institutions for Affordable Housing Provisions: A Review of Nigeria and Kenya Case Studies.* Retrieved from www.eprints-convenantuniversity.edu.ng/2683/1/

AfDB. (2009). *Oil and Gas in Africa.* New York: Oxford University Press Inc.

AfDB. (2011). *Africa Infrastructure Country Diagnostic 2011. Africa's Infrastructure: A Time for Transformation.* AfDB.

Afkarmena. (n.d.), *Fees & Special features.* Retrieved from https://www.afkarmena.com/en/page/fees-special-features/

Africa 4Tech org. (2016). *eHealth in Africa*. Retrieved from http://africa4tech.org/wp- content/themes/afourtech/papers/A4T%20-%20EHEALTH%20-%20Single.pdf

Africa Progress Report (APR). (2012). *Africa Progress Report. Jobs, Justice and Equity. Seizing Opportunities in Times of Global Change.* Africa Progress Panel.

African Legacy. (2000). *Hausaland Walled Cities & Towns - remote sensing studies*. Retrieved from https://csweb.bournemouth.ac.uk/africanlegacy/kano_walls.htm

African Media Agency. (2017). *Digitising East Africa's agricultural sector*. Retrieved from www.bizcommunity.com / sendToFriend.aspt/156413pdf

African Union Youth Volunteer Corps (AU-YVC). (2017). *Continental development program that promotes youth volunteerism in Africa*. Retrieved from www.neuvoo.com.ng/jobs/volunteering-jobs-in-Abj

Afrikstart. (2015). *Crowdfunding Africa*. Retrieved from http://afrikstart.com/report/wp-content/uploads /2016/09/Afrikstart-Crowdfunding-In-Africa-Report.pdf

Afrikstart. (2015). *Crowdfunding in Africa*. Retrieved from http://afrikstart.com/report/wp-content/.../Afrikstart-Crowdfunding-In-Africa-Report.pdf

Afrikstart. (2015). *Crowdfunding in Africa: Fundraising goes Digital in Africa: The emergence of Africa- Based Crowdfunding Platforms*. Retrieved from http://afrikstart.com/report/wp-content/uploads/2016/09/Afrikstart-Crowdfunding-In-Africa-Report.pdf

Afrikstart. (2016). *Afrikstart Crowdfunding in Africa Report*. Retrieved from http://afrikstart.com/report/wp-content/uploads/2016/09/Afrikstart-Crowdfunding-In-Africa-Report.pdf

AfrikStart. (2016). *Crowdfunding in Africa- Fundraising goes Digital in Africa: The Emergence of Africa-Based Crowdfunding Platforms*. Retrieved 5 8, 2017, from The AfrikStart Crowdfunding Africa:https://afrikstart.com/report/

Afrikstart. (2016*). Crowdfunding in Africa. Fundraising goes Digital in Africa: The emergence of Africa-Based Crowdfunding Platforms*. Retrieved from http://afrikstart.com/report/wp-content/uploads/2016/09/Afrikstart-Crowdfunding-In-Africa-Report.pdf

AfrikStart. (n.d.). *Crowdfunding in Africa- Fundraising goes Digital in Africa: The Emergence of Africa- Based Crowdfunding Platforms*. Retrieved from https://afrikstart.com/report/

Afrikstat. (2016). *Fundraising goes Digital in Africa: The emergence of Africa-Based Crowdfunding Platforms*. London: Afrikstart.

Afuah, A., & Tucci, C. L. (2013). Value Capture and Crowdsourcing. *Academy of Management Review*, *38*(3), 457–460. doi:10.5465/amr.2012.0423

Agrawal, A., Catalini, C., & Goldfarb, A. (2014). Some Simple Economics of Crowdfunding. National Bureau of Economic Research, (2014), 63-97.

Agrawal, A., Catalini, C., & Goldfarb, A. (2011). *Offline Relationships, Distance, and the Internet: The Geography of Crowdfunding*. Cambridge, MA: National Bureau of Economic Research. doi:10.3386/w16820

Ahmad, A. (2006). *Policies and Regulations for Expanding eUBanking to the Poor*. Academic Press.

Ahmad, A. N. (2010). Is twitter a useful tool for journalists? *Journal of Media Practice, 11*(2), 145-155.

Ahmed, J. (2012). *Theoretical Framework & Growing Demand of ESP in Saudi Arabia*. Retrieved from https://www.kau.edu.sa/Files/0053226/Researches/65162_36509.pdf

Ahmed, M. K. (2014). The ESP Teacher: Issues, Tasks and Challenges, *English for Specific Purposes World, 42*(14). Retrieved from http://www.esp-world.info/Articles_42/Documents/Ahmed.pdf

Aidid, A. (2017). *Crowdfunding in Africa: Opportunities and Challenges*. Accessed 08/07/17 from https://www.natlawreview.com/article/crowdfunding-africa-opportunities-and-challenges

Aidid, A. (2017). *Crowdfunding in Africa: Opportunities and Challenges*. Retrieved from https://www.covafrica.com/2017/02/crowdfunding-in-africa-opportunities-and-challenges/

Al Fraidan, A. (2012). Evaluation of Two ESP Courses. *Journal of Language Teaching and Research, 2*(5).

Alampay, E. (2010). *Mobile Banking, Mobile Money and Telecommunication Regulations*. Academic Press. 10.2139/ssrn.1618166

Alfehaid, A. F. T. (2011). *Developing An ESP Curriculum For Students Of Health Sciences Through Needs Analysis And Course Evaluation In Saudi Arabia*. Retrieved from https://lra.le.ac.uk/bitstream/2381/10289/1/2011alfehaidaftphd.pdf

Alharby, M. (2005). *ESP Target Situation Needs Analysis: The English Language Communicative Needs As Perceived By Health Professionals In The Riyadh Area*. Retrieved from http://faculty.ksu.edu.sa/majed/Documents/alharby_majid_200505_phd.pdf

Allen, S., Deragon, J. T., Orem, M., & Smith, C. F. (2009). *The Emergence of the Relationship Economy: The New Order of Things to Come*. Retrieved from http://www.happyabout.com/RelationshipEconomy.php

AlliedCrowds. (2015). *Developing World Crowdfunding-Sustainability through Crowdfunding*. Author.

AlliedCrowds. (2016a). *Developing World Crowdfunding Prosperity through Crowdfunding*. Author.

AlliedCrowds. (2016b). *Crowdfunding Annual Report January 2016*. Retrieved from http://alliedcrowds.com/reports

Alm, J. (2011). *Municipal Finance of Urban Infrastructure: Knowns and Unknowns*. Working Paper 1103. Department of Economics, Tulane University, New Orleans, LA.

Almerico, K. (2014, March 3). *Your Crowdfunding Campaign Is Doomed Without This*. Retrieved January 31, 2017, from Entrepreneur Middle East: https://www.entrepreneur.com/article/231882

Alsamani, A. S., & Daif-Allah, A. S. (2016). Introducing Project-based Instruction in the Saudi ESP Classroom: A Study in Qassim University. *English Language Teaching, 9*(1), 2016.

Andriani, L. (2013). *Social Capital: A Road map of Theoretical Frameworks and Empirical Limitations*. Working Papers in Management. Birkbeck University of London.

Annez, P. (2010). *Financing Indian Cities: Opportunities and Constraints in an Nth Best World*. The World Bank. Policy Research Working Paper 5474.

Anonymous. (2010). *About the Project*. Retrieved 04 01, 2017, from Yoza Project: https://m4lit.wordpress.com/about-the-project/

Anonymous. (2012). CCK releases 2nd quarter ICT sector statistics for 2011/2012. Communications Commission of Kenya.

Anonymous. (2013). *Vodacom Tanzania reports five million M-PESA subs; transactions top USD823m*. Retrieved 04 06, 2017, from TeleGeography: https://www.telegeography.com/products/commsupdate/articles/2013/05/02/vodacom-tanzania-reports-five-million-m-pesa-subs-transactions-top-usd823m/

Anonymous. (2015). *Why does Kenya lead the world in mobile money?* Retrieved 02 03, 2017, from Economist: http://www.economist.com/blogs/economist-explains/2013/05/economist-explains-18

Anonymous. (n.d.). *Search Traffic: Mobile Friendly Test Tool.* Retrieved December 2016, from Search Console Help: https://support.google.com/webmasters/answer/6352293?hl=en

Anozie, C. E. E. (2013). Christian Church: A Catalyst for Economic Development in Nigeria. *African Research Review, 7*(4), 274–287. doi:10.4314/afrrev.v7i4.17

Appsafrica. (2016). *Crowdfunding in Africa is gaining momentum.* Accessed 20/05/17 at https://www.appsafrica.com/crowdfunding-in-africa-is-gaining-momentum/

Appsafrica. (2016). *Crowdfunding in Africa is gaining momentum.* Available at: https://www.appsafrica.com/crowdfunding-in-africa-is-gaining-momentum/

Ardeman, D. (2016). *Why Chinese equity crowdfunding is taking its lead from the UK – and what challenges the sector faces.* Accessed 20/05/17 at http://www.cityam.com/money/crowdfunding

Arinola, O., & Obiako, N. (2017). *eHealth Africa (eHA) is collaborating with the World Health Organization (WHO), Bill and Melinda Gates Foundation (BMGF), AEEP (2014): Status Report Africa-EU Energy Partnership. Progress, achievements and future perspectives.* Retrieved from http://www.iass-potsdam.de/sites/default/files/files/study_march_2016_the_future_of_africas_energy_supply.pdf

Arvanitis, Y. (2015). Financing for innovation: What can be done for African SMEs? *AEB, 6*(6), 1–8.

ASICS. (2016). Annual Survey of India's City-Systems 2016: Shaping India's Urban Agenda. ASICS.

Athwal, N. (2016). *A beginner's guide to real estate crowdfunding.* Available online: https://www.landlordology.com/real-estate-crowdfunding/

Atkinson, A. B. (2015). *The colonial legacy: Income inequality in former British African colonies.* Research Brief based on the WIDER Working Paper 2014/45.

Babu Das Augustine. (2017, August 1). *Dubai launches a regulatory framework for crowdfunding platforms.* Retrieved from http://gulfnews.com/business/sectors/banking/dubai-launches-regulatory-framework-for-crowdfunding-platforms-1.2067534

Bafana, B. (2016). Africa's Cities of the Future: Proper Planning Key to Sustainable Cities. *Africa Renewal, 30*(April), 4–5. doi:10.18356/59905b7c-en

Bagchi, D. S. (2014, June 24). *Public Garden Maintainance Through PPP - A case of Ahemdabad.* Retrieved from https://dhwanishahbagchi.wordpress.com

Balogun, A. (2016). *Infrastructure development in Nigeria: Better late than never.* Retrieved from http://www.lexology.com/1166035/author/Adekalu_Balogun/

Bandyopadhyay, S. (2014, May). *Municipal Finance in India: Some Critical Issues.* Retrieved from International Center for Public Policy (Working Paper 14-21): http://scholarworks.gsu.edu/cgi/viewcontent.cgi?article=1010&context=icepp

Bandyopadhyay, S., & Rao, M. (2009). *Fiscal Health of Selected Indian Cities.* Policy Research Working Paper No. 4863. Washington, DC: World Bank.

Bångens, D. L., & Söderberg, B. (2008). *Mobile Banking – Financial Services for the Unbanked? Report, The Swedish Program for ICT in Developing Regions.* SPIDER.

Barber, B. (2004). *Strong Democracy: Participatory Politics for a New Age.* University of California Press.

Barker, A., Krull, G., & Mallinson, B. (2005). Proposed theoretical model for m-learning adoption in developing countries. *mLearn 2005, 4th world conference on m-learning.*

Barnett, C. (2015). Trends Show Crowdfunding To Surpass VC In 2016. *Forbes.*

Barry, J. S. (2014, April). Crowdsourcing in the 21st Century. *The CPA Journal*, 5.

Bassett, K. (2014, March). Prepare to Share. *Managementtoday.com*, 35-38.

Baud, I., & Navtej, N. (2008). Negotiated spaces for representation in Mumbai: Ward committees, advanced locality management and the politics of middle-class activism. *Environment and Urbanization, 20*(2), 483–499. doi:10.1177/0956247808096124

Bauwens, M. and Lievens, J. (2015). *Sauver le monde, Vers une société post-capitaliste avec le peer-to-peer.* Paris: Les liens qui liberent, Editorial.

Behrend, T. S., Sharek, D. J., Meade, A. W., & Wiebe, E. N. (2011). The viability of crowdsourcing for survey research. *Behavior Research Methods, 43*(3), 800–813. doi:10.3758/s13428-011-0081-0 PMID:21437749

Belcher, D. D. (2004). Trends in teaching English for specific purposes. *Annual Review of Applied Linguistics, 24*, 165–186. doi:10.1017/S026719050400008X

Belleflamme, P., Lambert, T., & Schwienbacher, A. (2010). *Crowdfunding: An Industrial Organization Perspective.* Prepared for the workshop Digital Business Models: Understanding Strategies, Paris, France.

Belleflamme, P., Lambert, T., & Schwienbacher, A. (2011) Crowdfunding: tapping the right crowd. Center for Operations Research and Econometrics (CORE).

Belleflamme, P., Lambert, T., & Schwienbacher, A. (2012). *Crowdfunding: Tapping the Right Crowd.* Retrieved from http://innovation-regulation2.telecom-paristech.fr/wp-content/uploads/2012/10/Belleflamme-CROWD-2012-06-20_SMJ.pdf

Belleflamme, P., Omrani, N., & Peitz, M. (2015). *The Economics of Crowdfunding Platforms.* Core Discussion Paper 2015/15, CORE, Voice du Roman Pays.

Belleflamme, P., Lambert, T., & Schwienbacher, A. (2013). Crowdfunding: Tapping the right crowd. *Journal of Business Venturing.*

Benevolo, L. (1967). *Origins of Modern Town Planning.* Cambridge, MA: MIT Press.

Benna & Garba. (2015). Population Growth and Rapid Urbanization in Developing World. IGI Global. doi:10.4018/978-1-5225-0187-9.ch014

Benna, U. G. (2013). Timbuktu, the African Medieval Knowledge City: The Role of Knowledge Development Actors. *Journal of Information & Knowledge Management, 12*(3).

Benna, U. G., & Garba, S. B. (Eds.). (2016). *Population Growth and Rapid Urbanization in the Developing World.* IGI Global. doi:10.4018/978-1-5225-0187-9

Berkey, J. P. (1992). *The transmission of Knowledge in Medieval Cairo: A Social History of Islamic Education.* Princeton University Press. doi:10.1515/9781400862580

Berliner, J. (1977). Internal migration: A comparative disciplinary view. In A. Brown & E. Neuberger (Eds.), *Internal migration: A comparative perspective* (pp. 443–446). New York: Academic Press. doi:10.1016/B978-0-12-137350-4.50028-7

Berndt, A. (2016). Crowdfunding in the African Context: A New Way to Fund Ventures. In Entrepreneurship and SME Management Across Africa (pp. 31-49). Academic Press.

Berndt, A., & Mbassana, M. (2016). Crowdfunding: the beliefs of Rwandan entrepreneurs. *East Africa Research Papers in Business, Entrepreneurship and Management*. Available at: http://ju.se/download/18.b50f80815532427699617f/1465522955791/EARP-BEM+2016-05+Adele.pdf

Berndt, A., & Mbassana, M. (2016). *Crowdfunding: The Beliefs of Rwandan Entrepreneurs*. Retrieved from https://www.researchgate.net/publication/310597267_Crowdfunding_The_Beliefs_of_Rwandan_Entrepreneurs

Best, J., Neiss, S., Swart, R., Lambkin, A., & Raymond, S. (2013). *Crowdfunding's potential for the developing world*. InfoDev. Retrieved from http://documents.worldbank.org/curated/en/409841468327411701/Crowdfundings-potential-for-the-developing-world

Bhaskar, U. (2017, May 15). *94 cities get rated as urban local bodies prepare for municipal bonds*. Retrieved May 21, 2017, from Livemint: http://www.livemint.com/Politics/KjJbJIc7eENNMAqTonjqcN/94-cities-get-Crisil-ratings-as-urban-local-bodies-prepare-f.html

Bhatia, S. (2016, December 16). *The Genesis and Rise of Crowdfunding*. Retrieved July 16, 2017, from Linkedin: https://www.linkedin.com/pulse/genesis-rise-crowdfunding-shobhit-bhatia-msc

Bijkerk, W. (2014). *Risks and Benefits of Crowd-funding*. Tokyo: International Organisation of Securities Commissions.

Bird, R. M. (1999). *Rethinking Subnational Taxes: A new Look at Tax Assignment*. IMF Working Paper WP99/165. IMF, Washington, DC.

Bollier, D. (2011). Intellectual Property in the Digital Age. In *Key Issues in the Arts and Entertainment Industry*. London: Goodfellow Publishers. Retrieved from http://bollier.org/ip-digital-age-book-chapter

Bosha, E. (2015). *Factors influencing continuous data collection for a public safety crowdsourcing smart city project* (Doctoral dissertation). University of Fort Hare, South Africa.

Boston Consulting Group (BCG). (2017). *Going Beyond The Rhetoric*. Retrieved from https://www.bcg.com/publications/2017/new-globalization-going-beyond-rhetoric.aspx

Botsman, R. (2012, August 20). *Welcome to the new reputation economy*. Retrieved 02 21, 2015, from http://www.wired.co.uk/magazine/archive/2012/09/features/welcome-to-the-new-reputation-economy?page=all

Botsman, R. (2013). *The Sharing Economy Lacks a Shared Definition*. Retrieved 02 12, 2015, from http://www.fastcoexist.com/3022028/the-sharing-economy-lacks-a-shared-definition

Botsman, R. (2014, September). Sharing's Not Just for Startups. *Harvard Business Review*, 23–25.

Botsman, R., & Rogers, R. (2010). *What's Mine Is Yours: The Rise of Collaborative Consumption*. New York: Harper Business.

Boum, E. (2016). *Crowdfunding in Africa: Fundraising goes Digital in Africa: The Emergence of Africa-Based Crowdfunding Platforms*. Johannesburg: Afrikstart.

Bourdieu, P. (1990) *Capital Social, Ecole et Space Culturel*. Paris: XXIe Siecle.

Brabham, D. C. (2009). Crowdsourcing the public participation process for planning projects. *Planning Theory*, *8*(3), 242–262. doi:10.1177/1473095209104824

Bradshaw, Y. (1987). Urbanization and underdevelopment: A global study of modernization, urban bias, and economic dependency. *American Sociological Review*, *52*(2), 224–239. doi:10.2307/2095451

Bright, J. (2015). *Why Africa may be on the verge of an Internet boom*. Retrieved from http://fortune.com/2015/02/16/nigeria- internet-startups/

BringBackOurGirls. (2017). *Map showing location of Chibok, Borno, etc*. Retrieved from https://www.pinterest.com/pin/433541901601586039/

Brown, J. S., & Duguid, P. (1991). Organizational learning and communities of practice: Toward a unified view of working, learning and innovation. *Organization Science*, *2*(1), 40–57. doi:10.1287/orsc.2.1.40

Brown, J. S., & Duguid, P. (2000). *The Social Life of Information*. Boston, MA: Harvard Business School Press.

Bruton, G., Khavul, S., Siegel, D., & Wright, M. (2014). New Financial Alternatives in Seeding Entrepreneurship: Microfinance, Crowdfunding, and Peer-to-Peer Innovations. *Entrepreneurship Theory and Practice*, 9–26.

Budiu, R. (2015, March 22). *The State of Mobile User Experience*. Retrieved January 26, 2017, from Nielsen Norman Group: https://www.nngroup.com/articles/mobile-usability-update/

Buhr, W. (2003). *What is infrastructure?VolkswirtschaftlicheDiskussionsbeiträge 107-03*. Universität Siegen, FakultätWirtschaftswissenschaften, Wirtschaftsinformatik und Wirtschaftsre.

Burtch, G., Ghose, A., & Wattal, S. (2013). An empirical examination of the antecedents and consequences of contribution patterns in crowd-funded markets. *Information Systems Research*, *24*(3), 499–519. doi:10.1287/isre.1120.0468

Burt, R. (2000). *The network structure of social capital. In Research in Organisational Behaviour* (Vol. 22). Greenwich, CT: JAI Press.

Busarovs, A. (2011). Crowdsourcing as user-driven innovation,New business Philosophy's model. *Journal of Business and Management*, *4*, 53–60.

Business Wire. (2017). *Mastercard Launches Mobile Marketplace to Digitize East Africa's Agricultural Sector*. Retrieved from http://www.businesswire.com/news/home/20170116005049/en/Mastercard-Launches-Mobile-Marketplace-Digitize-East-Africa%E2%80%99

Cambridge Centre for Alternative Finance (CCAF). (2017). *Africa and Middle East Alternative Finance Benchmarking Report*. Retrieved from https://www.jbs.cam.ac.uk/faculty-research/centres/alternative-finance/publications/africa-middle-east/#.Wd9nZFuCyvg

Cambridge Centre for Alternative Finance (CCAF). (2017). *Crowdfunding in East Africa*. Retrieved from https:// www.jbs.cam.ac.uk/faculty-research/centres/alternative-finance/ publications/crowdfunding-in-east-africa/#.WRc4_9wlFY0

Cambridge Centre for Alternative Finance (CCAF). (2017). *Crowdfunding in East Africa: Regulation and Policy for Market Development: Reducing poverty through financial sector development*. London: Cambridge Centre for Alternative Finance.

Cambridge Centre for Alternative Finance (CCAF). (2017). *The Africa and Middle East Alternative Finance Benchmarking Report*. London: Cambridge Centre for Alternative Finance.

Cambridge Centre for Alternative Finance (CCAF). (2017a). *Alternative Finance*. Retrieved from http://Jbs.cam.ac.uk

Cambridge Centre for Alternative Finance (CCAF). (2017b). *Africa and Middle East Alternative Finance Benchmarking Report*. Retrieved from https://www.jbs.cam.ac.uk/faculty-research/centres/alternative-finance/publications/africa-middle-east/#.Wbr9cbIjGT8

Campbell, S. (1996). Green Cities, Growing Cities, Just Cities? Urban Planning and the Contradictions of Sustainable Development. *Journal of the American Planning Association*, *62*(3), 296–312. doi:10.1080/01944369608975696

Canada Media Fund. (n.d.). *Using social media effectively for your crowdfunding campaign.* Retrieved January 31, 2017, from Canada Meida Fund: http://crowdfunding.cmf-fmc.ca/best_practices/using-social-media-effectively-for-your-crowdfunding-campaign

Cantino, V., Rossignoli, C., & Ricciardi, F. (2017). Organizational learning for the common good: an emerging approach to sustainability and resilience. In *IFKAD 2017 Special Tracks Proposal.* Retrieved from http://www.ifkad.org/Tracks/?track=01

Carrillo, F. J. (2002). Capital systems: implications for a global knowledge agenda. Journal of Knowledge Management, 6(4).

Carrillo, F. J. (2004). Capital cities: a taxonomy of capital accounts for knowledge cities. Journal of Knowledge Management, 8(5), 28-46. doi:10.1108/13673270410558738

Carrillo, F. J. (Ed.). (2006). Knowledge Cities. Approaches, Experiences and Perspectives. Burlington, MA: Butterworth-Heinemann (Elsevier).

Carrillo, J., Yigitcanlar, T., Garcia, B., & Lonnqvist, A. (2014). *Knowledge & the City. Concepts and Applications of Knowledge-Based Development.* Routledge.

Castells, M. (2004). *The Network Society: A Cross-Cultural Perspective.* Cheltenham, UK: Edward Edgar. doi:10.4337/9781845421663

CCAF. (2016). Financial Statements for the year ended March 31, 2016. Cambridge Centre for Alternative.

CCAF. (2017). *The Africa and the Middle East - Alternative Finance Benchmarking Report. Cambridge Centre for Alternative Finance, University of Cambridge Judge Business School.* Cambridge Centre for Alternative Finance.

Census of India. (2011). Primary Census Abstract for Slum. Author.

Certoma, C., Corsini, F., & Rizzi, F. (2015). Crowdsourcing urban sustainability. Data, people and technologies in participatory governance. *Futures*, *74*, 93–106. doi:10.1016/j.futures.2014.11.006

Cervantes, M.E., Casillas, L., Weigend, J., & Hoppenstedt, S (2016). *Open Source Cities: Monterrey 2021.* Prospectiva Estratégica, ITESM.

Chaligha, A. E. (2014). *Transparency and Accountability in Local Governance in Tanzania. Repoa Brief 45(2014).* Dar es Salaam: Repoa.

Chan, K. L. (2017). *The World's Most Powerful Languages.* Retrieved from https://knowledge.insead.edu/leadership-organisations/the-worlds-most-powerful-languages-6156

Chatzkel, J. (2004). Greater Phoenix as a knowledge capital. *Journal of Knowledge Management, 8*(5), 28-46.

Chenal, J. (2016). *Capitalizing on Urbanization: The Importance of Planning Infrastructure, and Finance for Africa's Growing Cities.* Available from https://www.brookings.edu/wp-content/uploads/2016/05/foresightafrica2016_ch4-1.pdf

Cheney, C. (2017). *What can the sharing economy bring to emerging markets?* Retrieved May 12, 2017, from https://www.devex.com/news/what-can-the-sharing-economy-bring-to-emerging-markets-89214

Cheney, C. (2017, March 9). *What can the sharing economy bring to emerging markets?* Retrieved 05 05, 2017, from https://www.devex.com/news/what-can-the-sharing-economy-bring-to-emerging-markets-89214

Cheung, C. M., Lee, M. K., & Rabjohn, N. (2008). The impact of electronic word-of-mouth. *Internet Research, 18*(3), 229–247. doi:10.1108/10662240810883290

Chibango, C. (2016). Prosperity Gospel, a Pathway out of a Socioeconomic Crisis? The Case of PHD Ministries of Walter Magaya, Zimbabwe. *Modern Research Studies, 3*(1), 55–82.

Chilton, S. (2009, November). Crowdsourcing is radically changing the geodata landscape: case study of OpenStreetMap. *Proceedings of the UK 24th International Cartography Conference.*

Chirisa, I., Bobo, T., & Matamanda, A. (2016). Policies and strategies to Manage Urban insecurity: Focus on selected African Cities. *Journal of Public Policy in Africa, 3*(2), 93–106.

Chuene, D., & Mtsweni, J. (2015, May). The adoption of crowdsourcing platforms in South Africa. In *IST-Africa Conference, 2015* (pp. 1–9). IEEE. doi:10.1109/ISTAFRICA.2015.7190561

Clark, B. (2011). *The History & Evolution of Crowdfunding.* Retrieved from http://mashable.com/2011/09/15/crowdfunding-history/#0u8WF.phe8qf

Clark, S. (2010). *Jerome Bruner: Teaching, Learning and the Spiral Curriculum.* Retrieved from https://sheldonclark.files.wordpress.com/2011/07/jerome-bruner-teaching-learning-and-the- spiral-curriculum2.pdf

Clarkson, N. (2015). *A brief History of Crowdfunding.* Retrieved from https://www.virgin.com/entrepreneur/brief-history-crowdfunding

Classy. (n.d.). *The Big Social Media Guide For Nonprofits.* Classy.

Cnaan, R. A., Handy, F., & Wadsworth, M. (1996). Defining who is a volunteer; Conceptual and empirical considerations. *Nonprofit and Voluntary Sector Quarterly, 25*(3), 364–383. doi:10.1177/0899764096253006

Cobo, C. (2013). Gobierno Abierto: de la transparencia a la inteligencia cívica. *Info DF*, 11.

Cohen, B., & Muñoz, P. (2016). *The Emergence of the Urban Entrepreneur.* Retrieved from https://books.google.co.in/books?id=tBYsDAAAQBAJ&pg=PA161&lpg=PA161&dq=World+Bank+Urban+Crowd+Funding&source=bl&ots=cpOt-2N89y&sig=fB3Pr86ywtrRP6-6AJRle-5_x4U&hl=en&sa=X&ved=0ahUKEwiwl_nqqvnTAhWIPY8KHWozCaYQ6AEIRDAF#v=onepage&q=World%20Bank%20Urban%20Crowd%20Funding&f=false

Coleman, J. S. (1988). Social capital and the creation of human capital. *American Journal of Sociology, 94*, 95–120. doi:10.1086/228943

Collaborative Consumption. (2015). Retrieved 02 10, 2015, from http://www.collaborativeconsumption.com/about/

Coopers, P. (2005). *Cities of the Future. Global competition Local leadership.* Available from www.pwc.com

Correia de Freitas, J., & Amado, M. (2013). *Crowdfunding in urban planning: Opportunities and Obstacles.* Conference Paper 2013.

Correia de Freitas, J., & Amado, M. (2013, July). Crowdfunding in urban planning: Opportunities and Obstacles. *RC43 Annual Conference,* 10-12.

Coxhead, A. (2012). ESP and Vocabulary. In The Handbook of English for Specific Purposes. John Wiley.

Crooks, A., Pfoser, D., Jenkins, A., Croitoru, A., Stefanidis, A., Smith, D., & Lamprianidis, G. et al. (2015). Crowdsourcing urban form and function. *International Journal of Geographical Information Science, 29*(5), 720–741. doi:10.1080/13658816.2014.977905

Crowdfunding Center. (n.d.). *AFKARMENA*. Retrieved from http://www.thecrowdfundingcenter.com/?page=platform&domain=afkarmena.com

CrowdfundingHub. (2016). *Current State of Crowdfunding in Europe: An Overview of the Crowdfunding Industry in more than 25 Countries: Trends, Volumes and Regulations*. CrowdfundingHub, Armsterdam.

Crowdfuning hub. (2017). *Current State of Crowdfunding in Europe. An overview of the Crowdfunding Industry in 27 Countries: Trends, Volumes, and Regulations*. Retrieved from http://www.crowdfundinghub.eu/

Crowdsourcing, LLC. (2012, May). *Crowd Funding Industry Report.* Research Report - Abridged Version. Author.

Cummings, S., Maile Petty, M., & Walker, B. (2014). Innovation is not the only thing. In C. Bilton & S. Cummings (Eds.), *Handbook of management and creativity* (pp. 97–127). Cheltenham, UK: Edward Elgar.

Cuso International. (2016). *E-Connect: Cuso International's E-Volunteering Guide*. Retrieved from http://www. cusointernational.org/docs/default-source/publications/Training-Resources/e-volunteering-toolkit.pdf?sfvrsn=4

DAAOA. (n.d.). The Trans-Saharan Gold Trade (Seventh–Fourteenth Centuries). In *Heilbrunn Timeline of Art History*. New York: The Metropolitan Museum of Art. Retrieved from http://www.metmuseum.org/toah/hd/gold/hd_gold.htm

Dabán, T., & Hélis, J. (2009). *A Public Financial Management Framework for Resource-Producing Countries.* IMF Working Paper, WP/10/72. International Monetary Fund.

Daily Trust. (2017). *FG to engage 200,000 community health volunteers*. Retrieved from www.dailytrust.com.ng/news/

Daucettee, J. (2015). *Crowdfunding for Public Goods and Philanthropy*. Retrieved from https://medium.com/the-digital-civil-society-lab/crowdfunding-for-public-goods-and-philanthropy-c7c7c5976898

Davenport, T., & Prusak, L. (1998). *Working Knowledge: How organisations manage what they know*. Boston: Harvard Business School Press.

Davies, R. (2014). Civic crowdfunding as a marketplace for participation in urban development. Center for Work, Technology and Organizations, Stanford University.

Davies, R. (2014). *Civic Crowdfunding: Participatory Communities, Entrepreneurs and the Political Economy of Place.* Center for Work, Technology and Organizations, MIT Center for Civic Media. 10.2139/ssrn.2434615

Davies, R. (2014, September 1). *Civic crowdfunding as a marketplace for participation in urban development*. Stanford.

Davies, R. (2014b, May 9). *Civic Crowdfunding – Four Things We Know, Two Things We Don't.* Retrieved January 31, 2017, from RodrigoDavies.com: http://rodrigodavies.com/blog/2014/05/09/civic-crowdfunding-four-things-we-know-two-things-we-dont.html

Davies, R. (2014c, Oct. 21). *Three Provocations for Civic Crowdfunding.* Retrieved from https://rodrigodavies.com/three-provocations-for-civic-crowdfunding-fdff45dd4008

Davis, K. (1965). The urbanization of the human population. *Scientific American, 13*(3), 41–53.

Debray, A., Kwon, H., & Gill, R. (2014). *Mobile Money opportunities for Mobile Operators.* White Paper, Huawei.

Deininger, K., & Byerlee, D. (2011). *Rising Global Interestin Farmland: Can It Yield Sustainable and Equitable Benefits?* Washington, DC: The World Bank. doi:10.1596/978-0-8213-8591-3

Deloitte. (2016). *Using the crowd in enterprise.* Retrieved from https://www2.deloitte.com/content/.../deloitte-uk-crowsourcing-using-the-crowd.pdf

Desai, S. (2014, August). Effects of latest trends on sharing economy. *Siliconindia*, 10.

Dewey, J. (1949). *Knowing and the Known*. American institute for Economic Research. Available on line at: http://www.aier.org/research

Doan, A., Ramakrishnan, R., & Halevy, A. Y. (2011). Crowdsourcing systems on the World-Wide Web. *Communications of the ACM*, *54*(4), 86–96. doi:10.1145/1924421.1924442

Dobbs, R., & Sankhe, S. (2010). *Comparing urbanization in China and India. McKinsey Quarterly.*

Douglas, D. (2012). ESP and Assessment. In The Handbook of English for Specific Purposes. John Wiley.

Doulingo.com. (2017). *Duolingo.com Traffic Statistics*. Retrieved from http://www.alexa.com/siteinfo/duolingo.com

Dowla, A. (2006). In credit we trust: Building social capital by Grameen Bank in Bangladesh. *Journal of Socio-Economics*, *35*(1), 102–122. doi:10.1016/j.socec.2005.12.006

Dubois, E., Schor, J., & Carfagna, L. (2014, Spring). Connected consumption a sharing economy takes hold. *Rotman Management*, 50-55.

Dudley-Evans, T., & St. John, M. J. (1998). *Developments in English for Specific Purposes: A Multidisciplinary Approach*. Cambridge, UK: Cambridge University Press.

Dutt, A. (2001). *Global urbanization: Trends, form and density gradients*. Allahabad: Professor R. N. Dubey Foundation.

Dvir, R. (2006). Knowledge City seen as a collage of Human Knowledge Moments. In Knowledge Cities. Approaches, Experiences and Perspectives. Burlington, MA: Butterworth-Heinemann (Elsevier). doi:10.1016/B978-0-7506-7941-1.50022-1

Dvir, R., & Pasher, E. (2004). Innovation engines for knowledge cities: an innovation ecology perspective. Journal of Knowledge Management, 8(5), 16-27.

Easley, D., & Kleinberg, J. (2010). *Networks, Crowds and Markets. Reasoning about a Highly Connected World*. Cambridge, UK: Cambridge University Press. doi:10.1017/CBO9780511761942

Edgar, J., Murphy, J., & Keating, M. (2016). Comparing Traditional and Crowdsourcing Methods for Pretesting Survey Questions. *SAGE Open*, *6*(4), 2158244016671770. doi:10.1177/2158244016671770

Edvardsson, B., & Olsson, J. (1996, April). The key concept for new service development. *Service Industries Journal*, *16*(2), 2. doi:10.1080/02642069600000019

Edvinsson, L. (2002). *Corporate Longitude*. Harlow: Pearson Education.

Edvinsson, L., & Grafstrom, G. (1999). *Accounting of Minds*. Stockholm, Sweden: Skandia.

Ellis, P., & Roberts, M. (2016). *Leveraging Urbanization in South Asia - Global Economic Prospects, 2016*. World Bank.

EMBARQ Network. (2017). *You too can build a sustainable city through crowdfunding*. Available online: http://www.smartcitiesdive.com/ex/sustainablecitiescollective/friday-fun-you-too-can-build-sustainable-city-through-crowdfunding/330406/

Endstrom, W. (n.d.). *Digital Persuasion: How Social Media Motivates Action and Drives Support for Causes*. Retrieved from Waggener Edstrom: http://waggeneredstrom.com/downloads/DSCA-Summary.pdf

Engeström, Y. (2004). New forms of learning in Co-configuration work. *Journal of Workplace Learning*, *16*(1/2), 11–21. doi:10.1108/13665620410521477

Ergazakis, K., Metaxiotis, K., & Psarras, J. (2004). Towards knowledge cities: conceptual analysis and success stories. Journal of Knowledge Management, 8(5), 5-15.

Erian, P. (2015). Social innovation. Seismic: shake up your city! Seismic. In The Civic Economy Opportunities and challenges for European cities. Academic Press.

Ericson. (2015). *Sub-Saharan Africa Ericsson Mobility Report. Market Overview.* Retrieved from www.ericsson.com/res/docs/2015/mobility-report/emr-nov-2015-regional-report-sub-saharan-africa.pdf

Estellés-Arolas, E., & González-Ladrón-de-Guevara, F. (2012). Towards an Integrated Crowdsourcing Definition. *Journal of Information Science, 38*(2), 189–200.

Estelles-Arolas, E., & Gonzalez-Ladron-De-Guevara, F. (2012). Towards an integrated crowdsourcing definition. *Journal of Information Science, 38*(2), 189–200. doi:10.1177/0165551512437638

Etzensperger, C. (2014). *Microfinance Market Outlook 2015.* Zurich: responsAbility Investments AG.

Eureeca. (n.d.). Retrieved from https://eureeca.com/Crowd-funding-pages/FrontEnd/home/FAQ/Investor/English

Fadel, S., & Rajab, H. (2017). *Investigating the English Language Needs of the Female Students at the Faculty of Computing and Information Technology at King Abdulaziz University in Saudi Arabia.* Retrieved from http://www.ccsenet.org/journal/index.php/elt/issue/view/1813

Feak, C. B. (2012). ESP and Speaking. In The Handbook of English for Specific Purposes. John Wiley.

Felber, C. (2012). *The economy of the common good.* Bilbao: Ed. Deusto.

Feresu, S. B. (Ed.). (2010). *Zimbabwe Environmental Outlook: Our Environment, Everybody's Responsibility. Executive Summary. The government of the Republic of Zimbabwe.* Harare: The Ministry Of Environment and Natural Resources Management.

Finke, R. (2003). *Spiritual Capital: Definitions, Applications, and New Frontiers.* Prepared for the *Spiritual Capital Planning Meeting.*

Finley, K. (2013). *Trust in the Sharing Economy: An Exploratory Study* (MA Thesis). University of Warwick.

Fjeldstad, O., Chambas, G., & Brun, J. (2014). *Local Government Taxation in sub-Saharan Africa: A Review and an Agenda for Research.* CMI Working Paper 2014:2. CMI.

Fleming, M. (2013, April 27). *UPDATE: Zach Braff's 'Wish I Was Here' Kickstarter Hits $2 Million Goal In 3 Days.* Retrieved April 09, 2017, from Deadline: http://deadline.com/2013/04/zach-braff-goes-kickstarter-route-for-wish-i-was-here-482485/

Florida, R. (1995). Towards the Learning Region. *Futures, 27*(5), 527–536. doi:10.1016/0016-3287(95)00021-N

Flörkemeier, T. (2012). *Local Food Systems and Community Supported Agriculture.* Freiburg: Albert-Ludwigs-Universität Freiburg.

Flowerdew, L. (2012). Needs Analysis and Curriculum Development in ESP. In The Handbook of English for Specific Purposes. John Wiley.

FORM 10-Q. (2016). *Quarterly Report Pursuant to Section 13 or 15(D) of the Securities Exchange Act of 1934:* LinkedIn Corporation.

Fox, J. (2008). *Accountability Politics: Power and Voice in Rural Mexico.* Oxford Studies in Democratization Series.

Freund, B. (2007). *The African City: A History*. Cambridge, UK: Cambridge University Press. doi:10.1017/CBO9780511618307

Fsdafrica.org. (2016). *East Africa Crowdfunding Landscape Study: Reducing Poverty Through Financial Sector Development*. Retrieved from https://www.fsdafrica.org/wp-content/uploads/2016/10/16-11-07-Crowdfunding_Report-final-1.pdf

Fuel a Dream. (2017). *Fuel a Dream - Suryoday Parivar Case-Study*. Retrieved July 15, 2017, from Lets Make a 8KM Canal for 700 Drought-Hit Farmers in 15 Days: https://www.fueladream.com/home/campaign/216

Fund for Unity. (2017). *Fund for Unity Crowd Funding Platform*. Retrieved from http://fundforunity.statueofunity.in/

Gallardo, J. (2001). *A Framework for Regulating Microfinance Institutions:The Experience in Ghana and the Philippines*. The World Bank.

Gallion, A. B., & Eisner, S. (1996). *The Urban Pattern*. Delhi, India: CBS Publishers.

Gándara, G. Y., & Osorio, F. (2014). *M étodos prospectivos. Manual para el estudio y la construcción del futuro*. Paidós.

García Nales, M. C. (2010). *Gobernanza local: alcances y limitaciones conceptuales*. San Luis Potosí: El Colegio de San Luis.

Garcia, B. (2007, October). Working and Learning in a Knowledge City: A Framework for Knowledge Workers. *Journal of Knowledge Management, 11*(5), 18–30. doi:10.1108/13673270710819771

Garg, S. (2007). Overview of Urban Infrastructure Finance in India. In Financing Cities: Fiscal Responsibility and Urban Infrastructure in Brazil, China, India, Poland and South Africa (pp. 108-157). The World Bank.

Gasparro, K. (2015). *Funding Municipal Infrastructure: Integrating Project Finance and Crowdfunding*. National Science Foundation.

Gellers, J. C. (2016). Crowdsourcing global governance: Sustainable development goals, civil society, and the pursuit of democratic legitimacy. *International Environmental Agreement: Politics, Law and Economics, 16*(3), 415–432. doi:10.1007/s10784-016-9322-0

Georgetown University & Waggener Edstrom. (2012). *Digital Persuation How Social Media Motivates Action and Drives Support for Causes*. Waggener Edstrom Worldwide and Georgetown University, School of Continuous studies, Center for Social Impact Communication.

Gerber, E. M., & Hui, J. S. (2012). *Crowdfunding: Motivations and Deterrents for Participation*. Retrieved from http://www.segal.northwestern.edu/media/pdf/2012/May /29/segal_report_12-02.pdf

Gerber, E. M., & Julie, H. (2013). *Crowdfunding: Motivations and deterrents for participation*. Retrieved from https://www.scholars.northwestern.edu/en/publications/crowdfunding-motivations-and-deterrents-for-participation

Gerber, E. M., Hui, J. S., & Kuo, P.-Y. (2012a). *Crowdfunding: Why People are Motivated to Participate*. Retrieved from http://www.segal.northwestern.edu/media/pdf/2012/May /29/segal_report_12-02.pdf

Gerstner, L. (2014, July). Cash In on the Sharing Economy. Money, 58-61.

Giddens, A. (1984). *The Constitution of Society: outline of the theory of structuration*. Berkeley, CA: University of California Press.

Giudici, G., Nava, R., Lamastra, C., & Vereco, C. (2012). *Crowdfunding: The New Frontier for Financing entrepreneurships?* Available at SSRN: http:// ssrn.com/abstract=2157429

Goh, C. M. (2012). ESP and Listening. In The Handbook of English for Specific Purposes. John Wiley.

Goldin, C. (2014). *Human Capital. Department of Economics Harvard University and National Bureau of Economic Research.*

Gollin-Kies, S. (2014). Methods reported in ESP research articles: A comparative survey of two leading journals. *English for Specific Purposes*, *36*, 27–34. doi:10.1016/j.esp.2014.04.001

Gonzalez, A. L., Izidoro, D., Willrich, R., & Santos, C. A. (2013, October). OurMap: Representing Crowdsourced Annotations on Geospatial Coordinates as Linked Open Data. CRIWG, 77-93.

Goodchild, M. F., & Glennon, J. A. (2010). Crowdsourcing geographic information for disaster response: A research frontier. *International Journal of Digital Earth*, *3*(3), 231–241. doi:10.1080/17538941003759255

Goodrich, R. (2013, February 26). *What is Crowdsourcing?* Retrieved 1 18, 2015, from http://www.businessnewsdaily.com/4025-what-is-crowdsourcing.html

Government of India (GoI). (2007). *Local governance: An inspiring journey into the future.* Government of India, Second administrative reform commission, 6th report.

Government of India (GoI). (2011). *Working Group on Environmental Sustainability of Indian Cities for the formulation of the 12th Five Year Plan. Ministry of Housing and Urban Poverty Alleviation Government of India (GoI). 2009. Report of the 13th Finance Commission.* New Delhi: Finance Commission India.

Government of India (GoI). (2015). *Housing for all (urban): Scheme guidelines 2015.* Ministry of Housing & Urban Poverty Alleviation. Government of India.

GPFI (Global Partnership for Financial Inclusion). (2016). *2016 Progress Report to G20 Leaders.* Retrieved from http://www.g20.utoronto.ca/2016/gpfi-progress-report.pdf

Gregson, J., & Jordaan, D. (2009). Exploring the Challenges and Opportunities of M-learning, Within an International Distance Education Programme. Mobile Learning: Transforming the Delivery of Education and Training.

Griffiths, H., Madden, P., & Howe, C. (2016). *Civic Crowdfunding - A guidebook for local authorities.* Retrieved September 6, 2017, from Catapult - Future Cities: http://about.spacehive.com/wp-content/uploads/2017/03/Civic-Crowdfunding_A-Guide-for-Local-Authorities.pdf

Griffiths, H. (2016). *Civic Crowdfunding: A guidebook for local authorities.* Future Cities Catapult.

Guardian. (2014). *Crowdfunding: Essential advice for charities.* Retrieved from https://www.theguardian.com/voluntary-sector- network/2014/sep/17/crowdfunding-charities-essential-advice-fundraising

Gundry, J. (2006). *Web 0.0 Social Media.* Paper from Knowledge Ability Ltd, Malmesbury, UK. Retrieved from www.knowab.co.uk/socialmedia.html

Gupta, A., Dalal, S., Basu, D., & Joseph, A. (2012). *Magarpatta City: Farmers direct investment (FDI).* Working paper No 384. Indian Institute of Management Bangalore.

Gupta, D. (2009, November 18). *JNNURM: Community participation fund.* Retrieved July 18, 2017, from India Water Portal: http://www.indiawaterportal.org/opportunities/jnnurm-community-participation-fund

GWEC. (2014). *Global Wind Energy Outlook 2014.* Greenpeace.

Halal, W. E. (2005). *Making sense of knowledge.* Bradford, UK: Emerald Publishing.

Hamari, J., Sjöklint, M., & Ukkonen, A. (2015). *The sharing economy: Why people participate in collaborative consumption.* Copenhagen: Social Science Research Network.

Hao, P. (2012). *Spatial evolution of urban villages in Shenzhen*. ITC dissertation number 205. ITC Printing Department.

Harriman. (2017, May 2). *Crowd Funding Municipal Projects; A Look at the Impact of CrowdFunded Infrastructure in Rotterdam*. Retrieved from http://harriman.com/inspirations/crowdfunding-municipal-projects-look-impact-crowdfunded-infrastructure-rotterdam/

Haski-Leventhal, D., & Bargal, D. (2008). The volunteer stages and transitions model: Organizational socialization of volunteers. *Human Relations*, *61*(1), 67–102. doi:10.1177/0018726707085946

Healey, P. (2010). *Making Better Places: The Planning Project in the Twenty-First Century*. Hampshire, UK: Palgrave Macmillan. doi:10.1007/978-1-137-01379-8

Helps, W. I., & Grant, E. S. (2013). *Crowdsourcing Curriculum Design*. Retrieved from http://micsymposium.org/mics_2013_Proceedings/submissions/mics20130_submission_23.pdf

Hemer, J. (2011). *A Snapshot on Crowdfunding*. Fraunhofer ISI Working Paper. Retrieved from http://www.legalefiscale.it/wp-content/uploads/2016/09/StudioCrowdfundig.pdf

Hensel, P. R., Allison, M. E., & Khanani, A. (2008). *Colonial Legacies and Territorial Claims*. Paper presented at the conference National Territory and Sovereignty: Sixty Years since the Founding of the Nation, Seoul, South Korea.

Herbst, J. (2008). *Government and Politics in Zimbabwe*. Harare: University of Zimbabwe Publications.

Herman, D. (2013). *Crowdfunding: Catalysing Growth, Investment and Access to Capital*. Toronto: Deepcentre.

Hijazi, A. T. (2014). *Islam in Perspective. Najashi: The King who supported Muslim emigrants*. Retrieved from http://www.arabnews.com/news/546951

Hirvela, A. (2012). ESP and Reading. In The Handbook of English for Specific Purposes. John Wiley.

Hossain, M., & Kauranen, I. (2015). Crowdsourcing: A comprehensive literature review. *Strategic Outsourcing*, *8*(1), 2–22. doi:10.1108/SO-12-2014-0029

Howard, E. (1902). *Garden Cities of Tomorrow*. London: Faber and Faber.

Howe, J. (2006). The Rise of Crowdsourcing. *Wired Magazine, 14*(6), 1-4.

Howe, J. (2006). The rise of crowdsourcing. *Wired Magazine*. Retrieved from http://www.wired.com/wired/archive/14.06/crowds_pr.html

Howe, J. (2008). *Crowdsourcing - How the Power of the Crowd is Driving the Future of Business*. Random House Business.

HPEC Report and Recommendations. (2011, September 29). *Urbanization in India - HPEC Report and Recommendations*. Isher Judge Ahluwalia.

Hufner, A. (2016). *Motivation for Financial Backing of Reward Crowdfunding Campaigns- Based on Data from Germany and Norway (A multiple case study)* (MS Thesis Report). University of Agder.

Hufner, A. (2016). *Motivation for Financial Backing of Reward Crowdfunding Campaigns- Based on Data from Germany and Norway (A multiple case study)* (MS Thesis). University of Agder.

Hui, J. S., Greenberg, M. D., & Gerber, E. M. (2014). *Understanding the role of Community in Crowdfunding Work*. Retrieved from https://egerber.mech.northwestern.edu/wp-content/uploads/2012/11/Gerber_UnderstandingtheRoleofCommunityinCrowdfundingWork.pdf

Human Service Solutions. (n.d.). *Advantages of Mobile Website Optimization*. Retrieved January 26, 2017, from Human Service Solutions: https://www.hswsolutions.com/services/mobile-web-development/advantages/

Hung-Yi, C. (n.d.). *Crowdfunding and its Interaction with Urban Development*. Nagoya University.

Hussain, A., & Lawrence, J. (2013). *The Islamic Development Bank Assisting Private Sector Growth in Africa*. Retrieved from http://www.klgates.com/the-islamic-development-bank-assisting-private-sector- growth-in-africa-11-05-2013/

Hustinx, L., Cnaan, R. A., & Handy, F. (2010). Navigating Theories of Volunteering: A Hybri Map for a Complex Phenomenon. *Journal for the Theory of Social Behaviour*, *40*(4), 410–434. doi:10.1111/j.1468-5914.2010.00439.x

Hutchinson, A. (2017, February 01). *Facebook Q4 Numbers – 1.86 Billion Active Users, 1.23 Billion Logging in Every Day*. Retrieved April 11, 2017, from Social Media Today: http://www.socialmediatoday.com/social-business/facebook-q4-numbers-186-billion-active-users-123-billion-logging-every-day

Hutchinson, T., & Waters, A. (1987). English for specific purposes: A learning-centered approach. Cambridge: Cambridge University Press. *Journal of Education and Practice*, *3*(6), 2012.

Huysman, M. H. (2003). Communities of Practice: Towards a second generation of Knowledge Management. Human Resource Development, 4(4).

Huysman, M., & Wulf, D. (2005). The role of Information Technology in building and sustaining the relational base of communities. The Information Society, (21), 81-89. doi:10.1080/01972240590925285

Huysman, M. H., & de Wit, D. (2004). Practices in Knowledge sharing: Towards a second generation of Knowledge Management. *Knowledge and Process Management*, *11*(2), 81–92. doi:10.1002/kpm.192

Hyland, K. (2012). ESP and Writing. In The Handbook of English for Specific Purposes. John Wiley.

Iannaccone, L. R., & Klick, J. (2003). *Spiritual Capital: An Introduction and Literature Review. Preliminary draft*. Paper prepared for the Spiritual Capital Planning Meeting.

IEA. (2014). *Africa Energy Outlook. A Focus on Energy Prospects in Sub-Saharan Africa*. IEA.

IIHS. (n.d.). *Urban Transport in India - Challenges and Recommendations*. Retrieved from www.iihs.co.in

Ilarde, M. J. (2014). *ESP Course Design and skills and strategies*. Retrieved from https://www.slideshare.net/jaysonilarde/esp-course-design-and-skills-and-strategies

infoDev. (2013a). *Crowdfunding's Potential for the Developing World. World Bank, Finance and Private Sector Development Department*. Washington, DC: Information for Development Program (infoDev)/The World Bank.

infoDev. (2013b). *Crowdfunding's Potential for the Developing World. Finance and Private Sector Development Department*. Available at: http://www.infodev.org/infodev-files/wb_crowdfundingreport-v12.pdf

InformAfrica.com. (2015). *African History: Facts about the Great Walls of Benin*. Retrieved from http://www.informafrica.com/african-history/african-history-facts-about-the-great-walls-of-benin/

Ingwe, R. (2017). Crowdsourcing-Based Geoinformation, Disadvantaged Urbanisation Challenges, Subsaharan Africa: Theoretical Perspectives and Notes. *Quaestiones Geographicae*, *36*(1), 5–14. doi:10.1515/quageo-2017-0001

Insider, C. (2014). *GlobalGiving is Raising Funds for Ebola Epidemic Relief*. Accessed 17/05/17 from https://www.crowdfundinsider.com/2014/08/47495-globalgiving-raising-funds-ebola-epidemic-relief/

Institute for Advanced Sustainability Studies (IASS). (2016). *The Future of Africa's Energy Supply*. Retrieved from http://www.iass- potsdam.de/sites/default/files/files/study_march_2016_the_future_of_africas_energy_supply.pdf

Instrgram. (2016, December 15). *600 Million and Counting*. Retrieved April 11, 2017, from Instagram: http://blog.instagram.com/post/154506585127/161215-600million

Internetworldstats. (2017). *Internet Usage Statistics For Africa*. Available at:http://www.internetworldstats.com/stats1.htm

IRENA. (2014). *RE-thinking Energy: Towards a new power system*. IRENA.

IRENA. (2015). *Renewable Energy Capacity Statistics 2015*. IRENA.

Jacob, K., Quitzow, R., & Bär, H. (2015). *Green Jobs: Impacts of a Green Economy on Employment. BMZ/GIZ*. Bonn: Eschborn.

Jain, J. K. (2015). *Crowd-Funding in Microfinance in India: Issues, Challenges and Opportunities. UK Government's Department for International Development (DFID) and Small Industries Development Bank of India (SIDBI)*. DFID and SIDBI.

Jain, J. K. (2015). *Crowd-Funding in Microfinance in India: Issues, Challenges and Opportunities. UK Government's Department for International Development (DFID) and Small Industries Development Bank of India*. SIDBI.

Jain, M., & Xie, X. (2017). The rise of informal urbanization in the Global South: A breach of urban planning or bridging the gap of urban infrastructure supply? In N. Schlitz & J. Poerting (Eds.), *Aktuelle Forschungsbeiträge zu Südasien: 7. Jahrestagung des AK Südasien, 27./28. Januar 2017*. Augsburg.

Jain, V., Chennuri, S., & Karamchandani, A. (2016). *Informal Housing, Inadequate Property Rights Understanding the Needs of India's Informal Housing Dwellers*. FSG Reimagining Social Change.

Jama, B., & Pizarro, G. (2008, June). Agriculture in Africa: Strategies to Improve and Sustain Smallholder Production Systems. *Annals of the New York Academy of Sciences*, *1136*(1), 218–232. doi:10.1196/annals.1425.034 PMID:18579884

Jekins, K. (2014, December 17). *How to send a crowdfunding promotion email that works (includes templates)*. Retrieved January 31, 2017, from Multitude: http://www.multitude.co.nz/mud/crowdfunding-promotion-email/

JNNURM Document. (2013, November 22). *Jawaharlal Nehru National Urban Renewal Mission (JNNURM)*. Retrieved from https://www.gktoday.in/jawaharlal-nehru-national-urban-renewal_06/

John, N. A. (2013). Sharing, collaborative consumption and Web 2.0. London: Media@LSE, London School of Economics and Political Science ("LSE").

Kacprowicz, M., & Borowiecka, B. (2014). *E-Volunteering Handbook*. Retrieved from http://e-volunteering.eu/wp-content/uploads/2014/11/evolunteering-handbook.pdf

Kamau, M., & Donoghue, D. (2015). *Transforming our World: The 2030 Agenda for Global Action. (Final draft of the outcome document for the US summit to adopt the Post-2015 Development Agenda)*. United Nations, Permanent Mission of the Republic of Kenya to the United Nations. Retrieved from https://www.uclg.org/sites/default/files/final_draft_outcome_document_un_sept_summit_july_8_1.pdf

Kamete, A. Y. (2002). Governance for sustainability? Balancing social and environmental concern in Harare. Chr. Michelsen Institute, Development Studies and Human Rights, Bergen.

Kapur, V. (2009). *Financing Urban Infrastructure in Small and Medium Towns- Pooled Bonds as an Instrument of Financial Inclusion*. Paper presented in a Seminar on Financing Urban Development, Chennai, India.

Karam, R., & Melchiori, M. (2013, October). A crowdsourcing-based framework for improving geo-spatial open data. In *Systems, Man, and Cybernetics (SMC), 2013 IEEE International Conference on* (pp. 468-473). IEEE. doi:10.1109/SMC.2013.85

Karuri-Sebina, G. (2016). *The State of South African Cities Report. South African Cities Network (SACN)*. Johannesburg, South Africa: SACN.

Kasarda, J., & Crenshaw, E. (1991). Third World urbanization: Dimensions, theories and determinants. *Annual Review of Sociology*, *17*(1), 467–501. doi:10.1146/annurev.so.17.080191.002343 PMID:12285403

Katz & Wagner. (2014). *The Rise of Innovation Districts: A New Geography of Innovation in America*. Academic Press.

Katz, B., & Wagner, J. (2014). *The Rise of Innovation Districts: A New Geography of Innovation in America*. Retrieved from https://www.brookings.edu/wp-content/uploads/2016/07/InnovationDistricts1.pdf

Keane, A. O., & Griffiths, H. (2017, March 20). *Civic Crowdfunding – A Guidebook for Local Authorities*. Retrieved July 23, 2017, from Spacelive - Catapult - Future Cities: https://about.spacehive.com/civic-crowdfunding-a-guidebook-for-local-authorities/

Keating, M., Rhodes, B., & Richards, A. (2013). Crowdsourcing: a flexible method for innovation, data collection, and analysis in social science research. *Social media, sociality, and survey research*, 179-201.

Kelly, J. (2009). *Challenges - Red Kayaks and Hidden Gold: The Rise, Challenges and 11 Value of Citizen Journalism*. Oxford, UK: Reuters Institute for the Study of Journalism. Retrieved from http://reutersinstitute.politics.ox.ac.uk/fileadmin/documents/Publications/Red_Kayaks_Hidden_Gold.pdf

Khan, A. (2017, April 18). *Maharashtra schools raise Rs 216 crore via crowd funding*. Retrieved from http://indianexpress.com/article/india/maharashtra-schools-raise-rs-216-crore-via-crowd-funding-4617328/

Kim, J. (2016). *Handbook on Urban Infrastructure Finance*. New Cities Foundation. Available from: http://bit.ly/NCFUrbanFinance

Kirby, E., & Worner, S. (2014). *Crowd-funding: An Infant Industry Growing Fast*. Academic Press.

Kirby, E., & Worner, S. (2014). *Crowdfunding: An Infant Industry Growing Fast*. Retrieved from http://www.iosco.org/research/pdf/swp/Crowd-funding-An-Infant-Industry-Growing-Fast.pdf

Kirby, E., & Worner, S. (2014). *Crowd-funding: an Infant Industry Growing Fast*. Madrid, Spain: International Organization of Securities Commissions. Retrieved from https://www.iosco.org/library/pubdocs/pdf/IOSCOPD459.pdf

Kiva. (2017). *Kiva.org*. Retrieved 05 13, 2017, from www.kiva.org

Kleinhans, R., van Ham, M., & Evans-Cowley, J. (2015). Using Social Media and Mobile Technologies to Foster Engagement and Self-organisation in Participatory Urban Planning and Neighbourhood Governance. *Planning Practice and Research*, *30*(3), 237–247. doi:10.1080/02697459.2015.1051320

Koch, J., & Siering, M. (2015). Crowdfunding Success Factors: The Characteristics of Successfully Funded Projects on Crowdfunding Platforms. *ECIS 2015 Completed Research Papers,* Paper 106.

Koch, C. (2014, May). Ready to join the sharing economy. *Director*, 66.

Koci, A. (2016). *ESP courses in Kosovo Higher Education System*. Retrieved from https://aab-edu.net/assets/uploads/2017/01/ICLLC2016_Book-of-Abstracts.pdf

Koerten, H., & van den Besselaar, P. (2015). Crowdsourcing and Citizen Science in biodiversity research http://www.synthesys.info/wp-content/uploads/2014/01/NA3-Del.-3.4-Crowdsourcing-report-Phase-1.pdf

Kostof, S. (1991). *The City Shaped: Urban Patterns and Meanings Through History*. London: Thames and Hudson.

KPMG. (2016). *Fintech in India A global growth story*. Retrieved from https://assets.kpmg.com/content/dam/kpmg/pdf/2016/06/FinTech-new.pdf

Krätli, G., & Ghislaine, L. (2011). *The Trans-Saharan Book Trade: Manuscript Culture, Arabic Literacy and Intellectual History in Muslim Africa*. London: Brill.

Kriščiūnas, K., & Daugeliene, R. (2006). The assessment models of knowledge-based economy penetration. *The Engineering Economist*, *50*(5), 36–46.

Krogman, H., & Khumalo, N. (2016). *Plugging Africa into e-commerce*. Retrieved from https://www.afdb.org/en/blogs/industrialisation-and-trade-corner/post/plugging-africa-into-e- commerce-16592/

Kumar, A., & Rai, A. K. (2014). Urbanization Process, Trend, Pattern and its Consequences in India. *Neo Geographia*, *3*(4), 54–77.

Lakaji. (2013). *Agricultural Growth Corridor Summit (AGCIS) Schematics*. Retrieved from http://www.nigerianextt.org/?page_id=334

Lake, R. (2015). *A Guide to Building a Portfolio with Crowdfunded Investments*. Retrieved 04 07, 2017, from Investopedia: http://www.investopedia.com/articles/personal-finance/120415/guide-building-portfolio-crowdfunded-investments.asp

Lakhani, K. R. (2013). Using the Crowd as an Innovation Partner. *Harvard Business Review*, *91*(4), 60–69. PMID:23593768

Lamberton, C. (2015). Consumer Sharing: Collaborative Consumption, from Theoretical Roots to New Opportunities. Cambridge Handbook of Consumer Psychology, 0, 1-54.

Lane, M. B. (2005). Public Participation in Planning: An Intellectual History. *The Australian Geographer*, *36*(3), 283–299. doi:10.1080/00049180500325694

Larralde, B., & Schwienbacher, A. (2012). Crowdfunding of Small Entrepreneurial Ventures. In D. Cumming (Ed.), *The Oxford Handbook of Entrepreneurial Finance* (Vol. 369). New York: Oxford University Press.

Latham & Watkins. (2016). *Africa's funding alternative. The continent accounts for less than one percent of global sukuk issuance. This may be about to change*. Academic Press.

Lave, J., & Wenger, E. (1991). *Situated Learning. Legitimate Peripheral Participation*. Cambridge, UK: Cambridge University Press. doi:10.1017/CBO9780511815355

Lawal, G. (2007). Corruption and Development in Africa: Challenges for Political and Economic Change. *Humanities and Social Sciences Journal*, *2*(1), 1–7.

Lawton, K., & Marom, D. (2010). *The Crowdfunding Revolution: Social Networking Meets Venture Financing*. Academic Press.

Lee, B. (2006). *A New Challenge Model of a Volunteer Program*. Retrieved from www.volunteerprogramme

Lee, J., Rabanal, P., & Sandri, D. (2010, January 15). U.*S. Consumption after the 2008 Crisis*. International Monetary Fund.

Lehner, O. M. (2013). Crowdfunding social ventures: a model and research agenda. *Venture Capital: An International Journal of Entrepreneurial Finance*, 289-311. DOI:10.1080/13691066.2013.782624

Levišauskait, K. (2010). *Investment Analysis and Portfolio Management*. Vytautas Magnus University Kaunas. Retrieved from http://www.bcci.bg/projects/latvia/pdf/8_IAPM_final.pdf

Lewkowicz, K. (2016, May 10). *April Email Market Share: Mobile Rises To 56%, Its Highest Point Yet*. Retrieved April 11, 2017, from Litmus: https://litmus.com/blog/mobile-rises-to-56-market-share-longest-sustained-growth-in-2016

Li, J. (2016). Equity Crowdfunding in China: Current Practice and Important Legal Issues. *The Asian Business Lawyer*, (18). Accessed 20/05/17 at https://ssrn.com/abstract=2842752

Liton, H. A. (2012). Developing EFL teaching and learning practices in Saudi colleges: A review. *International Journal of Instruction*, *5*(2), 129–152.

Lonavath, A. K. (2014). Structure of Family Size in Urban Areas: A study on Telangana, Coastal Andhra and Rayalaseema regions of Andhra Pradesh. *International Journal of Advanced Scientific and Technical Research, 1*(4), 1-9.

Lorenzo, F. (2005). *How is English for Specific Purposes (ESP) different from English as a Second Language (ESL), also known as general English?* Retrieved from www.usingenglish.com

Lushaba, L. S. (2009). *Development as Modernity, Modernity as Development*. Dakar: CODESRIA.

Luzar, C. (2013, January 21). *Effective Email Marketing For Crowdfunding Campaigns.* Retrieved January 31, 2017, from Crowdfund Insider: https://www.crowdfundinsider.com/2013/01/8555-email-marketing-crowdfunding/

Lydon, G. (2009). *On Trans-Saharan Trails: Islamic Law, Trade Networks, and Cross-Cultural Exchange in Nineteenth-Century Western Africa.* Cambridge University Press. doi:10.1017/CBO9780511575457

Lyman, T., Pickens, M., & Porteous, D. (2008). *Regulating Transformational Branchless Banking: Mobile Phones and Other Technology to Increase Access to Finance.* Consultative Group to Assist the Poor (CGAP) Focus Note 43, Consultative Group to Assist the Poor (CGAP) Focus Note 43.

Lynn, J. (2011). *Curriculum Development in Six Steps for Med-Ed.* Retrieved from https://medicine.osu.edu/education/Documents/curriculum_design_2010.pdf

Maathai, W. (2009). *The Challenges for Africa.* New York: Pantheon Books.

Macbeth, H., & Collinson, P. (2002). *Human Population Dynamics: CrossDisciplinary Perspectives.* Cambridge University Press. doi:10.1017/CBO9780511542480

Magala, C., & Rubagumya, A. (2005). *Why Pay? Motivators for Payments of Local Market Dues in Rwanda and Uganda.* Amsterdam: SNV.

Maggio, Saltarelli, & Stranack. (2016). *Crowdsourcing the Curriculum: A MOOC for Personalized, Connected Learning.* Retrieved from http://er.educause.edu/articles/2016/3/crowdsourcing-the-curriculum-a-mooc-for-personalized-connected-learning

Mahadevia, D., Bhatia, N., & Bhatt, B. (2014). *Resident Welfare Associations (RWAs) in BSUP Sites of Ahmedabad: Experiences of Mahila Housing SEWA Trust (MHA). CUE working Paper 25, September 2014.* Ahmedabad, India: Center for Urban Equity, CEPT University.

Mahajan, S. (2014). *Economics of South African Townships: Special Focus on Diepsloot.* Washington, DC: The World Bank.

Maisonneuve, N., Stevens, M., & Ochab, B. (2010). Participatory noise pollution monitoring using mobile phones. *Information Polity, 15*(1-2), 51-71.

Mandelli, S., Barbieri, J., Mattarolo, L., & Colombo, E. (2014). Sustainable Energy in Africa: A Comprehensive Data and Policy Review. *Renewable & Sustainable Energy Reviews*, *37*, 656–686. doi:10.1016/j.rser.2014.05.069

Mankiw, N. G. (2009). *Macroeconomics* (7th ed.). New York: Worth Publishers.

Mansour, E. Z. (2017). *Role of NGOs in development.* Retrieved from https://www.slideshare.net/MansourEsmaeilZaei/role-of-ngos-in-development

Marchand, F. (2015). Equity-based Crowdfunding Real Estate Markets: An institutional Comparison of Crowdfunding Real Estate Markets and Their Employment as Alternative Financing Tool for Real Estate between the Netherlands and the US. Unpublished P2 Report, Delft University of Technology.

Marmore Research. (2015). *Marmore Company Reports. Ooredoo (Qatar Telecommunications Company).* Retrieved from https://www.e-marmore.com/MarMore/media/TOCDownloadPDF/Ooredoo-Executive-summary.pdf

Mason, R. J. (2007). *Collaborative Land use Management: The Quieter Revolution in Place-Based Planning.* Rowan and Littlefield Publishers.

Massolution. (2015). *The Crowdfunding Industry Report.* Available at:http://www.crowdsourcing.org/editorial/global-crowdfunding-market-to-reach-344b-in-2015- predictsmassolutions-2015cf-industry-report/45376

Massung, E., Coyle, D., Cater, K. F., Jay, M., & Preist, C. (2013, April). Using crowdsourcing to support pro-environmental community activism. In *Proceedings of the SIGCHI Conference on Human Factors in Computing Systems* (pp. 371-380). ACM. doi:10.1145/2470654.2470708

Mathur, O., & Peterson, G. (2006). *State Finance Commission and urban fiscal decentralization in India. India urban initiatives.* Washington, DC: The Urban Institute.

Matofska, B. (2014). *What is the Sharing Economy?* Retrieved 12 08, 2014, from http://www.thepeoplewhoshare.com/blog/what-is-the-sharing-economy/

Matovu, G., Chirisa, I., & Matamanda, A. (2015). Local Development and Governance in Anglophone and Lusophone Africa and Its Relevance to the EU Agenda: Continuity with Change. *Journal of Public Policy in Africa*, *3*(1), 20–36.

Matthew, E. E., & Idowu, C. A. (2012). *Political corruption and national development in Nigeria.* Paper presented at the International Conference on Democracy, Governance and Curbing Corruption in sub-Saharan Africa, Cheyney University of Pennsylvania.

Matunhu, J. (2011). A Critique of Modernization and Dependency Theories in Africa: Critical Assessment. *African Journal of History and Culture*, *3*(5), 65–72.

Max-Neef, M. A. (1991). *Human Scale Development: Conception, Application and Further Reflections, Dag Hammarskjöld Foundation.* New York: The Apex Press.

Mayer, R. C. (1995). An Integrative Model of. *Academy of Management Review*, *20*(3), 709–734.

McAlpine, T. (2014, December). The Sharing Economy. *Credit Union Management*, 40-41.

McCormick, T. H., Lee, H., Cesare, N., Shojaie, A., & Spiro, E. S. (2017). Using Twitter for demographic and social science research: Tools for data collection and processing. *Sociological Methods & Research*, *46*(3), 390–421. doi:10.1177/0049124115605339

McGonigal, J. (2011). *Reality is broken: Why games make us better and how they can change the world.* New York: Penguin Press.

M-Changa. (n.d.). Retrieved from http://changa.co.ke/faq/

McKinsey Global Institute (MGI) Report. (2010). *India's Urban Awakening: Building Inclusive Cities and Sustainable Economic Growth.* Author.

McKinsey. (2015). Brighter Africa — The Growth Potential of the Sub-Saharan Electricity Sector. McKinsey & Company.

Mdlongwa, E. T. (2014). *Local government at the heart of poor service delivery.* Available at: http://www.psam.org.za/research/1460540011.pdf

Mehra, V. (2015). *Crowdfunding in Arab Region.* Retrieved from https://www.linkedin.com/pulse/crowdfunding-arab-region-vinod-kumar-mehra

Mehra, D. (2013). What has urban decentralization meant? A case study of Delhi. *Pacific Affairs, 86*(4), 813–833. doi:10.5509/2013864813

Melbourne City Council. (2002). *Melbourne City Plan 2010.* Melbourne City Council Official Documentation. Retrieved from http:www.melbourne.vic.gov.au/cityplan/infopage.cfm?tid=*1

Menon, S. (2016, September 9). *Crowd control: Sebi warning turns off crowdfunding tap for startups.* Retrieved July 17, 2017, from ET Rise by Economics Times: http://economictimes.indiatimes.com/small-biz/money/crowd-control-sebi-warning-turns-off-crowdfunding-tap-for-startups/articleshow/54202702.cms

Meyer, R. L. (2015). *Financing agriculture and rural areas in sub-Saharan Africa Progress, challenges and the way forward.* London: International Institute for Environment and Development.

MHRD. (2017, September). *Constitutional Provision.* Retrieved September 12, 2017, from Ministry of Human Resource Development (MHRD) under Government of India (GOI): http://mhrd.gov.in/article-243w

Microfinance. (2014). In *Wikipedia.* Retrieved 12 08, 2014, from http://en.wikipedia.org/wiki/Microfinance

Milaap. (2017). *Crowdfunding for India: Raise funds online for yourself, loved ones, charities and more.* Available online: https://milaap.org/

Ministry of Housing & Urban Affairs. (2016, May 17). *States asked to convert 3,784 urban areas into statutory Urban Local Bodies.* Retrieved from http://pib.nic.in/newsite/PrintRelease.aspx?relid=145405

Ministry of Land, Infrastructure, Transport and Tourism, Japan (MLIT). (2016). *An overview of spatial policy in Asian and European Countries: China.* Retrieved August 9, 2016, from http://www.mlit.go.jp/kokudokeikaku/international/spw/general/china/index_e.html

Mirbabaic, M., Stieglitz, S., & Volkeri, S. (2016, January). Volunteered Geographic Information and Its Implications for Disaster Management. In *System Sciences (HICSS), 2016 49th Hawaii International Conference on* (pp. 207-216). IEEE.

Misra, A., Gooze, A., Watkins, K., Asad, M., & Le Dantec, C. (2014). Crowdsourcing and its application to transportation data collection and management. *Transportation Research Record: Journal of the Transportation Research Board, 2414*, 1–8. doi:10.3141/2414-01

MohammedO. (2016). *The New Online Shoppers.* Retrieved from https://qz.com/478714/africas-emerging-consumer-class-is-a-boon-for-the-continents-online-retailers/

Mohan, M. (2016). Geospatial Information from Satellite Imagery for Geovisualisation of Smart Cities in India. *ISPRS - International Archives of the Photogrammetry. Remote Sensing and Spatial Information Sciences, 41, B8*, 979–985.

Mohanty, P., Misra, B., Goyal, R., & Jeromi, P. (2007). *Municipal Finance in India – An Assessment. Study No. 26.* Mumbai: Department of Economic Analysis and Policy, Reserve Bank of India.

Moleskis, M., & Canela, M. Á. (2016). Crowdfunding success: The case of kiva.org. Barcelona: IESE Business School.

Mollick, E. (2014). The dynamics of crowdfunding: An exploratory study. *Journal of Business Venturing, 29*(1), 1–16. doi:10.1016/j.jbusvent.2013.06.005

Monge, P. R., & Contractor, N. S. (2003). *Theories of Communication Networks.* New York: Oxford University Press. Retrieved from www.uiuc.edu/ph/www/nosh

Morales, J. A. (2013). *Sustainable Development By Means of a Collaborative Planning Framework. The Case of Municipal Housing in Guatemala City* (MSc Thesis). University of Twante.

Moravec, J. (2008). *Knowmads in Web 3.0.* Retrieved from http://www.educationfutures.com/2008/11/20/knowmads-in-society-30/

Moravia. (2017). *Translation services for a digital world.* Retrieved from https://www.moravia.com/

Morris, A. E. J. (Ed.). (1994). History of Urban Form: Before the Industrial Revolution. London: Prentice Hall.

Mosdell, T. (2006). Free basic services: The evolution and impact of free basic water policy in South Africa. In U. Pillay, R. Tomlinson, & J. Toit (Eds.), *Democracy and delivery: Urban policy in South Africa* (pp. 283–301). Cape Town: HSRC Press.

MOUD. (2015, April). *The Future of Urban Development and Services: Urban Development Recommendations for Government of India.* Retrieved July 19, 2017, from World Economics Forum: http://www3.weforum.org/docs/WEF_IU_FUDS_Urban_Development_Recommendations_Government_India_Report_2015.pdf

Muchadenyika, D., & Williams, J. J. (2016). Social Change: Urban Governance and Urbanization in Zimbabwe. *Urban Forum, 2016*(27), 253-274.

Mugumbate,, J., & Maushe,, F., & Nyoni. (2013). Ruralisation of Urban Areas: Reversing Development in Zimbabwe. *International Journal of Advanced Research in Management and Social Sciences, 2*(7), 13–30.

Müllerleile, T., Joenssen, D., & Müllerleile, A. (2014). Crisis, Co-Financing, and Crowdfunding: Igniting Regional Development. *Proceedings of International Conference for Entrepreneurship, Innovation and Regional Development.*

Muller, M., Soule, T., Daniel, S., Geyer, W., & Cheng, L.-T. (2013). Crowdfunding Inside the Enterprise: Employee Initiatives for Innovation and Collaboration. *Proceedings of the SIGCHI Conference on Human Factors in Computing Systems.* doi:10.1145/2470654.2470727

Mumford, L. (1961). *The City in History.* New York: Harcourt Brace Javanovich.

Munyanyi, W., & Mapfumo, A. (2016). Factors Influencing Crowdfunding Plausibility in Post Hyperinflationary Zimbabwe. *Journal of Entrepreneurship and Business Innovation, 3*(1), 18–27. doi:10.5296/jebi.v3i1.9244

Murray, S. (2007). *The World's Biggest Industry.* Retrieved 05 05, 2017, from https://www.forbes.com/2007/11/11/growth-agriculture-business-forbeslife-food07-cx_sm_1113bigfood.html

Murrell, P. (2001). The Economics of Sharing: A Transactions Costs Analysis of Contractual Choice in Farming. *The Bell Journal of Economics, 14*(1), 283–293. doi:10.2307/3003555

Mutiga, M. (2014). *Kenya's Banking Revolution Lights a Fire.* Retrieved 04 06, 2017, from The New York Times: https://www.nytimes.com/2014/01/21/opinion/kenyas-banking-revolution-lights-a-fire.html

MXit. (n.d.). *The First Mobile Messenger.* Retrieved 03 30, 2017, from MXit: http://www.mxit.com/index.html

Nagalakshmi, S., & Cecilia, G. U. (2014). Crowd Funding – An Emerging Trend in India. *International Journal of Scientific Research, 3*(4), 71–73. doi:10.15373/22778179/APR2014/206

Naija247News. (2017). *NPAC/TAC-Transformation of Nigeria's oil.* Retrieved from http://naija247news.com

Nallathiga, R. (2008). Trends and prespectives of urban public finance in select countries. *ICFAI Journal of Urban Policy*, 16-32.

Nallathiga, R. (2008). Trends and Perspectives of Urban Public Finance in Select Countries and India. *ICFAI Journal of Urban Policy*, *3*(1), 16–32.

Nead, N. (2017). *Nine Risks Associated with Crowdfunding.* Accessed 17/05/17 from http://crowdfund.co/nine-risks-associated-with-crowdfunding/

Nehemia, L. (1963). The Thirteenth- and Fourteenth-Century Kings of Mali. *Journal of African History, 4*(3), 341-353.

Nejak, E. L. (2016). *Top Indian Crowdfunding Platforms With local and Global Operations.* Retrieved from http://crowdsourcingweek.com/blog/indias-top-ten-crowdfunding-platforms/

Nekaj, E. L. (2016, August 18). *India's Top 10 Crowdfunding Platforms.* Retrieved from Crowd Source Week: http://crowdsourcingweek.com/blog/indias-top-ten-crowdfunding-platforms/

Nesta. (2012). *An Introduction to Crowdfunding*. Nesta.

Nesta. (2012). *An Introduction to Crowdfunding.* Retrieved from http://www.ema.eu/fileadmin/content/REALISE_IT_2/REALISE_IT_3/IntroToCrowdfunding.pdf

Newshandle. (2017). *Federal Government Partners WTO, CNN to boost development.* Retrieved from www.newshandle.com/nigeria-vanguard

NextGen Crowdfunding. (2017). *Explore a New Ear of Crowdfunding.* Retrieved from https://www.nextgencrowdfunding.com/companies/title-iii-crowdfunding-reg-cf-541/

Nicole. (2010). *Collaborative Consumption Will Save Us.* Retrieved 12 8, 2014, from http://www.aviewfromtheedge.net/blog/2010/11/01/collaborative-consumption-will-save-us/

Nigerianextt. (2017). *Nigeria Expanded Trade and Transport Project.* Retrieved from www.nigerianextt.org

Nigeriannext. (2013). *Don't miss these women initiatives in Nigeria!* Retrieved from www.nigeriannext.org

NITDA. (2017). *NITDA set up multi-million naira training centre for IDPs in Abuja.* Retrieved from http://www.herald.ng/nitda-set-up-multi-million-naira-training-centre-for-idps-inabuja/#leTddyJd1XUwK4ac.99

Njegomir, V., Tepavac, R., & Ivanisevic, N. (2017). Alternative Sources of Financing entrepreneurial undertakings in agriculture. *Economics of Agriculture*, *1*(64), 295–306.

Njoh, A. J. (2000). *The Impact of Colonial Heritage on Development in Sub-Saharan Africa.* Retrieved from www.msu.ac.zw/.../1299832433impact%20of%20colonial%20heritage%20on%20dvt

Njoh, A. J. (1999). *Urban Planning, Housing, and Spatial Structures in Sub-Saharan Africa.* Ashgate.

Nonaka, I. (1991). The Knowledge Creating Company. Harvard Business Review, 69(6), 96-105.

Nordicity. (2012). *Crowdfunding in a Canadian Context: Exploring the Potential of Crowdfunding in the Creative Content Industries*. Nordicity.

Novak, J. D., & Cañas, A. J. (2006). The Origins of the Concept Mapping Tool and the Continuing Evolution of the Tool. *Information Visualization Journal*, *5*(3), 175–184. doi:10.1057/palgrave.ivs.9500126

Novak, J., & Cañas, A. J. (2007). Theoretical Origins of Concept Map, How to construct them and their used in Education. *Reflecting Education*, *3*(1), 29–42.

Nyamwanza, L., Paketh, L., Mhaka, C., Makaza, F., & Moyo, N. (2015). An Evaluation of the Policies Instituted by the Government of Zimbabwe in Promoting Survival and Growth of SMEs: The Case of Glenview Area 8 SMEs. *International Journal of Novel Research in Marketing Management and Economics*, *2*(2), 35–44.

Nylund, M., & Gopalkrishnan, A. (2014). *Crowdsourcing in Media*. Retrieved from http://dspace.arcada.fi:8080/xmlui/handle/10478/64

Obeng-Odoom, F. (2015). The Social Spatial, and Economic Roots of Urban Inequality in Africa: Contextualizing Jane Jacobs and Henry George. *American Journal of Economics and Sociology*, *74*(3), 550–586. doi:10.1111/ajes.12101

Ochieng, L. (2016). *M-Pesa reports 27 pc jump in global users to 25 million*. Retrieved 04 06, 2017, from Daily Nation: http://www.nation.co.ke/business/M-Pesa-reports-27-pc-jump-in-global-users-to-25-million/996-3178018-5ykpjpz/index.html

OECD. (n.d.). *What is social capital? OECD Insights: Human Capital*. OECD.

Ojabo, D. (2016). *eHealth Africa Providing Technical Support to Help Curb Nigeria's Meningitis Outbreak*. Retrieved from https://www.ehealthafrica.org/latest/2017/5/8/ehealth-africa-providing-technical-support-to-help-curb-nigerias-meningitis-outbreak

Ojo, I. F. (2014). Article. *European Journal of Business Management, 2*(1). Retrieved from http://www. ejobm.org

Okpala, R. (2009). Regional Overview of the Status of Urban Planning and Planning Practice in Anglophone (Sub-Saharan) African Countries. In *UN Habitats* (p. 10). United Nations.

Olson, M. (1965). *The Logic of Collective Action: Public Goods and the Theory of Groups*. Cambridge, MA: Harvard University Press.

Omotosho, O. A., & Snyder, M. (2002). Considerations of Community: The context and Process of Volunteerism. *The American Behavioral Scientist*, *45*(5), 846–867. doi:10.1177/0002764202045005007

Open Knowledge Foundation. (2011). *Open Knowledge Foundation*. Available from: http://web.archive.org/web/20131109174520/http://opendcfinition.org/okd/esp anol/

Oranje, M. (2010). Post-Apartheid National Spatial Development Planning in South Africa- A Brief History. *European Spatial Research and Policy*, *17*(2), 55–70. doi:10.2478/s10105-010-0010-8

Ordanini, A. (2009, March 23). Crowd funding: Customers as investors. *The Wall Street Journal*.

Ordanini, A., Miceli, L., Pizzetti, M., & Parasuraman, A. (2011). Crowd-funding: Transforming customers into investors through innovative service platforms. *Journal of Service Management*, *22*(4), 443–470. doi:10.1108/09564231111155079

Ortmann, G. F., & King, R. P. (2010). Research on agri-food supply chains in Southern Africa involving small-scale farmers: Current status and future possibilities. *Agrekon*, *49*(4), 397–417. doi:10.1080/03031853.2010.526428

Osborne, M., Kearns, P., & Yang, J. (2013). Learning Cities: Developing Inclusive, Prosperous and Sustainable Urban Communities. International Review of Education, 59(4), 409-423.

Ostrom, E. (1990). *Governing the Commons: The Evolution of Institutions for Collective Action*. Cambridge, MA: Cambridge University Press. doi:10.1017/CBO9780511807763

Ostrom, E., & Hess, C. (2007). *Understanding knowledge as a commons: from theory to practice*. Cambridge, MA: MIT Press.

Otah, J. I. (2012). Dutch Disease and Nigeria oil Economy. *African Research Review*, *6*(1), 82–90.

Owyang, J., Samuel, A., & Grenville, A. (2014, Mar 02). *Are we becoming a collaborative economy? Possibly.* Retrieved 01 16, 2015, from http://www.slideshare.net/jeremiah_owyang/sharingnewbuying/1

Padmanabhan, A. (2016, March 27). *Crowdfunding Platforms in India for Tech Start-Ups.* Retrieved July 15, 2017, from Indian Engineering Design Forum: https://www.iedf.in/index.php/blog/item/crowdfunding-platforms-in-india-for-tech-start-ups

Paltridge, B. (2015). *Keynote: Developments in English for Specific Purposes Research.* Retrieved from http://jaltcue.org/files/OnCUE/OCJ9.2/OCJ9.2_pp73-85_Paltridge.pdf

Paltridge, B., & Starfield, S. (Eds.). (2012). *The Handbook of English for Specific Purposes.* Wiley- Blackwell. doi:10.1002/9781118339855

Papadopoulou, C. A., & Giaoutzi, M. (2014). Crowdsourcing as a tool for knowledge acquisition in spatial planning. *Future Internet*, *6*(1), 109–125. doi:10.3390/fi6010109

Paquet, S. (2010). *What are Emergent Cities?* Retrieved on 3 Nov 2010, from: http://emergentcities.sebpaquet.net/what-are-emergent-cities

Parkinson, J., & Taylor, K. (2003). Decentralized wastewater management in peri-urban areas in low-income countries. *Environment and Urbanization*, *15*(1), 75–89. doi:10.1177/095624780301500119

Parmar, N. (2013). *Today $249 for clay pots - tomorrow the region.* Retrieved from http://www.thenational.ae/business/industry-insights/finance/today-249-for-clay-pots-tomorrow-the-region

Partridge, A. (2015, July 1). *Crowdfunding City Futures?* URBACT in Ireland.

Pazowski, P., & Czudec, W. (2014). *Economic Prospects and Conditions of Crowdfunding.* Paper presented to the Management, Knowledge and Learning International Conferences, Portoroz, Slovenia.

Pearce, F. (1999). African Queen. *New Scientist*, (2203). Retrieved from http://www.yorku.ca/nhp/seminars/2004_05/Ribat.pdf

Pedersen, J., Kocsis, D., Tripathi, A., Tarrell, A., & de Vreede, G. J. (2013, January). Conceptual foundations of crowdsourcing: A review of IS research. In *System Sciences (HICSS), 2013 46th Hawaii International Conference on* (pp. 579-588). IEEE.

Pereira, A. (2017). *Homegrown Cities.* Available online: https://www.indiegogo.com/projects/homegrown-cities#/

Peterson, G. (2008). *Unlocking Land Values to Finance Urban Infrastructure: Land-Based Financing Options for Cities. Gridlines; No. 40.* World Bank.

Pethe, A., Nallathiga, R., Gandhi, S., & Tandel, V. (2014, February 15). *Re-thinking urban planning in India: Learning from the wedge between the de jure and de facto development in Mumbai.* Academic Press.

Philips, J. (2012). Open Innovation Typology. In P. Sloane (Ed.), *A Guide to Open Innovation and Crowdsourcing: Advice from Leading Experts* (pp. 22–36). Kogan Page.

Porter, M. (1995, May). The Competitive advantage of the Inner City. *Harvard Business Review.*

Porter, M. E., & Kramer, M. (2011, January). Creating Shared Value: How to reinvent capitalism—and unleash a wave of innovation and growth. Harvard *Business Review*, 1–17.

Portes, A. (1998). Social Capital: its origins and applications in modern sociology. Annual Review of Sociology, 24.

Prabhu, D. (2016, October 28). *Is Crowdfunding Legal in India? SEBI Regulations & It's Implications.* Retrieved July 16, 2017, from Linkedin: https://www.linkedin.com/pulse/crowdfunding-legal-india-sebi-regulations-its-deepak-prabhu

Pradhan, K. (2013). Unacknowledged urbanization: The new census towns of India. *Economic and Political Weekly, 48*(36), 43–51.

Press Information Bureau. (2016, May 17). *States asked to convert 3,784 urban areas into statutory Urban Local Bodies.* Retrieved from http://pib.nic.in/newsite/PrintRelease.aspx?relid=145405

Prinsha K. (2016). A Study on Crowd Funding and its Implications in India. *Indian Journal of Research - Paripex, 5*(1), 233-235.

Profugo.org. (2017). Retrieved from www.profugo.org/cite

Prpic, J., & Shukla, P. (2016, January). Crowd science: Measurements, models, and methods. In *System Sciences (HICSS), 2016 49th Hawaii International Conference on* (pp. 4365-4374). IEEE.

Putman, R. (Ed.). (2002). *Democracies in Flux: The Evolution of Social Capital in Contemporary Society.* Oxford, UK: Oxford University Press.

Putzier, K. (2015). Crowdfunding: A short history. *Tapping small-time investors is nothing new — it's older than the Statue of Liberty.* Retrieved from https://therealdeal.com/issues_articles/crowdfunding-a-short-history/

Pwiti, G., & Ndoro, W. (1999). The Legacy of Colonialism: Perceptions of the Cultural Heritage in Southern Africa, with Special Reference to Zimbabwe. *African Archaeological Review, 16*(3), 143–153. doi:10.1023/A:1021624632398

Quah, D. (2002). *Digital goods and the New Economy.* Centre for Economic Performance, London School of Economics. Available at: http://cep.lse.ac.uk/pubs/download/dp0563.pdf

Rabbat, N. (n.d.). *The Islamic City: Historicity and Abstraction.* Retrieved from https://archnet.org/system/publications/contents/10625/original/DTP103010.pdf?1468397437

Ramanathan, R., & Dasgupta, S. (2009). *Estimates of Urban Infrastructure Financing Requirements in India, 2006-2031.* Available from: http://www.cprindia.org/sites/default/files/working_papers/HPEC%20REPORT.pdf

Rao, G., & Bird, R. (2010). *Urban Governance and Finance in India.* Rotman School of Management Working Paper No. 1568858.

Rao, M. (2013). *Property Tax System in India: Problems and Prospects of Reform.* Working Paper No. 2013-114, National Institute of Public Finance and Policy.

RBI Executive Summary, . (2011). *Municipal Finance in India – An Assessment. Executive Summary on Performance of ULB's in India.* Retrieved from Reserve Bank of India: http://www.rbi.org.in/scripts/bs_viewcontent.aspx?Id=1157

REN21. (2015). *Renewables 2015. Global Status Report.* Paris: Renewable Energy Network for the 21st Century.

Report of a Symposium (RS). (2009). *Understanding Research, Science and Technology Parks: Global Best Practice.* Retrieved from http://www.nap.edu/catalog.php?record_id=12546

Report, M. (2015, March 31). *Massolution Posts Research Findings: Crowdfunding Market Grows 167% in 2014, Crowdfunding Platforms Raise $16.2 Billion.* Retrieved July 16, 2017, from Massolution - Crowd Powered Business: https://www.crowdfundinsider.com/2015/03/65302-massolution-posts-research-findings-crowdfunding-market-grows-167-in-2014-crowdfunding-platforms-raise-16-2-billion/

Reserve Bank of India. (2016, April). *Consultation Paper on Peer to Peer Lending*. Retrieved July 17, 2017, from Reserve Bank of India (RBI) - Database: https://www.rbi.org.in/scripts/bs_viewcontent.aspx?Id=3164

Reuters. (2017, February 9). *Twitter Misses Fourth-Quarter Revenue, User Growth Expectations*. Retrieved April 11, 2017, from Fortune Tech: http://fortune.com/2017/02/09/twitter-q4-2016/

Riaga, O. (2016, July 4). *Kenya's e-Commerce deemed to explode and offer new opportunities for Kenyan entrepreneurs*. Retrieved December 13, 2016, from Kenya Tech News: Retrieved from http://www.kachwanya.com/2016/07/04/kenya-e-commerce-landscape-deemed-explode-offer-new-opportunities-kenyan-entrepreneurs/

Rinne, A. (2012). *Shareable*. Retrieved 12 08, 2014, from http://www.shareable.net/blog/lessons-from-microfinance-for-the-sharing-economy

Roche-Saunders, G., & Hunt, O. (2017). *Crowdfunding for charities and social enterprises: Crowdfunding has created new opportunities for raising funds from the public*. Crowdfunding focus. Charity and Social Enterprise Update, Summer 2017.

Rogers, K. (2017). *"Ubuntu": What Does It Mean?* Retrieved from www.africanimpact.com/VolunteerinAfrica

Roocke, N. (2015). Crowdfunding - an option for projects in agriculture. *Australian Canegrower*, (26), 20.

Rosen, H. S. (2002). *Public Finance: Essay for the Encyclopedia of Public Choice*. CEPS Working Paper No. 80.

Roth, S., Kaivo-Oja, J., & Hirschmann, T. (2013). Smart regions: Two cases of crowdsourcing for regional development. *International Journal of Entrepreneurship and Small Business*, *20*(3), 272–285. doi:10.1504/IJESB.2013.056890

Rowan, D. (2011). *Rentalship Is the New Ownership in the Networked Age*. Retrieved 12 8, 2014, from http://www.wired.com/2011/02/rentalship-the-new-ownership/

Saad, E. N. (1983). *The Social History of Timbuktu: The Role of Muslim Scholars and Notables 1400 - 1900*. Cambridge, UK: Cambridge University Press.

Sahasranaman, A. (2014, June 6). *Financing Metropolitan Governments in Developing Countries*. Retrieved from IFMR Finance Foundation: http://financingcities.ifmr.co.in/blog/category/municipal-finance/

Salat, S., & Bourdic, L. (2013). Urban Complexity, Efficiency and Resilience. In Z. Morvaj (Ed.), Energy Efficiency—A Bridge to Low Carbon Economy. Academic Press.

Salat, S., & Bourdic, L. (2011). Factor 10: Multiplying by 10 Resource Productivity in the Urban World. *Proceedings of the World Sustainable Conference*.

Salau, M. B. (2011). *Ribats and the Development of Plantations in the Sokoto Caliphate: a Case Study of Fanisau*. Retrieved from www.yorku.ca/nhp/seminars/2004_05/Ribat.pdf

Sankhe, S., Vittal, I., Dobbs, R., Mohan, A., Gulati, A., Ablett, J., & Sethy, G. et al. (2010). *India's urban awakening: Building inclusive cities, sustaining economic growth*. McKinsey Global Institute.

Saqlain, S. (2016). *Developing Crowdfunding Ecosystems in the Middle East*. Retrieved 5 8, 2017, from Entrepreneur-Middle East: https://www.entrepreneur.com/article/278955

Sarin, A. (2008). *Mobile phone banking in Africa* [Youtube Video]. Retrieved 04 06, 2017, from Department for International Development (DFID): https://www.youtube.com/watch?v=TNrDv4PQdCc

Sassen, S. (2002). *Global networks, Linked Cities*. New York: Routledge.

Saunders, T., & Baeck, P. (2015). *Rethinking Smart Cities from the Ground Up*. London: Nesta.

Savage, D., & Dasgupta, S. (2007). *Governance framework for delivery of urban services*. India Infrastructure Report 2006.

Savage, Ch. (1990). *Fifth Generation Management. Integrating enterprises through human networking*. Bedford: Digital Press.

Sawant, A. (2017, May 2). *College students to crowdfund library project in rural Maharashtra*. Retrieved from http://www.dnaindia.com/india/report-college-students-to-crowdfund-library-project-in-rural-maharashtra-2424422

Saxton, G. D., Oh, O., & Kishore, R. (2013). Rules of Crowdsourcing Models, Issues, and Systems of Control. *Information Systems Management, 30*(1), 2–20. doi:10.1080/10580530.2013.739883

Schelling, T. (1960). *The Strategy of Conflict*. Cambridge, MA: Harvard University Press.

Schiller, B. (2014). *Pay For Your City: Crowdfunding For Civic Projects Is Unusually Successful*. Retrieved March 01, 2017, from Fast Company: https://www.fastcoexist.com/3031412/pay-for-your-city-crowdfunding-for-civic-projects-is-unusually-successful

Schulist, K. (2012). *Collaborative consumption: A new form of consumptionin a changing economy* (MBA Thesis). University of North Carolina.

Schuringa, T. (2013). *How Social Entrepreneurs and Civic Innovation Can Affect Smart Growth in New Jersey*. New Jersey Future.

Scott, B. (2005). *Introduction to conversation Theory: Applications in education and Epistemology*. Paper presented in the Higher Education Academy seminar: e-Learning, University of Manchester. Available on line at: http://www.omg.mcs.cranfield.ac.uk

SEBI (Securities and Exchange Board of India). (2014). *Consultation Paper on Crowdfunding in India*. Retrieved from http://www.aibi.org.in/PR%20- %20Consultation%20Paper%20on%20Crowdfunding%20in%20India.pdf

SEBI. (2017, March 11). *Consultation Paper on Crowdfunding in India*. Consultation Paper on Crowdfunding in India. SEBI.

Seltzer, E., & Mahmoudi, D. (2012). Citizen participation, open innovation, and crowdsourcing: Challenges and opportunities for planning. *CPL Bibliography, 28*(1), 3-18.

Seufert, A., & Seufert, S. (1998). Knowledge Creation and Transfer in Knowledge Networks. IO Management, 67, 77-84.

Seufert, A., Krogh, G. von, & Back, A. (1999). Towards knowledge networking. *Journal of Knowledge Management, 3*(3), 180-190. Retrieved on 3 October 2011: http://citeseerx.ist.psu.edu/viewdoc/download?doi=10.1.1.116.9649&rep=rep1&type=pdf

Seufert, A., Krogh, G. von, & Back, A. (2003). Unleashing the power of networks for knowledge management: putting knowledge networks into action. In Knowledge management and networked environments. Amacom.

Shah, A. (Ed.). (2007). *Public Sector Governance and Accountability Series - Participatory Budgeting*. Washington, DC: The World Bank.

Sharma, A. M. (2016). Crowd Funding: An online Financing option. International Journal in Multidisciplinary and Academic Research, 5(3).

Sharma, P. (2011). *Crowdsourcing in Higher Education IT*. Retrieved from http://er.educause.edu/articles/2011/9/crowdsourcing-in-higher-education-it

Shen, E. (2016). *China Equity Crowdfunding Market Research Report 2016 is issued; —Equity-for-Fee‖Model is Popular among Platforms*. Accessed 21/05/17 at http://en.pedaily.cn/Item.aspx?id=220799

Shira & Associates. (2017). *The Growing Potential of Crowdfunding in China*. Accessed 08/07/17 from https://www.eastwestbank.com/ReachFurther/News/Article/The-Growing-Potential-of-Crowdfunding-in-China

Siemens, G. (2006). *Knowing Knowledge*. Retrieved on 21st Nov 2006, from: http://www.elearnspace.org/Knowing-Knowledge_LowRes.pdf

Sihlongonyane, M. F. (2015). The Challenges of Theorising about the Global South: A View from and African Perspective. *Africa Insight*, *45*(2), 59–74.

Sithole, A. (2013). Corruption in Zimbabwe Urban Local Authorities: A Case of Gweru City Council. Asia. *Journal of Social Sciences and Humanities*, *2*(3), 2–33.

Smith, C. (2017, March 22). *388 Amazing Twitter Statistics and Facts (February 2017)*. Retrieved April 11, 2017, from DMR Stat | Gadgets: http://expandedramblings.com/index.php/march-2013-by-the-numbers-a-few-amazing-twitter-stats/

Smith, M. K. (2000). Curriculum theory and practice. In *The encyclopaedia of informal education*. Retrieved from www.infed.org/biblio/b-curric.htm

Smith, T. (2012). *Crowdfunding: A new source of finance for sustainability and renewable energy*. Retrieved August 16, 2017, from http://www.climatechangenews.com/2012/07/31/crowdfunding-anew-source-of-finance-for-sustainability-and-renewable-energy/

Solemon, B. (2013). *A review of the uses of crowdsourcing in higher education*. Retrieved from http://www.aessweb.com/pdf-files/ijass-si-3(9)-2066-2073.pdf

Soltész, K. (2010). Sustainable urban development and developing countries. *Curentul Juridic, The Juridical Current. Le Courant Juridique*, *43*, 144–152.

Sosense. (2015). *5 Crowdfunding models you should know*. Accessed 17/05/17 from https://www.sosense.org/5-crowdfunding-models-know/

Sridhar, G. (2015, April 14). *Crowd funding gaining pace for Amaravati project*. Retrieved from http://www.thehindubusinessline.com/news/national/crowd-funding-gaining-pace-for-amaravati-project/article8476414.ece

Srivastava, M., M, K. J., & Sagar, M. (2014). An Insight into Crowd Funding in India. *International Journal of Management and Social Science Research Review*, *1*(6), 56–62.

Stanley, C., Winschiers-Theophilus, H., Onwordi, M., & Kapuire, G. K. (2013, December). Rural communities crowdsource technology development: a Namibian expedition. In *Proceedings of the Sixth International Conference on Information and Communications Technologies and Development: Notes-Volume 2* (pp. 155-158). ACM. doi:10.1145/2517899.2517930

Statista. (2017). *Statista – The portal for statistics*. Retrieved from https://www.statista.com/

Statista. (2017). *The Statistics Portal: FinTech*. Retrieved from https://www.statista.com/outlook/377/112/crowdinvesting/south-africa#

Statista. (2017, January). *Most famous social network sites worldwide as of January 2017, ranked by number of active users (in millions)*. Retrieved April 11, 2017, from The statistics Portal (Statista): https://www.statista.com/statistics/272014/global-social-networks-ranked-by-number-of-users/

Statt, N. (2016, February 1). WhatsApp has grown to 1 billion users. More than doubling since Facebook acquired it. *The Verge*.

Steinberg, S. (2012). *The Crowdfunding Bible: How to Raise Money for any Start-up, Video Game, Or Project*. New York: Overload Entertainment, LLC.

Stevens, M., & D'Hondt, E. (2010, September). Crowdsourcing of pollution data using smartphones. *Workshop on Ubiquitous Crowdsourcing*.

Stewart, T. (1997). *Intellectual Capital: The new wealth of Organisations*. New York: Doubleday/ Currency.

Stiver, A., Barroca, L., Minocha, S., Richards, M., & Roberts, D. (2014). *Civic crowdfunding research: Challenges, opportunities, and future agenda. In New media & society* (pp. 1–23). The Open University. Retrieved from http://oro.open.ac.uk/41478/1/CivicCrowdfunding_NMS_December2014.pdf

Storey, C. W. (2007). *Insights into Language Curriculum Development*. Retrieved from http://e-flt.nus.edu.sg/v4n12007/storey.pdf

Stratigea, A., Papadopoulou, C. A., & Panagiotopoulou, M. (2015). Tools and Technologies for Planning the Development of Smart Cities. *Journal of Urban Technology*, *22*(2), 43–62. doi:10.1080/10630732.2015.1018725

Strecker, E. (2013, March 13). *'Veronica Mars' reaches Kickstarter goal*. Retrieved April 09, 2017, from Entertainment: http://ew.com/article/2013/03/13/veronica-mars-movie-is-a-go-kickstarter/

Sundararajan, A. (2014). *Peer-to-Peer Businesses and the Sharing (Collaborative) Economy: Overview, Economic Effects and Regulatory Issues*. New York: NYU Stern School of Business.

Surowiecki, J. (2005). *The Wisdom of Crowds*. Anchor Books. Retrieved from https://www.ehealthafrica.org/latest/2017/3/30/ehealth-africa-transforms-disease-surveillance-and-response-in-sierra-leone

Surowiecki, J. (2004). *The Wisdom of Crowds*. Anchor Books.

Sustainable Cities International. (2012). *Indicators for Sustainability: How Cities are Monitoring and Evaluating their Success*. Vancouver, Canada: SCI.

Sutton, R. I., & Straw, B. M. (1995). What theory is not. *Administrative Science Quarterly*, *40*(3), 371–38. doi:10.2307/2393788

Swilling, M. (2010). *Africa 2050: Growth, resource productivity and decoupling*. Policy Brief for the 7th meeting of the International Panel for Sustainable Resource Management of the United Nations Environment Programme.

Sy & Copley. (2017). *Closing The Financing Gap For African Energy Infrastructure: Trends, Challenges, And Opportunities*. Brookings Institute Report.

Talbot, P. (2017). *English for Specific Purposes (ESP): An Objectives-Oriented Approach*. Retrieved from https://www.linkedin.com/pulse/english-specific-purposes-esp-objectives-oriented-approach-talbot

Tandel, V., Hiranandani, K., & Kapoor, M. (2016, July 28). *What's In A Definition? A Study on Implications and Suitability of Urban Definitions in India through its Employment Guarantee Programme*. Retrieved May 18, 2017, from IDFC: http://www.idfcinstitute.org/site/assets/files/9615/tandel_et_al_28th_july_whats_in_a_definition.pdf

Technologies, B. (2017, June 7). *Parched Indian Villages Uses Crowd Funding to Build Canal*. Retrieved July 14, 2017, from Bloomberg Technologies: https://www.bloomberg.com/news/articles/2016-08-08/parched-india-village-uses-crowdfunding-to-build-canal

The Economist. (2013, March 9). *The rise of the sharing economy*. Retrieved 01 10, 2015, from http://www.economist.com/news/leaders/21573104-internet-everything-hire-rise-sharing-economy

The Hindu. (2017, February 10). *SEBI to form panel to facilitate crowdfunding*. Retrieved July 16, 2017, from The Hindu: http://www.thehindu.com/todays-paper/tp-business/SEBI-to-form-panel-to-facilitate-crowdfunding/article17280456.ece

The World Bank Group. (2014). *UN World Urbanization Prospects (WUP), 2014 - Final Report*. Department of Economic and Social Affairs, Population Division.

The World Bank Group. (2015, September 24). *Leveraging Urbanization in India*. Retrieved September 13, 2017, from Leveraging Urbanization in India: http://www.worldbank.org/en/country/india/brief/leveraging-urbanization-india

Thuan, N. H., Antunes, P., & Johnstone, D. (2016). Factors influencing the decision to crowdsource: A systematic literature review. *Information Systems Frontiers*, *18*(1), 47–68. doi:10.1007/s10796-015-9578-x

Thundafund. (n.d.). Retrieved from https://blog.thundafund.com/how-does-thundafund-work/faqs/

Tilburg, D. A. (2015, October 22). *Civic Crowdfunding is Not About the Money*. Retrieved January 31, 2017, from VOOR JE BUURT: https://www.voorjebuurt.nl/civiccrowdfundingisnotaboutthemoney/

Times of India. (2017, May 27). *Crowdfunding helps Latur youths get internet connectivity to home village*. Retrieved from http://timesofindia.indiatimes.com/city/pune/crowdfunding-helps-latur-youths-get-internet-connectivity-to-home-village/articleshow/58866158.cms

Timm. (2016, April 13). *South Africa's FSB to rule on Crowdfunding by June 30*. News, Venturebun.

Tiwari & Rao. (2016). *Housing Markets and Housing Policies in India*. Asian Development Bank Institute. No. 565.

Tiwari, K. (2009, May 7). *Amul watering AMC, Auda parks*. Retrieved May 19, 2017, from Amul watering AMC, Auda parks: http://www.dnaindia.com/india/report-amul-watering-amc-auda-parks-1253682

Todes, A. (2008). Rethinking spatial planning. *SSB/TRP/MDM*, *2008*(53), 10-14.

Toister, J. (2014). *Instructional Design: Adult Learners*. Retrieved from https://www.lynda.com/Higher-Education-tutorials/Instructional-Design-Essentials-Adult-Learners

Tomei, L. (2004). *An Examination of Cognitivism: The Psychology of Knowledge and Strategies*. Retrieved 04 28, 2017, from Learning Theories -- A Primer Exercise: http://faculty.rmu.edu/~tomei/ed711psy/c_ausub.htm

Toto Same, A. (2008). *Mineral-Rich Countries and Dutch Disease: Understanding the Macroeconomic Implications of Windfalls and the Private Prospects: The Case of Equatorial Guinea*. Washington, DC: The World Bank.

Trucano, M. (2011, February 16). *Mobile learning in developing countries in 2011: What's new, what's next?* Retrieved November 16, 2016, from EDUTECH, The World Bank IBRD-IDA: http://blogs.worldbank.org/edutech/water/mlearning2011-whatsnew

Tshabalala, S. (2015). *Why South Africa's largest mobile network, Vodacom, failed to grow M-Pesa*. Retrieved 04 06, 2017, from Quartz Africa: https://qz.com/467887/why-south-africas-largest-mobile-network-vodacom-failed-to-grow-mpesa/

Tuomi, I. (2002). The Future of Knowledge Management. *Lifelong Learning in Europe (LLinE)*, *7*(2), 69-79. Available at: http://www.meaningprocessing.com/personalPages/tuomi/articles/FutureOfKnowledgeManagement.pdf

Tuomi, I. (2004a). *Future Challenges of the European Knowledge Society*. Paper presented at Institute for Prospective Technological Studies. Available at: http://www.meaningprocessing.com/personalPages/tuomi/articles/TheFutureOfTheEuropeanKnowledgeSociety.pdf

Tuomi, I. (2004b). *Knowledge sharing and the idea of Public Domain.* Paper presented at the Unesco 21st Century Dialogue on Building Knowledge Societies. Available at: http://www.meaningprocessing.com/personalPages/tuomi/articles/KnowledgeSharingAndTheIdeaOfPublicDomain.pdf

UN DESA. (2014). *World Urbanization Prospects: The 2014 Revision, Highlights.* New York: United Nations, Department of Economic and Social Affairs, Population Division.

UN Habitat. (2016). Urbanization and Development: Emerging Futures. World Cities Report 2016. Author.

UN. (2015). *World Population Prospects: The 2015 revision. Key findings and advance tables.* New York: Department of Economic and Social Affairs, Population Division, United Nation.

UNCTAD. (2015). *The Information Economy Report 2015: Unlocking the Potential of E-Commerce for Developing Countries.* Retrieved from http://unctad.org/en/PublicationsLibrary/ier2015_en.pdf

UNDESA. (2012). *World Urbanization Prospects: The 2011 Revision.* New York: UNDESA.

UNDESA. (2014). *World Urbanization Prospects.* Retrieved from https://esa.un.org/unpd/wup/publications/files/wup2014-highlights.Pdf

UNDESA. Population Division. (2014). World Urbanization Prospects. New York: United Nations Department of Economic and Social Affairs, Population Division.

UNDP. (2015). *United Nations - 17 Sustainable Development Goals (SDGs).* Retrieved May 5, 2017, from Goal 11: Make cities inclusive, safe, resilient and sustainable: http://www.un.org/sustainabledevelopment/cities/

UNDP. (2017). *Averting Famine in Northeast Nigeria, Somalia, South Sudan and Yemen.* UN Development Programme.

UNDP. (2017). *Rebuilding North-East Nigeria.* Retrieved from http://www.ng.undp.org/content/nigeria/en/home/our-work/crisispreventionandrecovery.html

UNECA. (2014). *Contribution to the 2014 United Nations Economic and Social Council (ECOSOC) Integration Segment.* Nairobi: ECOSOC.

UNESCO. (2017). *Ancient Kano City Walls and Associated Sties.* Retrieved from http://whc.unesco.org/en/tentativelists/5171/

UN-Habitat. (2009). *Guide to Municipal Finance.* Nairobi: UN-Habitat.

UN-HABITAT. (2010). *State of African Cities 2010.* Nairobi: UN-HABITAT.

UN-HABITAT. (2013). State of The World's Cities 2012/2013: Prosperity of Cities. UN-Habitat.

UN-Habitat. (2014). *The State of African Cities 2014 - Re-imagining sustainable urban transitions.* Nairobi: UN-Habitat.

UN-Habitat. (n.d.). Retrieved from https://unhabitat.org/un-habitat-at-a-glance/#

UNIDO. (2016). *Ecoindustrial Parks In Developing And Emerging Countries.* Retrieved from https://www.unido.org/fileadmin/user_media_upgrade/Resources/Publications/Envionment/2016

United Nations (UN). (2017). *World urbanization prospects: The 2017 revision.* New York: Department of Economic and Social Affairs.

United Nations Development Programme (UNDP). (2002). Developing Capacity through Technical Cooperation: Country Experiences. London: Overseas Development Institute.

United Nations Volunteers (UNV) programme. (2015). *Delivering at Grassroots*. Retrieved from https://www.unv.org/annual-report-2015/

United Nations. (2015, September 25). *Sustainable Developmwnt Goals (SDGs)*. Retrieved November 8, 2016, from 17 Sustainable Developmwnt Goals (SGDs) to Transform Our World: http://www.un.org/sustainabledevelopment/sustainable-development-goals/

Urban Development Corporation (UDC) Detroit. (2017). *Volunteer*. Retrieved from http://urbandevelopmentcorp.org/volunteers/

USAID Nigeria. (2015). *LAKAJI Corridor*. Retrieved from http://www.nigerianextt.org/?pageid=334

Ushahidi. (n.d.). Retrieved from https://www.ushahidi.com/support/ushahidi-overview

Vachelard, J., Gambarra-Soares, T., Augustini, G., Riul, P., & Maracaja-Coutinho, V. (2016). *A Guide to Scientific Crowdfunding*. Retrieved from http://journals.plos.org/plosbiology/article?id=10.1371/journal.pbio.1002373

Vadgama, C., Khutwad, A., Damle, M., & Patil, S. (2015). Smart Funding Options for Developing Smart Cities: A Proposal for India. *Indian Journal of Science and Technology*, *8*(34). doi:10.17485/ijst/2015/v8i34/85418

Vanguard. (2017). Retrieved from www.vanguardngr.com

Varma, V. (2017, June 7). *Can crowdfunding help build a canal? A village in parched Marathwada thinks so!* Retrieved July 14, 2017, from The Indian Express: http://indianexpress.com/article/india/india-news-india/crowdfunding-in-india-marathwada-drought-canal-farmers-2838988/

Varnelis, K. (2010). *The meaning of network culture*. Retrieved on 14th January 2010, from: http://www.eurozine.com/articles/2010-01-14-varnelis-en.html

Vaughan, R., & Hawksworth, J. (2014). *The sharing economy:how will it disrupt your business?* PWC.

Venable, N. (n.d.). *Spike Lee's Kickstarter Campaign Was Mostly Funded By Rich People*. Retrieved April 09, 2017, from Cinema Blend: http://www.cinemablend.com/new/Spike-Lee-Kickstarter-Campaign-Was-Mostly-Funded-By-Rich-People-39104.html

Vercellone, C., Bria, F., Fumagalli, A., Gentilucci, E., Giuliani, A., Griziotti, G., & Vattimo, P. (2015). *Managing the commons in the knowledge economy*. Retrieved from https://www.nesta.org.uk/publications/d-cent-managing-commons-knowledge-economy

Vidal, J. (2015). *Ethiopia dam will turn Lake Turkana into 'endless battlefield', locals warn*. Available at: http://www.theguardian.com/ global-development/2015/jan/13/ethiopiagibe-iii-dam-kenya

Villano, M. (2014, December). The sharing economy 2.0. *Entrepreneur*, 56-58 .

Voor je buurt. (n.d.). *About Voor Je Buurt Civic Crowdfunding*. Last visited January 31, 2017. https://www.voorjebuurt.nl/about/

Vosloo, S. (2014). *BBC –Future – Future of education in Africa is mobile*. Retrieved 11 16, 2016, from BBC: http://www.bbc.com/future/story/20120823-what-africa-can-learn-from-phones

Vygotsky, L. S. (1986). *Thought and Language*. Cambridge, MA: MIT Press.

Waag. (2015). *Waag*. Retrieved from https://waag.org/en/blog/hackablecity

Wadhwa, K. (2013). *Wikipedia Zero Getting Wikipedia to the people who need it most*. Retrieved 03 30, 2017, from Blog.Wikimedia.org: https://blog.wikimedia.org/2013/02/22/getting-wikipedia-to-the-people-who-need-it-most/

Wang, D. (n.d.). *Optimizing Campaign Length.* Retrieved April 11, 2017, from Shopify: The Ultimate Guide to Crowdfunding: https://www.shopify.com/guides/crowdfunding

Wang, L., & Shen, J. (2014). Changing spatial planning in China's five-year planning system. *Urban Design and Planning, 167*(5DP5), 189–195. doi:10.1680/udap.14.00008

Wang, Y., Wang, Y., & Wu, J. (2009). Urbanization and informal development in China: Urban villages in Shenzhen. *International Journal of Urban and Regional Research, 33*(4), 957–973. doi:10.1111/j.1468-2427.2009.00891.x

Wankel, C. (2009). Management education using social media. *Organizational Management Journal, 6*(4), 251–262. doi:10.1057/omj.2009.34

Ward, C., & Ramachandran, V. (2010). *Crowdfunding the next hit: Microfunding online experience goods.* Workshop on Computational Social Science and the Wisdom of Crowds, Whistler, Canada.

Watson, V. (2009). 'The planned city sweeps the poor away. . .'. Urban planning and 21st century urbanization. *Progress in Planning, 72*(3), 151–193. doi:10.1016/j.progress.2009.06.002

Weber, M. (1958). *The City.* New York: The Free Press, Macmillan Publishing Co.

WEC. (2013). World Energy Scenarios — Composing Energy. World Energy Council.

WEF. (2016). *Africa's energy poverty is keeping its people poor.* Retrieved from https://www.weforum.org/agenda/2016/09/africa-s-energy-poverty-is-keeping-its-people-poor

Wei, L., & Paul, M. (2014). China's Central Bank Leads Effort to Regulate Internet Finance. *WSJ.* Accessed 21/05/17 at http://online.wsj.com/news/articles/SB10001424052702303874504579376111028523376

Wenger, E. (1998). *Communities of Practice: Learning, Meaning and Identity.* Cambridge, UK: Cambridge University Press. doi:10.1017/CBO9780511803932

Wesler, K. W. (1998). *Historical archaeology in Nigeria.* Africa World Press. Retrieved from https://www.lw.com/thoughtLeadership/africas-funding-alternative

WeslerKit, W. (1998). Historical Archaeology in Nigeria. Africa World Press.

Westlake, S., Baeck, P., & Bone, J. (2016). *Another Year of Growth For P2P Lending and Crowdfunding in the UK.* Nesta.

Wicks, M. (2013). *Crowdfunding: An introduction.* Victoria: Blue Beetle Books Inc.

Wikipedia. (2017). *Violent Extremism.* Retrieved from https://en.wikipedia.org/wiki/Violent_extremism retrieved 20/04/17

Wiley, D. (2011). *Project Management for Instructional Designers. Iterating Towards Openess.* Retrieved Jan 10, 2013, from http://opencontent.org/blog/archives/2119

Williamson, W., & Parolin, B. (2012). Review of web-based communications for town planning in local government. *Journal of Urban Technology, 19*(1), 43–63. doi:10.1080/10630732.2012.626702

Wilson, J. (2017). *Volunteerism Research: A Review Essay.* Retrieved from www.//journals.sagepub.com

Wilson, J. (2017). *Volunteerism Research: A Review Essay.* Retrieved from www.http://www.journals.sagepub.com

Wishart, N. (2006). *MicroUpayment systems and their application to mobile networks: Examples of Mobile enabled services in the Philippines.* Infodev.

Wolfe, D. (2004). The role of Higher Education in Regional Innovation and Cluster Development. In *Creating Knowledge, Strengthening Nations*. Toronto: Toronto University Press. Available on line at http://www.utoronto.ca /progris/pdf_files/higher_education_UofTPress.pdf

Work Foundation. (2002). *Manchester: Ideopolis? Developing a Knowledge Capital*. London: Prepared by Andy Westwood and Max Nathan. The Work Foundation.

Work Foundation. (2005). *The Ideopolis: Knowledge City Consortium*. Research Project. Available at: http://theworkfoundation.com/research/ideopolis.jsp

World Bank Data. (2016). *Gross national income per capita 2016, Atlas method and PPP*. Retrieved from http://databank.worldbank.org/data/download/GNIPC.pdf

World Bank Document. (2013). *Crowdfunding's Potential for the Developing World*. Washington, DC: World Bank.

World Bank. (2002). *Global Development Learning Network*. Available at: www.globalknowledge.org

World Bank. (2010). *Volunteer Technology Communities: The World Bank Open Development*. Retrieved from https://www.gfdrr.org/sites/gfdrr/files/publication/Volunteer%20Technology%20Communities%20-%20Open%20Development_0.pdf

World Bank. (2011). *Water Supply and Sanitation in Uganda: Turning Finance into Services for 2015 and Beyond*. Nairobi: World Bank.

World Bank. (2011). *World Bank and Energy in Africa. The World Bank, 2011. Web. 20 Sept. 2012 2012*. World Bank Fact Sheet.

World Bank. (2013). *Annual Report 2013*. Author.

World Bank. (2013). *Crowdfunding's Potential for the Developing World*. Retrieved from http://documents.worldbank.org/curated/en/409841468327411701/pdf/840000WP0Box380cr owdfunding0study00.pdf

World Bank. (2013). *Crowdfunding's Potential for the Developing World*. Washington, DC: World Bank.

World Bank. (2013). *Diaspora Remittances Must Open the Door to Financial Inclusion*. Retrieved from http://www.worldbank.org/en/news/feature/2013/10/10/diaspora-remittances-must-open-the-door-to-financial-inclusion

World Bank. (2013). *Doing Business 2014: Smarter Regulations for Small and Medium-Size Enterprises*. Washington, DC: World Bank Group.

World Bank. (2014). *Annual Report 2014*. Author.

World Bank. (2015). *Annual Report 2015*. Author.

World Bank. (2015). *Crowdfunding in Emerging Markets: Lessons from East African Startups*. Retrieved from https://www.infodev.org/infodev-files/crowdfunding-in-east-africa.pdf

World Bank. (2015). *Crowdfunding in Emerging Markets: Lessons from East African Startups*. Washington, DC: World Bank.

World Bank. (2016). *From oil to cities: Nigeria's next transformation. Directions in Development*. Washington, DC: World Bank Group. Retrieved from http://documents.worldbank.org/curated/en/711661468010811972/From-oil-to-cities-Nigeria-s-next-transformation

World Bank. (2016). *From oil to cities: Nigeria's next transformation*. Retrieved from http://documents.worldbank.org/curated/en/711661468010811972/pdf/106150-PUB-ADD-DOI-ISBN-SERIES-OUO-9.pdf

World Capital Institute (WCI). (2007). *The Most Admired Knowledge City (MAKCi) Report.* World Capital Institute & Teleos. Available at: http://www.worldcapitalinstitute.org/makci/history

World Economic Forum (WEF). (2016). *The Future of Jobs and Skills in Africa: Preparing the Region for the Fourth Industrial Revolution.* https://www.weforum.org/reports/the-future-of-jobs-and- skills-in-africa-preparing-the-region-for-the-fourth-industrial-revolution

World Urban Campaign. (2014). *Crowd Funding – A collective option for urban sustainable development.* Retrieved from http://www.worldurbancampaign.org/civic-crowdfunding-collective-option-urban-sustainable-development

Worldometers. (2017, July). *India Population (LIVE) 1,343,205.* Retrieved from http://www.worldometers.info/world-population/india-population/

Writer, S. (2016). *These are the biggest townships in South Africa.* Available online: https://businesstech.co.za/news/general/132269/these-are-the-biggest-townships-in-south-africa/

Wu, R. (2015, August 10). *How to Use Social Media for Crowdfunding Campaigns.* Retrieved January 31, 2017, from Social Media Examiner: http://www.socialmediaexaminer.com/social-media-for-crowdfunding/

Yle's Strategy for 2016–2020. (2016). Retrieved from https://yle.fi/aihe/artikkeli/2016/01/13/yles-strategy-2016-2020

Yomken. (n.d.). Retrieved from https://www.yomken.com/about#faq

Yoo, Y. G., & Choe, Y. C. (2014). Current Status of Korean Crowdfunding Industry and its Applicability to Agrifood Sector. *Advanced Science and Technology Letters*, *49*, 213–221. doi:10.14257/astl.2014.49.41

Younes & Fatimah. (2016). *Investigating the Factors Leading to Speaking Difficulties: Both Perspectives of EFL Saudi Learners and Their Teachers.* Retrieved from https://papers.ssrn.com/sol3/papers.cfm?abstract_id=2814824

Yuen, M. C., King, I., & Leung, K. S. (2011, October). A survey of crowdsourcing systems. In *Privacy, Security, Risk and Trust (PASSAT) and 2011 IEEE Third International Conference on Social Computing*, 766-773. doi:10.1109/PASSAT/SocialCom.2011.203

ZBC. (2016). *PhD Ministries conduct clean-up campaign.* Available at: http://www.ZBC.co.zw/index.php/news-categories/local-news/71738-phd-ministries-conducts-clean-up-campaign-

Zhang, T., Yip, C., Wang, G., & Zhang, Q. (2014). *China crowdfunding report: How to leverage crowdfunding to support China's social and environmental SGB's.* China Impact Fund.

Zhang, T., Yip, C., Wang, G., & Zhang, Q. (2014). *China Crowdfunding Report: How to Leverage Crowdfunding to Support China's Social and Environmental SGBs.* Beijing: China Impact Fund.

Zhang, T., Yip, C., Wang, G., & Zhang, Q. (2014). *China Crowdfunding Report: How to leverage Crowdfunding to support China's Social and Environmental SGBs.* Dao Ventures & China Impact Fund.

Zhao, Y., & Han, Q. (2016). Spatial crowdsourcing: Current state and future directions. *IEEE Communications Magazine*, *54*(7), 102–107. doi:10.1109/MCOM.2016.7509386

Zhao, Y., & Zhu, Q. (2014). Evaluation on crowdsourcing research: Current status and future direction. *Information Systems Frontiers*, *16*(3), 417–434. doi:10.1007/s10796-012-9350-4

Zheng, S., Long, F., Fan, C., & Gu, Y. (2009). Urban Villages in China: A 2008 Survey of Migrant Settlements in Beijing. *Eurasian Geography and Economics*, *50*(4), 425–446. doi:10.2747/1539-7216.50.4.425

Zhou, G., & Chilunjika, A. (2013). The Challenges of Self-Financing Local Authorities: The Case of Zimbabwe. *International Journal of Humanities and Social Science*, *3*(11), 233–245.

Zhou, X., & Zhao, M. (2017). Comparison of Territorial Spatial Planning System between China and Japan and Its Enlightenment. *Journal of Service Science and Management*, *10*(01), 54–71. doi:10.4236/jssm.2017.101005

Zoomaaal. (n.d.). Retrieved from https://zoomaal.com/help/how

Zucker, L. (1986). Production of Trust: Institutional Sources of Economic. In B. M. Cummings (Ed.), *Research in Organization Behavior* (pp. 53–111). Greenwich, CT: JAI Press.

Zu, Yu. (2004). Changing urbanization processes and in-situ rural-urban transformation: reflections on China's settlement definitions. In T. Champion & G. Hugo (Eds.), *New forms of urbanization: Beyond the urban-rural dichotomy* (pp. 207–228). Aldershot, UK: Ashgate Publishing Limited.

Zweig, J. (2013). *live.ca*. Retrieved 02 10, 2015, from http://www.liveca.ca/pay-no-tax-how-the-cra-knows-youre-cheating/

About the Contributors

Umar G. Benna earned his MRP and Ph. D. from the University of North Carolina in 1975 and is the Distinguished Professor of the Nigerian Universities Commission and is a SPURS Fellow at MIT, USA. He has a multidisciplinary background in architecture and city and regional planning. He has integrated academic and research pursuits with intense professional and administrative experience locally and internationally. Dr. Benna has over 45 years of teaching experience in universities in Nigeria, Saudi Arabia, Germany and USA. His research interests include urbanization issues in developing countries, urban activity systems, the role of large-scale projects on cities and regions, and the impact of new technologies on cities and regions. His professional activities – with Benna Associates – include architecture and urban design as well as the planning of new university campuses, master planning of many cities in Nigeria and Saudi Arabia. Urban administration experience came in the form of membership of the board of directors of the development authorities of Nigerian cities, Federal Housing Authority and similar agencies. Dr. Benna is principal partner in Benna Associates, Nigeria.

* * *

Ismaila Rimi Abubakar is associate professor in the department of urban and regional planning, University of Dammam, Saudi Arabia. He obtained a Master of Science in Computing from the Robert Gordon University, a Master of City and Regional Planning from KFUPM, and a PhD Urban and Regional Planning from Florida State University. He previously taught in the department of urban and regional planning, Ahmadu Bello University Zaria, Nigeria. His main research interests are urban sustainability, new towns development, urban services delivery, urban growth management, informal sector and GIS.

Rabiu Bena holds Masters Degree in Urban and Regional Planning. He is a registered Town Planner, and corporate Member, Nigerian Institute of Town Planners. He holds postgraduate Diploma in Education and is a registered teacher. He is currently a Principal Lecturer in the Department of Urban and Regional Planning, and was the Pioneer Director, Department of Physical Planning of Waziri Umaru Federal Polytechnic, Birnin Kebbi, Nigeria.

Jyoti Chandiramani has more than 30 years of experience in teaching and research. She is presently the Director of Symbiosis School of Economics and the Dean Faculty of Humanities and Social Sciences at the Symbiosis International University, Pune – India. She teaches Urban Economic Development, Trade, Aid & Development, and International Organization and Regional Cooperation at the Masters level. In 2007, She was awarded a short-term scholarship at the University of DePauw, Indianapolis –to study Liberal Arts Education. In 2013, she was a part of the Indian delegation to Pakistan (Lahore) for the Tenth South Asian Economic Students Meet (SAESM), and in 2015. Recently, she was invited to the 5th ASEM Rectors' Conference and as a Mentor for the Students' Forum (ARC5), organized by Charles University in Prague and the Asia-Europe Foundation (ASEF) at Prague in 2016.Besides writing a couple of textbooks, she has jointly edited a book with Ramanath Jha on 'Perspectives in Urban Development: Issues in Infrastructure, Planning, and Governance.' Her areas of research interest in urban include Urban Infrastructure, Urban Transport, Urban Poverty and presently working on Pune centric cases. Besides, she keenly studies and follows trends in International Development Cooperation – from the MDGs to the SDGs.

Innocent Chirisa: DPhil, MSc, BSc Hons. Rural & Urban Planning, (University of Zimbabwe), DipLMISR (IHS, Erasmus University), MZIRUP (Zimbabwe), Full Professor teaching Urban and Environmental Planning courses in the Department of Rural & Urban Planning, University of Zimbabwe. Currently is serving as the Deputy Dean of the Faculty of Social Studies, University of Zimbabwe. Also he is currently serving as the Acting Chairman of the Department of Rural & Urban Planning, University of Zimbabwe Prof Chirisa was recently appointed as a Research Fellow, Department of Urban and Regional Planning, University of Free State, Bloemfontein, South Africa for the period 2016 to 2020.

Umar Lawal Dano, Ph.D., is an Assistant Professor at the University of Dammam under the College of Architecture and Planning. He earned his PhD from Universiti Teknologi Petronas, Malaysia. His research interests include the applications of GIS, remote sensing and Multi-criteria Decision Analysis (Analytic Hierarchy Process and Analytic Network Process) in flood disaster forecasting. Dr. Umar has authored and co-authored many research papers indexed in ISI and Scopus and has attended a number of international conferences. He is an active member of SSSI Australia and APCBEES Hong Kong.

Blanca C. Garcia (MSc, PhD; University of Manchester, UK) is an Associate Professor at the Public Policy Department in the Northern Borderlands Research College (Colegio de la Frontera Norte, COLEF) a National Research Center with a unit based in Monterrey, Northern Mexico. She works under the flag of Knowledge City schemes, particularly interested in looking at the convergence of place, social capital, and social learning as key dynamics of Knowledge-based Development (KBD) in city-regions. Blanca also acts as the community broker for the knowledge-based development international consultation exercise known as MAKCi Awards for WCI, an international think-thank which convenes a Knowledge Cities World Summit on an annual basis. Blanca has also joined the PASCAL International Observatory initiative, a UK-based global alliance who gathers, informs and converses with decision makers to design and implement regional development strategies that balance economic growth, social equity, and environmental sustainability. Blanca has contributed to the growing KBD literature with publications on Knowledge City case studies and KBD applications for a number of editorial houses, such as Elsevier-Heinemann, Routledge, Inderscience and IGI Global brands.

Manisha Jain is a postdoc in the department of Resource Efficiency of Settlement Structures at the Leibniz Institute of Ecological Urban and Regional Development, Dresden, Germany. She holds a PhD in Urban and Regional Planning from Stuttgart University, Germany. Manisha Jain has practiced architecture and planning in India for more than six years. Her research focuses on the spatial analysis of the settlement structure, dynamics of urban growth, models and instruments of growth management and the role of infrastructure provision in growth management.

Artem Korzhenevych is the head of a research area at the Leibniz Institute of Ecological Urban and Regional Development, Dresden, Germany and Professor of Regional, Urban and Environmental Economics at the Technical University of Dresden. Artem Korzhenevych is a specialist in economic modelling, in particular in the areas of transport and regional economics, environmental and climate policies. Artem Korzhenevych received an M.A. (Economics) degree from the National University of Kyiv-Mohyla Academy (Ukraine) and a doctoral degree from Kiel University (Germany).

Abraham R. Matamanda graduated from the University of Zimbabwe with a BSc degree in Rural and Urban Planning in 2013 and went on to obtain a Masters in Social Ecology in 2015. Currently he is a PhD student at the University of the Free State in the department of Urban and Regional Planning focusing on urban form and social challenges in The Global South. Abraham has published in international peer reviewed journals and the issues that he has addressed include poverty and housing, housing and informality, water and sanitation issues as well as on ecological planning through the lenses of ecosystem services derived from wetlands. Basically, his researches focus on urban sustainability, environmental planning and management, rural development and the planning of cities and towns.

Liaison Mukarwi holds a Bachelor of Science Honours Degree in Rural and Urban Planning from the University of Zimbabwe. His areas of research interest have a strong inclination towards Regional and Urban Planning. He is actively engaged in research in the area of urban studies with focus on Urban Management and Governance, Environmental Design, Housing and Community Issues, Transport and Sustainability issues. Liaison Mukarwi had been a research assistant for several consultant research work in Transport, Waste Management and Urban Governance. He is an upcoming researcher who had written more than 5 articles and papers published in refereed international journals, or presented at peer reviewed conferences and seminars.

Gargi Patil completed her Masters in Economics from Fergusson College, Pune, in May 2014. In September 2014, she enrolled as full-time research scholar at Symbiosis International University (SIU), and is currently working as Visiting Faculty in the Department of Economics. Her area of research is Urban Finance and her PhD thesis is based on the same. She has attended a number of conferences and seminars and has papers published in a few journals. Recently, she has published a paper titled "A comparative study of select States in India with respect to sources of Tax Revenue" at a National Conference held in Jawaharlal Nehru University, New Delhi. Her area of interest includes Urban Economics, Public Policy and Micro Economics.

Hamza O. Salami obtained a PhD in Computer Science and Engineering from King Fahd University of Petroleum and Minerals, Dhahran, Saudi Arabia in 2014. He is currently an Assistant Professor at the Department of Computer Science and Engineering, University of Hafr Al Batin, Hafr Al Batin, Saudi Arabia. Dr Salami's research interests include metaheuristic search techniques, data mining and software retrieval.

N. Sridharan is an urban and regional planner with Economics and Finance background. Having an experience of more than 33 years in the field of teaching and consultancy in the field of urban and regional planning, he has worked with the Government of India, Private organisation, and in School of National Importance. He has been the Former Director of one of the National Institution of School of Planning and Architecture(SPA), Vijayawada, Andhra Pradesh, and currently Director of SPA-Bhopal one of the three SPAs in India. He has published several articles in leading journals in National and International Journals. His research interest includes: urban governance, peri-urban development, RURBAN, and financing development.

Muhammad A. Sulaiman obtained his Ph.D. in Computer Science from the Universiti Malaysia Sarawak (UNIMAS), Malaysia in 2017. Since 2012, he has been working as a Technical Research Assistant (IT professional) in King Fahd University of Petroleum & Minerals, Saudi Arabia. Sulaiman's research interest among other things includes the role of digital technology analysis of social equity and inclusiveness of development issues.

Adamu M. Yangora studied ICT in Swinburne University of Technology, Melbourne, Australia. Pursuing postgraduate research in the field of Knowledge Management at Universiti Malaysia Sarawak (UNIMAS).

Index

S

T

U

V

www.ingramcontent.com/pod-product-compliance
Lightning Source LLC
LaVergne TN
LVHW062135300926
849161LV00010B/2539
* 9 7 8 1 5 2 2 5 3 9 5 2 0 *